INTERNATIONAL

SECOND CANADIAN EDITION

RELATIONS

JOSHUA S. GOLDSTEIN

American University, Washington, D.C. and
University of Massachusetts, Amherst

JON C. PEVEHOUSE

University of Chicago

Canadian Edition by
SANDRA WHITWORTH

of York University, based on *International Relations,*
2006–2007 Edition, by Joshua S. Goldstein
and Jon C. Pevehouse

PEARSON
Longman

Toronto

To our families

—J.S.G. & J.C.P.

To my students, who have taught me so much

—S.W.

Library and Archives Canada Cataloguing in Publication

Goldstein, Joshua S., 1952–
    International relations / Joshua S. Goldstein, Jon C. Pevehouse,
Sandra Whitworth.—2nd Canadian ed.

Includes bibliographical references and index.
ISBN 978-0-321-49839-7

    1. International relations—Textbooks.   I. Pevehouse, Jon C.   II. Whitworth, Sandra, 1959–   III. Title.

JZ1242.G64 2007   327   C2007-904559-6

ISBN-13: 978-0-321-49839-7
ISBN-10: 0-321-49839-9

Vice President, Editorial Director: Gary Bennett
Senior Acquisitions Editor: Laura Paterson Forbes
Executive Marketing Manager: Judith Allen
Developmental Editor: Jody Yvonne
Production Editor: Katie Hearn
Copy Editor: Sally Glover
Proofreader: Karen Alliston
Production Coordinator: Janis Raisen
Composition: Integra
Photo Research: Amanda McCormick
Art Director: Julia Hall
Cover Design: Miguel Angel Acevedo
Interior Design: Julia Hall
Cover Image: Getty Images

Photo credits appear on page 559, which constitutes an extension of this copyright page.

1 2 3 4 5   11 10 09 08 07

Printed and bound in the United States of America.

PEARSON
Longman

Contents

Preface

Canadians are in a unique and interesting position when confronting international relations (IR). Both the study and practice of IR in Canada have been conducted in the shadow of one of the world's superpowers—the United States. Canada is not only a contiguous neighbour to the U.S. but shares many ideological and social commitments with that neighbour, as well as defence and security arrangements, a robust trading relationship and important diplomatic ties. Likewise, Canadian students of international relations more commonly read U.S. texts and scholarly journals of IR than they will Canadian sources, for no other reason than that there are far *more* texts and journals that originate in the U.S. than in Canada.

Canada's relationship with the United States was once characterized by Prime Minister Pierre Elliott Trudeau as being like that of "a mouse in bed with an elephant." Nonetheless, Canada's engagements with global-level politics, in both practical and scholarly terms, have sometimes shared the U.S. position but at other times charted a very different course from that of its southern neighbour. In foreign policy terms, while Canada supported the U.S. after the horrific attacks of September 11, 2001, it later refused to participate in the invasion of Iraq in 2003 but participated in Afghanistan, now under the authority of NATO. Canadian governments have long been committed to multilateralism and institutions like the United Nations, whereas the U.S. has been far more critical and considerably less enthusiastic about many of these institutions.

Likewise, while the U.S. has been reluctant to ratify some international human rights conventions (such as the Convention on the Elimination of Discrimination Against Women, or CEDAW), environmental protections (such as the Kyoto Accord) or disarmament agreements (like the 1999 Landmines Ban), Canada has often taken the lead in pursuing these kinds of instruments. Canadian and U.S. governments have long shared a commitment to freeing up trade and enhancing globalization, but they sometimes differ on the nuances of how this is to be accomplished.

In terms of scholarship, it is probably not unfair to describe the Canadian IR academic community as more heterogeneous in theoretical orientation than its counterpart in the United States. As will be described in later chapters, the study of IR has been dominated by an approach that is called "realism," and this has been particularly true in the United States. This does not mean that there are not many realist scholars of IR in Canada—indeed there are; nor does it mean that scholars working from theoretical perspectives other than realism do not exist in the United States—indeed they do. But in part because of the different practical orientation of decision-makers in Canada, and in part because of the particular contributions that some IR theorists in Canada have made, there is a greater tendency in Canadian university classrooms to ensure that students are exposed to the range of theoretical debate around questions of global politics, and that they come to appreciate that realism is one theoretical approach among many in IR.

It is for these reasons that IR textbooks written in the U.S. for American university students are not entirely appropriate for a Canadian audience. Those textbooks may be empirically rigorous and theoretically sound, but they "speak to" a different context than is found in Canada. This textbook takes one of the best introductory textbooks on IR available today, Joshua Goldstein's *International Relations,* and develops it for Canadian readers. This has been accomplished in two interrelated ways. First, examples of the role of Canada, and Canadians, in global-level politics have been introduced throughout the text. This has not meant eliminating information about the United States—the U.S. will always be an important part of the study of IR, and is treated as such in this edition. Rather, it has meant the introduction of Canadian-relevant historical information, data and policy concerns. What is clear in this second Canadian edition of *International Relations* is that Canadian activity in the world, whether on the part of our politicians, policy-makers, diplomats, scholars, activists or citizens, is an important element in the workings of global politics.

The second way in which this text has been written for Canadian students has been to develop some of the theoretical coverage, provide greater exposure to Canadian IR theorists (as well as theorists from other parts of the world) and in particular to make clear throughout the text the kinds of debates that take place between IR theorists on the variety of issues they engage, from war and peace to political economy, through international law, to development and underdevelopment and the environment. This is done in a variety of ways: through the "Thinking Theoretically" boxes and the "Changing World Order" boxes, as well as discussions in the text.

The rich complexity of international relationships—political, economic, social and cultural—provides a fascinating puzzle for all students of IR to try to understand. The puzzle is not just intellectually challenging; it is also emotionally powerful. It contains human-scale stories in which the subject's grand themes—war and peace, tragedy and triumph, conflict, inequality and community—are played out. International relations is also relevant to our daily lives as never before; today's students will graduate into a global economy in which no nation stands alone and in which their understanding of the world is more sophisticated than any generation that preceded them. This book links the conceptual apparatus of the field to the people who make up international relations and those whose lives are at stake.

Pedagogical Elements

This book's aim is to present the current state of knowledge in IR in a comprehensive and accessible way—to provide a map of the subject covering its various research communities in a logical order. This map is organized around the subfields of international security, international organizations and political economy, and North-South issues and the environment.

These subfields, although separated physically in this book, are integrated conceptually and overlap in many ways. No longer does one set of principles apply to military affairs, another set to economic relations and a third to development issues, as was sometimes argued during the Cold War. This book connects the subfields of IR to the real world by using concrete examples to illustrate theories. Many people in the television generation find information—especially abstract concepts—easier to grasp when linked with pictures. Thus, the book uses photographs extensively to illustrate important points. Photo captions reinforce main themes from each section of the text and link them with the scenes pictured.

In a subject like IR, where knowledge is tentative and empirical developments can overtake theories, critical thinking is a key skill for university and college students to develop. At various points in the text, conclusions are left open-ended to let students reason their way through an issue. The questions at the end of each chapter are designed to engage students in thinking critically about the contents of the chapter.

The use of quantitative data also encourages critical thinking. Basic data, presented simply and appropriately at a global level, allow students to form their own judgments and to reason through the implications of different policies and theories. The text uses global-level data (showing the whole picture) and conveys information graphically where appropriate.

Many people come to the study of IR with little background in world geography and history. The first chapter of this book presents background material on these topics. A historical perspective places recent decades in the context of the evolution of the modern international system. The global orientation of the book reflects the diversity of IR experiences for different actors, including those in the global South.

Three levels of analysis—individual, domestic and interstate—have often been used to sort out the multiple influences operating in international relations. This book adds a fourth: the global level. Global-level phenomena such as the United Nations, the world environment, the global political economy and global telecommunications and culture receive special attention.

IR is a large subject that offers many directions for further exploration. The footnotes in this book suggest further reading on various topics; unless otherwise noted, they are not traditional source notes. Each chapter ends with questions on thinking critically, a chapter summary, a list of key terms and a list of chapter-related weblinks.

This edition adds some new features. One focuses on "Canadian Scholarship in International Relations" and provides information about the kind of scholarly work being conducted in International Relations at Canadian universities. These are placed in each chapter throughout the text, and may be helpful for students as they search for programs of study at the graduate level in International Relations. They are intended to be representative of university scholarship in Canada and, though not completely exhaustive, do provide a good illustration of the breadth of work being done by Canadian scholars in International Relations. As well, Chapter 15 includes a list of weblinks to university programs in International Relations across the country. This edition also provides a feature entitled "Careers in International Relations" to help students begin to think about career paths in this field. These pages, devoted to careers in government and diplomacy, in nongovernmental organizations and in international business, appear at the end of Chapters 8, 10 and 12. They include books and website links to further pursue the issue. Finally, Research Questions have been added at the end of each chapter. These questions encourage students to use Pearson's Research Navigator™ to delve deeper into issues introduced in the chapter. The questions are also helpful as potential essay topics.

Structure of the Book

The book is divided into four parts. In Part One the study of International Relations is examined, first (in Chapter 1) by conveying the state of the IR field as well as its geographic and historical context. Chapter 2 then examines realist approaches to the study of IR, followed (in Chapter 3) by liberal and (in Chapter 4) critical approaches. Parts Two, Three and Four cover substantive topics: international security in Part Two, international organizations and international political economy in Part Three, and North-South issues and the environment in Part Four. Parts Two, Three and Four, although convenient for organization, overlap substantively and theoretically, as noted in several places.

The three chapters of Part Two begin with the foreign policy process and the roles of substate actors in Chapter 5. Chapter 6 introduces the main sources of international conflict, including ethnic, territorial and economic conflicts, and terrorism. The conditions and manner in which such conflicts lead to the use of violence are discussed in Chapter 7, on military force.

Part Three begins with Chapter 8, which shows how international agreements, treaties, organizations and law, and especially the United Nations, have evolved to become major influences in IR. Chapter 9 introduces again some of the theoretical concepts in political economy and discusses the most important topic in international political economy, namely, trade relations. Chapter 10 describes the politics of international money, banking and multinational business operations. Chapter 11 explores the processes of international integration, telecommunications and cultural exchange on both a regional scale—the European Union—and a global one.

Part Four opens with Chapter 12, which addresses global North-South relations, with particular attention to poverty in the global South. Chapter 13 then considers alternatives for economic development in the context of international business, debt and foreign aid. Chapter 14 examines some of the most pressing issues of IR today: the environment and population growth. Chapter 15—a brief postscript—reflects on the book's central themes and encourages critical thinking about the future.

Supplements

The following instructor supplements are available for downloading from a password-protected section of Pearson Education Canada's online catalogue (vig.pearsoned.ca). Navigate to your book's catalogue page to view a list of those supplements that are available. See your local sales representative for details and access.

Instructor's Manual: This resource, available to instructors using this textbook, includes chapter overviews, learning objectives, and detailed lecture outlines to help structure discussions and classroom presentations.

Test Item File: Available in Microsoft Word format, this test bank includes over a thousand questions and includes multiple-choice, short answer, essay, and map questions.

PowerPoints: The PowerPoint presentations to accompany *International Relations*, Second Canadian Edition, provide instructors with an interesting and useful way to cover the key concepts in each chapter and will help enhance classroom lectures.

Companion Website: Students are invited to use the learning resources at the Companion Website for *International Relations*, Second Canadian Edition, by visiting **www.pearsoned.ca/goldstein.** There you will find useful chapter summaries, practice tests, theoretical simulations, and relevant Web destinations. You will also be able to explore the implications of the information revolution for international relations as the Companion Website provides opportunities to expand your understanding of the issues raised in the Information Revolution boxes found throughout the text.

Pearson Education Canada/CBC Video Library: The second Canadian edition of *International Relations* is accompanied by a selection of videos from the CBC and an associated video guide. The videos are designed to provoke class discussion and complement the topics addressed in the text, and the video guide will help instructors integrate the videos into their lectures.

Video Case Studies for International Relations and Comparative Politics (0-205-57436-X): This DVD contains 19 video clips from ITN (UK) programs offering reports and insights on recent world affairs (2006 and 2007) such as Warlords in Somalia; Corruption in Kenya; Devolution in the UK; France's Future; and Mexico's Drug Economy. Instructors can use these excellent 2–5 minute clips as discussion starters in the classroom.

Pearson Advantage and Innovative Solutions Team

Pearson Advantage   For qualified adopters, Pearson Education is proud to introduce the Pearson Advantage. The **Pearson Advantage** is the first integrated Canadian service program committed to meeting the customization, training, and support needs for your course. Our commitments are made in writing and in consultation with faculty. Your local Pearson Education sales representative can provide you with more details on this service program.

Content Media Specialists   Pearson's Content Media Specialists work with faculty and campus course designers to ensure that Pearson technology products, assessment tools, and online course materials are tailored to meet your specific needs. This highly qualified team is dedicated to helping schools take full advantage of a wide range of educational technology, by assisting in the integration of a variety of instructional materials and media formats.

Acknowledgments

Thanks go to Emily Saso for research assistance on the first Canadian edition. Maya Eichler and Roshan Jahangeer provided research assistance for the second Canadian edition. Maya also reviewed and updated the material for the "Careers in International Relations" feature and Roshan tracked down information on Canadian programs and scholarship in International Relations for the "Focus on Canadian Scholarship" feature. Others who were very helpful in tracking down sources for me for both editions include Marshall Beier, Lori Crowe, Eric Helleiner, Keith Krause, Nicole LaViolette, Ananya Mukherjee-Reed, Leo Panitch and Alejandra Roncallo. I would also like to thank Elizabeth Dauphinee, Tami Jacoby and Cristina Masters for advice and suggestions. The team at Pearson Education Canada who assisted me with the book in both its editions— Lori Will, Christine Cozens, Jody Yvonne, John Polanszky, Söğüt Güleç, Lisa Berland, Tara Tovell, Katie Hearn, Laura Forbes, Sally Glover and others behind the scenes—both initiated this timely project and were enormously helpful in seeing it to completion. I have been encouraged by students for over 18 years to develop a textbook of IR; to them go my largest thanks. Among the many colleagues who contributed ideas that influenced this textbook, the following reviewers, in particular, made many useful suggestions:

Isabella Bakker, York University

Mark Baron, University of Calgary

Vincent Della Salla, Carleton University

Alistair D. Edgar, Wilfrid Laurier University

David G. Haglund, Queen's University

Nancy Kokaz, University of Toronto

Ed Lavalle, Capilano College

Logan Masilamani, Simon Fraser University

David Mutimer, York University

Julian Schofield, Concordia University

Yasmine Shamsie, Wilfrid Laurier University

Elliot Tepper, Carleton University

Russell Alan Williams, Memorial University

Sandra Whitworth

To the Student

The topics studied by scholars are like a landscape with many varied locations and terrains. This textbook is a map that can orient you to the main topics, debates and issue areas in International Relations. Scholars use specialized language to talk about their subjects. This text is also a phrase book that can translate such lingo and explain the terms and concepts that scholars use to talk about IR. However, IR is filled with many voices speaking many tongues. The text translates some of those voices—of prime ministers and professors, free-traders and feminists—to help you sort out the contours of the subject and the state of knowledge about its various topics. But, ultimately, the synthesis presented in this book is the authors' own. Both you and your professor may disagree with many points. Thus, this book is only a starting point for conversations and debates.

With map and phrase book in hand, you are ready to explore a fascinating world. The great changes taking place in world politics have made the writing of this textbook an exciting project. May you enjoy your own explorations of this realm.

A Note on Nomenclature

In International Relations, names are politically sensitive; different actors may call a territory or an event by different names. This book cannot resolve such conflicts; it has adopted the following naming conventions for the sake of consistency. The United Kingdom of Great Britain (England, Scotland, Wales) and Northern Ireland are usually called Britain. Burma, renamed Myanmar by its military government, is generally referred to as Burma or Burma/Myanmar. Cambodia, renamed Kampuchea by the Khmer Rouge in the 1970s, is called Cambodia. The 1991 U.S.-led multinational military campaign that retook Kuwait after Iraq's 1990 invasion is called the Gulf War. The war between Iran and Iraq in the 1980s is called the Iran-Iraq War (not the "Gulf War" as some called it at the time). The U.S. war against Iraq in 2003 is usually called the Iraq War. The country of Bosnia and Herzegovina is generally shortened to Bosnia (with apologies to Herzegovinians). The former Yugoslav Republic of Macedonia is called Macedonia. The People's Republic of China is referred to as China. The former Zaire is now Democratic Congo. Elsewhere, country names follow common usage, dropping formal designations such as "Republic of."

A Great Way to Learn and Instruct Online

The Pearson Education Canada Companion Website is easy to navigate and is organized to correspond to the chapters in this textbook. Whether you are a student in the classroom or a distance learner you will discover helpful resources for in-depth study and research that empower you in your quest for greater knowledge and maximize your potential for success in the course.

Companion Website

[www.pearsoned.ca/goldstein]

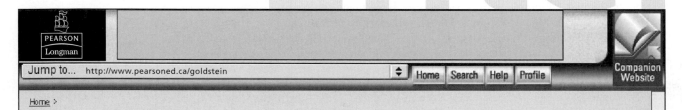

Enter

PEARSON Longman

Jump to...   http://www.pearsoned.ca/goldstein   ⬍   Home | Search | Help | Profile

Companion Website

Home >

Companion Website

International Relations, Second Canadian Edition, by Goldstein, Pevehouse and Whitworth

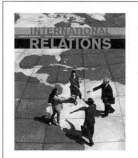

Student Resources

The modules in this section provide students with tools for learning course material. These modules include:

- Chapter Summary
- Multiple-Choice Quiz
- True/False Quiz
- Pattern Match
- Short Essay
- Long Essay
- Simulation
- Information Revolution
- Let's Debate the Issue
- Weblinks

In the quiz modules students can send answers to the grader and receive instant feedback on their progress through the Results Reporter.

Instructor Resources

A link to this book on the Pearson Education Canada online catalogue (vig.pearsoned.ca) provides instructors with additional teaching tools. Downloadable PowerPoint Presentations and an Instructor's Manual are just some of the materials that may be available. The catalogue is password protected. To get a password, simply contact your Pearson Education Canada Representative or call Faculty Sales and Services at 1-800-850-5813.

Introduction

A vote is taken at the UN
Security Council.

THE STUDY OF IR

Our world is large and complex. International relations is a fascinating topic because it concerns peoples, institutions and cultures throughout the world. The scope and complexity of the interactions among these groups make international relations a challenging subject to master. There is always more to learn. This book is only the beginning of the story.

The field of **international relations (IR)** at one time concerned strictly the relationships among the world's governments. This is no longer true today. Contemporary scholars and students of IR study international organizations, multinational corporations, social movements, nongovernmental organizations, individuals, as well as the world's governments. IR also is concerned with economics, culture and domestic politics; issues of gender, race, ethnicity and class; and geographical and historical factors that influence politics at the global level. The subject of IR overlaps several other fields.

The purpose of this book is to introduce the field of IR, to organize in a logical way what is known and theorized about IR, and to convey key concepts and ideas. This first chapter defines IR as a field of study, introduces the actors of interest and reviews the geographical and historical contexts within which IR occurs.

international relations (IR)
The relationships among the world's state governments and the connection of those relationships with other actors (such as the United Nations, multinational corporations and individuals), with other social relationships (including economics, culture and domestic politics) and with geographic and historical influences.

IR and Daily Life

Sometimes international relations is portrayed as a distant and abstract ritual conducted by a small group of people such as prime ministers, generals and diplomats. This picture is not an accurate one. Although leaders do play a major role in international affairs, many other people participate as well. University students and other citizens participate in international relations every time they vote in an election or work on a political campaign, any time they buy a product or service traded in world markets and each time they watch the news. The choices we make in our daily lives ultimately affect the world we live in. Are the clothes and electronic products you purchase made in a country that is poorer than your own? Under what conditions? Do your elected leaders prefer diplomacy or military solutions to international conflict? Do you drive a car to work or take public transit? Every person faces unique choices as an individual human being. Through those choices, each person makes a unique contribution, however small, to the world of international relations.

REFLECTIONS OF WAR
IR touches our lives in many ways. Canadian veterans mark the D-Day memorial in 2004.

In turn, IR profoundly affects the daily lives of university students and other citizens. Prospects for finding jobs after graduation depend on the global economy and international economic competition. For middle-class Canadians with university degrees, these jobs also are more likely than ever to entail international travel or communication. And the rules of the world trading system affect the goods that students consume, from mobile phones to gasoline.

Although international economics pervade life on a daily basis, war dominates the lives of most Canadians far less frequently. Still, it can cast a long shadow. In major wars, of course, students and their friends and families may go off to battle and their lives may change irreversibly. In Canada today, people involved in the armed forces may be deployed on peacekeeping missions or sent into battle settings such as Afghanistan, which can have an enormous impact on their lives. New Canadians may have emigrated to Canada to flee armed conflict. Even in peacetime, war can be a pervasive influence. Children play with war toys; TV and films reproduce and multiply images of war; and a sizeable sector of the world economy is structured around military production.

As technology advances, the world is shrinking year by year. Better communication and transportation capabilities are constantly expanding the ordinary citizen's contact with people, products and ideas from other countries. Globalization is internationalizing us.

IR as a Field of Study

IR as a field of study—separate from the study of diplomatic history or economics or politics more generally—is a relatively recent enterprise. The very first Chair of International Relations was established at the University of Wales in Aberystwyth in 1919. Though IR as a field had its beginnings in the United Kingdom, it was in the United States that the study of IR really took hold after World War II—with the creation of programs, university departments and research institutes all focused on developing expertise in the study of global-level politics.[1] Today, universities around the world have courses and programs devoted to the study of IR.

---

[1] Martin Hollis and Steve Smith, *Explaining and Understanding International Relations* (Oxford: Clarendon, 1991). Stanley Hoffmann, "An American Social Science: International Relations," *Daedalus* 106.3 (1977): 41–60.

IR as a field of study, whether taught in Canada, the U.K., Mexico or Thailand, has always had uncertain boundaries.[2] As a part of political science, IR is about *politics at the global level*—the decisions of governments concerning their actions toward other governments, the activities of international institutions, global trade and armed conflict, protest movements, international financial institutions, environmental issues, global trafficking in minerals or people and international human rights, to name a few of the issues that students in IR will study. Some universities offer separate degrees or departments of IR. Most, however, teach IR under the discipline of political science.

One level of politics that is international in nature is not generally included in the field of IR: the domestic politics of foreign countries. It is considered to be a separate field of political science called *comparative politics*. Comparative politics overlaps with IR to the considerable extent that domestic politics influence foreign policy in many countries, and many actors at the global level (businesses, nongovernmental organizations, social movements) are involved in both local-level and global-level politics. Despite these overlaps, IR as a field tends to avoid issues that concern domestic politics in Canada, the United States or other countries *except* to the extent that they affect politics at the global level.

The scope of the field of IR may also be defined by the *subfields* it encompasses. Traditionally, the study of IR has focused on questions of war and peace—considered the subfield of **international security.** Subjects that dominated the study of IR in the past, especially in the 1950s and 1960s—the movements of armies and diplomats, the crafting of treaties and alliances, the development and deployment of military capabilities—continue to hold a central position in the field. However, in the 1990s, after the Cold War, the subfield of security studies broadened beyond its traditional focus on military forces and the superpower arms race. Regional conflicts began to garner more attention, and ethnic conflicts became more prominent. Scholars of foreign policy processes increasingly saw themselves as part of a broader security studies community. Meanwhile, interdisciplinary peace studies programs, which emerged in the 1980s at many universities, sought to expand concepts of "security" further—as did feminist scholars. While the study of war, weapons and military forces continues to be the core concern of international security studies, these trends have expanded the boundaries of the subfield.[3]

In the 1970s and 1980s, as economics became increasingly central to international relations, the subfield of **international political economy (IPE)** grew and became the counterpoint to international security studies as a second main subfield of IR. Scholars of IPE study trade and financial relations among nations and the international institutions that support these relations, such as the World Trade Organization and the International Monetary Fund. Since the 1990s, growing attention has been paid also

international security A subfield of international relations (IR) that focuses on questions of war and peace.

international political economy (IPE) The study of the politics of trade, monetary and other economic relations among nations, and their connection to other transnational forces.

---

[2] Peter J. Katzenstein, Robert O. Keohane and Stephen D. Krasner, eds., *Exploration and Contestation in the Study of World Politics* (Cambridge, MA: MIT P, 1999). John Macmillan and Andrew Linklater, eds., *Boundaries in Question: New Directions in International Relations* (London: Pinter, 1995).

[3] Stephen M. Walt, "The Renaissance of Security Studies," *International Studies Quarterly* 35.2 (1991): 211–40. Barry Buzan, *People, States and Fear: An Agenda for International Security Studies in the Post–Cold War Era,* 2nd ed. (Boulder, CO: Rienner, 1991). Keith Krause and Michael C. Williams, eds., *Critical Security Studies* (Minneapolis: U of Minnesota P, 1997). Ronnie D. Lipschutz, ed., *On Security* (NY: Columbia UP, 1995). Stuart Croft and Terry Terriff, eds., *Contemporary Security Policy: Critical Reflections on Twenty Years of Change* (Ilford, UK: Frank Cass, 2000).

to global North-South interactions between rich and poor nations (see pp. 475–486), including such topics as economic dependency, debt, foreign aid and technology transfer. As the East-West confrontation of the Cold War recedes into history, North-South issues are becoming more salient, as are problems of international environmental management and global telecommunications. The subfield of IPE is expanding accordingly. Of course, different professors see the scope and structure of the field of IR in different ways.

IR scholars now recognize the close connections of IPE to security (after decades of treating them as separate and different issues). The same principles and theories that help us understand international security (covered in Part Two) also help us understand IPE (Part Three), and development and the environment. Economics is important in security affairs, and vice versa. The organization of this book may seem to propose that a divide exists between the subfields, but in reality they are interwoven.

Theories

IR scholars want to understand why and how international events occur in the way they do. Why did a particular war break out? Why did a certain trade agreement benefit one nation or group of people more than another? How have some countries come to be so much richer than others? These questions can be answered in several ways. One kind of answer can be found by tracing the immediate, short-term sequence of events and decisions that led to a particular outcome. For instance, the outbreak of a war might be traced to a critical decision made by a particular leader. This kind of answer is largely *descriptive*—it seeks to describe how particular forces and actors operate to bring about a particular outcome.

Another answer to these types of questions results from seeking general explanations and longer-term, more indirect causes. For example, the outbreak of a war might be seen as an instance of a general pattern in which arms races lead to war. Conversely, wars may occur because particular interests within a state see it as to their advantage to push their state to engage in armed conflict (arms producers, for example). These kinds of answers are *theoretical* because they place the particular event in the context of a more general pattern applicable across many cases.

Understanding IR requires both descriptive and theoretical knowledge. It would do little good only to describe events without being able to generalize or draw lessons from them. Nor would it do much good to formulate purely abstract theories without being able to apply them to the finely detailed and complex world in which we live.

IR has long been a rather practical discipline. There is a close connection between scholars in colleges, universities and thinktanks and policy-making communities working in governments. This is especially true in the United States (for instance, Professor Condoleezza Rice became U.S. president Bush's National Security Advisor in 2001 and Secretary of State in 2005), but it also occurs in other countries. Some professors serve in government, and sometimes when policy-makers retire from political life they turn to research and teaching (for instance, Canada's former Minister of Foreign Affairs and International Trade, Lloyd Axworthy, joined the University of British Columbia when he left politics in 2000 and then became president of the University of Winnipeg in 2004). Professors also publicize their ideas about global politics through newspaper columns or

Focus on Canadian Scholarship

In each chapter, information about some of the specific research and scholarship conducted at Canadian universities which is of relevance to each chapter topic will be provided. This will acquaint Canadian students with the kinds of IR scholarship being done at universities across the country, and will be a useful resource for those students considering continuing their studies in International Relations. These descriptions, though representative, will not be exhaustive and it is important for students to explore available information about programs of study that emphasize International Relations as well as any research being conducted by individual faculty. To help you get started, a list of Canadian programs, with weblinks, is provided in Chapter 15 on page 544.

TV interviews. In many cases, they are seeking to influence their government's foreign policies or even just the opinion of average citizens.

IR is an unpredictable realm of turbulent processes and events that catch experts by surprise—such as the fall of the Berlin Wall in 1989, for example. Most IR scholars are modest about their ability to make accurate predictions—and with good reason. The best theories provide only a rough guide to understanding what actually occurs in IR or to predicting what will happen next.

Perhaps because of this complexity and unpredictability, IR scholars do not agree on a single set of theories to explain IR or even on a single set of concepts through which to discuss the field. Throughout these discussions, no single theoretical framework has the support of all IR scholars.[4]

One way to look at the variety of theories is to distinguish three broad theoretical perspectives or paradigms: realist, liberal-pluralist and critical. A paradigm, for our purposes here, means a group of theories that: (1) share a vision of what the world looks like; (2) share some sense of what to study in that world (states? transnational organizations or businesses? social movements? economic classes?); and (3) share certain values about the purpose or goal of theorizing about global-level politics. In some sense, each is a lens through which the world looks different and different things seem important. At the same time, the three perspectives can complement each other, and certainly theorists within each of the paradigms engage with one another and are sometimes influenced by each other. Each broad paradigm contains different specific theories, and debate and disagreement can take place within the paradigms as much as between them. But in each, there is a general shared consensus about what the world looks like, what we should study in that world and what our purpose or goals are in making theory in IR.

The *realist* paradigm sees the world as characterized primarily by conflict. Realists believe that the most important actors in world politics are states and state decision-makers, and that the purpose of theorizing is to provide insights to help guide those decision-makers as they try to decide what they must do on the global stage. This paradigm generally values maintenance of the status quo and discounts the element of large-scale change in IR. It focuses on the laws of power politics, which are considered

---

[4] Tim Dunne, Milya Kurki and Steve Smith, *International Relations Theories: Discipline and Diversity* (UK: Oxford, 2007).

timeless and universal. Realist perspectives find their most fertile ground in the sub-field of international security, with its logic of military power. Relative position with regard to other states is more important than the absolute condition of a state, because in the anarchic world, with its ever-present possibility of war, winning and losing matter above all. Realist perspectives tend to see conflict—or the potential for conflict—as the natural order of things; a sometimes necessary evil for which one should always be prepared. They see international trade as a potential source of national power, a view expressed in IPE as *mercantilism* (the accumulation of national war chests, or the equivalent, through control of trade).

The *liberal-pluralist* paradigm sees the world as characterized more by cooperative relations than conflicting ones. Liberal pluralists believe we should look at the activities of states and the many other actors involved in global politics: individuals, multinational corporations, international institutions and nongovernmental organizations. The purpose of theorizing, by this view, is to provide practical advice, but not only to state decision-makers; rather, advice can be provided to any of the actors in global politics—states, businesses, individual actors and others. Liberal pluralists do not deny that conflicts occur, but they argue that cooperative interactions among states, peoples and institutions far outnumber conflicting relations. This is harder to see in international relations partly because the drama of war and armed conflict captures our attention in a way that cooperative relations do not. But for liberal pluralists, we could not travel, communicate or trade with people from other parts of the world if there were not an intricate web of agreements and institutions in place that allowed us to do so. The liberal-pluralist paradigm values reform of the status quo through an evolutionary process of incremental change. Theories that build on the liberal tradition often focus on the mutual benefits to be gained in IR through interdependence and reciprocity. Gaining wealth in absolute terms is more important from this perspective than gaining power relative to other countries. Liberal approaches find their most fertile ground in the IPE subfield because of the potential for mutual gain in trade and exchange, with each nation exploiting its comparative advantage in particular products and services. Liberal approaches tend to value *freedom*, especially free trade and free exchange of ideas. They tend to see war not as a natural tendency but as a mistake to be prevented or at least minimized by international agreements and organizations.

The *critical* paradigm sees the world as characterized primarily by inequalities: inequalities among states, peoples, races, genders, classes, ethnic groups and others. Critical theorists believe we must look at those inequalities and at the activities of the peoples, states or groups who have been marginalized in both the practice and study of IR. These people or groups are the most affected by international relations, but they have not been in a position to call the tune. For critical theorists, the purpose of theorizing about IR is to contribute to a transformation of global politics, and in particular to transform and rectify relations of inequality. Critical theorists may disagree on which inequalities are the most important: some focus on class inequality, others on inequalities of wealth between states, and others still on relations of inequality between genders or races. However, what they all share is a view of the world that does not take existing power relations for granted, but rather asks, "How did this world come about and whose interests does it serve?"[5] These perspectives often focus on the unfair and exploitive aspects of international relationships, and on efforts to radically change those relationships. Critical approaches

---

[5] Cynthia Enloe, *Bananas, Beaches and Bases: Making Feminist Sense of International Politics* (Berkeley: U California P, 1990). Robert Cox, "Social Forces, States and World Orders: Beyond International Relations Theory," *Approaches to World Order*, R.W. Cox, with Timothy J. Sinclair (Cambridge UP, 1996).

have found resonance in areas of IR scholarship dealing with North-South relations and global development because of the evident injustice of grinding poverty suffered by a majority of the world's people. Critical approaches tend to value *justice*. They often see war as a product of underlying exploitative economic relationships, or as perpetrated to serve particular interests.

Although each paradigm has found resonance or been more influential in different areas of IR (realism in international security, liberal pluralism in IPE and critical theories in North-South relations and development issues), this does not mean that they are each silent about the issues that tend to be dominated by one or another of the paradigms. For example, critical theorists have a great deal to say about security and IPE issues, and liberal pluralism engages with questions of development and international security. Likewise, variants of realism engage with questions of IPE and North-South issues. Chapters 2, 3 and 4 discuss the paradigms in more detail. In addition, throughout this textbook, the manner in which each paradigm engages with specific substantive issues of IR will be highlighted, both in the text and in the "Thinking Theoretically" boxes.

Theoretical debates in the field of IR are fundamental, but unresolved. They leave IR scholarship in a turbulent condition, racing to try to make sense of a rapidly changing world in which old ideas work poorly. Students of global politics must begin to confront not only the various issues of IR, but to think through which—if any—of the theoretical paradigms within IR provides the most persuasive account of different events in world politics. In some cases, students may find that none of the theories answer their questions sufficiently; in other cases, students may find that part of each theory is useful. The goal of this book is to lay out the current state of knowledge without exaggerating the successes of the discipline or any particular approach.

ACTORS AND INFLUENCES

Who are the actors in IR? The international stage is crowded with actors large and small who are intimately interwoven into global-level politics. These actors are governments and the people within them who make decisions about foreign policy. They are also

Thinking Theoretically

Theories provide possible ways to understand events in IR. These boxes on "thinking theoretically" will encourage you to examine possible theoretical (generalizable) explanations for several prominent cases. For example, consider some of the biggest tests of response to aggression in the post–Cold War era—Kuwait, Rwanda, the former Yugoslavia, 9/11, nuclear tests in India and Pakistan, sabre-rattling in North Korea and the U.S. invasion of Iraq. As you read about these cases throughout this text, ask yourself: What accounts for the different responses by various states to these events? How would each of the paradigms interpret these events? Whose views were included in the formal responses and whose were excluded?

Theoretical knowledge accumulates through a repeated cycle of generalizing and then testing or interpreting events. For any given puzzle, various theories might explain the result (though none perfectly) as a case of a more general principle or category. Each theory also logically predicts other outcomes, and some of these alternatives can be tested empirically. A laboratory science, controlling all but one variable, can test theoretical predictions efficiently. Obviously IR does not have this luxury and must untangle many variables and elements operating simultaneously. Since knowledge of IR is tenuous in this way, it is especially important to think critically and creatively about IR events and consider several different theoretical explanations before deciding which (if any) provides the best explanation.

individual leaders and citizens. They are bureaucratic agencies in foreign ministries. They are multinational corporations and terrorist groups. They are international institutions such as the United Nations and the International Monetary Fund, and the people who staff these organizations. They are women and men, ethnic groups and social movement activists.

State Actors

state An inhabited territorial entity controlled by a government that exercises its sovereignty.

United Nations (UN) An organization of nearly all world states, created after World War II to promote collective security.

A **state** is a territorial entity controlled by a government and inhabited by a population. A state government answers to no higher authority; it exercises *sovereignty* over its territory—to make and enforce laws, to collect taxes and so forth. This sovereignty is recognized (acknowledged) by other states through diplomatic relations and usually by membership in the **United Nations (UN).** (The concepts of state sovereignty and territoriality are elaborated in Chapter 2.) The population inhabiting a state forms a *civil society* to the extent it has developed participatory institutions of social life. All or part of the population that shares a group identity may consider itself a *nation* (see "Nationalism, 1500–the Present" later in this chapter). The state's government is a *democracy* to the extent that the government is controlled by the members of the population rather than imposed on them.[6] (Note that the word *state* in IR does not mean a state in the United States or in any other country.)

In political life, and to some extent in IR scholarship, the terms *state*, *nation* and *country* are used imprecisely, usually to refer to the decisions of state governments. It is common to discuss states as if they were people, as in "France supports the UN resolution" or "the United States attacked Iraq." In reality, states take such actions as the result of complex internal processes. It is also unlikely that everyone living within a state agrees with every decision made by their government—not all Americans, for example, agreed with the U.S. decision to invade Iraq; not all Canadians agree with the Canadian government's decision to stay out of Iraq. Ultimately, only individual human beings are true actors making conscious decisions and we need to exercise caution when treating states as if they were people.

With few exceptions, each state has a capital city—the seat of government from which it administers its territory—and often a single individual who acts in the name of the state. We may refer to this person simply as the "state leader." Often he or she is the *head of government* (such as a prime minister) or the *head of state* (such as a president or a king or queen). In some countries, such as the United States, the same person is head of state and government. In other countries, such as Canada, the Queen and her representative (the Governor General) have become more figurehead or symbolic positions (though technically they can still be called upon in certain instances). In any case, the most powerful political figure is the one we refer to as "state leader," and these figures have been important individual actors in IR since the days when kings or queens ruled territories by decree. The state actor includes the individual leader as well as bureaucratic organizations (such as foreign ministries) that act in the name of the state.

international system The set of relationships among the world's states, structured by certain rules and patterns of interaction.

The **international system** is the set of relationships among the world's states, structured according to certain rules and patterns of interaction. Some such rules are

---

[6] See World Development Indicators Database, World Bank, 1 July 2006, available at http://siteresources. worldbank.org/DATASTATISTICS/Resources/GDP_PPP.pdf.

explicit, some implicit. They include who is considered a member of the system, what rights and responsibilities the members have, and what kinds of actions and responses normally occur between states. The international system is discussed in detail in Chapter 2.

The modern international system has existed for less than 500 years. Before then, people were organized into more mixed and overlapping political units such as city-states, empires and feudal fiefs. In the past 200 years the idea has spread that nations—groups of people who share a sense of national identity, usually including a language and culture—should have their own states (see "Nationalism, 1500–the Present" later in this chapter). In fact, however, few large states today are considered **nation-states.** Russia, India, the United States and Canada are all states in which several "nations" could be said to exist. Additionally, since World War II, the decolonization process in much of Asia and Africa has brought about the development of many new states, not all of which can be considered nation-states. One question in IR (as well as in Comparative Politics) is how well do states "manage" the diversity of nations within their borders? A major source of conflict and war is the frequent mismatch between perceived nations and actual state borders. When people identify with a nationality that their state government does not represent, they may fight to form their own state and thus to gain sovereignty over their territory and affairs. This substate nationalism is only one of several growing trends that undermine the present-day system of states. Other such trends include the globalization of economic processes, the power of telecommunications and the proliferation of ballistic missiles.

The independence of former colonies and, more recently, the breakup of large multi-national states into smaller states (the Soviet Union, Yugoslavia and Czechoslovakia)

nation-states States whose populations share a sense of national identity, usually including a language and culture.

United States President George W. Bush and Canadian Prime Minister Stephen Harper meet in Cancun, Mexico, in 2006.

have increased the number of states in the world. The exact total depends on the status of a number of quasi-state political entities, and it keeps changing as political units split apart or merge. The UN had 192 members in 2007.

Some other political entities are often referred to as states or countries although they are not formally recognized as such. Taiwan is the most important of these. It operates independently in practice but is claimed by China (a claim recognized formally by outside powers and, until recently, by Taiwan itself), and is not a member of the UN. Formal colonies and possessions still exist, although their status may change in the future. They include Puerto Rico (U.S.), Bermuda (British), French Guiana, the Netherlands Antilles (Dutch), the Falkland Islands (British) and Guam (U.S.). Hong Kong reverted from British to Chinese rule in 1997, and retains a somewhat separate economic identity under China's "one country, two systems" formula. The small former Portuguese colony of Macau also recently reverted to Chinese rule. The status of the Vatican (Holy See) in Rome is ambiguous. Counting these various territorial entities as states brings the world total to about 200 state or quasi-state actors.

There are also several would-be states (such as Kurdistan and Western Sahara) that do not fully control the territory they claim and are not universally recognized. Since smaller states may continue to split away from larger ones (for instance, if Québec were ever to separate from Canada), the number of states is likely to grow.

The size of the world's states varies dramatically, from China and India—with more than 1 billion people each—to microstates such as Nauru with populations of less than 20 000. With the creation of many small states in recent decades, the majority now have fewer than 10 million people each, and more than half of the remainder have 10 to 50 million each. The 15 states with populations above 70 million people together make up about two-thirds of the world's population.

gross domestic product (GDP) The size of a state's total annual economic activity.

States also differ tremendously in the size of their total annual economic activity— **gross domestic product (GDP)**[7]—from the $12 trillion U.S. economy to those of tiny states such as the Pacific island of Vanuatu ($600 million). The world economy is dominated by a few states, just as world population is. The United States alone accounts for one-fifth of the world economy; together with four other great powers it accounts for more than half (see pp. 18–21). The world's 15 largest economies—which make up three-quarters of the world economy—are the United States, China, Japan, India, Germany, United Kingdom, France, Italy, Brazil, Russia, Spain, Canada, South Korea, Mexico and Indonesia.[8]

A few of these large states possess especially great military and economic strength and influence, and are sometimes called *great powers*. They are defined and discussed in Chapter 2. For realists, the *great-power system* may be defined as the set of relationships among great powers, and their rules and patterns of interaction (a subset of the

---

[7] Gianfranco Poggi, *The State: Its Nature, Development, and Prospects* (Palo Alto, CA: Stanford UP, 1991). Hendrik Spruyt, *The Sovereign State and Its Competitors: An Analysis of Systems Change* (Princeton, NJ: Princeton UP, 1994).

[8] GDP is the total of goods and services produced by a nation; it is very close to the gross national product (GNP), which many international organizations and governments now describe as Gross National Income, or GNI. Such data are difficult to compare across nations with different currencies, economic systems and levels of development. In particular, comparisons of GDP in capitalist and socialist economies, or in rich and poor countries, should be treated cautiously. GDP data used in this book are mostly from the World Bank. GDP data are adjusted through time and across countries for "purchasing-power parity" or PPP (how much a given amount of money can buy).

international system). Great powers have special ways of behaving and of treating each other that do not apply to other states. The most powerful of great powers, those with truly global influence, have been called *superpowers*. This term generally meant the United States and the Soviet Union during the Cold War, but most IR scholars now consider the United States to be the world's only superpower (if indeed it still is one). Countries such as Canada are sometimes described as middle powers: too small to be great powers, but too big to be marginal. Smaller and weaker states also are important in IR, but taken singly most of them do not affect outcomes in IR to nearly the extent that major states or middle powers do.

Nonstate Actors

National governments may be important actors in IR, but they are strongly conditioned, constrained and influenced by a variety of actors that are not states. These **nonstate actors** may be grouped in several categories. First, groups and interests exist within states that attempt to influence the state's foreign policy. These are *substate actors*. For instance, the American automobile and tobacco industries have distinct interests in American foreign economic policy (to sell cars or cigarettes abroad; to reduce imports of competing products made abroad). They are politically mobilized to influence those policies through political action committees, lobbying and other means. Similarly, the Canadian fishing industry tries to influence the Canadian government to enforce fishing quotas against foreign fishers. They do not want to see their own conservation efforts lost to overfishing by other countries in or near Canadian waters.

> **nonstate actors** Actors other than state governments who operate either below the level of the state (that is, within states) or across state borders.

The actions of substate economic actors—companies, consumers, workers, investors—help to create the context of economic activity in which international political events play out, and within which governments must operate. Day in and day out, people extract natural resources, produce and consume goods and buy and sell products and services. These activities of substate actors take place in what is now clearly a world economy—a global exchange of goods and services woven together by a worldwide network of communication and culture.

Increasingly, then, actors operating below the state level also operate across state borders, becoming *transnational actors*. Businesses that buy, sell or invest in a variety of countries are a good example. The decision of a company to do business with or in another state changes the relationship between the two states, making them—especially from the perspective of liberal

IN THE ACTION
Nonstate actors participate in IR alongside states, although generally in less central roles. Nongovernmental organizations (NGOs) such as the Catholic Church are becoming increasingly active in IR. Here, Pope Benedict meets Iraq's Jalal Talabani, 2005.

pluralists—more interdependent and creating a new context for decisions the governments make about each other.

The thousands of multinational corporations (MNCs) are important transnational actors. The interests of a large company doing business globally do not correspond with any one state's interests. Such a company may sometimes even act against its home government's policies. MNCs often control greater resources, and operate internationally with greater efficiency, than many small states. MNCs may prop up (or even help to create) friendly foreign governments, as the United Fruit Company did in Guatemala in the 1950s and the International Telephone and Telegraph Company did in Chile in the early 1970s. But MNCs also provide poor states with much-needed foreign investment and tax revenues. MNCs in turn depend on states to provide protection, well-regulated markets and a stable political environment. MNCs as international actors receive special attention in Chapters 10 and 13.

nongovernmental organizations (NGOs)
Transnational groups or entities (such as the Catholic Church, Greenpeace and the International Olympic Committee) that interact with states, multinational corporations (MNCs), other NGOs and intergovernmental organizations (IGOs).

Another type of transnational actor is the **nongovernmental organization (NGO),** thousands of which pull and tug at international relations every day. These private organizations, some of considerable size and resources, interact with states, MNCs and other NGOs. Increasingly NGOs are being recognized, in the UN and other forums, as legitimate actors along with states, though they are not considered equal to them. Examples of NGOs include the Catholic Church, Greenpeace and the International Olympic Committee. Some of these groups have a political purpose, some a humanitarian one, some an economic or technical one. Sometimes NGOs combine efforts through transnational advocacy networks.[9] NGOs do not follow a single pattern.

global social movements
Nonstate groups that organize transnationally, usually to protest around an issue or event (such as the environment, peace, women's issues, human rights and globalization).

Global social movements are also increasingly important actors in international relations. These include antiwar protesters, environmental activists, women's movements, human rights activists and the many elements associated with the antiglobalization protests that were seen in Seattle, Washington, Québec City, Prague, Genoa and Heiligendamm. Social movements are not formally institutionalized in the way that NGOs are, although some social movements have transformed into formal NGOs (for example, Greenpeace had its roots in environmental activism). Social movements have a variety of goals: some are aimed at reforming current global practices, others at completely transforming the system. Social movement activists successfully shut down World Trade Organization talks in Seattle in 1999—a dramatic example of the impact such movements can have.

Contemporary *international terrorist networks* are not NGOs or social movements, but they operate in similar ways—interacting both with states and directly with relevant populations and institutions. The spectacularly destructive attacks on the United States on September 11, 2001, demonstrated the increasing power that technology gives terrorists as nonstate actors. Just as Greenpeace can travel to remote locations and beam video of its environmental actions to the world, or social movements can organize thousands to arrive at world trade talks through email and websites, so too can the al Qaeda network place suicide bombers in world cities, coordinate their operations and finances through the internet and global banking system, and reach a global audience with videotaped appeals. "Global reach," once an exclusive capability of great powers, now is available to many others, for better and worse.

---

[9] Margaret E. Keck and Kathryn Sikkink, *Activists Beyond Borders: Advocacy Networks in International Politics* (Ithaca, NY: Cornell UP, 1998). Ann M. Florini, ed., *The Third Force: The Rise of Transnational Civil Society* (Washington, DC: Carnegie Endowment for International Peace, 2000). Union of International Associations, *Yearbook of International Associations 2000–2001* (Munich: K.G. Saur Verlag).

Finally, states often take actions through, within or in the context of **intergovernmental organizations (IGOs)**—organizations whose members are national governments. The UN and its agencies are IGOs. So are most of the world's economic coordinating institutions, such as the World Bank and the International Monetary Fund (IMF). IGOs fulfill a variety of functions, and they vary in size from just a few states to virtually the whole UN membership. For example, the Organization of Petroleum Exporting Countries (OPEC) seeks to coordinate the production and pricing policies of its 11 member states. The World Trade Organization (WTO) sponsors negotiations on lowering trade barriers worldwide and enforces trade rules.

Military alliances such as NATO and political groupings such as the African Union are also IGOs. The hundreds of IGOs now operating on the world scene (several times more than the number of states) all have been created by their member states to provide some function that those states find useful.

Together, IGOs and NGOs are referred to simply as international organizations (IOs). By one count there are now over 25 000 NGOs and over 5000 IGOs. In this world of interlaced connections, of substate actors and transnational actors, states are still important. To some extent, however, they are being gradually pushed aside as corporations, groups and individuals deal ever more directly with each other across borders, and as the world economy becomes globally integrated (see Chapter 11).

> **intergovernmental organizations (IGOs)** Organizations (such as the United Nations and its agencies) whose members are state governments.

The Information Revolution

Both state and nonstate actors are strongly affected by the current revolution in information technologies. The new information-intensive world promises to reshape international relations profoundly. Technological change dramatically affects actors' relative capabilities and even preferences. Nobody knows where those changes will take us. Already, information capabilities are the central motor of "globalization." Telecommunications and computerization allow economics, politics and culture alike to operate on a global scale as never before. The ramifications of information technology for various facets of IR will be discussed in each chapter of this book.

Levels of Analysis

The many actors involved concurrently in IR contribute to the complexity of competing explanations and theories. One way scholars of IR deal with this multiplicity of influences, actors and processes is to categorize them into different *levels of analysis* (see Table 1.1). IR scholars have proposed various level-of-analysis schemes, most often with three main levels (and sometimes a few sublevels between), including an individual level, state level and system level.[10]

The *individual* level of analysis concerns the perceptions, choices and actions of individual human beings. Great leaders influence the course of history, as do individual citizens, thinkers, soldiers and voters. Without Lenin, it is said, there might have been no Soviet Union. If a few more university students had voted for Nixon rather than Kennedy in the razor-close 1960 election, the Cuban Missile Crisis might have ended differently. United Nations peacekeeping may never have evolved without Canada's Lester B. Pearson.

---

[10] J. David Singer, "The Level-of-Analysis Problem in International Relations," *World Politics* 14.1 (1961): 77–92. Kenneth Waltz, *Man, the State and War* (NY: Columbia UP, 1959).

Table 1.1 Levels of Analysis

Many influences affect the course of international relations. Levels of analysis provide a framework for categorizing these influences and thus for suggesting various explanations of international events. Examples include

Global Level

North-South gap	Technological change
World regions	Information revolution
European imperialism	Global telecommunications
UN System	Worldwide scientific and business
World environment	communities

Interstate Level

Power	IGOs
Balance of power	Diplomacy
Alliance formation and dissolution	Summit meetings
Wars	Bargaining
Treaties	Reciprocity
Trade agreements	

Domestic Level

Nationalism	Political parties and elections
Ethnic conflict	Public opinion
Type of government	Gender
Democracy	Economic sectors and industries
Dictatorship	Military-industrial complex
Domestic coalitions	Foreign policy bureaucracies

Individual Level

Great leaders	Learning
Crazy leaders	Assassinations, accidents of history
Decision-making in crises	Citizens' participation (voting, rebelling,
Psychology of perception and decision	going to war, etc.)

The study of foreign policy decision-making, which is discussed in Chapter 5, pays special attention to individual-level explanations of IR.

The *domestic* (or *state* or *societal*) level of analysis concerns the aggregations of individuals within states that influence state actions in the international arena. Such aggregations include interest groups, political organizations and government agencies. These groups operate differently (with different international effects) in various kinds of societies and states. For instance, democracies and dictatorships may act differently from one another, and democracies may act differently in an election year than they do at other times. The politics of ethnic conflict and nationalism, bubbling up from within states, play an increasingly important role in relations among states. Economic sectors within states, including the military-industrial sector, can influence governments to take actions in the international arena that are good for business. Within governments, foreign policy agencies often fight bureaucratic battles over policy decisions.

The Information Revolution

In each chapter, "Information Revolution" boxes pose critical-thinking questions about the impacts of rapid changes in information technology on IR. To explore the questions, go to www.pearsoned.ca/goldstein.

The *interstate* (or *international* or *systemic*) level of analysis concerns the influence of the international system on outcomes. This level of analysis therefore focuses on the interactions of states themselves, without regard to their internal makeup or the particular individuals who lead them. The interstate level pays attention to the geographic locations of states and their relative power positions in the international system.

A fourth level can also be added—the *global* level of analysis.[11] It seeks to explain international outcomes in terms of global trends and forces that transcend the interactions of states themselves. This level of analysis deserves particular attention because of the growing importance of global-level processes. The evolution of human technology, the global political economy, certain worldwide beliefs and our human relationship to the natural environment are all processes that influence international relations at a global level. The global level is also increasingly the focus of IR scholars studying transnational integration through worldwide scientific, technical and business communities (see Chapter 11). Another pervasive global influence is the lingering effect of historical European imperialism—Europe's conquest of Latin America, Asia and Africa (see "Imperialism, 1500–the Present" later in this chapter).

Levels of analysis offer varying explanations for international events. For example, there are many possible explanations for the 1999 Kosovo War between Serbia and NATO. At an individual level, the war might be attributed to the irrational gambles and mistaken judgments of Serbia's leader, Slobodan Milosevic. At a domestic level, the war could be attributed to the fragmentation of Yugoslavia's multiethnic federation, which left Kosovo—and its largely Albanian population—as a province of the aggressively nationalistic Serbia. At the interstate level, the war might be attributed to the balance-of-power process in which a state (Serbia) eventually galvanizes a countercoalition of states (NATO) to contain it. At a global level, the war could be attributed to Serbia's resistance to economic incorporation into Western capitalism, a process that had begun over a decade before with IMF austerity measures.[12]

Although IR scholars often focus their study on one level of analysis, other levels bear on a problem simultaneously. There is no single correct level for a given question of global politics, and moreover, levels usually overlap one another. Levels of analysis suggest multiple explanations and approaches to consider in trying to understand a given event. They remind scholars and students to look beyond the immediate and superficial aspects of an event to explore the possible influences of more distant causes. IR is such a complex

[11] Robert C. North, *War, Peace, Survival: Global Politics and Conceptual Synthesis* (Boulder, CO: Westview, 1990).

[12] Paul Phillips, "Why Were We Bombing Yugoslavia?" *Studies in Political Economy* 60 (Autumn 1999): 85–98.

process that there is rarely any single cause that completely explains an outcome. Table 1.1 lists some of the processes operating at each level of analysis. Note that the processes at higher levels tend to operate more slowly than those at lower levels. Individuals come and go from office often, while the structure of the international system or the nature of global capitalism changes more slowly.

The rest of this chapter explores two contextual aspects of globalization that shape the issue areas discussed in subsequent chapters—(1) relations among the world's major regions, especially the rich North and poor South; and (2) the evolution of the international system over the past century.

World Geography

International relations takes place in the context of geography. To highlight the insights afforded by a global level of analysis, this book is based on a division of the world into nine regions. These *world regions* differ from each other in the number of states they contain and in each region's particular mix of cultures, geographical realities and languages, but each represents a geographical corner of the world, and together they reflect the overall larger divisions.

North-South gap The disparity in resources (income, wealth and power) between the industrialized, relatively rich countries of the West (and the former Communist bloc) and poorer countries in Africa, the Middle East and much of Asia and Latin America.

The global **North-South gap** between the relatively rich industrialized countries of the North and the relatively poor countries of the South is the most important geographical element at the global level of analysis. The division of regions used in this book have been drawn to separate (with a few exceptions) the rich countries from the poor. The North includes both the West (the rich countries of North America, Western Europe and Japan) and the old East (the former Soviet Union and its bloc of allies).[13] The South includes Latin America, Africa, the Middle East and much of Asia. The South is sometimes called the "third world" (third after the so-called "first world" of the West and the "second world" of the former Communist bloc)—however, this is a term that, although still used by many people, is considered problematic. Likewise, countries in the South are referred to as "developing" countries or "less-developed" countries (LDCs), in contrast to the "developed" countries of the North. Each of these terms describes the global South as "less than" the North (" *third* World," "*less*-developed country"). This textbook will use the terms global South and global North to describe these areas of the world.

Several criteria beyond income levels help distinguish major geographically contiguous regions. Countries with similar economic levels, cultures and languages have been kept together where possible. States with a history of interaction, including historical empires or trading zones, are grouped together. Finally, countries that might possibly unify in the future—notably South Korea with North Korea and China with Taiwan—are kept in the same region. Of course, no scheme works perfectly, and some states are pulled toward two regions.

The overall world regions are shown in Figure 1.1. The global North is divided into *North America* (the United States and Canada); *Western Europe* (mainly European Union

---

[13] Note that geographical designations such as the "West" and the "Middle East" are European-centred. From Korea, for example, China and Russia are to the west and Japan and the United States are to the east. On world-level geography, see Michael Kidron, Ronald Segal and Angela Wilson, *The State of the World Atlas*, 5th ed. (NY: Penguin, 1995); Andrew Boyd, *An Atlas of World Affairs*, 9th ed. (NY: Routledge, 1994). On the synthesis of world-level geography and social and political phenomena, see Dan Smith, *The State of War and Peace Atlas* (Penguin, 1996); and Joni Seager, *The State of Women in the World Atlas* (Penguin, 1997).

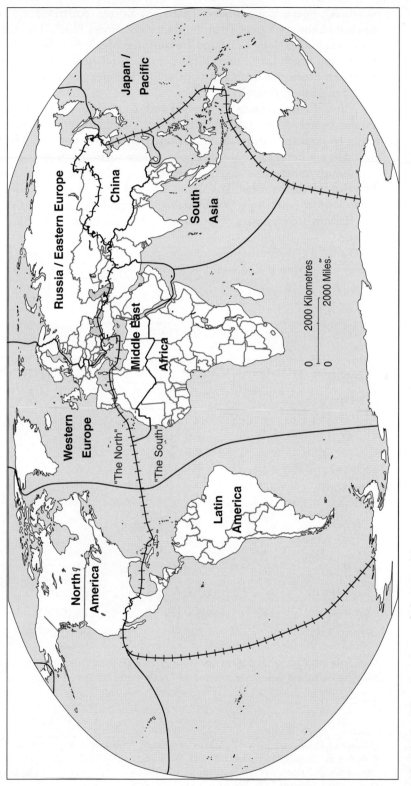

Figure 1.1 Nine Regions of the World

members); *Japan/Pacific* (mainly Japan, the Koreas, Australia and New Zealand); and *Russia and Eastern Europe* (mainly the former Soviet bloc). The South is divided into *China* (including Hong Kong and Taiwan); the *Middle East* (from North Africa through Turkey and Iran); *Latin America* (Mexico, Central America, the Caribbean and South America); *South Asia* (Afghanistan through Indonesia and the Philippines); and *Africa* (below the Sahara desert).

Most of these regions correspond with commonly used geographical names, but a few notes may help. *East Asia* refers to China, Japan and Korea. *Southeast Asia* refers to countries from Burma through Indonesia and the Philippines. Russia is considered a European state, although a large section (Siberia) is in Asia. The *Pacific Rim* usually means East and Southeast Asia, Siberia and the Pacific coast of North America and Latin America.[14] *South Asia* only sometimes includes parts of Southeast Asia. Narrow definitions of the *Middle East* exclude both North Africa and Turkey. The *Balkans* are the states of southeastern Europe, bounded by Slovenia, Romania and Greece.

Table 1.2 shows the approximate population and economic size (GDP) of each region in relation to the world as a whole. As the table indicates, income levels per

Table 1.2 Comparison of World Regions

Region	Population (Millions)	GDP (Trillion $)	GDP per Capita (Dollars)
The North			
North America	300	$13	$43,000
Western Europe	400	12	30,000
Japan/Pacific	200	6	26,000
Russia & E. Europe	400	4	7,000
The South			
China	1,300	8	6,000
Middle East	400	2	6,000
Latin America	500	5	9,000
South Asia	2,000	7	3,400
Africa	700	2	2,400
Total North	**1,300 (21%)**	**35 (59%)**	**27,000**
Total South	**4,900 (79%)**	**25 (41%)**	**5,000**
World Total	**6,200**	**$60**	**$9,700**

Note: Data adjusted for purchasing-power parity. 2004 GDP estimates (in 2005 dollars) are from Table 1.2; those for Russia and Eastern Europe, and for China, should be treated especially cautiously.

---

[14] James C. Hsiung, ed., *Asia Pacific in the New World Politics* (Boulder, CO: Rienner, 1993). Gerald Segal, *Rethinking the Pacific* (NY: Oxford UP, 1991). Derek McDougall, *The International Politics of the New Asia Pacific* (Boulder, CO: Rienner, 1997). Fu-Chen Lo and Yue-man Yeung, eds., *Emerging World Cities in Pacific Asia* (Tokyo: UN University Press, 1997).

capita are, overall, about five times higher in the North than in the South. *The North contains only 20 percent of the world's people but 60 percent of its goods and services.* The other 80 percent of the world's population, in the South, have only 40 percent of the goods and services.

Within the region of the global North, Russia and Eastern Europe lag behind in income levels, and suffered declines in the 1990s. In the global South, the Middle East, Latin America and (more recently) China have achieved somewhat higher income levels than have Africa and South Asia, which remain extremely poor. Even in higher-income regions, income is distributed quite unevenly and many people remain very poor. Some observers have noted that "first world" and "third world" divisions tend to ignore the ways in which there are "third worlds" in otherwise "first world" countries, and vice versa.[15] Note that more than half of the world's population lives in the densely populated (and poor) regions of South Asia and China.

IR scholars have no single explanation of the tremendous North-South gap in wealth and poverty (see Chapter 13). Some see it as part of a natural process of uneven growth in the world economy. Others tie it to the history of imperialism by European states, as well as by Russia, the United States and Japan. Some see the gap as a reflection of racism—the North is predominantly white whereas most of the South populations are nonwhite.

Using the nine world regions as an organizing framework, the world's states and territories are listed in Table 1.3, with an estimate of the total size of each state's economy (GDP). Reference maps with greater detail appear after the Subject Index.

Geographic divisions of the world, based on either territory or GDP, do not tell us everything there is to know about global politics. No single map or table would tell us all that we need to know, but different types of maps can signal different ways to think about how the world is configured. In Figure 1.2 (pp. 22–23), the representation of women in governments around the world, as of 2002, is depicted. This map is interesting for a number of reasons, not least because it challenges some of the assumptions held by people living in the North. Notice that many countries of the South have equal or better representation of women in government than do countries in the North. According to this map, for example, Botswana, Tanzania, Angola and Peru all have more women in government than the United States; Malawi, Mozambique, Uganda, Argentina and Rwanda have more women in government than both the U.S. and Canada. Maps such as this one provide us with information about different parts of the world, and also confront stereotypes that are associated with some of the world's traditional geographic and economic divisions.

Although geography provides one context in which IR takes place, history provides another. The world as we perceive it developed over many years, step by step. The past 500 years, known as the "modern age," are of special interest in IR. This has been the age of the international system of sovereign states. The remainder of this chapter briefly reviews the historical development of that system and its context. Special attention is given to the relations between Europe and the rest of the world, where the roots of the present North-South gap can be found.

---

[15] Chandra Talpade Mohanty, "Women Workers and Capitalist Scripts: Ideologies of Domination, Common Interests and the Politics of Solidarity," *Feminist Genealogies, Colonial Legacies, Democratic Futures*, ed. M. Jacqui Alexander and Chandra Talpade Mohanty (New York: Routledge, 1997) 3–29.

Table 1.3 States and Territories with Estimated Total 2004 GDP
(in Billions of 2005 U.S. Dollars)

North America

United States	12,000	Canada	1,000	Bahamas	5

Western Europe

Germany[a]	2,400	Switzerland	300	Luxembourg[a]	30
Britain[a]	1,900	Austria[a]	300	Iceland	10
France[a]	1,800	Portugal[a]	200	Malta[a]	8
Italy[a]	1,700	Greece[a]	200	Andorra	1
Spain[a]	1,000	Denmark[a]	200	Monaco	1
Netherlands[a]	500	Norway	200	Liechtenstein	1
Belgium[a]	300	Finland[a]	200	San Marino	1
Sweden[a]	300	Ireland[a]	200		

Japan/Pacific

Japan	3,900	Guam/Marianas[b]	3	Nauru	0
South Korea	1,000	Solomon Islands	1	Marshall Islands	0
Australia	600	Samoa	1	Palau	0
New Zealand	100	Vanuatu	1	Kiribati	0
North Korea	20	Tonga	1	Tuvalu	0
Papua New Guinea	20	Micronesia	0		
Fiji	5	American Samoa[b]	0		

Russia and Eastern Europe

Russia[c]	1,400	Croatia	60	Albania	20
Poland[a]	500	Uzbekistan[c]	50	Georgia[c]	10
Ukraine[c]	300	Lithuania[a]	50	Macedonia	10
Czech Republic[a]	200	Slovenia[a]	40	Armenia[c]	10
Romania	200	Azerbaijan[c]	40	Kyrgyzstan[c]	10
Hungary[a]	200	Turkmenistan[c]	40	Tajikistan[c]	8
Kazakhstan[c]	100	Bosnia and Herzegovina	30	Moldova[c]	7
Slovakia[a]	80	Serbia-Montenegro	30	Mongolia	5
Belarus[c]	70	Latvia[a]	30		
Bulgaria	60	Estonia[a]	20		

China

China	7,300	Hong Kong[b]	300	Macau[b]	9
Taiwan[b]	600				

Middle East

Turkey	600	Tunisia	80	Lebanon	30
Iran	500	Iraq	70	Jordan	30
Saudi Arabia	300	Syria	70	Qatar	20
Egypt	300	United Arab Emirates	70	Yemen	20
Algeria	200	Libya	50	Cyprus[a]	20
Israel/Palestine	200	Kuwait	50	Bahrain	10
Morocco/W. Sahara	100	Oman	40		

Latin America

Brazil	1,500	Uruguay	30	Netherlands Antilles[b]	2
Mexico	1,000	Paraguay	30	Virgin Islands[b]	2
Argentina	500	Bolivia	30	Bermuda[b]	2
Colombia	300	Cuba	30	Suriname	2
Chile	200	Panama	20	French Guiana[b]	1
Venezuela	200	Honduras	20	St. Lucia	1
Peru	200	Trinidad & Tobago	20	Belize	1
Puerto Rico[b]	80	Nicaragua	20	Antigua & Barbuda	1
Dominican Republic	70	Haiti	20	Grenada	1
Guatemala	50	Jamaica	10	St. Vincent & Grenadines	1
Ecuador	50	Martinique[b]	5	St. Kitts & Nevis	1
Costa Rica	40	Barbados	5	Dominica	0
El Salvador	40	Guyana	3		

South Asia

India	3,400	Vietnam	200	Laos	10
Indonesia	800	Singapore	100	Brunei	7
Thailand	500	Sri Lanka	80	Bhutan	2
Philippines	400	Burma (Myanmar)	70	Maldives	1
Pakistan	300	Nepal	40	East Timor	0
Bangladesh	300	Cambodia	30		
Malaysia	300	Afghanistan	20		

Africa

South Africa	500	Mauritius	20	Lesotho	5
Nigeria	200	Botswana	20	Central African Republic	5
Sudan	70	Burkina Faso	20	Somalia	5
Ethiopia	60	Equatorial Guinea	20	Eritea	5
Ghana	50	Chad	20	Sierra Leone	5
Cameroon	40	Mali	10	Congo Republic	4
Democratic Congo	40	Rwanda	10	Reunion[b]	3
Kenya	40	Niger	10	Cape Verde	3
Uganda	40	Namibia	10	Liberia	3
Angola	30	Zambia	10	Gambia	3
Côte d'Ivoire (Ivory Coast)	30	Gabon	9	Djibouti	2
Zimbabwe	30	Togo	9	Guinea-Bissau	1
Tanzania	30	Benin	8	Comoros Islands	1
Mozambique	20	Malawi	7	Seychelles	1
Guinea	20	Mauritania	7	São Tomé & Principe	0
Senegal	20	Swaziland	6		
Madagascar	20	Burundi	5		

[a]European Union.

[b]Nonmember of UN (colony or territory).

[c]Commonwealth of Independent States (former USSR).

Note: GDP data are inexact by nature. Estimates for Russia and Eastern Europe, China, and other nonmarket or transitional economies are particularly suspect and should be used cautiously. Numbers below 0.5 are listed as 0.

Sources: Data are authors' estimates based on World Bank. Data are at purchasing-power parity. See footnote 9 on p. 12.

Women in Government

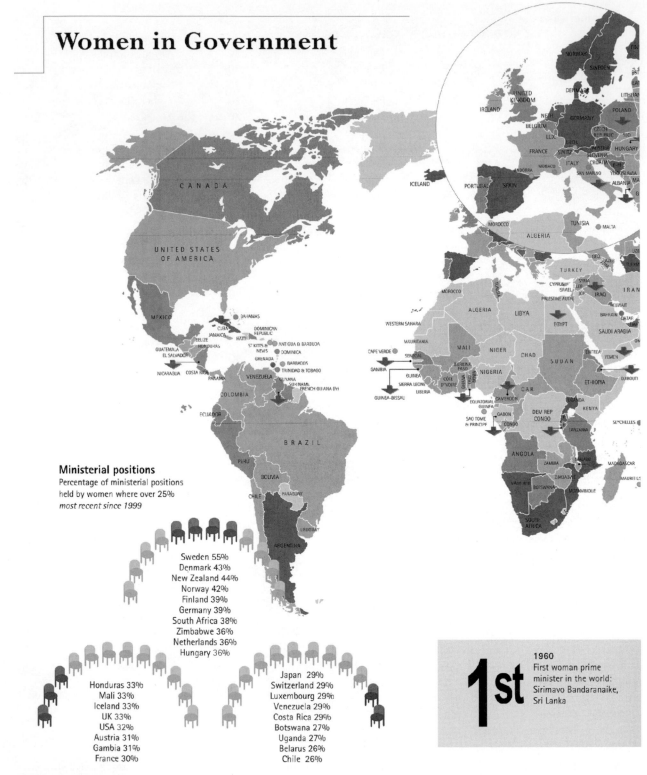

Ministerial positions
Percentage of ministerial positions
held by women where over 25%
most recent since 1999

Sweden 55%
Denmark 43%
New Zealand 44%
Norway 42%
Finland 39%
Germany 39%
South Africa 38%
Zimbabwe 36%
Netherlands 36%
Hungary 36%

Honduras 33%
Mali 33%
Iceland 33%
UK 33%
USA 32%
Austria 31%
Gambia 31%
France 30%

Japan 29%
Switzerland 29%
Luxembourg 29%
Venezuela 29%
Costa Rica 29%
Botswana 27%
Uganda 27%
Belarus 26%
Chile 26%

1st
1960
First woman prime
minister in the world:
Sirimavo Bandaranaike,
Sri Lanka

Figure 1.2 Women in Government

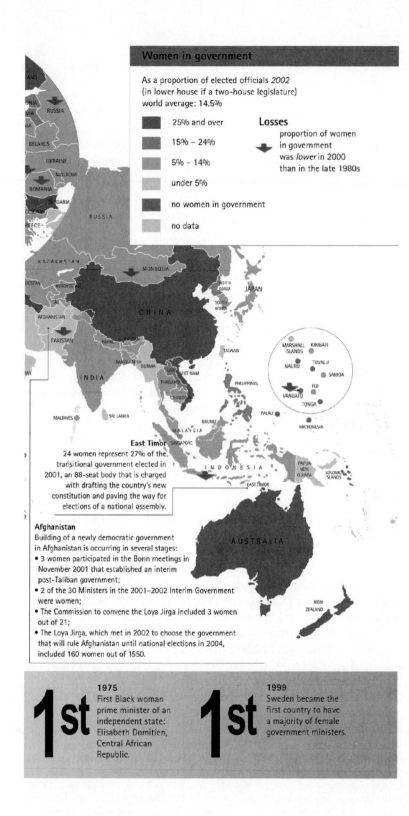

Women in government

As a proportion of elected officials *2002*
(in lower house if a two-house legislature)
world average: 14.5%

- 25% and over
- 15% – 24%
- 5% – 14%
- under 5%
- no women in government
- no data

Losses
proportion of women
in government
was *lower* in 2000
than in the late 1980s

East Timor
24 women represent 27% of the
transitional government elected in
2001, an 88-seat body that is charged
with drafting the country's new
constitution and paving the way for
elections of a national assembly.

Afghanistan
Building of a newly democratic government
in Afghanistan is occurring in several stages:
- 3 women participated in the Bonn meetings in
  November 2001 that established an interim
  post-Taliban government;
- 2 of the 30 Ministers in the 2001–2002 Interim Government
  were women;
- The Commission to convene the Loya Jirga included 3 women
  out of 21;
- The Loya Jirga, which met in 2002 to choose the government
  that will rule Afghanistan until national elections in 2004,
  included 160 women out of 1550.

1st
1975
First Black woman
prime minister of an
independent state:
Elisabeth Domitien,
Central African
Republic.

1st
1999
Sweden became the
first country to have
a majority of female
government ministers.

HISTORY

The turn of the millennium found the world breaking free of the logic of the two world wars and the Cold War that dominated the twentieth century. New possibilities are emerging everywhere, both good and bad. With so much change occurring, one might wonder whether history is still relevant to understanding the world. It is. The basic structures and principles of international relations, even in the current era, are deeply rooted in historical developments. Our discussion of these developments—necessarily only a series of brief sketches—begins with a long-term perspective and gradually focuses on more recent history.

World Civilizations to the Present Day

The present-day international system is the product of Western civilization, centred in Europe. The international system as we know it developed among the European states of 300 to 500 years ago, was exported to the rest of the world, and has in the past century subsumed virtually all of the world's territory into sovereign states. It is important to keep in mind that other civilizations existed in other world regions for centuries before Europeans ever arrived. These cultural traditions continue to exert an influence on IR, especially when their styles and expectations come into play in international interactions.[16]

North American students should note that much of the world differs from North America in that before Europeans arrived, cultures in this region did not have extensive agriculture, large cities, irrigation and the other trappings of "civilization." Its indigenous cultures were largely exterminated or pushed aside by European settlers. Today's North American population is overwhelmingly descended from immigrants. In other regions, however, the European conquest followed many centuries of advanced civilization—more advanced than that of Europe in the case of China, India, Japan, the Middle East and Central America. In most of the world (especially in Africa and Asia), European empires integrated indigenous populations rather than pushing them aside. Today's populations are descended primarily from indigenous inhabitants, not immigrants. These populations are therefore more strongly rooted in their own cultural traditions and history than are most Canadians or Americans.

European civilization evolved from roots in the eastern Mediterranean—Egypt, Mesopotamia (Iraq) and especially Greece. Of special importance for IR is the classical period of Greek city-states around 400 B.C., which exemplified some of the fundamental principles of interstate power politics (reflected in Thucydides's classic account of the Peloponnesian Wars between Athens and Sparta). By that time, states were carrying out sophisticated trade relations and warfare in a broad swath of the world from the Mediterranean through India to East Asia. Much of this area came under Greek influence following the conquests of Alexander the Great (around 300 B.C.), then was ruled by the Roman Empire (around A.D. 1), followed by an Arab caliphate (around A.D. 600).

---

[16] Isaac Asimov, *Asimov's Chronology of the World: The History of the World from the Big Bang to Modern Times* (NY: HarperCollins, 1991). Geoffrey Barraclough, ed., *The Times Atlas of World History* (Maplewood, NJ: Hammond, 1978). William Hardy McNeill, *The Pursuit of Power* (Chicago: U Chicago P, 1982). Janet Abu-Lughod, *Before European Hegemony: The World System, A.D. 1250–1350* (NY: Oxford UP, 1989). Marshall G. S. Hodgson, *The Venture of Islam: Conscience and History in a World Civilization* (Chicago: U Chicago P, 1974). Adda Bozeman, *Politics and Culture in International History* (Princeton, NJ: Princeton UP, 1960). Raymond Cohen and Raymond Westbrook, eds., *Amarna Diplomacy: The Beginnings of International Relations* (Baltimore: Johns Hopkins UP, 1999).

China remained an independent civilization throughout this time. In the "warring states" period, at about the same era as the Greek city-states, sophisticated states (organized as territorial political units) first used warfare as an instrument of power politics. This is described in the classic work *The Art of War*, by Sun Tzu.[17] By about A.D. 800, when Europe was in its "dark ages" and Arab civilization in its golden age, China under the T'ang dynasty was a highly advanced civilization quite independent of Western influence. Japan, strongly influenced by the Chinese, flowered on its own in the centuries leading up to the Shoguns (around A.D. 1200). Japan isolated itself from Western influence under the Tokugawa shogunate for several centuries, ending after 1850 when the Meiji restoration began Japanese industrialization and international trade. Latin America also had flourishing civilizations—the Mayans around A.D. 100 to 900 and the Aztecs and Incas around 1200—independent of Western influence until conquered by Spain in approximately 1500. In Africa, the great kingdoms flowered after A.D. 1000 (and as early as A.D. 600 in Ghana) and were highly developed when European slave traders arrived on the scene around 1500.

The Arab caliphate of about A.D. 600 to 1200 plays a special role in the international relations of the Middle East. Almost the entire region was once united under this empire, which arose and spread with the religion of Islam. European invasions—the Crusades—were driven out. In the sixteenth to nineteenth centuries, the eastern Mediterranean came under the Turkish-based Ottoman Empire, which gave relative autonomy to local cultures if they paid tribute. This history of empires continued to influence the region in the twentieth century. For example, *Pan-Arabism* (or Arab nationalism), especially strong in the 1950s and 1960s, saw the region as potentially one nation again, with a single religion, language and identity. During the Gulf War, Iraq's Saddam Hussein likened himself to the ruler who drove away Crusaders a thousand years before. Today, the strength of Islamic fundamentalism throughout the region, as well as the emotions attached to the Arab-Israeli conflict, reflect the continuing importance of the historic Arab empire.

Europe itself began its rise to world dominance around 1500, after the Renaissance (when the Greek and Roman classics were rediscovered). The Italian city-states of the period employed the rules of interstate power politics, as described by an adviser to Renaissance princes named Niccolò Machiavelli. Feudal units were merged into large territorial nation-states under single authoritarian rulers (monarchs). The military revolution of the period created the first modern armies.[18] European monarchs put cannons on sailing ships and began to "discover" the world. The development of the international system, of imperialism, of trade and war, were all greatly accelerated by the *Industrial Revolution* after 1750. Ultimately, the European conquest of the world brought about a single world civilization, albeit with regional variants and subcultures.[19]

---

[17] Sun Tzu, *The Art of War*, trans. Samuel B. Griffith (NY: Oxford UP, 1963).

[18] Michael Howard, *War in European History* (NY: Oxford UP, 1976). Geoffrey Parker, *The Military Revolution: Military Innovation and the Rise of the West, 1500–1800*, 2nd ed. (NY: Cambridge UP, 1996). Jeremy Black, ed., *The Origins of War in Early Modern Europe* (Edinburgh: Donald, 1987). Janice E. Thomson, *Mercenaries, Pirates, and Sovereigns: State-Building and Extraterritorial Violence in Early Modern Europe* (Princeton, NJ: Princeton UP, 1994).

[19] Geoffrey Barraclough, *An Introduction to Contemporary History* (NY: Penguin, 1964). Carlo M. Cipolla, *Guns, Sails and Empires* (NY: Pantheon, 1965). Perry Anderson, *Lineages of the Absolutist State* (London: N.L.B., 1974). Fernand Braudel, *Civilization and Capitalism, 15th–18th Century*, 3 vols. (NY: Harper & Row, 1984). Hedley Bull and Adam Watson, eds., *The Expansion of International Society* (NY: Oxford UP, 1984).

In recent decades, world regions formerly dominated by Europe have gained independence, with their own sovereign states participating in the international system. Independence came earlier in the Americas (around 1800). In Latin America, most of the nineteenth century was absorbed with wars, border changes, the rise and fall of dictatorships and republics, a chronic foreign debt problem, revolutions and recurrent military incursions by European powers and the United States to recover debts.

The Great-Power System, 1500–the Present

The modern state system is often dated (particularly by realists) from the *Peace of Westphalia* in 1648, which established the principles of independent, sovereign states that continue to shape the international system today. These rules of state relations did not, however, originate at Westphalia; they took form in Europe in the sixteenth century. Key to this system was the ability of one state, or a coalition of states, to balance the power of another so that it could not gobble up smaller units and create a universal empire.

This power-balancing system placed special importance on a handful of great powers with strong military capabilities, global interests and outlooks and intense interactions with each other. (Great powers are defined and discussed on pp. 65–67.) A system of great-power relations has existed since close to A.D. 1500, with the structure and rules of that system remaining fairly stable through time, although the particular members change. The structure is a balance of power among the six or so most powerful states, which form and break alliances, fight wars and make peace, letting no single state conquer the others.

The most powerful states in sixteenth-century Europe were Britain (England), France, Austria-Hungary and Spain. The Ottoman Empire (Turkey) recurrently fought with European powers, especially with Austria-Hungary. Today, that historic conflict between the (Islamic) Ottoman Empire and (Christian) Austria-Hungary is a source of ethnic conflict in the former Yugoslavia (the edge of the old Ottoman Empire).

In Europe, Austria-Hungary and Spain were allied under the control of the Hapsburg family, which also owned the territory of the Netherlands. The Hapsburg countries (which were Catholic) were defeated by mostly Protestant countries in northern Europe—France, Britain, Sweden and the newly independent Netherlands—in the *Thirty Years' War* of 1618–1648.[20] The 1648 Treaty of Westphalia established the basic rules that have defined the international system ever since—the sovereignty and territorial integrity of states as equal and independent members of an international system. Since then, states defeated in war might be stripped of some of their territories but were generally allowed to continue as independent states rather than being subsumed into the victorious state.

In the eighteenth century, the power of Britain increased as it industrialized, and Britain's great rival was France. Sweden, the Netherlands and the Ottoman Empire all declined in power, but Russia and later Prussia (the forerunner of modern-day Germany) emerged as major players. In the *Napoleonic Wars* (1803–1815), which followed the French Revolution, France was defeated by a coalition of Britain, the Netherlands, Austria-Hungary, Spain, Russia and Prussia. The *Congress of Vienna* (1815) ending that war reasserted the principles of state sovereignty in reaction to the challenges of the French Revolution and Napoleon's empire.[21] In the *Concert of Europe* that dominated the

---

[20] Theodore K. Rabb, ed., *The Thirty Years' War* (NY: UP of America, 1981).

[21] Henry A. Kissinger, *A World Restored* (1957; Boston: Houghton Mifflin, 1973).

following decades, the five most powerful states tried, with some success, to cooperate on major issues to prevent war—a possible precedent for today's UN Security Council. In this period, Britain became a balancer, joining alliances against whatever state emerged as the most powerful in Europe.

By the outset of the twentieth century, three new rising powers had appeared on the scene: the United States (which had become the world's largest economy), Japan and Italy. The great-power system became global rather than just European. Powerful states were industrializing, extending the scope of their world activities and the might of their militaries. After Prussia defeated Austria and France in wars, a larger Germany emerged to challenge Britain's position.[22] In *World War I* (1914–1918), Germany and Austria-Hungary were defeated by a coalition that included Britain, France, Russia, Italy and the United States. After a 20-year lull, Germany, Italy and Japan were defeated in *World War II* (1939–1945) by a coalition of the United States, Britain, France, Russia (the Soviet Union) and China. The five winners of World War II make up the permanent membership of today's UN Security Council.

After World War II, the United States and the Soviet Union, which had been allies in the war against Germany, became adversaries for 40 years in the Cold War. Europe was split into rival blocs—East and West—with Germany itself split into two states. The rest of the world became contested terrain where each bloc tried to gain allies or influence, often by sponsoring opposing sides in regional and civil wars. The end of the Cold War, marked by the collapse of the Soviet Union in 1991, returned the international system to a more cooperative arrangement of the great powers, somewhat similar to the Concert of Europe in the nineteenth century. However, new strains emerged among the European-American-Japanese "allies" once they no longer faced a common threat from the Soviet Union.[23] Some of those relations became particularly strained when the United States decided to invade Iraq in 2003 with the support of some of its allies (the U.K. and Japan, for example) but not others (Canada and France).

Imperialism, 1500–the Present

European imperialism (described more fully in Chapter 12) got its start in the fifteenth century with the development of oceangoing sailing ships, in which a small crew could transport a sizeable cargo over a long distance. Portugal pioneered the first voyages of exploration beyond Europe. Spain, France and Britain soon followed. With superior military technology, Europeans gained control of coastal cities and of supply outposts along major trade routes. Gradually this control extended further inland—first in Latin America, then North America and later throughout Asia and Africa.

In the sixteenth century, Spain and Portugal had extensive empires in Central America and Brazil, respectively. Britain and France had colonies in North America and the Caribbean. The imperialists bought slaves in Africa and shipped them to Mexico and Brazil, where they worked in tropical agriculture and mining silver and gold. The wealth produced was exported to Europe, where monarchs used it to buy armies and build states.

---

[22] William L. Langer, *European Alliances and Alignments, 1871–1890* (NY: Knopf, 1931).

[23] Daniel Unger and Paul Blackburn, eds., *Japan's Emerging Global Role* (Boulder, CO: Rienner, 1993). Tsuneo Akaha and Frank Langdon, eds., *Japan in the Posthegemonic World* (Boulder, CO: Rienner, 1993). Takashi Inoguchi and Daniel I. Okimoto, eds., *The Political Economy of Japan*. Vol. 2: *The Changing International Context* (Palo Alto, CA: Stanford UP, 1988).

These empires decimated indigenous populations and cultures, causing immense suffering. Over time, the economies of colonies developed with the creation of basic transportation and communication infrastructure, factories and so forth. However, these economies were often moulded to the needs of the colonizers rather than the local populations.

Decolonization began with the British colonists in the United States who declared independence in 1776. Most of Latin America gained independence a few decades later. The new states in North America and Latin America were, of course, still run by the descendants of Europeans—to the disadvantage of Native Americans and African slaves.

New colonies were still being acquired by Europe through the end of the nineteenth century, culminating in a scramble for colonies in Africa in the 1890s (resulting in arbitrary territorial divisions as competing European armies rushed inland from all sides). India became Britain's largest and most important colony in the nineteenth century. Latecomers such as Germany and Italy were frustrated to find few attractive territories remaining in the world when they tried to build overseas empires in the late nineteenth century. Ultimately, only a few non-European areas retained their independence: Japan, most of China, Iran, Turkey and a few others. Japan began building its own empire, as did the United States, at the end of the nineteenth century. China became weaker and its coastal regions fell under the domination, if not the formal control, of European powers.

In the wave of decolonization after World War II, it was not local colonists (as in the Americas) but indigenous populations in Asia and Africa who won independence. Decolonization continued through the mid-1970s until almost no European colonies remained. Most of the newly independent states have faced tremendous challenges and difficulties in the postcolonial era. Because long-established economic patterns continue despite political independence, some refer to the postcolonial era as *neocolonial*. Although the global North no longer imports slave labour from the South, it continues to rely on the South for cheap labour, energy and minerals and the products of tropical agriculture. However, the North in turn makes vital contributions in capital investment, technology transfer and foreign assistance (see Chapter 13).

The collapse of the Soviet Union and its bloc, which reduced Russia to its size of a century earlier, can be seen as an extension of the post–World War II wave of decolonization and self-determination. There, as in much of the global South, imperialism has left ethnic conflict in its wake as new political units come to terms with territorial divisions created in distant imperial capitals.

Nationalism, 1500–the Present

nationalism The identification with and devotion to the interests of one's nation. It usually involves a large group of people who share a national identity and often a language, culture, or ancestry.

Many people consider **nationalism**—devotion to the interests of one's nation—to be the most important force in world politics in the last two centuries. A nation is a population that shares an identity, usually including a language and culture. For instance, most of the 60 million inhabitants of France speak French, eat French cuisine, learn French history in school and are represented (for better or worse) by the national government in Paris. But nationality is a difficult concept to define precisely. To some extent, the extension of political control over large territories like France created a commonality necessary for nationhood—so it could be said that states create nations. At the same time, however, the perceived existence of a nation has often led to the creation of a corresponding state as a population wins sovereignty over its own affairs—nations creating states.

Around A.D. 1500, countries such as France and Austria began to bring entire nations together into single states. These new nation-states were very large and powerful; they overran smaller neighbours. Over time, many small territorial units were conquered and incorporated into nation-states.[24] Eventually the idea of nationalism itself became a powerful force and ultimately contributed to the disintegration of large, multinational states such as Austria-Hungary (in World War I), the Soviet Union and Yugoslavia.

The principle of *self-determination* implies that people who identify as a nation should have the right to form a state and exercise sovereignty over their affairs. Self-determination is a widely praised principle in international affairs today (not historically), though it is generally secondary to the principles of sovereignty (noninterference in other states' internal affairs) and territorial integrity, with which it frequently conflicts. Self-determination does not give groups the right to change international borders, even those imposed arbitrarily by colonialism, in order to unify a group with a common national identity. Generally, though not always, self-determination has been achieved by violence. When the borders of (perceived) nations do not match those of states, conflicts almost inevitably arise. Today such conflicts are widespread—in Northern Ireland, Québec, Israel-Palestine, India-Pakistan, Sri Lanka, Tibet, Sudan and many other places.[25] In some cases, these conflicts are addressed through democratic means; in others, through repression and violence.

The Netherlands helped to establish the principle of self-determination when it broke free of Spanish ownership around 1600 and set up a self-governing Dutch republic. The struggle over control of the Netherlands was a leading cause of the Thirty Years' War (1618–1648), in which states mobilized their populations in new ways. For instance, Sweden drafted one out of every ten men for long-term military service, while the Netherlands used the wealth derived from global trade to finance a standing professional army.

This process of popular mobilization intensified greatly in the French Revolution and the subsequent Napoleonic Wars, when France instituted a universal draft and a centrally run "command" economy. Its motivated citizen armies, composed for the first time of Frenchmen rather than mercenaries, marched longer and faster. People participated in part because they were patriotic. Their nation-state embodied their aspirations and brought them together under a common national identity.

The United States, meanwhile, had followed the example of the Netherlands by declaring independence from Britain in 1776. The U.S. nation held together in the Civil War of the 1860s and developed a surprisingly strong sense of nationalism, considering the size and diversity of the country. Latin American states gained independence early in the nineteenth century, and Germany and Italy unified their nations out of multiple political units (through war) later that century. As a Dominion of Britain, Canada was expected to follow the British government, particularly on matters of foreign affairs. It was only with the Statute of Westminster of 1931 that the Canadian government could sign its own treaties and act independently of the British House of Lords.[26]

---

[24] Ernest Gellner, *Nations and Nationalism* (Ithaca, NY: Cornell UP, 1983). Charles Tilly, *Coercion, Capital and European States*, A.D. 990–1990 (Oxford: Blackwell, 1990). E. J. Hobsbawm, *Nations and Nationalism since 1780: Programme, Myth, Reality* (NY: Cambridge UP, 1990). James Mayall, *Nationalism and International Society* (NY: Cambridge UP, 1990). Liah Greenfeld, *Nationalism: Five Roads to Modernity* (Cambridge, MA: Harvard UP, 1992).

[25] David Carment and Patrick James, eds., *Wars in the Midst of Peace: The International Politics of Ethnic Conflict* (Pittsburgh: U Pittsburgh P, 1997).

[26] J. L. Granatstein, "Introduction," *Canadian Foreign Policy: Historical Readings*, ed. J. L. Granatstein (Toronto: Copp Clark Pitman, 1993) 1–4.

Before World War I, socialist workers from various European countries banded together as workers to fight for their rights. In the war, however, most abandoned such solidarity and instead fought for their own nations; nationalism proved a stronger force than socialism. Before World War II, nationalism helped Germany, Italy and Japan to build political orders based on *fascism*—an extreme authoritarianism girded by national chauvinism. And in World War II it was nationalism and patriotism (not communism) that rallied the Soviet people to sacrifice millions in order to turn back Germany's invasion.

Over the past 50 years, nations by the dozens have gained independence and state-hood. Jews worked persistently in the first half of the twentieth century to create the state of Israel, and Palestinians have aspired in the second half to create a Palestinian state. While multinational states such as the Soviet Union and Yugoslavia have frag-mented in recent years, ethnic and territorial units such as Ukraine, Slovenia and East Timor have established themselves as independent nation-states. Others, such as Kosovo and Kurdistan, are seeking to do so. The continuing influence of nationalism in today's world is evident. More than ever, it is a major factor in international conflict and war.

National identity is psychologically reinforced on a daily basis by symbols such as national flags, rituals like singing a national anthem and other practices designed to rein-force the identification of a population with its nation and government. In truth, people have multiple identities and belong to various circles, from their immediate family through their town, ethnic or religious group, nation or state and humanity as a whole (see pp. 378–381). Nationalism has been remarkably successful in establishing national identity as a people's primary affiliation in much of the world. (In many places a sense of local affiliation remains important, however.)

Nationalism harnesses the energies of large populations based on their patriotic feelings toward a nation. The feeling of "we the people" is hard to sustain if the people are excluded from participating in government. This participation is so important that even authoritarian governments often go through the motions of holding elections (even with only one candidate or party). Democracy can be a force for peace, con-straining the power of state leaders to commit their nations to war, but popular influ-ence over governments can also increase conflict with other nations, especially when ethnic tensions erupt.

Over time, democratic participation has broadened to more countries and more peo-ple within those countries (nonlandowners, women, etc.). The trend toward democracy seems to be continuing in most regions of the world in recent years—in Russia and Eastern Europe, Africa, Latin America and Asia. Both nationalism and democracy remain great historical forces exerting strong influences in IR.

The World Economy, 1750–the Present

industrialization The use of fossil-fuel energy to drive machinery and the accumulation of such machinery along with the products created by it.

In 1750, Britain, the world's most advanced economy, had a GDP of about $1200 per capita (in today's U.S. dollars)—less than the present level of most of the global South. However, Britain today produces more than 10 times as much per person (and with a much larger population). This accomplishment is due to **industrialization**—the use of energy to drive machinery and the accumulation of such machinery along with the prod-ucts created by it. The Industrial Revolution started in Britain in the eighteenth century (notably with the inventions of a new steam engine in 1769, a mechanized thread-spinner in 1770 and the cotton gin in America in 1794), and was tied to Britain's emerging leadership role in the world economy. Industrialization—a process at the world level of analysis—spread to other advanced economies.[27]

By around 1850, the wooden sailing ships of earlier centuries had been replaced by larger and faster coal-powered iron steamships. Coal-fuelled steam engines also drove factories producing textiles and other commodities. The great age of railroad building was evolving. These developments not only increased the volume of world production and trade, but also tied distant locations more closely together economically. The day trip across France by railroad contrasted with the same route a hundred years earlier, when it took three weeks to complete. In this period of mechanization, however, factory conditions were extremely harsh, especially for women and children operating machines.

Britain dominated world trade in this period. Because Britain's economy was the most technologically advanced in the world, its products were competitive worldwide. Thus British policy favoured **free trade.** In addition to its central role in world trade, Britain served as the financial capital of the world, managing an increasingly complex world market in goods and services in the nineteenth century. British currency, pounds sterling (silver), became the world standard. International monetary relations were still based on the value of precious metals, as they had been in the sixteenth century when Spain bought its armies with Mexican silver and gold.

free trade The flow of goods and services across national boundaries unimpeded by tariffs or other restrictions; in principle (if not always in practice), free trade was a key aspect of Britain's policy after 1846 and of U.S. and Canadian policy after 1945.

By the outset of the twentieth century, however, the world's largest and most advanced economy was no longer Britain but the United States. The industrialization of the U.S. economy was fuelled by territorial expansion throughout the nineteenth century, adding vast natural resources. The U.S. economy was attracting huge pools of immigrant labour from the poorer fringes of Europe. The United States led the world in converting from coal to oil and from horse-drawn transportation to motor vehicles. New technological innovations, from electricity to airplanes, also helped push the U.S. economy into a dominant world position.

In the 1930s, Canadian and world economies suffered a severe setback in the Great Depression. The protectionist Hawley-Smoot Act adopted by the United States in 1930, which imposed tariffs on imports, contributed to the severity of the depression by provoking retaliation and reducing world trade.

Following World War II, the capitalist world economy was restructured under U.S. leadership. Today's international economic institutions, such as the World Bank and International Monetary Fund (IMF), date from this period. The United States provided massive assistance to resuscitate Western European economies (through the Marshall Plan) as well as Japan's. World trade greatly expanded, and the world market became ever more closely woven together through air transportation and telecommunications. Electronics emerged as a new leading sector, and technological progress accelerated throughout the twentieth century.

The economies of the Soviet Union and Eastern Europe, organized on communist principles of central planning and state ownership, stood apart from this world capitalist economy in the years after World War II. The Soviet economy had some notable successes in rapidly industrializing the country in the 1930s, surviving the German assault in the 1940s, and developing world-class aerospace and military production capability in the 1950s and 1960s. The Soviet Union launched the world's first satellite (*Sputnik*) in 1957, and in the early 1960s its leaders boasted that communist economies would outperform capitalist ones within decades. Instead, the Soviet bloc economies stagnated under the

---

[27] Douglass C. North and Robert Paul Thomas, *The Rise of the Western World: A New Economic History* (NY: Cambridge UP, 1973). E. J. Hobsbawm, *Industry and Empire: From 1750 to the Present Day* (Harmondsworth, UK: Penguin-Pelican, 1969). James D. Tracy, ed., *The Political Economy of Merchant Empires: State Power and World Trade, 1350–1750* (NY: Cambridge UP, 1991).

weight of bureaucracy, ideological rigidity, environmental destruction, corruption and extremely high military spending. In the 1990s, the former Soviet republics and their Eastern European neighbours tried—with much difficulty and mixed success—to make a transition to some form of capitalist market economy.

Today there is a single integrated world economy that almost no country can resist joining. However, the imperfections and problems of that world economy are evident in the periodic crises and recessions of recent years—in Russia and Eastern Europe, Japan and other Asian economies, and at times in the mature industrialized countries of North America and Western Europe. Above all, the emergence of a global capitalist economy has sharpened disparities between the richest and poorest world regions. While countries such as Canada and the United States enjoy unprecedented prosperity, Africa's increasing poverty has created a human catastrophe on a continental scale.

Just as the world economy climbed out of depressions in the 1890s and 1930s, it appears that a new wave of technological innovation is pulling the advanced industrialized countries into a new phase of growth—possibly one that is more information-intensive and resource-efficient. Much less clear is whether technological change will bypass or empower the global South (see Chapters 12 and 13).

The Two World Wars, 1900–1950

World War I (1914–1918) and World War II (1939–1945) occupied only 10 years of the twentieth century but greatly shaped its character. Nothing comparable has happened since, and the two wars remain a key reference point for our world today. Along with just two other cases in history—the Thirty Years' War and the Napoleonic Wars—the two world wars were global or hegemonic conflicts in which almost all major states participated in an all-out struggle over the future of the international system.[28]

For many people, World War I symbolizes the tragic irrationality of war. It fascinates scholars of IR because it was catastrophic and seems unnecessary and perhaps even accidental. After a century of relative peace, the great powers marched into battle for no good reason. There was even a popular feeling that Europe would be uplifted and reinvigorated by a war—that young men could once again prove their manhood on the battlefield in a glorious adventure. Such ideas were soon crushed by the immense pain and evident pointlessness of it all.

Previous to the two world wars, the only major conflict had been the Franco-Prussian war of 1870–1871, when Germany executed a swift offensive using railroads to rush forces to the front. That war ended quickly, decisively, and with a clear winner (Germany). People expected that a new war would follow the same pattern. All the great powers made plans for a quick railroad-borne offensive and rapid victory—what has been called the *cult of the offensive*. Under these doctrines, one country's mobilization for war virtually forced its enemies to mobilize as well, and it was believed that the first to strike would win. Thus, when a Serbian nationalist assassinated Archduke Ferdinand of Austria in 1914 in Sarajevo, a minor crisis escalated and mobilization plans pushed Europe to all-out war.[29]

---

[28] Michael Dockrill, *Atlas of Twentieth Century World History* (NY: HarperCollins, 1991). Niall Ferguson, *The Pity of War: Explaining World War I* (NY: Basic, 1999). John Keegan, ed., *The Times Atlas of the Second World War* (NY: HarperCollins, 1989). Gerhard L. Weinberg, *A World at Arms: A Global History of World War II* (NY: Cambridge UP, 1994).

[29] Stephen Van Evera, "The Cult of the Offensive and the Origins of the First World War," *International Security* 9 (1984): 58–107. Jack Lewis Snyder, *The Ideology of the Offensive: Military Decision Making and the Disasters of 1914* (Ithaca, NY: Cornell UP, 1984). Miles Kahler, "Rumors of War: The 1914 Analogy," *Foreign Affairs* 58.2 (1979/80): 374–96.

Contrary to expectation, the war was neither short nor decisive, and certainly not glorious. It was bogged down in *trench warfare* along a fixed front. For example, in 1917 at the Battle of Passchendaele (Belgium), the British fired 4.5 tonnes of artillery shells per metre of front line over an 18-kilometre-wide front, and then lost 400 000 men in a failed ground attack in three months. The horrific conditions were worsened by chemical weapons and by the attempts of Britain and Germany to starve each other's population into surrender. However, the first world war was also one in which countries like Canada "came into their own," in part through participating in historic battles such as that at Vimy Ridge in 1917, a battle which saw the Canadian Corps successfully take the ridge after previous failures by the British and French. The cost, however, was high, with over 3500 Canadian troops killed and a further 7000 wounded.

Other states crumbled, and Russia was one of the first. Revolution at home removed Russia from the war in 1917 (and led to the founding of the Soviet Union). The entry of the United States on the anti-German side of the war that year quickly turned the tide. In the *Treaty of Versailles* of 1919, Germany was forced to give up territory, pay reparations, limit its future armaments and admit guilt for the war. German resentment against the harsh terms of Versailles would contribute to Adolf Hitler's rise to power in the 1930s. After World War I, U.S. president Woodrow Wilson led the effort to create the **League of Nations,** a forerunner of today's UN. The U.S. Senate, however, would not approve U.S. participation, and the League did not prove effective. U.S. isolationism between the world wars, along with declining British power and Russia's withdrawal into revolution, left a power vacuum in world politics.

In the 1930s, Germany and Japan stepped into that vacuum, embarking on aggressive expansionism that ultimately led to World War II. Japan had already occupied Taiwan and Korea, after defeating China in 1895 and Russia in 1905. During World War I, Japan gained some German colonies in Asia and in 1931 occupied Manchuria (northeast China) and set up a puppet regime. In 1937, Japan invaded the rest of China and began a brutal occupation that continues to haunt Chinese-Japanese relations. Japanese leaders planned a *coprosperity sphere* in which an industrialized Japan would control the natural resources of East and Southeast Asia.

Meanwhile, in Europe in the 1930s, Nazi Germany under Hitler had rearmed, intervened to help fascists win the Spanish Civil War, and grabbed territory from its neighbours under the rationale of reuniting ethnic Germans in those areas with their homeland. Hitler was emboldened by the weak response of the international community and League of Nations to aggression by fascist regimes in Italy and Spain. In an effort to appease German ambitions, Britain agreed to let Germany occupy part of Czechoslovakia in the **Munich Agreement** of 1938. Appeasement has since had a negative connotation in IR, because the Munich Agreement seemed only to encourage Hitler's further conquests.

In 1939, Germany invaded Poland, and Britain joined the war against Germany in response. World War II was an important turning point for Canada. In World War I, Britain declared war on Germany on behalf of Canada, but by World War II, Canada joined the war as a fully sovereign nation. By formally allying itself with Britain and France, Canada was engaging in war as an independent nation for the first time.[30]

Hitler signed a nonaggression pact with his archenemy Joseph Stalin of the Soviet Union and threw his full army against France, occupying most of it quickly. Hitler then double-crossed Stalin and invaded the Soviet Union in 1941. This offensive was ultimately

League of Nations
Established after World War I and a forerunner of today's United Nations, the League of Nations achieved certain humanitarian and other successes but was weakened by the absence of U.S. membership and its own lack of effectiveness in ensuring collective security. See also *collective security.*

Munich Agreement A symbol of the failed policy of appeasement, this agreement, signed in 1938, allowed Nazi Germany to occupy a part of Czechoslovakia. Rather than appease German aspirations, it was followed by further German expansions, which triggered World War II.

---

[30] D. W. Middlemiss and J. J. Sokolsky, *Canadian Defence: Decisions and Determinants* (Toronto: Harcourt, 1988).

bogged down and turned back after several years, but the Soviet Union took the brunt of the German attack and suffered by far the greatest share of the 60 million deaths caused by World War II. This trauma continues to be a powerful memory that shapes views of IR in Russia and Eastern Europe.

The United States joined World War II against Germany in 1942, with its economy producing critically important weapons and supplies for Allied armies. The United States played an important role with Britain in the strategic bombing of German cities—including the firebombing of Dresden in February 1945, which caused 100 000 civilian deaths. In 1944, after crossing the English Channel on June 6 (*D-Day*), British, American and Canadian forces pushed into Germany from the west while the Soviets pushed from the east. A ruined Germany surrendered and was occupied by the Allied powers.

At its peak, Nazi Germany and its allies occupied much of Europe. Under its fanatical policies of racial purity, Germany rounded up and exterminated 6 million Jews and millions of others, including homosexuals, Gypsies and communists. These mass murders, now known as the Holocaust, along with the sheer scale of war unleashed by Nazi aggression, are considered among the greatest *crimes against humanity* in history. Many German officials faced justice in the *Nuremberg Tribunal* after the war (see pp. 286–290). The pledges of world leaders after that experience to "never again" allow **genocide**—the systematic extermination of a racial or religious group—have been called into question as genocide recurred in the 1990s in Bosnia and Rwanda.

genocide The intentional and systematic attempt to destroy a national, ethnic, racial or religious group, in whole or part. It was confirmed as a crime under international law by the UN Genocide Convention (1948). See also *crimes against humanity* and *dehumanization*.

While war was raging in Europe, Japan fought its own conflict with the United States and its allies over control of Southeast Asia. Japan's expansionism in the 1930s served only to underscore the dependence on foreign resources that it was intended to solve: the United States punished Japan by cutting off U.S. oil exports. Japan then destroyed much of the U.S. Navy in a surprise attack at *Pearl Harbor* (Hawaii) in 1941, and seized desired territories (including Indonesia, whose oil replaced that of the United States). The United States, however, built vast new military forces and retook a series of Pacific islands in subsequent years. The strategic bombing of Japanese cities by the U.S. culminated in the only historical use of nuclear weapons in war—the destruction of the cities of *Hiroshima* and *Nagasaki* in August 1945—which triggered Japan's quick surrender.

The lessons of the two world wars seem contradictory. Many people have concluded from the failure of the Munich Agreement in 1938 to appease Hitler that only a hard-line foreign policy with preparedness for war will deter aggression and prevent conflict. Yet in 1914 it was just such hard-line policies that apparently led Europe into a disastrous war, which might have been avoided by appeasement. Evidently the best policy would be sometimes harsh and at other times conciliatory, but IR scholars have not discovered a simple formula for choosing (see "The Causes of War" in Chapter 6).

The Cold War, 1945–1990

The United States and the Soviet Union became the two superpowers of the post–World War II era.[31] Each had an ideological mission (capitalist democracy versus communism), networks of alliances and client states in the global South and a deadly arsenal of nuclear

---

[31] John Lewis Gaddis, *We Now Know: Rethinking Cold War History* (NY: Oxford UP, 1997). Vladislav Zubok and Constantine Pleshakov, *Inside the Kremlin's Cold War: From Stalin to Krushchev* (Cambridge, MA: Harvard UP, 1996). Raymond Garthoff, *Détente and Confrontation: American-Soviet Relations from Nixon to Reagan* (Washington, DC: Brookings, 1985). Deborah Welch Larson, *Anatomy of Mistrust: U.S.-Soviet Relations during the Cold War* (Ithaca, NY: Cornell UP, 1997). Marc Trachtenberg, *A Constructed Peace: The Making of the European Settlement, 1945–1963* (Princeton, NJ: Princeton UP, 1999).

weapons. Europe was divided, with massive military forces of the United States and its *North Atlantic Treaty Organization (NATO)* allies on one side and massive forces of the Soviet Union and its *Warsaw Pact* allies on the other. Germany itself was split, with three-quarters of the country—and three-quarters of the capital city of Berlin—occupied by the United States, Britain and France. The remainder, surrounding West Berlin, was occupied by the Soviet Union. Crises in Berlin in 1948 and 1961 led to armed confrontations but not war. In 1961, East Germany built the Berlin Wall separating East from West Berlin. It symbolized the division of Europe by what Winston Churchill had called the "iron curtain."

Despite the hostility of East-West relations during the **Cold War,** a relatively stable framework of relations emerged, and conflicts never escalated to all-out war. At a U.S.-Soviet-British meeting at *Yalta* in 1945, when the defeat of Germany was imminent, the Western powers acknowledged the Soviet army's presence in Eastern Europe, allowing that area to remain under Soviet influence. Although the Soviet bloc did not join Western economic institutions such as the IMF, all the world's major states joined the UN. Signatories to the United Nations Charter pledged to try to save future generations from the scourge of war; to reaffirm faith in fundamental human rights; to establish conditions under which justice and respect for international law can be maintained; and to promote social progress. The United Nations (unlike the ill-fated League of Nations) managed to maintain almost universal membership and adherence to basic structures and rules throughout the Cold War era.

> **Cold War** The hostile relations, punctuated by occasional periods of improvement, or détente, between the two superpowers—the U.S. and the U.S.S.R.—from 1945 to 1990.

The central concern of the West during the Cold War was that the Soviet Union might gain control of Western Europe—either through outright invasion or through communists' taking power in the area's war-weary and impoverished countries. This could have put the entire industrial base of the Eurasian landmass (from Europe to Siberia) under one state. The *Marshall Plan*—U.S. financial aid to rebuild European economies—responded to these fears, as did the creation of the NATO alliance. Half of the entire world's military spending was devoted to the European standoff. Much spending was also devoted to a superpower nuclear arms race, which saw each superpower produce tens of thousands of nuclear weapons (see pp. 72–74).

Through the policy of **containment,** adopted in the late 1940s, the United States sought to halt the expansion of Soviet influence on several levels at once—military, political, ideological and economic. The United States maintained an extensive network of military bases and alliances worldwide. Virtually all of U.S. foreign policy in subsequent decades, from foreign aid and technology transfer to military intervention and diplomacy, came to serve the goal of containment.

> **containment** A policy adopted in the late 1940s by which the United States sought to halt the global expansion of Soviet influence on several levels—military, political, ideological and economic.

The *Chinese communist revolution* in 1949 led to a Sino-Soviet alliance (*Sino* means "Chinese"). However, China became fiercely independent in the 1960s following the **Sino-Soviet split,** when China opposed Soviet moves toward *peaceful coexistence* with the United States.[32] In the late 1960s, young radicals opposed to both superpowers ran China during the chaotic and destructive *Cultural Revolution*. Feeling threatened by Soviet power, China's leaders developed a growing affiliation with the United States during the 1970s, starting with a dramatic visit to China by U.S. president Nixon in 1972. This visit led to U.S.-Chinese diplomatic relations in 1979, and ended a decades-long argument in the U.S. foreign policy establishment about "who lost China" to communism in 1949. During the Cold War, China generally tried to play a balancing role against whichever superpower seemed most threatening at the time.

> **Sino-Soviet split** A rift in the 1960s between the communist powers of the Soviet Union and China, fuelled by China's opposition to Soviet moves toward peaceful coexistence with the United States.

---

[32] David Allan Mayers, *Cracking the Monolith: U.S. Policy against the Sino-Soviet Alliance, 1949–1955* (Baton Rouge: Louisiana State UP, 1986). Ilpyong J. Kim, ed., *Beyond the Strategic Triangle* (NY: Paragon, 1992).

In 1950, the *Korean War* broke out when communist North Korea attacked and overran most of U.S.-allied South Korea. The United States and its allies (under UN authority obtained after the Soviets walked out of the Security Council in protest) counterattacked and took over most of North Korea. China sent masses of "volunteers" to help North Korea, and the war bogged down near the original border until a 1953 truce ended the fighting. The Korean War hardened U.S. attitudes toward communism and set a negative tone for future East-West relations, especially for U.S.-Chinese relations in the 1950s. U.S. leaders considered using nuclear weapons during the Korean War, but ultimately decided against it.

summit meeting A meeting between heads of state, often referring to leaders of great powers, as in the Cold War superpower summits between the United States and the Soviet Union or today's meetings of the Group of Eight on economic coordination.

The Cold War thawed temporarily after Stalin died in 1953 and Eisenhower was elected and promised to bring an end to the Korean conflict. The first **summit meeting** between superpower leaders took place in Geneva in 1955. However, the Soviet Union sent tanks to crush a popular uprising in Hungary in 1956 (an action it repeated in 1968 in Czechoslovakia), and the Soviet missile program that orbited *Sputnik* in 1957 alarmed the United States. The shooting down of a U.S. spy plane (the *U-2*) over the Soviet Union in 1960 scuttled a summit meeting between superpower leaders Nikita Khrushchev and Dwight D. Eisenhower. Meanwhile, after Fidel Castro's communist revolution in 1959 in Cuba, the United States attempted a counterrevolution in the botched 1961 *Bay of Pigs* invasion.

Cuban Missile Crisis (1962) A superpower crisis, sparked by the Soviet Union's installation of medium-range nuclear missiles in Cuba, that marks the moment when the United States and the Soviet Union came closest to nuclear war.

These hostilities culminated in the **Cuban Missile Crisis** of 1962, when the Soviet Union installed medium-range nuclear missiles in Cuba. The Soviet Union's aims were to reduce their strategic nuclear inferiority, to counter the deployment of U.S. missiles on Soviet borders in Turkey, and to deter another U.S. invasion of Cuba. U.S. leaders, however, considered the missiles threatening and provocative. As historical documents revealed years later, nuclear war was quite possible. Several U.S. policy-makers favoured military strikes before the missiles became operational, when in fact some nuclear weapons in Cuba were already operational and commanders were authorized to use them in the event of a U.S. attack.[33] Instead, President John F. Kennedy imposed a naval blockade to force their removal. The Soviet Union backed down on the missiles, and the United States promised not to invade Cuba in the future. Leaders on both sides were shaken, however, by the possibility of nuclear war. They signed the *Limited Test Ban Treaty* in 1963, prohibiting atmospheric nuclear tests, and began to cooperate in cultural exchanges, space exploration, aviation and other areas.

Despite these moments of tension, the Cold War was described by some observers as a "long peace" because war never actually broke out between the United States and the Soviet Union. However, the two superpowers often jockeyed for position in the global South, supporting **proxy wars** in which they typically supplied and advised opposing factions in civil wars. The alignments were often arbitrary. For instance, the United States backed the Ethiopian government while the Soviets backed next-door rival Somalia in the 1970s; when an Ethiopian revolution caused the new government to seek Soviet help, the United States switched to support Somalia instead. The Cold War may have been a period of relative peace for the superpowers, but it was a period of profound violence for many states and peoples of the South.[34]

proxy wars Wars in the global South—often civil wars—in which the United States and the Soviet Union jockeyed for position by supplying and advising opposing factions.

---

[33] James A. Nathan, ed., *The Cuban Missile Crisis Revisited* (NY: St. Martin's, 1992). Ernest May and Philip Zelikow, eds., *The Kennedy Tapes: Inside the White House during the Cuban Missile Crisis* (Cambridge, MA: Harvard UP, 1997).

[34] Amitav Acharya, "Beyond Anarchy: Third World Instability and International Order after the Cold War," *International Relations Theory and the Third World,* ed. Stephanie G. Neuman (NY: St. Martin's, 1998) 159–211.

One flaw of U.S. policy in the Cold War period was to view regional conflicts through East-West lenses. Its preoccupation with communism led the United States to support unpopular pro-Western governments in a number of poor countries—nowhere more disastrously than during the *Vietnam War* in the 1960s. The war in Vietnam divided U.S. citizens and ultimately failed to prevent a communist takeover. The fall of South Vietnam in 1975 appeared to signal U.S. weakness, especially combined with U.S. set-backs in the Middle East: the 1973 Arab oil embargo against the United States and the 1979 overthrow of the U.S.-backed Shah of Iran by Islamic fundamentalists.

In this period of apparent U.S. weakness, the Soviet Union invaded Afghanistan in 1979. However, like the United States in Vietnam, the Soviet Union could not suppress rebel armies supplied by the opposing superpower. The Soviets ultimately withdrew after almost a decade of war that considerably weakened the Soviet Union. Meanwhile, President Ronald Reagan built up U.S. military forces and supported rebel armies in the Soviet-allied states of Nicaragua and Angola (and one faction in Cambodia) as well as in Afghanistan. Superpower relations slowly improved after Mikhail Gorbachev, a reformer, took power in the Soviet Union in 1985. But some battlegrounds of the global South (notably Afghanistan and Angola) continued to suffer through brutal civil wars (fought with leftover Cold War arms) into the new century.

In retrospect, it seems that both superpowers exaggerated Soviet strength. In the early years of the nuclear arms race, U.S. military superiority was absolute, especially in nuclear weapons. The Soviets managed to match the United States over time, with A-bombs to H-bombs to multiple-warhead missiles. By the 1970s the Soviets had achieved strategic parity, meaning that neither side could prevent its own destruction in a nuclear war. Behind this military parity, however, lay a Soviet Union lagging far behind the West in everything else—sheer wealth, technology, infrastructure and citizen/worker motivation.

In June 1989, massive pro-democracy demonstrations in China's capital of Beijing (Tiananmen Square) were put down violently by the communist government. Hundreds were shot dead in the streets. Around 1990, as the Soviet Union stood by, one after another Eastern European country replaced its communist government under pressure of mass demonstrations. The toppling of the Berlin Wall in late 1989 symbolized the end of the Cold War division of Europe. Germany formally reunified in 1990. The Soviet leader, Gorbachev, allowed these losses of external power (and more) in hopes of concentrating on Soviet domestic restructuring under his policies of *perestroika* (economic reform) and *glasnost* (openness in political discussion). In 1991, however, the Soviet Union itself broke apart. Russia and many of the other former republics struggled throughout the 1990s against economic and financial collapse, inflation, corruption, war and military weakness, although they remained political democracies. China remained a communist authoritarian government but liberalized its economy and avoided military conflicts. In contrast to the Cold War era, China developed close ties with both the United States and Russia, and joined the world's liberal trading regime.

Scholars do not agree on the important question of why the Cold War ended.[35] One view is that U.S. military strength under President Reagan forced the Soviet Union into bankruptcy as it tried to keep up in the arms race. A different position is that the Soviet Union suffered from internal stagnation over decades and ultimately imploded because of

---

[35] Rey Koslowski and Friedrich Kratochwil, "Understanding Change in International Politics: The Soviet Empire's Demise and the International System," *International Organization* 48.2 (1994): 215–48. Stephen G. Brooks and William C. Wohlforth, "Power, Globalization, and the End of the Cold War: Reevaluating a Landmark Case for Ideas," *International Security* 25.3 (2000/2001): 5–53. Karin Fierke, *Changing Games, Changing Strategies: Critical Reflections in Security* (Manchester, UK: Manchester UP, 1998).

weaknesses in its system of governance that had little to do with external pressure. Indeed, some scholars think the Soviet Union might have fallen apart earlier without the United States as a foreign enemy to bolster its government's legitimacy with its own people.

The Post–Cold War Era, 1990–2007

The post–Cold War era began with a bang, while the Soviet Union was still disintegrating. In 1990, perhaps believing that the end of the Cold War had left a power vacuum in its region, Iraq occupied its neighbour Kuwait in an aggressive grab for control of Middle East oil. Western powers were alarmed—both at the example that such aggression, if unpunished, could set in a new era, and about the direct threat to energy supplies for the world economy. The United States mobilized a coalition of the world's major countries (with almost no opposition) to oppose Iraq. Working through the UN, the U.S.-led coalition applied escalating sanctions against Iraq—from condemnation to embargoing Iraq's oil exports to threats and ultimatums.

When Iraq did not withdraw from Kuwait by the UN's deadline, the United States and its allies easily smashed Iraq's military and evicted its army from Kuwait in the *Gulf War*. The coalition did not occupy Iraq or overthrow its government. The costs of the Gulf War were shared among the participants in the coalition, with Britain and France making military commitments while Japan and Germany made substantial financial contributions. The pass-the-hat financing for this war was an innovation, one that worked fairly well but also eventually produced criticisms in countries such as Germany and Japan, both of which have never been invited to become members of the UN Security Council but are encouraged to contribute financially to UN-supported missions.[36]

The final collapse of the Soviet Union followed mere months after the Gulf War. The 15 republics of the Union—of which Russia under President Boris Yeltsin was just one—had begun taking power from a weakened central government, declaring themselves as sovereign states. This process raised complex problems ranging from issues of national self-determination to the reallocation of property. A failed military coup attempt in 1991—and the prominent role of Russian president Yeltsin in opposing it—accelerated the collapse of the Soviet Union.[37] Soon both capitalism and democracy were adopted as the basis of the economies and political systems of the former Soviet states. The republics became independent states and formed a loose coordinating structure—the *Commonwealth of Independent States (CIS)*. Of the former Soviet republics, only the three small Baltic states are nonmembers.

Western relations with Russia and the other republics have been mixed since the 1990s. Due to their own economic problems, and because of the sense that Russia needed internal reform more than external aid, Western countries provided only limited aid for the region's harsh economic transition, which drastically reduced living standards. Russia's brutal suppression of its secessionist province of Chechnya in 1995 and 1999 provoked Western fears of an expansionist, aggressive Russian nationalism, especially after the success of ultranationalists in Russian parliamentary elections earlier in the decade. Russian leaders feared that NATO expansion into Eastern Europe would place threatening Western military forces on Russia's borders, creating a new division of

---

[36] Lawrence Freedman and Efraim Karsh, *The Gulf Conflict: 1990–1991* (Princeton, NJ: Princeton UP, 1993).

[37] Michael McFaul, *Russia's Unfinished Revolution: Political Change from Gorbachev to Putin* (Ithaca, NY: Cornell UP, 2001). James H. Billington, *Russia Transformed: Breakthrough to Hope: Moscow, August 1991* (NY: Free Press, 1992). Marshall I. Goldman, *What Went Wrong with Perestroika* (NY: Norton, 1994).

Europe. Meanwhile, Japan and Russia could not resolve a lingering, mostly symbolic, territorial dispute.[38]

Despite these problems, overall the world's great powers increased cooperation after the Cold War. Russia was accepted as the successor state to the Soviet Union and took its seat on the Security Council. Russia and the United States agreed to major reductions in their nuclear weapons programs, and carried them out in the 1990s.

Just after the Gulf War in 1991, the former Yugoslavia broke apart, with several of its republics declaring independence. Ethnic Serbs, who were minorities in Croatia and Bosnia, seized about a third of Croatia and two-thirds of Bosnia as territory to form a "Greater Serbia" with the neighbouring republic of Serbia. In those territories, with help from Serbia, which controlled the Yugoslav army, Serb forces massacred hundreds of thousands of non-Serb Bosnians and Croatians and expelled millions more to create an ethnically pure state. Croatian militias in Bosnia emulated these tactics, though on a smaller scale.

The international community recognized the independence of Croatia and Bosnia, admitting them to the UN and passing dozens of Security Council resolutions to protect their territorial integrity and civilian populations. But in contrast to the Gulf War, the great powers showed no willingness to bear major costs to protect Bosnia. Instead they tried to contain the conflict by assuming neutral roles as peacekeepers and intermediaries. The UN sent almost 40 000 peacekeepers to Bosnia and Croatia, at a cost of more than $1 billion per year. NATO threatened military action repeatedly, only to back down when costs appeared too high, as when Serb forces took peacekeepers hostage and threatened to kill them if NATO attacked.[39] In 1995, Serbian forces overran two UN-designated "safe areas" in eastern Bosnia, expelling the women and slaughtering thousands of the men. Finally, two weeks of NATO air strikes (the alliance's first-ever military engagement), along with losses to Croatia on the ground, induced Serb forces to come to terms. The treaty to end the war (the Dayton Agreement) formally held Bosnia together but granted Serb forces autonomy on half of its territory, while placing about 60 000 heavily armed (mostly NATO) troops on the ground to maintain a ceasefire. More than 40 000 Canadians have served in Bosnia in either UN or NATO missions since 1992, and 24 Canadians lost their lives.

In contrast to their indecision early in the Bosnia crisis, Western powers acted decisively in 1999 when Serbian forces carried out "ethnic cleansing" in the Serbian province of Kosovo, predominantly populated by ethnic Albanians. NATO launched an air war that escalated over ten weeks, and came under criticism from Russia and China for acting without explicit UN authorization and interfering in Serbia's internal affairs. (The international community and the UN considered Kosovo, unlike Bosnia, to be a part of Serbia.) In the end, Serbian forces withdrew from Kosovo and the UN has controlled the

---

[38] G. John Ikenberry, *After Victory* (Princeton, NJ: Princeton UP, 2000). Raymond L. Garthoff, *The Great Transition: American-Soviet Relations and the End of the Cold War* (Washington, DC: Brookings, 1994). John Lewis Gaddis, *The United States and the End of the Cold War: Implications, Reconsiderations, Provocations* (NY: Oxford UP, 1992). Robert Jervis and Seweryn Bialer, eds., *Soviet-American Relations after the Cold War* (Durham, NC: Duke UP, 1991). Bennett Ramberg, ed., *Arms Control without Negotiation: From the Cold War to the New World Order* (Boulder, CO: Rienner, 1993). Francis Fukuyama, *The End of History and the Last Man* (NY: Free Press, 1992).

[39] James Gow, *Triumph of the Lack of Will: International Diplomacy and the Yugoslav War* (NY: Columbia UP, 1997). David Rieff, *Slaughterhouse: Bosnia and the Failure of the West* (NY: Simon & Schuster, 1995). Noel Malcolm, *Bosnia: A Short History* (NY: New York UP, 1994). Roy Gutman, *A Witness to Genocide* (NY: Macmillan, 1993). Steven L. Burg and Paul S. Shoup, *The War in Bosnia-Herzegovina: Ethnic Conflict and International Intervention* (Armonk, NY: Sharpe, 1999).

province since, with the question of independence to be decided by the UN Security Council in 2007.[40] Meanwhile, Serbian strongman Slobodan Milosevic was indicted for war crimes by the UN tribunal for the former Yugoslavia, and was eventually delivered to the tribunal in 2001, after losing power. He died in 2006 near the end of a lengthy trial.

Other Western interventions since 1990 include a UN mission in Cambodia, where the United Nations launched one of its largest multidimensional peacekeeping missions to literally rebuild the Cambodian state, only to see one of the Cambodian political parties launch a coup and then conduct a highly questionable set of elections several years later. In Somalia, a U.S.-led coalition sent tens of thousands of troops to suppress factional fighting and deliver relief supplies to a large starving population. However, when those forces were drawn into the fighting and sustained casualties, the United States abruptly pulled out, with the UN following by 1995.[41] In Rwanda in 1994, the genocide of more than half a million civilians—massacred in just a few weeks—was virtually ignored by the international community, despite the efforts of the Canadian force commander of the UN mission, Lieutenant-General Roméo Dallaire, to draw the world's attention to the horrors that were taking place. The great powers, burned by failures in Somalia and Bosnia, decided that their vital interests were not at stake. In 1997, the Rwanda conflict spilled into neighbouring Zaire (now the Democratic Republic of Congo), where rebels overthrew a corrupt dictator. Neighbouring countries were drawn into the fighting but the international community steered clear even as living conditions worsened and millions of civilians died. The U.S. military intervened in Haiti to restore the elected president, but the situation there remained bleak for years afterward. In 2004, rebels forced Aristide from office and U.S., French and Canadian forces moved in to provide stability under a United Nations–authorized mission.

In Russia, Yeltsin resigned at the end of 1999 and his designated successor, Prime Minister Vladimir Putin, took office and was elected president a few months later. Despite the leadership change, Russian-American relations faced the continuing challenges of conflicting interests in multiple areas. Not only has the U.S. provided little aid, in Russia's perspective, but it was pushing NATO's boundaries eastward, promoting new oil pipelines to bypass Russian territory in moving oil from former Soviet republics to Western consumers, and planning to rapidly deploy ballistic missile defences and withdraw from the ABM Treaty (see p. 275).

While these U.S.-Russian tensions reflect lingering problems from earlier times, new rifts opened in 2001 between the United States and much of the rest of the world. The United States stood nearly alone against the rest of the international community on a range of issues—on the one hand supporting missile defences and on the other opposing the Kyoto treaty on global warming, a treaty to enforce the prohibition on biological weapons, a proposal to curb international small-arms sales, a proposed International Criminal Court (to replace the ad hoc war-crimes tribunals of the 1990s) and a proposal to curb tobacco marketing in poor countries. Signalling aspects of this shifting alignment, Russia and China signed a treaty of friendship in 2001, and European countries helped vote the United States off two important UN commissions.

---

[40] Andrew J. Bacevich and Eliot A. Cohen, *War over Kosovo* (NY: Columbia UP, 2002). Peter R. Prifti, *Confrontation in Kosovo: The Albanian-Serb Struggle, 1969–1998* (NY: Columbia UP, 1999). Julie A. Mertus, *Kosovo: How Myths and Truths Started a War* (Berkeley: U California P, 1999). Miranda Vickers, *Between Serb and Albanian: A History of Kosovo* (NY: Columbia UP, 1998).

[41] Walter S. Clarke and Jeffrey I. Herbst, eds., *Learning from Somalia: The Lessons of Armed Humanitarian Intervention* (Boulder, CO: Westview, 1997). Helen Fogarassy, *Mission Improbable: The World Community on a UN Compound in Somalia* (Lanham, MD: UP America, 1999).

These divisive issues receded for a time, however, when the United States was attacked by terrorists on September 11, 2001. The attack destroyed the World Trade Center in New York and a wing of the Pentagon in Washington, killing thousands of Americans and citizens of about 60 other countries. The attacks mobilized support for the United States by a very broad coalition of states, not only out of sympathy but out of a realization that terrorism threatens the interstate system itself. President G.W. Bush declared a "war on terrorism" that was expected to last years and span continents, employing both conventional and unconventional means. In late 2001, U.S., Canadian and British forces and their Afghan allies ousted the Taliban regime in Afghanistan, which had supported the al Qaeda network (led by Osama bin Laden) responsible for attacks on the United States. Canada continues to be involved in Afghanistan in both security and reconstruction efforts (as of June 2007 some 2500 troops were stationed in Afghanistan and 60 Canadians had lost their lives there since 2002).

Then, in 2003, the United States and the United Kingdom invaded Iraq based on the belief that President Saddam Hussein had been amassing weapons of mass destruction, which he intended to use against the U.S., Israel or other allies. The attack on Iraq went ahead without United Nations approval and without the support of many of the U.S. and Britain's allies, including Canada, France and Germany. No weapons of mass destruction were ever uncovered, and though the original offensive to oust Saddam Hussein went relatively smoothly for the United States, the continued occupation of Iraq has resulted in thousands of casualties for both coalition forces and Iraqi citizens. Sectarian violence between Shi'ite and Sunni communities (rival wings of Islam) pushed the country to the brink of civil war. Estimates of Iraqi deaths since the invasion began have ranged from tens of thousands to more than 600 000. The war inflamed anti-American and anti-Western sentiment in many regions of the world, most particularly in Muslim countries such as Egypt and Pakistan. The revelation in 2004 that U.S. personnel had abused Iraqi prisoners at Abu Ghraib prison outside Baghdad inflamed anti-U.S. sentiments even further. Tensions between Muslim and Western countries heightened in 2006 after the publication of anti-Muslim cartoons in a Danish newspaper sparked riots from Africa to South Asia. The execution of Saddam Hussein in Iraq on December 30, 2006, after being convicted of crimes against humanity by a special Iraqi tribunal for his part in the murder of 148 Iraqi Shi'ites in 1982, also heightened tensions.

Some observers now say that the next site of U.S. confrontation in the Middle East will be Iran. The U.S. was already concerned when North Korea restarted its nuclear enrichment program, producing possibly half a dozen nuclear bombs in 2003 and testing one in 2006, but it returned to a more diplomatic posture with North Korea and began a move toward providing light-water nuclear reactors in return for North Korea's cessation of its enrichment and weapons program.[42] Iran also began a nuclear enrichment program in 2006, but diplomatic measures have been limited. The UN Security Council voted in late 2006 to block the sale of nuclear-related technology or equipment to Iran and also froze the assets of a number of companies and individuals associated with the nuclear program. Iran, in turn, ignored deadlines set by the UN. In early 2007, opinion within the U.S. administration seemed mixed, with some U.S. decision-makers seeking to avoid another military confrontation in the region and others arguing that regime change in Iran may be the logical next step after what had happened in Iraq.

---

[42] Leon V. Sigal, "The Lessons of North Korea's Test," *Current History* (November 2006): 363–64.

CHANGE IN THE AIR
Peaceful trends mark the post–Cold War era, but war and terrorism continue. Here, women begin to remove their burqa coverings after the liberation of Kabul, Afghanistan, in December 2001.

The post–Cold War era may seem to be a conflict-prone period in which savage wars flare up with unexpected intensity around the world, in places such as Iraq, Bosnia and Rwanda—even New York City. It is true that the era is complex and unpredictable, leaving some policy-makers and IR theorists susceptible to Cold War nostalgia—longing for a time when world politics followed simpler rules based on a bipolar world order. Despite these new complexities, however, *the post–Cold War era has been more peaceful than the Cold War.* World military spending decreased by about one-third from its peak in the 1980s, although it has risen again since 2001. Old wars have ended faster than new ones have begun. Latin America and Russia/Eastern Europe have nearly extinguished significant interstate war in their regions, joining a zone of peace already encompassing North America, Western Europe, Japan/Pacific and China.

Warfare is diminishing even in the arc of conflict from Africa through the Middle East to South Asia. Since 1990, long, bloody wars have ended in South Africa, Mozambique, Angola, Democratic Congo, southern Sudan and Ethiopia-Eritrea, as did the Cold War conflicts in Central America. More recent wars in Sri Lanka, Ivory Coast, Rwanda, Indonesia and the Philippines have also largely wound down. After the Cold War, world order did not spiral out of control with rampant aggression and war. However, the Israeli-Palestinian conflict, which saw rising expectations of peace in the 1990s, worsened in 2000 after a proposed deal fell through. With the 2006 Palestinian election victory of the Islamist party Hamas, which refuses to recognize Israel, hopes for a durable peace faded and internal divisions between Hamas and Fatah (a secular Palestinian party tied to the Palestinian Liberation Organization) have brought Palestine to a civil war. In 2006 Israel fought a brief and intense war with Hezbollah guerrillas in southern Lebanon, which resulted in over 1000 deaths, mostly Lebanese. The continuing war in Iraq has threatened broader stability of the Middle East.

At the same time, the United States and the United Kingdom remained embroiled in Iraq, and terrorist actions against the United Nations and any state seen to support the U.S. in Iraq—even if they had not contributed troops to the Iraqi invasion, such as Turkey—were on the rise. In some cases, such as with Spain, governments that had supported the United States were democratically removed after terrorists attacked Spanish citizens. Other countries, such as Italy, have also withdrawn, and the United Kingdom began withdrawing troops in 2007.

In international economic relations, the post–Cold War era is one of globalization. Countries worldwide are integrating into a world market, for better or worse. New hubs of economic growth are emerging, notably in parts of Asia, where remarkable economic gains occurred in the 1990s (notwithstanding a sharp setback in 1997). At the same time, disparities between the rich and poor are growing, both globally and within individual countries (including Canada). Globalization has created backlashes among people who are adversely affected or who believe their identities are threatened by foreign influences.

The resurgence of nationalism and ethnic-religious conflict—occasionally in extremely brutal form—results partly from that backlash, as did the protest movement against capitalist-led globalization—such as at the failed 1999 Seattle meeting of the World Trade Organization and great-power summit meetings in Québec (2000), Genoa, Italy (2001) and Heiligendamm, Germany (2007).

With increasing globalization, transnational concerns such as environmental degradation and disease have become more prominent. Global warming looms as an ever more present danger, underscored in 2005 by the toll of Hurricane Katrina on New Orleans and the accelerating melting of arctic ice. In 2006, a virulent bird flu spread worldwide, faster than expected, and triggered panicky efforts to prepare for a possible human pandemic if the flu virus mutates and spreads person-to-person.

China is becoming more central to world politics at the beginning of the twenty-first century. Its size and rapid growth make China a rising power—a situation that some scholars liken to Germany's rise a century earlier. Historically, such shifts in power relations have caused instability in the international system. China is the only great power that is not a democracy. Its poor record on human rights makes it a frequent target of Western criticism from both governments and NGOs.

China holds (but seldom uses) veto power in the UN Security Council, and it has a credible nuclear arsenal. It adjoins several regional conflict areas (Korea, Southeast Asia, India and Central Asia) and affects the global proliferation of missiles and nuclear weapons. It claims disputed territory in the resource-rich South China Sea, but has not fought a military battle in 25 years. China also claims the mountainous country of Tibet, though many people around the world dispute that claim. In 2004, then-Canadian prime minister Paul Martin rankled Chinese authorities by agreeing to meet with the Dalai Lama, the spiritual leader of Tibet. With the transfer of Hong Kong from Britain in 1997, China acquired a valuable asset and turned its hopes on someday reintegrating Taiwan as well under the Hong Kong formula of "one country, two systems." China is the only great power from the global South. Its population size and rapid industrialization from a low level make China a big factor in the future of wide-scale environmental trends such as global warming. All these elements make China an important actor in the coming decades.

It remains to be seen whether, in the coming years, the international system can provide China with appropriate status and respect to reflect its rising power and historical importance, and whether China in turn can conform with international rules and norms. The decision to hold the 2008 Olympic games in Beijing, which was greeted with tremendous popular enthusiasm when announced in 2001, may affect these long-term processes, as might the Chinese leadership's decisions about whether to encourage or discourage the rising tide of nationalism among China's young people as communist ideology loses its hold.

The transition into the post–Cold War era has been a turbulent time, full of international changes and new possibilities (both good and bad).[43] It is likely, however, that basic rules and principles of IR—those that scholars have long struggled to understand—will continue to apply even though their contexts and outcomes may change. Central to sorting through these changing contexts and outcomes is understanding the different theoretical approaches to the study of International Relations, which we will now address.

---

[43] Max Singer and Aaron B. Wildavsky, *The Real World Order: Zones of Peace, Zones of Turmoil* (Chatham, NJ: Chatham House, 1996). Stanley Hoffmann, *World Disorders: Troubled Peace in the Post–Cold War Era* (Lanham, MD: Rowman & Littlefield, 1998).

The Changing World Order

A New Era?

"World order" refers to the rules that govern—albeit in a messy and ambiguous way—the most important relationships of the interstate system in general and the world's great powers in particular. Aspects include balance of power, spheres of influence, shared beliefs, key treaties and institutions, principles like sovereignty, practices like free trade and so forth. Historically, transformations of the world order and the rise of new guiding principles have occurred after terrible great-power wars. However, the end of the Cold War (1945–1990) brought a more peaceful transition in world order.

In the 1990s, world order lacked a strong direction or guiding principle—notwithstanding the attempt by President Bush (senior) to codify a "new world order." State and nonstate actors adapted incrementally to changing relationships and technologies. The world seemed to pick its way through the world-order challenges of the 1990s, from the Gulf to former Yugoslavia, a falling Russia and a rising China, learning by trial and error what worked. The idea of "human security" emerged, a notion promoted in particular by Canada. Overall, the reduced warfare and more stable great-power relations of the 1990s—along with the steadily cheap oil prices that resulted partly from the Gulf War—underwrote a period of unprecedented prosperity in North America, Europe and China.

At the same time, however, in the late 1990s Southeast Asia experienced one of the worst financial crises since the Depression, and this had an impact on economies around the world. Although Yugoslavia had descended into hellish war, Russia and the rest of Eastern Europe hung on through a long depression without imploding. Western military interventions, following a painful learning curve, suppressed ultranationalism in Yugoslavia before it spread as a model. Indeed, democracy was the growing model in the 1990s. Unprecedented world trade and technical integration fuelled prosperity in Canada and other Western economies.

In 2001 the United States suffered the worst foreign attack on U.S. territory in history. The destruction of the World Trade Center—a prominent symbol of American wealth and power, and the defining feature of New York City's skyline—caused direct and indirect damage estimated in the order of $100 billion. The attack came as a U.S. recession was already underway after the collapse of a speculative bubble in internet stocks.

World Trade Center, New York, September 2001.

The terrorist attacks altered international relationships. Tensions between the great powers eased for a time, and unprecedented cooperation began. Borders became tighter—a security asset but an economic liability and an infringement on civil liberties, with racial profiling used to target people of Muslim heritage. The U.S. military became more active in more countries, and began operating from Central Asian military bases. In Afghanistan, the might of a technologically advanced superpower turned the tide of a low-tech war, sweeping out terrorists and their collaborators. As the war began to wane in Afghanistan, a new apparent threat emerged in Iraq. On the assumption that Saddam Hussein was amassing weapons of mass destruction, the U.S. formed a new coalition (this time with less widespread and less enthusiastic support from its allies) and invaded Iraq in 2003. By mid-2004, cheap oil had all but disappeared, and economists debated whether this signalled a looming recession or merely a period of short-term adjustment.

Do these changes mean a new world order? Were the 1990s just an unstable interim that ended as abruptly as it began? Or were the 2001 attacks a temporary aberration in the world order as it had evolved over the prior decade? Is a new order taking shape slowly as various episodes take us along a lengthy learning curve—September 11 being only one in a series of good and bad experiences? As the new world order takes form, what are its salient features? Its winners and losers? The prospects for war and peace? "The Changing World Order" boxes throughout the book will examine these questions.

Thinking Critically

1. Pick a current area in which interesting international events are taking place. Can you think of possible explanations for those events from each of the four levels of analysis? (See Table 1.1, p. 14.) Do explanations from different levels provide insights into different aspects of the events?

2. For a given state that was once a *colony,* can you think of ways in which the state's current foreign policies might be influenced by its history of colonialism? What of a state that was once a *colonizer*?

3. The Cold War is over, but its influences linger. Can you think of three examples in which the Cold War experience continues to shape the foreign policies of today's states?

4. In what ways do international economics affect our daily lives? Is this true for all people in all places? Or do economic processes like globalization affect some regions more than others?

5. What do you expect will be the character of the twenty-first century? Peaceful? War-prone? Orderly? Chaotic? Why do you have the expectations you do, and what clues from the unfolding of events in the world might tell you whether your guesses were correct?

Chapter Summary

- IR affects daily life profoundly; we all participate in IR.

- IR is a field of political science, concerned mainly with explaining and understanding political outcomes in international security affairs and the international political economy.

- Theories complement descriptive narratives in explaining international events and outcomes, but scholars do not agree on a single set of theories or methods for use in studying IR.

- States are important actors in IR; the international system is based on the sovereignty of (about 200) independent territorial states.

- States vary greatly in size of population and economy, from tiny microstates to great powers.

- Nonstate actors such as multinational corporations (MNCs), nongovernmental organizations (NGOs), global social movements and intergovernmental organizations (IGOs) exert a growing influence on international relations.

- The worldwide revolution in information technologies will profoundly reshape the capabilities and preferences of actors in IR in ways that we do not yet understand.

- Four levels of analysis—individual, domestic, interstate and global—suggest multiple explanations (operating simultaneously) for outcomes observed in IR.

- The global level of analysis draws attention especially to technological change and the global gap in wealth between the industrialized North and the South.

- A variety of world civilizations were conquered by Europeans over several centuries and forcefully absorbed into a single global international system initially centred in Europe.

- The great-power system, an idea particularly important for realists, is made up of about half a dozen states (with membership changing over time as state power rises and falls).

- Great powers have restructured world order through recurrent wars, alliances and the reign of hegemons (states that temporarily gain a preponderance of power in the international system). The most important wars have been the Thirty Years' War, the Napoleonic Wars, World War I and World War II. Periods of hegemony include Britain in the nineteenth century and the United States after World War II.

- European states colonized most of the rest of the world during the past five centuries. Latin American countries gained independence shortly after the United States (about 200 years ago), while those in Africa, Asia and the Middle East became independent states only in the decades after World War II.

- Nationalism strongly influences IR; conflict often results from the perception of nationhood leading to demands for statehood or for the adjustment of state borders.

- Democracy is a force of growing importance: more states are becoming democratically governed, and democracies rarely fight each other in wars.

- The world economy has generated wealth at an accelerating pace in the past two centuries and is increasingly integrated on a global scale, although with huge inequalities.

- World Wars I and II dominated the twentieth century, yet seem to offer contradictory lessons about the utility of hard-line or conciliatory foreign policies.

- For most of the 60 years since World War II, world politics revolved around the East-West rivalry of the Cold War. This bipolar standoff created stability and avoided great-power wars, including nuclear war, but had harmful consequences for states of the global South that became proxy battlegrounds.

- The post–Cold War era that began in the 1990s held hope of general great-power cooperation despite the appearance of new ethnic and regional conflicts.

- The post–Cold War era is also the era of globalization.

- A "war on terrorism"—with broad international support but uncertain scope and duration—began in 2001 after terrorist attacks on the United States.

- The United States and Britain, without the support of the UN and key allies such as Canada, France and Germany, invaded Iraq in 2003 to oust Iraqi leader Saddam Hussein, who was later executed in 2006 after being found guilty of crimes against humanity for his part in the murder of 148 Iraqi Shi'ites in 1982.

Key Terms

international relations (IR)   1

international security   3

international political economy (IPE)   3

state   8

United Nations (UN)   8

international system   8

nation-states   9

gross domestic product (GDP)   10

nonstate actors   11

nongovernmental organizations (NGOs)   12

global social movements   12

intergovernmental organizations (IGOs)   13

North-South gap   16

nationalism   28

industrialization   30

free trade   31

League of Nations   33

Munich Agreement   33

genocide   34

Cold War   35

containment   35

Sino-Soviet split   35

summit meeting   36

Cuban Missile Crisis   36

proxy wars   36

Research Navigator Question

Use the Link Library for History—World History on Research Navigator™ and explore several of the sites that focus on the Thirty Years' War. For International Relations scholars, what matters most about the Thirty Years' War is its settlement, and specifically the ways in which the principle of sovereignty is embedded in the Peace of Westphalia. But in these historical accounts a more detailed picture of the Thirty Years' War emerges. Are there other lessons to be learned from the Thirty Years' War in addition to the one most often cited by scholars of International Relations?

Weblinks

One way to get a sense of both events going on in the world and different perspectives on those events is to visit media and news outlets from around the world. Following are a few sites you should bookmark and visit now and again as you go through the text. An internet search will find media outlets for numerous other countries. Do these media sources cover the same news items, and in the same way, as your own local media?

allAfrica:
http://allafrica.com

Aljazeera English Language Site:
http://english.aljazeera.net/HomePage

Bangkok Post:
http://www.bangkokpost.net

BBC World News Service:
http://news.bbc.co.uk

The Japan Times:
http://www.japantimes.co.jp

The Jerusalem Post:
http://www.jpost.com

The Mail & Guardian (South Africa):
http://www.mg.co.za

The New York Times:
http://www.nytimes.com

People's Daily (China):
http://english.people.com.cn

Phnom Penh Post:
http://www.PhnomPenhPost.com

Pravda (Russia):
http://english.pravda.ru

The Times of India:
http://timesofindia.indiatimes.com

Realist Approaches

2

Maj. Andrew Zdunich of Canada talks to elders in the village of Leyvani, Afghanistan, in 2004.

THEORETICAL APPROACHES IN INTERNATIONAL RELATIONS

Engaging with theoretical approaches in international relations is both indispensable and difficult. It is indispensable because everyone in IR operates from a theoretical perspective (or some combination of perspectives). Every academic book or article, media report, policy-maker or student is commenting or writing from a theoretical perspective. No one is just presenting "the facts"; rather, they are interpreting what those facts mean through the lens of a theoretical approach. Part of the job of studying IR is to become familiar with the different theoretical perspectives that observers of IR use, and to be aware of the different implications of adopting one perspective over another. Students also need to think through, in an analytical way, the reasons they do, or do not, find arguments made in IR persuasive. Having a sense of the theoretical perspective in which an argument is based is one part of that analytical investigation.

But becoming familiar with and identifying the different paradigms can be difficult. Not everyone makes their theoretical perspective(s) explicit, and some people may even be unaware that their point of view has a basis in a theoretical approach. Some observers of international relations use different theoretical approaches to explain or understand different events; others may try to combine elements of various approaches into a single new theory (this is difficult to accomplish without becoming contradictory). Many theoretical approaches are also quite fluid: they are adapted and modified by the people who use them, often in an effort to respond to criticisms, some of which originate in competing paradigms.

There are many more theories of IR than can be covered here. What is offered in these chapters is an introduction to some of the main approaches in the study of IR. This text organizes those approaches into three main paradigms: realist, liberal-pluralist and critical theories (see this chapter as well as Chapters 3 and 4). These paradigms or categories group together theories that share some broad agreement about what the world looks like, how we should study it and what the purpose of theory should be.

Even categorizing *where* one specific theory should go is sometimes debated (some actual theorists of IR, for example, may consider themselves critical theorists and find that they are described here as liberal, or vice versa). Students of theory in IR need to become familiar with the different perspectives and begin to think through which perspective, if any, they find most convincing. They also need to know that this is at best an inexact science, and that debate exists in IR as much about the theories themselves as the issues the theories seek to address.

REALISM

Realism (or *political realism*) is a school of thought that explains international relations in terms of power (see "Defining Power," pp. 52–53). The exercise of power by states toward each other is sometimes called *realpolitik,* or simply *power politics*. Realism has a long history, and it dominated the study of IR from the end of World War II until the early 1970s when alternative approaches began to emerge. Even as other theoretical approaches were developed, realism remained very important to the study of international relations. Some schools of international relations or political science continue to teach IR as though realism is still the only theoretical approach. This is particularly true in the United States, where realist thought first developed and had an important impact on both scholarship and policy-making.

Realism as we know it developed in reaction to a tradition that realists called **idealism** (of course, idealists themselves do not consider their approach unrealistic). Idealism emphasizes international law, morality and international organization over power alone as key influences on international events. Idealists think human nature is basically good. With good habits, education and appropriate international structures, human nature can become the basis of peaceful and cooperative international relationships. Idealists see the international system as one based on a community of states with the potential to work together to overcome mutual problems (see Chapter 3).

For idealists, the principles of IR must flow from morality. More than 2000 years ago, the Chinese writer Mo Ti stated that everyone "knows that [murder] is unrighteous," yet "when murder is committed in attacking a country it is not considered wrong; it is applauded and called righteous." For Mo Ti, this made no sense. "If a man calls black black if it is seen on a small scale, but calls black white when it is seen on a large scale, then he is one who cannot tell black from white."[1] Idealists were particularly active in the period between World Wars I and II, in response to the painful experience of World War I. U.S. president Woodrow Wilson and other idealists placed their hopes for peace in the League of Nations as a formal structure for the community of nations.

Those hopes were dashed when that structure proved helpless to stop German and Japanese aggression in the 1930s. Since World War II, realists have blamed idealists for

realism (political realism)
A broad intellectual tradition that explains international relations mainly in terms of power.

idealism An approach that emphasizes international law, morality and international organization, rather than power alone, as key influences on international relations.

---

[1] Sun Tzu, *The Art of War*, trans. Samuel B. Griffith (NY: Oxford UP, 1963) 22.

looking too much at how the world *ought* to be instead of how it *really* is. Sobered by the experiences of World War II, realists set out to understand the principles of power politics without succumbing to wishful thinking. Realism provided a theoretical foundation for the Cold War policies of containment and the determination of U.S. policy-makers not to appease the Soviet Union and China.

Realists ground themselves in a long tradition. The Chinese strategist *Sun Tzu*, who lived two thousand years ago (at the time of Mo Ti), advised the rulers of states how to survive in an era when war had become a systematic instrument of power for the first time (the "warring states" period). Sun Tzu argued that moral reasoning was not very useful to the state rulers of the day, who were faced with armed and dangerous neighbours. Sun Tzu showed rulers how to use power to advance their interests and protect their survival.

At roughly the same time, in Greece, *Thucydides* wrote an account of the Peloponnesian War (431–404 B.C.) focusing on relative power among the Greek city-states. He stated that "the strong do what they have the power to do and the weak accept what they have to accept."[2] Much later, in Renaissance Italy (around 1500), *Niccolò Machiavelli* urged princes to concentrate on expedient actions to stay in power and to pay attention to war above all else. Today the adjective *Machiavellian* refers to excessively manipulative power manoeuvres.[3]

In the seventeenth century, English philosopher *Thomas Hobbes* discussed the free-for-all that exists when government is absent and people seek their own self-interest. He called it the "state of nature" or "state of war" (in contrast to what we would now call the rule of law). Hobbes favoured a strong monarchy to prevent the condition, but in international affairs, according to realists, there is no such central authority (see pp. 60–63).

In the nineteenth century, German military strategist *Karl von Clausewitz* said that "war is a continuation of politics by other means." U.S. admiral *Alfred Mahan* promoted naval power as the key means of achieving national political and economic interests. In these historical figures, realists see evidence that the importance of power politics is timeless and cross-cultural.

After World War II, scholar *Hans Morgenthau* argued that international politics is governed by objective, universal laws based on national interest defined as power (not on psychological motives of decision-makers). He reasoned that no nation had "God on its side" (a universal morality) and that all nations must base their actions on prudence and practicality.

Realists tend to treat political power as separate from and dominant over morality, ideology and other social and economic aspects of life. For realists, ideologies do not matter much, nor do religions or other cultural factors states may use to explain their actions. Realists see states with very different religions or ideologies or economic systems as quite similar in their actions with regard to national power.[4]

---

[2] Thucydides, *History of the Peloponnesian War*, trans. R. Warner (NY: Penguin, 1972) 402.

[3] Niccolò Machiavelli, *The Prince, and the Discourses*, trans. Luigi Ricci, revised by E. R. P. Vincent (NY: Modern Library, 1950). Friedrich Meinecke, *Machiavellism: The Doctrine of Raison d'État and Its Place in Modern History*, trans. D. Scott (New Haven, CT: Yale UP, 1957).

[4] Hans J. Morgenthau and Kenneth W. Thompson, *Politics among Nations: The Struggle for Power and Peace*, 6th ed. (NY: Knopf, 1985). Edward Hallett Carr, *The Twenty Years' Crisis, 1919–1939: An Introduction to the Study of International Relations* (1939; London: Macmillan, 1974). Raymond Aron, *Peace and War: A Theory of International Relations*, trans. R. Howard and A. B. Fox (NY: Doubleday, 1966).

Focus on Canadian Scholarship

Scholars at Canadian universities who have explored or developed realist thinking in IR include **Frank Harvey** of Dalhousie University, who researches nuclear and conventional deterrence and strategic stability and is particularly interested in the "illusions" of multilateral security in the face of globalized terrorism. Also at Dalhousie, **Dan Middlemiss** has focused on Canadian defence policy. **David Dewitt** at York University along with colleague **John Kirton** at the University of Toronto developed the idea of Canada as a "principal power." **David Bercuson,** a historian at the University of Calgary, focuses on Canadian military and diplomatic history and strategic studies. **Paul Buteux** at the University of Manitoba focuses on nuclear force modernization in NATO. **Albert Legault** at the University of Québec at Montréal does work on conflict, arms control and terrorism, and **Charles-Philippe David,** also at UQAM, focuses on U.S. foreign and defence policy. **Michel Fortmann** at the University of Montréal works on

IR theory and foreign policy. **David Haglund** at Queen's University is interested in American foreign policy, Canadian foreign policy and transatlantic relations. At the University of Windsor, Andrew Richter examines Canadian military strategy and nuclear weapons. **Elinor Sloan** of Carleton University focuses on U.S. and Canadian security and defence policies and military force transformation, and her colleague **Brian Schmidt** is working on a book on realism. At Carleton's Norman Paterson School of International Affairs, **Fen Hampson** researches international negotiation and conflict resolution. **Michael Brecher** at McGill University focuses on theories of crisis and protracted conflicts. At the University of Guelph, **Ian Spears** has examined power sharing agreements in the aftermath of civil war and is interested in the prospects for conflict and conflict resolution in African states. **Paul T. Mitchell** at the Canadian Forces College is interested in network-centric warfare and small navies.

Realists share several assumptions about how IR works. They assume that IR can be best (though not exclusively) explained by the choices of states operating as autonomous actors rationally pursuing their own interests in a system of sovereign states. Sometimes the realist framework is summarized in three propositions: (1) *states* are the most important actors (the state-centric assumption); (2) they act as *rational* individuals in pursuing power; pursuing power is in the national interest (the unitary rational-actor assumption); and (3) they act in the context of an international system lacking central government (the *anarchy* assumption).

Neorealism, sometimes called *structural realism*, is an adaptation of realism developed by theorists such as Kenneth Waltz.[5] Neorealism explains patterns of international events in terms of the system structure—the international distribution of power—rather than the internal makeup of individual states. Neorealists sought to move away from arguments rooted in human nature (in Morgenthau's phrase, the universal "desire of man to attain maximum power") and instead put emphasis on the structure of the international system, which is anarchic. Compared with traditional realism, neorealism aims to be more scientific in the sense of proposing general laws to explain events, but critics of neorealism argue that it has lost some of the richness of traditional realists, who took account of many complex elements (geography, willpower, diplomacy, etc.).[6]

neorealism A version of realist theory that emphasizes the influence of the system's structure on state behaviour, and particularly the international distribution of power. See also *realism.*

[5] Kenneth N. Waltz, *Theory of International Politics* (Reading, MA: Addison-Wesley, 1979). See also Kenneth N. Waltz, "Realist Thought and Neorealist Theory," in Robert L. Rothstein, ed., *The Evolution of International Theory* (South Carolina: U of South Carolina Press, 1991).

[6] Robert O. Keohane, ed., *Neorealism and Its Critics* (NY: Columbia UP, 1986). Barry Buzan, Charles Jones and Richard Little, *The Logic of Anarchy: Neorealism to Structural Realism* (NY: Columbia UP, 1993). Frank W. Wayman and Paul F. Diehl, eds., *Reconstructing Realpolitik* (Ann Arbor: U Michigan P, 1994). John A. Vasquez, *The Power of Power Politics: From Classical Realism to Neotraditionalism* (UK: Cambridge UP 1999).

It is important to note that while there is a general coherence within realism and broad agreement on some of the theory's principal assumptions (the primacy of the state, the rational pursuit of power, and the anarchy of the international system), there is also considerable debate among realists today. "Postclassical" realists, for example, argue that states will sometimes prioritize economic over military capacity. Others argue that contemporary realism needs to take into account both "offensive" realism and "defensive" realism (the latter suggesting that states are often willing to settle for the "status quo" distribution of power if it means avoiding an unnecessary conflict). There has also been considerable debate about the role of institutions, with some neorealists insisting that institutions have no independent effect on state behaviour, whereas many others argue that institutions do in fact matter and have an impact on the decision-making in which states engage.[7]

There is also considerable debate among realists about the specific policy options pursued by states. Because of realism and neo-realism's emphasis on power and security, many observers assume that this means realists are themselves proponents of war, but it is an incorrect assumption. Realists can be critics of war and of the use of force and are sometimes vocal critics of their own government's policies. Hans Morgenthau, for example, was an outspoken critic of the U.S. conflict in Vietnam. In 2002, prior to the U.S. invasion of Iraq, a group of 33 American scholars of IR took out a one-page advertisement in the *New York Times* and wrote that "military force should be used only when it advances U.S. national interests. War with Iraq does not meet this standard." Many of the signatories were prominent American realist and neo-realist thinkers, including Kenneth Waltz, John Mearsheimer, Alexander George and Stephen Walt, among others.[8]

POWER

Power is a central concept in international relations—the central one for realists—but one that is surprisingly difficult to define or measure.

Defining Power

power The ability or potential to influence others' behaviour, as measured by the possession of certain tangible and intangible characteristics.

Power is often defined as the ability to get another actor to do what it would not otherwise have done (or not to do what it would have done).[9] A variation on this idea is that actors are powerful to the extent that they affect others more than others affect them. These definitions treat power as influence. If actors get their way a lot, they must be powerful.

One problem with this definition is that we seldom know what a second actor would have done in the absence of the first actor's power. There is a danger of circular logic: power explains influence, and influence measures power. Thus it is hard to use power to explain why international events occur (the aim of realism). A related problem is that common usage treats power as a thing rather than a process: states "have" power.

---

[7] John J. Mearsheimer, "The False Promise of International Institutions," *International Security* 14.1 (1994/95): 4–49. Randall L. Schweller and David Priess, "A Tale of Two Realisms: Expanding the Institutions Debate," *Mershon International Studies Review* 41.1 (May 1997): 1–32. Robert Jervis, "Realism, Neoliberalism, and Cooperation: Understanding the Debate," *International Security* 24.1 (Summer 1999): 42–63.

[8] "War with Iraq Is Not in America's National Interests," *The New York Times* 26 Sept. 2002. Cited from Mohammed Nuruzzaman, "Beyond the Realist Theories: 'Neo-Conservative Realism' and the American Invasion of Iraq, *International Studies Perspective* 7.3 (August 2006): 239–53. This article also provides a summary of realist and neorealist thought as well as an application of current realist thinking to the Iraq War.

[9] Robert A. Dahl, *Modern Political Analysis,* 2nd ed. (Englewood Cliffs, NJ: Prentice Hall, 1970).

These problems are resolved if we recall that power is not influence itself, but the ability or potential to influence others. IR scholars believe that such potential is based on specific (tangible and intangible) characteristics or possessions of states—such as size, levels of income, armed forces and so forth. This is *power* as *capability*. Capabilities are easier to measure than influence and less circular in logic.

Measuring capabilities to explain how one nation influences another is not simple, however. It requires summing up various kinds of potentials. States possess varying amounts of population, territory, military forces and so forth. Some realists consider the best single indicator of a state's power to be its total GDP, which combines overall size, technological level and wealth. But even GDP is at best a rough indicator.

Furthermore, beyond tangible capabilities, power depends on intangible elements. Capabilities give a state the potential to influence others only to the extent that political leaders can mobilize and deploy them effectively and strategically. This depends on national will, diplomatic skill, popular support for the government (its legitimacy) and so forth. Some scholars emphasize the *power of ideas*—the ability to maximize the influence of capabilities through a psychological process. This process includes the domestic mobilization of capabilities—often through religion, ideology or (especially) nationalism. International influence is also gained by being an actor who forms rules of behaviour and changes how others see their own national interests. If a state's own values become widely shared among other states, it will easily influence others. For example, the United States has influenced many other states to accept the value of free markets and free trade. Canada often has sought to influence other states to support diplomacy and international organizations. This has been called *soft power*.[10]

A state can have power only relative to other states. *Relative power* is the ratio of the power that two states can bring to bear against each other. It matters little to realists whether a state's capabilities are rising or declining in absolute terms, only whether they are falling behind or overtaking the capabilities of rival states.

Even realists recognize the limits to explanations based on power. At best, power provides a general understanding of typical or average outcomes. In actual IR there are many other elements at work, including an element of accident or luck. The more powerful actor does not always prevail. Power provides only a partial explanation.[11]

Estimating Power

The logic of power suggests that in wars, the more powerful state will generally prevail. Thus, estimates of the relative power of the two antagonists should help explain the outcome of each war. These estimates could take into account the nations' relative military capabilities and the popular support for each government, among other factors. Most important, however, is the total size of each nation's economy—the total GDP—which reflects both population size and the level of income per person (per capita). With a healthy enough economy, a state can buy a large army, popular support (by providing consumer goods) and even allies.

---

[10] Joseph S. Nye, Jr., *Bound to Lead: The Changing Nature of American Power* (NY: Basic Books, 1990). See also Lloyd Axworthy, *Navigating a New World: Canada's Global Future* (Toronto: Knopf, 2004).

[11] John M. Rothgeb, Jr., *Defining Power: Influence and Force in the Contemporary International System* (NY: St. Martin's, 1992). Ralph Pettman, *International Politics: Balance of Power, Balance of Productivity, Balance of Ideologies* (Boulder, CO: Rienner, 1991). Robert W. Cox, *Production, Power, and World Order: Social Forces in the Making of History* (NY: Columbia UP, 1987). George Liska, *The Ways of Power: Patterns and Meaning in World Politics* (Cambridge, UK: Blackwell, 1990). Richard Stoll and Michael D. Ward, eds., *Power in World Politics* (Boulder, CO: Rienner, 1988). Michael P. Sullivan, *Power in Contemporary International Politics* (Columbia, SC: U South Carolina P, 1990).

For example, when the United States invaded Iraq in 2003 it was the most powerful state in world history, and Iraq had been weakened by two costly wars and a decade of sanctions. The power disparity was striking. In GDP, the United States held an advantage of more than a hundred to one; in population, more than ten to one. U.S. forces were larger and much more capable technologically. In 2003, the United States lacked some of the power elements it had possessed during the 1991 Gulf War—the moral legitimacy conferred by the UN Security Council, a broad coalition of allies (including the most powerful states regionally and globally) and partners willing to pay for most of the costs of the war. Despite these shortfalls, U.S. military power was able to carry out the objective of regime change in Iraq within a month and with low U.S. casualties.

And yet, four years later, the U.S. forces' grip on Iraq remained tenuous as an anti-American insurgency proved far stronger than expected and religious divisions threatened to tear Iraq apart. At the same time, the war weakened support for American policies around the world. The difficulties encountered by the world's superpower in trying to establish stable political control in Iraq demonstrate that power—getting others to do what you want—includes many elements beyond just military might or GDP. Neither can predict who will win a war.

Elements of Power

State power is a mix of many ingredients, including natural resources, industrial capacity, moral legitimacy, military preparedness and popular support of government. All these elements contribute to an actor's power, but most realists acknowledge that there is no precise equation to determine which combination of elements produces the greatest measure of power.

Elements that an actor can draw on over the *long term* include total GDP, population, territory, geography and natural resources. These attributes change slowly. Less tangible long-term power resources include political culture, patriotism, education of the population and strength of the scientific and technological base. The credibility of its commitments (reputation for keeping its word) is also a power resource that can be nurtured over time, as is the ability of one state's culture and values to consistently shape the thinking of other states (the power of ideas). Power resources shape an actor's potential power.

Other capabilities allow actors to exercise influence in the *short term*. Military forces are such a capability—perhaps the most important kind. The size, composition and preparedness of two states' military forces matter more in a short-term military confrontation than do their respective economies or natural resources. Another short-term capability is the military-industrial capacity to quickly produce

THE ECONOMICS OF POWER
Military power rests on economic strength, roughly measured by GDP. The large U.S. economy supports U.S. military dominance. In the 2003 Iraq War, the United States could afford to send a large and technologically advanced military force to the Middle East. Here, U.S. forces enter Iraq in March 2003.

weapons. The quality of a state's bureaucracy is another type of capability, allowing the state to gather information, regulate international trade or participate in international conferences. Less tangibly, the *support* and *legitimacy* that an actor commands from constituents and allies in the short term are capabilities that the actor can use to gain influence, as is the *loyalty* of a nation's army and politicians to their leader.

Given the limited resources that any actor commands, there are always trade-offs among possible capabilities. Building up military forces diverts resources that might be put into foreign aid, for instance. Or buying a population's loyalty with consumer goods reduces resources available for building up military capabilities. To the extent that one element of power can be converted into another, it is *fungible*. Generally, money is the most fungible capability because it can buy other capabilities.

Realists tend to see *military force* as the most important element of national power in the short term, and they see other elements, such as economic strength, diplomatic skill or moral legitimacy as being important to the extent that they are fungible to military power. Such fungibility of nonmilitary elements of power into military ones is considerable, at least in the long term. Well-paid soldiers fight better, as do soldiers imbued with moral fervour for their cause or soldiers using high-technology weapons. Skilled diplomats can avoid unfavourable military confrontations or provoke favourable ones. Moral foreign policies can help sway public opinion in foreign countries and cement alliances that increase military strength. Realists tend to treat these dimensions of power as important mainly because of their potential military impact. Chairman Mao Zedong of China said, "All power grows out of the barrel of a gun."

The different types of power capabilities can be contrasted by considering the choice to possess tanks or gold. One standard power capability that states want is the battle tank. In land warfare to control territory, the tank is arguably the most powerful instrument available, and the leading defence against it is another tank. One can assess power on this dimension by counting the size and quality of a state's tank force (an imprecise but not impossible exercise). A different power capability of time-honoured value is the stockpile of gold (or its modern-day equivalent in hard currency reserves; see Chapter 9). Gold represents economic power and is a power resource, whereas tanks represent military power and are a power capability.

In the long term, gold is better because it can be turned into tanks (it is fungible), where it might be hard to turn tanks into gold. However, in the short term, the tanks might be better because if an enemy tank force invades one's territory, gold will not stop them; indeed they will soon take the gold for themselves. For example, in 1990 Iraq (which had gone for tanks) invaded its neighbour Kuwait (which had gone for gold). In the short term, Iraq proved much more powerful: it plundered Kuwait and occupied it.

Morality can contribute to power, by increasing the will to use power and by attracting allies. States have long clothed their actions, however aggressive, in rhetoric about peaceful and defensive intentions. For instance, the 1989 U.S. invasion of Panama was named "Operation Just Cause" and the United States' response to the September 11, 2001, attacks is called "Operation Enduring Freedom." Military capabilities are most effective in the context of justifications that make state actions seem moral. Of course, if a state uses moralistic rhetoric to cloak self-interest too often, it loses credibility even with its own population.

The use of geography as an element of power is called **geopolitics.** It is often tied to the logistical requirements of military forces (see Chapter 6). Frequently, state leaders use maps in thinking about international power positions and alignments. In geopolitics, as in real estate, the three most important considerations are location, location, location. States increase their power to the extent they can use geography to enhance their military

geopolitics The use of geography as an element of power, and the ideas about it held by political leaders and scholars.

capabilities, such as by securing allies and bases close to a rival power or along strategic trade routes, or by controlling key natural resources. In general, power declines as a function of distance from a home state, although technology seems to be making this decline less steep.

A recurrent geopolitical theme for centrally located, largely land-locked states such as Germany and Russia is the threat of being surrounded. The 1979 Soviet invasion of Afghanistan was seen by some Western leaders as a step toward Soviet expansion southward to the Indian Ocean, driven by the motive to secure a port free of ice year-round. Militarily, centrally located states often face a *two-front problem*. For states less centrally located, such as Britain or the United States, different geopolitical problems appear. These states have been called "insular" in that bodies of water protect them against land attacks.[12] Their geopolitical problem in the event of war is having to move soldiers and supplies over long distances to reach the scene of battle.

RATIONALITY

rational actors Actors conceived as single entities that can "think" about their actions coherently, make choices, identify their interests and rank the interests in terms of priority.

Most realists (and many nonrealists) assume that those who wield power behave as **rational actors** in their efforts to influence others.[13]

This rationality implies that the actor exercising power is a single entity that can "think" about its actions coherently and make choices. This is called the *unitary actor* assumption, or sometimes the *strong leader* assumption, and is used to describe the nature of states as international actors. Although useful, this simplification does not capture the complexity of how states actually arrive at decisions (see Chapter 5).

national interest The interests of a state overall (as opposed to particular parties or factions within the state).

The assumption of rationality also implies that states and other international actors can identify their interests and put priorities on them. Realists assume that the exercise of power attempts to advance the **national interest**—the interests of the state itself. Again, the assumption is a simplification, because the interests of particular politicians, parties, economic sectors or regions of a country often conflict.

What are the interests of a state? Are they the interests of domestic groups (see Chapter 5)? The need to prevail in conflicts with other states (see Chapter 6)? The need to cooperate with the international community for mutual benefit (see Chapter 8)? There is no simple answer. Some realists simply define the national interest as maximizing power—a debatable assumption.

cost-benefit analysis A calculation of the costs incurred by a possible action and the benefits it is likely to bring.

This understanding of rationality also implies that actors are able to perform a **cost-benefit analysis**—calculating the costs incurred by a possible action and the benefits it is likely to bring. Applying power incurs costs and should produce commensurate gains. As with the problem of estimating power, one has to add up different dimensions in such a calculation. For instance, states presumably do not initiate wars that they expect to lose, except in cases where they stand to gain political benefits, domestic or international, that outweigh the costs of losing the war. But it is not easy to tally intangible political benefits

---

[12] Ludwig Dehio, *The Precarious Balance: Four Centuries of the European Power Struggle*, trans. Charles Fullman (Germany: 1948; NY: Vintage Books, 1962). George Modelski and William R. Thompson, *Seapower in Global Politics, 1494–1993* (Seattle: U Washington P, 1988). Joshua S. Goldstein and David P. Rapkin, "After Insularity: Hegemony and the Future World Order," *Futures* 23.9 (1991): 935–59.

[13] Michael E. Brown, Owen R. Coté, Jr., Sean M. Lynn-Jones and Steven E. Miller, eds., *Rational Choice and Security Studies* (Cambridge, MA: MIT P, 2000). David A. Lake and Robert Powell, eds., *Strategic Choice and International Relations* (Princeton, CT: Princeton UP, 1999). Michael Nicholson, *Rationality and the Analysis of International Conflict* (NY: Cambridge UP, 1992). Jeffrey Friedman, ed., *The Rational Choice Controversy: Economic Models of Politics Reconsidered* (New Haven, CT: Yale UP, 1996).

against the tangible costs of a war. Even victory in war may not be worth the costs paid. Rational actors can miscalculate costs and benefits, especially when using faulty information. Finally, human behaviour and luck can be unpredictable.

The ancient realist Sun Tzu advised that the best general was not the most courageous or aggressive one, but the one who could coolly calculate the costs and benefits of alternative courses of action. The best war was a short one, in Sun Tzu's view, because wars are costly. Better yet was to take another state intact without fighting—by intimidation, deception and the disruption of enemy alliances. Capturing an enemy army was better than fighting it. If fighting was necessary, it was to occur on another state's territory so that the army could live off the land. Attacking cities was too destructive and thus reduced the benefits of war.

These three assumptions about rationality—that states are unitary actors, that they have coherent interests, and that they can make cost-benefit calculations—are simplifications that not all IR scholars accept. But realists consider these simplifications useful because they allow scholars to explain in a general way the actions of diverse actors. Power in IR has been compared with money in economics as a universal measure. In this view, just as firms compete for money in economic markets, states compete for power in the international system.[14]

In order to provide a general explanation of state actions, realism makes a fourth assumption, implicit in the parallel to economics. This is the assumption that all states (or their leaders) have basically the same values and interests—*intersubjective preferences*. (The outcomes valued by an actor are called preferences or *utility*.) Economists assume that everyone prefers more money to less. Realists assume that all states prefer more power to less.

This assumption has been criticized. If a state leader prefers upholding his or her honour by fighting a losing war rather than being dictated to by a foreign leader, such an action is rational in terms of the leader's own preferences. Similarly, the suicidal charges of Iranian teenagers against Iraqi positions in the Iran-Iraq war were rational for the teenagers, who believed that as martyrs, they would go directly to heaven. Such preferences are hardly universal, however.

Despite these criticisms, realists argue that rational-actor models capture not all but the most important aspects of IR. These simplified models provide the foundations for a large body of IR research that represents international bargaining relationships mathematically. By accepting the limitations of the four assumptions of rationality, IR scholars can build very general and abstract models of international relationships.

Game Theory

Game theory is a branch of mathematics concerned with predicting bargaining outcomes. A game is a setting in which two or more players choose among alternative moves, either once or repeatedly. Each combination of moves (by all players) results in a set of payoffs (utility) to each player. The payoffs can be tangible items such as money or any intangible items of value. Game theory aims to deduce likely outcomes (what moves players will make), given the players' preferences and the possible moves open to them. Games are sometimes called formal models.

game theory A branch of mathematics concerned with predicting bargaining outcomes. Games such as Prisoner's Dilemma and Chicken have been used to analyze various sorts of international interactions.

Game theory was first used extensively in IR in the 1950s and 1960s by scholars trying to understand U.S.-Soviet nuclear war contingencies. Moves were decisions to use nuclear weapons in certain ways, and payoffs were outcomes of the war. The use of game theory to study international interactions has become more extensive among IR scholars in recent years, especially among realists, who accept the assumptions about rationality. To analyze a game mathematically, one assumes that each player chooses a move rationally, to maximize its payoff.

---

[14] Kenneth N. Waltz, *Theory of International Politics* (Reading, MA: Addison-Wesley, 1979).

Different kinds of situations are represented by different classes of games, as defined by the number of players and the structure of the payoffs. One basic distinction is between **zero-sum games,** in which one player's gain is by definition equal to the other's loss, and *non-zero-sum games*, in which it is possible for both players to gain (or lose). In a zero-sum game there is no point in communication or cooperation between the players because their interests are diametrically opposed. In a non-zero-sum game, coordination of moves can maximize the total payoff to the players, although each may still manoeuvre to gain a greater share of that total payoff.

A *two-person game* has only two players; because it is simple and easy to analyze mathematically, this is the most common type of game studied. An *N-person* game has more than two players, and the moves typically result in coalitions of players, with the members of the winning coalition dividing the payoff among themselves in some manner. In most games, all the players make a move simultaneously. They may do so repeatedly, in a *repeated game* (or an *iterated game, sequential game* or *supergame*). In a few games, the players alternate moves so that each knows the other's move before deciding on its own.

Analysis of a game entails searching for a *solution*—a set of moves by all the players such that no player can increase its payoff by changing its move. It is the outcome at which rational players will arrive. Some simple games have one solution, but many games have multiple solutions or no single stable solution.

A category of games with a given structure—in terms of the relationships between moves and payoffs—is sometimes given a name that evokes a story or metaphor representing the nature of the games. Each such game yields an insight or lesson regarding a type of international bargaining situation.[15]

The most commonly studied game is called *Prisoner's Dilemma (PD)*, in which rational players will choose moves that produce an outcome where all players are worse off than under a different set of moves. They all could do better, but as individual rational actors they are unable to achieve this outcome. How can this be?

🌐 Thinking Theoretically

For game theorists, the Prisoner's Dilemma represents some of the basic elements of world politics as faced by state leaders: high risks and the imperative to make decisions quickly in situations of uncertainty. The one-shot PD game (a game played only once, not unlike the decision demanded of prisoners themselves) is thought to best represent the realist vision of IR.

However, game theorists have shown that in an iterated PD game (one played repeatedly with the same players), the possibility of reciprocity can make it rational to cooperate. Now, players reason that they will meet one another in future games and a cooperative move in the present may be reciprocated by an opponent in future. Some suggest that this represents a more liberal view of the world: states and other actors interact with one another repeatedly, and can learn from each other's behaviour and adjust their own behaviour accordingly.

Critical theorists are unlikely to be involved in elaborating on game theory, but they would still have questions to pose of game theorists. Some might be: Who decides the rules of the game? Who determines the payoff matrix?

---

[15] Barry O'Neill, "A Survey of Game Theory Models on Peace and War," *Handbook of Game Theory*, ed. R. Aumann and S. Hart, vol. 2 (Amsterdam: North-Holland, 1994). Robert Powell, *In the Shadow of Power: States and Strategies in International Politics* (Princeton, NJ: Princeton UP, 1999). James D. Morrow, *Game Theory for Political Scientists* (Princeton, NJ: Princeton UP, 1995). Roger B. Myerson, *Game Theory: Analysis of Conflict* (Cambridge, MA: Harvard UP, 1991). Steven J. Brams, *Superpower Games: Applying Game Theory to Superpower Conflict* (New Haven, CT: Yale UP, 1985).

The original story tells of two prisoners questioned separately by a prosecutor. The prosecutor knows they committed a bank robbery but has only enough evidence to convict them of illegal possession of a gun unless one of them confesses. The prosecutor tells each prisoner that if he confesses and his partner doesn't, he will go free. If his partner confesses and he doesn't, he will get a long prison term for bank robbery (while the partner goes free). If both confess, they will get a somewhat reduced term. If neither confesses, they will be convicted on the gun charge and serve a short sentence. The story assumes that neither prisoner will have a chance to retaliate later, that only the immediate outcomes matter and that each prisoner cares only about himself.

This game has a single solution: both prisoners will confess. Each will reason as follows: "If my partner is going to confess, then I should confess too, because I will get a slightly shorter sentence that way. If my partner is not going to confess, then I should still confess because I will go free instead of serving a short sentence." The dilemma is that by following their individually rational choices, both prisoners will end up serving fairly long sentences when they could have both served short ones by cooperating (keeping their mouths shut).

In IR, the PD game has been used to gain insight into arms races. Consider the decisions of India and Pakistan about whether to build sizeable nuclear weapons arsenals. Both have the ability to do so. In 1998, when India detonated underground nuclear bombs to test weapons designs, Pakistan promptly followed suit. Now, neither side can know whether the other is secretly building up an arsenal, unless they reach an arms control agreement with strict verification provisions. To analyze the game, we assign values to each possible outcome—often called a *preference ordering*—for each player. This is not simple: if we misjudge the value a player puts on a particular outcome, we may draw wrong conclusions.

The following preferences regarding possible outcomes are plausible: the best outcome would be that oneself but not the other player had a nuclear arsenal (the expense of building nuclear weapons would be justified because one could then use them as leverage); second best would be for neither to go nuclear (no leverage, but no expense); third best would be for both to develop nuclear arsenals (a major expense without gaining leverage); worst would be to forgo nuclear weapons oneself while the other player developed them (and thus be subject to blackmail).

The game can be summarized in a *payoff matrix* (see Table 2.1). The first number in each cell is India's payoff, and the second number is Pakistan's. To keep things simple, four indicates the highest payoff, and one the lowest. As is convention, a decision to refrain from building nuclear weapons is called "cooperation," and a decision to proceed with nuclear weapons is called "defection." The dilemma here parallels that of the prisoners just discussed. Each state's leader reasons: "If they go nuclear, we must; if they don't, we'd

Table 2.1 Payoff Matrix in India-Pakistan PD Game

| | | Pakistan | |
		Cooperate	Defect
India	Cooperate	(3,3)	(1,4)
	Defect	(4,1)	(2,2)

Note: First number in each group is India's payoff, second is Pakistan's. The number four is highest payoff, one lowest.

be crazy not to." The model seems to predict an inevitable Indian-Pakistani nuclear arms race, although both states would do better to avoid one. And, indeed, a costly and dangerous arms race is currently underway.

IR scholars have analyzed many other games beyond PD. For example, *Chicken* represents two male teenagers speeding toward a head-on collision. The first to swerve is "chicken." Each reasons: "If he doesn't swerve, I must; but if he swerves, I won't." The player who first commits irrevocably not to swerve ("throwing away the steering wheel") will win. Similarly, in the 1962 Cuban Missile Crisis, some scholars argued that President Kennedy "won" by seeming ready to risk nuclear war if Khrushchev did not back down and remove Soviet missiles from Cuba. (There are, however, alternative explanations of the outcome of the crisis.)

Through analysis of these and other games, IR researchers try to predict what rational actors would do in various situations. Games can capture and simplify the fundamental dynamics of various bargaining situations. However, a game-theoretic analysis is only as good as the assumptions that go into it. In particular, the results of the analysis depend on the preferences that players are assumed to have about outcomes. It is difficult to test either the assumptions or the predictions of a formal model against the realities of IR, which are much more complex in practice.

THE INTERNATIONAL SYSTEM

For realists, states interact within a set of well-defined and long-established "rules of the game" governing what is considered a state and how states treat each other. Together these rules shape the international system as we know it.[16]

Anarchy and Sovereignty

anarchy In IR theory, the term implies not complete chaos but the lack of a central government that can enforce rules.

Realists emphasize that the rules of the international system create **anarchy**—a term that implies not complete chaos or absence of structure, but rather the lack of a central government that can enforce rules.[17] In domestic society within states, governments can enforce contracts, deter participants from breaking rules, and use their monopoly on legally sanctioned violence to enforce a system of law. Both democracies and dictatorships provide central government enforcement of a system of rules. Lack of such a government among states is what realists mean by anarchy. No central authority enforces rules and ensures compliance with norms of conduct. The power of one state is countered only by the power of other states. They must rely on *self-help*, which they supplement with allies and the (sometimes) constraining power of international norms.

Some people think that only a world government can solve this problem. Others think that short of world government, adequate order can be provided by international organizations and agreements (see Chapter 8). Most realists, however, think that IR cannot escape

---

[16] Barry Buzan and Richard Little, *International Systems in World History: Remaking the Study of International Relations* (Oxford: Oxford UP, 2000). Evan Luard, *Conflict and Peace in the Modern International System: A Study of the Principles of International Order* (London: Macmillan, 1988). Martin Wight, *Systems of States* (Leicester: U Leicester P, 1977).

[17] Hedley Bull, *The Anarchical Society: A Study of Order in World Politics* (NY: Columbia UP, 1977). Michael Taylor, *Anarchy and Cooperation* (NY: Wiley, 1976). Harvey Starr, *Anarchy, Order, and Integration: How to Manage Interdependence?* (Ann Arbor: U Michigan P, 1997).

from a state of anarchy and will continue to be dangerous as a result.[18] In this anarchic world, realists emphasize prudence as a great virtue in foreign policy. States should pay attention not to the intentions of other states but rather to their capabilities. As Sun Tzu advised, do not assume that other states will not attack but instead be ready if they do.

Despite its anarchy, the international system is far from chaotic. The great majority of state interactions closely adhere to **norms of behaviour**—shared expectations about what behaviour is considered proper.[19] Norms change over time, slowly, but the most basic norms of the international system have changed little in recent centuries.

Sovereignty—traditionally the most important norm—means that a government has the right, at least in principle, to do whatever it wants in its own territory. States are separate, autonomous and answer to no higher authority (due to anarchy). In principle, all states are equal in status if not in power. Sovereignty also means that states should not interfere in the internal affairs of others. Although states do try to influence each other (exert power) on matters of trade, alliances, war and so on, they should not meddle in the internal politics and decision processes of other states. For example, it would be inappropriate for Russia or the United States to endorse a candidate for Canadian prime minister. (This rule is often bent in practice.)[20]

The principles of state sovereignty were exemplified during the era of South Africa's apartheid regime—a regime that excluded the majority of South Africa's population, blacks, from any political, social or economic rights. Many Western states claimed to be opposed to apartheid but insisted that they could do nothing because it was an "internal affair." During the 1980s, many people around the world called for sanctions to be imposed on South Africa, a call that many countries resisted, claiming it would have been a violation of South Africa's sovereignty. For defenders of sovereignty, change in South Africa would have to come from within, not imposed from without.

In practice, states have a progressively harder time warding off interference in their affairs. Such "internal" matters as human rights or self-determination are, increasingly, seen as concerns for the international community. In the Helsinki agreements that codified East-West détente in the Cold War, the Soviet Union and Eastern Europe promised to respect human rights within their own borders (an internal affair). When the international community failed to respond to the 1994 Rwandan genocide, many viewed it as a horrifying and catastrophic failure. Furthermore, the integration of global economic markets and telecommunications makes it easier than ever for ideas to penetrate state borders.

States are based on territory. Respect for the territorial integrity of all states, within recognized borders, is an important principle of IR. Many of today's borders are the result of past wars (in which winners took territory from losers) or were imposed arbitrarily by third parties such as colonizers. Borders can therefore create many problems—the splitting of nations or ethnic groups into different states, the creation of oddly shaped states that may lack resources or access to ports, and so forth (see pp. 165–173). Despite these imperfections, the international system places a high value on respect for internationally recognized borders. Almost all of the world's land territory falls under the

norms (of behaviour) Shared expectations about what behaviour is considered proper.

sovereignty A state's right, at least in principle, to do whatever it wants within its own territory; traditionally sovereignty is the most important international norm.

---

[18] John J. Mearsheimer, *The Tragedy of Great Power Politics* (NY: Norton, 2001).

[19] Dorothy Jones, *Code of Peace: Ethics and Security in the World of the Warlord States* (Chicago: U Chicago P, 1991). Thomas M. Franck, *The Power of Legitimacy among Nations* (NY: Oxford UP, 1990).

[20] Stephen D. Krasner, *Sovereignty: Organized Hypocrisy* (Princeton, NJ: Princeton UP, 1999). Charles W. Kegley, Jr. and Gregory A. Raymond, *Exorcising the Ghost of Westphalia: Building World Order in the New Millennium* (Upper Saddle River, NJ: Prentice Hall, 2002). Gene M. Lyons and Michael Mastanduno, eds., *Beyond Westphalia: State Sovereignty and International Intervention* (Baltimore: Johns Hopkins UP, 1995).

sovereign control of existing states; very little is considered "up for grabs" (high seas are outside any state's territory; see Chapter 14).

The territorial nature of the interstate system reflects the origins of that system in an age when agrarian societies relied on agriculture to generate wealth. In today's world, where trade and technology rather than land create wealth, the territorial state may be less important. Information-based economies are linked across borders instantly, and the idea of the state having a hard shell now seems archaic. The accelerating revolution in information technologies may dramatically affect the territorial state system in the coming years.

Membership in the international system rests on general recognition (by other states) of a government's sovereignty within its territory. This recognition is extended formally through diplomatic relations and by membership in the UN. It does not imply that a government has popular support but only that it controls the state's territory and agrees to assume its obligations in the international system—to accept internationally recognized borders, to assume the international debts of the previous government and to refrain from interfering in other states' internal affairs.

States have developed norms of diplomacy to facilitate their interactions. An embassy is considered to be territory of its home state, and not the country where it is located (see pp. 282–285).

Diplomatic norms recognize that states try to spy on each other. It is up to each state to keep others from being successful at it. In 2002, China discovered that its new presidential aircraft—a Boeing 767 refurbished in Texas—was riddled with sophisticated listening devices. China did not make an issue of it (the plane

STILL SOVEREIGN TERRITORY
Sovereignty and territorial integrity are central norms governing the behaviour of states. They give states control within established borders. Embassies are considered the home country's territory. Here, the ruined Russian Embassy grounds in the capital of Afghanistan become a refuge to 15 000 people displaced by war (2002).

security dilemma A situation in which states' actions taken to assure their own security (such as deploying military forces) are perceived as threats to the security of other states.

had not gone into service), and a U.S.-China summit went forward the following month.

Realists acknowledge that the rules of IR often create a **security dilemma**—a situation in which states' actions taken to assure their own security (such as deploying military forces) tend to threaten the security of other states.[21] The responses of those other states (such as deploying their own military forces) in turn threaten the first state. The dilemma parallels the Prisoner's Dilemma game discussed earlier. It is a prime cause of arms races in which states waste large sums of money on mutually threatening weapons that do not ultimately provide security. The current debate over developing missile defences hinges in part on whether such defences would cause a worried China or Russia to deploy more nuclear weapons—another case of a security dilemma.

[21] Robert Jervis, "Cooperation under the Security Dilemma," *World Politics* 30.2 (1978): 167–214.

The security dilemma is a negative consequence of anarchy in the international system. Realists tend to see it as unsolvable, whereas liberals think it can be solved through the development of norms and institutions (see Chapters 3 and 8).

As we shall see in later chapters, changes in technology and norms are undermining the traditional principles of territorial integrity and state autonomy in IR. Some IR scholars consider states to be practically obsolete as the main actors in world politics as they integrate into larger entities or fragment into smaller units.[22] Other scholars find the international system and state units quite stable in structure.[23] For realists, one of its most enduring features is the balance of power.

Balance of Power

In the anarchy of the international system, the most reliable brake on the power of one state is the power of other states. The term **balance of power** refers to the general concept of one or more states' power being used to balance that of another state or group of states. The term is used in several ways and is imprecisely defined. Balance of power can refer to any ratio of power capabilities between states or alliances; or it can mean only a relatively equal ratio. Alternatively, balance of power can refer to the process by which counterbalancing coalitions have repeatedly formed in history to prevent one state from conquering an entire region.[24]

The theory of balance of power argues that such counterbalancing occurs regularly and maintains the stability of the international system. The system is stable in that its rules and principles stay the same: state sovereignty does not collapse into a universal empire. This stability does not, however, imply peace; it is rather a stability maintained by means of recurring wars that adjust power relations.

Alliances (see Chapter 8) play a key role in the balance of power. Building up one's own capabilities against a rival is a form of power balancing, but forming an alliance against a threatening state is often quicker, cheaper and more effective. When such a counterbalancing coalition has a geopolitical element—physically hemming in the threatening state—the power-balancing strategy is called *containment*. In the Cold War, the United States encircled the Soviet Union with military and political alliances to prevent Soviet territorial expansion.

Sometimes a particular state deliberately becomes a balancer (in its region or the world),

balance of power The general concept of one or more states' power being used to balance that of another state or group of states. The term can refer to (1) any ratio of power capabilities between states or alliances, (2) a relatively equal ratio, or (3) the process by which counterbalancing coalitions have repeatedly formed to prevent one state from conquering an entire region.

The Information Revolution

Cyberspace versus Sovereignty?

The interstate system is based on states' sovereignty within their territories. In the 1990s, the astounding growth of the internet and World Wide Web created "cyberspace"—a world of business relationships and communities with shared personal interests, in which geography is irrelevant. How is the growth of cyberspace changing state sovereignty?

To explore this question, go to www.pearsoned.ca/goldstein.

---

[22] James N. Rosenau, *Along the Domestic-Foreign Frontier: Exploring Governance in a Turbulent World* (NY: Cambridge UP, 1997). Yale H. Ferguson and Richard W. Mansbach, *Polities: Authority, Identities, and Change* (Columbia, SC: U South Carolina P, 1996).

[23] Daniel Drache, *Borders Matter: Homeland Security and the Search for North America* (Halifax: Fernwood, 2004). Robert Gilpin, *War and Change in World Politics* (NY: Cambridge UP, 1981).

[24] Edward V. Gulick, *Europe's Classical Balance of Power* (Ithaca, NY: Cornell UP, 1955). Emerson M. S. Niou, Peter C. Ordeshook and Gregory F. Rose, *The Balance of Power: Stability and Instability in International Systems* (NY: Cambridge UP, 1989). Thomas R. Cusack and Richard J. Stoll, *Exploring Realpolitik: Probing International Relations Theory with Computer Simulation* (Boulder, CO: Rienner, 1990).

shifting its support to oppose whatever state or alliance is strongest at the moment. Britain played this role on the European continent for centuries, and China played it in the Cold War. But states do not always balance against the strongest actor. Sometimes smaller states "jump on the bandwagon" of the most powerful state; this has been called *bandwagoning* as opposed to balancing. For instance, after World War II a broad coalition did not form to contain U.S. power; rather most major states, including Canada, joined the U.S. bloc. States may seek to balance threats rather than raw power; U.S. power was greater than Soviet power but was less threatening to Europe, Canada and Japan (and later to China as well).[25] Furthermore, small states create variations on power-balancing themes when they pit rival great powers against each other. For instance, during the Cold War Cuba received massive Soviet subsidies by putting itself in the middle of the U.S.-Soviet rivalry.

In the post–Cold War era of U.S. dominance, balance-of-power theory would predict closer relations among Russia, China and even France—great powers that are not close U.S. military allies. These predictions appear to be on the mark. Russian-Chinese relations have improved dramatically in such areas as arms trade and demilitarization of the border. France vigorously contested U.S. positions on global trade negotiations and discussions of NATO's command structure, and sometimes sided with Russia and China in the UN Security Council, notably before the 2003 Iraq War. French leaders have complained repeatedly of U.S. "hyperpower." Europe and Japan opposed U.S. positions on a range of proposed treaties in 2001, including missile defence, biological weaponry, small arms trade and global warming. (Public opinion in European countries disapproved in large majorities of Bush Administration international policies in mid-2001).[26] Only the appearance of a common enemy—international terrorists—brought the great powers back together in September 2001.

But the 2003 Iraq War resulted in strong public, and in many cases governmental, opinion against U.S. predominance. In 2003, as the United States used military force in Iraq, world public opinion revealed widespread anti-U.S. sentiment. In Indonesia, Pakistan, Turkey and Nigeria—which contain half of the world's Muslim population— more than 70 percent worried that the United States could become a threat to their own country, a worry shared by 71 percent of Russians. In Indonesia, Pakistan, Turkey and Jordan, less than a quarter of the population supported the U.S. war on terrorism. A survey of 38 000 people in 44 nations showed a dramatic drop in support for the United States from 2002 to 2003. Some of that anti-U.S. sentiment appeared to be abating in 2005, but world public support for the U.S. and its policies slipped again in 2006. Of traditional U.S. allies, Canadian public support for the U.S. declined most significantly since 2002. Support for the U.S.-led war on terror among Canadian respondents fell by 23 percentage points in this period, and the number of Canadians who believe that the U.S. considers Canadian interests when conducting foreign policy declined further, from 25 percent in 2002 to 19 percent in 2006. This may be partly attributed to the result of the 2004 U.S. presidential election: three-quarters of Canadians polled reported a less favourable view of the U.S. as a result of President Bush's re-election.[27]

---

[25] Stephen M. Walt, *The Origins of Alliances* (Ithaca, NY: Cornell UP, 1987).

[26] *New York Times* 24 Apr. 1997: A3. "Going It Alone," *Washington Post* 4 Aug. 2001: A15. Adam Clymer, "Surveys Find European Public Critical of Bush Policies," *New York Times* 16 Aug. 2001: A6.

[27] Pew Global Attitudes Project, "America's Image Slips, but Allies Share U.S. Concerns Over Iran, Hamas," released 13 June 2006, available at http://pewglobal.org/reports/display.php?PageID=825.

Great Powers and Middle Powers

Power, of course, varies greatly from one state to another. The *most powerful* states in the system exert most of the influence on international events and therefore get the most attention from IR scholars. By almost any measure of power, a handful of states possess the majority of the world's power resources. At most, a few dozen states have any real influence beyond their immediate locality. These are called the great powers and middle powers in the international system.

Although there are no firm definition lines, **great powers** are generally considered the half dozen or so most powerful states. Until the past century, the great-power club was exclusively European. Sometimes great powers' status is formally recognized in an international structure, such as the nineteenth-century Concert of Europe or the UN Security Council. In general, great powers may be distinguished by the criterion that they can be defeated militarily only by another great power. Great powers also tend to share a global outlook based on national interests far from their home territories.[28]

great powers Generally, the half dozen or so most powerful states; the great-power club was exclusively European until the twentieth century. See also *middle powers*.

The Changing World Order
The Bush Doctrine

According to some observers, the events of September 11, 2001, changed the world forever. However, many realists might disagree, arguing that the world is still characterized by conflict, insecurity and uncertainty. While it is true that the sources of insecurity have shifted to nonstate actors (terrorists), those actors still rely on states for support. This is one reason the United States' response to September 11 emphasized that "states are responsible for what goes on inside their borders." Any states harbouring terrorists would be targeted themselves. This has been described as the "Bush Doctrine."

Even states that do not harbour terrorists have been subjected to greater scrutiny by the U.S., and this has been particularly true of Canada. The world's "longest undefended border" is one that terrorists could use to gain access to U.S. territory, and initial reports after the September 11 attacks suggested that the hijackers had entered the United States through Canada (this later proved to be untrue). U.S. policy-makers also worry about Canada's apparently more open immigration policy. Additionally, during the post–Cold War era, the Canadian government allowed its military to shrink significantly and shifted its emphasis to peacebuilding missions rather than the continental defence of North America.

Realist commentators on Canadian foreign policy have argued that while the world may not have changed as a result of September 11, 2001, U.S. foreign policy has been transformed because of its heightened insecurity. The United States is the single most powerful state in the world today, which means Canada should adapt to a changing world order informed by this fact. By this view, Canadians need to recognize that on most issues their interests are the same as those of the U.S., and so Canada should work with, rather than against, the United States. This would mean, among other things, that Canada should refrain from open expressions of criticism against the U.S. and instead use "quiet diplomacy"; it should expand its armed forces; it should direct foreign aid more narrowly than it has in the past—in particular in support of countries that are important to Canada's national security interests; and, though Canada should continue to promote international institutions, it should see those institutions as instruments to achieve national interests, not as ends in themselves.*

Are these realist suggestions the best responses for Canada as it negotiates the changing world order? Can you think of other responses? What would your arguments be in support of one or another set of policy options?

*Denis Stairs, David J. Bercuson, Mark Entwistle, J. L. Granatstein, Kim Richard Nossal and Gordon S. Smith, *In the National Interest: Canadian Foreign Policy in an Insecure World* (Canadian Defence and Foreign Affairs Institute, 2003).

---

[28] Jack S. Levy, *War in the Modern Great Power System, 1495–1975* (Lexington: UP Kentucky, 1983).

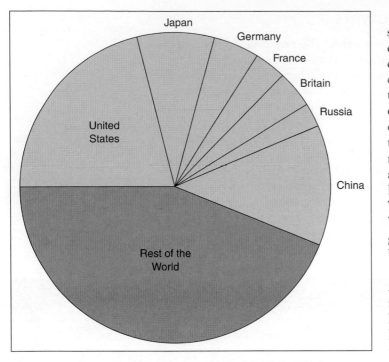

Figure 2.1 Great Power Shares of World GDP, 2004 (purchasing-power method)

The great powers generally have the world's strongest military forces and the strongest economies to pay for military and for other power capabilities. These large economies in turn rest on some combination of large populations, plentiful natural resources, advanced technology and educated labour forces. Because power is based on these underlying resources, membership in the great-power system changes slowly. Only rarely does a great power—even one defeated in a massive war—lose its status, because its size and long-term economic potential change slowly. Thus Germany and Japan, decimated in World War II, are powerful today, and Russia, after gaining and then losing the rest of the Soviet Union, is still considered a great power.

What states are great powers today? Although definitions vary, seven states appear to meet the criteria: the United States, China, Russia, Japan, Germany, France and Britain (see Figure 2.1). Together they account for more than half of the world's total GDP and two-thirds of its military spending. They include the five permanent members of the UN Security Council, who are also the members of the "club" openly possessing large nuclear weapons arsenals (several other states have smaller or undisclosed nuclear arsenals). Notable on this list are the United States and China. The United States is considered the world's only superpower because of its world leadership role since World War II and its dominant military might.

China has the world's largest population, rapid economic growth (8–10 percent annually over 15 years) and a large though not very modern military that includes a credible nuclear arsenal. China is likely to play a central role in world politics in the twenty-first century. Japan and Germany are economic great powers, but have played constrained roles in international security affairs since World War II. Nonetheless, both have large and capable military forces, which they have begun to deploy abroad, and both would like seats on the UN Security Council. Russia, France and Britain were winners in World War II and have been active military powers since. Although much reduced in stature since the height of their colonial power, they still qualify as great powers.

The slow change in great-power status is evident. Britain and France have been great powers for 500 years, Russia and Germany for more than 250 years, the United States and Japan for about 100 years and China for 50 years. Only six other states were ever (but no longer are) considered great powers: Italy, Austria (Austria-Hungary), Spain, Turkey (the Ottoman Empire), Sweden and the Netherlands.

middle powers States that rank somewhat below the great powers in terms of their influence on world affairs (for example, Canada, Brazil and India). See also *great powers.*

Middle powers rank somewhat below the great powers in terms of their influence on world affairs. Some are large but not highly industrialized; others have specialized capabilities but are small. Some aspire to regional dominance, and many have considerable influence in their regions. Even more than with great powers, it is hard to establish a bottom criterion for distinguishing middle powers.

The top rungs of middle powers are easier to identify. India (US$4 trillion) and Brazil (US$1.6 trillion) are both regional giants that some scholars see as rising powers and possible new great powers in this century. In terms of total GDP, Italy and Canada are just below the range of France and Britain and some would consider them great powers. Both states belong to the Group of Eight (G8) economic powers (along with the United States, Germany, Japan, France, Britain and Russia—which joined in 1998). Mexico, Indonesia, South Korea, Australia and Spain all have GDPs greater than half a trillion dollars and are active middle powers. Below this level, GDP estimates become more closely bunched and the order of national economies becomes much harder to sort out.

A list of middle powers (on which not everyone would agree) might include the following states. The first tier would include large states with substantial economic activity, fairly strong military forces and considerable regional political influence: Canada, Italy, India, Brazil, Mexico, South Korea, Australia, Iran and Turkey. A second tier could include important regional actors with somewhat smaller economies or with strong capabilities on specific dimensions of power: Taiwan, Indonesia, Spain, Ukraine, Argentina, Israel, Saudi Arabia, Egypt, Pakistan, South Africa and Kazakhstan. A third tier might include smaller rich states along with middle-sized, middle-income ones and regional "activists" that exercise power beyond their size: the Netherlands, Belgium, Sweden, Greece, Poland, Nigeria, Venezuela, Vietnam, Syria, Iraq, Serbia and North Korea.

Middle powers have not received as much attention in IR as have great powers. These states do, however, often come into play in specific regional conflicts or as mediators on various issues. A number of realist scholars argued during the Cold War that some middle powers—and in particular, Canada—should be termed "principal powers." Principal powers, they argued, were states at the top of the international hierarchy, closer in status to countries like France or Germany than true middle powers like Australia or Brazil. In part, the idea of Canada as a principal power came out of the observation in the Cold War's declining decade that power was becoming more diffuse and nonhegemonic, thus making room for important states like Canada to take more prominent roles in international relations. It is less clear in the post–Cold War period, in which the United States has established itself as the preponderant global power, whether the idea of Canada as a principal power still applies (if it ever did).[29]

Smaller, weaker states (not even of middle-power strength) also are often at the centre of specific conflicts and crises, but their own actions have only minor influence on world politics. The actions of great powers and middle powers in those conflicts and crises have more impact.

Power Distribution

With each state's power balanced by other states, the most important characteristic of an international system in the view of many realists (but particularly neorealists) is the *distribution* of power. Power distribution as a concept can apply to all the states in the world or to just one region, but most often it refers to the great-power system (with most of the world's total power capabilities).

Sometimes international power distribution (world or regional) is described in terms of polarity (a term adopted from physics), which refers to the number of independent power centres in the system. This concept encompasses both the underlying power of various participants and their alliance groupings.

---

[29] David Dewitt and John Kirton, *Canada as a Principal Power* (Toronto: Wiley, 1983). See also David R. Black and Heather A. Smith, "Notable Exceptions? New and Arrested Direction in Canadian Foreign Policy Literature," *Canadian Journal of Political Science* 26.4 (December 1993).

multipolar system An
international system with
typically five or six centres of
power that are not grouped
into alliances.

In a **multipolar system** there are typically five or six centres of power, which are not grouped into alliances. Each state participates independently and on relatively equal terms with the others. They may form a coalition of the whole for mutual security through coordination of efforts. In the classical multipolar balance of power, the great-power system itself was stable but wars were frequently used as power-adjusting mechanisms.

At the other extreme, a unipolar system has a single centre of power around which all others revolve. The dominance of a single state tends to reduce the incidence of war; it performs some of the functions of a government, somewhat reducing anarchy in the international system.

A bipolar system has two predominant states or two great rival alliance blocs. Tight bipolar systems, such as the East-West standoff in the 1950s, may be distinguished from looser ones such as that developed when China and (to a lesser extent) France split off from their alliance blocs in the 1960s. IR scholars do not agree about whether bipolar systems are relatively peaceful or warlike. The U.S.-Soviet standoff seemed to provide stability and peace to great-power relations, but rival blocs in Europe before World War I did not.

In a tripolar system there are three great centres of power. Such a configuration is fairly rare; there is a tendency for a two-against-one alliance to form. Aspects of tripolarity can be found in the "strategic triangle" of the United States, the Soviet Union and China during the 1960s and 1970s.[30] Some scholars imagine that in the coming decades a tripolar world will emerge, with rival power centres in North America, Europe and East Asia. Others point to the rise of both China and India in the near future, serving as two poles to the United States' third.

Some IR scholars have argued that peace is best preserved by a relatively equal power distribution (multipolarity), since no country can be given an opportunity to win easily. However, the empirical evidence for this theory is not strong. The opposite proposition has more support: peace is best preserved by unipolarity, and next best by bipolarity.

Such is the focus of power transition theory.[31] This theory holds that the largest wars result from challenges to the top position in the status hierarchy, when a rising power is surpassing (or threatening to surpass) the most powerful state. When this happens, power is relatively equally distributed, and these are the most dangerous times for major wars. Status quo powers doing well under the old rules will try to maintain them, whereas challengers feeling locked out by the old rules may try to change them.[32] If a challenger does not start a war to displace the top power, the latter may provoke a "preventive" war to stop the rise of the challenger before it becomes too great a threat.[33]

When a rising power's status (formal position in the hierarchy) diverges from its actual power, the rising power may suffer from relative deprivation: its people may feel they are not doing as well as others or as they deserve, even though their position may be improving in absolute terms. The classic example is Germany's rise in the nineteenth century, which gave it great-power capabilities even though it was left out of colonial

[30] Randall Schweller, *Deadly Imbalances: Tripolarity and Hitler's Strategy of World Conquest* (NY: Columbia UP, 1998). Gerald Segal, *The Great Power Triangle* (NY: St. Martin's, 1982).

[31] A. F. K. Organski, *World Politics* (NY: Knopf, 1958). A. F. K. Organski and Jacek Kugler, *The War Ledger* (Chicago: U Chicago P, 1980). Jacek Kugler and Douglas Lemke, eds., *Parity and War: Evaluations and Extensions of the War Ledger* (Ann Arbor: U Michigan P, 1996).

[32] Edward D. Mansfield, "The Concentration of Capabilities and the Onset of War," *Journal of Conflict Resolution* 36.1 (1992): 3–24. William R. Thompson and Karen Rasler, "War and Systemic Capability Reconcentration," *Journal of Conflict Resolution* 32.2 (1988): 335–66. Charles F. Doran, *Systems in Crisis: New Imperatives of High Politics at Century's End* (NY: Cambridge UP, 1991).

[33] Jack S. Levy, "Declining Power and the Preventive Motivation for War," *World Politics* 40.1 (1987): 82–107.

territories and other signs of status. Some neorealists have raised concerns that the rise of China in coming decades, and whether it is satisfied with its place in the global hierarchy, may be the largest determinant of future conflicts.[34]

According to power transition theory, then, peace among great powers results when one state is firmly in the top position, and the positions of others in the hierarchy are clearly defined and correspond with their actual underlying power.

Hegemony

For neorealists, **hegemony** is the holding by one state of a preponderance of power in the international system, so that it can single-handedly dominate the rules and arrangements by which international political and economic relations are conducted.[35] Such a state is called a *hegemon*. (Usually hegemony means domination of the world, but sometimes it refers to regional domination.) From a distinctly nonrealist perspective, the Italian Marxist theorist Antonio Gramsci used "hegemony" to refer not simply to dominance, but to the complex of ideas that rulers use to gain consent for their legitimacy and keep subjects in line.[36] By extension, such a meaning in IR refers to the hegemony of ideas like democracy and capitalism, and to the global dominance of U.S. culture (see pp. 408–410).

Most studies of hegemony point to two examples: Britain in the nineteenth century and the United States after World War II. Britain's predominance followed the defeat of its archrival France in the Napoleonic Wars. Both world trade and naval capabilities were firmly in British hands, as "Britannia ruled the waves." U.S. predominance followed the defeat of Germany and Japan (and the exhaustion of the Soviet Union, France, Britain and China in the effort). In the late 1940s, the U.S. GDP was more than half the world's total; U.S. vessels carried the majority of the world's shipping; the U.S. military could single-handedly defeat any other state or combination of states; and only the United States had nuclear weapons. U.S. industry led the world in technology and productivity, and U.S. citizens enjoyed the world's highest standard of living.

As the extreme power disparities resulting from major wars slowly diminish (states rebuild over years and decades), hegemonic decline may occur, particularly when hegemons have overextended themselves with costly military commitments. IR scholars do not agree about whether U.S. hegemony is in decline or becoming more entrenched.[37] And beyond the U.S. and British examples, IR scholars do not agree on which historical cases were instances of hegemony. Some see the Netherlands in the early seventeenth century, or Spain in the sixteenth, as cases of hegemony.

The theory of hegemonic stability (see pp. 84–86) holds that hegemony provides some order in the international system, reduces anarchy and provides some functions similar to a

hegemony The holding by one state of a preponderance of power in the international system, so that it can single-handedly dominate the rules and arrangements by which international political and economic relations are conducted. See also *hegemonic stability theory*.

---

[34] Ronald L. Tammen, "The Impact of Asia on World Politics: China and India Options for the United States," *International Studies Review* 8 (2006): 563–80.

[35] Ethan B. Kapstein and Michael Mastanduno, *Unipolar Politics* (NY: Columbia UP, 1999). Mark Rupert, *Producing Hegemony: The Politics of Mass Production and American Global Power* (NY: Cambridge UP, 1995). Lea Brilmayer, *American Hegemony: Political Morality in a One-Superpower World* (New Haven, CT: Yale UP, 1994). David P. Rapkin, ed., *World Leadership and Hegemony* (Boulder, CO: Rienner, 1990).

[36] Antonio Gramsci, *The Modern Prince and Other Writings* (NY: International, 1959). Stephen Gill, ed., *Gramsci, Historical Materialism and International Relations* (NY: Cambridge UP, 1993).

[37] Paul Kennedy, *The Rise and Fall of the Great Powers: Economic Change and Military Conflict from 1500 to 2000* (NY: Random House, 1987). W. R. Mead, *Mortal Splendor: The American Empire in Transition* (Boston: Houghton Mifflin, 1987). Bruce Russett, "The Mysterious Case of Vanishing Hegemony," *International Organization* 39.2 (1985): 207–31.

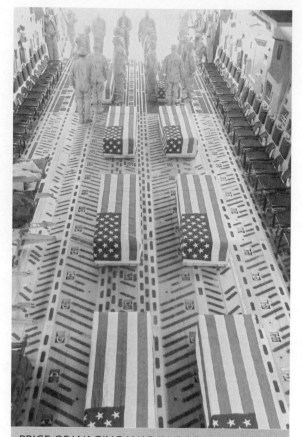

PRICE OF WAGING WAR IN IRAQ
The United States is the world's most powerful single actor. Its ability and willingness to assume a role as hegemon—as after World War II—are important factors that have shaped world order, but the role of the U.S. today is still uncertain and will be affected by its willingness to absorb casualties. Here, soldiers return from Afghanistan in 2004.

central government—deterring aggression, promoting free trade and providing a hard currency that can be used as a world standard. Hegemons can help to resolve or at least keep in check conflicts among middle powers or small states.

From the perspective of less powerful states, of course, such hegemony may seem an infringement of state sovereignty, and the order it creates may seem unjust or illegitimate. For instance, China chafed under U.S.-imposed economic sanctions for 20 years after 1949, feeling itself encircled by U.S. military bases and hostile alliances led by the United States. To this day, Chinese leaders use the term *hegemony* as an insult, and the theory of hegemonic stability does not impress them.

Even in the United States itself there is considerable ambivalence about U.S. hegemony. U.S. foreign policy has historically alternated between *internationalist* and *isolationist* moods.[38] It was founded as a breakaway from the European-based international system, and its growth in the nineteenth century was based on industrialization and expansion within North America. The United States acquired overseas colonies in the Philippines and Puerto Rico but did not relish a role as an imperial power. In World War I, the country waited three years to weigh in—and refused to join the League of Nations afterward. U.S. isolationism peaked in the 1930s; public opinion polls late in that decade showed 95 percent of the U.S. public opposed to participation in a future great European war, and about 70 percent opposed to joining the League of Nations or joining with other nations to stop aggression.[39]

Internationalists, such as Presidents Theodore Roosevelt and Woodrow Wilson, favoured U.S. leadership and activism in world affairs. These views seemed vindicated by the failure of isolationism to prevent World War II (or to allow the United States to stay out of it). U.S. leaders after the war became alarmed by the threat of Soviet (and then Chinese) communism and drummed up U.S. public opinion to favour a strong internationalism during the Cold War. The United States became an activist, global superpower. Despite an introspective period after the Vietnam War, the United States has largely continued this internationalist stance. That commitment became only stronger after the attacks on the World Trade Center and Pentagon in September 2001.[40]

---

[38] Frank L. Klingberg, "The Historical Alternation of Moods in American Foreign Policy," *World Politics* 4.2 (1952): 239–73. Fareed Zakaria, *From Wealth to Power: The Unusual Origins of America's World Role* (Princeton, NJ: Princeton UP, 1998).

[39] Lloyd A. Free and Hadley Cantril, *The Political Beliefs of Americans* (Piscataway, NJ: Rutgers UP, 1967).

[40] Michael E. Brown, Owen R. Cote, Jr., Sean M. Lynn-Jones and Steven E. Miller, eds., *America's Strategic Choices*, rev. ed. (Cambridge, MA: MIT P, 2000). Richard N. Haass, *The Reluctant Sheriff: The United States after the Cold War* (Washington, DC: Brookings, 1997). John G. Ruggie, *Winning the Peace* (NY: Columbia UP, 1996). Kenneth A. Oye, Robert J. Lieber and Donald Rothchild, eds., *Eagle in a New World: American Grand Strategy in the Post–Cold War Era* (NY: HarperCollins, 1992).

STRATEGY

Actors use strategy to pursue good outcomes in bargaining with one or more other actors. States deploy power capabilities as leverage to influence one another's actions.[41] Bargaining is interactive, and requires an actor to take account of other actors' interests even while pursuing its own.[42] Sometimes bargaining communication takes place through actions rather than words.

Statecraft

Classical realists emphasize *statecraft*—the art of managing state affairs and effectively manoeuvring in a world of power politics among sovereign states. Power strategies are plans actors use to develop and deploy power capabilities to achieve goals.

A key aspect of strategy is choosing the kinds of capabilities to develop, given limited resources, in order to maximize international influence. This requires foresight because the capabilities required to manage a situation may need to be developed years before that situation presents itself, yet the means chosen often will not be fungible in the short term. Central to this dilemma is determining what kind of standing military forces to maintain in peacetime—enough to prevent a quick defeat if war breaks out, but not so much as to overburden one's economy (see pp. 225–231).

Strategies also shape policies for when a state is willing to use its power capabilities. The *will* of a nation or leader is hard to estimate. Even if leaders make explicit their intention to fight over an issue, they might be bluffing.

The strategic actions of China in recent years exemplify the concept of strategy as rational deployment of power capabilities. China's central foreign policy goal is to prevent the independence of Taiwan, which China considers an integral part of its territory (as does the United Nations). Taiwan's government was set up to represent all of China in 1949, when the nationalists took refuge there after losing to the communists in China's civil war. Since the international community's recognition of the Beijing government as "China," Taiwan has attempted to operate more and more independently, with many Taiwanese favouring independence. China may not have the military power to invade Taiwan successfully, but it has declared repeatedly that it will go to war if Taiwan declares independence. So far, even though such a war might be irrational on China's part, the threat has deterred Taiwan from formally declaring independence. China might lose such a war, but would certainly inflict immense damage on Taiwan. In 1996, China held war games near Taiwan, firing missiles over the sea. The United States sent two aircraft carriers to signal China that its exercises must not go too far.

In not risking war by declaring independence, Taiwan has instead engaged in diplomacy to gain influence in the world. It lobbies the U.S. Congress, asks for admission to the UN and other world organizations and grants foreign aid to countries that recognize Taiwan's government (24 mostly small, poor countries worldwide as of 2007).

China has used its own diplomacy to counter these moves. It breaks diplomatic relations with countries that recognize Taiwan and punishes any moves in the direction of Taiwanese independence. Half the countries that recognize Taiwan are in the Caribbean and Central America, leading to a competition for influence in the region.

---

[41] Robert C. North, *War, Peace, Survival: Global Politics and Conceptual Synthesis* (Boulder, CO: Westview, 1990).

[42] Glenn H. Snyder and Paul Diesing, *Conflict among Nations: Bargaining, Decision Making, and System Structure in International Crises* (Princeton, NJ: Princeton UP, 1977).

China has tried to counter Taiwanese ties with those countries by manipulating various positive and negative leverages. For example, in Panama, where China is a major user of the Panama Canal, Taiwan has cultivated close relations, invested in a container port and suggested hiring guest workers from Panama in Taiwan. But China has implicitly threatened to restrict Panama's access to Hong Kong or to reregister China's many Panamanian-registered ships in the Bahamas instead. (Bahamas broke with Taiwan in 1997 after a Hong Kong conglomerate, now part of China, promised to invest in a Bahamian container port.) Similarly, when the Pacific microstate of Kiribati recognized Taiwan in late 2003 to gain Taiwanese aid, China broke off relations and removed a Chinese satellite-tracking station from Kiribati. Since the tracking station played a vital role in China's military reconnaissance and growing space program—which had recently launched its first astronaut—its dismantling underscored China's determination to give Taiwan priority even at a cost to other key national goals.

Two of the five vetoes China has ever used in the UN Security Council were to block peacekeeping forces in countries that extended recognition to Taiwan. These vetoes demonstrate that if China believes its interests in Taiwan are threatened, it can play a spoiler role on the Security Council. When the former Yugoslav republic of Macedonia recognized Taiwan in 1999 (in exchange for $1 billion in aid), China vetoed a UN peacekeeping mission there at a time of great instability in next-door Kosovo. By contrast, when its interests in Taiwan are secure, China cooperates on issues of world order. For example, although China opposed the 1991 Gulf War, it did not veto the UN resolution authorizing it.

These Chinese strategies mobilize various capabilities, from missiles to diplomats to industrial conglomerates, in a coherent effort to influence the outcome of China's most important international issue. Strategy thus amplifies China's power.[43]

Some individual actors too are better than others at using their capabilities strategically. For instance, in the late 1970s U.S. president Jimmy Carter used the great-power capabilities available to him, but his own strategic and interpersonal skills seem to have been the key to success in the Camp David agreements (which achieved the U.S. foreign policy goal of an Egyptian-Israeli treaty). Good strategies bring together power capabilities for maximum effect, but poor strategies make inefficient use of available capabilities. Of course, even the most skillful leader never has total control of an international situation, but can make best use of the opportunities available while minimizing the effects of bad luck.

Reciprocity, Deterrence and Arms Races

To have the best effect, strategic bargaining over IR outcomes should take into account the other actor's own goals and strategies. Only then can one predict which forms of leverage may induce the other actor to take the actions one desires. But this can be a problem: often states do not know each others' true intentions but can only observe each others' actions and statements (which may be lies).

---

[43] *Current History* 96.611 (Sept. 1997), spec. issue on China. Larry Rohter, "Taiwan and Beijing Duel for Recognition in Central America," *New York Times* 5 Aug. 1997: A7. Quansheng Zhao, *Interpreting Chinese Foreign Policy: The Micro-Macro Linkage Approach* (NY: Oxford UP, 1996). Chih-yu Shih, *China's Just World: The Morality of Chinese Foreign Policy* (Boulder, CO: Rienner, 1992). Paul M. Evans and B. Michael Frolic, eds., *Reluctant Adversaries: Canada and the People's Republic of China, 1949–1970* (Toronto: U Toronto P, 1991).

One very effective strategy for influencing another actor whose plans are not known is reciprocity—a response in kind to the other's actions.[44] A strategy of reciprocity uses positive forms of leverage as promises of rewards (if the actor does what one wants), simultaneously using negative forms of leverage as threats of punishment (if the actor does not refrain from doing what one does not want). Reciprocity is effective because it is easy to understand. After one has demonstrated one's ability and willingness to reciprocate—gaining a reputation for consistency of response—the other actor can easily calculate the costs of failing to cooperate or the benefits of cooperating.

Reciprocity can be an effective strategy for achieving cooperation in a situation of conflicting interests. If one side expresses willingness to cooperate and promises to reciprocate the other's cooperative actions, the other side has great incentive to work out a cooperative bargain. And because reciprocity is relatively easy to interpret, the vow of future reciprocity often need not be stated explicitly.[45]

Reciprocity can also help achieve cooperation in the sense of refraining from an undesired action. This is the intent of the strategy of **deterrence**—the threat to punish another actor if it takes a certain negative action (especially attacking one's own state or allies). The slogan "peace through strength" reflects this approach. If deterrence works, its effects are almost invisible; its success is measured in attacks that did not occur.[46]

Generally, advocates of deterrence believe that conflicts are more likely to escalate into war when one party is weak. In this view, building up military capabilities usually convinces the stronger party that a resort to military leverage would not succeed, so conflicts are less likely to escalate into violence. A strategy of **compellence,** sometimes used after deterrence fails, refers to the use of force to make another actor take some action (rather than refrain from taking one).[47] Generally it is harder to get a state to change course (the purpose of compellence) than it is to get it to refrain from changing course (the purpose of deterrence).

One strategy used to try to compel compliance by another state is *escalation*—a series of negative sanctions of increasing severity applied in order to induce another actor to take some action. In theory, less severe actions establish credibility—showing the first actor's willingness to exert its power on the issue—and the pattern of escalation establishes the high costs of future sanctions if the second actor does not cooperate.

reciprocity A response in kind to another's actions; a strategy of reciprocity uses positive forms of leverage to promise rewards and negative forms of leverage to threaten punishment.

deterrence The threat to punish another actor if it takes a certain negative action (especially attacking one's own state or allies).

compellence The use of force to make another actor take some action (rather than refrain from taking one); sometimes used after deterrence fails.

---

[44] Robert O. Keohane, "Reciprocity in International Relations," *International Organization* 40.1 (1986): 1–27. Deborah Welch Larson, "The Psychology of Reciprocity in International Relations," *Negotiation Journal* 4 (1988): 281–301. Robert Jervis, "Security Regimes," *International Regimes*, ed. Stephen D. Krasner (Ithaca, NY: Cornell UP, 1983). Stephen R. Rock, *Why Peace Breaks Out: Great Power Rapprochement in Historical Perspective* (Chapel Hill, NC: U North Carolina P, 1989). George W. Downs and David M. Rocke, *Optimal Imperfection? Domestic Uncertainty and Institutions in International Relations* (Princeton, NJ: Princeton UP, 1995).

[45] Joshua S. Goldstein and John R. Freeman, *Three-Way Street: Strategic Reciprocity in World Politics* (Chicago: U Chicago P, 1990). Joshua S. Goldstein, "Great-Power Cooperation under Conditions of Limited Reciprocity: From Empirical to Formal Analysis," *International Studies Quarterly* 39.4 (1995): 453–77. Joshua S. Goldstein and Jon C. Pevehouse, "Reciprocity, Bullying, and International Cooperation: Time-Series Analysis of the Bosnia Conflict," *American Political Science Review* 91.3 (1997): 515–29.

[46] Frank C. Zagare, *Perfect Deterrence* (NY: Cambridge UP, 2000). Avery Goldstein, *Deterrence and Security in the 21st Century* (Palo Alto, CA: Stanford UP, 2000). Ted Hopf, *Peripheral Visions: Deterrence Theory and American Foreign Policy in the Third World, 1965–1990* (Ann Arbor: U Michigan P, 1994). Paul K. Huth, *Extended Deterrence and the Prevention of War* (New Haven, CT: Yale UP, 1988). Robert Jervis, Richard Ned Lebow and Janice Gross Stein, *Psychology and Deterrence* (Baltimore: Johns Hopkins UP, 1985). Alexander L. George and Richard Smoke, *Deterrence in American Foreign Policy: Theory and Practice* (NY: Columbia UP, 1974).

[47] Thomas C. Schelling, *The Strategy of Conflict* (Cambridge, MA: Harvard UP, 1960).

These should induce the second actor to comply, assuming that it finds the potential costs of the escalating punishments to be greater than the costs of compliance. But escalation can be quite dangerous. During the Cold War, many IR scholars worried that conventional war could lead to nuclear war if the superpowers tried to apply escalation strategies.

An **arms race** is a reciprocal process in which two (or more) states build up military capabilities in response to each other. Since each wants to act prudently against a threat, the attempt to reciprocate leads to a runaway production of weapons by both sides. The mutual escalation of threats erodes confidence, reduces cooperation and makes it more likely that a crisis (or accident) could cause one side to strike first and start a war rather than waiting for the other side to strike. The arms race process was illustrated vividly in the U.S.-Soviet nuclear arms race, which created arsenals of tens of thousands of nuclear weapons on each side.[48] However, as will be discussed in later chapters, liberal and critical understandings of arms races focus on the economic factors involved, most particularly those associated with the interests of the military industrial complex.

arms race A reciprocal process in which two (or more) states build up military capabilities in response to each other.

THE ECONOMIC VARIANT OF REALISM

This chapter has focused on realist analyses of questions of international security. Indeed, this is where realism seems to exhibit its greatest strength. But realism also offers an analysis of economic issues. **Mercantilism** (or economic nationalism) is the economic variant of realism. Mercantilism shares with realism most of its central assumptions: that states are the most important actors in IR, and that they act rationally in the pursuit of power in an anarchic international system. For mercantilists, the economy should always be subservient to politics, and economic relations are important only insofar as they contribute to the wealth (and therefore power) of the state. Mercantilists are thus concerned about trading relations with other states: increasing interdependence between states can produce vulnerabilities and make one country dependent on another for important goods. Mercantilists tend to recommend policies of self-sufficiency over interdependence.[49] Mercantilism will be discussed more fully in Chapter 9.

mercantilism An economic theory and a political ideology opposed to free trade; it shares with realism the belief that each state must protect its own interests without seeking mutual gains through international organizations. See also *liberalism*.

This chapter has focused on realism and some of its concerns, such as the interests of states, distribution of power among states and bargaining between states. Consistent with the realist framework, the chapter has treated states as unitary actors, much as one would analyze the interactions of individual people. The actions of state leaders have been treated as more or less rational in terms of pursuing definable interests through coherent bargaining strategies.

However, realism is not the only way to frame the major issues of international security. Chapter 3 re-examines these themes from a liberal perspective, followed by critical theoretical perspectives in Chapter 4.

---

[48] Walter Isard and Charles H. Anderton, "Arms Race Models: A Survey and Synthesis," *Conflict Management and Peace Science* 8 (1985): 27–98. S. Plous, "Perceptual Illusions and Military Realities: The Nuclear Arms Race," *The Journal of Conflict Resolution* 29.3 (1985): 363–90. Michael D. McGinnis and John T. Williams, "Stability and Change in Superpower Rivalry," *American Political Science Review* 83 (1989): 1101–24.

[49] Robert Gilpin, *Global Political Economy: Understanding the International Economic Order* (Princeton, NJ: Princeton UP, 2001).

Thinking Critically

1. Using Table 1.3 on pp. 20–21 (with GDP as a measure of power) and the maps at the back of the book, pick a state and speculate about what coalition of nearby states might form with sufficient power to oppose the state if it became aggressive.

2. Choose a recent international event and list the power capabilities that participants used as leverage in the episode. Which capabilities were effective, and which were not? Why?

3. Given the distinction between zero-sum and non-zero-sum games, can you think of a current international situation that is a zero-sum conflict? One that is non-zero-sum?

4. If you were the leader of a small state in Africa, bargaining with a great power about an issue where your interests diverged, what leverage and strategies could you bring into play to improve the outcome for your state?

5. Given changes in international power distribution and the end of the Cold War order, where do you think the threats to peace will come from in the future? Through what means could states respond to those threats?

6. The modern international system came into being at a time when agrarian societies relied primarily on farmland to create wealth. Now that most wealth is no longer created through farming, is the territorial nature of states obsolete? How might the diminishing economic value of territory change the ways in which states interact?

Chapter Summary

- Realism explains international relations in terms of power.

- Realists and idealists differ in their assumptions about human nature, international order and the potential for peace.

- Power can be conceptualized as influence or as capabilities that can create influence.

- The most important single indicator of a state's power is its GDP.

- Short-term power capabilities depend on long-term resources, both tangible and intangible.

- Realists consider military force the most important power capability.

- Rational-actor approaches treat states as though they were individuals acting to maximize their own interests. These simplifications are debatable but allow realists to develop concise and general models and explanations.

- Game theory draws insights from simplified models of bargaining situations.

- International anarchy—the absence of world government—means that each state is a sovereign and autonomous actor pursuing its own national interests.

- The international system traditionally places great emphasis on the sovereignty of states, their right to control affairs in their own territory and their responsibility to respect internationally recognized borders.

- Seven great powers account for more than half of the world's total GDP and two-thirds of its military spending.

- Power transition theory says that wars often result from shifts in relative power distribution in the international system.

- Hegemony—the predominance of one state in the international system—can help provide stability and peace in international relations, but with some drawbacks.

- Reciprocity can be an effective strategy for reaching cooperation in ongoing relationships but carries a danger of turning into runaway hostility or arms races.
- Mercantilism, the economic variant of realism, shares many of realism's central assumptions (in particular about primacy of states, power and anarchy) and applies them to economic issues.
- Mercantilists tend to suggest policies of economic nationalism.

Key Terms

realism   49
idealism   49
neorealism   51
power   52
geopolitics   55
rational actors   56
national interest   56
cost-benefit analysis   56
game theory   57
zero-sum games   58
anarchy   60
norms (of behaviour)   61

sovereignty   61
security dilemma   62
balance of power   63
great powers   65
middle powers   66
multipolar system   68
hegemony   69
reciprocity   73
deterrence   73
compellence   73
arms race   74
mercantilism   74

Research Navigator Question

Using Research Navigator™, find article AN 14854212, an article by Jack Snyder entitled "One World, Rival Theories." In the article, Snyder examines realism, liberalism and constructivism, and argues among other things that each of these theories serves as a powerful check on the others. In small groups, review the article and choose individuals who will present each of these approaches. What is your assessment of Snyder's final conclusions?

Weblinks

In addition to reading this text, you can read many scholarly journals of international relations. You should become familiar with some of these journals, either online or through your library. Following are links to the home pages of a number of relevant journals, but your university library may also have electronic subscriptions to some or all of these (which would give you access to all the articles in the journal), so you should also ask at your library or explore your library's website.

Foreign Affairs:
http://www.foreignaffairs.org

International Journal of the Canadian Institute of International Affairs:
http://www.ciia.org/ij.htm

Belfer Center for Science and International Affairs:
http://bcsia.ksg.harvard.edu/publications.cfm?program=ISP

International Studies Quarterly:
http://www.isq.unt.edu

Journal of Military and Strategic Studies:
http://www.jmss.org

Liberal Approaches

3

ALTERNATIVES TO REALISM

LIBERAL PLURALISM
Traditional Liberal
  Critiques
Immanuel Kant
The Invisible Hand
Woodrow Wilson
Neoliberal Institutionalism
Collective Goods
International Regimes

Hegemonic Stability
Collective Security
The Democratic Peace

CONSTRUCTIVISM

PEACE STUDIES
Broadening the Focus
Conflict Resolution
War and Militarism
Positive Peace

Peace Movements
Nonviolence

**ECONOMIC
LIBERALISM**

Lilian Thuram, a football star from the Barcelona Football Club, visits Liberia in support of the country's Sport for Peace Programme.

ALTERNATIVES TO REALISM

Although realism has tended to dominate the study of international relations, especially in the U.S., it is not the only approach to the study of IR. Many alternatives exist, some with very different visions of what the world looks like, how the world should be studied and what the purpose of theory is. The many alternative theories that exist will be grouped in this chapter and the next under two paradigms: liberal pluralism (discussed in this chapter) and critical theory (discussed in Chapter 4).

Realism is the most *homogeneous* of the three paradigms. This does not mean that there is no debate among realists as they elaborate on their theory and its application to particular issues or events. As noted in Chapter 2, debate exists and is sometimes quite heated. However, realists tend to identify as either realist or neorealist (or the economic variant, mercantilist), and most realists share the same basic assumptions of realism regarding the primacy of the state, the pursuit of power and the anarchy of international relations.

Liberal pluralists are less homogeneous than realists. They may self-identify using a number of terms, such as liberal, pluralist, liberal pluralist, liberal internationalist, neoliberal, liberal institutionalist, peace researcher, economic liberal and others. Depending on what elements of liberalism are emphasized, there are also more potential contradictions between some liberals. For example, on questions of the environment, economic liberals might argue that market forces should determine responses to industrial pollutants. If an industry is allowed to become profitable, its own research and entrepreneurship will eventually develop and implement pollution controls. Neoliberal internationalists, by contrast, would have more faith in establishing rules and regulations through international institutions. They would promote accords and other mechanisms to be administered through organizations like the UN in an effort to address industrial pollutants sooner rather than later. The theories and theorists grouped within the liberal-pluralist paradigm do share a number of assumptions, but this paradigm contains a more diverse group of theories than that found in realism.[1]

LIBERAL PLURALISM

In the broadest terms, liberal pluralism differs from realism in a number of important respects. It suggests that while states are important actors in IR, there are many more actors that operate in the global system. These include individuals, institutions, multinational corporations, NGOs and social movements. Liberals also emphasize the cooperative features of global interaction over conflictual ones. Finally, liberals are interested in producing policy-relevant advice, but may provide that advice to many actors and not simply states alone.

Traditional Liberal Critiques

Since the time of Mo Ti and Sun Tzu in ancient China, idealism (an early precursor to liberal pluralism) has provided a counterpoint to realism. This long tradition of idealism in IR holds that morality, law and international organization can form the basis for relations among states; human nature is not evil; peaceful and cooperative relations among states are possible; and states can operate as a community rather than merely as autonomous self-interested agents.[2]

Traditionally, liberals have offered five major lines of criticism against key assumptions of realism. First, liberals argue that the assumption of international *anarchy* is no more than a partial truth. Of course, international interactions are structured by power relations, but for liberals, order also evolves through norms and institutions based on reciprocity and cooperation, and even on law.

Second, liberals criticize the notion of states as *unitary actors*, each with a single set of coherent interests. As the study of foreign policy reveals (Chapter 5), state actions often do not reflect a single individual set of preferences. Rather, state behaviour is shaped by internal bargaining among and within bureaucracies, interest groups and other actors with divergent goals and interests. Nonstate actors—individuals, NGOs, IGOs and ethnic groups, among others—further confound the idea that IR can be reduced to the interactions of a small number of well-defined state actors pursuing national interests.

Third, realism's conception of *rationality* is problematic. For realists, rationality is seeking narrow self-interest whereas liberal rationality is to seek to share in long-term collective benefits.

Just as liberal conceptions of rationality differ from the realist account, liberals also differ from realists in their approach to power. Realists define power as the ability to get

---

[1] For a more detailed review of theoretical approaches in IR, see Tim Dunne, Milya Kurki and Steve Smith, eds., *International Relations Theories: Discipline and Diversity* (Oxford UP, 2007). Jill Steans and Lloyd Pettiford, *International Relations: Perspectives and Themes*, 2nd ed. (UK: Pearson Education, 2005). Scott Burchill, Richard Devetak, Andrew Linklater, Matthew Paterson, Christian Reus-Smit and Jacqui True, eds., *Theories of International Relations* (NY: Palgrave, 2001).

[2] Terry Nardin and David R. Mapel, eds., *Traditions of International Ethics* (NY: Cambridge UP, 1992). David Long and Peter Wilson, eds., *Thinkers of the Twenty Years' Crisis: Inter-War Idealism Reassessed* (NY: Oxford UP, 1995).

another actor to do something—or as the capabilities required to so influence an actor (see pp. 5–6). This is power *over* others—a concept that some liberals consider inherently oppressive, and rooted in a need to control or dominate others. This is the power of the bully to make others comply. But are bullies really the most powerful actors? Do they achieve the best outcomes? And do we really live in an international world populated by bullies?

An alternative definition is based not on power over others but on power to accomplish desirable ends. This kind of power often derives from capitalizing on common interests rather than gaining an edge in bargaining over conflicting interests. Such empowerment often entails the formation of coalitions and partnerships, or the mobilization of the resources of multiple actors for a common purpose. For many liberals, this is a truer, more useful concept of power.

Finally, for liberals, *military force* as a form of leverage does not seem nearly as all-important as realism implies. It is a costly way to influence other actors (see Chapter 7) as compared with diplomacy, conflict resolution, peacekeeping and other nonmilitary means. International organizations, laws and norms create stable contexts for bargaining, making nonmilitary leverage increasingly effective as international organization develops (see Chapter 8).

In addition to these general criticisms of realism, some liberals have argued that changes in the way IR works have made realist assumptions obsolete. Realism may once have been "realistic," when European kings and queens played war and traded territories as property. But states are now interconnected, a reality contradicting the assumptions of autonomy and sovereignty. Borders are becoming fluid, making territorial integrity increasingly untenable. The evolution of norms regarding the use of force has substantially changed the ways in which military force contributes to international power. This line of argument has been prominent in liberal interdependence approaches to IR since the 1970s, but the roots of liberal thinking go back much further.

Immanuel Kant

Liberal theories of IR try to explain how peace and cooperation are possible. Over 200 years ago, the German philosopher Immanuel Kant conceived several answers.[3] The first was that peace depends on the internal character of governments—specifically that republics, in which citizens hold the head of state in check, will be more peaceful than autocracies. For Kant, citizens—unlike monarchs—bear the direct costs of going to war and therefore will be reluctant to do so.[4] A variation on Kant's view, namely that *democracies* do not fight *each other*, is the basis of present-day democratic peace theory, discussed later in this chapter.

Kant also argued that states could develop the organizations and rules to facilitate cooperation and avoid war, specifically by forming a world federation resembling today's United Nations. Since past treaties ending great-power wars had never lasted permanently, Kant proposed a federation (league) of the world's states. Through such a federation, Kant proposed, the majority of states could unite to punish any one state that committed aggression. This union would safeguard the collective interests of all the nations together against the narrow self-interest of one nation that might otherwise profit from aggression. The

---

[3] Immanuel Kant, *Perpetual Peace*. Edited by Lewis White Beck. Indianapolis: Bobbs-Merrill, 1957 [1795].

[4] Tim Dunne, "Liberalism," in John Baylis and Steve Smith, eds., *The Globalization of World Politics: An Introduction*, 3rd ed. (Oxford UP: 2005) 186–203.

federation would also protect the self-determination of small nations that all too easily became pawns in great-power games.

Kant also discussed universal or cosmopolitan rights—laying the groundwork for modern conceptions of human rights that form a corner piece of modern liberal thought. He was also an advocate of free trade, another important element of liberal thought.

The Invisible Hand

Liberal theory in IR has also been greatly influenced by developments in liberal economic thinking.[5] The political economist Adam Smith argued in 1776 that in pursuing their own self-interest via the free market (which he argued was guided by the invisible hand of supply and demand), individuals would contribute to a larger good, and a harmony of interests would emerge. Richard Cobden, writing in the nineteenth century, developed the ideas of liberal economists and applied them to the behaviour of states interacting with one another, in particular focusing on the idea that trade promotes peace. This idea relies on the presumption that trade increases wealth, cooperation and global well-being while making conflict less likely in the long term—since governments will not want to disrupt any process that adds to the wealth of their state.[6]

HAPPY FAMIILY
Liberals emphasize the potential for rivalries to evolve into cooperative relationships as states recognize that achieving mutual benefits is cost-effective in the long run. For example, the U.S. and Soviet/Russian space programs began cooperating in the 1960s, and today many countries participate in building the International Space Station. Here, U.S. shuttle commander Eileen Collins says goodbye to Space Station commander Sergei Krikalev while astronauts from the United States, Japan and Australia look on, 2005.

Woodrow Wilson

U.S. president Woodrow Wilson was considered one of the early and strongest advocates for the idea, like that proposed by Kant, of a federation of states. Wilson was instrumental in creating the League of Nations in 1919 at the end of World War I (although the United States would never ratify the Treaty of Versailles, which both ended World War I and established the League). In his "Fourteen Points" address to the U.S. Congress in 1918, Wilson spelled out the need for a general association of nations. He also explicitly advocated for free trade and self-determination of many of the occupied nations of Europe, and established the idea of collective security, which will be discussed later in the chapter.

---

[5] *Ibid.*

[6] Norman Angell, *The Foundations of International Polity* (London: William Heinemann, 1914). Philip A. Schrodt, "Democratic Peace or Liberal Peace: The Debate," *International Studies Review* 6.2 (2004): 292.

Neoliberal Institutionalism

In the 1980s, a new liberal critique of realism emerged. The approach stressed the importance of international institutions in reducing the inherent conflict that realists assume in an international system. The reasoning for this approach is based on the core liberal idea that seeking long-term mutual gains is often more rational than maximizing individual short-term ones. The approach became known as "neoliberal institutionalism" or **neoliberalism** for short.

The neoliberal approach differs from earlier liberal approaches in that it concedes to realism in several important assumptions—among them, that states are unitary actors rationally pursuing their own self-interests. Neoliberals say to realists, "Even if we grant your assumptions about the nature of states and their motives, your pessimistic conclusions do not follow." States achieve cooperation fairly often because it is in their interest to do so, and they can learn to use institutions to ease the pursuit of mutual gains and the reduction of possibilities for cheating or taking advantage of another state.

Despite the many sources of conflict in IR, states do cooperate most of the time. Neoliberal scholars ask how this is possible in an anarchic world.[7] They try to show that even in a world of unitary rational states, neorealist pessimism about international cooperation is not valid. States can create mutual rules, expectations and institutions to promote behaviour that enhances (or at least doesn't destroy) the possibilities for mutual gain.

Neoliberals use the *Prisoner's Dilemma (PD)* game (see pp. 57–60) to illustrate the argument that cooperation is possible. Each actor can gain by individually defecting, but both lose when both defect. The narrow, self-serving behaviour of each player leads to a bad outcome for both, one they could have improved by cooperation. Similarly, in IR states often have a mix of conflicting and mutual interests. The dilemma can be resolved if the game is played over and over again; in an accurate model of IR, states deal with each other in repeated interactions.

A strategy of strict reciprocity after an initial cooperative move (nicknamed **tit for tat**) can bring about mutual cooperation in a repeated PD game, because the other player must conclude that any defection will merely provoke a like defection in response.[8] The strategy parallels the just war doctrine (see pp. 285–286), which calls for states never to initiate war but to use it in response to war. In international trade, such a strategy calls for opening one's markets but selectively closing them in response to another state's closing its markets (see pp. 319–323).

Reciprocity is an important principle in IR that helps encourage international cooperation despite the absence of central authority. Through reciprocity, rather than a world government, norms and rules are enforced. In international security, reciprocity underlies the gradual improvement of relations sought by arms control agreements and peacekeeping missions. In international political economy (IPE), where cooperation can create great benefits through trade, the threat to restrict trade in retaliation for unfair practices is a strong incentive to comply with rules and norms.

neoliberalism Short for "neoliberal institutionalism," an approach that stresses the importance of international institutions in reducing the inherent conflict that realists assume in an international system; with reasoning based on the core liberal idea that seeking long-term mutual gains is often more rational than maximizing individual short-term ones. See also *liberalism*.

tit for tat A strategy of strict reciprocity (matching the other player's response) after an initial cooperative move; it can bring about mutual cooperation in a repeated Prisoner's Dilemma game, since it ensures that defection will not pay.

---

[7] David A. Baldwin, ed., *Neorealism and Neoliberalism: The Contemporary Debate* (NY: Columbia UP, 1993). Charles W. Kegley, Jr., ed., *Controversies in International Relations Theory: Realism and the Neoliberal Challenge* (NY: St. Martin's, 1995). Joseph S. Nye, Jr., rev. of "Neorealism and Neoliberalism," *World Politics* 40.2 (1988): 235–51. John Gerard Ruggie, ed., *Multilateralism Matters: The Theory and Praxis of an Institutional Forum* (NY: Columbia UP, 1993). Helen Milner, rev. of "International Theories of Cooperation among Nations: Strengths and Weaknesses," *World Politics* 44.3 (1992): 466–94. Kenneth A. Oye, ed., *Cooperation under Anarchy* (Princeton, NJ: Princeton UP, 1986).

[8] Robert Axelrod, *The Evolution of Cooperation* (NY: Basic, 1984). Robert Axelrod and Robert O. Keohane, "Achieving Cooperation under Anarchy: Strategies and Institutions," *Cooperation under Anarchy*, ed. Oye (see previous footnote) 226–54. Robert Axelrod, *The Complexity of Cooperation: Agent-Based Models of Competition and Collaboration* (Princeton, NJ: Princeton UP, 1997).

Although reciprocity is an important norm, it is just one among many that mediate states' interactions. For example, diplomatic practices and participation in international organizations (IOs) are strongly governed by shared expectations about the rules of correct behaviour. As situations such as the Prisoner's Dilemma crop up in IR, states rely on a context of rules, norms, habits and institutions that make it rational for all sides to avoid the self-defeating outcomes that would result from pursuing narrow, short-term self-interests. Neoliberals study historical and contemporary cases in IR to see how institutions and norms have affected the possibilities for overcoming dilemmas and achieving international cooperation. Thus, for neoliberals the emergence of international institutions is key to understanding how states achieve a superior type of rationality that includes long-term self-interest and not just immediate self-interest.

Collective Goods

For many liberals, IR revolves around a key problem: How can a group serve its *collective* interests when doing so requires its members to forgo their *individual* interests? For example, it costs less to drive a polluting car than to pay for emission controls, and the air that the car owner breathes is hardly affected by his or her own car. The air quality is a collective good. If too many car owners pollute, all will breathe dirty air. But if just a few pollute, they will breathe fairly clean air; the few who pollute are **free riders**, because they benefit from someone else's provision of the collective good.

free riders Those who benefit from someone else's provision of a collective good without paying their share of costs.

At the international level, every country has an interest in stopping global warming, a goal that can be achieved only by many countries acting together. Yet each country also has an individual interest in burning fossil fuels to keep its economy going. Similarly, all members of a military alliance benefit from the strength of the alliance, but each member has a separate interest in minimizing its own contributions of troops and money. Individual nations can advance their own short-term interests by seizing territory, cheating on trade agreements and refusing to contribute to international efforts like peacekeeping or vaccination campaigns. But if all nations acted this way, they would find themselves worse off, in a chaotic and vicious environment where mutual gains from security and trade would disappear.

This problem of shared versus conflicting interests among members of a group is called different names in different contexts—the problem of "collective action," "free riding," "burden sharing," the "tragedy of the commons," a "mixed interest game," or the "Prisoner's Dilemma," to name a few. The issue is generally referred to as the **collective goods problem**, that is, the problem of how to provide something that benefits all members of a group regardless of what each member contributes to it.

collective goods problem The problem of how to provide something that benefits all members of a group regardless of what each member contributes to it.

In domestic society, many collective goods problems are solved by governments, which enforce rules for the common good. Governments can punish free riders who are tempted to avoid contributing. They can also pass laws against polluting cars or force citizens to pay taxes to support collective goods such as national defence, highways or schools. In the international system, the absence of central government sharpens the difficulties created by collective goods. It is difficult to maintain multilateral cooperation when each government is tempted by its own possibility of free riding.

In general, collective goods are easier to provide in small groups than in large ones.[9] In a small group, the defection (free riding) of one member is harder to conceal, has a

---

[9] Todd Sandler, *Global Collective Action* (Cambridge UP, 2004). Mancur Olson, *The Logic of Collective Action* (1965; Cambridge, MA: Harvard UP, 1971).

greater impact on the overall collective good and is easier to punish. The advantage of small groups helps explain the importance of the great-power system in international security affairs. It is one reason why the G8 (Group of Eight) industrialized countries have frequent meetings to try to coordinate their economic policies, instead of relying only on groups such as the World Bank or WTO (each of which has more than a hundred member states). Small groups do not solve the problem entirely, however. Whether in small groups or large, the world's states lack a government to enforce contributions to collective goods; states must look elsewhere.

International Regimes

Because of the contradictory interpretations that parties to a conflict usually have, it is difficult to resolve such conflicts without a third party to arbitrate or an overall framework to set common expectations for all parties. These considerations underlie the creation of IOs in the international security field (see Chapter 7). Norms of behaviour are at least as important in international economics as in international security because of the great gains to be realized by maintaining a stable framework for smoothly carrying on large economic transactions.

An **international regime** is a set of rules, norms and procedures around which the expectations of actors converge on a certain issue (whether arms control, international trade or Antarctic exploration).[10] The convergence of expectations means that participants in the international system have similar ideas about what rules will govern their mutual participation: each expects to play by the same rules. (This meaning of *regime* is not the same as that referring to the domestic governments of states, especially governments that are considered illegitimate or are in power for only a short time.)

Regimes can help solve collective goods problems by increasing transparency—because everyone knows what everyone is doing, cheating is more costly. The current revolution in information technologies is strengthening regimes in this aspect in particular. Also, with better international communication, states can identify conflicts and negotiate solutions through regimes more effectively.

Regimes are an important and widespread phenomenon in IR. Several will be discussed in the remaining chapters on international security. For example, the Missile Technology Control Regime (see p. 214) is a set of rules and expectations governing the international trade of missiles. In IPE, regimes are even more central. The frameworks within which states carry on trade-monetary relations, communications and environmental protection policies are key to realizing the benefits of mutual cooperation in these areas.

IR scholars may view regimes in several different ways, and the concept has been criticized as too vague. However, the most common view of regimes combines elements of realism and liberalism. States are considered the important actors, and seen as autonomous units maximizing their own interests in an anarchic context. Regimes do not play a role in issues where states can realize their interests directly through unilateral applications of leverage. Rather, regimes come into existence to overcome collective goods dilemmas by coordinating the behaviours of individual states. Although states continue to pursue their own interests, they create frameworks to coordinate their actions with those of other states if and when such coordination is necessary to realize self-interest (that is, in collective goods dilemmas). Thus, regimes help make cooperation possible even in an international system based on anarchy—exactly the point neoliberals focus on.

international regime A set of rules, norms and procedures around which the expectations of actors converge on a certain international issue (such as oceans or monetary policy).

---

[10] Stephen D. Krasner, ed., *International Regimes* (Ithaca, NY: Cornell UP, 1983). Charles Lipson, "Why Are Some International Agreements Informal?" *International Organization* 45.4 (1991): 495–538. Andreas Hasenclever, Peter Mayer and Volker Rittberger, *Theories of International Regimes* (NY: Cambridge UP, 1997).

The Information Revolution

Empowering Regimes?

Liberal international regimes codify norms and help solve collective goods problems. "Transparency" reduces cheating or free riding (such as on a treaty, alliance or cartel) because all states know what the others are doing. As evolving information technologies "illuminate" the world, will international regimes be strengthened and work better, or will information technologies become primarily an instrument of power in states' hands, as realists might argue?

To explore this question, go to www.pearsoned.ca/goldstein.

Regimes do not replace basic calculations of costs and benefits by states; they just open up new possibilities with more favourable benefit-cost ratios. Regimes do not constrain states, except in a very narrow and short-term sense. They facilitate and empower national governments faced with issues where collective goods problems would otherwise prevent them from achieving their ends. Regimes can be seen as *intervening variables* between the basic causal forces at work in IR—for realists, the relative power of state actors—and outcomes such as international cooperation (or lack thereof). Regimes do not negate the effects of power: more often they codify and normalize existing power relations. For example, the ballistic missile regime previously mentioned (see p. 83) protects a status quo in which only a few states have such missiles. If the regime works, it will keep less-powerful states from gaining leverage that could be used against more powerful states.

Hegemonic Stability

hegemonic stability theory The argument that regimes are most effective when power in the international system is most concentrated. See also *hegemony.*

Since regimes depend on state power for their enforcement, some IR scholars argue that regimes are most effective when power in the international system is most concentrated—when there is a hegemon to keep order (see "Hegemony" on pp. 69–70). This theory is known as **hegemonic stability theory.**[11] When one state has the predominant power, it can enforce rules and norms unilaterally, avoiding the collective goods problem. More specifically in this view, hegemons can maintain global free trade and promote world economic growth.

This theory attributes the peace and prosperity of the decades after World War II to U.S. hegemony, which created and maintained a global framework of economic relations supporting relatively stable and free international trade, as well as a security framework that prevented great-power wars. By contrast, the Great Depression of the 1930s and the outbreak of World War II have been attributed to the power vacuum in the international system at the time—Britain was no longer able to act as a hegemon, and the United States was unwilling to begin doing so.[12]

Why should a hegemon care about enforcing rules for the international economy that are in the common good? According to hegemonic stability theory, a hegemon has the same interests as the common good of all states. As the largest international traders, hegemons have an inherent interest in the promotion of integrated world markets, where they tend to dominate. As the state most advanced in productivity and technology, a hegemon does not

[11] Robert O. Keohane, "The Theory of Hegemonic Stability and Change in International Economic Regimes, 1967–1977," *Change in the International System,* ed. Ole R. Holsti, R. M. Siverson and A. L. George (Boulder, CO: Westview, 1980). Timothy J. McKeown, "Hegemonic Stability Theory and 19th Century Tariff Levels in Europe," *International Organization* 37.1 (1983): 73–91.

[12] Charles P. Kindleberger, *The World in Depression, 1929–1939* (Berkeley: U California P, 1973). David A. Lake, *Power, Protection, and Free Trade: International Sources of U.S. Commercial Strategy, 1887–1939* (Ithaca, NY: Cornell UP, 1988).

The Changing World Order
Hegemony, Stability and the Study of IR

Most observers of international relations would acknowledge that the post–September 11, 2001, world is dominated by U.S. power more than at any previous time, and that the United States appears much more willing to use its power internationally than it has in recent years. The international system has become unipolar.

For liberals and realists who promote the idea of hegemonic stability theory, the rise of a strong hegemonic power will increase stability and peace in the world order. This seemed to be true after World War II when the United States was similarly dominant, and during the nineteenth century when Britain dominated. Of course, the prospect that a self-interested United States could impose its will on others without restraint makes other great powers nervous. However, the theory is that as a great trading power, the United States has a strong interest in a stable and peaceful international system where participants play by the rules. Ultimately, U.S. promotion of such a world order is also in other countries' interests. If this prediction holds true, the peaceful trends of the 1990s (see pp. 38–43) will accelerate in the 2000s.

Critical theorists, and some liberals, would dispute this view and argue instead that the increasing power of the United States has led to a very limited understanding of world politics and a tendency to see the world through a distinctly U.S. lens. We see this in both the dominant approach to the study of IR and the foreign policies being adopted by the U.S. and its allies. Such views privilege militarized responses to current events and seek to abandon (whenever they are not useful) the international institutions that were created in the post–World War II period. These responses, according to this more critical view, will only result in more rather than less violence.*

These are two decidedly different views of the changing world order. One sees U.S. predominance as something that will lead to greater stability and order, the other that it will instead result in more violence. Think through a number of contemporary events taking place in international relations. Which view do they support?

*Steve Smith, "The United States and the Discipline of International Relations: Hegemonic Country, Hegemonic Discipline," *International Studies Review* 4.2 (2002): 67–85.

---

fear competition from industries in other states; it fears only that its own superior goods will be excluded from competing in them. Thus hegemons favour free trade and use their power to achieve it. Hegemony, then, provides both the ability and the motivation to maintain regimes that provide a stable political framework for free international trade, according to hegemonic stability theory. This theory is not, however, accepted by all IR scholars.[13]

What happens to regimes when hegemons lose power and decline? Regimes do not always decline with the power of the hegemons that created them. Rather, they may take on a life of their own. Although hegemony may be crucial in *establishing* regimes, it is not necessary for *maintaining* them.[14] Once actors' expectations converge around the rules embodied in a regime, they realize that the regime serves their own interests. Working through the regime becomes a habit, and national leaders may not give serious consideration to breaking out of the established rules.

This persistence of regimes was demonstrated in the 1970s, when U.S. power declined following its decades of hegemony in the years since 1945. Diminished U.S. power was

---

[13] Lloyd Gruber, *Ruling the World: Power Politics and the Rise of Supernational Institutions* (Princeton, NJ: Princeton UP, 2000). Joanne Gowa, "Rational Hegemons, Excludable Goods, and Small Groups: An Epitaph for Hegemonic Stability Theory?" *World Politics* 41.3 (1989): 307–24. Duncan Snidal, "The Limits of Hegemonic Stability Theory," *International Organization* 39.4 (1985): 580–614.

[14] Robert O. Keohane, *After Hegemony: Cooperation and Discord in the World Political Economy* (Ithaca, NY: Princeton UP, 1984). Joanne Gowa, "Bipolarity, Multipolarity, and Free Trade," *American Political Science Review* 83.4 (1989): 1227–44.

evident in the loss of the Vietnam War, the rise of OPEC and the malaise of the U.S. economy. Some IR scholars expected that the entire framework of international trade and monetary relations established after World War II would collapse once the United States was no longer able to enforce the rules of that regime, but that did not happen. International economic regimes adjusted somewhat and survived.

In part, that survival is attributable to the embedding of regimes in permanent *institutions* such as the UN, NATO and the International Monetary Fund. As the rules of the game persist over time and become habitual, institutions develop around them. These institutions become the tangible manifestation of shared expectations as well as the machinery for coordinating international actions based on those expectations. In international security affairs, the UN, NATO and other IOs provide a stable framework for resolving disputes (Chapter 8). IPE is even more institutionalized, again because of the heavier volume of activity and the wealth that can be realized from cooperation.[15]

Collective Security

collective security The formation of a broad coalition of most major actors in an international system for the purpose of jointly opposing aggression by any actor; sometimes seen as presupposing the existence of a universal organization (such as the United Nations) to which both the aggressor and its opponents belong. See also *League of Nations*.

A major application of liberal conceptions of international security affairs is the concept of **collective security**—the formation of a broad coalition of most major actors in an international system for the purpose of jointly opposing aggression by any actor. The rationale for this approach was laid out by Kant and proposed in the ideas of Woodrow Wilson's "Fourteen Points" speech, as noted on page 80.

After the horrors of World War I, the *League of Nations* was formed to address member states' collective security. It was flawed in two ways: its membership did not include all the great powers (nor the most powerful one, the United States), and its members proved unwilling to bear the costs of collective action to oppose aggression when it occurred in the 1930s, starting with Japan and Italy. After World War II, the United Nations was created as the League's successor to promote collective security (see Chapter 8).

Several regional IGOs also currently perform collective security functions (deterring aggression) as well as economic and cultural ones. In Latin America and the United States, there is the *Organization of American States (OAS)*. The Middle East (including North Africa) has the *Arab League*. In Africa (also including North Africa), there is the *African Union*.

The success of collective security depends on two components. First, members must keep their commitments to the group. When a powerful state commits aggression against a weaker one, it often is not in the immediate interest of other powerful states to go to war over the issue. It can be very costly to suppress a determined aggressor.

A second requisite for collective security is that enough members must agree on what constitutes aggression. In international relations, it is often hotly debated as to whether a state has acted aggressively or defensively. The UN Security Council is structured so that aggression is defined by what all five permanent members, as well as at least four of the other 10 members, can agree on (see "The Security Council" on pp. 258–262). However, this collective security system does not work against aggression by a great power. When the Soviet Union invaded Afghanistan, or the United States mined the harbours of

---

[15] Paul Taylor and A. J. R. Groom, eds., *International Institutions at Work* (NY: St. Martin's, 1988). John Gerard Ruggie, ed., *Multiculturalism Matters: The Theory and Praxis of an Institutional Form* (see footnote 7 in this chapter). Robert O. Keohane, "International Institutions: Two Approaches," *International Studies Quarterly* 32.4 (1988): 379–96.

Nicaragua, or France blew up the Greenpeace ship *Rainbow Warrior,* the UN could do nothing—because those states can veto Security Council resolutions.[16]

Both requirements were met in the case of Kuwait in 1990–1991. The aggressor, Iraq, was a member of the UN, as was the victim, Kuwait. It was the first time since the founding of the UN that one member had invaded, occupied and annexed another member—attempting to erase it as a sovereign state. The invasion was so blatant a violation of Kuwaiti sovereignty and territorial integrity that the Security Council had little trouble labelling it aggression. The aggression was flagrant, the rules of world order were being redefined as the Cold War ended and, of course, the West's oil supply was threatened. In a series of resolutions, the Council condemned Iraq, applied mandatory economic sanctions (requiring all UN members to stop trading with Iraq) and ultimately authorized the use of force by a multinational coalition. Collective security worked in this case because the conquest of Kuwait brought all the great powers together and because they were willing to bear the costs of confronting Iraq. (China abstained on the resolution authorizing force and did not contribute to the coalition, but it did not veto the resolution.)

In 2002–2003, the United States could not convince the UN that collective security was being threatened by Iraq. The U.S. claimed that Iraq possessed weapons of mass destruction and planned to use them against the U.S. or its allies. The Security Council debated Iraq's failure to abide by its promise to disclose all of its weapons of mass destruction. Iraq claimed they had all been destroyed after the Gulf War, but the U.S. insisted Iraq retained significant stockpiles. In early 2003, a resolution authorizing military force was withdrawn after France promised to veto it; Germany, Russia and China had also all strongly opposed the resolution and a war against Iraq. When the UN did not act, the U.S. formed a "coalition of the willing" that included the United Kingdom and Australia (but not Canada), and invaded Iraq. Saddam Hussein's regime was overthrown, but no weapons of mass destruction were ever found (thus confirming the UN's reluctance to support armed intervention in the name of collective security).

The concept of collective security has been broadened in recent years. Toward the end of the Cold War, the liberal premises of international community and mutual state interests provided the foundations for a new idea called *common security* (or "mutual security")—the notion that because the security of all states, enemies as well as friends, is interdependent, the insecurity of one state makes all states less secure.[17] A local dispute in one part of the world can threaten another part; economic and ethnic rivalries can spill over into violent conflicts; the costs of preparing for war can bankrupt great powers even in peacetime. This new reality—if state leaders recognized it—would resolve the security dilemma (see p. 62), because a state's own security interests would be (indirectly) *diminished* if it threatened another state.

The theory and practice of common security were promoted during the late 1980s by Soviet president Gorbachev, who won the Nobel peace prize for his accomplishments (although he was swept from office when the Soviet Union collapsed). Gorbachev argued that as states became more closely connected economically and culturally, it was futile and wasteful to arm against each other, especially with nuclear weapons.

---

[16] Joseph Lepgold and Thomas G. Weiss, eds., *Collective Conflict Management and Changing World Politics* (Albany: SUNY P, 1998).

[17] Palme Commission [Independent Commission on Disarmament and Security Issues], *Common Security: A Programme for Disarmament* (London: Pan, 1982). Emma Rothschild, "What Is Security?" *Daedalus* 124.3 (1995): 53–98. Barry Buzan, Ole Waever and Jaap de Wilde, *Security: A New Framework for Analysis* (Boulder, CO: Rienner, 1997).

Focus on Canadian Scholarship

Scholars working at Canadian universities whose work either explores or is informed by issues raised in liberalism include **Stéphane Roussel** at the University of Québec at Montréal, who works on questions of liberal institutionalism. At Carleton University's Norman Paterson School of International Affairs, **David Long** has examined the impact of liberal thought on IR theory and his colleague **James Ron** works on human rights while **Brian Tomlin** focuses on bargaining and dispute resolution. At the University of Western Ontario, **Charles Jones** works on issues of international justice and cosmopolitanism and his colleague **H. Peter Langille** works in peace studies and is interested in questions of Canadian defence policy and human, common and cooperative security. **Edna Keeble** at St. Mary's University focuses on women's human rights. At the University of British Columbia, **Katharina Coleman** examines state interest in international legitimacy and is interested in why states choose to launch peace

enforcement operations within the framework of international organizations. **William Coleman** at McMaster University has assessed constructivist applications to the emergence of agricultural biotech regimes. At the University of Calgary, **Antonio Francheset** focuses on ethics and global governance, human security and the application of cosmopolitan political morality to international legal rules. **Emanuel Adler** at the University of Toronto has explored questions of identity and peace and constructivist IR theory. Also at the University of Toronto, **Lou Pauly** studies global liberalism and political order. **Norrin Ripsman** at Concordia University examines domestic sources of foreign security policy in democratic states and peacemaking by democracies. At the University of Lethbridge, **Chris Kukucha** works on alternative dispute resolution. At Wilfrid Laurier University, **Rhonda Howard-Hassmann** focuses on international human rights, and at Acadia University, **Marshall Conley** is interested in peace studies and human rights.

human security Expands the notion of security away from a focus on states to one that examines all the complex ways in which people are made secure, including through human rights protections; access to education, food and shelter; availability of health services; and a sustainable environment.

Another elaboration of security has been developed by Canadian scholars and policymakers (though the term itself did not originate in Canada). The idea of **human security** expands the notion of security away from one that is focused on states to a view of security that examines all the complex ways in which people are made secure, including through human rights protections; access to education, food and shelter; availability of health services; and a sustainable environment. Human security (see also pp. 137–139) acknowledges that a world in which states are secure is not necessarily one in which people are secure. A considerable amount of violence takes place within states, and not just between them, and it is usually states that are the biggest perpetrators of human rights abuses. State policies can also be responsible for poverty, disease, famine and environmental disasters. By this view, the foreign policy of states such as Canada should aim to promote remedies that enhance human security over and above state security.[18]

Liberals have sought to reform rather than radically reshape the international system as we know it. They have tried to overhaul the realist model but not to reject its terms of reference entirely (this is one reason that realists and liberals can continue to debate and to understand one another's arguments even while disagreeing. Another reason they can understand each other, as discussed in the next chapter, is that both would fall into the category of "problem-solving theories"). Liberal scholars and liberal state leaders alike have argued that international cooperation and the avoidance of violence are ultimately better for states themselves, more rational for state leaders to pursue and more likely to promote peace and prosperity.

---

[18] Elizabeth Ridell-Dixon, "Canada's Human Security Agenda: Walking the Talk?" *International Journal* 60.4 (Autumn 2005): 1067–92. Denis Stairs, "The Changing Office and the Changing Environment of the Minister of Foreign Affairs in the Axworthy Era," *Canada Among Nations 2001: The Axworthy Legacy*, ed. Fen Osler Hampson, Norman Hillmer and Maureen Appel Molot (Toronto: Oxford UP, 2001).

The Democratic Peace

As noted on page 79, Immanuel Kant argued that lasting peace would depend on states' becoming republics, with legislatures to check the power of monarchs (or prime ministers) in calling for war. He thought that checks and balances in government would act as brakes on the use of military force. IR scholars have examined whether empirical data support the idea that democracy is linked with a kind of foreign policy fundamentally different from that of authoritarianism.[19] One theory they considered was that democracies are generally *more peaceful* than authoritarian governments (fighting fewer or smaller wars). This turned out *not* to be true. Democracies

ELECTORAL UPSET
Upsurges of democratic movements throughout the world in recent years testify to the power of the idea of democracy. Since democracies rarely fight each other, worldwide democratization might lead to lasting peace, but democratization also brings surprises. In free elections in 2006, Palestinians fed up with a corrupt administration elected the militant and violent Islamic party Hamas, whose candidates here campaign with green crescents, a symbol of Islam.

fight as many wars as do authoritarian states. Indeed, the three most war-prone states of the past two centuries (according to political scientists who count wars) were France, Russia and Britain. Britain was a democracy throughout, France for part of that period and Russia not at all.

What *is* true about democracies is that although they fight wars against authoritarian states, *they almost never fight each other*. No major historical cases contradict this generalization, which is known as the **democratic peace.** Why this is so is not entirely clear. As there have not been many democracies for very long, the generalization could be just a coincidence, though this seems unlikely. It may be that democracies

democratic peace The proposition, strongly supported by empirical evidence, that democracies almost never fight wars against each other (although they do fight against authoritarian states).

---

[19] Bruce Russett and John Oneal, *Triangulating Peace: Democracy, Interdependence, and International Organizations* (NY: Norton, 2000). Joanne Gowa, *Ballots and Bullets: The Elusive Democratic Peace* (Princeton, NJ: Princeton UP, 1999). Spencer R. Weart, *Never at War: Why Democracies Will Not Fight One Another* (New Haven, CT: Yale UP, 1998). Miriam Fendius Elman, ed., *Paths to Peace: Is Democracy the Answer?* (Cambridge, MA: MIT P, 1997). Bruce Russett, *Grasping the Democratic Peace: Principles for a Post–Cold War World* (Princeton, NJ: Princeton UP, 1993). James Lee Ray, *Democracy and International Conflict: An Evaluation of the Democratic Peace Proposition* (Columbia: U South Carolina P, 1995). Michael W. Doyle, "Liberalism and World Politics," *American Political Science Review* 80 (1986): 1151–70. Zeev Maoz, "The Controversy over the Democratic Peace: Rearguard Action or Cracks in the Wall?" *International Security* 22.1 (1997): 162–98. John M. Owen, *Liberal Peace, Liberal War: American Politics and International Security* (Ithaca, NY: Cornell UP, 1997).

The Information Revolution

Democratization accelerated worldwide in the 1990s, potentially enlarging the zone of "democratic peace" since democracies rarely fight one another. New information technologies may allow citizens greater access to political processes, including those that cross borders. However, these technologies may also give those with wealth and power new means of influence, as when state-controlled media whip up nationalism or when advertising promotes Western products and values in the global South. Will the information revolution usher in global democracy and peace, or sharpen divisions?

To explore this question, go to www.pearsoned.ca/goldstein.

avoid severe conflicts with each other as they tend to be capitalist states whose trade relations create strong interdependence (war would be costly since it would disrupt trade). Or, citizens of democratic societies (whose support is necessary for wars to be waged) may simply not see the citizens of other democracies as enemies. By contrast, authoritarian governments of other states can be seen as enemies. Peace among democracies gives empirical support to a long-standing liberal claim that, because it is rooted in the domestic level of analysis, contradicts a fundamental premise of realism—that the most important explanations in IR are to be found at the interstate level.

Over the past two centuries, democracy has become more and more widespread as a form of government, a trend that is changing the nature of the foreign policy process worldwide. Many states do not yet have democratic governments (the most important of these is China). Existing democracies are imperfect in various ways—from political apathy in countries like Canada and the United States and corruption in Japan to autocratic traditions in Russia. Nonetheless, the trend is toward democratization in most of the world's regions.

We do not know where trends toward democracy will lead, but because it is now conceivable that someday all or most of the world's states will be democratically governed, wars may become less frequent. As Kant envisaged, an international community based on peaceful relations may emerge. However, although mature democracies almost never fight each other, a period of *transition* to democracy may be more prone to war than either a stable democracy or a stable authoritarian government.[20] This seems to be particularly true when states are emerging from civil conflict.[21] Therefore, the process of democratization does not necessarily bode well for peace in the short term.

A further caution is in order. The generalization about democracies almost never fighting each other is historically valid but not necessarily applicable in the future. By way of analogy, there was a generalization during the Cold War that communist governments never yield power peacefully. That generalization held up until suddenly a series of communist governments did just that around 1990. As the world has more democracies for a longer period of time, the generalization about their almost never fighting each other also might not hold up.

---

[20] Jack Snyder, *From Voting to Violence: Democratization and Nationalist Conflict* (NY: Norton, 2000). Michael D. Ward and Kristian S. Gleditsch, "Democratizing for Peace," *American Political Science Review* 92.1 (1998): 51–61.

[21] Roland Paris, *At War's End: Building Peace after Civil Conflict* (NY: Cambridge UP, 2004). Roland Paris, "Bringing the Leviathan Back In: Classical Versus Contemporary Studies of the Liberal Peace," *International Studies Review* 8 (2006): 425–40.

CONSTRUCTIVISM

Constructivism is a recently popular approach in IR that focuses on the nature of norms, identity and social interaction between various actors in global politics. Some variants of constructivism are more liberal in orientation and some are more critical; one author has described constructivism as a "middle ground" between traditional and critical approaches.[22] At base, constructivism sees the activities of IR as a "world of our making" and in this way highlights the potential for agency or action in IR (as opposed to a world determined exclusively by the structure of the system, as neorealists contend).[23] It is an approach that can provide powerful insights into the world of IR.

Constructivism is interested in how actors define their national interests, the threats to those interests and their relationships to one another. Realists (and neoliberals) tend to simply take state interests as given. Thus, constructivism puts IR in the context of broader social relations.[24]

One constructivist approach focuses on how people use language to make or "construct" the social world and how the social world in turn shapes individuals. Rules (including legal rules and nonlegal norms) are seen as crucial because they stand between people and society, enabling the two-way process of construction to be an ongoing one. Rules are statements telling people how they should behave under certain conditions, and this version of constructivism analyzes rules in terms of the kinds of "speech acts" that comprise them. Anarchy, sovereignty, regimes and other basic IR concepts are then seen in terms of how they relate to rules in this broad sense.

A different constructivist approach considers how states' interests and identities are shaped by rule-governed (or norm-governed) interactions. Most liberals tend to see rules and norms mainly as mediators and coordinators of states' self-interested behaviour. For constructivists, however, norms do more than help states to pursue their selfish interests in mutually beneficial ways and to overcome collective goods problems. Rather, norms affect how states conceive of their interests and, indeed, identities, in the first place. Thus, the state's conception of its interests, its presentation of itself on the international stage and its behaviour all might change as a result of interstate interactions. States, like people, come to see themselves as others do.

Constructivists reject the assumption that states always want more rather than less power and wealth, or the assumption that state interests exist independently of a context of interactions. Rather, constructivists assume that complex cultures shape state behaviour regarding international security and military force. For example, a small state asked to mediate a conflict between two larger states might acquire a new identity as a peacemaker or mediator, and with that new identity would come an interest in *acting* as a peacemaker would.

Constructivists hold that these state identities are complex, changing and arise from interactions with other states—often through a process of *socialization*. Some constructivist scholars contend that over time, states can conceptualize one another in such a way

constructivism A recently popular approach in IR that focuses on the nature of norms, identity and social interaction between various actors in global politics.

---

[22] K.M. Fierke, "Constructivism," in Tim Dunne, Milya Kurki and Steve Smith, eds., *International Relations Theories: Discipline and Diversity* (Oxford UP, 2007) 166–87.

[23] Nicolas Onus, *World of Our Making: Rules and Rule in Social Theory and International Relations* (Columbia, SC: U of South Carolina Press, 1989).

[24] Alexander Wendt, *Social Theory of International Politics* (Cambridge UP, 1999). See also Christian Reus-Smit, *The Moral Purpose of the State: Culture, Social Identity, and Institutional Rationality in International Relations* (Princeton, NJ: Princeton, 1999). Martha Finnemore, *National Interests in International Society* (Ithaca, NY: Cornell UP, 1996). Jutta Weldes, Mark Laffey, Hugh Gusterson and Raymond Duval, eds., *Cultures of Insecurity: States, Communities and the Production of Danger* (Minneapolis: U Minnesota P, 1999).

that there is no danger of a security dilemma, arms race or other effects of anarchy. They point to Europe as an example—a continent that was the centre of two military conflicts in the first half of the twentieth century that killed millions. By the end of that century, war had become unthinkable. European identities are now intertwined with the European Union, not with the violent nationalism that led to two world wars. For constructivists, power politics, anarchy and military force cannot explain this change. Institutions, regimes, norms and changes in identity are better explanations.[25]

States may also come to value and covet something like status or reputation, which are social rather than material concepts. Switzerland, for example, values its role as a neutral, nonaligned state (it belongs to neither the European Union nor NATO, and joined the UN only in 2002). This status as a neutral gives Switzerland prestige and power—not material power such as money or guns, but a normative power to intervene diplomatically in important international affairs. Similarly, Canada's foreign policy contains its own identity-driven imperatives, usually revolving around peacekeeping and humanitarian operations, though more recently this has begun to shift as Canadian decision-makers attempt to construct a more assertive identity for Canada on the global stage.

Another field of constructivist research relies heavily on international norms and their power to constrain state action. While realists (and neoliberals) contend that states make decisions based on a *logic of consequences* (what will happen to me if I behave a certain way?), constructivist scholars note that there is a powerful *logic of appropriateness* (how should I behave in this situation?).[26] For example, some cases of humanitarian intervention or peacekeeping—military intervention by one state or states to protect citizens or subjects of another—seem difficult to explain in realist terms; they very seldom serve the strategic interests of the intervening state. A constructivist explanation might point to changing norms about which kinds of people are worthy of protection. In the nineteenth century, European powers occasionally intervened to protect Christian subjects of the Ottoman Empire from massacres, but generally ignored non-Christian victims. However, as decolonization enshrined the principle of self-determination and as human rights became widely valued, the scope of humanitarian intervention expanded.[27]

How are international norms spread around the world? In an age of global communication and relative ease of transportation, there are many possibilities. Constructivists emphasize different sets of actors who spread norms. Some contend that individuals, labelled *norm entrepreneurs*, change ideas and encourage certain types of norms through travel, writing and meeting with elites. Some point to broad-based social movements and nongovernmental organizations, such as the anti-apartheid movement encouraging the development of a global norm of racial equality. Others show how international organizations (such as the UN or NATO) can diffuse norms of what is appropriate and inappropriate behaviour. In each case, however, it is new ideas and norms, rather than power and self-interest, driving state behaviour.[28]

[25] Jeffrey Checkel, "Social Learning and European Identity Change." *International Organization* 55.3 (2000): 553–88.

[26] James G. March and Johan Olsen, "The Institutional Dynamics of International Political Orders," *International Organization* 52.4 (1998): 943–69.

[27] Martha Finnemore, *Purpose of Intervention* (Ithaca: Cornell UP, 2004).

[28] Margaret Keck and Kathryn Sikkink, *Activists Beyond Borders: Advocacy Networks in International Politics* (Ithaca: Cornell UP, 1998). Audie Klotz, *Norms in International Relations: The Struggle against Apartheid* (Ithaca: Cornell UP, 1995).

Research in the constructivist tradition has expanded rapidly in recent years. Scholars have examined the role of the European Union in socializing elites in new member states. Others have investigated how international organizations gain authority through expertise (e.g., the IMF on international financial issues) to make decisions that run counter to what member states desire. Finally, constructivist scholars have begun to investigate how notions of identity and symbolism are important for understanding terrorist movements and counter-terrorism policy.[29]

PEACE STUDIES

Another approach that challenges some fundamental concepts behind realism is *peace studies*. As with constructivism, peace studies contains elements of liberal thought, but also contains some elements of critical theory as discussed in Chapter 4. Some peace studies scholars emphasize possibilities for reform of the international system, others seek a more fundamental transformation in both the way we think about world politics and what should be done to promote peace. Many universities have created interdisciplinary peace studies programs through which scholars and students organize discussions and courses about peace.[30] Typically, such programs include not only political scientists but psychologists who have studied conflict, physicists who have studied nuclear weaponry, religious scholars who have studied practical morality and so forth. With these various disciplinary backgrounds, scholars of peace studies tend to be more eclectic than political scientists and much more broad-minded in the topics they consider worthy of study in international security affairs.[31]

Broadening the Focus

Peace studies seeks to shift the focus of IR away from the interstate level of analysis and toward a broad conception of social relations at the individual, domestic and global levels. Peace studies connects war and peace with individual responsibility, economic inequality, gender relations, cross-cultural understanding and with other aspects of social relationships. The discipline seeks the potential for peace not in the transactions of state leaders but in the transformation of entire societies (through social revolution) and in transnational communities (bypassing states and ignoring borders to connect people and groups globally).[32]

Another way in which peace studies seeks to broaden the focus of inquiry is to reject the supposed objectivity of traditional (realist and liberal) approaches. Most scholars of

---

[29] Jeffrey Checkel, "International Institutions and Socialization in Europe: Introduction and Framework," *International Organization* 59.4 (2005): 801–26. Michael Barnett and Martha Finnemore, *Rules for the World* (Ithaca: Cornell UP, 2004). David Leheny, "Symbols, Strategies, and Choices for International Relations Scholarship after September 11," *Dialogue IO* 1.1 (2003): 57–70.

[30] David P. Barash, *Introduction to Peace Studies* (Belmont, CA: Wadsworth, 1991). Michael T. Klare, ed., *Peace and World Security Studies: A Curriculum Guide*, 6th ed. (Boulder, CO: Rienner, 1994). Paul Smoker, Ruth Davies and Barbara Munske, eds., *A Reader in Peace Studies* (NY: Pergamon, 1990). George A. Lopez, ed., "Peace Studies: Past and Future," *Annals of the American Academy of Political and Social Science* 504 (Newbury Park, CA: Sage, 1989).

[31] Ursula Franklin, *The Real World of Technology*, rev. ed. (Toronto: Anansi, 1999).

[32] Francesca M. Cancian and James William Gibson, *Making War/Making Peace: The Social Foundations of Violent Conflict* (Belmont, CA: Wadsworth, 1990). Anatol Rapoport, *Peace: An Idea Whose Time Has Come* (Ann Arbor: U Michigan P, 1992). Johan Galtung, *Peace by Peaceful Means: Peace and Conflict, Development and Civilization* (Thousand Oaks, CA: Sage, 1996).

peace studies think that a good way to gain knowledge is to participate in actions, such as peace movements—and not just to observe objectively. This approach seeks to integrate theory with practice.

Peace studies scholars participate in the practice of seeking peace because they want to use their theories and knowledge to influence the world they live in. They are not interested just in describing the world as it is, but in exploring how it should or could be and helping make it that way. The main reason for studying war and peace, in this view, is to lessen war and promote the chances for peace. This lack of objectivity is called a **normative bias** because scholars impose their personal norms and values on the subject. Some political scientists (especially realists) dismiss peace studies because it lacks scientific objectivity about outcomes.

Scholars in peace studies are quick to convey, however, that realism too has normative biases and makes policy prescriptions. Realists (from Sun Tzu to Henry Kissinger) even take jobs as advisers to state leaders, urging them to follow the principles of realism. Because realism's assumptions—that actors pursue only their own interests, that violence is a normal and acceptable way to achieve ends, that order is more important than justice—are debatable as objective statements of fact; they might better be seen as value statements. Realism, then, becomes more of an ideology than a theory.

Thus scholars in peace studies defend both their broader approach to the subject and their willingness to bring their own values into play in their studies. These characteristics of peace studies can be seen in its approach to war—the central topic in international security affairs.

normative bias The personal norms and values that IR scholars bring to their studies, such as a preference for peace rather than war.

Conflict Resolution

The development and implementation of peaceful strategies for settling conflicts—using alternatives to violent forms of leverage—is known by the general term **conflict resolution.** These methods are at work, and are competing with violent methods, in virtually all international conflicts. The use of conflict resolution has been increasing of late, becoming more sophisticated and succeeding more often.[33]

Most conflict resolution uses a third party whose role is **mediation** between two conflicting parties.[34] Most of today's international conflicts have one or more mediating parties working regularly to resolve the conflict without violence. There is no hard-and-fast rule dictating what kind of third party mediates what kind of conflicts. Presently the UN is the most important mediator on the world scene. Some regional conflicts are mediated through regional organizations, single states or even private individuals. For instance, the former president of Costa Rica, Oscar Arias, won the

conflict resolution The development and implementation of peaceful strategies for settling conflicts.

mediation The use of a third party (or parties) in conflict resolution.

[33] Lester R. Kurtz, ed., *Encyclopedia of Violence, Peace, and Conflict*, 3 vols. (San Diego: Academic, 1999). Ho-Won Jeong, *Conflict Resolution: Dynamics, Process, and Structure* (Brookfield, VT: Ashgate, 2000). Antonia Handler Chayes and Abram Chayes, *Planning for Intervention: International Cooperation in Conflict Management* (Cambridge, MA: Kluwer Law, 1999). Michael S. Lund, *Preventing Violent Conflicts: A Strategy for Preventive Diplomacy* (Washington, DC: U.S. Institute of Peace, 1996). Dennis J. D. Sandole and Hugo Van der Merwe, eds., *Conflict Resolution: Theory and Practice* (NY: St. Martin's, 1993). Hugh Miall, *The Peacemakers: Peaceful Settlement of Disputes since 1945* (NY: St. Martin's, 1992). Raimo Väyrynen, ed., *New Directions in Conflict Theory: Conflict Resolution and Conflict Transformation* (Newbury Park, CA: Sage, 1991). John W. Burton, *Conflict Resolution and Prevention* (NY: St. Martin's, 1990).

[34] Chester A. Crocker, Fen Osler Hampson and Pamela Aall, eds., *Herding Cats: The Management of Complex International Mediation* (Washington, DC: U.S. Institute of Peace, 1999). Jacob Bercovitch, ed., *Resolving International Conflicts: The Theory and Practice of Mediation* (Boulder, CO: Rienner, 1996). Thomas Princen, *Intermediaries in International Conflict* (Princeton NJ: Princeton UP, 1992).

1987 Nobel peace prize for mediating a multilateral agreement among Central American presidents to end several brutal wars in the region.[35]

The level of the mediator's involvement varies. Some mediation is strictly *technical*—a mediator may take an active but strictly neutral role in facilitating communication between two states that lack other channels of communication.[36] For example, Pakistan secretly passed messages between China and the United States before the breakthrough in U.S.-Chinese relations in 1971. Such a role is sometimes referred to as offering the mediator's *good offices* to a negotiating process. In facilitating communication, a mediator listens to each side's ideas and presents them in a way the other side can hear. The mediator works to change each side's view of difficult issues. In this role, the mediator is like a translator between the two sides or a therapist helping them work through psychological problems in their relationship.

Mediators may also actively *propose solutions* based on an assessment of each side's demands and interests. Such solutions may be compromises, may recognize the greater validity of one side's position (or power) or may be creative ideas that meet the needs of both parties. A fifty-fifty compromise is not always the best or fairest solution—it may simply reward the side with the more extreme starting position.

KEEPING THE PEACE
Proponents of peacekeeping argue that it is a way to use militaries in zones of conflict in decidedly nonmilitaristic ways.

If both sides agree in advance to abide by a solution devised by a mediator, the process is called *arbitration*. In that case, both sides present their arguments to an arbitrator, who decides on a "fair" solution. For example, the Israelis and Egyptians submitted their border dispute over the hotel at Taba (see p. 166) to arbitration when they could not come to an agreement on their own. Similarly, Chile and Argentina presented their border problems to a panel of Latin American judges in the 1980s and 1990s. When Serbian and Bosnian negotiators could not agree on who should govern the city of Brcko, they turned the issue over to arbitration rather than hold up the entire 1995 Dayton Agreement. Arbitration often uses a panel of three people, one chosen by each side unilaterally and a third on whom both sides agree. In 2002, such a panel (with the UN choosing the third member) delineated the Ethiopian-Eritrean border following a costly war.

In many situations, two conflicting parties could benefit from a solution other than war but lack the trust and communication channels to find such a solution. Neutral mediation with various degrees of involvement can bring about awareness of the two parties' common interests. When heads of state do not see their common interests, ordinary citizens might try to raise awareness of such mutual interests on both sides. Travel and discussion by private

---

[35] Jack Child, *The Central American Peace Process, 1983–1991: Sheathing Swords, Building Confidence* (Boulder, CO: Rienner, 1992).

[36] Janice Gross Stein, ed., *Getting to the Table: The Processes of International Prenegotiation* (Baltimore: Johns Hopkins UP, 1989).

individuals and groups toward this end has been called *citizen diplomacy*, and it occurs fairly regularly (though not very visibly) when conflicting states are stuck in a cycle of hostility.[37]

Conflicting parties (and mediators) can also work to *restructure* terms of bargaining—in effect extending the possible solutions for one or both sides so that their interests overlap. Often a mediator can come up with a win-win solution.[38] This may be as simple as providing the means for one or both parties to *save face* when giving up some demand. In other cases, creative solutions may satisfy both parties. For instance, at the Camp David negotiations, Egypt insisted on regaining sovereignty over all its territory in the Sinai desert. Israel insisted on security against the threat of attack from the Sinai. The win-win solution was a return of the territory to Egyptian sovereignty but with most of it demilitarized so that Egypt could not use it to stage an attack. A win-win solution often trades off two disputed items on which the states place different priorities. Each side can then prevail on the issue that it considers important while yielding on an issue it does not care as much about.

Another way to create mutual interests is to break a conflict into pieces (fractionation) and start with those pieces for which a common interest and workable solution can be found. These may initially be largely symbolic *confidence-building* measures but can gather momentum as the process proceeds. A gradual increase in trust reduces the risks of nonviolent settlements relative to cost and creates an expectation that the issues at stake can be resolved nonviolently.

War and Militarism

Most scholars in peace studies reject realists' willingness to treat war as normal or their willingness to be objective about the merits of war or peace. Peace studies resonates with Benjamin Franklin's observation that "there never was a good war or a bad peace."[39] In particular, peace studies scholars object to realists' willingness to treat nuclear weaponry as another instrument of state military power. In general, peace studies tries to call into question the nature of war and its role in society.

militarism The glorification of war, military force and violence and the structuring of society around war—for example, the dominant role of a military-industrial complex in a national economy.

Peace studies scholars argue that war is not a natural expression of power but one closely tied to militarism in some cultures.[40] **Militarism** is the glorification of war, military force and violence through TV, films, books, political speeches, toys, games, sports and other such avenues. Militarism also refers to the structuring of society around war—for example, the dominant role of a military-industrial complex in a national economy, the dominance of national security issues in domestic politics and so forth. Militarism is thought to underlie the propensity of political leaders to use military force.

Historically, militarism has had a profound influence on the evolution of societies. War has often been glorified as a "manly" enterprise that ennobles the human spirit (especially before World War I, which succeeded in changing that perspective). Even Mahatma Gandhi (discussed later) conceded that "war is an unmitigated evil. It certainly does one

---

[37] Gale Warner and Michael Shuman, *Citizen Diplomats: Pathfinders in Soviet-American Relations and How You Can Join Them* (NY: Continuum, 1987).

[38] Roger Fisher and William Ury, with Bruce Patton, *Getting to Yes: Negotiating Agreement without Giving In* (NY: Penguin, 1983).

[39] Benjamin Franklin, letter to Josiah Quincy, 11 September 1773.

[40] Lt. Col. Dave Grossman, *On Killing: The Psychological Cost of Learning to Kill in War and Society* (Boston: Little, Brown, 1995). Elise Boulding, ed., *New Agendas for Peace Research: Conflict and Security Reexamined* (Boulder, CO: Rienner, 1992).

good thing, however: it drives away fear and brings bravery to the surface."[41] By this view, not only evil acts are brought forth by war, but also exemplary acts of humanity—sacrifice, honour, courage, altruism on behalf of loved ones and bonding with a community larger than oneself.

The culture of modern states—and of realism—celebrates and rewards these qualities of soldiers, just as hunter-gatherer cultures created rituals and rewards to induce participation in warfare. Many countries have holidays in honour of warriors, provide them (or their survivors) with veterans' benefits, and bury them in special cemeteries where their individual identities are symbolically submerged into a larger collective identity. Because militarism seems so pervasive and is so strongly associated with the state, many scholars in peace studies question whether the very nature of states must change before lasting peace will be possible.

The United States is considered by some scholars to be a particularly militarized society. In

SHADOW OF WAR
Militarism in a culture, or the lack thereof, can influence foreign policy. In societies at war, children's psychological trauma contributes to intergroup conflicts decades later. Generations of Palestinians have grown up in a society permeated by violent conflict with Israel. This boy holds a Palestinian gunman's assault rifle during fighting in Bethlehem, 2001.

the 1950s, children hid under school desks to practise for a nuclear attack. In the 1960s and 1970s, the Vietnam War dominated the experiences of young people. In the 1980s, fear of nuclear war returned, in 1991 the Gulf War began, and 2003 saw the start of the Iraq War. The Junior Reserve Officer Training Program, a Pentagon-designed military training program, has been adopted by school boards across the U.S., in part because it comes with extra funding from the Defense Department (especially important for underfunded public schools).[42] Scholars in peace studies have made a connection between U.S. uses of military force and the American gun mania, high murder rate, Wild West myths, television violence and other aspects of American life conveying that violence is socially acceptable.

Peace studies seeks examples of less-militarized cultures to show that realism's emphasis on military force is not universal or necessary. Some point to countries such as Canada and Ireland, which have devoted themselves more to peacekeeping than war-making (though both have used peacekeeping as part of their rationales to maintain military

---

[41] Mohandas K. Gandhi, *Non-Violence in Peace and War*, vol. 1 (1942; NY: Garland, 1972) 270.

[42] Cynthia Enloe, *Maneuvers: The International Politics of Militarizing Women's Lives* (Berkeley: U of California P, 2000).

forces, and Canada was involved in the two world wars of the twentieth century and is currently involved in Afghanistan). Costa Rica has had no army for 50 years (just lightly armed forces), even during the 1980s when wars occurred in neighbouring Nicaragua and Panama. Japanese culture since World War II has developed strong norms against war and violence. Public opinion, even more than Japan's constitution, makes it difficult for political leaders to consider military force a viable instrument of foreign policy, which is a dramatic reversal of Japan prior to World War II. All kinds of society seem to have the potential for warfare under some conditions (see Chapter 6), and so distinctions such as "warlike" are only relative.

Positive Peace

In peace studies, just as war is seen as a pervasive aspect of society as a whole, so can peace be reconceptualized in a broader way.[43] According to peace studies scholars, peace should be defined as more than just the absence of war. The mere absence of war does not guarantee that it will not recur. As Kant pointed out, every peace treaty ending a European great-power war in the sixteenth through eighteenth centuries merely set the stage for the next war. Nor can the absence of great-power war in the Cold War be considered true peace: proxy wars in the global South killed millions of people while a relentless arms race wasted vast resources. Because realism assumes the normalcy of military conflicts, it recognizes only a negative definition of peace—the temporary absence of war.

positive peace A peace that resolves the underlying reasons for war; not just a ceasefire but a transformation of relationships, including elimination or reduction of economic exploitation and political oppression.

By contrast, **positive peace** refers to a peace that resolves the underlying reasons for war—peace that is not just a ceasefire but a transformation of relationships. Under positive peace, not only do state armies stop fighting each other, they stop arming, stop forming death squads against internal protest and reverse the economic exploitation and political oppression that scholars in peace studies believe are responsible for social conflicts that lead to war.

Proponents of the positive peace approach see broad social and economic issues—assumed by realists to be relatively unimportant—as inextricably linked with positive peace. Some scholars define poverty, hunger and oppression as forms of violence—which they call **structural violence** because they are caused by the structure of social relations rather than by direct actions such as shooting people. Structural violence in this definition kills and harms many more people each year than do war and other forms of direct political violence. Positive peace is usually defined as including the elimination of structural violence because it is considered a source of conflict and war.

structural violence A term used by some scholars to refer to poverty, hunger, oppression and other social and economic sources of conflict.

In this view, negative peace that merely prevents violence may actually lock in place an unjust status quo. That injustice is epitomized in the global North-South disparity (see Chapter 13), with its massive structural violence against the South. Thus, a narrow, negative definition of peace is seen as inadequate because it conflicts with the achievement of justice, which in turn is necessary for positive peace.

Advocates of positive peace also criticize militaristic culture. The "social construction of war"—a complex system of rules and relations that ultimately supports the existence of war—touches our lives in many ways: from children's war toys to patriotic rituals in schools; from teenagers' gender roles to military training for young men; from the taxes we pay to the sports we play. The positive peace approach seeks to change the whole system, and not just one piece of it.

---

[43] Robert Elias and Jennifer Turpin, eds., *Rethinking Peace* (Boulder, CO: Rienner, 1994). Linda Rennie Forcey, ed., *Peace: Meanings, Politics, Strategies* (NY: Praeger, 1989). Istvan Kende, "The History of Peace: Concept and Organizations from the Late Middle Ages to the 1870s," *Journal of Peace Research* 26.3 (1989): 233–47. Kenneth E. Boulding, *Stable Peace* (Austin: U Texas P, 1978).

More controversial within peace studies is the question of whether positive peace requires that states' authority be subordinated to a **world government.**[44] The creation of a world government has long been debated by scholars and pursued by activists; many plans have been drawn up, though none have succeeded. Some scholars believe progress is being made (through the UN) toward the eventual emergence of a world government. Others think the idea is impractical or even undesirable (merely adding another layer of centralized control, when peace demands decentralization and freedom).

world government
A centralized world governing body with strong enforcement powers.

Peace Movements

Scholars in peace studies also examine how to achieve the conditions for positive peace. Approaches vary, from building a world government to strengthening democratic governance, or from redistributing wealth to strengthening spiritual communities. Most in peace studies share a skepticism that, if left to themselves, state leaders would ever achieve positive peace. Rather, they believe the practice of IR will change only as a result of pressures from individuals and groups.

peace movements
Movements against specific wars or against war and militarism in general, usually involving large numbers of people and forms of direct action, such as street protests.

The most commonly studied method of exerting such pressure is through **peace movements**—people taking to the streets in protest against war and militarism.[45] Such protests occur in many, though not all, states involved in wars. Peace studies scholars believe that people all over the world want peace more than governments do.

In addition to mass demonstrations, common *tactics* of peace movements include getting antiwar messages into the media, participating in civil disobedience (nonviolently breaking laws and inviting arrest to show one's beliefs) and occasionally organizing consumer boycotts. Favourite *targets* of peace movements include conscription, government buildings, taxes and nuclear test sites. Like other interest groups, peace movements participate in elections and lobbying (see pp. 146–148). Peace movements also try to educate the public by spreading information about a war or arms race that the government may be downplaying or suppressing.

Peace activists often disagree on goals. Some who are more *internationalist* in orientation see international organizations (today, the UN) as the best hope for peace, and have supported wars against aggression. *Pacifists* oppose all wars, and sometimes distrust international organizations whose members are state governments.[46]

A motorist drives past an anti-war protest in downtown Peterborough, Canada, as demonstrators voice their concerns regarding the occupation of Iraq and Afghanistan.

---

[44] Wesley T. Wooley, *Alternatives to Anarchy: American Supranationalism since World War II* (Bloomington: Indiana UP, 1988).

[45] Steve Breyman, *Why Movements Matter: The West German Peace Movement and U.S. Arms Control Policy* (Albany: SUNY P, 2001). Cecelia Lynch, *Beyond Appeasement: Interpreting Interwar Peace Movements in World Politics* (Ithaca, NY: Cornell UP, 1999). April Carter, *Peace Movements: International Protest and World Politics since 1945* (White Plains, NY: Longman, 1992).

[46] Dwight D. Eisenhower, *Ike's Letters to a Friend, 1941–1958*, Robert Griffith, ed. (Lawrence: UP Kansas, 1984).

In Japan, peace movements are extremely broad-based (enjoying wide popular support) and are pacifist in orientation (as a result of reaction against militarism before and during World War II). In the Soviet Union and Eastern Europe during the Cold War, official state-sponsored peace groups linked international peace to the struggle against Western imperialism while unofficial peace groups linked peace to the struggle for human rights and democracy at home. In Canada, peace groups have protested specific policies, such as cruise missile testing, and militarism more generally.

These divergent tendencies in peace movements come together at peak times in opposition to particular wars or arms races. Beyond this reactive mode of politics, however, peace movements have often had trouble defining a long-term direction and agenda. Scholars of peace studies are interested in studying the successes and failures of peace movements to understand how popular influence on foreign policy can affect state decisions.

Nonviolence

nonviolence/pacifism
A philosophy based on a unilateral commitment to refrain from using any violent forms of leverage. More specifically, pacifism refers to a principled opposition to war in general rather than simply to particular wars.

The philosophies of **nonviolence** and **pacifism** are based on a unilateral commitment to refrain from using any violent forms of leverage in bargaining. No state today follows such a strategy; indeed, it is widely believed that in the modern world, a state that adopts a nonviolent philosophy would risk exploitation or conquest.[47]

Pacifism nonetheless figures prominently in debates concerning the peaceful resolution of conflicts and the achievement of positive peace. Many states contain substantial numbers of citizens, often organized into popular movements, who believe that only pacifism—an ironclad commitment to renounce violence—can change the nature of IR so as to avoid future wars. As pacifist A. J. Muste put it: "There is no way to peace; peace is the way." Japan has a sizeable pacifist movement, and pacifists have historically formed the hard core of the peace movement in Canada, the United States and Western Europe.

Religious faith has often provided a foundation for philosophies of nonviolence and pacifism. Despite the millions killed in the name of religion throughout history, many pacifists draw inspiration from the teachings of religious figures, including Jesus Christ and Buddha.

The term *pacifism* has fallen out of favour because it has been taken to imply passivity in the face of aggression. The more popular term, nonviolence, reflects especially the philosophy and practice of *Mahatma Gandhi*, who led India's struggle for independence from the British Empire before 1948. Gandhi emphasized that nonviolence must be *active* in seeking to prevent violence, to resolve conflicts without violence and especially to stand up against injustice enforced violently. Gandhi organized Indians to resist the British colonial occupation without resorting to violence, even when British troops shot down unarmed Indian protesters.

As a tool of the *powerless* standing up against injustices by the powerful, nonviolence is often the most cost-effective approach—because the costs of violent resistance would be prohibitive.[48] Thus, nonviolence has traditionally been promulgated by people with the

---

[47] Richard B. Miller, *Interpretations of Conflict: Ethics, Pacifism, and the Just-War Tradition* (Chicago: U Chicago P, 1991).

[48] Peter Ackerman and Jack DuVall, *A Force More Powerful: A Century of Nonviolent Conflict* (NY: St. Martin's, 2001). Paul Wehr, Heidi Burgess and Guy Burgess, eds., *Justice without Violence* (Boulder, CO: Rienner, 1994). Ralph Crow, Philip Grant and Saad E. Ibrahim, eds., *Arab Nonviolent Political Struggle in the Middle East* (Boulder, CO: Rienner, 1990).

greatest stake in social change but the least access to the instruments of large-scale violence. In the United States, the philosophy of nonviolence spread widely in the 1960s in the civil rights movement, especially through the work of Martin Luther King, Jr. The powerful, unfortunately, have fewer practical incentives to adopt nonviolence because they have greater access to types of leverage that rely on violence.

ECONOMIC LIBERALISM

The economic variant of liberal pluralism is called *economic liberalism*. Economic liberals are interested in the institutions and regimes that establish the rules of the game in IPE (such as the IMF, World Bank and World Trade Organization), but are most interested in the institution of the market. For economic liberals (unlike mercantilists, discussed in Chapter 2 and Chapter 9), the state should allow markets to function freely. In other words, states should seek to open up trading relations and financial markets rather than restrict them to serve political ends. For economic liberals, when institutions like the IMF and WTO seek to accomplish these ends (and by most accounts, they do), they are important elements of the global political economy. When institutions interfere with the market, however, they detract from growth and efficiency and can even impact on the peaceful relations between states. The economic liberal argument will be discussed in greater detail in Chapter 9.

This chapter and the previous one have reviewed the two mainstream paradigms in the study of international relations, realism and liberal pluralism. Some of the central debates in IR have been conducted within and between variants of these approaches. However, an equally important paradigm—and one that has received considerable attention over the past 20 years, is that of critical IR theory, and is the focus of Chapter 4.

Thinking Critically

1. U.S.-Canadian relations seem better explained by liberalism than realism, yet realist scholars of Canadian foreign policy would debate this. Discuss the contrasting tenets of realism and liberalism, showing how each applies to the relationship.

2. Choose a "collective goods" problem that faces state leaders today (for example, global warming) and explore the reaction of two different states to the issue. How do these states' policies differ from those advocated by interested lobby groups, NGOs or social movements? Do any of the suggested responses resolve the collective goods problem in the issue you chose?

3. Explore the U.S.-led invasion and occupation of Iraq from a realist and a constructivist perspective. Which account is more persuasive, in your opinion? What would a constructivist focus on in examining the government of Canada's decision not to become involved in that conflict? Contrast this with the Canadian government's position on Afghanistan. Does the same explanation help make sense of these two different cases?

4. Peace studies claims that the internal characteristics of states (at the domestic level of analysis) strongly affect the propensity for war or potential for lasting peace. For one society, show how internal characteristics—social, economic and/or cultural—influence that society's external behaviour.

Chapter Summary

- The central claims of realism, regarding anarchy, state actors, rationality, power and the utility of military force, have been challenged on a variety of grounds.

- Liberals dispute the realist notion that narrow self-interest is more rational than mutually beneficial cooperation.

- Neoliberalism argues that even in an anarchic system of autonomous rational states, cooperation can emerge through the building of norms, regimes and institutions.

- Collective goods are benefits received by all members of a group regardless of their individual contribution. Shared norms and rules are important in getting members to pay for collective goods.

- International regimes—convergent expectations of state leaders about the rules for issue areas in IR—help provide stability in the absence of a world government.

- Hegemonic stability theory suggests that the holding of dominant power by one state lends stability to international relations and helps create regimes.

- In a collective security arrangement, a group of states agrees to respond together to aggression by any participating state; the UN and other IGOs perform this function.

- Human security expands the notion of security away from one focused on states to one that examines all the complex ways in which people are made secure.

- Constructivists reject realist assumptions about state interests, tracing those interests in part to international rules and norms.

- Peace studies programs are interdisciplinary and seek to broaden the study of international security to include social and economic factors ignored by realism.

- Peace studies acknowledges a normative bias—that peace is good and war is bad—and a willingness to put theory into practice by participating in politics.

- Mediation and other forms of conflict resolution are alternative means of exerting leverage on participants in bargaining. Increasingly these means are succeeding in settling conflicts without (or with no further) use of violence.

- For scholars in peace studies, militarism in many cultures contributes to states' propensity to resort to force in international bargaining.

- Positive peace implies not just the absence of war but addressing conditions that scholars in peace studies connect with violence—especially injustice and poverty.

- Peace movements try to influence state foreign policies regarding military force; such movements are of great interest in peace studies.

- Nonviolence—the renunciation of force—can be an effective means of leverage, especially for poor or oppressed people with few other means available.

- Economic liberalism is the economic variant of liberal pluralism.

Key Terms

neoliberalism   81
tit for tat   81
free riders   82
collective goods problem   82
international regime   83
hegemonic stability theory   84

collective security   86
human security   88
democratic peace   89
constructivism   91
normative bias   94
conflict resolution   94

Research Navigator Question

Log on to Research Navigator and use Content Search under the Political Science database to search for an article about Kant and liberal IR theory. Answer the following question: Are liberal states inherently peaceful? Note that you will need to define what is meant by "peaceful."

Weblinks

Below are links to additional scholarly journals that focus on issues of interest to liberal pluralism:

Global Governance:
http://www.arts.ualberta.ca/globalgovernance

Human Rights Quarterly:
http://muse.jhu.edu/journals/human_rights_quarterly

International Organization:
http://www.cambridge.org/journals/journal_catalogue.asp?mnemonic=INO

International Studies Perspectives:
http://www.blackwellpublishing.com/journal.asp?ref=1528-3577&site=1

Review of International Studies:
http://titles.cambridge.org/journals/journal_catalogue.asp?mnemonic=ris

Critical Approaches

4

Afghanistan's first presidential election, 2004.

DIVERSITY AND POWER

In Chapters 2 and 3, it was noted that realist theory is the most homogeneous of the approaches to IR theory and that liberalism is more heterogeneous. Realists, in other words, share more common assumptions and orientations toward understanding the world than do liberals. Liberals often disagree with one another about the most important actors in global politics and the policy prescriptions that flow from their analyses. However, of the three paradigms, critical theory is the *most* heterogeneous. It includes Marxists, critical theorists, Gramscian theorists, dependency theorists, world system theorists, neo-Marxists, socialists, feminists, poststructuralists, anti-racist scholars, post-modernists, queer theorists, postcolonial scholars and others. Critical theorists do not share a view of what the world looks like so much as a disposition toward it. Each asks, "How did the world come about, and whose interests does it serve?" Many focus on the way in which more mainstream approaches to IR preclude asking certain questions and direct us to a view of the world that is taken as "given" or "natural." For critical theorists, the kinds of questions posed by realists and liberals are very narrow, and thus they conclude that numerous actors and issues are ignored in the study of global politics. When we focus, for example, on state leaders or the heads of multinational corporations, we rarely reflect on the ways in which the majority of the world's population—those at the margins of authority—are continuously impacted by the workings of global politics. Critical theorists attempt to reveal the diversity of the issues and actors that "inhabit" a more broadly conceived IR.

Critical theorists are also concerned with power, but they understand power very differently than do either realists or liberals. Most critical theorists in one way or another emphasize the relations of inequality that characterize the world and our study of it (though they may not all use terms like "inequality"). Moreover, they often disagree about which inequalities matter the most. Orthodox Marxists, for example, may resist theories that draw attention away from a class analysis of contemporary capitalism and global politics, while anti-racist and feminist scholars may balk at a Marxist's insistence that class forms the starting point for analysis. Many of the critical theorists also, of course, attempt to build bridges between different forms of analysis, and try to understand the various ways in which relations of inequality, in all its guises, are mutually sustaining.[1]

One of the first scholars to write about critical theory in international relations was Canadian political scientist Robert W. Cox. Cox distinguished two types of theory: problem-solving and critical theory. **Problem-solving theory** takes the world as it is and attempts to make institutions and relationships work more smoothly within that given framework. Critical theory, by contrast, "stands apart from the prevailing order of the world and asks how that order came about."[2] **Critical theory** questions the very framework (the very world) that problem-solving theory takes for granted, and is concerned with relations of inequality and the issues that go unsaid or are made invisible in more mainstream approaches to IR. Part of that questioning is related to the political commitments of critical theory, following as it does Marx's observation that the point is not simply to understand the world but to change it.

Cox's elaboration of critical theory was informed by the work of Antonio Gramsci, and has been described as falling within the realm of Gramscian political economy. Other influences come from the Frankfurt School of critical theory as developed by social theorists such as Jürgen Habermas, Theodor Adorno and Max Horkheimer. Further influence came out of postmodernism, feminism, Marxism, post-positivism, dependency theory, anti-racism and postcolonialism and more. There is enormous debate among critical theorists about which relations of inequality are the most important in any given time or place. There is also debate among some of these scholars about whether all of these influences really should be grouped under the term "critical." Postmodernism, for example, aims at deconstructing the taken-for-granted assumptions of all social phenomena, including IR, and in this way is deeply critical. However, postmodernists are also usually very reluctant to define "emancipation" as their goal (in part because they believe all such claims should be deconstructed), so they are viewed by some observers as falling outside the realm of critical theory. For our purposes, all theories that follow Cox's original distinction—that is, those theories that do not take the world as "given"—will be grouped into this category, but students of IR should be aware of these kinds of debates. As one author has suggested, critical theory is best described as a "constellation" of theories rather than a single unified one.[3]

problem-solving theory Theory that takes the world as it is and attempts to make institutions and relationships work more smoothly within that given framework. Problem-solving theory is usually contrasted with critical theory, which stands apart from the prevailing order of the world and asks how that order came about.

critical theory Theory that questions the very framework (the very world) that problem-solving theory takes for granted, and is concerned with relations of inequality and the issues that are unexplored or made invisible within more mainstream approaches to IR.

---

[1] For a detailed review of theoretical approaches in IR, see Jill Steans and Lloyd Pettiford, *International Relations: Perspectives and Themes* (UK: Pearson Education, 2001). Scott Burchill, Richard Devetak, Andrew Linklater, Matthew Paterson, Christian Reus-Smit and Jacqui True, eds., *Theories of International Relations* (NY: Palgrave, 2001).

[2] Robert W. Cox with Timothy J. Sinclair, *Approaches to World Order* (Cambridge: Cambridge UP, 1996). See also Robert W. Cox (with Michael G. Schechter), *The Political Economy of a Plural World: Critical Reflections on Power, Morals and Civilization* (London: Routledge, 2002) and Mark Neufeld, *The Restructuring of International Relations Theory* (Cambridge: Cambridge UP, 1995).

[3] Richard Wyn Jones, "Introduction: Locating Critical International Relations Theory," *Critical Theory and World Politics*, ed. Richard Jones (Boulder, CO: Rienner, 2001). See also Claire Turenne Sjolander and Wayne S. Cox, eds., *Beyond Positivism: Critical Reflections on International Relations* (Boulder, CO: Rienner, 1994). Michael J. Shapiro and Hayward R. Alker, eds., *Challenging Boundaries: Global Flows, Territorial Identities* (Minneapolis: U Minnesota P, 1996).

Focus on Canadian Scholarship

Canadian universities have many scholars working in Critical International Relations theory. As noted, one of the founding figures of Critical IR Theory is **Robert Cox** at York University. His work on Gramscian Political Economy has been further explored and developed by his colleague at York, **Stephen Gil**. Also at York University, **Anna Agathangelou** works on empire and contemporary imperialism, and feminist and postcolonial pedagogies. At Carleton University in Ottawa, **Fiona Robinson** works on questions of ethics and feminist theory. At McMaster University, **J. Marshall Beier** explores questions of indigeneity and alternative conceptions of security. A cross-country collaborative effort involving **Claire Turenne Sjolander** at the University of Ottawa, **Heather Smith** at the University of Northern British Columbia and **Deborah Stienstra** at the University of Manitoba produced a study on feminist approaches to Canadian foreign policy. Turenne

Sjolander has also worked with **Wayne Cox** of Queen's University on questions of epistemology in International Relations. **Dan O'Meara** at the University of Québec at Montréal works on issues of the political economy of conflict and Africa, and his colleague, **Alex Macleod**, also at UQAM, does work on International Relations theory and security issues. At Trent University, **Mark Neufeld** has explored questions of restructuring IR theory. **Tami Jacoby** at the University of Manitoba has conducted research on Israeli and Palestinian women's activism, and at the University of New Brunswick in St. John, **Lesley Jeffrey** examines sex trafficking. At UNB Fredericton **Thom Workman** and **David Bedford** have examined the impact of the Iroquois Great Law of Peace on IR theory and practice. At the University of Victoria, **Rob Walker** is interested in theories of modernity, the practices of spatio-temporality and the rearticulation of political boundaries.

This chapter will examine several theoretical traditions within the constellation of critical theory. Chapter 12 will elaborate further on some of the critical theory interventions in IPE. It is important to note that "critical theory" should not be treated synonymously with critical analysis or criticism. *All* theories make criticisms of one another, and of events that take place or issues that arise in the world of global politics. *All* students and scholars of IR also develop critical analyses—they explain why (or why not) any given argument is persuasive or convincing. Critical theory does not have a monopoly on either criticism or critical analysis (any more than realism has a monopoly on reality).

Understanding IR[4]

As diverse as critical theory is, most variants of it are united in their rejection of positivism.[5] Positivism has dominated the study of International Relations since its formal inception, and it is a view that the social world, like the natural one, is comprised primarily of regularities—events or processes that occur repeatedly and in a similar fashion across time and place. For positivists, the scientific method used to study the natural world is thus equally appropriate to the study of the social world, and therefore applicable to the study of global politics. By this account, the role of the social scientist is to observe the regularities of IR and formulate hypotheses that speculate on the cause of an event or process. The hypothesis is then tested against the "real world" to determine whether it is

---

[4] This subheading is taken from the title of Martin Hollis and Steve Smith, *Explaining and Understanding International Relations* (Oxford: Clarendon Press, 1991).

[5] Positivism itself is complex, and for students interested in a fuller account than is possible here, see Steve Smith, Ken Booth and Marysia Zalewski, eds., *International Theory: Positivism and Beyond* (Cambridge: Cambridge UP, 1996). Much of this section is drawn from this book, in addition to Hollis and Smith, *Explaining and Understanding International Relations*.

confirmed (or, more accurately, not "falsified") based on its relationship to observed reality. Like natural scientists, social scientists must determine the appropriate tests for hypotheses, and likewise decide on appropriate measures for determining whether a hypothesis can be confirmed.

Not all realists or liberal theorists of IR follow strict or even self-conscious positivism; in fact, most do not. Most do share the basic philosophic assumptions of positivism; that the role of theory is to help explain causes of events in order to predict when these events will occur again, and that there is an objective world "out there" that is knowable and separable from us as individuals and theorists.[6] By this view, theories are largely neutral and their explanatory effect is determined by observing the extent to which they correspond to an objective and external reality.

Most critical theorists reject these assumptions, and in particular argue that the relationship between the observer (the theorist) and the external world is far more complex than positivism allows. Critical theorists argue that the external world is not easily separable from the theorist, and in fact, our existing knowledge and theories help us to interpret and make sense of the world. This means that objectivity is impossible because all knowledge about the world is mediated by our prior assumptions and political commitments. Put most provocatively, for critical theorists who adopt a **post-positivist** position, our theories are constitutive of the world as we know it and do not stand apart from the world any more than we as individuals do.

For critics of Critical IR, the rejection of objectivity and the idea that there is a world "out there" existing independently of us as theorists or individuals is a fundamental weakness of this approach—critical theory, according to this criticism, cannot tell us very much about the workings global politics. Proponents of critical theory disagree, arguing that their very different orientation toward what the world is (ontology) and how to study it (epistemology) does not mean critical theorists cannot study or seek to *understand* that world. Where critical theorists depart from their mainstream counterparts is that few are willing to attempt to objectively *explain* the causes of events or processes in global politics in the same way positivists do.

Moreover, critical theorists also insist that because theories are never neutral—in one of Robert Cox's classic phrases, "Theory is always for someone and for some purpose"—it is more appropriate to acknowledge one's perspective and standpoint openly. By this view, theories that are presented as though they do not originate from a particular perspective in time and space are merely ideology disguised as theory. It is for this reason that many critical theorists examine the role of theory in maintaining existing relations of power, and the possibilities of using theory to promote change in global politics.[7]

post-positivism Entails reflecting on the assumptions and political commitments that inform our theories and acknowledging that theories help to constitute the world as we know it.

MARXIST THOUGHT

Most critical theorists owe an intellectual debt (some more direct than others) to the analyses of capitalism developed in the nineteenth century by Karl Marx and Friedrich Engels. Marx and Engels focused primarily on the development of capitalism in the domestic societies of Europe and rarely discussed the international realm. However, Marxist critiques of capitalism have implications for IR and have been adapted and applied by

---

[6] See Kenneth Waltz, *Theory of International Politics* (New York: Random House, 1979).

[7] Robert W. Cox, "Social Forces, States and World Orders: Beyond International Relations Theory," *Millennium, Journal of International Studies* 10.2 (Summer 1981): 126–55. See also Richard Devetak, "Critical Theory," *Theories of International Relations*, 3rd ed., ed. Scott Burchill et al. (UK: Palgrave Macmillan, 2005).

numerous scholars to the study of global politics. For Marxists, the central unit of analysis is class, and more specifically, class relations. By this view, societies are constituted and the primary relations of power between members are conducted via the way in which production (work) is organized. Under capitalism, class relations are by definition unequal, as those who control the means of production (capitalists) always ensure that the relations of exchange work against those who have only their labour power to sell (workers). It is capitalists' incessant pursuit of profit that drives the growth and wealth achieved under capitalism, but ultimately for Marxists, that wealth is accomplished through the increasing immiseration of workers. Understanding societies in terms of the ways relations of production are organized and eventually transformed came to be called **historical materialism**, one of the unique contributions of Marxist thought.[8]

historical materialism
A unique contribution of Marxist thought which understands societies in terms of the ways in which relations of production are organized and eventually transformed.

The implications for IR of Marxist thought are numerous, not least because Marx and Engels saw capitalist relations of production as breaking down the barriers between nation states and homogenizing all nations and societies around the globe. As they wrote in *The Communist Manifesto*:

> The bourgeoisie has through its exploitation of the world-market given a cosmopolitan character to production and consumption in every country. . . . In place of the old local and national seclusion and self-sufficiency, we have intercourse in every direction, universal interdependence of nations. . . . National one-sidedness and narrow-mindedness become more and more impossible. . . . [9]

In this way, Marx and Engels were early theorists of globalization. For Marx and Engels, capitalism contained the "seeds of its own destruction," in part because they predicted that capitalism would see cycles of dramatic growth and collapse, with each succeeding crisis more severe than the last. The costs of these crises would be borne primarily by workers, who over time would organize against capitalism and overthrow it, instituting in its place a socialist society, to be eventually followed by communism.

One of the explicit and early adaptations of Marxist thought to International Relations was provided by V. I. Lenin, founder of the Soviet Union, and it was directed at the recurring crises of capitalism. In his monograph entitled *Imperialism the Highest Stage of Capitalism*, Lenin argued that imperialism resulted from crises of capitalism: European capitalists invested in colonies where they could continue to earn large profits, which were in part used to buy off the working class at home. One limit Lenin saw was that after the scramble for colonies in the 1890s, few areas of the world were left to be colonized. Imperialist expansion could occur only at the expense of other imperialist states, leading to inter-imperialist competition and wars, such as World War I.[10] Lenin also anticipated that these efforts would assuage the European working class for only so long, and could not prevent the eventual collapse of capitalism as workers across the globe mobilized against it.

Marxist thought has been subject to much critique—both by those who seek to dismiss it and by others who have sought to develop it. Perhaps the most common criticism has been against Marxism's single most important failure: the (thus far) incorrect prediction that capitalism would be overthrown and replaced by socialism and eventually communism. Even in societies where communist principles have been adopted (see Chapter 12), the historical trajectory of that adoption has not followed the analysis suggested by Marx and

---

[8] D. McLennan, ed., *Karl Marx: Selected Writings* (Oxford UP, 1977).

[9] Cited from Andrew Linklater, "Marxism," *Theories of International Relations*, ed. Scott Burchill (NY: Palgrave, 2001) p. 123.

[10] V. I. Lenin, "Imperialism the Highest Stage of Capitalism," *Essential Works of Lenin* (1916; NY: Bantam, 1966): 177–270.

Engels. For contemporary critical theorists, classic Marxist thought is sometimes described as too "economistic," reducing all social and political relations to class relations and ignoring other intersecting axes of power and inequality. Some critics also focus on Marx's use of the scientific method—he was as committed a positivist as many of his more traditional counterparts (and was critiqued by fellow positivists for his failures in that role).

Despite these criticisms, it is worth underlining some of the important lines of continuity between early Marxist thought and current critical approaches in IR. The first is the position of interrogation taken by Marxism—capitalism was assumed to be neither natural nor inevitable and its historical trajectory and possible transformation were considered appropriate lines of inquiry. Also important in Marxist thought is the acknowledgment of the relationship between knowledge and forms of power. Marx presented his ideas as scientific, but also argued that traditional economic analyses served to obfuscate existing relations of power—that they were ideas and forms of analysis that represented the interests of ruling classes but were presented as though they were universal. Marx did not reject objectivity as such, but he did underscore the extent to which ideas that were presented as objective were in fact ideological. Finally, Marx also insisted on the importance of drawing links between theory and practice, or praxis. He argued that the point of theory was not simply to analyze the world, but to change it—a commitment that most critical theorists retain today.

Gramscian IR

Marxist thought has contributed directly to a number of theories within IR, including world systems theory and dependency theory (both of which will be discussed in Chapter 12). However, the further development of Marxism through the work of the Italian Marxist Antonio Gramsci, followed by the adaptation of Gramsci's ideas by scholars such as Robert Cox, Stephen Gill, Craig Murphy and others, has had the most direct connection to critical theory as it pertains to IR. Cox was one of the first theorists to draw attention to the applicability of some of Gramsci's ideas to IR. This was seen as innovative (and remains contested)[11] because Gramsci had very little to say about IR. His most important work, *Prison Notebooks*, contained writings Gramsci did largely in secret while imprisoned by Italian fascists between 1929 and 1935. He was concerned primarily with the relationship between civil society and the state, specifically the Italian state, and was concerned about the possibilities of progressive politics in the face of fascism.

Although Gramsci grappled with questions different from those faced by IR scholars, some of the concepts he developed have been usefully applied to the discipline.[12] Gramsci was interested in changing social order and the ways in which "common sense" or "shared mental frameworks" become dominant in any given time or place. He was committed to historical materialism, but did not think that ideas flowed directly from one's class position; rather, they were the product of struggle and contestation. For Gramsci, the ability to present a set of particular interests as universal is a requisite of power, and he argued

---

[11] See for example Randall D. Germain and Michael Kenny, "Engaging Gramsci: International Relations Theory and the New Gramscians," *Review of International Studies* 24.1 (1998): 3-21, and replies by Craig Murphy, "Understanding IR: Understanding Gramsci," *Review of International Studies* 24.3 (1998): 417–25 and Mark Rupert, "(Re-)Engaging Gramsci: A Response to Germain and Kenny," *Review of International Studies* 24.3 (1998): 427–34.

[12] See Robert W. Cox, "Gramsci, Hegemony, and International Relations: An Essay in Method," in R. W. Cox and T. Sinclair, *Approaches to World Order*, pp. 124–43; see also Stephen Gill, ed., *Gramsci, Historical Materialism and International Relations* (Cambridge: Cambridge UP, 1993).

Gramscian hegemony
A view that contrasts with realist definition of hegemony; recognizes that those with power rule through a mixture of coercion and consent and that hegemony functions when the relations of power that sustain a given social order recede into the background of consciousness.

that those in power rule through a mixture of coercion and consent. This concept informed the important notion of **Gramscian hegemony** (in contrast to the realist account of hegemony discussed in Chapter 2). In Gramsci's view, a social system is hegemonic not when force must be used to sustain it, but rather when those who are ruled consent to that rule. Hegemony functions, in short, when the relations of power that sustain a given order recede into the background of consciousness.

IR scholars such as Cox have used Gramsci's notion of hegemony to apply not only to particular national situations, but to world orders. For Cox, an important question in IR is to ask why some world orders are stable in specific historical moments while at other times they are not. Likewise for Cox, the neorealist response to this question (world orders are stable when they are led by strong states) was insufficient because it could not explain why in some periods strong states refused to lead the system (the United States in the post–World War II period) or why in other instances the presence of a strong state contributed to disorder (the post–September 11 period). Nor did it make connections between the political and economic workings of global politics. For Cox and other Gramscians (sometimes also called neo-Gramscians), it is important to examine the configuration of forces that make up world orders. These are the existing material conditions, including military power, economic conditions and class relations. World orders also comprise prevailing ideas and norms that are universalized throughout the system and the activities of international organizations, which function as the process through which prevailing ideas are developed and dispersed. For Cox, hegemonic order is that in which there exists a fit between power, ideas and institutions.

Cox and other neo-Gramscians are interested in hegemonic order, but are equally interested in the possibilities for counter-hegemonic forces to transform world orders. Scholars such as Stephen Gill have outlined the current "organic crisis" of contemporary neoliberalism—a situation in which power is exerted through supremacy rather than hegemony. Although that power can be expressed and made present in numerous subtle ways, what Gill underscores is the extent to which a world order based on supremacy is more vulnerable to transformative forces than a hegemonic one. Some of these forces may be authoritarian, but others may be more grounded in a progressive commitment to issues of justice, ecology and culture.[13] Gramscian IR theorists thus attempt to address current configurations of power with more subtlety than do either realists or traditional Marxists, and also remain committed to questions of praxis or action within IR.

FEMINISM

Feminist scholarship has also always been committed to political action, and has cut a broad swath across academic disciplines, from literature to psychology to history. In recent years, it has made inroads in international relations, once considered one of the fields most resistant to feminist arguments. Feminist scholarship in IR has produced a rapidly growing literature in the past two decades.[14]

---

[13] Stephen Gill, "Globalisation, Market Civilization and Disciplinary Neoliberalism," *Millennium: Journal of International Studies* 24.3 (1995): 169–99.

[14] V. Spike Peterson and Anne Sisson Runyan, *Global Gender Issues*, 2nd ed. (Boulder, CO: Westview, 1999). J. Ann Tickner, *Gendering World Politics: Issues and Approaches in the Post–Cold War Era* (NY: Columbia UP, 2001). Jill Steans, *Gender and International Relations: An Introduction* (Piscataway, NJ: Rutgers UP, 1998). Sandra Whitworth, *Feminism and International Relations* (NY: St. Martin's, 1994). Joshua S. Goldstein, *War and Gender: How Gender Shapes the War System and Vice Versa* (Cambridge UP, 2001).

A GUY THING
Feminists from various traditions argue that the gender makeup of international summits is important. Here, leaders of the G8 states—the United States, Canada, France, Japan, Britain, Italy, Russia and Germany—meet with the leaders of Nigeria, Senegal, Ethiopia, Tanzania and South Africa, along with the heads of the World Bank, UN, African Union and European Union in 2005. All 20 are men. (In 2006, a woman was elected leader of Germany.)

Feminist scholarship encompasses a variety of strands of work, but all have in common the insight that gender matters in understanding how IR works, and this is true in issues of war and security, global political economy, North-South relations and international institutions. Feminist scholarship seeks to uncover hidden assumptions about gender in how we study a subject such as IR. What mainstream scholars traditionally claim to be universal often turns out to be true only of males.

Some feminists examine how *women* interact with, or are affected by, international relations. Others argue that *gender* informs all aspects of IR in one way or another, whether women are present or not. Examining gender (as opposed to sex) means looking at the assumptions about women and men that prevail in any given time or place, and the material condition of both women's and men's lives. Gender also acknowledges that women's and men's lives are shaped not only by their sex, but by their class, race, ethnicity, sexuality and geographic location.

Some feminists have argued that the core assumptions of realism—especially of anarchy and sovereignty—reflect a masculine worldview based on the ways in which *males* tend to interact and to see the world. Or, more accurately, the way males are *expected* to interact and see the world, because not even all men are able to live up to the expectations associated with masculinity. In this view, the realist approach simply assumes the male as norm when discussing foreign policy decision-making, state sovereignty or the use of military force.

Beyond revealing the hidden assumptions about gender in a field of scholarship, feminists often *challenge traditional concepts of gender* as well. In IR, these traditional concepts revolve around the assumptions that men fight wars and run states, whereas

CRITICAL MASS
Standpoint feminists see women as inherently less warlike than men and more adept at making peace because of their potential and actual experiences as mothers. Low representation of women in governments makes this theory hard to test. In an exception, Chile's first woman president, Michelle Bachelet, appointed women as half the members of her cabinet in 2006.

women are either uninformed or uninterested in the topics and issues of global politics. Such gender roles are based in the broader construction of masculinity as suitable to *public* and political spaces, and femininity with the sphere of the *private* and domestic. An example of gendered construction was provided by White House Chief of Staff Donald Regan at a 1985 Reagan-Gorbachev summit meeting when he commented that women do not care about the throw weights of ICBMs (see p. 211) and would rather watch Nancy Reagan. Later he said that U.S. women would not support sanctions against white-ruled South Africa because they would not want to lose their diamonds (a South African export). Feminists call into question, at a minimum, the stereotypes of women as caring more about fashion and jewellery than arms control and apartheid.

Beyond the basic agreement that gender is important, there is no single feminist approach to IR, but several such approaches. Although they are interwoven (all paying attention to gender or to the status of women), they often run in different directions. On some core issues, the different strands of feminism have conflicting views, creating interesting debates *within* feminism.

standpoint feminism
A strand of feminism that believes gender differences are not just socially constructed and that views women as inherently less warlike than men (on average).

One strand, **standpoint feminism,** focuses on valorizing the feminine—that is, valuing the unique contributions of women *as* women. Standpoint feminists argue that most of global politics has been both created and analyzed from the standpoint of men, and that we need to bring the standpoint of women to bear on IR because women have a unique contribution and point of view. Given their greater experience with nurturing and human relations, women are seen as potentially more effective than men (on average) in conflict resolution as well as in group decision-making. Standpoint feminists believe there are real differences between the genders that are not just social constructions and cultural indoctrination (although these contribute to gender roles, too). Some standpoint feminists believe there is a core biological essence to being male or female (sometimes called *essentialism*), others think that women's differences are more culturally than biologically determined. In either case, feminine perspectives create a *standpoint* from which to observe, analyze and criticize the traditional perspectives of IR.[15]

Another strand, **liberal feminism,** rejects these claims as being based on stereotyped gender roles. Liberal feminists see the "essential" differences in men's and women's abilities or perspectives as trivial or nonexistent—men and women are equal. They deplore the exclusion of women from positions of power in IR but do not believe that including women would change the nature of the international system. Liberal feminists seek to include women more often as subjects of study—such as female state leaders, female soldiers and other women operating outside the traditional gender roles in IR.

A third approach adds to feminism some insights from postmodernism, discussed later in this chapter. **Post-positivist feminism** tends to reject the assumptions about gender made by both standpoint and liberal feminists. While standpoint feminists consider gender differences to be important and fixed, and liberal feminists consider those differences to be trivial, post-positivist feminists are more interested in the ways in which representations of difference may impact upon, or be used to legitimize, certain events in IR.

liberal feminism A strand of feminism that emphasizes gender equality and views the "essential" differences in men's and women's abilities or perspectives as trivial or nonexistent.

post-positivist feminism An effort to combine feminist and postmodernist perspectives with the aim of uncovering the hidden influences of gender in IR and showing how arbitrary the construction of gender roles is.

The Masculinity of Realism

Standpoint feminism provides a perspective from which to re-examine the core assumptions of realism—especially the assumption of autonomy—from which flow the key realist concepts of sovereignty and anarchy. To realists, the international system consists of autonomous actors (states) that control their own territory and have no right to infringe on another's. Do these concepts rest on a "masculine" view of the world? If so, what would a "feminine" approach to international security be like? Some standpoint feminists have argued that realism emphasizes autonomy and separation because men find separation easier to deal with than interconnection.

This view rests on a psychological theory that boys and girls grow up with different views of separateness and connection.[16] In this theory, because a child's primary caretaker in the early years is almost always female, girls form their gender identity around the perception of *similarity* with their caretaker (and by extension the environment in which they live), but boys perceive their *difference* from the caretaker. From this experience, boys develop social relations based on individual *autonomy*, but girls' relations are based on *connection*. As a result, women are held to be more likely than men to fear abandonment, whereas men are more likely to fear intimacy.

In *moral* reasoning, according to this research, boys tend to apply abstract rules and stress individual rights (reflecting their sense of separation from the situation), but girls pay more attention to the concrete contexts of different situations and to the responsibility of group members for each other. In playing *games*, boys resolve disputes through arguments about rules and then keep playing, but girls are more likely to abandon a game rather than argue over the rules and risk the social cohesion of their group. In *social relations*, boys form and dissolve friendships more readily than girls, who are more likely to

---

[15] Robert O. Keohane, "International Relations Theory: Contributions of a Feminist Standpoint," *Millennium* 18.2 (1989): 245–53.

[16] Carol Gilligan, *In a Different Voice: Psychological Theory and Women's Development* (Cambridge, MA: Harvard UP, 1982). Nancy Chodorow, *The Reproduction of Mothering* (Berkeley: U California P, 1978).

HER ROLE AND HIS
Feminist scholars emphasize the importance of gender roles in IR, especially the traditional distinction between males in political-military roles and females in domestic-family roles. Here in Sarajevo, a UN soldier provides cover as a Bosnian citizen runs along "sniper's alley" (1994).

stick loyally with friends. All these gender differences in children reflect the basic concept that for girls, connection matters more than independence, but for boys the reverse is true.

Realism, of course, rests on the concept of states as separate, autonomous actors that make and break alliances freely while pursuing their own interests (but not interfering in each other's internal affairs). Such a conception of autonomy parallels the masculine psyche just described. Thus, some feminists find in realism a hidden assumption of masculinity. Furthermore, the sharp distinction that realists draw between international politics (anarchic) and domestic politics (ordered) parallels the distinction in gender roles between the public (masculine) and private (feminine) spheres. Thus, realism constructs IR as a man's world.

By contrast, an international system based on *feminine* principles might give greater importance to the *interdependence* of states rather than to their autonomy, stressing the responsibility of people to care for each other with less regard for states and borders. In the struggle between the principles of human rights and of sovereignty (noninterference in internal affairs), human rights would receive priority. In the choice of forms of leverage when conflicts arise between states, violence might be less prevalent. The concept of national security might be based on human security (see pp. 137–139) rather than narrow self-interest.

The realist preoccupation with the interstate level of analysis presumes that the logic of war itself is autonomous and can be separated from other social relationships such as economics, domestic politics, sexism and racism. Standpoint feminism, however, reveals the *connections* of these phenomena with war. It suggests new avenues for understanding war at the domestic and individual levels of analysis—underlying causes that realists largely ignore.

Thinking Theoretically

Feminist theories provide explanations that differ from both realist and liberal theories. In the case of response to aggression, such as in Kuwait and Bosnia, feminists might call attention to the importance of gender roles such as the desire on the part of state leaders to prove their manhood by standing up to the bad guys.

In the case of Kuwait, President George H. W. Bush had long been criticized as being a "wimp" (an insult to his manhood), and his determination to respond to Iraq's aggression became a personal battle with Saddam Hussein. A key moment in Bush's decision process was said to be when Britain's prime minister, Margaret Thatcher—a woman—urged him to act firmly, saying, "Don't go all wobbly on us, George."

Some of the initial reaction to the attacks against the United States on September 11 also indicated that a swift, tough and manly reaction was demanded. Former Defense Intelligence Agency officer Thomas Woodrow wrote that, "To do less [than use tactical nuclear capabilities against the bin Laden camps in the desert of Afghanistan] would be rightly seen . . . as cowardice on the part of the United States." Journalist Steve Dunleavy commented that, "This should be as simple as it is swift—kill the bastards. A gunshot between the eyes, blow them to smithereens, poison them if you have to. As for cities or countries that host these worms, bomb them into basketball courts." Not to be outdone, George W. Bush sought to establish his credentials when he said of Osama bin Laden: "Wanted Dead or Alive."

For feminists, this kind of masculinist frame can lead decision-makers down paths that could, and should, be avoided. In turn, it likely forecloses other policy options precisely because they are not "manly" enough. Some observers suggested that the U.S. government could make an enormously profound statement after September 11 by "bombarding Afghanistan with massive supplies of food instead of warheads. Such an approach would surely earn America's commander-in-chief the media label of wimp—and much worse. Obviously, it's the sort of risk that the president wouldn't dare to take."*

* Thomas Woodrow, "Time to Use the Nuclear Option," *Washington Times* 14 Sept. 2001. Steve Dunleavy, *New York Post* 12 Sept. 2001. Norman Solomon, "The 'Wimp' Factor: Goading to Shed Blood," *Media Beat* 28 Sept. 2001. See also Sandra Whitworth, "11 September and the Aftermath," *Studies in Political Economy* 67 (Spring 2002): 33–38. Krista Hunt, "The Strategic Co-optation of Women's Rights: Discourse in the 'War on Terrorism,'" *International Feminist Journal of Politics* 4.1 (2002): 116–21. "Forum: The Events of 11 September 2001 and Beyond," *International Feminist Journal of Politics* 4.1 (2002): 95–115.

From this feminist perspective, neoliberalism has gone backward from traditional liberalism by accepting the realist assumption that the important actors are separate, unitary states, and downplaying substate and transnational actors—including women. Neoliberalism's definition of cooperation as rule-based interactions among autonomous actors also reflects masculinist assumptions.

Gender in War and Peace

In addition to its emphasis on autonomy and anarchy, realism stresses military force as the key form of leverage in IR. Here, too, many standpoint feminists see in realism a hidden assumption of masculinity. They see war as not only a male occupation, but the quintessentially male occupation. In this view, men are inherently the more warlike sex, and women the more peaceful. Thus, although realism may accurately portray the importance of war and military force in IR as we now know it, this merely reflects the male domination of the international sphere to date—not a necessary, eternal or inescapable logic of relations among states.[17]

---

[17] Lois Ann Lorentzen and Jennifer Turpin, eds., *The Women and War Reader* (NY: New York UP, 1998). Jean Bethke Elshtain and Sheila Tobias, eds., *Women, Militarism, and War: Essays in History, Politics, and Social Theory* (Lanham, MD: UP of America, 1989).

Standpoint feminists find plenty of evidence to support the idea of war as a masculine pursuit. Anthropologists have found that in all known cultures, males are the primary (and usually the only) combatants in warfare, despite the enormous diversity of those cultures in so many other ways. (Of course, voting and political leadership were also male domains for most of history, yet feminists would hardly call those activities essentially masculine.)

One supposed link between war and masculinity is the male sex hormone testosterone (along with related hormones), which some biologists have connected with aggressive behaviour in animals. However, testosterone does not *cause* aggression. Rather, social interactions "feed back" to affect testosterone levels (winners' testosterone rises while losers' levels fall). Thus testosterone is a link in a complex system of relationships between the organism and the social environment. Complex behaviours such as aggression and war cannot be said to be biologically *driven* or predetermined, because humanity's most striking biological capability is flexibility.

Even some feminists who see gender differences as strictly cultural, and not biological at all, view war as a masculine construction. In one theory, for example, war may fill a void left for men by their inability to give birth; war provides a meaning to life and, through heroism, gives men an opportunity to transcend their individual isolation and overcome their fear of death—an opportunity that women potentially get through childbirth. In addition, heroism on the battlefield, especially before modern mechanized war, promised men a form of immortality, as their deeds would live on in collective memory.[18]

By contrast, women are usually portrayed by standpoint feminists as more peaceful creatures than men—whether because of biology, culture or (most likely) both. These feminists emphasize women's unique abilities and contributions as *peacemakers*. They stress women's roles as *mothers* and potential mothers. Given their caregiving roles, women are presumed to be more likely than men to oppose war and more likely to find alternatives to violence in resolving conflicts.[19]

Both biologically and anthropologically, there is no firm evidence connecting women's caregiving functions (pregnancy and nursing) with any behaviour such as reconciliation or nonviolence—although females have been studied less than males. The role of women varies considerably from one society to another. Although they rarely take part in combat, women sometimes provide logistical support to male warriors and sometimes help to drive the men into a war frenzy by dancing, shaming nonparticipating males and other activities supportive of war. Yet in other cultures, women restrain the men from war or play special roles as mediators in bringing wars to an end.

The idea of women as peacemakers has a long history. In ancient Athens, the (male) playwright Aristophanes speculated in his play *Lysistrata* about how women might end the unpopular Peloponnesian War with Sparta, then in progress. In the play, a young woman named Lysistrata organizes the Athenian and Spartan women to withhold sex from the men until the latter stop the war (the women also make off with the war treasury). In short order, the men come to their senses and make peace.[20]

---

[18] Nancy C. M. Hartsock, "Masculinity, Heroism, and the Making of War," *Rocking the Ship of State: Toward a Feminist Peace Politics*, ed. Adrienne Harris and Ynestra King (Boulder, CO: Westview, 1989) 133–52.

[19] Virginia Woolf, *Three Guineas* (1938; London: Hogarth, 1977). Ruth Roach Pierson, *Women and Peace: Theoretical, Historical and Practical Perspectives* (London: Croom Helm, 1987). M. K. Burguieres, "Feminist Approaches to Peace: Another Step for Peace Studies," *Millennium* 19.1 (1990): 1–18. Birgit Brock-Utne, *Educating for Peace: A Feminist Perspective* (NY: Pergamon, 1985). Betty Reardon, *Sexism and the War System*. (NY: Teachers College, 1985). Micaela De Leonardo, rev. of "Morals, Mothers, and Militarism: Antimilitarism and Feminist Theory," *Feminist Studies* 11 (1985): 599–617.

[20] Aristophanes, *Lysistrata*, ed. Jeffrey Henderson (NY: Oxford UP, 1987).

Women have formed their own organizations to work for peace on many occasions. In 1852, *Sisterly Voices* was published as a newsletter for women's peace societies. Bertha von Suttner persuaded Alfred Nobel in 1892 to create the Nobel peace prize (which Suttner won in 1905). In 1915, during World War I, Jane Addams and other feminists convened an international women's peace conference at the Hague. They founded the Women's Peace Party (now called the Women's International League for Peace and Freedom).[21]

After World War I, the *suffrage* movement won the right for women to vote. Standpoint feminists thought that women would vote for peace and against war, changing the nature of foreign policy, but women generally voted as their husbands did. Similarly, decades later when women participated in liberation struggles against colonialism in the global South, some feminists thought such participation would lead to different kinds of foreign policies in the newly independent countries, but in general such changes did not materialize (partly because women were often pushed aside from political power after the revolution).

Public opinion polling on foreign policy issues partially vindicates standpoint feminists. In most Western countries in which people are polled on such issues, a **gender gap** shows women to be less supportive than men when asked about military action. Meanwhile, feminists in recent decades have continued to organize women's peace organizations.[22] In the 1980s, Women's Action for Nuclear Disarmament (WAND) opposed the nuclear arms buildup, and women encamped for years at Britain's Greenham Common air base. In Israel, the "women in black" held vigils to protest their government's military actions against Palestinians. In 1995, the UN-sponsored Beijing Conference on Women brought together women activists from around the world, and helped deepen feminists' engagement with global issues such as North-South inequality.

gender gap Refers to polls showing women lower than men on average in their support for military actions (as well as for various other issues and candidates).

Through these varied actions, standpoint feminists began developing a feminist practice of international relations that could provide an alternative to the masculine practice of realism. The motto of the UN Educational, Scientific, and Cultural Organization (UNESCO) is "Since war begins in the minds of men, it is in the minds of men that the foundations for peace should be sought." For standpoint feminists, war does indeed begin in the minds of men, but the foundations for peace would be better sought in the minds of women.

Women in IR

Liberal feminists are skeptical of standpoint feminist critiques of realism. They believe that when women are allowed to participate in IR, they play the game basically the same way men do, with similar results. They think that women can practise realism—based on autonomy, sovereignty, anarchy, territory, military force and all the rest—just as well as men can. Liberal feminists therefore tend to reject the critique of realism as masculine. They, along with other feminists, contend that standpoint arguments about the fundamental differences between women and men may appeal to prevailing stereotypes, but they do not tell us much about women's experiences in world politics or how gender impacts IR.

[21] Marie Louise Degen, *The History of the Woman's Peace Party* (1939, Johns Hopkins UP; NY: Burt Franklin Reprints, 1974).

[22] Amy Swerdlow, "Pure Milk, Not Poison: Women Strike for Peace and the Test Ban Treaty of 1963," *Rocking the Ship of State*, ed. Harris and King (see footnote 18 in this chapter) 225–37. Carolyn M. Stephenson, "Feminism, Pacifism, Nationalism, and the United Nations Decade for Women," *Women and Men's Wars*, ed. Judith Stiehm (Oxford: Pergamon, 1983) 341–48. Gwyn Kirk, "Our Greenham Common: Feminism and Nonviolence," *Rocking the Ship of State*, ed. Harris and King (see footnote 18 in this chapter) 115–30.

Liberal feminism focuses on the integration of women into the overwhelmingly male preserves of foreign policy-making and the military. In most states, these occupations are typically at least 90 percent male. For instance, in 1995, the world's diplomatic delegations to the UN General Assembly were 80 percent male overall, and the heads of those delegations were 97 percent male. The Canadian military, with one of the highest proportions of women anywhere in the world or in history, is still 85 percent male.[23]

For liberal feminists, the main effect of this gender imbalance on the nature of IR—that is, apart from its effects on the status of women—is to waste talent. Since liberal feminists think that women have the same capabilities as men, the inclusion of women in traditionally male occupations (from state leader to foot soldier) would bring additional capable individuals into those areas. Gender equality would thus increase national capabilities by giving the state a better overall pool of diplomats, generals, soldiers and politicians.

In support of their argument that, on average, women handle power just as men do, liberal feminists point to the many examples of women who have served in such positions. No distinctly feminine feature of their behaviour in office distinguishes these leaders from their male counterparts. Rather, they have been diverse in character and policy. Of course, women in traditionally male roles may have been selected (or self-selected) on the basis of their suitability to such roles; they may not act the way "average" women would act. Still, they do show that individuals cannot be judged accurately using group characteristics alone.

Female state leaders do not appear to be any more peaceful, or any less committed to state sovereignty and territorial integrity, than are male leaders. It has even been suggested that women in power tend to be more warlike to compensate for being females in traditionally male roles.

Only one female has led a great power in the past century—Britain's Margaret Thatcher in the 1980s. She went to war in 1982 to recover the Falkland/Malvinas Islands from Argentina (at issue were sovereignty and territorial integrity). Among middle powers, Indira Gandhi likewise led India in war against Pakistan in 1971, as did Israel's Golda Meir against Egypt and Syria in 1973. But Benazir Bhutto of Pakistan and Corazón Aquino of the Philippines struggled to control their own military forces in the late 1980s. Turkey's Tansu Çiller led a harsh war to suppress Kurdish rebels in the mid-1990s. But Violetta Chamorro of Nicaragua kept the peace between factions that had fought a brutal civil war in the 1980s. The president of Sri Lanka, Chandrika Bandaranaike Kumaratunga, and her mother, the prime

FLOWER GIRLS
Consistent with the premise of liberal feminism, the first female U.S. secretary of state, Madeleine Albright, was at least as hard-line as her male colleagues. She advocated the use of force in Bosnia and the expansion of NATO in Eastern Europe. Here, however, she told refugee girls from Afghanistan (where the Taliban faction harshly restricted women) that women worldwide "are all the same, and we have the same feelings"—a line more consistent with difference feminism (1997).

---

[23] Joni Seager, *The Penguin Atlas of Women in the World*, 2nd ed. (London: Penguin, 2003).

minister, tried to make peace with separatist rebels, but returned to war when that initiative failed. Indonesia's president Megawati Sukarnoputri has tried to hold together a fractious Indonesia in recent years. Other states, such as Finland, Norway, Iceland and (briefly) Canada, have had female leaders when war and peace were not major political issues in those countries. Overall, women state leaders, like men, seem capable of leading in war or in peace as circumstances demand.[24]

Liberal feminists believe that female soldiers, like female politicians, have a range of skills and abilities comparable to men's. Again, the main effect of including more women from a liberal feminist position would be to improve the overall quality of military forces.[25]

Although women have served with distinction in military forces, they have been excluded from combat roles in almost all those forces. (It is a myth that women in the Israeli army serve in combat infantry roles.) In some countries, military women are limited to traditional female roles such as nursing and typing. Even where women may hold nontraditional positions such as mechanics and pilots, most women remain in the traditional roles. And certain jobs still remain off-limits—on submarines or in combat infantry, for instance. Thus there are relatively few cases by which to judge women's abilities in combat.

Those cases include historical examples of individual women who served in combat (sometimes disguised as men, sometimes not). In the fifteenth century, Joan of Arc rallied French soldiers to defeat England, turning the tide of the Hundred Years' War. (The English burned her at the stake as a witch after capturing her.) In recent years, female U.S. soldiers have found themselves in combat in both the Gulf and Iraq Wars (present-day mobile tactics and fluid front lines make it hard to separate combat from support roles). Women pilot helicopters and planes, have been killed, and have been taken prisoner. Images from Iraq of rescued POW Jessica Lynch were used extensively by the U.S. as evidence of the stoic courage exhibited by female soldiers. By contrast, the release of images depicting a female U.S. soldier involved in the physical and sexual torture of Iraqi prisoners showed that women can also be equal partners in the ruthless side of soldiering.

Women have repeatedly participated in combat in rebel forces fighting guerrilla wars in Vietnam, Nicaragua and elsewhere, as well as in terrorist or paramilitary units in countries such as Peru, Germany, Italy and Palestine. Women in Eritrea's guerrilla forces became part of that country's regular army after independence and then served in front-line combat units during the Eritrea-Ethiopia war in the late 1990s. All these cases suggest that (at least some) women are able to hold their own in combat. Women have also served on peacekeeping missions, and governments such as Canada that are actively involved in peacekeeping missions make no distinction between male and female soldiers.

Some argue that women are more vulnerable (that is, to rape) if taken as POWs. Again liberal feminists disagree. All POWs are vulnerable, and both male and female

[24] Claire T. Sjolander, Deborah Stienstra and Heather A. Smith, eds., *Feminist Approaches to Canadian Foreign Policy* (Toronto: Oxford UP, 2003). Francine D'Amico and Peter R. Beckman, eds., *Women in World Politics: An Introduction* (Westport, CT: Bergin & Garvey, 1995). Barbara J. Nelson and Najma Chowdhury, eds., *Women and Politics Worldwide* (New Haven, CT: Yale UP, 1994). Michael A. Genovese, ed., *Women as National Leaders: The Political Performance of Women as Heads of Government* (Thousand Oaks, CA: Sage, 1993). Nancy E. McGlen and Meredith Reid Sarkees, *Women in Foreign Policy: The Insiders* (NY: Routledge, 1993).

[25] Linda Grant De Pauw, *Battle Cries and Lullabies: Women in War from Prehistory to the Present* (Norman, OK: U Oklahoma P, 1998). Linda Bird Francke, *Ground Zero: The Gender Wars in the Military* (NY: Simon & Schuster, 1997). Judith Hicks Stiehm, ed., *It's Our Military, Too!* (Philadelphia: Temple UP, 1996). Antonia Fraser, *The Warrior Queens* (NY: Knopf, 1989). Elisabetta Addis, Valerie E. Russo and Lorenza Ebesta, eds., *Women Soldiers: Images and Realities* (NY: St. Martin's, 1994). Eva Isaksson, ed., *Women and the Military System* (NY: St. Martin's, 1988).

FIGHTING FEMALES
Female soldiers have performed as well as males in military tasks, as predicted by liberal feminists. But in state armies, women are barred from virtually all infantry combat units worldwide. Guerrilla forces more often include women, such as these soldiers of the Tamil Tigers rebels in Sri Lanka, 2002.

POWs can be sexually abused. One of the female soldiers who had been captured during the Gulf War commented that the only difference between male and female POWs is no one thinks to ask the male soldiers if they were raped, whereas it is the first question asked of females.

The main reason military forces give for their exclusion of women from combat is fear about what effect their presence might have on the male soldiers, whose discipline and loyalty have traditionally been thought to depend on male bonding and single-minded focus (based on prevailing assumptions about women and men). Opponents of women in the military claimed vindication, ironically, with a series of high-profile cases of sexual discrimination, harassment, adultery and rape in the U.S. military in the mid-1990s and early 2000s. For example, by February 2004 reports had emerged from Iraq that more than 100 female U.S. soldiers had reported being sexually assaulted by fellow soldiers. The presence of females in the ranks, critics argue, was breaking down discipline and morale. Liberal feminists reject such arguments and argue that group bonding in military units does not depend on gender segregation. (After all, similar rationales were once given for racial segregation in U.S. military forces.)[26] Thus, a heated public debate continues on the question of women in the military.

The effects of war on noncombatant women has also received growing attention.[27] Attacks on women in Algeria, Rwanda, Bosnia and Afghanistan pointed to a possible new trend toward women as military targets. Systematic rape was used as a terror tactic in Bosnia and Rwanda, and the Japanese army in World War II operated an international network of sex slaves known as "comfort women." Rape has long been treated as a normal, if regrettable, byproduct of war, but recently certain instances of rape have been declared war crimes (see p. 286) by the international war crimes tribunal for the former Yugoslavia.

In sum, liberal feminists reject the argument that women bring uniquely feminine assets or liabilities to foreign and military affairs. They do not critique realism as essentially masculine in nature but do criticize state practices that exclude women from participation in international politics and war.

In addition to the liberal and standpoint strands of feminism, the third strand, postmodern feminism, is connected with the rise of postmodernism in the social sciences.

---

[26] Julian Borger, "U.S. Soldiers Accused of Raping 100 Colleagues," *The Guardian* 26 Feb. 2004. Mary Fainsod Katzenstein and Judith Reppy, eds., *Beyond Zero Tolerance: Discrimination in Military Culture* (Lanham, MD: Rowman & Littlefield, 1999).

[27] United Nations Secretary-General Study, *Women, Peace and Security* (New York: United Nations, 2002). Wenona Giles and Jennifer Hyndman, *Sites of Violence: Gender and Conflict Zones* (Berkeley: U of California P, 2004).

Post-positivist Feminism

Post-positivist feminism seeks to deconstruct realism (and liberalism) with the specific aim of uncovering the pervasive hidden influences of gender in IR while showing how arbitrarily gender roles are constructed. Post-positivist feminists agree with standpoint feminists that realism carries hidden meanings about gender roles but deny that there is any fixed, inherent meaning in either male or female genders. Rather, feminist post-positivists look at the interplay of gender and power in a more open-ended way. Post-positivist feminists criticize liberal feminists for trying merely to integrate women into traditional structures of war and foreign policy. They also criticize standpoint feminists for glorifying traditional feminine virtues.

In studying war, post-positivist feminists have challenged the archetypes of the (male) "just warrior" and the (female) "beautiful soul." They argue that women are not just passive bystanders or victims in war, but active participants in a system of warfare tied to both genders. Women act not only as nurses and journalists at the "front" but as mothers, wives and girlfriends on the "home front."[28] These scholars believe that stories of military forces should not omit the roles of prostitutes at military bases, that stories of armed conflict should not omit the details of women's activism in zones of conflict, nor should stories of diplomacy omit the roles of diplomats' wives.[29]

Post-positivist feminists reject not only realism but also some alternative approaches that emphasize the protection of women and other noncombatants. Just war doctrine (see pp. 285–286) is considered too abstract—a set of concepts and rules that does not do justice to the richness of each historical context and the varied roles of individual men and women within it.[30] Liberal pluralism is considered too problem-solving in orientation, and unsophisticated in its analysis

SEX IN THE SUBTEXT
Feminist post-positivists try to reveal hidden subtexts connecting gender with IR, such as the roles of sex and death in the constructions of masculinity by U.S. airmen in England, 1944.

---

[28] Jean Bethke Elshtain, *Women and War*, 2nd ed. (Chicago: U Chicago P, 1995). Gail Braybon and Penny Summerfield, *Out of the Cage: Women's Experiences in Two World Wars* (NY: Pandora, 1987).

[29] Cynthia Enloe, *Bananas, Beaches, and Bases: Making Feminist Sense of International Politics* (Berkeley: U California P, 1989). Wenona Giles, Malathi de Alwis, Edith Klein and Neluka Silva, eds., *Feminists under Fire: Exchanges across War Zones* (Toronto: Between the Lines, 2003). Simona Sharoni, *Gender and the Israeli-Palestinian Conflict: The Politics of Women's Resistance* (Syracuse, Syracuse UP, 1995). Tami Jacoby, *Women in Zones of Conflict* (Montreal: McGill-Queen's UP, forthcoming). Jan Jindy Pettman, *Worlding Women: A Feminist International Politics* (NY: Routledge, 1996). Katherine H. S. Moon, *Sex among Allies: Military Prostitution in U.S.–Korea Relations* (NY: Columbia UP, 1997).

[30] Elshtain, *Women and War* (see footnote 28 in this chapter). Sara Ruddick, *Maternal Thinking: Towards a Politics of Peace* (London: Women's Press, 1989).

of the relations of power between women and men—relations of power that will not be transformed simply by "getting more women in" to governments and militaries.

Many post-positivist feminists also engage with questions of masculinity, but they take a very different view of masculinity than that offered by standpoint feminists. By this view there is no single masculinity or femininity, but rather multiple masculinities and femininities. There are forms of masculinity, for example, that privilege physical strength and machismo attitudes as well as those that privilege rational thought or entrepreneurial spirit. In different times or places, communities or institutions, any one vision of masculinity may dominate over others, or, for some theorists of masculinity, become hegemonic.[31]

Post-positivist feminists have tried to deconstruct the language of realism, especially where it reflects influences of gender and sex. For instance, the first atomic bombs had male gender (they were named "Fat Man" and "Little Boy"); the coded telegram informing Washington, D.C., that the first hydrogen bomb had worked said simply, "It's a boy" (presumably being born a girl would have indicated a failure). The plane that dropped the atomic bomb on Hiroshima (the *Enola Gay*) had female gender; it was named after the pilot's mother. Likewise, the French atom-bomb test sites in the South Pacific were all given women's names.[32] Similarly, pilots have pasted pinup photos of nude women onto conventional bombs before dropping them. In all these cases, post-positivist feminists would note that the feminine gender of vehicles, targets or decorations amplifies the masculinity of the weapon itself. These efforts find sex and gender throughout the subtexts and analyses of realism. The hidden meanings not explicitly addressed in the text are often called the **subtext.**

subtext Meanings that are implicit or hidden in a text rather than explicitly addressed. See also *postmodernism.*

For example, the terms *power* and *potency* refer to both state capability and male virility. Military force depends on phallic objects—weapons designed to shoot projectiles, penetrate targets and explode. In basic training, men chant, "This is my rifle [holding up rifle], this is my gun [pointing to crotch]; one's for killing, the other's for fun."[33] Nuclear weapons are also repeatedly spoken of in sexual terms, perhaps due to their great "potency." Female models are hired to market tanks, helicopter missiles and other "potent" weapons to male procurement officers at international military trade shows.[34] The phallic character of weapons has seemingly persisted even as technology has evolved from spears to guns to missiles.

Realism and liberalism ignore all the sexual aspects of weaponry, limiting themselves to such issues as a weapon's explosive power, its range and other technical information about its use as state leverage. But if sexual assumptions enter into decisions about whether and when to use bombs or other military forces, or where and how to establish colonies, then realism and liberalism cannot adequately explain those decisions.[35] Post-positivist feminism thus reveals another reality—the desire of male politicians and

[31] Marysia Zalewski and Jane Parpart, eds., *The "Man" Question in International Relations* (Boulder, CO: Westview Press, 1998). R. W. Connell, *Masculinities* (Berkeley: U California P, 1995). Marieke de Goede, "Mastering 'Lady Credit': Discourses of Financial Crisis in Historical Perspective," *International Feminist Journal of Politics* 2.1 (2000): 73. Charlotte Hooper, *Manly States: Masculinities, International Relations and Gender Politics* (NY: Columbia UP, 2001). Lily Ling, "Hypermasculinity on the Rise, Again: A Response to Fukuyama on Women and World Politics," *International Feminist Journal of Politics* 2.2 (2000): 278–86. Abouali Farmanfarmaian, "Did You Measure Up? The Role of Race and Sexuality in the Gulf War," *Collateral Damage: The New World Order at Home and Abroad*, ed. C. Peters (Boston: South End, 1992) 111–38.

[32] Carol Cohn, "Sex and Death in the Rational World of Defense Intellectuals," *Signs* 12 (1987): 687–718.

[33] Gwynne Dyer, *War* (NY: Crown, 1985).

[34] Center for Defense Information [Washington, DC], "Weapons Bazaar," slide show (1985).

[35] Anne McClintock, *Imperial Leather: Race, Gender and Sexuality in the Colonial Conquest* (NY: Routledge, 1995).

soldiers to exhibit, or be perceived to exhibit, sexual competency—which competes with the realities of realism and neoliberalism and their focus on maximizing national interests (narrowly or broadly construed).

Some post-positivist feminists point out that the more likely reason militaries prefer gender segregation is that the creation of soldiers depends on a series of myths, including the superiority of one's nation (and usually race), the celebration of violence and the promise that women maintain the home front while soldiers "man" the battlefront. As feminist author Cynthia Enloe writes: "If male aircraft pilots can't have a few drinks and send women down a hotel corridor gauntlet, how are they supposed to militarily bond with one another? And if a woman who isn't sexually attracted to even benign versions of male heterosexuality is permitted to openly express her sexual indifference to masculinized pilots, then what's the prize waiting at the end of the war?"[36]

By radically shifting the focus and approach of IR scholarship, post-positivist feminists hope to challenge traditional understandings of IR, rationality and the kinds of questions that can be asked about global-level politics.

POSTMODERNISM

Postmodernism, like Marxist thought and feminism, is a broad approach to scholarship that has left its mark on various academic disciplines, especially the study of literature. Because of their literary roots, postmodernists pay special attention to *texts* and to *discourses*—how people write and talk about their subject (IR).[37] Postmodern critiques of realism thus often concentrate on analyzing realists' words and arguments or those presented by policy-makers.[38]

postmodernism An approach that denies the existence of a single fixed reality, and pays special attention to texts and discourses—that is, how people write and talk about a subject.

Deconstructing Realism

A central idea of postmodernism is that there is no single, objective reality but a multiplicity of experiences and perspectives that defy easy categorization. Postmodernists explicitly reject positivism and insist that all concepts or norms must be deconstructed in order to understand the relations of power that exist through various discursive practices. This section will merely convey some important postmodern themes, necessarily oversimplified, and show how postmodernism can help illuminate some problems of realism.

From a postmodern perspective, realism cannot justify its claim that states are the central actors in IR and that states operate as unitary actors with coherent sets of objective interests (which they pursue through international power politics). Postmodern critics of realism see nothing objective about state interests, and certainly nothing universal (in that one set of values or interests applies to all states).

More fundamentally, postmodernism calls into question the whole notion of states as actors. States have no tangible reality as such; they are "fictions" that we collectively

---

[36] Cynthia Enloe, "The Right to Fight: A Feminist Catch-22," *Ms.* July–Aug 1993: 84–87. See also Deborah Harrison and Lucie Laliberté, *No Life Like It: Military Wives in Canada* (Toronto: Lorimer, 1994). Deborah Harrison, *The First Casualty: Violence against Women in Canadian Military Communities* (Toronto: Lorimer, 2002).

[37] Pauline Marie Rosenau, *Post-Modernism and the Social Sciences: Insights, Inroads, and Intrusions* (Princeton, NJ: Princeton UP, 1992).

[38] Richard K. Ashley and R. B. J. Walker, "Speaking the Language of Exile: Dissident Thought in International Studies" [Introduction to special issue], *International Studies Quarterly* 34.3 (1990): 259–68. Yosef Lapid, "The Third Debate: On the Prospects of International Theory in a Post–Positivist Era," *International Studies Quarterly* 33.3 (1989): 235–54. James Der Derian, *On Diplomacy: A Genealogy of Western Estrangement* (NY: Basil Blackwell, 1987).

construct to make sense of the actions of large numbers of individuals. For postmodernists, the stories told about the actions and policies of states are just that—stories. Actions and activities in global politics are all filtered through an interpretive process that distorts the actual experiences of those involved.[39] More importantly, states and others actively "make" the world around them. In contrast to the realist claim that says states respond to objective threats that exist in the world and always seek to ensure their own survival, many postmodern thinkers argue that states actively construct those threats. States do not have to justify their actions (military interventions or wars) if there is widespread agreement that real dangers and threats exist in the world.[40] When those dangers disappear, as when the Soviet Union disintegrated in the early 1990s, then new "dangers" are necessary to legitimize some foreign policy decisions.

Postmodernists seek to "deconstruct" constructions such as states, the international system and the associated stories and arguments (texts and discourses) with which realists portray the nature of international relations. To *deconstruct* a text—a term borrowed from literary criticism—means to tease apart the words in order to reveal hidden meanings, looking for what might be omitted or included only implicitly. Like post-positivist feminists, postmodernists examine the subtexts of analyses, actions and events.

What is the subtext in the stories realists tell about IR? What does realism omit from its accounts of IR? We have just discussed one major omission—women and gender. Furthermore, in its emphasis on states, realism omits the roles of individuals, domestic politics, economic classes, MNCs and other nonstate actors. In its focus on the great powers, realism omits the experiences of countries of the global South. In its attention to military forms of leverage, it omits the roles of various nonmilitary ones.

Realism focuses so narrowly because its aim is to reduce IR to a simple, coherent model. The model is claimed to be objective, universal and accurate. To postmodernists, the realist model is none of these things; it is a biased model that creates a narrow and one-sided story for the purpose of promoting the interests of powerful actors. Postmodernists seek to "trouble" or call into question this model along with any other model (including neoliberalism) that tries to represent IR in simple, objective categories. The rationale for doing so is not simply to celebrate the diversity of experiences that make up IR, though for some postmodernists this is certainly a goal. More importantly, postmodernists seek to disrupt the "moral certitude" that too often accompanies state actions and the analyses made of those actions. Postmodernist thought is often criticized for being "nihilistic," for refusing to take an ethical stand on issues of global politics. However, much postmodern writing in IR is very explicitly ethical, particularly insofar as it raises concerns about the kinds of actions that are adopted or foreclosed by states and presented as inevitable.[41]

---

[39] Michael J. Shapiro, "Textualizing Global Politics," *International/Intertextual Relations: Postmodern Readings of World Politics*, ed. James Der Derian and Michael J. Shapiro (NY: Lexington, 1989) 11–22. Michael J. Shapiro and Hayward R. Alker, eds., *Challenging Boundaries: Global Flows, Territorial Identities* (Minneapolis: U Minnesota P, 1996).

[40] David Campbell, *Politics without Principle: Sovereignty, Ethics, and the Narratives of the Gulf War* (Boulder, CO: Rienner, 1993). Anders Stephanson, *Kennan and the Art of Foreign Policy* (Cambridge, MA: Harvard UP, 1989). William Chaloupka, *Knowing Nukes: The Politics and Culture of the Atom* (Minneapolis: U Minnesota P, 1992).

[41] R. B. J. Walker and Saul H. Mendlovitz, eds., *Contending Sovereignties: Redefining Political Community* (Boulder, CO: Rienner, 1990). R. B. J. Walker, *Inside/Outside: International Relations as Political Theory* (NY: Cambridge UP, 1993). Cynthia Weber, *Simulating Sovereignty: Intervention, the State and Symbolic Exchange* (NY: Cambridge UP, 1995). Jim George, *Discourses of Global Politics: A Critical (Re)Introduction to International Relations* (Boulder, CO: Rienner, 1994).

Postcolonialism

Postmodern and post-positivist theorists engage in the ways in which discursive constructions of men and women, states and militaries, laws and institutions, all impact how we understand and engage with politics at the global level. Postcolonial theorists draw on these insights and argue further that imperialism constitutes one of the crucial moments, or processes, through which modern identities became established. For postcolonial theorists, the project of theorizing in IR should be to explore the intersectionality of race, class, gender and imperialism. It is through the colonial encounter, by this view, that the widespread and naturalized identities emerged that shape how we think about the world and each other. These include the following kinds of binaries: developed/undeveloped, core/periphery, rational/irrational, male/female, First World/Third World, modern/traditional, civilized/ backward, white/black, advanced/barbaric. Importantly, for postcolonial theorists, representations of the "South" or the "colonial other" have less to do with the South than they do with "our" world. Depictions of the "other," in other words, tell us what we think about "ourselves" (usually the words found on the "superior" side of the binaries).[42]

Postcolonial theorists also argue that IR itself is part of the colonial project. The failure of mainstream approaches like realism and liberalism to explore imperialism, inequality and difference is not, by this view, an innocent omission. Emphasizing differences between states rather than the many profound differences and inequalities that mark the world (both within and between states) is a way to make some sets of questions accepted and legitimate (war and peace, trade, finance) while others are cast to the margins (racism and colonialism). It is, moreover, a parochial and impoverished way to understand the enormous diversity and complexity of the contemporary world.[43]

The contemporary colonial project, by this view, is not carried only by warriors but by a variety of practices and actors, including those that liberals would argue are on the "benign" or more overtly positive side of global politics, such as the UN and the functioning of international law. Peacekeeping and humanitarian interventions are also subject to interrogation by postcolonial theorists as part of the "civilizing mission" of Western institutions, often informed by overtly racist assumptions about the peoples of countries to which such missions are deployed.[44] Postcolonialism offers some of the most profound critiques of IR found within the "constellation" of critical theories.

In sum, through a variety of methods and concepts, critical theorists challenge mainstream accounts of international relations. They seek to replace oversimplified models

[42] Geeta Chowdhry and Sheila Nair, eds., *Power, Postcolonialism and International Relations* (London: Routledge, 2002). Roxanne Lynn Doty, *Imperial Encounters: The Politics of Representation in North-South Relations* (Minneapolis: U Minnesota P, 1996). Edward Said, *Orientalism* (NY: Vintage, 1979). Edward Said, *Culture and Imperialism* (NY: Knopf, 1993).

[43] Naeem Inayatullah and David L. Blaney, *International Relations and the Problem of Difference* (NY: Routledge, 2004). J. Marshall Beier, *International Relations in Uncommon Places: Indigeneity, Cosmology, and the Limits of International Theory* (NY: Palgrave MacMillan, 2005).

[44] Sherene Razack, *Dark Threats and White Knights: The Somalia Affair, Peacekeeping and the New Imperialism* (Toronto: U Toronto P, 2004). Jayan Nayar, "Orders of Inhumanity," *Reframing the International: Law, Culture and Politics*, ed. Richard Falk, Edwin J. Lester Ruiz and R. B. J. Walker (NY: Routledge, 2002). Anne Orford, "Feminism, Imperialism and the Mission of International Law," *Nordic Journal of International Law* 71.2 (2002): 275–96. Anne Orford, "Muscular Humanitarianism: Reading the Narratives of the New Interventionism," *European Journal of International Law* 10.4 (1999): 679–711.

with one in which multiple realities coexist—realities of gender and sexuality, race and class, and imperialism and colonialism. They seek to better understand IR by listening to voices silenced by power—the voices of women, of oppressed ethnic minorities and of "others" whose interests and actions are not done justice to by states or by theories of IR that focus exclusively on states or other more traditional actors, such as international organizations or MNCs.

With this chapter and the previous two as theoretical background, the next four chapters will cover the major topics in international security studies, broadly defined. Questions in the domain of foreign policy studies are the subject of Chapter 5.

Thinking Critically

1. Think about the difference between the concept of hegemony as used by realists (as described in Chapter 2) and the concept as used by Gramscians. How would a neo-Gramscian conception of hegemony be applied to understand the U.S.-led invasion and occupation of Iraq? Would this differ from how the realist notion of hegemony might be used to understand the same event?

2. Would IR operate differently if most leaders of states were women? What would the differences be? What evidence (beyond gender stereotypes) supports your answer?

3. How would a feminist or postcolonial understanding of militarism impact how you see international relations? Could these approaches also change the way policies are made in IR? Would they want to?

4. Watch a half-hour news broadcast or documentary that is devoted to an IR issue or event. Write down the terms and phrases that are used to describe the event. What subtexts are at play in the coverage of the issue? How do those subtexts contribute to the way the issue is understood?

5. Deconstruct this book by identifying implicit themes, subjects not covered and hidden biases.

6. Write your own critical-thinking question concerning the topics discussed in this chapter. What are the merits of your question? How would you go about answering it?

Chapter Summary

- Critical theorists share a disposition toward the world and ask: How did this world come about and in whose interests does it serve?

- Critical approaches focus on power, but understand power differently than do either realists or liberals by emphasizing inequalities.

- Critical theorists are concerned with the issues and actors that are excluded in an examination of IR when conducted from a more mainstream (realist or liberal) perspective.

- Most critical theorists reject the idea of objectivity in the positivist sense, but still argue that their analyses contribute to understandings of IR.

- Many critical theorists owe an intellectual debt to Marxist theory.

- A direct development of Marxist thought has been in Gramscian IR theory, which retains Marxism's commitment to historical materialism but seeks to avoid problems of economism.

- For Gramscians, hegemony is a condition in which the relations of power that sustain a given world order recede into the background of consciousness, often accomplished via international institutions.

- Feminist scholars of IR agree that gender is important in understanding IR but diverge into several strands regarding their concept of the role of gender.

- Standpoint feminists argue that real (not arbitrary) differences between men and women exist. Men think about social relations more often in terms of autonomy (as do realists), but women think in terms of connection.

- Standpoint feminists argue that men are on average more warlike than women. Although individual female participants (such as state leaders) may not reflect this difference, the participation of large numbers of women would change the character of the international system, making it more peaceful.

- Liberal feminists disagree that women have substantially different capabilities or tendencies as participants in IR. They argue that women are equivalent to men in virtually all IR roles. As evidence, liberal feminists point to historical and present-day female leaders and soldiers.

- Postmodern critics reject the entire framework and language of realism, with its unitary state actors. Postmodernists argue that no simple categories can capture the multiple realities experienced by participants in IR.

- Post-positivist feminists seek to uncover gender-related subtexts implicit in realist discourse, including sexual themes connected with the concept of power.

- Postcolonial theorists explore the intersectionality of race, class, gender and imperialism.

Key Terms

problem-solving theory   105
critical theory   105
post positivism   107
historical materialism   108
Gramscian hegemony   110
standpoint feminism   112

liberal feminism   113
post-positivist feminism   113
gender gap   117
subtext   122
postmodernism   123

Research Navigator Question

Using Research Navigator™, find article AN 12733052 on "Women, Peace and Security." Review the discussion of the importance of UN Security Council Resolution 1325. Using the information from this article, prepare a 10-minute speech on the resolution, explaining its history and significance as clearly and concisely as possible. Imagine that you are giving your speech to a small audience of people who are interested in your topic but have no prior background knowledge of either the UN or the issue itself.

Weblinks

Below are links to additional scholarly journals that focus on issues of interest to critical theory:

Alternatives: Global, Local, Political:
http://www.rienner.com/viewbook.cfm?BOOKID=1585

International Feminist Journal of Politics:
http://www.tandf.co.uk/journals/titles/14616742.asp

Millennium: Journal of International Studies:
http://www.lse.ac.uk/Depts/intrel/millenn

Review of International Political Economy:
http://www.jhu.edu/~ripe

Review of International Studies:
http://titles.cambridge.org/journals/journal_catalogue.asp?mnemonic=ris

Foreign Policy

5

Secretary of State Condoleezza Rice at confirmation hearings, 2005.

MAKING FOREIGN POLICY

Looking at states as unitary actors is useful up to a point, but not very accurate. A state is not a single conscious being; its actions are a composite of individual human choices—by its citizenry, political leaders, diplomats and bureaucrats—aggregated through its internal structures. This chapter looks at the state from the inside out, in an attempt to understand the processes and structures *within* states that make them take the actions they do toward other states.

Foreign policies are the strategies used by governments to guide their actions in the international arena (various alternative definitions have been proposed). Foreign policies spell out the objectives state leaders have decided to pursue in a given relationship or situation as well as the general means by which they intend to pursue those objectives. In important ways, foreign policy is at the intersection of domestic politics and international relations. As Lester Pearson once commented, "Foreign policy is merely domestic policy with its hat on."[1]

Every day, states take actions in international affairs. Diplomats are appointed to posts, given instructions for their negotiations or recalled home. Trade negotiators agree to reduce their demands by a few percent. Military forces are moved around and occasionally sent into battle. Behind each of these actions are decisions by foreign policy bureaucrats in national capitals (including but not limited to the top state leaders). These decisions in turn generally reflect the overall policies states have developed to govern their relationships with other states.

---

[1] Quoted in a speech by Stephen Harper, reported in James Travers, "Putting a Swagger into Foreign Policy," *The Toronto Star* 17 March 2007.

The study of foreign policies includes understanding the various states' substantive policies; for example, understanding why Canada supported the United States during the first Persian Gulf War in 1991 and did not support them in the Iraq War of 2003. In general, IR scholars are interested in the **foreign policy process**—how policies are arrived at, and implemented, in various states.[2]

foreign policy process
The process by which foreign policies are arrived at and implemented.

States establish various organizational structures and functional relationships to create and carry out foreign policies. Officials and agencies collect information about a situation through various channels; they write memoranda outlining possible options for action; they hold meetings to discuss the matter; some of them meet privately to decide how to steer the meetings. Such activities, broadly defined, are what is meant by "the foreign policy process." IR scholars are especially interested in exploring whether certain kinds of policy processes lead to certain kinds of decisions—whether certain processes produce better outcomes (for the state's self-defined interests) than do others.

Foreign policy outcomes result from multiple forces working simultaneously at the various levels of analysis. The outcomes depend on individual decision-makers, on the type of society and government they are working within and on the international and global context of their actions. Since the study of foreign policy concentrates on forces within the state, its main emphasis is on the individual and domestic levels of analysis.

Comparative foreign policy is the study of foreign policy in various states in order to discover whether similar types of societies or governments consistently have similar types of foreign policies (comparing across states or across time periods for a single state). Such studies have focused on three characteristics in particular: size, wealth and extent of democratic participation in government.[3] An alternative approach categorizes societies according to their relative populations, natural resources and levels of technology.[4]

A major focus of such studies is whether certain characteristics of a state or society predispose it to be warlike or aggressive. In particular, during the Cold War, scholars debated whether communism or capitalism was inherently more warlike in nature. However, no simple rule has been found to predict a state's warlike tendencies based on attributes such as size, wealth and type of government. There is great variation among states, and even within a single state over time. Both capitalist and communist states have proven capable of naked aggression or peaceful behaviour, depending on circumstances.

Some political scientists have tried to interpret particular states' foreign policies in terms of each one's *political culture and history*. For example, some observers insist that Canada's multicultural heritage (a mosaic rather than a melting pot), its large immigrant population, its official bilingualism and its commitment to liberal democracy and human rights informs its foreign policy stance. This stance has tended toward what is called liberal internationalism: respect for (and sometimes a direct hand in creating) multilateral institutions such as the United Nations, NATO, the World Bank and the International Criminal Court; and historically greater emphasis on peacekeeping than war-making.[5] These

---

[2] Kim Richard Nossal, *The Politics of Canadian Foreign Policy* (Scarborough: Prentice Hall Canada, 1997). Laura Neack, *The New Foreign Policy: U.S. and Comparative Foreign Policy in the 21st Century* (Lanham, MD: Rowman & Littlefield, 2003). Deborah J. Gerner, "Foreign Policy Analysis: Exhilarating Eclecticism, Intriguing Enigmas," *International Studies Notes* 16.3 (1991): 4–19.

[3] Steven W. Hook, *Comparative Foreign Policy* (Upper Saddle River, NJ: Prentice Hall, 2002). James N. Rosenau, *The Scientific Study of Foreign Policy,* 2nd ed. (London: Frances Pinter, 1980).

[4] Robert C. North, *The World That Could Be* (Palo Alto, CA: Stanford Alumni Association, 1976).

[5] Pierre S. Pettigrew, "Canada's International Personality," *International Journal* 60.3 (Summer 2005): 623–34. Jennifer M. Welsh, "Fulfilling Canada's Global Promise," *Policy Options* (February 2005): 56–59. See also Jennifer M. Welsh, *At Home in the World: Canada's Global Vision for the 21st Century* (Toronto: Harper Perennial, 2005).

commitments might help explain the question posed earlier—Canada supported the United States during the first Persian Gulf War in 1991 and did not support the United States in the Iraq War of 2003 because in the former instance the United Nations endorsed the invasion of Iraq but did not do so in 2003. For Canadian decision-makers, UN approval for military interventions is of utmost importance, and then-prime minister Jean Chrétien confirmed as much when he said in a speech explaining the Canadian decision that respect for multilateralism is part of "Canada's distinctive international personality."[6]

However, it is also worth noting that political culture and history explanations are not always straightforward. One may have predicted that Canada's cultural and historical connections to both the U.S. and Britain would supersede its commitment to multilateralism. As was noted at the time, never before on a matter of such importance had Canada distanced itself from both of its "Anglo-Saxon" allies at once. Other factors may also influence a decision—in this case not only Canada's respect for the UN, but strong public opinion against the Iraq War in Québec, which was in the midst of a provincial election at the time.[7] Many factors may contribute to any particular foreign policy decision.

Most studies of foreign policy have not focused on the comparison of policies of different states; they have instead concentrated on understanding more generally the kinds of processes used in various states to reach (and implement) foreign policies. Scholars have tried to probe the effects of these processes on the resulting outcomes.

The foreign policy process is a process of *decision-making*. States take actions because people in governments choose those actions. People whose job it is to make decisions about international relations—*decision-makers*—have to go through the same kinds of processes, in one way or another, that anyone would go through, even in a decision as simple as deciding what to eat for dinner.

Decision-making is a *steering* process in which adjustments are made as a result of feedback from the outside world. Decisions are carried out by actions taken to change the world, and then information from the world is monitored to evaluate the effects of actions. These evaluations—along with information about other, independent changes in the environment—become part of the

FRESH LEADERSHIP
Foreign policy outcomes result from processes at several levels of analysis. For example, the sudden change in Palestinian leadership after Yasser Arafat's death in 2004 tested the importance of the individual level (which changed radically) versus larger social structures and conflicts (which did not). Here, Mahmoud Abbas votes in the fair elections in 2005 that elected him president. Abbas opposes violence against Israel and hoped to restart peace talks to establish a Palestinian state. However, legislative elections in 2006 brought to power the violently anti-Israeli party Hamas, halting peace talks and suggesting that the domestic and interstate levels of analysis can trump the individual level.

---

[6] Quoted from Srdjan Vucetic, "Why Did Canada Sit out of the Iraq War? One Constructivist Analysis," *Canadian Foreign Policy* 13.1 (2006): 146.

[7] David G. Haglund, "Canada and the Anglosphere: In, Out, or Indifferent?" *Policy Options* (February 2005): 72–76.

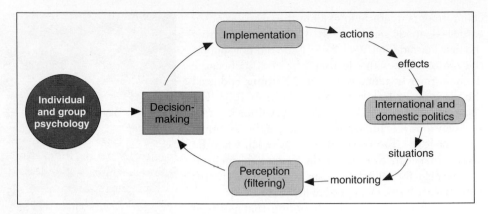

Figure 5.1 Decision-Making as Steering

next round of decisions (see Figure 5.1). The steering process, with its external feedback, is based on the *goals* of the decision-maker. On the way to achieving to these goals, decision-makers set *objectives* as discrete steps to be reached. Objectives fall along a spectrum from core long-term objectives to very short-term practical ones.

MODELS OF DECISION-MAKING: THE RATIONAL ACTOR MODEL

rational actor model (of decision-making)
A model in which decision-makers calculate the costs and benefits of each possible course of action, then choose the one with the highest benefits and lowest costs.

A common starting point for studying the decision-making process is the **rational actor model.**[8] In this model, decision-makers calculate the costs and benefits of each possible course of action, then choose the one with the highest benefits and lowest costs. This model is favoured by realists. For some scholars, the state is seen as generating decisions in a manner analogous to the decision-making process undertaken by an individual. Whether it is understood as actual individuals involved in decision-making, or by analogy to individual decision-making, the rational actor model envisions a number of steps in the decision-making process:

1. *Clarify goals* in the situation.
2. *Order them* by importance (in case different goals conflict).
3. *List the alternatives* available to achieve the goals.
4. *Investigate the consequences* (probable and possible outcomes) of those alternatives.
5. *Choose* the course of action that will produce the best outcome (in terms of reaching one's goals).

The choice may be complicated by *uncertainty* about the costs and benefits of various actions. In such cases, decision-makers must attach probabilities to each possible outcome of an action. Some decision-makers are relatively *accepting of risk*, whereas others are *averse to risk*. These factors affect the importance that decision-makers place on the various outcomes that could result from an action. For example, U.S. president George W. Bush's decision to

---

[8] It, along with the organizational process and bureaucratic politics models discussed later, derives from Graham Allison; see Graham T. Allison and Philip Zelikow, *Essence of Decision: Explaining the Cuban Missile Crisis*, 2nd ed. (NY: Longman, 1999). Jonathan Bendor and Thomas H. Hammond, "Rethinking Allison's Models," *American Political Science Review* 86.2 (1992): 301–22.

invade Iraq showed high acceptance of risk. The potential benefits were great (including seizing possible weapons of mass destruction), and Bush was willing to risk the lives of U.S. and coalition military personnel on the chance that such a gamble might pay off.

The rational actor model may imply that decision-making is simpler than is actually the case. A decision-maker may hold different conflicting goals simultaneously. The goals of different individuals involved in making a decision may diverge, as may the goals of different state agencies. The rational model of decision-making thus is somewhat complicated by uncertainty and the multiple goals of decision-makers.

Although the rational model is the common starting point for thinking about foreign policy decision-making, there are many reasons to question whether decisions can be considered rational. The nonrational elements in decision-making are best understood from a *psychological* analysis of individual and group decision-making processes.[9]

Individual Decision-Makers

Individuals are the only true actors in IR. Every international event is the result, intended or unintended, of decisions made by individuals. IR does not just happen. President Harry Truman, who made the decision to drop U.S. nuclear bombs on two Japanese cities in 1945, understood this. He had a sign on his desk: "The buck stops here." If he chose to use the bomb (as he did), more than 100 000 civilians would die. If he chose not to, the war might drag on for months with tens of thousands of U.S. casualties. Truman had to choose. Some people applaud his decision; others condemn it. For better or worse, Truman had to decide, and to take responsibility for the consequences, as an individual. Similarly, the decisions of individual citizens, though they may not seem important when considered individually, are what create the great forces of world history.

The study of individual decision-making revolves around the question of rationality. To what extent are national leaders (or citizens) able to make rational decisions in the national interest—if indeed such an interest can be defined—and thus conform to a realist view of IR? Individual rationality is not equivalent to state rationality: states might filter individuals' irrational decisions so as to arrive at rational choices, or states might distort individually rational decisions and end up with irrational state choices. Realists tend to assume that both states and individuals are rational and that the goals or interests of states correlate with those of leaders. This assumption partly reflects the role of strong individuals such as monarchs and dictators in many states, where the rationality and interests of the leader determine those of the state.

The most simplified rational-actor models go so far as to assume that interests are the same from one actor to another. If this were so, individuals could be substituted for each other in various roles without significantly changing history. States would all behave similarly to each other (or rather, the differences between them would reflect different resources, geography and similar features, not differences in the nature of national interests). Many realists make this type of assumption, but it is at best a great oversimplification.[10] In truth, individual decisions reflect the *values* and *beliefs* of the decision-maker.

How can IR scholars characterize an individual's values and beliefs? Sometimes beliefs and values are spelled out in ideological autobiographies such as Hitler's *Mein Kampf*.

[9] Philip E. Tetlock, "Psychological Advice on Foreign Policy: What Do We Have to Contribute?" *American Psychologist* 41 (1986): 557–67. Zeev Maoz, *Domestic Sources of Global Change* (Ann Arbor: U Michigan P, 1996).

[10] James M. Goldgeier, *Leadership Style and Soviet Foreign Policy: Stalin, Khrushchev, Brezhnev, Gorbachev* (Baltimore: Johns Hopkins UP, 1994). Barbara Farnham, *Roosevelt and the Munich Crisis: A Study of Political Decision-Making* (Princeton, NJ: Princeton UP, 1997).

Thinking Theoretically

In 1988 during the Canadian federal election campaign, the Liberal Party promised to tear up the Free Trade Agreement between the U.S. and Canada if elected. Although the Liberals and the New Democratic Party (also opposed to free trade) together received a combined majority of the popular vote in that election, the Progressive Conservative Party, which supported free trade, won more seats in Parliament. The Free Trade Agreement subsequently went into effect on January 1, 1989. However, five years later, when the Liberals under Prime Minister Jean Chrétien formed the Canadian government, their position on free trade changed. Once elected, the Liberal Party not only retained the agreement but signed the North American Free Trade Agreement (NAFTA) and sought to expand it to the entire Western Hemisphere (with the exception of Cuba) under the Free Trade Agreement of the Americas (FTAA). What theories might help explain this switch? A variety of explanations might be drawn from the three theoretical perspectives.

One theory, the organizational process model, holds that government bureaucracies churn out policy in a routine manner, with only incremental change as political leaders come and go. The liberal pluralist (not to be confused with the Liberal Party) elements of this model include its understanding of the state as a complex organization cross-cut by numerous departments and agencies, its emphasis on substate actors, and its view of change as incremental. This reasoning could explain the continuity in Canadian policy on free trade, even when a new leader and party came in with fresh ideas. The relevant departments "educated" the Liberal Party and Prime Minister Chrétien, and policy remained relatively unchanged.

A different theoretical approach, drawing on realist themes, explains decisions such as free trade agreements as actions taken rationally (benefits exceed costs) in the pursuit of national interests. For realists, these interests tend to be defined—rather narrowly—as access to tangible power resources such as territory, energy supply, wealth, strategic military bases and the like. By this line of reasoning, the Liberals did not change the Canadian position on free trade because Canadian interests had not changed. For realists, neither political rhetoric nor changes in government matter as much as basic national interests and capabilities. The Liberal prime minister Jean Chrétien made roughly the same cost-benefit calculation as had the Progressive Conservative prime minister Brian Mulroney.

A critical theory perspective might suggest that mainstream political parties like the Liberal Party usually have close ties with—and depend on the support of—Canadian business and other elites within Canadian society. Those interests support either what is good for business or, more broadly, what facilitates the continued and smooth functioning of capitalism. For critical theorists, no matter what political parties may say as part of their election platforms, when they are in power, they will make decisions that support those business and elite interests.

The difficulty in the study of international relations is that there are no "experiments" in which theories can be tested against each other. Often scholars and students of IR can only make judgments based on how persuasive a case each perspective presents. This means assessing the coherence of the argument and the quality of the evidence mounted in support of contending positions. Which position do you find most convincing?

Other times IR researchers try to infer beliefs through a method called *content analysis*—analyzing speeches or other documents to count the number of times key words or phrases are repeated, and in what contexts. Scholars of IR have also described *operational codes*—routines and methods that mediate between beliefs and practical actions. They have traced out such operational codes, for example, for Soviet communist leaders.[11] Other scholars have created computer-based models of beliefs.[12]

---

[11] Alexander L. George, "The 'Operational Code': A Neglected Approach to the Study of Political Leaders and Decision Making," *International Studies Quarterly* 13.2 (1969): 199–222.

[12] Charles S. Taber, "POLI: An Expert System Model of U.S. Foreign Policy Belief Systems," *American Political Science Review* 86.4 (1992). Valerie M. Hudson, ed., *Artificial Intelligence and International Politics* (Boulder, CO: Westview, 1991).

The goals of individuals differ, as do the ways in which they pursue those goals. Individual decision-makers not only have differing values and beliefs, but unique personalities—personal experiences, intellectual capabilities and personal styles of making decisions. Some IR scholars study individual psychology to understand how personality affects decision-making. *Psychoanalytic approaches* hold that personalities reflect the subconscious influences of childhood experiences. For instance, some scholars believe that Canadian prime minister Pierre Elliott Trudeau's adolescent fears of being left behind and his sense that he was neither physically strong nor intellectually bright (despite all evidence to the contrary) contributed to a later refusal to back down in a fight. During the 1970 October Crisis, Trudeau earned the admiration of many foreign leaders for his refusal to yield to terrorist demands of the Front de Libération du Québec (FLQ), but his suspension of civil liberties earned him much criticism at home.[13]

U.S. president Clinton's early years in office drew much criticism for his zigzagging foreign policy. A notable Clinton personality trait was his readiness to compromise. Clinton himself has noted that his experience of growing up with a violent, alcoholic stepfather shaped him into a "peacemaker, always trying to minimize the disruption."[14]

Beyond individual *idiosyncrasies* in goals or decision-making processes, there are at least three *systematic* ways in which individual decision-making diverges from the rational actor model. First, decision-makers suffer from **misperceptions and selective perceptions** (taking in only some kinds of information) when they compile information on the likely consequences of their choices.[15] Decision-making processes must by necessity reduce and filter the incoming information on which a decision is based; the problem is that such filtration often is biased. **Information screens** are subconscious filters through which people screen information about the world around them. Often they simply ignore any information that does not fit their expectations. Information is also filtered out as it passes from one person to another in the decision-making process. For example, prior to the September 2001 terrorist attacks, U.S. intelligence agencies failed to adequately interpret available evidence, in part because too few analysts were fluent in Arabic.

Second, the rationality of individual cost-benefit calculations is undermined by emotions that decision-makers feel while thinking about the consequences of their actions—an effect referred to as *affective bias*. (Positive and negative affect refer to feelings of liking or disliking someone.) As hard as a decision-maker tries to be rational, the decision-making process is bound to be influenced by strong feelings held about the person or state toward which the decision is directed. (Affective biases also contribute to information screening, as positive information about disliked people or negative information about liked people is filtered out.)

Third, *cognitive biases* are systematic distortions of rational calculations based not on emotional feelings but simply on the limitations of the human brain in making choices. The most important seems to be the attempt to produce *cognitive balance*—or to reduce *cognitive dissonance*. These terms refer to people's tendency to maintain mental models of the world that are logically consistent (this seldom succeeds entirely). For instance, after

misperceptions and selective perceptions The selective or mistaken processing of the available information about a decision; one of several ways—along with affective and cognitive bias—in which individual decision-making diverges from the rational model.

information screens The subconscious or unconscious filters through which people screen information about the world around them.

---

[13] Richard Gwyn, *The Northern Magus: Pierre Trudeau and Canadians* (Toronto: McClelland & Stewart, 1980).

[14] Nancy Collins, "A Legacy of Strength and Love," interview with President Clinton, *Good Housekeeping* 221.5 (Nov. 1995): 113–15.

[15] Robert Jervis, *Perception and Misperception in International Politics* (Princeton, NJ: Princeton UP, 1976). Robert Jervis, *The Logic of Images in International Relations* (NY: Columbia UP, 1989).

deciding whether to intervene militarily in a conflict, a state leader will very likely adjust his or her mental model to downplay the risks and exaggerate the gains of the chosen course of action.[16]

One implication of cognitive balance is that decision-makers place greater value on goals that they have put much effort into achieving—the *justification of effort*. This is especially true in a democracy, where politicians must face their citizens' judgment at the polls and therefore do not want to admit failures. British and American involvement in Iraq may have trapped decision-makers in this way. After sending hundreds of thousands of troops halfway around the world, it will be difficult for U.S. or British leaders to admit to themselves that the costs of the war may be greater than the benefits.

Decision-makers also achieve cognitive balance through *wishful thinking*—an overestimate of the probability of a desired outcome. A variation of wishful thinking is to assume that an event with a *low probability* of occurring will *not* occur. This could be a dangerous way to think about catastrophic events such as accidental nuclear war.

Cognitive balance often leads decision-makers to maintain a hardened image of an *enemy* and to interpret all the enemy's actions in a negative light (since the idea of bad people doing good things would create cognitive dissonance).[17] Obviously, this cognitive bias overlaps with the affective bias felt toward such enemies.

A *mirror image* refers to two sides in a conflict maintaining very similar enemy images of each other ("we are defensive, they are aggressive," etc.). This happens frequently in ethnic conflicts. A decision-maker may experience psychological *projection* of his or her own feelings onto another actor. For instance, if (hypothetically) Indian leaders wanted to gain nuclear superiority over Pakistan but found that goal inconsistent with their image of themselves as peaceful and defensive, the resulting cognitive dissonance might be resolved by believing that Pakistan was trying to gain nuclear superiority (the example works as well with the states reversed).

Another form of cognitive bias, related to cognitive balance, is the use of *historical analogies* to structure one's thinking about a decision. This can be quite useful or quite misleading, depending on whether the analogy is appropriate.[18] As each historical situation is unique in some way, when a decision-maker latches on to an analogy and uses it as a shortcut to a decision, the rational calculation of costs and benefits may be cut short as well. For example, U.S. leaders used the analogy of Munich in 1938 to convince themselves that appeasement of communism in the Vietnam War would lead to increased communist aggression in Asia. In retrospect, the differences between North Vietnam and Nazi Germany made this a poor analogy. Vietnam then became a potent analogy that helped convince U.S. leaders to avoid involvement in certain overseas conflicts, including Bosnia; this was called the "Vietnam syndrome" in U.S. foreign policy.

---

[16] Yaacov Y. I. Vertzberger, *The World in Their Minds: Information Processing, Cognition, and Perception in Foreign Policy Decisionmaking* (Palo Alto, CA: Stanford UP, 1990). Richard Hermann, "The Empirical Challenge of the Cognitive Revolution: A Strategy for Drawing Inferences about Perceptions," *International Studies Quarterly* 32.2 (1988): 175–204. Martha L. Cottam, *Foreign Policy Decision Making: The Influence of Cognition* (Boulder, CO: Westview, 1986).

[17] Sam Keen, *Faces of the Enemy: Reflections of the Hostile Imagination* (San Francisco: Harper & Row, 1986).

[18] George W. Breslauer and Philip E. Tetlock, eds., *Learning in U.S. and Soviet Foreign Policy* (Boulder, CO: Westview, 1991). Yuen Foong Khong, *Analogies at War: Korea, Munich, Dien Bien Phu, and the Vietnam Decisions of 1965* (Princeton, NJ: Princeton UP, 1992).

All these psychological processes—misperception, affective biases and cognitive biases—interfere with the rational assessment of costs and benefits in making a decision.[19] Two specific modifications to the rational model of decision-making have been proposed to accommodate psychological realities.

First, the model of *bounded rationality* takes into account the costs of seeking and processing information. Nobody thinks about every single possible course of action when making a decision. Instead of **optimizing,** or picking the very best option, people usually work on the problem until they come up with a "good enough" solution that meets some minimal criteria; this is called **satisficing,** or finding a satisfactory solution.[20] The time constraints faced by top decision-makers in IR—who are constantly besieged with crises requiring their attention—generally preclude their finding the very best response to a situation. Time constraints were described by U.S. defense secretary William Cohen in 1997: "The unrelenting flow of information, the need to digest it on a minute-by-minute basis, is quite different from anything I've experienced before. . . . There's little time for contemplation; most of it is action."[21]

Second, *prospect theory* provides an alternative explanation (rather than simple rational optimization) of decisions made under risk or uncertainty.[22] According to this theory, decision-makers go through two phases. In the editing phase, they frame the options available and the probabilities of various outcomes associated with each option. In the evaluation phase, they assess the options and choose one. Prospect theory holds that evaluations take place by comparison with a *reference point,* which is often the status quo but might be some past or expected situation. The decision-maker asks if she or he can do better than that reference point, but the value placed on outcomes depends on how far from the reference point they are. The theory also holds that individuals *fear losses* more than they relish gains. Decision-makers are therefore often willing to forgo opportunities rather than risk a setback.

Individual decision-making thus follows an imperfect and partial kind of rationality at best. Not only do the goals of different individuals vary, but decision-makers face a series of obstacles in receiving accurate information, constructing accurate models of the world and reaching decisions that further their own goals. The rational model is at best only a simplification and must be supplemented by an understanding of individual psychological processes that affect decision-making.

optimizing Picking the very best option; contrasts with satisficing, or finding a satisfactory but less than best solution to a problem. The model of "bounded rationality" postulates that decision-makers generally satisfice rather than optimize.

satisficing The act of finding a satisfactory or "good enough" solution to a problem.

Human Security

For all the constraints on individual decision-making, it is also clear that individuals can have an enormous impact on the foreign policy direction taken by particular states. As noted on page 13, without Canada's Lester B. Pearson, the UN may have never developed the practice of peacekeeping. Pearson was also associated with the idea of "Pearsonian

---

[19] Barbara W. Tuchman, *The March of Folly: From Troy to Vietnam* (NY: Knopf/Random House, 1984). Richard B. Parker, *The Politics of Miscalculation in the Middle East* (Bloomington: Indiana UP, 1993). Andrew Bennett, *Condemned to Repetition? The Rise, Fall, and Reprise of Soviet-Russian Military Interventionism, 1973–1996* (Cambridge, MA: MIT, 1999).

[20] Herbert A. Simon, *Models of Bounded Rationality* (Cambridge, MA: MIT, 1982).

[21] *Washington Post* 5 March 1997: A22.

[22] James W. Davis, *Threats and Promises: The Pursuit of International Influence* (Baltimore: Johns Hopkins UP, 2000). Rose McDermott, *Risk-Taking in International Politics: Prospect Theory in American Foreign Policy* (Ann Arbor: U Michigan P, 1998). Barbara Farnham, ed., *Avoiding Losses/Taking Risks: Prospect Theory and International Conflict* (Ann Arbor: U Michigan P, 1994). Jack S. Levy, "Prospect Theory, Rational Choice, and International Relations," *International Studies Quarterly* 41.1 (1997): 87–112.

internationalism"—a foreign policy commitment to international economic cooperation—and North Atlantic defence and international institutions like the United
Nations.[23]

The Canadian foreign policy emphasis on human security in more recent years is a good
illustration of the importance of individuals as decision-makers. Human security became a
foreign policy priority of the Canadian government under former minister of Foreign Affairs
Lloyd Axworthy. Human security signals a departure from the strictly state-based understanding of conflict and security that tends to dominate IR. During the Cold War, there was at least
some consensus that the term *security* meant national security. Scholars of international
relations focused on causes of war, sources of threat and means of addressing those threats.
Advocates of the notion of human security argue that security should include a broader
definition of what makes people secure. In addition to thinking about violence and conflict,
scholars and policy-makers who talk about human security also focus on freedom from want
(economic and social justice issues) and political freedoms such as human rights.[24]

Some discussions of human security originated from a 1994 report by the United
Nations Development Program (UNDP) that was then picked up by policy-makers like
Axworthy. In that report, the UNDP identified seven elements of security: economic
security, food security, health security, environmental security, community security,
personal security and political security. Some of these elements can be addressed through
more traditional military means, but others require attention to questions of human rights
and sustainable economic development. Human security also demands that decision-
makers consider the specific impact of more traditional forms of conflict on particularly
vulnerable groups, such as the elderly, children and women.[25]

Axworthy made an explicit decision to shape Canadian foreign policy with an emphasis on human security. As part of its pursuit of a human security agenda, the Department of
Foreign Affairs and International Trade under Axworthy's leadership established the
Canadian Consortium on Human Security at the University of British Columbia to
provide research and policy advice on human security. Canada was also actively involved
in the convention to ban landmines as part of its commitment to promoting human security, another initiative that Axworthy made a priority. Canada also focused—via its human
security agenda—on the control of small arms and efforts to protect refugees, on addressing
issues of women and children in armed conflict and the establishment of the International
Criminal Court (see p. 286). Canada was centrally involved in the International
Commission on Intervention and State Sovereignty and the development of the principle
of "the Responsibility to Protect," which outlines both the legal and ethical grounds for
humanitarian intervention.

Axworthy is so closely associated with human security that subsequent Liberal
ministers of foreign affairs who continued his agenda are sometimes described as
"Axworthians."[26] By contrast, and in an effort to put its own stamp on Canadian foreign
policy, the Conservative government under Prime Minister Stephen Harper seems to be

---

[23] Yves Fortier, "Canada and the United Nations: A Half Century Partnership," The O.D. Skelton Memorial
Lecture, 6 March 1996, Montréal, Québec, available at http://www.international.gc.ca/department/skelton/
lecture96-en.asp.

[24] Fen Osler Hampson, *Madness in the Multitude: Human Security and World Disorder* (Toronto: Oxford UP, 2002).

[25] Fen Osler Hampson, *Madness in the Multitude* (see note above). Fen Osler Hampson, Norman Hillmer and
Maureen Appel Molot, *Canada among Nations: The Axworthy Legacy* (Toronto: Oxford UP, 2001).

[26] David Bosold and Wilfried von Bredow, "Human Security: A Radical or Rhetorical Shift in Canada's Foreign
Policy?" *International Journal* 61.4 (Autumn 2006): 829–44.

moving away from an emphasis on human security. In 2007, the government withdrew funding from the Canadian Consortium on Human Security, raised defence spending and was working to establish closer ties with the U.S.[27] What is clear from Canada's adoption of, and more recent retreat from, a human security agenda is that individuals can have an enormous impact on the foreign policy direction of any particular state.

Not even an absolute dictator, however, makes decisions all alone. State decisions result from the interactions of groups of people. Leaders surround themselves with advisers to help them think about decisions. Decision-making bodies—from committees and agency task forces to legislatures and political parties—all rely on the interactions of relatively small groups of people reasoning or arguing together. The psychology of group dynamics, discussed below, thus has great influence on the way foreign policy is formulated.

MODELS OF DECISION-MAKING: THE ORGANIZATIONAL PROCESS AND BUREAUCRATIC POLITICS MODELS

Liberal pluralist analysts (and some realists) argue that the state is more complex than is suggested by the rational actor model. From this perspective, governments are complex organizations with many departments and agencies, each charged with particular areas of responsibility. In Canada, for example, the Departments of National Defence and of Foreign Affairs and International Trade are both involved in Canada's relationship to the rest of the world, but in different aspects: one is charged with the defence of the nation and the other focuses on peace, diplomacy and trade.

Organizational Process Model

Once the state is understood to be a complex organization, the manner in which that organization generates decisions is understood quite differently. One alternative to the rational actor model is called the **organizational process model.** In this model, foreign policy decision-makers generally skip the labour-intensive process of identifying goals and alternative actions in response to every situation as it arises, relying instead on standardized responses or *standard operating procedures* for most decisions. For example, the Department of Foreign Affairs and International Trade receives upwards of a thousand reports or inquiries from its embassies around the world every day and sends out as many responses or instructions in return. The vast majority of those cables, phone calls and emails are never seen by the top decision-makers (the minister of Foreign Affairs, the minister of International Trade or the prime minister); instead, they are handled by low-level decision-makers who apply general principles—or who simply try to make the least controversial, most standardized decision. These low-level decisions may not even reflect the high-level policies adopted by top leaders, but rather have a life of their own. The organizational process model implies that much of foreign policy results from "management by muddling through."[28]

organizational process model A decision-making model in which policy-makers or lower-level officials rely largely on standardized responses or standard operating procedures.

---

[27] James Travers, "Putting Swagger into Foreign Policy" (see note 1 above). John Kirton, "Harper's Foreign Policy Success," *International Insights* 4.4 (November 28, 2006), available at http://www.igloo.org/ciia/Publications/internat.

[28] Deborah D. Avant, *Political Institutions and Military Change: Lessons from Peripheral Wars* (Ithaca, NY: Cornell UP, 1995). Jack S. Levy, "Organizational Routines and the Causes of War," *International Studies Quarterly* 30.2 (1986): 193–222.

What is distinctive about decisions generated through the organizational process model is their preprogrammed character. Departments or agencies within a government do not wait to respond to events as they happen; rather, they prepare "standard" responses that can be implemented when the need arises. These standard operating procedures allow the coordination of hundreds of individuals within an organization, but do not address new situations very well.

Bureaucratic Politics or Government Bargaining Model

bureaucratic politics model A decision-making model that sees foreign policy decisions as flowing from a bargaining process among various government agencies that have somewhat divergent interests in the outcome ("where you stand depends on where you sit"). Also called the *government bargaining model*.

Another alternative to the rational model is the **bureaucratic politics model** (also called the *government bargaining model*). This model envisions the state as a complex organization, but suggests that what is distinctive about foreign policy decision-making is the bargaining process among various government agencies with somewhat divergent interests in the outcome.[29] In 1996, the Canadian government became actively involved in supporting a ban on anti-personnel landmines, a particularly insidious weapon that annually claimed some 26 000 casualties, many of which were civilians. In Canada, the push to achieve the ban came from the Department of Foreign Affairs and International Trade (or DFAIT) under Axworthy's leadership. The Department of National Defence, by contrast, resisted the ban, arguing in part that landmines were legitimate weapons and could not be eliminated until "effective and humane alternatives" could be found. In the end, DFAIT's position was the most successful, and a Convention to Ban Anti-Personnel Landmines was signed by 122 countries in Ottawa in December, 1997.[30]

The bureaucratic politics model emphasizes not just the impact of individuals, but the way in which certain agencies or departments within government traditionally clash. An endless tug-of-war shapes the foreign policies that emerge. In an extreme example of interagency rivalry, the U.S. State Department and the CIA backed opposite sides in a civil war in Laos in 1960.

In general, bureaucracies promote policies for which their own capabilities would be effective and their power would increase. There is a saying in this model that "where you stand" on an issue "depends on where you sit" (in the bureaucratic structure). In the example of the landmines debate above, the Department of National Defence claimed that any issue concerning a weapon fell exclusively within its area of responsibility, and so DND ought to determine the policy stance of the Canadian government on that issue. DND failed in persuading the prime minister, or the government in general, to adopt its position. One can often predict just from the job titles of participants how they will argue on a policy issue. The government bargaining model pays special attention to the interagency negotiations that result from conflicts of interest between agencies of the same government. The conflicting and overlapping interests of agencies can be complex, especially in large governments such as those of the great or middle powers, with dozens of agencies that deal with international relations. And although representatives of bureaucratic agencies usually promote the interests of their own bureaucracies, sometimes heads of agencies try to appear loyal to their state leader by forgoing the interests of their own agencies.

---

[29] David A. Welch, "The Organizational Process and Bureaucratic Politics Paradigms: Retrospect and Prospect," *International Security* 17.2 (1992): 112–46.

[30] Maxwell A. Cameron, Robert J. Lawson and Brian W. Tomlin, *To Walk without Fear: The Global Movement to Ban Landmines* (Toronto: Oxford UP, 1998).

Units within agencies have similar tensions. In many countries, military services (army, navy, air force) pull in somewhat different directions, even if they ultimately unite to battle a foreign ministry. Bureaucrats working in particular units or projects become attached to them. Officials responsible for a new weapons system will lose bureaucratic turf, and perhaps their jobs, if the weaponry's development is cancelled.

Of special concern in many states is the institutional interest that military officers have in maintaining a strong military. If civilian state leaders allow officers' salaries to fall or the size of the military forces to be cut, they may face institutional resistance from the military—or in an extreme case, a military takeover of the government (see pp. 234–237). These issues were factors in attempted military coups in the Philippines, Venezuela and other states in the 1990s. Even falling short of dramatic examples such as coups, military leaders' support or criticism of their governments can be highly controversial, especially in liberal democracies where they are expected to answer to civilian leaders. In Canada, Chief of Defence Staff Rick Hillier was criticized in early 2007 for making comments deemed "highly political" and "inappropriate" when he alluded to problems of reduced defence spending under Liberal governments. In October 2006, the chief of the army in the U.K. stunned his government by criticizing its continued presence in Iraq, arguing that British troops stationed there were heightening the U.K.'s security problems.[31]

WHERE DID WE GO WRONG?
Small groups isolated from outsiders may be blind to the consequences of their actions. The murder of several Somali men by Canadian soldiers was investigated in a commission of inquiry.

---

[31] "Liberal MP Slams Hillier as Conservative 'Prop'" CBC News 17 Feb. 2007, available at http://www.cbc.ca/canada/story/2007/02/16/coderre-hillier.html. "Government stunned by Army chief's Iraq blast," *The Daily Mail* 13 Oct. 2006, available at http://www.dailymail.co.uk/pages/live/articles/news/news.html?in_article_id=410163&in_page_id=1770.

In general, bureaucratic rivalry as an influence on foreign policy challenges the notion of states as unitary actors in the international system. Such rivalries suggest that a state does not have any single set of goals—a national interest—but that its actions may result from the bargaining of subunits, each with its own set of goals.[32] Furthermore, such a perspective extends far beyond bureaucratic agencies because other substate actors have their own goals, which they seek to advance by influencing foreign policy.

Group Dynamics

Both the organizational process and bureaucratic politics models signal that the larger organization, or group, is an important consideration in understanding foreign policy decision-making. This view necessarily raises questions about the implications of group psychology for foreign policy decision-making. In one respect, groups promote rationality by balancing out the blind spots and biases of any individual. Advisers or legislative committees may force a state leader to reconsider a rash decision, and the interactions of different individuals in a group may result in the formulation of goals that more closely reflect state interests rather than individual idiosyncracies. However, group dynamics also introduce new sources of irrationality into the decision-making process. These fall into two general categories: the psychological dynamics that occur within groups, and the ways that the structure of group decision-making processes can bias outcomes.

Group Psychology The most significant psychological problem for groups is the tendency to reach decisions without accurately assessing consequences, since individual members tend to go along with ideas they think others support. This is called **groupthink.**[33] The basic phenomenon is illustrated by a simple psychology experiment. A group of six people is asked to compare the lengths of two lines projected onto a screen. When five of the people are secretly instructed to say that line A is longer—even though anyone can see that line B is actually longer—the sixth person is likely to agree with the group rather than believe her or his own eyes.

Unlike individuals, groups tend to be overly optimistic about the chances of success and are thus more willing to take risks. Participants tend to suppress doubts about questionable undertakings because everyone else seems to think an idea will work. Because groups diffuse responsibility from individuals, nobody feels accountable for actions.

In a spectacular case of groupthink, President Ronald Reagan's close friend and director of the U.S. Central Intelligence Agency (CIA), William Casey, bypassed his own agency and ran covert operations spanning three continents using the National Security Council (NSC) staff in the White House basement. The NSC sold weapons to Iran in exchange for the freedom of U.S. hostages held in Lebanon, and then used the Iranian payments to illegally fund Nicaraguan Contra rebels. The *Iran-Contra scandal* resulted when these operations, managed by an obscure NSC aide named Oliver North, became public. Because the operation was secret, the small group involved was cut off from skeptical views, and its few participants seem to have talked themselves into thinking that the operation was a smart idea. They discounted risks such as being discovered and

groupthink The tendency of individual members of a group to go along with ideas they think other group members support, leading to the adoption of decisions that conform to group sentiment but not necessarily to the available evidence (and in extreme cases, that contravene legal or ethical norms).

[32] Richard D. Anderson, Jr., Margaret G. Hermann and Charles F. Hermann, "Explaining Self-Defeating Foreign Policy Decisions: Interpreting Soviet Arms for Egypt in 1973 through Process or Domestic Bargaining Models?" (Comment and Response), *American Political Science Review* 86.3 (1992): 759–67.

[33] Irving L. Janis, *Victims of Groupthink: A Psychological Study of Foreign-Policy Decisions and Fiascoes* (Boston: Houghton Mifflin, 1972). Paul Hart, Eric K. Stern and Bengt Sundelius, eds., *Beyond Groupthink: Political Group Dynamics and Foreign Policy-Making* (Ann Arbor: U Michigan P, 1997).

exaggerated the benefits of opening channels to Iranian moderates (who proved elusive). The involvement of a top authority figure surely reassured other participants.

A U.S. Senate intelligence committee concluded in 2004 that the CIA succumbed again to groupthink when it collected and presented evidence in support of the U.S. invasion of Iraq. The report claimed that the agency had used overstated, misleading and incorrect information to convince the president, the Senate and U.S. allies that Saddam Hussein was amassing weapons of mass destruction. Analysts within the CIA ignored information that contradicted their presumptions about Iraqi weapons, and focused only on evidence that supported their conclusions. Calling it "the most devastating intelligence failure in the history of the nation," the senators who authored the report said that this case of groupthink resulted in an avoidable war, with significant loss of life on all sides. It also inflamed anti-American sentiment around the world, making the U.S. and its citizens more, rather than less, vulnerable.[34]

Decision Structure   The *structure of a decision-making process*—the rules for who is involved in making a decision, how voting is conducted and so forth—can affect the outcome, especially when a group has *indeterminate preferences* because no single alternative appeals to a majority of participants. Experienced participants in foreign-policy formation are familiar with techniques for manipulating decision-making processes to favour outcomes they prefer. A common technique is to control a group's formal *decision rules*, which include the items of business the group discusses and the order in which proposals are considered (especially important when participants are satisficing). Probably most important is the ability to *control the agenda* and thereby structure the terms of debate. A group's voting procedures also affect the choices it makes. Procedures requiring more votes for adoption tend to favour conservative approaches to policy, whereas those allowing adoption with a mere plurality of votes tend to foster more frequent changes in policy.

The structure of decision-making is reflective of the composition of a decision group. Who is represented? Often the group is composed of individuals cast in particular *roles*. (Some IR scholars treat role as a distinct level of analysis between the individual and domestic levels.) Roles can be institutional—a participant may represent a viewpoint shared by her or his particular group; for example, an intelligence agency. Different roles within particular groups can be based on factions, mediators, swing voters and so forth. One adviser might often play the role of introducing new ideas, another the role of defending the status quo, and a third the role of staying neutral so as to gain the leader's ear last.

State leaders often rely on an inner circle of advisers in making foreign policy decisions. In Canada, the formal inner circle is the Cabinet, a group of ministers which, in principle, collectively makes foreign policy decisions. Some groups depend heavily on *informal* consultations in addition to formal meetings. A leader may create a "kitchen cabinet"—a trusted group of friends who discuss policy issues with the leader even though they have no formal positions in government. For instance, Israel's Golda Meir held many such discussions at her home, sometimes literally in her kitchen. Russian president Boris Yeltsin relied on the advice of his bodyguard, who was a trusted friend. Canadian prime minister Lester B. Pearson often made foreign policy decisions together with his minister of External Affairs, Paul Martin (father of former prime minister Paul Martin), and together they informed Cabinet colleagues.[35]

---

[34] Janice Tibbetts, "CIA's 'group-think' blamed for U.S. decision to go to war," *Ottawa Citizen* 10 July 2004: A9.

[35] Kim Richard Nossal, *The Politics of Canadian Foreign Policy* (see footnote 2 in this chapter). During Pearson's time, the ministry of Foreign Affairs was called the Department of External Affairs.

Informal settings may be used in another way—to shake up formal decision groups and draw participants away from their usual bureaucratic roles. Soviet premier Leonid Brezhnev took President Richard Nixon on a speedboat ride before settling down for discussions at Brezhnev's dacha (villa) in the countryside in 1972.

Crisis Management

The difficulties in reaching rational decisions, both for individuals and groups, are heightened during a crisis.[36] *Crises* are foreign policy situations in which outcomes are very important and time frames are compressed. There is no firm boundary between crisis and routine policy-making. If a situation drags on for months or loses the dedicated attention of the top political leaders, it is no longer considered a crisis. Crisis decision-making is harder to understand and predict than normal foreign policy-making.

In a crisis, decision-makers operate under tremendous time constraints. The normal checks on unwise decisions may not operate. Communications become shorter and more stereotyped, and information that does not fit a decision-maker's expectations is more likely to be discarded simply because there is no time to consider it. In framing options, there is a tendency to restrict choices, again to save time, and a tendency to overlook creative options while focusing on the most obvious ones.

Groupthink occurs easily during crises. During the 1962 Cuban Missile Crisis, U.S. president John F. Kennedy created a small, closed group of advisers who worked together intensively for days on end, cut off from outside contact and discussion. Even the president's communication with Soviet leader Nikita Khrushchev was rerouted through Kennedy's brother Robert and the Soviet ambassador, cutting out the State Department. Recognizing the danger of groupthink, Kennedy would leave the room from time to time—removing the authority figure from the group—to encourage free discussion. Through this and other means, the group managed to identify a third option (a naval blockade) beyond their first two choices (bombing missile sites or doing nothing).

Participants in crisis decision-making are not only rushed, they experience severe psychological *stress*. As most of us have experienced personally, people do not often make decisions wisely when under stress. Stress amplifies the biases just discussed. Decision-makers tend to overestimate the hostility of adversaries and to underestimate their own hostility toward them. Dislike easily turns to hatred, and anxiety to fear. More and more information is screened out in order to come to terms with decisions being made and to restore cognitive balance. Crisis decision-making also leads to physical exhaustion. *Sleep deprivation* sets in within days as decision-makers use every hour to stay on top of a crisis. University students who have "pulled an all-nighter"—or several in a row—know that within days, people deprived of sleep lose touch with reality, experience everything as exaggerated and suffer from depression and even hallucinations. Unless decision-makers are careful about getting enough sleep, vital foreign policy decisions may be made under such conditions. In addition to sleep deprivation, physiological stress comes from drugs used by top policy-makers—often nicotine and caffeine in high doses, and sometimes alcohol.

Because of the importance of sound decision-making during crises, voters pay great attention to the psychological stability of their leaders. Before Israeli prime minister Yitzhak Rabin won a 1992 election, he faced charges that he had suffered a one-day

---

[36] Michael Brecher and Jonathan Wilkenfeld, *A Study of Crisis* (Ann Arbor: U Michigan P, 2000). David Houghton, *U.S. Foreign Policy and the Iran Hostage Crisis* (NY: Cambridge UP, 2001). James L. Richardson, *Crisis Diplomacy: The Great Powers since the Mid-Nineteenth Century* (NY: Cambridge UP, 1994). Richard Ned Lebow, *Between Peace and War: The Nature of International Crisis* (Baltimore: Johns Hopkins UP, 1981).

nervous breakdown when he'd headed the armed forces just before the 1967 war. Not so, he responded; he'd been smart enough to realize that the crisis had caused both exhaustion and acute nicotine poisoning, and he'd needed a day of rest in order to go on and make good decisions.

Whether in crisis mode or following normal routines, individual decision-makers do not operate alone. Their decisions are shaped by the government and society in which they work. Foreign policy is constrained and shaped by substate actors ranging from government agencies to political interest groups and industries.

Substate Actors

Foreign policy is shaped not only by the internal dynamics of individual and group decision-making but also by the states and societies within which decision-makers operate.

Bureaucracies The substate actors closest to the foreign policy process are the state's bureaucratic agencies maintained for developing and carrying out foreign policy. Different states maintain different foreign policy bureaucracies but share some common elements.

Virtually all states maintain a *diplomatic corps*, or *foreign service*, of diplomats working in *embassies* in foreign capitals (and in *consulates* in noncapital foreign cities), as well as diplomats who remain at home to help coordinate foreign policy. States appoint *ambassadors* as their official representatives to other states and to international organizations. Diplomatic activities are organized through a *foreign ministry* or the equivalent (for example, Foreign Affairs and International Trade Canada, the U.S. State Department or the Foreign and Commonwealth Office in the U.K., known more widely in abbreviated form as the Foreign Office).

In many democracies, some diplomats are *political appointees* who come and go with changes in government leaders (often as patronage for past political support). Others are *career diplomats*, who come up through the ranks of the foreign service and tend to outlast changes in administration. Skilled diplomats are assets that increase a state's power.

Diplomats provide much of the information that goes into developing foreign policies, but their main role is to carry out rather than create policies. Nonetheless, foreign ministry bureaucrats can often make foreign relations so routine that top

WORKING UNDER STRESS
Crisis management can take a high psychological and physiological toll. President Eduard Shevardnadze of Georgia appears to show this strain in 1992—at the beginning of years of civil war and perpetual crisis in that country. Shevardnadze, formerly Gorbachev's foreign minister, returned to lead his native Georgia when the Soviet Union dissolved. He eventually resigned from office in November 2003, following a wave of popular protest.

leaders and political appointees can come and go without greatly altering the country's relations. The national interest is served, the bureaucrats believe, by the stability of overall national goals and positions in international affairs.

Tension is common between state leaders and foreign policy bureaucrats. Career diplomats try to orient new leaders and their appointees, and to control the flow of information they receive (creating information screens). Politicians, for their part, struggle to exercise power over formal bureaucratic agencies because the latter can be too "bureaucratic" (cumbersome, overly routine, conservative) to control easily. Also, these agencies are often staffed (at least at lower levels) by career officials who may not owe loyalty to political leaders.

Sometimes, state leaders appoint a close friend or key adviser to manage the foreign policy bureaucracy. President George Bush (senior) did this with his closest friend, James Baker. Chinese leader Mao Zedong put his loyal ally, Zhou Enlai, in charge of foreign policy.

Interest Groups Foreign policy-makers operate not in a political vacuum but in the context of the political debates in their society. In all states, societal pressures influence foreign policy, although policies are aggregated and made effective through varying channels in different societies. In pluralistic democracies, interested parties influence foreign policy through interest groups and political parties. Similar influences occur in dictatorships, though less visibly. Thus foreign policies adopted by states generally reflect a process of domestic coalition formation.[37] Of course, international factors also have a strong influence on domestic politics.[38]

interest groups Coalitions of people who share a common interest in the outcome of some political issue and who organize themselves to try to influence the outcome.

Interest groups are coalitions of people who share a common interest in the outcome of some political issue and who organize themselves to try to influence the outcome. For instance, French farmers have a big stake in international negotiations in the European Union (which subsidizes agriculture) and in world trade talks (which set agricultural tariffs). The farmers exert political pressure on the French government through long-established and politically sophisticated associations and organizations. They lobby for desired legislation and contribute to politicians' campaigns. More dramatically, when their interests have been threatened in the past, French farmers have turned out in large numbers across the country to block roads, stage violent street demonstrations and threaten to grind the national economy to a halt unless the government adopted their position. Similarly (but often less dramatically), interest groups form around businesses, labour unions, churches, veterans, senior citizens, members of an occupation or citizens concerned about an issue such as the environment.

Lobbying is the process of talking with legislators or officials to influence their decisions on some set of issues. Three important elements that go into successful lobbying are the ability to gain a hearing with busy officials, the ability to present cogent arguments for one's case and the ability to trade favours in return for positive action on an issue. These favours—legal and illegal—range from campaign contributions through dinners at nice restaurants and trips to golf resorts to securing illicit sexual liaisons and paying bribes.

---

[37] Tony Smith, *Foreign Attachments: The Power of Ethnic Groups in the Making of American Foreign Policy* (Cambridge, MA: Harvard UP, 2000). Helen Milner, *Interests, Institutions, and Information: Domestic Politics and International Relations* (Princeton, NJ: Princeton UP, 1997). Peter B. Evans, Harold K. Jacobson and Robert D. Putnam, eds., *Double-Edged Diplomacy: International Bargaining and Domestic Politics* (Berkeley: U California P, 1993). Bruce Bueno de Mesquita and David Lalman, *War and Reason: Domestic and International Imperatives* (New Haven, CT: Yale UP, 1992). Jack L. Snyder, *Myths of Empire: Domestic Politics and International Ambition* (Ithaca, NY: Cornell UP, 1991).

[38] Elizabeth Riddell-Dixon, *The Domestic Mosaic: Interest Groups and Canadian Foreign Policy* (Toronto: Canadian Institute of International Affairs, 1985). Peter Gourevitch, "The Second Image Reversed: International Sources of Domestic Politics," *International Organization* 32.4 (1978): 881–911.

Focus on Canadian Scholarship

Numerous scholars focus on questions of foreign policy in various Canadian universities. **Kim Richard Nossal,** at Queen's University, has focused on Canadian and Australian foreign and defence policy as well as humanitarian intervention and international sanctions. At the University of Alberta, **Tom Keating** studies Canada and world order, foreign policy and internationalism, and public opinion and foreign policy. **Michael Tucker**, at Mount Allison University, examines Canadian foreign policy and Canada and the new world order. **Peggy Falkenheim Meyer,** at Simon Fraser University, works on comparative foreign policy with a focus on Russian relations with Japan, China and the Korean peninsula. Also at Simon Fraser, **Alex Moens** focuses on U.S. foreign policy and foreign policy of the European Union. At the University of Laval, **Louis Balthazar** has worked on U.S. foreign policy. At York University, **Ann Denholm Crosby** has examined the Ottawa Process to ban landmines as well as defence decision-making. **Steven Holloway,** at St. Francis Xavier University, has explored Canadian foreign policy and defining the national interest. **Don Barry,** at the University of Calgary, has explored the history of Canada's Department of External Affairs as well as Canada-U.S. relations. **Stéphane Paquin** of the University of Sherbrooke examines Canadian and Québec foreign policies. At the Canadian Forces College, **Christopher Spearin** researches non-state actors, mercenaries, the privatization of security and Canadian foreign and defence policy, and his colleague, **Pierre Pahlavi,** is interested in public diplomacy. At the University of Saskatchewan,

Kalowatie Deonandan examines U.S. foreign policy and its impact on Canadian policy. **George A. MacLean,** at the University of Manitoba, has explored Canada-U.S. relations as well as U.S. president Bill Clinton's foreign policy in Russia. At the University of Winnipeg, **Samantha Arnold** researches questions around the disciplinary practices of U.S. foreign policy and Canadian public diplomacy. Also at the University of Winnipeg, **Tanya Narozhna** specializes in human security and terrorism. At Dalhousie University, **Dennis Stairs** has explored foreign and defence policy as well as Canada-U.S. relations, and his colleague **Brian Bow** examines Canada-U.S. relations and Canadian diplomacy. **Stephen Clarkson** of the University of Toronto examines Canada within a North American framework as well as the specific foreign (and domestic) policies of Pierre Elliott Trudeau. Also at the University of Toronto, **David Welch** has developed a theory of Foreign Policy Change, and **Beth A. Fischer** has written on U.S. foreign policy during the Reagan era. **Andrew Cooper,** at the University of Waterloo, has focused on Canada as a middle power and Canadian diplomacy. **Barry Bartman** of the University of Prince Edward Island examines the foreign policies of small states. At the University of Western Ontario, **Elizabeth Riddell-Dixon** examines interest groups and Canadian foreign policy as well as the democratization of foreign policy decision-making and Canadian policy toward the United Nations. Also at Western, **Erika Simpson** focuses on Canadian policies of humanitarian intervention and principles of liberal internationalism in Canadian foreign and defence policies.

In many states, corruption is a major problem in governmental decision-making (see pp. 473–475), and interest groups may induce government officials by illegal means to take certain actions.

Ethnic groups within one state often form interest groups concerned about their ancestral nation outside that state. Many members of ethnic groups, or diaspora communities, feel strong emotional ties to their relatives in other countries; because the rest of the population generally does not care about such issues one way or the other, even a small ethnic group can have considerable influence on policy toward a particular country. Such ethnic ties are emerging as a powerful foreign policy influence. The effect is especially strong in the United States, which is ethnically mixed and has a pluralistic, interest-group form of democracy. For example, Cuban Americans organize to influence U.S. policy toward Cuba, as do Greek Americans on Greece, Jewish Americans on Israel and African Americans on Africa. Although ethnic groups do not exert the same organized pressure in countries such as Canada, they sometimes try to influence foreign

MAKING THEMSELVES HEARD
Foreign policies are affected by the pulling and tugging of various domestic interest groups. European farmers and truckers have tried to influence policies by repeatedly blocking rail and road traffic. Here, Belgian truckers block a border crossing to Germany, 2000.

policy or are called upon by government for advice and input. For example, after the massacre of pro-democracy protesters in Beijing's Tiananmen Square in June 1989, the Department of External Affairs assembled members of the Canadian Chinese community along with Chinese scholars, businesspeople and nongovernmental organization (NGO) representatives to help the Canadian government determine a policy response to the massacre.[39] Ethnic communities can also pull decision-makers in different directions. In the summer of 2006, conflict between Israel and Hezbollah, located in Lebanon, led to lobbying by both Jewish and Lebanese diaspora communities in Canada. The Canadian government issued statements calling Israeli air strikes against Lebanon "measured" while at the same time mounting a massive evacuation campaign of some 15 000 individuals from Lebanon.[40]

Interest groups have goals and interests that may or may not coincide with the national interest as a whole (if indeed such an interest can be identified). As with bureaucratic agencies, the view of the state as a unitary actor can be questioned. The head of General Motors once said that "what's good for General Motors is good for the country, and vice versa." This is not self-evident. Nonetheless, defenders of interest group politics argue that while various interest groups push and pull in different directions, ultimate decisions generally reflect the interests of society as a whole.

Public Opinion

public opinion In IR, the range of views on foreign policy issues held by the citizens of a state.

Interest groups and other substate actors often seek to influence **public opinion**—the range of views on foreign policy issues held by the citizens of a state. Public opinion has greater influence on foreign policy in democracies than in authoritarian governments. Even dictators must pay attention to what citizens think. No government can rule by force alone: it needs legitimacy to survive. It must convince people to accept (if not to

---

[39] Bernard M. Frolic, *Canada and the People's Republic of China: Twenty Years of a Bilateral Relationship 1970–1990* (Ottawa: Lowe-Martin, 1992).

[40] "Lebanon Exodus: The Largest-Ever Evacuation of Canadian Citizens," *Foreign Affairs and International Trade Canada,* n.d., available at http://geo.international.gc.ca/cip-pic/pdf/Lebanon%20Exodus.pdf. "Middle East in Crisis: Timeline of Recent Events," CBC News 14 Aug. 2006, available at http://www.cbc.ca/news/background/middleeast-crisis. See also Elizabeth Ridell-Dixon, "Domestic Demographics and Canadian Foreign Policy" (Calgary: Canadian Defence and Foreign Affairs Institute, 2003), available at http://www.cdfai.org/PDF/Domestic%20Demographics%20and%20Canadian%20Foreign%20Policy.pdf.

like) its policies, because ultimately, policies are carried out by ordinary people—soldiers, workers, petty bureaucrats.

Due to a need for public support, even authoritarian governments expend great effort on *propaganda*—the public promotion of their official line—to win support for foreign policies. States use television, newspapers and other media in this effort. For instance, when China invited U.S. president Richard Nixon to visit in 1972, the Chinese government mounted a major propaganda campaign to explain to its people that the United States was not so bad after all. In many countries, the state owns or controls major mass media such as television and newspapers, mediating the flow of information to its citizens; however, new information technologies with multiple channels are beginning to make this difficult.

In democracies, where governments must stand for election, public opinion is even more important. An unpopular war can force a leader or party from office, or a popular war can help secure a government's mandate to continue in power, as happened to Margaret Thatcher in Britain after the 1982 Falkland Islands War. A key influence on public opinion is the content of scenes appearing on television: U.S. soldiers were sent to Somalia to assist in relief efforts in 1992 after television news showed the heartrending results of civil war and famine there. Later, television news showed an American soldier's body being dragged through the streets by members of a Somali faction after a deadly firefight that killed 18 U.S. soldiers, and public opinion in the U.S. shifted quickly against the Somalia operation.

Journalists serve as the gatekeepers of information passing from foreign policy elites to the public. The media and government often conflict, because of the traditional role of the press as a watchdog and critic of government actions and powers. The media try to uncover and publicize that which the government wants to hide, especially in situations involving scandal. Foreign policy decision-makers often rely on the media for information about foreign affairs; many world leaders turn to media outlets such as CNN to find out about events going on around the world.

Yet the media, in turn, depends on the government for information; the size and resources of foreign policy bureaucracies dwarf those of the press. This advantage gives the government great power to *manipulate* journalists by feeding them information in order to shape the news and influence public opinion. Government decision-makers can create dramatic stories in foreign relations—through summit meetings, crises, actions and so forth. Bureaucrats can also *leak* secret information to the press in order to support their own point of view and win bureaucratic battles. Finally, the military and the press have a running battle about journalists' access to military operations; for instance, in the invasion of Grenada and the Gulf War, U.S. military censors limited media coverage. In both Afghanistan and Iraq, militaries have adopted the practice of "embedding" journalists with particular military units. This provides them with access to information but also raises questions about whether their objectivity has been compromised.[41]

In democracies, where the flow of information and opinions is not tightly restricted by the state, public opinion can be accurately measured through *polling*—analyzing the responses of a sample group to questionnaires to infer the opinions of a larger population. This is impossible to do in societies where secret police monitor any expressions of opposition to state policies, but in societies where individuals feel free to speak out, polling has developed into an important part of the foreign policy-making process. In Canada, some of the larger polling firms include Ipsos-Reid, Decima Research, Ekos and Angus Reid, among others.

---

[41] See Graham Thomson, "Behind the wire: Embedded journalists in Afghanistan are expected to be part of the team— whether they like it or not," *The Ottawa Citizen* 12 May 2007: B2.

Occasionally a foreign policy issue is decided directly by a referendum of the entire citizenry, a tradition that is strong in countries such Switzerland and Denmark, for example.[42] In 2005, referendums in France and the Netherlands rejected a proposed constitution for the European Union, despite the support of major political leaders for the change (see p. 394).

Even in the most open democracies, states do not merely *respond* to public opinion. Decision-makers enjoy some autonomy to make their own choices, and they are pulled in various directions by bureaucracies and interest groups, whose views often conflict with the direction favoured by public opinion at large. Furthermore, public opinion is seldom unified on any policy, and sophisticated polling can show that particular segments of the population (regions of the country, genders, income groups, races, etc.) often differ in their perceptions of foreign policy issues—so a politician may respond to the opinion of one constituency rather than the whole population. Public opinion varies considerably over time on many foreign policy issues. States use propaganda or try to manipulate the media to keep public opinion from diverging too much from state policies.

In democracies, public opinion generally has *less effect on foreign policy than on domestic policy*. National leaders traditionally have additional latitude to make decisions in the international realm. This derives from the special need of states to act in a unified way to function effectively in the international system, as well as from the traditions of secrecy and diplomacy that remove IR from the realm of ordinary domestic politics. In Canada in 1982, for example, a public outcry erupted over news that the Canadian government planned to allow the United States Air Force to test cruise missiles over Canadian territory. Public protests, rallies and opinion polls that showed the majority of Canadians were opposed could not alter the Trudeau government's plans to go ahead with the testing.[43] In the nuclear age, IR was further distanced from everyday political life in the nuclear states by the public's willingness to trust experts and officials to deal with the technical and frightening issues of nuclear strategy. Over time, however, peace movements have sometimes pushed governments toward disarmament (see "Peace Movements" on pp. 99–100).

In the case of Japan, public opinion is a major political force restraining the government's military spending, its commitment of military forces beyond Japan's borders and especially the development of nuclear weapons (which is within Japan's technical abilities). The ruling party has slowly but steadily pushed to increase Japan's military spending and allowed Japanese military forces to expand their role modestly (in the 1980s, to patrol Asian sea lanes vital to Japanese trade; in the 1990s, to participate in UN peacekeeping operations; and more recently to send logistical and noncombat military personnel to Iraq in 2003 as part of the U.S.-led coalition). Repeatedly, these efforts have been slowed or rebuffed by strong public opinion against the military. In Japan, people remember the horrible consequences of militarism in the 1930s and World War II, culminating in the nuclear bombings of 1945. They are suspicious of any increase in the size or role of military forces, and are dead set against Japan's having nuclear weapons. In this case, public opinion constrains the state's conduct of foreign policy, and has slowed the pace of change.

The *attentive public* in a democracy is that minority of the population that stays informed about international issues. This segment varies with any given issue, but there is a core of people who care in general about foreign affairs and follow them closely. This is the element of the public that, in many ways, governments most seek to influence and

---

[42] John T. Rourke, Richard P. Hiskes and Cyrus Ernesto Zirakzadeh, *Direct Democracy and International Politics: Deciding International Issues through Referendums* (Boulder, CO: Rienner, 1992).

[43] Kim Richard Nossal, *The Politics of Canadian Foreign Policy* (see footnote 2 in this chapter).

secure the consent of for foreign policy decisions.[44] The most active members of the attentive public on foreign affairs constitute a foreign policy *elite*—people with power and influence who affect foreign policy. This elite includes people within governments as well as outsiders such as businesspeople, journalists, lobbyists and professors of political science. Public opinion polls show that elite opinions sometimes (but not always) differ considerably from those of the general population, and sometimes even from those of the government.[45]

Governments sometimes adopt foreign policies for the specific purpose of generating public approval and hence gaining domestic legitimacy.[46] This is the case when a government undertakes a war or foreign military intervention at a time of domestic difficulty, to distract attention and gain public support—taking advantage of the **rally 'round the flag syndrome** (the public's increased support for government leaders during wartime, at least in the short term). Citizens who would ordinarily criticize their government's policies on education or health care will often refrain from criticism when the government is at war and the lives of the nation's soldiers are on the line. In the U.S., President Bush (senior) enjoyed extremely high popularity ratings during both the 1989 Panama and the 1991 Gulf wars, as did President Bush (junior) during the war in Afghanistan in late 2001.

However, wars that go on too long, or are not successful, can turn public opinion against the government and even lead to a popular uprising to overthrow the government. In Argentina in 1982, the military government led the country into war with Britain over the Falkland/Malvinas Islands. At first, Argentineans rallied around the flag, but after losing the war they rallied around the cause of getting rid of their military government, replacing it with a new civilian government that prosecuted the former leaders. In 2006, U.S. president Bush's popularity, which had soared early in the Iraq War, plummeted as the war dragged on and voters threw his party out of power in Congress.

> **rally 'round the flag syndrome** The public's increased support for government leaders during wartime, at least in the short term.

MODELS OF DECISION-MAKING: ELITE ANALYSIS AND INSTRUMENTAL MARXISM

Another alternative model of decision-making focuses on the class or elite background of decision-makers (called either the **elite model** or **instrumental Marxism,** a more critical variant). Elite theorists and instrumental Marxists argue that decision-makers within governments or state agencies share a common business or class background, and that their decisions will reflect their business or class interests. For instance, European imperialism benefited banks and big business, which made huge profits from exploiting cheap labour and resources in overseas colonies.

Proponents of this perspective argue that it not only explains large processes, such as imperialism, but also specific foreign policy decisions. In 1951 in Guatemala, the election

> **elite model** (or its more critical variant, **instrumental Marxism**) The view that decision-makers within governments or state agencies share a common business or class background, and that their decisions will reflect their business or class interests.

[44] Noam Chomsky, "The Manufacture of Consent," *The Chomsky Reader* (NY: Pantheon Books, 1987).

[45] Richard Sobel, *The Impact of Public Opinion on U.S. Foreign Policy since Vietnam* (NY: Oxford UP, 2001). Ole R. Holsti, *Public Opinion and American Foreign Policy* (Ann Arbor: U Michigan P, 1996). Shoon Murray, *Anchors against Change: American Opinion Leaders' Beliefs after the Cold War* (Ann Arbor: U Michigan P, 1996). Miroslav Nincic, "A Sensible Public: New Perspectives on Popular Opinion and Foreign Policy," *Journal of Conflict Resolution* 36.4 (1992): 772–89.

[46] T. Clifton Morgan and Kenneth N. Bickers, "Domestic Discontent and the External Use of Force," *Journal of Conflict Resolution* 36.1 (1992): 25–52. Bruce Bueno de Mesquita, Randolph M. Siverson and Gary Woller, "War and the Fate of Regimes: A Comparative Analysis," *American Political Science Review* 86.3 (1992): 638–46.

of a socialist president, Jacobo Arbenz, caused some alarm in the United Fruit Company (UFC), a U.S.-based company with extensive land holdings in Guatemala. Arbenz had pledged his government to buy back Guatemalan land from UFC. At that time, John Foster Dulles was the U.S. Secretary of State and his brother Allen Dulles was the head of the Central Intelligence Agency (CIA). Before becoming secretary of state, John Foster Dulles had represented the United Fruit Company through his former law firm, and Allen Dulles had served on the company's board of trustees. For elite theorists and instrumental Marxists, it was the particular interest in UFC held by the Dulles brothers that explains the June 1954 U.S.-sponsored coup in Guatemala, a coup that used American planes to bomb the capital, and CIA-trained Guatemalans as personnel. The Arbenz government was overthrown, and the military dictatorship that replaced it quickly abandoned any plans for land reform.[47]

The Military-Industrial Complex

During the Cold War, Marxists and elite theorists frequently argued that U.S. foreign policy and that of its Western allies were driven by the profit motive of arms manufacturers.[48] Even a U.S. president expressed concern about the **military-industrial complex,** a huge, interlocking network of governmental agencies, industrial corporations and research institutes working together to supply a nation's military forces. Because of the domestic political clout of these actors, the complex was a very powerful influence on foreign policy in *both* the United States and the Soviet Union during the Cold War. Some of that influence remains, though it has diminished. The military-industrial complex was a response to the growing importance of technology (nuclear weapons, electronics, etc.) and logistics in Cold War military planning.

States at war have long harnessed their economic and technological might for the war effort. During the Cold War, military procurement occurred on a massive scale in "peacetime" as the superpowers raced to develop new high-technology weapons. This race created a special role for scientists and engineers in addition to the more traditional role of industries that produce war materials. In response to the launch of the Soviet satellite *Sputnik* in 1957, the United States increased spending on research and development and created new science education programs. By 1961, President Dwight Eisenhower warned in his farewell speech that the military-industrial complex was gaining "unwarranted influence" in U.S. society and that militarization could erode democracy in the United States. The threat to democracy was that the interests of the military-industrial complex in the arms race conflicted with the interests of ordinary citizens in peace, while the size of the complex gave it more political clout than ordinary citizens could muster.

The complex encompasses a variety of constituencies, each of which has an interest in military spending. *Corporations* that produce goods for the military profit from government contracts, as do military *officers* whose careers advance by building bureaucratic empires around new weapons systems. Universities and scientific institutes that receive military research contracts—a major source of funding for scientists in Russia and the United States—also profit.

military-industrial complex A huge, interlocking network of governmental agencies, industrial corporations and research institutes, all working together to promote and benefit from military spending.

---

[47] Nick Cullather, *Secret History: The CIA's Classified Account of Its Operations in Guatemala, 1952–1954* (Palo Alto, CA: Stanford UP, 1999). Walter LaFeber, *Inevitable Revolutions: The United States in Central America,* 2nd ed. (NY: Norton, 1993). Stephen Schlesinger and Stephen Kinzer, *Bitter Fruit: The Untold Story of the American Coup in Guatemala* (NY: Doubleday, 1982).

[48] V. Konobeyev, "The Capitalist Economy and the Arms Race," *International Affairs* [Moscow] 8 (1982): 28–48.

Subcontractors and parts suppliers for big weapons projects are usually spread around the country, so that local citizens and politicians join the list of constituents benefiting from military spending. This is true in the U.S. as well as in Canada. Recently, a similar phenomenon has emerged in the European Union, where weapons development programs have been parcelled out to several European states. A new fighter jet is less likely to be cancelled if one country gets the contract for the wings, another for the engines and so forth.

Executives in military industries, as the people who best understand their field, are often appointed as government officials responsible for military procurement decisions for a time and then return to their companies—a practice called the *revolving door*. In democracies, military industries also try to influence public opinion through *advertising* that ties their products to patriotic themes. In the U.S., military industries also give generous *campaign contributions* to national politicians who vote on military budgets, and sometimes bribes to Pentagon officials as well.[49] Changes in Canadian electoral laws in 2003 put tight restrictions on the amount that any corporation, union or individual can donate to a single political party, thus limiting the kind of influence that can be exerted through campaign financing.

When the Cold War ended, the military-industrial complex in both superpowers endured cutbacks in military budgets. In Russia, military industries formed the backbone of a political faction seeking to slow economic reforms and continue government subsidies to state-owned industries. The faction succeeded in replacing Russia's reformist prime minister with an industrial manager in late 1992. In the United States, meanwhile, the lingering influence of the military-industrial complex may help explain why Congress kept funding certain Cold War weapons (such as the Seawolf submarine and B-2 bomber) after their purpose seemingly disappeared.

Although the Canadian arms industry is not as large as that found in the United States or Russia, Canada's role as a producer of weapons may impact on some foreign policy decisions, and has also attracted criticism. The Canadian Association of Defence and Security Industries estimates that defence industries in Canada generate over $7 billion in revenues, approximately 30 percent of which is from exports to the United States and 37 percent from exports to the rest of the world. Critics charge that Canadian interest in projects like the U.S. National Missile Defense plan stems more from the benefits derived to the defence industry than any real impact on national security (estimated at between one-quarter to over $1 billion annually).[50] Although no scholarly studies have yet been conducted to test this relationship, such benefits suggest that the military-industrial complex in Canada may exert some leverage on foreign policy decisions.

Canada's involvement in the arms industry also draws criticisms from other sources. The human rights organization Amnesty International, for example, criticized the Canadian government in 2003 for exporting arms to a number of authoritarian and military regimes. In one case, helicopters made in Canada were exported to the United States, which then sent them on to Colombia. Under federal guidelines, the government would not have allowed the helicopters to be sold directly to Colombia because of its human rights abuses, but the sale was permitted because the final destination appeared to be the United States.[51]

---

[49] James Der Derian, *Virtuous War: Mapping the Military-Industrial-Media-Entertainment Network* (Boulder, CO: Westview, 2001). Jennifer Washburn, "When Money Talks, Congress Listens," *Bulletin of the Atomic Scientists* 53.4 (July-Aug. 1997): 40.

[50] Canadian Association of Defence and Security Industries, "A Defence and Security Industrial Strategy for Canada," CADSI Policy Backgrounder, n.d., available at https://www.defenceandsecurity.ca/public/docs/2007/April/CADSI%20Policy%20Document%20-%20Industrial%20Strategy%20for%20Canada.pdf. Stephen James-Kerr, "Meet Canada The Global Arms Dealer," *Znet*, 23 May 2003.

[51] Amnesty International, *A Catalogue of Failures: G8 Arms Exports and Human Right Violations* 19 May 2003, available at http://web.amnesty.org/pages/ENG-IOR300032003.

Making and Writing Foreign Policy

Some critical theory approaches to international relations examine foreign policies not to determine how particular foreign policies are made, but to explore what foreign policy "makes possible" for states. From this perspective, for example, it is not simply that the military-industrial complex exerts influence on state decision-makers to make particular choices. Rather, the depiction of some states or actors as dangerous, backward or barbarous makes certain foreign policy choices possible (such as deterrence, intervention, imperialism) and affects how we understand particular states, like the United States.

This approach suggests, for example, that there was nothing natural or inevitable about the U.S. treating the Soviet Union as a declared enemy in the post–World War II period. In fact, much evidence existed to suggest that the Soviet Union had largely defensive rather than offensive foreign policy goals. But understanding or depicting the Soviet Union as a particularly deadly enemy permitted not only a massive military buildup and the suppression of dissent (during the McCarthy era of the 1950s), but also provided the legitimacy for the U.S. to become hegemonic over the Western international system. By this view, then, when the Cold War collapsed, the United States went in search of new enemies: drugs, rogue states and "madmen" like Saddam Hussein.[52]

This approach to foreign policy analysis is dramatically different from the rational actor model, operational processes model, bureaucratic politics model and even the elite and instrumental Marxist model. It argues that we should question, or deconstruct, our taken-for-granted assumptions about foreign policies, and that the construction of some groups or individuals as "enemies" tells us as much about who "we" are in world politics as it does about those purported enemies.

Important work on foreign policy from this perspective since the September 11 attacks on the U.S. has focused on the surveillance of borders and the targeting of potential terrorists. This work examines how efforts aimed at promoting the "security" of, for example, Canadian citizens, also ultimately "secures" a particular identity of what it is to be a Canadian citizen. Given the racially biased focus of most border surveillance mechanisms, the argument can be made that "Canadianness" is discursively constructed through these policies as white, Western and Christian, whereas threats to Canada and "Canadianness" come from foreigners (both outside and within Canada) who are non-white, non-Western and Muslim. This impacts who is targeted through border control policies and who "we" understand to be dangerous. By this view it is no coincidence that noncitizens held under Security Certificates (see "The Changing World Order" box in this chapter) and Canadian citizens arrested under Canada's 2001 Anti-Terrorism Act (one Ottawa man in 2004 and 18 Toronto-area men in 2006) are all Muslim and persons of colour.[53]

---

[52] David Campbell, *Writing Security: United States Foreign Policy and the Politics of Identity* (Minneapolis: U Minnesota P, 1992). Roxanne Lynn Doty, *Imperial Encounters: The Politics of Representation in North-South Relations* (Minneapolis: U Minnesota P, 1996). David Mutimer, *The Weapons State: Proliferation and the Framing of Security* (Boulder, CO: Rienner, 2000). Charles E. Nathanson, "The Social Construction of the Soviet Threat: A Study in the Politics of Representation," *Alternatives* XIII (1988): 443–83.

[53] Nandita Sharma, "White Nationalism, Illegality and Imperialism: Border Controls as Ideology," in Krista Hunt and Kim Rygiel, eds., *(En)Gendering the War on Terror: War Stories and Camouflaged Politics* (Aldershot: Ashgate Publishing, 2006) 121–143. Kim Rygiel, "Protecting and Proving Identity: the Biopolitics of Waging War through Citizenship in the Post-9/11 Era," in *Ibid.* 147–167.

The Changing World Order

Foreign and Domestic Policy/Us and Them/Security versus Liberty

World order and domestic politics affect each other. The war on terrorism, for example, has been aimed at both external and internal terror threats. While countries launched offensive military operations in other nations such as Afghanistan and Iraq, they also focused on monitoring and in some cases detaining and arresting potential terror suspects within their borders, sometimes resulting in violations of individual rights and freedoms in the pursuit of security. Canada has seen several such high-profile cases. One involved Maher Arar, a Syrian-born Canadian who was arrested while travelling through the United States in 2002. He was identified by U.S. authorities through intelligence provided by the RCMP, information which later proved to be incorrect. He was deported to Syria, where he endured torture and abuse until he was returned to Canada over a year later. Arar's name was eventually cleared, and in 2007 he received a formal apology from Prime Minister Stephen Harper as well as financial compensation stemming from Canada's role in his ordeal.

In another case, a joint RCMP and Citizenship and Immigration Canada investigation dubbed "Project Thread" resulted in the August 2003 arrests of 24 suspected terrorists, all of whom were living in Canada on student visas. These suspects were eventually released without being formally charged, but most were also deported to Pakistan, their country of origin, where they feared further detention and possibly torture because of the attention drawn to them in Canada where their names were never publicly cleared.

The Project Thread detainees were held on what is called a "Security Certificate"—a seldom-used legal device that the Canadian government began to employ with some frequency after the September 11 attacks on the U.S. Security certificates are used to remove a person considered a security threat to Canada; they can be used only against foreign nationals or permanent residents, not Canadian citizens. Those subjected to a Security Certificate can be held indefinitely without being formally charged. They are not entitled to review or hear the evidence against them, thus making cross-examination of witnesses or evidence impossible.

Proponents of Security Certificates argue that they are a necessary safeguard for national security. Critics argue that they are a violation, among other things, of an individual's right to a fair trial. In February 2007, the Supreme Court of Canada ruled unanimously that Security Certificates were unconstitutional but permitted the Canadian government a year to revise its anti-terrorism legislation. Most of those still held on Security Certificates were released after the Supreme Court decision, but some still face possible deportation. As with Arar and the Project Thread suspects, Canadian lawyers have raised concerns that these individuals will face torture and abuse if they are deported.

The changing world order affects not only a country's foreign policy orientation but also its domestic laws. These examples provide a controversial illustration of that relationship for critical theorists pointing to questions of identity and the discursive construction of "citizens" and "enemies." They also raise a perennial debate in IR between realists and liberals: What is the proper balance between security and liberty?

The attempt to explain foreign policy in a general and *theoretical* way has met with only limited success. In varied ways, the approaches described in this chapter can all be equally persuasive, depending on the policy and the circumstances. Foreign policy is a complex outcome of a complex process. It results from the struggle of competing themes, competing domestic interests and competing government agencies. No single individual, agency or guiding principle determines the outcome. Yet foreign policy does achieve a certain overall coherence. States do form foreign policy on an issue or toward a region; it is not just an incoherent collection of decisions and actions taken from time to time. Out of the turbulent internal processes of foreign policy formation come relatively coherent interests and policies.

Of course, those aggregate state interests and policies frequently come into conflict with the interests and policies of other states. Such conflicts are the subject of the next chapter.

Thinking Critically

1. India and Pakistan are neighbours and enemies. Given the problems of misperception and bias in foreign policy decision-making, what steps would you propose that each government adopt to keep these problems from interfering in the rational pursuit of national interests?

2. Sometimes aggressive international actions are attributed to a "madman," such as Iraq's Saddam Hussein or Nazi Germany's Adolf Hitler. Do you agree that such leaders (each of whose actions severely damaged his state's well-being) must be "mad"? What other factors could account for their actions? How else might the charge of "madness" be understood?

3. Imagine a sudden, unexpected crisis caused by an event such as the explosion of a nuclear weapon (of unknown origin) in Moscow. Given the dangers inherent in crisis decision-making, what steps could the leaders of affected states take to prevent the situation from spinning out of control? Which of these steps might be taken *before* any crisis occurred, to prepare for a future crisis?

4. Traditionally, foreign policy elites have faced only sporadic pressure from mass public opinion. Is the role of television or the internet changing this relationship?

5. How do states balance their foreign and domestic policy concerns? Choose a particular foreign policy with which you are familiar and consider its impact on domestic policies.

Chapter Summary

- Foreign policies are strategies governments use to guide their actions toward other states. The foreign policy process is the set of procedures and structures that states use to arrive at and implement foreign policy decisions.

- In the rational actor model of decision-making, officials choose the action whose consequences best help to meet the state's established goals.

- The actions of individual decision-makers are influenced by their personalities, values and beliefs as well as by common psychological factors that diverge from rationality. These factors include misperception, selective perception, emotional biases and cognitive biases (including the effort to reduce cognitive dissonance).

- *Human security* is a foreign policy emphasis formed by particular individual decision-makers within the Canadian government and which illustrates the kinds of impacts individuals can have on foreign policy decisions.

- Another view of decision-making focuses not on the actions of individuals, but sees governments as complex organizations with multiple departments and agencies charged with various features of a country's foreign policy. In the organizational process model, decisions result from routine administrative procedures, and in the government bargaining (or bureaucratic politics) model, decisions result from negotiations among governmental agencies with different interests in the outcome.

- These models signal that foreign policy decisions are also influenced by the psychology of groups (including "groupthink"), the procedures used to reach decisions and the roles of participants.

- During crises, the potential for misperception and error are amplified.

- Struggles over the direction of foreign policy are common between professional bureaucrats and politicians, as well as among government agencies.

- Domestic constituencies (interest groups) have distinct interests in foreign policies and often organize politically to promote those interests.

- Public opinion influences governments' foreign policy decisions (more so in democracies than in authoritarian states), but governments also manipulate public opinion.

- An elite or instrumental Marxist model of decision-making focuses on the ways in which foreign policies tend to reflect the interests of particular business or capitalist class interests.

- Another critical approach focuses on the interests of military-industrial complexes consisting of military industries and others with an interest in high military spending.

- Some critical approaches to foreign policy do not explore how policy is made, but rather what particular policies "make possible" for states; this approach tends to deconstruct foreign policies and the many taken-for-granted assumptions associated with them.

Key Terms

foreign policy process   130
rational actor model   132
misperceptions and selective
    perceptions   135
information screens   135
optimizing   137
satisficing   137
organizational process model   139

bureaucratic politics model   140
groupthink   142
interest groups   146
public opinion   148
rally 'round the flag syndrome   151
elite model (instrumental Marxism)   151
military-industrial complex   152

Research Navigator Question

Research Navigator.com
RESOURCES FOR COLLEGE RESEARCH ASSIGNMENTS

Using Research Navigator™, find article AN 15113448 by Jennifer Welsh. This article explores the status of Canada as a middle power. Summarize (in two paragraphs) Welsh's argument about why Canada should aspire to an active internationalism, then find one or two newspaper articles that either confirm or refute this view.

Weblinks

The following links are a sampling of government departments, journals and research centres that are concerned with questions of foreign policy:

Canadian Foreign Policy:
http://www.carleton.ca/npsia/cfpj

Canadian Institute of International Affairs:
http://www.ciia.org

Foreign Affairs and International Trade Canada:
http://www.international.gc.ca/index.aspx

Foreign Policy in Focus:
http://www.fpif.org/index.html

U.S. Department of State:
http://www.state.gov

International Conflict

6

Israeli security wall under construction, 2002.

THE WARS OF THE WORLD

Although the frequency of war has been decreasing in recent years, it remains a very important area of study in IR. This chapter will focus on current and historical wars to explore the causes of international conflicts.

Of the roughly 12 wars in progress in 2007, the largest are in Iraq, western Sudan (Darfur) and Afghanistan. All but Chechnya are in the global South, and all but Colombia are in a zone of active fighting spanning parts of Africa, South Asia and the Middle East.

In five smaller zones, with the exception of Colombia, dozens of wars in recent decades have ended. Some of the countries in these zones still face difficult postwar years, with the possibility of sliding back into violence as Sri Lanka did in 2006–2007 after a 2002 ceasefire had held for several years. In southern Sudan, a 2005 peace agreement lasted more than a year before a battle killed hundreds. However, most peace agreements in the world's postwar zones are holding up.

War and other violent actions taken in international conflicts are aimed at settling conflicts on favourable terms by inflicting violence as a negative form of leverage. States also have alternative means of leverage and strategies that are often more effective than war in resolving conflicts (ending them on mutually acceptable terms).

Types of War

Many different activities are encompassed by the general term *war*. Consequently, it is not easy to say how many wars are going on in the world at any given time. Political scientists can count the number of militarized disputes or the number of international conflicts that regularly entail violence. Most lists of wars set some minimum criteria—for instance, a minimum of a thousand battle deaths—to distinguish the large-scale violence implied by war from the more common lower-level violence that occurs in many international conflicts. Criteria that are not often used include formal declarations of war (now largely obsolete) or other legal standards. For example, Japan and the Soviet Union never signed a treaty ending World War II but are not considered to be at war.

Wars are very diverse. Different types of war tend to arise from different situations and play varied roles in conflict bargaining. Beginning with the largest wars (which obviously meet the criteria), we may distinguish the following main categories.

Hegemonic war is a war over control of the entire *world order*—the rules of the international system as a whole, including the role of world hegemony (see "Hegemony" on p. 69). This class of war (with variations in definition and conception) is also known as *world war, global war, general war* or *systemic war*.[1] The last hegemonic war was World War II. This kind of war could probably not occur again without destroying civilization.

Total war is warfare by one state waged to conquer and occupy another. The goal is to reach the capital city and force the surrender of the government, which can then be replaced with one of the victor's choosing (see pp. 173–174). In rare cases, the victor annexes the loser into its own state, as Iraq tried to do with Kuwait. Total war as we know it began with the massively destructive Napoleonic Wars, which introduced large-scale conscription and geared the entire French national economy toward the war effort. The practice of total war evolved with industrialization, which further integrated all of society and economy into the practice of war. The last total war among great powers was World War II, which ended with Germany and Japan in ruins, occupied by the Western alliance.

In total war, with the entire society mobilized for the struggle, the entire society of the enemy is considered a legitimate target. For instance, in World War II Germany attacked British civilians with V-2 rockets, while British and U.S. strategic bombing killed 600 000 German civilians (and hundreds of thousands more Japanese) in an effort to weaken morale.

Limited war includes military actions carried out to gain some objective short of the surrender and occupation of the enemy. For instance, the U.S.-led war against Iraq in 1991 retook the territory of Kuwait but did not go on to Baghdad to topple Saddam Hussein's government. Many border wars have this character: after occupying the land it wants, a state may stop short and defend its gains.

Raids are limited wars that consist of a single action—a bombing run or a quick incursion by land. In 1981 Israeli warplanes bombed an Iraqi nuclear research facility to stop Iraq from making progress toward the development of nuclear weapons. (Without this raid, Iraq might have had nuclear weapons when it invaded Kuwait in 1990.) The action had a narrow objective—destruction of the facility—and was over within hours. Raids fall into the grey area between wars and nonwars because their destruction is limited and they are over quickly. Raiding that is repeated or that fuels a cycle of retaliation usually becomes a limited war or what is sometimes called "low-intensity conflict."

Civil war refers to war between factions within a state trying to create or prevent a new government for the entire state or some territorial part of it. (The aim may be to change the entire system of government, to merely replace the people in it or to split a region off as a new state.) The U.S. Civil War of the 1860s is a good example of a secessionist civil war, as is the

hegemonic war War for control of the entire world order—the rules of the international system as a whole. Also known as *world war, global war, general war,* or *systemic war.*

total war Warfare by one state waged to conquer and occupy another; modern total war originated in the Napoleonic Wars, which relied on conscription on a mass scale.

limited war Military actions that seek objectives short of the surrender and occupation of the enemy.

civil war A war between factions within a state trying to create or prevent a new government for the entire state or some territorial part of it.

---

[1] Jack S. Levy, "Theories of General War," *World Politics* 37.3 (1985): 344–74. William R. Thompson, *On Global War: Historical-Structural Approaches to World Politics* (Columbia: U South Carolina P, 1988).

war of Eritrea province in Ethiopia (now the internationally recognized state of Eritrea) in the 1980s. The war in El Salvador in the 1980s is an example of a civil war for control of the entire state (not secessionist). Civil wars are often among the most brutal wars—sometimes brother fighting brother, often with no clearly defined front lines. People fighting fellow citizens act no less cruelly than those fighting people from another state. The 50 000 or more deaths in the civil war in El Salvador, including many from massacres and death squads, were not based on ethnic differences. (Of course, many of today's civil wars have an element of ethnic conflict.)

guerrilla war Warfare without front lines and with irregular forces operating in the midst of, and often hidden or protected by, civilian populations.

Guerrilla war, which includes certain kinds of civil wars, is warfare without front lines. Irregular forces operate in the midst of, and often hidden or protected by, civilian populations. The purpose is not to directly confront an enemy army but rather to harass and punish it in the hope of gradually limiting its operation and effectively liberating territory from its control. U.S. military forces in South Vietnam fought against Viet Cong guerrillas in the 1960s and 1970s, with rising frustration. The United States could occupy a location in daylight, but by night the guerrillas would slip back and reclaim control.

counterinsurgency An effort to combat guerrilla armies, often including programs to "win the hearts and minds" of rural populations so that they stop sheltering guerrillas.

Efforts to combat such a guerrilla army—**counterinsurgency**—often include programs to "win the hearts and minds" of rural populations so that they stop sheltering guerrillas.

In guerrilla war, without a fixed front line, there is much territory that neither side controls; both sides exert military leverage over the same places at the same time. Thus, guerrilla wars are extremely painful for civilians. The situation is doubly painful because conventional armies fighting against guerrillas and paramilitaries often cannot distinguish them from civilians and punish both together. As a result, civilians constitute between 75 and 90 percent of the casualties in armed conflict. Civilians also are usually targeted differently, depending on whether they are men or women: men are more likely to be killed or abducted to serve as soldiers in guerrilla forces while women often face sexual assault, the risk of being trafficked and loss of livelihood.[2] Warfare is increasingly irregular and guerrilla-style; it is less and less often a conventional open clash of large state armies.[3]

Not all wars fit neatly into one of these categories, and some wars fit into more than one. The Iraq War of 2003, for example, seems to be a total war, at least insofar as its aim was to overthrow the Iraqi government, and civilians were inevitably targeted during the campaign. However, the United States and its coalition partners did not mobilize their entire societies in pursuit of this aim, and also insisted that their goal was to see a democratically elected government. For these reasons it could be labelled a limited war. At the same time, as resistance against the occupation grew, insurgents focused on the newly installed government and violence between Shi'ite and Sunni communities increased—leading many commentators to define the situation in Iraq as a civil war. The strategies used in Iraq (as in Afghanistan) also contain all the elements of a guerrilla war, with no single "battlefield" and a real fluidity between combatants and civilians.

In recent years, scholars and policy-makers have been interested in the difficult transition from war to peace around the world—postwar reconciliation, conflict resolution, transitional governments representing opposing factions, economic reconstruction and so forth. Important new work in this area examines how the "new" wars of the post–Cold War period, most particularly those in sub-Saharan Africa, may represent a

---

[2] Simon Chesterman, ed., *Civilians in War* (Boulder: Rienner, 2001). United Nations Secretary General Study, *Women, Peace and Security* (NY: United Nations, 2002).

[3] Ariel E. Levite, Bruce W. Jentleson and Larry Berman, eds., *Foreign Military Intervention: The Dynamics of Protracted Conflict* (NY: Columbia UP, 1992). Michael Klare and Peter Kornbluh, eds., *Low-Intensity Warfare: Counterinsurgency, Proinsurgency, and Antiterrorism in the Eighties* (NY: Random/Pantheon, 1991). Edward E. Azar and Chung-in Moon, eds., *National Security in the Third World: The Management of Internal and External Threats* (Aldershot, UK: Elgar, 1988).

complex configuration of processes of social transformation, with different factions interested in and benefiting from the continuation of the conflict rather than its resolution. This alternative view sees contemporary armed conflict as inextricably connected to the inclusions and exclusions associated with contemporary forms of capitalism, which makes efforts to bring these conflicts to an end enormously more complex than originally envisaged (and not normally amenable to military intervention).[4]

THE CAUSES OF WAR

The Roman writer Seneca said nearly 2000 years ago, "Of war men ask the outcome, not the cause."[5] This is not true of political scientists. They ask two fundamental questions: Why do international actors (states and nonstate actors alike) come into conflict with each other? And why do those conflicts sometimes lead to violence and war?

Conflict among states, for realists in particular, is not an unusual condition. **Conflict** may be defined as a difference in preferred outcomes in a bargaining situation. International conflicts will always exist. In such conflict bargaining, states develop capabilities that give them leverage to obtain more favourable outcomes than they could without such leverage. Whether fair or unfair, the ultimate outcome of the bargaining process is a **settlement** of the particular conflict.

conflict A difference in preferred outcomes in a bargaining situation.

The question of why war breaks out can be approached in different ways. Descriptive approaches, favoured by historians, tend to focus narrowly on specific direct causes of the outbreak of war, which vary from one war to another.[6] For example, one could say that the assassination of Archduke Ferdinand in 1914 "caused" World War I. More general, theoretical approaches, favoured by many political scientists, tend to focus on the search for general explanations, applicable to a variety of contexts, about why wars break out.[7] For example, one can view the cause of World War I as shifts in the balance of power among European states, with the assassination being only a catalyst.

settlement The outcome of a bargaining process.

Theories about War

Broad generalizations about the causes of war have been elusive. Wars do not have a single or simple cause. Some scholars distinguish *necessary* causes (conditions that must exist for a war to occur, but might not trigger one) from *sufficient* causes (conditions that will trigger war but are responsible for only some wars).[8] Many theories about war have been

---

[4] Mark Duffield, *Global Governance and the New Wars: The Merging of Development and Security* (London: Zed Books, 2001).

[5] Hercules Furens Seneca, *Seneca's Tragedies*, vol. 1, trans. Frank Justus Miller (London: Heinemann, 1917).

[6] Michael Howard, *The Invention of Peace: Reflections on War and the International Order* (New Haven, CT: Yale, 2001). Robert I. Rotberg and Theodore K. Rabb, eds., *The Origin and Prevention of Major Wars* (NY: Cambridge UP, 1989).

[7] John A. Vasquez, ed., *What Do We Know About War?* (Lanham, MD: Rowman Littlefield, 2000). Zeev Maoz and Azar Gat, eds., *War in a Changing World* (Ann Arbor: U Michigan P, 2001). Dale C. Copeland, *The Origins of Major War* (Ithaca, NY: Cornell UP, 2001). Stephen Van Evera, *Causes of War: Power and the Roots of Conflict* (Ithaca, NY: Cornell, 1999). Michael E. Brown, Owen R. Coté, Jr., Sean M. Lynn-Jones and Steven E. Miller, eds., *Theories of War and Peace* (Cambridge, MA: MIT P, 1998). Hidemi Suganami, *On the Causes of War* (NY: Oxford UP, 1996). John A. Vasquez, *The War Puzzle* (NY: Cambridge UP, 1993). Seyom Brown, *The Causes and Prevention of War* (NY: St. Martin's, 1987). Kalevi J. Holsti, *Peace and War: Armed Conflicts and International Order* (NY: Cambridge UP, 1991). Geoffrey Blainey, *The Causes of War* (London: Macmillan, 1973).

[8] Benjamin A. Most and Harvey Starr, *Inquiry, Logic and International Politics* (Columbia: U South Carolina P, 1989).

proposed, but few have universal validity. Levels of analysis can help us organize these theories or explanations of war.[9] Wars have been viewed as resulting from forces and processes operating on each level.

The Individual Level At the *individual* level of analysis, the question of why conflicts become violent revolves around the familiar issue of rationality. One theory, consistent with realism, holds that the use of war and other violent means of leverage in international conflicts is normal and reflects *rational* decisions of national leaders; that "wars begin with conscious and reasoned decisions based on the calculation, made by *both* parties, that they can achieve more by going to war than by remaining at peace."[10]

An opposite theory holds that conflicts often escalate to war as a result of *deviations* from rationality in the individual decision-making processes of national leaders. These potentials were discussed in Chapter 5—information screens, cognitive biases, groupthink and so forth. A related theory holds that the education and mentality of whole populations of individuals determine whether conflicts become violent. In this view, public nationalism or ethnic hatred—or even an innate tendency toward violence in human nature—may pressure leaders to solve conflicts violently. Some activists and IR researchers (especially peace researchers, as discussed in Chapter 3) believe that the re-education of populations can result in fewer conflicts escalating to violence.

Neither of these theories holds up very well. Some wars clearly reflect rational calculations of national leaders, whereas others were clearly mistakes that cannot be considered rational. Certainly there are individual leaders who seem prone to turn to military force to try to settle conflicts on favourable terms, but no reliable guide has been discovered to predict who will be a more warlike or more peaceful leader. A warlike leader can become peaceful, as in the case of Egypt's Anwar Sadat, for example. Individuals of varied cultural backgrounds and religions lead their states into war, as do both male and female leaders.

The Domestic Level The *domestic* level of analysis draws attention to those characteristics that may make states or societies more or less prone to use violence in resolving conflicts. During the Cold War, the Soviet Union and its allies frequently said that the aggressive and greedy *capitalist* states were prone to using violence in international conflicts, whereas Western leaders claimed that the expansionist, ideological and totalitarian nature of *communist* states made them especially apt to turn to violence. In truth, both types of society have used violence regularly in international conflicts.

Rich industrialized states and poor agrarian ones both use war at times. In fact, anthropologists have found that a wide range of *preagricultural* hunter-gatherer societies are even prone to warfare under certain circumstances.[11] Thus the potential for warfare seems to hold across cultures, types of society and time periods—although the importance and frequency of war vary greatly from case to case.

---

[9] Jack S. Levy, "The Causes of War: A Review of Theories and Evidence," *Behavior, Society, and Nuclear War*, ed. P. E. Tetlock et al., vol. 1 (NY: Oxford UP, 1989).

[10] Michael Howard, *The Causes of Wars and Other Essays* (Cambridge: Harvard UP, 1984) 22. Emphasis in original.

[11] Lawrence H. Keeley, *War before Civilization: The Myth of the Peaceful Savage* (NY: Oxford UP, 1996). Robert L. O'Connell, *Ride of the Second Horseman: The Birth and Death of War* (NY: Oxford UP, 1995). Barbara Ehrenreich, *Blood Rites: Origins and History of the Passions of War* (NY: Metropolitan/Holt, 1997). Carol R. Ember and Melvin Ember, "Resource Unpredictability, Mistrust, and War: A Cross-Cultural Study," *Journal of Conflict Resolution* 36.2 (1992): 242–62. Robert A. Rubinstein and Mary LeCron Foster, eds., *The Social Dynamics of Peace and Conflict: Culture in International Security* (Boulder, CO: Westview, 1988).

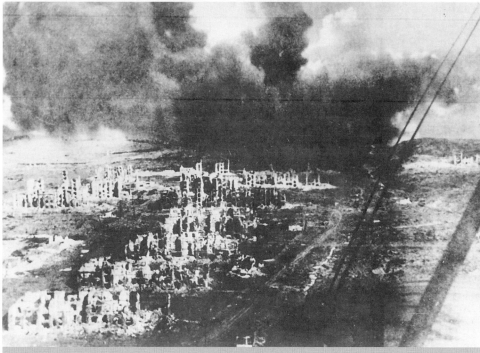

WHY WAR?
Political scientists do not agree on a theory of why great wars like World War II occurred and cannot predict whether they might happen again. The city of Stalingrad (Volgograd) was decimated during Germany's invasion of the Soviet Union, 1943.

Few useful generalizations can be made about what kinds of domestic society are more prone or less prone to war (given that all are war-prone to some extent). A given society may change greatly over time. For example, Japan was prone to using violence in international conflicts before World War II, but averse to such violence since. The !Kung bush people in Angola and Namibia—a hunter-gatherer society—were observed by anthropologists in the 1960s to be extremely peaceful, yet anthropologists in the 1920s had observed them engaging in murderous inter-group violence.[12] Political scientists have not yet identified any general principles to explain why some societies at some times are more peaceful than others or why they might change.

The Interstate Level   Theories at the *interstate* level are favoured by realists and explain war in terms of power relations among major actors in the international system. For example, power transition theory holds that conflicts generate large wars at times when power is relatively equally distributed and a rising power is threatening to overtake a declining hegemon in overall position. This level, too, has competing theories that seem incompatible. Deterrence, as we have seen, is intended to stop wars by building up power and threatening its use, but the theory of arms races holds that wars are caused, not prevented, by such actions. As noted in Chapter 2, no general formula exists to tell us in what circumstances each of these principles holds true.

---

[12] Irenaus Eibl-Eibesfeldt, *The Biology of Peace and War: Men, Animals, and Aggression* (NY: Viking, 1979).

Lacking a reliable method to predict what configurations of power among states will lead to war, some political scientists have tried to estimate the statistical *probabilities* that one or another type of interstate relationship might lead to such conflict.[13] Current research focuses on the effects of democracy, government structure, trade and related factors in explaining the escalation or settlement of "militarized interstate disputes."[14]

Scholars use quantitative and statistical methods to test various ideas about international conflict, including analyzing data about wars, weapons and arms races.[15] For example, researchers are analyzing conflicts between democracies to determine why they almost never escalate to war. The quality of available data is a major problem for statistical studies of infrequent occurrences such as wars.

The Global Level   At the *global* level of analysis, a number of theories of war have been proposed. There are several variations on the idea that major warfare in the international system is *cyclical*. One approach links large wars with *long economic waves* (also called *Kondratieff cycles*) of about 50 years' duration in the world economy. Another approach links the largest wars with a 100-year cycle based on the creation and decay of world orders (see "Hegemony" on pp. 69–70). These cycle theories at best explain only general tendencies toward war in the international system over time.[16]

A somewhat opposite approach is the theory of linear long-term change—that war as an outcome of conflict is becoming less likely over time due to the worldwide development of both technology and international norms. Some IR scholars argue that war and military force are becoming *obsolete* as leverage in international conflicts because these means of influence are not very effective in today's highly complex, interdependent world. A parallel line of argument holds that today's military technology is too powerful to use in most conflicts; this is especially applicable to nuclear weapons.

A possibly complementary theory traces the obsolescence of war to the evolution of international norms against the use of force. War was once seen as a normal way to resolve disputes but is now considered distasteful. An analogy has been drawn with the practices of slavery and duelling—once considered normal but now obsolete.[17]

Thus, at all levels of analysis, competing theories offer very different explanations for why some conflicts become violent and others do not. For these reasons, political scientists cannot yet predict with any confidence which of the world's many international

[13] Quincy Wright, *A Study of War* (1942; Chicago: U Chicago P, 1965). Lewis F. Richardson, *Arms and Insecurity* (Pittsburgh: Boxwood, 1960). Daniel S. Geller and J. David Singer, *Nations at War: A Scientific Study of International Conflict* (NY: Cambridge UP, 1998). John A. Vasquez and Marie T. Henehan, eds., *The Scientific Study of Peace and War: A Text Reader* (Lanham, MD: UP America/Lexington, 1999). Manus I. Midlarsky, ed., *Handbook of War Studies II* (Ann Arbor: U Michigan P, 2000). Claudio Cioffi-Revilla, *The Scientific Measurement of International Conflict: Handbook of Datasets on Crises and War, 1495–1988 A.D.* (Boulder, CO: Rienner, 1990).

[14] Stuart A. Bremer and Thomas R. Cusack, *The Process of War: Advancing the Scientific Study of War* (Newark, NJ: Gordon & Breach, 1995). J. David Singer and Paul F. Diehl, eds., *Measuring the Correlates of War* (Ann Arbor: U Michigan P, 1990). Melvin Small and J. David Singer, *Resort to Arms: International and Civil Wars, 1816–1980* (Beverly Hills: Sage, 1982).

[15] Peter Wallensteen, ed., *Peace Research: Achievements and Challenges* (Boulder, CO: Westview, 1988). Peter Van Den Dungen, "Jean De Bloch: A 19th Century Peace Researcher," *Peace Researcher* 15.3 (1983): 21–27.

[16] Joshua S. Goldstein, *Long Cycles: Prosperity and War in the Modern Age* (New Haven, CT: Yale UP, 1988). George Modelski, *Long Cycles in World Politics* (Seattle: U Washington P, 1987).

[17] John Mueller, *Retreat from Doomsday: The Obsolescence of Major War* (NY: Basic, 1989).

conflicts will lead to war. We can gain insight, however, by studying various types of conflicts to better understand what states are fighting about.

CONFLICTS OF INTEREST

The following sections discuss six types of international conflict. Three are conflicts over tangible material interests:

1. Territorial border disputes, including secession attempts
2. Conflicts over who controls national governments
3. Economic conflicts over trade, money, natural resources, drug trafficking and other such economic transactions

   The other three types of conflict concern less-tangible clashes of ideas:

4. Ethnic conflicts
5. Religious conflicts
6. Ideological conflicts

These six types of conflict are not mutually exclusive, and overlap considerably in practice. For example, the conflicts between Russia and Ukraine after the 1991 Soviet breakup were complex. The two new states had a *territorial* dispute over the Crimean peninsula, which Soviet leader Nikita Khrushchev had transferred to Ukraine in the 1950s. There and elsewhere, *ethnic* Russians living in Ukraine, and Ukrainians in Russia, experienced ethnic conflict. There are *religious* differences between Ukrainian and Russian forms of Christianity. The two states also had *economic* conflicts over trade and money after the Soviet breakup, which created new borders and currencies. These multiple conflicts did not lead to the use of military force, however. In 2005, the opposition took control of Ukraine's government (after a flawed election was rerun in response to weeks of mass street protests). Russian president Putin, who had campaigned for the incumbent party in Ukraine, protested vigorously but did not seriously consider military force. It should be kept in mind that the types of conflict discussed here come into play in combination rather than separately.

Again, conflict is not the same as war—most conflicts do not entail the use of violence. Conflicts of interest lie at the heart of many instances of international bargaining, from trade negotiations to arms control. Only sometimes do they turn violent.

Territorial Disputes

Among the international conflicts that concern tangible "goods," those concerning territory have special importance thanks to the territorial nature of the state (see "Anarchy and Sovereignty" on pp. 60–63). Conflicts over control of territory are of two varieties: territorial disputes (about where borders are drawn) and conflicts over control of entire states within existing borders (discussed next under "Control of Governments"). Consider first differences over where borders between two states should be drawn—that is, over which state should control a disputed territory.

Because states value home territory with an almost fanatical devotion, border disputes tend to be among the most intractable in IR. States will seldom yield territory in exchange for money or any other positive reward; nor do they quickly forget territory they may have lost involuntarily. For example, in 2002, Bolivian public opinion opposed a gas export pipeline through Chile to the sea because Chile had seized the coastline from Bolivia in 1879.

GOING SEPARATE WAYS
Efforts by a region to secede from a state are a frequent source of international conflict, but international norms generally treat such conflicts as internal matters unless they spill over borders. Increasingly, autonomy agreements are solving secession conflicts. Here, Indonesian troops leave Aceh province in 2005 after separatists disarmed under a limited self-rule agreement.

irredentism A form of nationalism whose goal is to regain territory lost to another state; it can lead directly to violent interstate conflicts.

The goal of regaining territory lost to another state is called **irredentism.** This form of nationalism can lead directly to serious interstate conflicts.[18]

Due to their association with the integrity of states, territories are prized far beyond any inherent economic or strategic value they hold. For example, after Israel and Egypt made peace in 1978, it took a decade to settle a border dispute at Taba, a tiny plot of beachfront on which Israeli developers had built a hotel just slightly across the old border. The two states finally submitted the issue for binding arbitration, and Egypt ended up in possession. For Egypt, regaining every centimetre of territory was a matter of national honour and a symbol of the sovereignty and territorial integrity that defined Egyptian statehood.

An exception to this attitude toward territories used to exist with regard to colonies and other territorial possessions. Because these were not part of the home territory or associated with the idea of the nation, they were valued only as property to be won, lost, sold or traded in political deals and wars. France and Russia sold their territories in Louisiana and Alaska, respectively, to the United States. Such territories are valued for their natural

---

[18] Paul F. Diehl, ed., *A Road Map to War: Territorial Dimensions of International Conflict* (Nashville, TN: Vanderbilt, 1999). Paul F. Diehl and Gary Goertz, *Territorial Changes and International Conflict* (NY: Routledge, 1992). Arie Marcelo Kacowicz, *Peaceful Territorial Change* (Columbia: U South Carolina P, 1994). Naomi Chazan, ed., *Irredentism and International Politics* (Boulder, CO: Rienner, 1991).

resources or geopolitical location. Since 1704, Britain has possessed the tiny Rock of Gibraltar, which commands the entrance to the Mediterranean; the United States has owned the Pacific island of Guam, used for military bases, since 1898. Today, with few colonies remaining, most of the world's territory is now home to some state.

The value states put on home territory appears to remain undiminished despite the apparent reduction in its inherent value over time as technology has developed. Historically, territory was the basis of economic production—in agriculture and in the extraction of raw materials. Even in Sun Tzu's time, it was said that "land is the foundation of the state." It was in these agrarian societies that the international system developed. Winning and losing wars meant gaining or losing territory, with which came wealth and hence long-term power. Today, however, wealth is derived much more from trade and technology than from agriculture. The costs of most territorial disputes appear to outweigh any economic benefits that the territory in question could provide. There are exceptions, however, such as the capture of diamond-mining areas in several African countries by rebels who use diamond revenues to finance war. In 2002, 40 states created a program of UN certification for legitimate diamonds, trying to keep "conflict diamonds" off the international market. (See also "Trafficking," pp. 175–177.)

Means of Controlling Territory   Historically, military means have been the most effective leverage for controlling territory, and wars have often redrawn the borders of states. Military forces can seize control on the ground in a way that is hard to contest by any means except other military forces. For example, when Saddam Hussein redrew the borders of Iraq to include Kuwait, his opponents found no better means to dislodge him (economic sanctions, diplomatic isolation, negotiations and so on) than military force. The 2003 invasion of Iraq by the United States and Britain was not ostensibly aimed at controlling Iraqi territory, but did topple Saddam Hussein's regime.

Since World War II, however, a strong norm has developed in the international system *against* trying to alter borders by force. Such attempts are considered grave matters by the international community. Thus, when Iraq annexed Kuwait and erased its borders, most states viewed the act as intolerable. By contrast, it is considered a lesser offence for one state to merely topple another's government and install a puppet regime, even if done violently. The principle is: Governments come and go; borders remain.

Secession   Efforts by a province or region to secede from an existing state create a special type of conflict over borders. Secession is the effort of a substate area to draw its own international borders, forming a new state. Dozens of secession movements have occurred around the world, in varying sizes and political effectiveness, but have rarely succeeded.

For instance, in the 1990s, the predominantly Albanian population of the Serbian province of Kosovo fought a war to secede from Serbia. NATO intervention, including sustained bombing of Serbia (not approved by the UN), led to the withdrawal of Serbia's army from Kosovo and its replacement with European and American peacekeeping troops—who have been there ever since. The majority of Kosovars want to secede, and feel the international system should give them self-determination. Serbians argue, however, that Kosovo is historically and presently under Serbian sovereignty, and must be respected as such by the international community. In 2006, the UN and the great powers mediated negotiations in an attempt to settle the conflict either by forcing Serbia to accept Kosovo's independence or by forcing Kosovars to remain citizens of Serbia, with regional autonomy but not sovereignty. A decision was expected in 2007.

Wars of secession can be large and deadly, and can easily spill over international borders or pull in other countries. A spillover is especially likely if members of an ethnic or a religious group span two sides of a border, constituting the majority group in one state and a majority in a nearby region of another state, but a minority in the other state as a whole. This pattern occurs in Bosnia-Serbia, Moldova-Russia, Iraq-Iran and India-Pakistan. In some cases, secessionists want to merge territories with a neighbouring state (as in the effort to carve out a "greater Serbia"), which amounts to a redrawing of an international border. International norms frown on such an outcome. (Ethnic and religious conflict are discussed later in this chapter.)

The strong international norms of sovereignty and territorial integrity treat secession movements as domestic problems that are of little concern to other states. Even when secession conflicts occasionally spill over international borders, the international community tends to treat the matter lightly as long as the cross-border incursion is temporary. The general principle seems to be: "We existing states all have our own domestic problems and disaffected groups or regions, so we must stick together behind sovereignty and territorial integrity."

Messy border problems have been created in a few recent cases of multinational states being broken up into pieces. In such cases, borders that were previously internal became international; given the relative youth of these borders, they may be more vulnerable to challenge.

Certainly this is the case in the former Yugoslavia, where ethnic groups had intermingled and intermarried, leaving mixed populations in most of the Yugoslav republics. When Yugoslavia broke up in 1991–1992, several republics declared their independence as separate states. Two of these, Croatia and Bosnia, held minority populations of ethnic Serbs. Serbia seized effective control of significant areas of Croatia and Bosnia that contained Serbian communities or linked such populations geographically. Non-Serbian populations were driven out of these areas or massacred— **ethnic cleansing.** Then, when Croatia reclaimed most of its territory in 1995, Serbian populations in turn fled the region. Ethnic nationalism proved stronger than multiethnic tolerance in both Serbia and Croatia, making borders problematic.

The breakup of a state need not lead to violence, however. Serbia split from Montenegro (another of the former Yugoslav republics) in 2006. Czechoslovakia split into the Czech Republic and Slovakia in a cooperative and civil manner. And the breakup of the Soviet Union did not lead to violent territorial disputes between republics in *most* cases, even where ethnic groups were split across new international borders (such as Ukraine-Russia).

The norm against forceful redrawing of borders does not apply to cases of decolonization. For example, when Portugal's empire crumbled in 1975, its colony of East Timor was brutally invaded and annexed by neighbouring Indonesia. Because East Timor was not a UN member state (most states did not recognize its independence), Indonesia got away with this move (although the move was not officially recognized by most states). The problem was treated mainly as one of human rights. However, the international community never formally recognized Indonesia's control over East Timor, and decades later East Timor achieved independence, joining the UN in 2003.

The transfer of Hong Kong from British to Chinese control in 1997 also illustrates how colonial territory is dispensable (Britain's perspective) while home territory is nearly sacred (China's perspective). The views of the inhabitants of a territory do not carry much weight in either perspective. The peaceful transfer of Hong Kong is one of the few recent cases of territory changing hands in the international system.

Increasingly, autonomy has become a realistic compromise between secession and full control by a central government. In 2005, spurred partly by the devastating tsunami a year earlier, separatists in the Aceh province of Indonesia disbanded, giving up on independence and instead participating in regional elections in 2006. The Indonesian government

ethnic cleansing Forced displacement of an ethnic group or groups from a particular territory, accompanied by massacres and other human rights violations; it has occurred after the breakup of multinational states, notably in the former Yugoslavia.

withdrew its 24 000 troops from Aceh and offered the province limited self-rule along with 70 percent of the oil, gas and mineral wealth it generates.

Interstate Borders   Border disputes between existing states are taken more seriously by the international community, but are less common than secessionist conflicts. Thanks to the norm of territorial integrity, few important border conflicts remain among long-established states. At one time, huge chunks of territory were passed between states at the stroke of a pen (on a peace treaty or marriage contract). However, wholesale redrawing of borders in this manner has not occurred among established states for 50 years. Since the end of World War II, only a minuscule amount of territory has changed hands between established states through force. Efforts that have been made to do so have failed. For instance, when Iraq attacked Iran in 1980, one objective was control of the Shatt-al-Arab waterway (with access to the Persian Gulf), because of its commercial and strategic value. But 10 years and a million deaths later, the Iran-Iraq border was back where it started. Bits of land have changed hands in recent decades through war, but it is remarkable how small those bits have been. (This does not apply to the formation of new states and the fragmenting of old ones.)

Furthermore, when territorial disputes do occur between established states, they *can* be settled peacefully, especially when the involved territory is small compared with the states disputing it. The Soviet Union agreed to China's boundary preferences in 1986 after the two states had disputed ownership of minor river islands for years (a dispute which included military skirmishes in 1969). El Salvador and Honduras took their border disputes to the World Court for adjudication in 1992, and in 1994, a panel of Latin American judges settled a century-long border dispute over some mountainous terrain between Argentina and Chile. The 3–2 ruling, reached after the countries submitted the dispute for judicial arbitration, awarded the territory to Argentina and provoked howls of protest from Chile. Despite the strong feelings evoked by the loss of territory, Argentina and Chile had settled 22 of 24 remaining border disputes peacefully during the previous 10 years (after nearly going to war in 1978 over disputed islands).

The possibility of peaceful resolution of territorial disputes was highlighted in 2006 with the withdrawal of Nigerian troops from the potentially oil-rich Bakassi Peninsula, which Nigeria is ceding to Cameroon's sovereignty. The resolution of the dispute, dating from colonial times, follows more than a decade of painstaking progress through the World Court, the personal mediation of the UN Secretary General when Nigeria initially rejected the court's decision and the promise of outside powers to monitor implementation of the agreement. Why would Nigeria—a country with nine times Cameroon's population, more than triple its GDP and a much stronger military—voluntarily cede territory? Doing so would run counter to the predictions of realism in particular and the dominance principle in general. Liberal theories could more aptly explain this outcome: Nigeria acted in its own self-interest, since turning the dispute over to the World Court and bringing in the UN to assist with implementation brought the kind of stability needed for foreign investment to develop the area's resources—primarily oil.

Lingering Disputes   Today, only a few of the world's interstate borders are disputed. Nonetheless, those that persist are important sources of international conflict. Among the most difficult are the borders of *Israel*, which have never been firmly defined and recognized by its neighbours. The 1948 ceasefire lines resulting from Israel's war of independence were expanded in the 1967 war, then contracted again on the Egyptian border with the Camp David peace treaty of 1978. The remainder of the territories occupied in 1967—the *West Bank* near Jordan, the *Gaza Strip* near Egypt and the *Golan Heights* of Syria—are central to the Arab-Israeli conflict. Since 1993, Israeli-Palestinian agreements have tried to move toward Palestinian autonomy in parts of the West Bank and Gaza Strip, and negotiations seemed headed toward the creation of a state of Palestine in all or most of the occupied territories, and peace with Israel. However, the 2000 "Camp David II" summit failed—over how to divide Jerusalem and other emotional issues—and a new phase of violence and hate began.

Another major border dispute is in *Kashmir,* where India, Pakistan and China intersect. The India-held part of Kashmir is predominantly inhabited by Muslims, a group that is the majority in Pakistan but a minority in India. A *Line of Control* divides the disputed province. Pakistan accuses India of oppressing Kashmiris and thwarting an international agreement to decide Kashmir's future by a popular referendum. India accuses Pakistan of aiding and infiltrating Islamic radicals who carry out attacks in Indian-occupied Kashmir. The two countries have been to war twice over the issue, and nearly did so again in 2002—with both sides holding dozens of nuclear-armed missiles that some experts estimated would kill more than 10 million people. Perhaps chastened by this experience, the two countries improved relations in 2003 and began a ceasefire that stopped the incessant low-level fighting along the Line of Control, although not the fighting between Indian authorities and insurgents. In 2004, India agreed to begin a slow withdrawal of troops from the region, and in 2005 a major earthquake led to improved relations as a result of the need to coordinate relief efforts.

Peru and Ecuador fought border skirmishes in 1995 over a nearly inaccessible stretch of mountainous terrain, part of a sizeable area signed over to Peru following its victory in a brief war with Ecuador in 1941. The conflict, which involved no tangible assets worth fighting over, illustrated once again the almost mystical power of territory as a symbol of national honour and the continuing usefulness of nationalism in generating political support for state leaders (the popularity of both presidents increased as the conflict escalated). International mediation cooled off the dispute after a month of fighting.

Many of the world's other remaining interstate territorial disputes—and often the most serious ones—concern the control of small islands, which can provide strategic advantages, natural resources (such as offshore oil) or fishing rights. The tiny disputed *Spratly Islands* in the South China Sea, whose surrounding waters may hold substantial oil reserves, are claimed in part or in full by China, Taiwan, Vietnam, the Philippines, Malaysia and Brunei (see Figure 6.1). All of those states except Brunei have resorted to military occupation at times to stake their claims, but in 2002 the countries agreed to avoid conflicts over the islands, and they remain calm. About half of the world's trade tonnage passes near the Spratly Islands, including Persian Gulf oil and other key resources headed for Japan, China, South Korea and Taiwan.

Japan and China also dispute tiny islands elsewhere, as do Japan and South Korea. These disputes involve low economic stakes, but have become a focus of nationalist sentiments on both sides, fuelled partly by memories of World War II, when Japan occupied China and Korea. In 2004, South Korea issued four postage stamps depicting a tiny island also claimed by Japan. They sold out within hours. In 2005, after Japan spent half a billion dollars preserving Okinotori—an uninhabited coral reef with two tiny protrusions smaller than a house and just inches

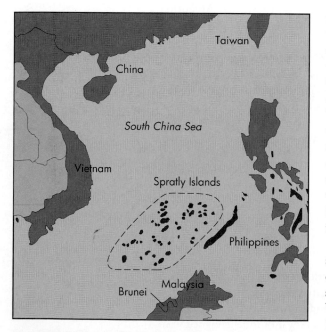

Figure 6.1 Disputed Islands

The Spratly Islands exemplify contemporary conflicts over territory and natural resources around islands. All or part of the Spratlys are claimed by China, Vietnam, Malaysia, Brunei, the Philippines and Taiwan.

above sea level—China declared it not an "island" (with a surrounding economic zone) but just a "rock" (which, without economic activity, does not qualify as such a zone).

A number of smaller conflicts exist around the globe. In the Middle East, Iran and the United Arab Emirates dispute ownership of small islands near the mouth of the Persian Gulf. In 2002, Spain sent soldiers to oust a handful of Moroccan troops from islands off Morocco's coast. In South America, Argentina and Britain still dispute control of the *Falkland Islands* (*Islas Malvinas*), over which they fought a war in 1982. In 2005, then-minister of defence Bill Graham drew attention to a long-standing dispute between Canada and Denmark over Hans Island, a small uninhabited island located between Ellesmere Island and Greenland. Sovereignty of the island had been contested since 1973, but was never resolved. Canadian troops landed on the island, planted a Canadian flag and built an Inuit stone marker, followed a week later by Graham's visit. Denmark protested the unannounced visit, but both Danish and Canadian authorities promised to seek a resolution to the dispute. Given that islands are surrounded by economic zones, international conflicts over islands will undoubtedly continue in the coming years.

Territorial Waters   States treat **territorial waters** near their shores as part of their national territory. Definitions of such waters are not universally agreed upon, but norms have developed in recent years, especially after the *UN Convention on the Law of the Sea (UNCLOS)* (see pp. 514–516). Waters within three nautical miles (5.6 kilometres) of shore have traditionally been recognized as territorial, but beyond that there are disputes about how far out national sovereignty extends and for what purposes. UNCLOS generally allows a 12-nautical mile (22.2-kilometre) limit for shipping, and a 200-nautical mile (370.4-kilometre) *exclusive economic zone (EEZ)* covering fishing and mineral rights (but allowing for free navigation by all). EEZs cover a third of the world's oceans.

Due to EEZs, sovereignty over a single tiny island can be accompanied by rights to as much as 259 000 square kilometres of surrounding ocean. These zones overlap greatly, and shorelines do not run in straight lines; thus numerous questions of interpretation arise about how to delineate territorial and economic waters. For example, Libya claims ownership of the entire Gulf of Sidra, treating it as a bay; the United States treats it as a curvature in the shoreline and insists that most of it is international waters. In 1986, the United States sent warships into the Gulf of Sidra to make its point. U.S. planes shot down two Libyan jets that challenged their manoeuvres.

In 1994–1995, Canada sent its navy to harass Spanish fishing boats just beyond the 200-nautical mile zone (affecting fish stocks within the zone). Canada and the U.S. have held long-standing disputes (joined with efforts at cooperation) over the Gulf of Maine, a semi-enclosed body of water bordered by Maine, Massachusetts, New Hampshire, New Brunswick and Nova Scotia. In the Sea of Okhotsk, Russia's EEZ includes all but a small "doughnut hole" of international waters in the middle (see p. 514). Non-Russian boats have fished intensively in the "hole," which of course depletes fish stocks in Russia's EEZ.

Arctic waters have been a consistent security issue for Canada. During the Cold War, concern focused on Soviet proximity to Canada via the Arctic Circle. Canada has faced other challenges to its sovereignty in the Arctic; in 1985, for example, a U.S. Coast Guard icebreaker traversed the Northwest Passage without seeking Canadian permission, precipitating a greater Canadian Forces presence in Canadian Arctic waters.[19]

territorial waters The waters near states' shores, generally treated as part of national territory. The UN Convention on the Law of the Sea provides for a 12-nautical mile territorial sea (and exclusive national jurisdiction over shipping and navigation) and a 200-nautical mile exclusive economic zone (EEZ) covering fishing and mineral rights (but allowing for free navigation by all). See also *high seas* and *UN Convention on the Law of the Sea (UNCLOS)*.

---

[19] Ron Purver, "The Arctic in Canadian Security Policy, 1945 to the Present," *Canada's International Security Policy*, ed. David B. Dewitt and David Leyton-Brown (Scarborough, ON: Prentice Hall, 1995). Philip J. Briggs, "The Polar Sea Voyage and the Northwest Passage Dispute," *Armed Forces and Society* 16.3 (Spring 1990): 437–52.

Canada views the Northwest Passage as an internal waterway, while the U.S. considers it international. Central to the debate is concern over international shipping. The Northwest Passage may eventually become fully navigable during summer months as Arctic ice continues to melt, cutting 5000 nautical miles from shipping routes between Europe and Asia. The U.S. and Canada are also involved in a dispute over the extension of the border between Alaska and the Yukon into the Beaufort Sea (Canada contends that it extends in a straight line while the U.S. contends it is slanted to the east). There are also resource issues at stake, depending on how these conflicts are resolved. Canada's debate over Arctic sovereignty is not focused solely on the U.S.: the Hans Island dispute with Denmark discussed above figures into this issue, and Canada also disagrees with Russia about the mapping of the Russian continental shelf, which affects the reach of its territorial waters. As some observers note, however, the question for Canada and the Arctic is not simply one of sovereignty but also one of surveillance and enforcement. The Arctic region is enormous, covering some 1.5 million square miles, making it very difficult to oversee.[20]

Airspace above a state is considered the territory of the state. Any airplane that wants to fly over a state's territory must have the state's permission. For example, in a 1986

airspace The space above a state that is considered its territory, in contrast to outer space, which is considered international territory.

STRUGGLE FOR CONTROL
Conflicts over who controls a national government, especially armed rebellions, can easily become internationalized. In 2003, U.S. and British forces overthrew Saddam Hussein's government in Iraq by force. Here, a statue of Saddam is toppled in central Baghdad (with a live worldwide television audience) after U.S. forces took the city in April 2003.

[20] Rob Huebert, "Northern Interests and Canadian Foreign Policy," Online Publication of the Canadian Defence and Foreign Affairs Institute, 2003, available at http://cdfai.org/PDF/NORTHERN%20INTER-ESTS%20AND%20CANADIAN%20FOREIGN%20POLICY.pdf. Levon Sevunts, "Northwest Passage redux," *The Washington Times* 12 June 2005, available at http://www.washingtontimes.com/specialreport/20050612-123835-3711r.htm.

raid on Libya, U.S. bombers based in Britain had to fly a long detour over the Atlantic Ocean because France (between Britain and Libya) would not grant permission for U.S. planes to use its airspace during the mission.

Outer space, by contrast, is considered international territory, much like oceans. International law does not define exactly where airspace ends and outer space begins. However, orbiting satellites fly higher than airplanes, move very fast and cannot easily change direction to avoid flying over a country. Also, very few states have the capability to shoot down satellites, though many can shoot airplanes. Since satellites have become useful intelligence-gathering tools for all the great powers, and since all satellites are extremely vulnerable to attack, a norm of demilitarization of outer space has developed. No state has ever attacked the satellite of another, and doing so would constitute a severe provocation.

Control of Governments

Despite the many minor border disputes that continue to plague the world, most of the struggles to control territory do not involve altering borders. Rather, they are conflicts over which governments ought to control entire states.

In theory, states do not interfere in each other's governance. In practice, they often have strong interests in the governments of other states and use a variety of means of leverage to influence who holds power in those states. When one state wants to alter or replace the government of a second state, a conflict obviously exists between the two governments. In addition, the first state may come into conflict with other parties that oppose changing the second state's government. Conflicts over governments take many forms, some mild and some severe, some deeply entwined with third parties and some more or less bilateral. Sometimes a state merely exerts subtle influences on another state's elections; at other times, a state supports rebel elements seeking to overthrow the second state's constitutional order.

During the Cold War, the U.S. and Russia actively promoted changes of government in countries of the global South through covert operations and support of rebel armies. The civil wars in Angola, Afghanistan and Nicaragua are good examples. Both superpowers committed weapons, money, military advisers and so forth in hopes of influencing the composition of the countries' governments.

Occasionally, one state invades another in order to change its government. The Soviet Union invaded Czechoslovakia in 1968; the United States did so in Grenada in 1983 and in Iraq in 2003. It can be hard for new governments created under these circumstances to gain legitimacy both domestically and internationally. People generally resent having foreigners choose their government for them—even if they didn't like the old government—and the international community frowns on such overt violations of national sovereignty. For instance, the government installed in Afghanistan after the Soviet invasion of 1979 was seen as a Soviet puppet and was finally toppled after a dozen years of rule marked by constant war.

And in Cambodia—where the Khmer Rouge government's atrocities led many people inside and outside the country to welcome the Vietnamese invasion that installed a new Cambodian government in 1979—the new government could not consolidate its international position for more than a decade. It did not gain Cambodia's seat in the UN, and the United States and China sent assistance to rebel groups that fought a long and bloody civil war against the Vietnamese-backed Cambodian government. (In the 1990s, the UN mediated a ceasefire and implemented a peace plan under which the UN basically ran the government while organizing elections.)

International conflicts over the control of governments—along with territorial disputes—are likely to lead to the use of violence. They involve core issues of the status and integrity of states, the stakes tend to be high and the interests of involved actors are often diametrically opposed. Other types of conflict are more widespread and sometimes less likely to lead to violence, such as economic conflict among states.

Economic Conflict

Economic competition is the most pervasive form of conflict in international relations due to the pervasiveness of economic transactions. Every sale made and every deal reached across international borders involves a resolution of conflicting interests. Costa Rica wants the price of coffee, one of its exports, to increase; Canada, an importer of coffee, wants the price to go down. Angola wants foreign producers of Angolan oil to receive fewer profits from oil sales; those companies' home states want them to generate more profits. In a global capitalist market, all economic exchanges involve some conflict of interest.

However, such economic transactions also involve a strong element of mutual economic gain in addition to the element of conflicting interests (see Chapters 4 and 9). This is a view most favoured by liberals, and particularly economic liberals. Mutual gains provide the most useful leverage in bargaining over economic exchanges: states and companies enter into economic transactions because they profit from doing so. The use of violence would for the most part interrupt and diminish such profit by more than could be gained by its use.

For liberals, then, economic conflict now seldom leads to violence because military forms of leverage are no longer very effective in economic conflicts. With the tight integration of the world economy and the high cost of military actions, the use of force is seldom justified to solve an economic issue. Thus, most economic conflicts are not issues in international security. They are discussed further in Chapters 8 through 13.

Such restraint has not always existed. In the sixteenth century, England's Sir Francis Drake intercepted Spanish ships bringing gold and silver from Central America and garnered the loot in the name of queen and country—a practice known as *privateering*. In the seventeenth century, England fought several naval wars against the Netherlands. An English general, when asked the reason for England's declaration of war in 1652, replied, "What matters this or that reason? What we want is more of the trade the Dutch now have."[21] In 1861, France, Britain and Spain invaded Mexico when it failed to pay international debts.

For critical theorists, economic relations bear on international security in a variety of ways. For some critical theorists, war has been an intrinsic part of capitalism and imperialism. This includes both wars fought between colonial powers over imperial possessions and the brutally one-sided wars of imperial conquest in which lands were occupied, peoples enslaved and resources looted.[22] Realists, too, sometimes make links between economics and security. The **theory of lateral pressure** connects economic competition with security concerns. This theory holds that the economic growth of states leads to geographic expansion as they seek natural resources beyond their borders (by various means, peaceful and violent). As great powers expand economic activities outward,

lateral pressure (theory of) The theory that the economic and population growth of states fuels geographic expansion as they seek natural resources beyond their borders, which in turn leads to conflicts and sometimes war.

---

[21] Michael Howard, *War in European History* (NY: Oxford UP, 1976) 47.

[22] Eric J. Hobsbawm, *Age of Extremes* (London: Little, Brown, 1994). Robbie Robertson, *Three Waves of Globalization: A History of a Developing Global Consciousness* (London: Zed Books, 2003).

competition leads to conflicts and sometimes war. The lateral pressure theory has been used to explain both World War I and the expansion of Japan prior to World War II.[23]

Another kind of economic conflict that affects international security concerns the *military-industrial complex* and the interests associated with the production of military equipment, especially high-technology weapons such as fighter aircraft or missiles. By this view, the arms trade is related to the outbreak of international violence in ways more complicated than simply making weapons available to belligerents. The countries responsible for exporting weapons are rarely the countries in which armed conflict takes place. If a country is an exporter of arms, and if its industrial base depends on the manufacture of weapons, then, as some critical theorists note, that country has an interest in ensuring there is always a market for their goods. In other words, it is in the interest of weapons exporters—most of which are northern, industrialized states—to make sure there is always a war being fought somewhere.[24]

Another source of economic conflict revolves around the distribution of wealth within and among states. As discussed in Chapter 13, there are tremendous disparities of wealth in our world, disparities that create a variety of international security problems with the potential for violence.

Revolutions in poor countries are often fuelled by disparities of wealth within a country as well as its poverty relative to other countries. In turn, these revolutions frequently attract other states as supporters of one side or the other in a civil war. If successful, revolutions can abruptly change a state's foreign policy, leading to new alliances and power alignments.

Critical approaches to international relations drawn from Marxist thought treat class struggle between rich and poor people as the basis of interstate relations. According to these approaches, capitalist states adopt foreign policies that serve the interests of the rich owners of companies. Conflicts and wars between the global North and South—rich states versus poor states—are seen as reflections of the domination and exploitation of the poor by the rich—imperialism in direct or indirect form. For example, most Marxists saw the Vietnam War as a U.S. effort to suppress revolution in order to secure continued U.S. access to cheap labour and raw materials in Southeast Asia. The 1991 Gulf War and the 2003 war in Iraq were seen in similar terms, though with a focus on access to oil. Many Marxists portray conflicts among capitalist states as competition over the right to exploit poor areas. Soviet founder V. I. Lenin portrayed World War I as a fight over the imperialists' division of the world.

Trafficking   Trafficking today takes many forms, and includes trafficking in resources such as gems and timber, drugs and people.

Gems, timber and other resources may be trafficked by belligerents in a conflict as a means to finance their efforts. Sometimes conflicts are civil (internal) in scope, but because they are related to the global political economy through shadow or war economies, they are also international. In some cases, continued fighting is the goal, rather than "defeating an enemy," because ongoing institutionalized violence serves as an

---

[23] Nazli Choucri and Robert C. North, *Nations in Conflict: National Growth and International Violence* (San Francisco: Freeman, 1975). Richard K. Ashley, *The Political Economy of War and Peace: The Sino-Soviet-American Triangle and the Modern Security Problematique* (London: Pinter, 1980). Nazli Choucri, Robert C. North and Susumu Yamakage, *The Challenge of Japan: Before World War II and After* (NY: Routledge, 1993).

[24] Marilyn Waring, *Counting for Nothing: What Men Value and What Women Are Worth*, 2nd ed. (Toronto: U Toronto P, 1999). Dr. Helen Caldicott, *The New Nuclear Danger: George W. Bush's Military-Industrial Complex* (NY: New Press, 2002).

effective cover and vehicle for the extraction and trafficking of resources.[25] Many contemporary conflicts are fought over access to resources, such as in the Democratic Republic of the Congo and Sierra Leone. Some observers of global politics predict that resource wars over timber, gems, strategic minerals and oil will become the most common sources of international conflict in the coming decades.[26]

Trafficking in persons is more often an effect of contemporary conflict than it is a cause, but it can certainly exacerbate conflicts. In some cases, children are trafficked during conflicts, often to serve as combatants. Women and children have also been trafficked for purposes of prostitution, sexual exploitation, forced labour and slavery. Trafficked women and children can become part of the barter of war, traded between camps of rebels and soldiers. When resource extraction is a defining part of local conflict, trafficked women and children can be forced to work in mines or in other elements of the extraction process.[27]

Drug trafficking supplies illegal products that are treated as a security threat because of their effect on national (and military) morale and efficiency, and because military forces participate regularly in operations against the heavily armed drug traffickers.[28] Conflicts over drugs are generally between state and nonstate actors, but other states can be drawn in because traffickers may cross national borders and their activities may involve corrupt state officials.

The international ramifications of drug trafficking are evident in the efforts of the U.S. government to prevent *cocaine cartels* based in Colombia from supplying cocaine to U.S. cities. Cocaine derives from coca plants mostly grown by peasant farmers in mountainous areas of Peru, Bolivia and Colombia. Processed in simple laboratories in the jungle, the drug is moved from Colombia through other countries, such as Panama, before arriving in the United States. In each of the states involved (including the United States), drug smugglers bribe corrupt officials, including some military or police officers, to stay clear. Other state officials in each country are working with U.S. law enforcement agencies and the U.S. military to crack down on the cocaine trade. The crackdown inevitably brings negative side effects. In 2001, Peruvian jets working with U.S. radar trackers shot down a small plane over the Andes that turned out to be carrying U.S. missionaries, and not cocaine traffickers, as thought.

The truth is that the populations in several of these countries, especially in cocaine-producing regions, benefit substantially from the drug trade. For peasant farmers in Bolivia or residents of the Colombian cocaine cartels' home provinces, the cocaine trade may be their only access to a decent income. This dilemma worsened in 2001 as coffee prices dropped to their lowest level in decades. Similarly, in 2003 many Ethiopian coffee farmers switched to growing the drug *khat* for export when low coffee prices left them unable to feed themselves. Benefits to corrupt state officials or rebel

---

[25] Mats Berdal and David M. Malone, eds., *Greed and Grievance: Economic Agendas in Civil Wars* (Boulder, CO: Rienner, 2000). Mark Duffield, *Global Governance and the New Wars* (London: Zed Books, 2001).

[26] Michael T. Klare, *Resource Wars: The New Landscape of Global Conflict* (NY: Holt, 2001).

[27] Integration of the human rights of women and the gender perspective: Violence against women: Report of the Special Rapporteur on violence against women, Ms. Radhika Coomaraswamy, on trafficking in women, women's migration and violence against women, submitted in accordance with Commission on Human Rights resolution 1977/44, UN Economic and Social Council (29 Feb. 2000), E/CN.4/2000/68.

[28] LaMond Tullis, *Unintended Consequences: Illegal Drugs and Drug Policies in Nine Countries* (Boulder, CO: Rienner, 1995). Francisco E. Thoumi, *Political Economy and Illegal Drugs in Colombia* (Boulder, CO: Rienner, 1994). Celia Toro, *Mexico's "War" on Drugs: Causes and Consequences* (Boulder, CO: Rienner, 1995).

armies are also substantial. In rural Peru and Colombia, leftist guerrillas have funded operations by controlling peasants' production of coca.

The cocaine trade thus creates several conflicts between the United States and the states of the region. Most of these interstate conflicts are resolved through positive forms of leverage, such as financial or military aid. State officials are often willing to make common cause with the United States because they are threatened by drug traffickers, who control great wealth and power, and who, being outlaws, have few incentives against using violence.

Because of the long history of U.S. military intervention in Latin America, state cooperation with U.S. military forces is a sensitive political issue. Governments in the region must respect a delicate balance between the need for U.S.

DRUG WARS
Because drug trafficking crosses national borders and involves guns and money, it is a source of interstate conflict. The United States invaded Panama to halt dictator Manuel Noriega's collusion with traffickers shipping illegal drugs to the United States. Here, U.S. forces train in Panama near a billboard advertising the United States' own drug export to Panama (tobacco), 1989.

help and the need to uphold national sovereignty. In some countries, governments have faced popular criticism for allowing the "Yankees" to "invade" in the name of the drug war. In one case, the U.S. military literally did invade. In 1989, U.S. forces invaded Panama, arrested its leader, dictator Manuel Noriega, and convicted him in U.S. courts of complicity in drug trafficking through Panama.

The growing world trade in *heroin* created similar conflicts in the late 1990s. Most of the raw material (opium poppies) came from two poor and conflict-ridden countries with authoritarian governments, Afghanistan and Burma. Afghan production of opium poppies doubled after 1998, making it the supplier of three-quarters of the world total. In 2007, Afghanistan remains the predominant source, with record high poppy production levels, despite the establishment of a pro-Western government after the Taliban was ousted in 2001. With no viable alternatives, local farmers often have no choice but to grow poppies and are deeply resentful (and left economically vulnerable) when Canadian or other NATO forces attempt to eradicate crops.

CONFLICTS OF IDEAS

Conflicts over tangible issues (whether territory, government or resources) often are associated with conflicts over ideas. In many cases, it is difficult to identify which element is the most important contributing factor in any given conflict. Although conflicts over ideas are inseparable from their more tangible elements, such as ethnic, religious or ideological differences, each is described separately here.

Figure 6.2 Kurdish Area

Ethnic populations often span international borders. The shaded region shows the approximate area of Kurdish settlements.

ethnic groups Large groups of people who share ancestral, language, cultural, or religious ties and a common identity.

Ethnic Conflict

Ethnic conflict is described by some observers as quite possibly the most important source of conflict in the numerous wars currently being fought throughout the world.[29] **Ethnic groups** are large groups of people who share ancestral, language, cultural or religious ties and a common *identity* (individuals identify with the group). Ethnic groups often form the basis for *nationalist* sentiments. Not all ethnic groups identify as nations; for instance, within Canada various ethnic groups coexist (though sometimes uneasily) with a common *national* identity as Canadians. In locations where millions of members of a single ethnic group live as the majority population in their ancestors' land, they usually think of themselves as a nation. In most such cases they aspire to have their own state with formal international status and territorial boundaries.[30]

Territorial control is closely tied to the aspirations of ethnic groups for statehood. Any state's borders will deviate to some extent (sometimes substantially) from the actual location of ethnic communities. Members of an ethnic group may be left outside its state's borders, and members of other ethnic groups may be kept within that state's borders. The resulting situation can be dangerous, with part of an ethnic group controlling a state and another part living as a minority within another state controlled by a rival ethnic group. Frequently the minority group suffers discrimination in the other state and the "home" state tries to rescue or avenge them.

Other ethnic groups lack any home state. Kurds share a culture, and many aspire to create a state of Kurdistan. Kurds reside in four states—Turkey, Iraq, Iran and Syria—all of which strongly oppose giving up control of part of their own territory to create a Kurdish state (see Figure 6.2). In recent years, rival Kurdish guerrilla armies have fought both Iraqi and Turkish military forces and each other. In the late 1990s, Turkey repeatedly sent large military forces into northern Iraq to attack Kurdish guerrilla bases.[31] Kurds enjoyed autonomy in part of northern Iraq under U.S. protection in the 1990s and may receive quasi-autonomous status in postwar Iraq.

In ethnic conflicts there are often pressures to redraw borders by force. For example, the former Soviet republic of Moldova is inhabited mostly by ethnic Romanians but also by a number of ethnic Russians, who primarily reside at the eastern end of the state (farthest from Romania). A river separates a strip of land at the east end from the rest of Moldova, and ethnic Russians make up the majority in that strip of territory. When Moldova became independent in 1991 and began asserting its Romanian identity—even considering a merge with Romania—the Russians living on the eastern strip of land sought to break away and make the river a new international border. Armed conflict ensued, and Russia and Romania threatened to intervene. Eventually a ceasefire and peacekeeping arrangements were implemented, with no formal change in borders.

---

[29] Ted Robert Gurr, *Peoples versus States: Minorities at Risk in the New Century* (Washington, DC: U.S. Institute of Peace, 2000). Stephen M. Saideman, *The Ties That Divide* (NY: Columbia UP, 2001). Milton J. Esman, *Ethnic Politics* (Ithaca, NY: Cornell UP, 1995). Stephen Iwan Griffiths, *Nationalism and Ethnic Conflict* (NY: Oxford UP, 1993). Donald L. Horowitz, *Ethnic Groups in Conflict* (Berkeley: U California P, 1985). Donald Rothchild, *Managing Ethnic Conflict in Africa: Pressures and Incentives for Cooperation* (Washington, DC: Brookings, 1997).

[30] Lars-Erik Cederman, *Emergent Actors in World Politics: How States and Nations Develop and Dissolve* (Princeton, NJ: Princeton UP, 1997).

[31] Henri J. Barkey and Graham E. Fuller, *Turkey's Kurdish Question* (Lanham, MD: Rowman & Littlefield, 1998).

When ethnic populations are minorities in territories controlled by rival ethnic groups, they may be driven from their land or (in rare cases) systematically exterminated. By driving out the minority ethnic group, a majority group can assemble a more unified, more contiguous and larger territory for its nation-state, as ethnic Serbs did through "ethnic cleansing" after the breakup of Yugoslavia.

Outside states often worry about the fate of "their people" living as minorities in neighbouring states. For instance, Albania is concerned about the ethnic Albanians who make up the majority population in the Serbian province of Kosovo. If Kosovo became independent of Serbia (or merged with Albania), then Serbia would worry about the minority of ethnic Serbs living in Kosovo. Similar problems have fuelled wars between Armenia and Azerbaijan (in the former Soviet Union) and between India and Pakistan. Before World War II, Adolf Hitler used the fate of ethnic German communities in Poland and Czechoslovakia to justify German territorial expansion into those neighbouring states. It appears likely that the dangerous combination of ethnic conflict and territorial disputes will lead to more wars in the future.

TELLING THE WORLD
Canadian lieutenant-general Roméo Dallaire served as the United Nations commander in Rwanda in 1994, and was unable to convince the United Nations to prevent the slaughter of over half a million Tutsis and moderate Hutus.

In extreme cases, such as Hitler's Germany, governments use genocide—systematic extermination of ethnic or religious groups in whole or in part—to try to destroy scapegoated groups or political rivals. In Rwanda, where the Hutu group is the majority and the Tutsi group the minority, a Hutu-nationalist government slaughtered more than half a million Tutsis (and Hutus opposed to the government) in a matter of weeks in 1994. The weak international response to this atrocity reveals the frailty of international norms of human rights compared with norms of noninterference in other states' internal affairs—at least when no strategic interests are at stake. The former United Nations commander in Rwanda, retired Canadian lieutenant-general Roméo Dallaire, has also suggested that the world community's indifference to the genocide was in no small measure a result of the racism of Northern decision-makers toward a country populated by black Africans.[32]

Many are concerned that the world may be standing idle again as genocide is perpetrated in the Darfur region of Sudan. Following the resolution of a peace agreement ending a decades-long civil war in the south of Sudan, rebels in the western Darfur region began to protest their exclusion from the agreement. In response, the government helped Arab (Muslim) militias raid black African (but also Muslim) Darfur villages, wantonly killing, raping and burning. Millions of refugees lived on the edge and have fled the

---

[32] Roméo Dallaire, *Shake Hands with the Devil: The Failure of Humanity in Rwanda* (Toronto: Random House Canada, 2003).

DRIVING OUT THE OUT GROUP
Ethnocentrism based on an in-group bias can promote intolerance and ultimately dehumanization of an out-group, as was the case in the Bosnian and Rwandan genocides, South African apartheid, the persecution of Jews and other minorities in Nazi Germany and slavery in the United States. Ethnic conflicts play a role in many international conflicts. Canadians, as part of a multiethnic society, view such conflicts somewhat differently than citizens of more homogeneous great powers. In 2006, the slaughter and expulsion of black farmers in Darfur, Sudan, by government-sponsored Arab militias continued even after some international officials called it "genocide"—a term that invokes obligations under international law. This Darfur woman returned to what had been her home after fleeing an attack in October, 2004.

region, some into towns or refugee camps within Sudan, others into bordering Chad. Some countries have openly called it genocide. In late 2004, the government and some of the Darfur rebels reached a tentative peace agreement to be monitored by the African Union and the United Nations. But Sudan blocked a robust UN peacekeeping force, and the war crimes in Darfur continued into 2007.

Often, in former colonies whose borders were drawn arbitrarily, some ethnic groups span two or more states while others share a state with groups that are traditionally rivals or enemies. For example, Nigeria includes 250 ethnic groups, the largest being two Muslim groups in the north and two Christian groups in the south. Although Nigeria's ethnic populations are slowly developing an overarching national identity as Nigerians, old tensions continue to disrupt politics. After a northern-dominated military government was replaced by an elected president from the south in 1999, as Nigeria democratized, ethnic violence killed hundreds of people. In cases of genocide and less extreme scapegoating, ethnic hatred does not erupt naturally, but is provoked and channelled by politicians to strengthen their own power. In late 2005, for example, Iran's Islamist president, looking to consolidate his power domestically as the international community pressured Iran over its nuclear program, called the Holocaust a "myth" (and in 2006 held an international conference on that topic) and said Israel should be "wiped off the map."

The Cold War, with its tight system of alliances and authoritarian communist governments, seems to have helped to keep ethnic conflicts in check. In the multinational states of the Soviet Union and Yugoslavia, the existence of a single strong state (willing to oppress local communities) kept a lid on ethnic tensions and enforced peace between neighbouring communities. The breakup of these states allowed ethnic and regional conflicts to take centre stage, sometimes bringing violence and war. Many realist and neo-realist commentators predicted that the end of the Cold War might result in rising ethnic conflict. Critical theorists would argue that ethnic conflict is often used to camouflage underlying causes of conflict, and depicts those who face ethnic conflict as "barbarians" and thus, as Dallaire suggested about Rwanda, not worthy of the international community's attention. Of course, not all ethnic groups have trouble getting along. After the fall of communism, most of the numerous ethnic rivalries in the former Soviet Union did not lead to warfare, and in Czechoslovakia and elsewhere ethnic relations were relatively peaceful.

Causes of Ethnic Hostility   Why do ethnic groups frequently dislike each other? Often there are long-standing historical conflicts over specific territories or natural resources, or over one ethnic group's economic exploitation or political domination of another. Over time, ethnic conflicts may transcend these concrete historical causes and take on a life of their own. They become driven not by tangible grievances (though these may persist) but by the kinds of processes described by social psychology that are set in motion when one group of people has a prolonged conflict with another and experiences violence at the hands of the other group.[33]

The ethnic group is a kind of extended *kinship* group—a group of related individuals sharing ancestors. Even when kinship relations are not very close, a *group identity* makes a person act as though the other members of their ethnic group are family. For instance, African Canadian men who call each other "brother" express group identity as kinship. Likewise Jews around the world treat each other as family even though each community has intermarried over time and may have more ancestors in common with local non-Jews than with distant Jews. Perhaps, as technology allows far-flung groups to congregate in cyberspace, there will be less psychological pressure to physically collect ethnic groups in a territorial nation-state.

Ethnocentrism, or *in-group bias*, is the tendency to see one's own group in favourable terms and an *out-group* in unfavourable terms. Some scholars believe that ethnocentrism has roots in a biological propensity to protect closely related individuals, but this idea is somewhat controversial.[34] More often, in-group bias is understood in terms of social psychology.

No *minimum criterion* of similarity or kin relationship is needed to evoke the group identity process, including in-group bias. In psychological experiments, even trivial

ethnocentrism (in-group bias) The tendency to see one's own group (in-group) in favourable terms and an out-group in unfavourable terms.

---

[33] Betty Glad, ed., *Psychological Dimensions of War* (Newbury Park, CA: Sage, 1990).

[34] Paul Shaw and Yuwa Wong, *Genetic Seeds of Warfare: Evolution, Nationalism, and Patriotism* (Boston: Unwin Hyman, 1989). J. Groebel and R. A. Hinde, eds., *Aggression and War: Their Biological and Social Bases* (NY: Cambridge UP, 1989). Albert Somit, "Humans, Chimps, and Bonobos: The Biological Bases of Aggression, War, and Peacemaking" [review essay]. *Journal of Conflict Resolution* 34.3 (1990): 553–82. Diane McGuinness, ed., *Dominance, Aggression, and War* (NY: Paragon, 1987).

differentiations can evoke these processes. If people are assigned to groups based on a known but unimportant characteristic (such as preferring, say, circles to triangles), before long the people in each group show in-group bias and find they don't much care for the other group's members.[35]

In-group biases are far stronger when another group looks different, speaks a different language or worships in a different way (or all three). All too easily, an out-group can be dehumanized and stripped of all human rights. This **dehumanization** includes the common use of animal names—"pigs," "dogs" and so forth—for members of the out-group. U.S. propaganda in World War II depicted Japanese people as apes. Especially in wartime, when people see members of an out-group killing members of their in-group, dehumanization can be extreme. The restraints on war that have evolved in regular interstate warfare, such as not massacring civilians (see "War Crimes" on pp. 286–290), are easily discarded in inter-ethnic warfare.

dehumanization
Stigmatization of enemies as subhuman or nonhuman, leading frequently to widespread massacres or, in the worst cases, destruction of entire populations. See also *crimes against humanity* and *genocide*.

truth commissions
Commissions used by new governments to hear testimony from periods of war; used to find truthful accounts of past occurrences in exchange for asylum from punishment for participants.

In several countries in the 1990s where long internal wars led to dehumanization and atrocities—notably in South Africa—new governments used **truth commissions** to help society heal and move forward. The commissions' role was to hear honest testimony from the period, to bring to light a truthful account of what happened during these wars, and in exchange to offer most of the participants asylum from punishment. Sometimes international NGOs helped facilitate the process. However, human rights groups objected to a settlement in Sierra Leone in 1999 that brought into the government a faction that had routinely cut off civilians' fingers as a terror tactic. (Hostilities did end, however, in 2001.) In 2006, Colombian right-wing militia leaders called from jail for the creation of a truth commission where they could confess their role in a long civil war (and receive amnesty). Thus, after brutal ethnic conflicts give way to complex political settlements, most governments try to balance the need for justice and truth with the need to keep all groups on board.

The Information Revolution
Nations and States

Many current international conflicts result from the mismatch of states' territorial borders with the actual distributions of ethnic or national populations. As technology allows communities to transcend geography, can national identity connect dispersed populations without generating territorial conflicts?

To explore this question, go to www.pearsoned.ca/goldstein.

Experience in Western Europe shows that education over time can help traditionally hostile nations such as France and Germany overcome ethnic animosities. After World War II, governments rewrote the textbooks with which a new generation would learn its people's histories. Previously, each state's textbooks had glorified its own past deeds, played down its misdeeds and portrayed its traditional enemies in unflattering terms. In a continent-wide project, new textbooks that gave a more objective and fair rendition were created. This project helped pave the way for European integration in subsequent decades. By contrast, many educators in Israel and Palestine report that textbooks and other teaching tools continue to depict the other side as a barbaric, irrational enemy while their own side (and this is true of each "side") is portrayed as a rational, just and innocent party in the conflict.

The existence of a threat from an out-group promotes the cohesion of an in-group, thereby creating a somewhat self-reinforcing process of ethnic division. However, ethnocentrism also often causes members of a group to view themselves as

---

[35] H. Tajfel and J. C. Turner, "The Social Identity Theory of Intergroup Behavior," *Psychology of Intergroup Relations*, 2nd eds., ed. S. Worchel and W. Austin (Chicago: Nelson-Hall, 1986) 7–24.

Thinking Theoretically

Ethnic Hutu extremists in the government of Rwanda in 1994 carried out an organized genocide, giving orders throughout the country to kill ethnic Tutsis and those Hutu who had opposed the government. In short, about 500 000 men, women and children were massacred, mostly by machete, and their bodies dumped into rivers; thousands at a time washed up on lakeshores in neighbouring Uganda. What theories could help explain this event?

Hutu hatred toward Tutsis might reflect the concrete interests and experiences of the two groups, especially since the minority Tutsis had earlier held power over the Hutu, and Belgian colonialism had exploited local rivalries. Realists might try to explain how the interests of Hutu extremists were served by exterminating their rivals for power. This explanation is undermined, however, by the outcome: the Hutu extremists lost power as a result of the episode.

We might instead view Hutu-Tutsi hatred as part of a pattern of age-old ethnic hatreds in the post–Cold War era, especially in so-called backward areas such as Africa.

This "age-old-hatreds" theory was often articulated by Western politicians in the case of Bosnia, portraying the Balkans, like Africans, as "backward" and conflict-prone. However, this theory is even weaker than the realist explanation, since one of the world's most civilized, "advanced" states, Germany, exterminated Jews even more efficiently than Rwanda did Tutsis—the difference being simply that the "advanced" society could kill with industrial chemicals instead of at knifepoint.

Social psychology theories would view the Rwandan genocide as pathological—a deviation from rationality and social norms. In-group biases based on fairly arbitrary group characteristics are amplified by a perceived threat from an out-group, exaggerated by history, myth and propaganda (including schooling). Such feelings can be exploited by politicians pursuing their own power. A key threshold is crossed when the out-group is dehumanized, and norms of social interaction, such as not slitting children's throats, can then be disregarded.

disunited (because they see their own divisions so closely) and the out-group as monolithic (because they see it only from outside). This usually reflects a group's sense of vulnerability. Furthermore, overstating the threat posed by an enemy is a common method used by political leaders to bolster their own position within an in-group. In the Arab-Israeli conflict, Israelis tend to see themselves as fragmented into dozens of political parties and diverse immigrant communities pulling in different directions, while they see Arabs as a monolithic bloc united against them. Meanwhile, Arab Palestinians see themselves as fragmented into factions and weakened by divisions among the Arab states, while Israelis appear monolithic in their view.

Over time, rival ethnic groups may develop a pattern of *feuding*. Each side retaliates for actions of the other in a continuing circle of violence. Reflecting in-group bias, each side often believes it is acting defensively and that the other side "started it."

Ethnic conflicts are hard to resolve because they are not about "who gets what" but about "I don't like you." To cast the conflict in a bargaining situation, each side places value on the other's loss of worth (making a zero-sum game; see p. 58). A person inflamed with hatred of an enemy is willing to *lose* value in absolute terms—to lose money, the support of allies or even life—to deprive the enemy of value as well. Suicide bombers exemplify this fanatical hatred. Almost all means of leverage used in such conflicts are negative, and bargains are very hard to reach. As such, ethnic conflicts tend to drag on without resolution for generations.

Ethnic groups are only one point along a spectrum of kinship relations—from nuclear families through extended families, villages, provinces and nations up to the entire human race. Loyalties fall at different points along the spectrum. Again, there is no minimum criterion for in-group identity. For instance, experts have said that of all the African countries, Somalia was likely immune from ethnic conflicts because all Somalis were from the same ethnic group and spoke the same language. Then, in 1991–1992, a ruinous civil war erupted between members of different clans (based on extended families), leading to mass starvation and the intervention of foreign military forces (which withdrew in 1995 after a humiliating failure to tame the violence).

It is unclear why people tend to strongly identify with one level of group identity.[36] In Somalia, loyalties are to clans; in Serbia, they are to ethnic groups; in Canada and elsewhere, multiethnic states have people's primary loyalty. States reinforce their citizens' sense of identification through flags, anthems, pledges of allegiance, patriotic speeches and so forth. Perhaps someday people will shift loyalties even further, developing a *global identity* as humans first and members of states and ethnic groups second.

Religious Conflict

One reason ethnic conflicts often transcend material grievances is that they find expression as *religious* conflicts. Since religion can be the core of a community's value system, people whose religious practices differ are easily disdained and treated as unworthy or even inhuman. When compared with ethnic and territorial conflicts, religion often surfaces as the central and most visible division between groups. For instance, most Indians are Hindus and most Pakistanis are Muslims. Most people in Azerbaijan are Muslims; Armenians are Christians. The majority of Croats are Roman Catholic Christians, whereas most Serbs are Orthodox Christians and most Bosnians and Albanians are Muslims.

Nothing inherent in religion mandates conflict, and in many places, members of different religious groups coexist peacefully. However, religious differences hold the potential for conflict, and for making existing conflicts more intractable, because they inherently involve core values, which are held as absolute truth.[37] This is increasingly true for *fundamentalist* movements, which have gained strength in recent decades. The reasons for the spread of fundamentalism are disputed, but it is clearly a global-level phenomenon. Fundamentalist movements in Christianity, Islam, Judaism, Hinduism and other religions have become larger and more powerful in recent decades. In India, Hindu fundamentalists have provoked violent clashes and massacres that have reverberated internationally. In 2002, Hindu nationalist extremists killed nearly a thousand Muslims in India's Gujarat state, where the Hindu nationalist party controls the state government. In Israel, Jewish fundamentalists have used violence, including the assassination of Israel's prime minister in 1995, to derail Palestinian-Israeli peace negotiations.

secular (state) A state created apart from religious establishments and in which there is a high degree of separation between religious and political organizations.

Such movements challenge the values and practices of **secular** political organizations—those created apart from religious establishments (the separation of religion and state). Among the secular practices threatened by fundamentalist movements are the rules of the international system, whereby states are treated as formally equal and sovereign whether they are "believers" or "non-believers." As transnational belief systems, religions are often viewed as a higher law than state laws and international treaties. Iranian Islamist fundamentalists train and support Islamic fundamentalists in other states, such as Algeria, Egypt, Jordan and Lebanon. Jewish fundamentalists build

---

[36] Jill Krause and Neil Renwick, eds., *Identities in International Relations* (NY: St. Martin's, 1996).

[37] R. Scott Appleby, *The Ambivalence of the Sacred: Religion, Violence, and Reconciliation* (Lanham, MD: Rowman & Littlefield, 1999).

settlements in Israeli-occupied territories and vow to cling to the land even if their government evacuates it. Christian fundamentalists in the United States try to convince their government to withdraw from the UN Population Fund because of that organization's views on family planning. In one way or another, all these actions run counter to the secular norms of the international system.[38]

Currently, violent conflicts are underway in the name of all the world's major religions. Special attention is due to conflicts involving Islamic groups and states. Islamist actors are active participants in eight of the world's 12 wars in progress (see p. 158). In addition, the U.S. "war on terrorism" is directed at a network of Islamic terror groups, and not against terrorism in general. To understand these groups, we must start with a broader understanding of Islamist movements, most of which are not violent.

Islam, the religion practised by **Muslims** (or *Moslems*), is broad and diverse. Its divergent populations include Sunni Muslims, Shi'ite Muslims and many smaller branches and sects. The areas of the world that are predominantly Islamic stretch from Nigeria to Indonesia, centred in the Middle East. Most countries with mainly Muslim populations belong to the Islamic Conference, an IGO (see Figure 6.3 on p. 186). Islam has been frequently stereotyped in European and North American political discourse, especially at times of conflict such as the 1973 oil embargo, the 1979 Iranian revolution, the 1991 Gulf War, the 2003 war in Iraq and the ongoing so-called war on terrorism. Islam is no more conflict-prone than other religions.

Islamist groups advocate a government and society based on Islamic law. These groups vary greatly in the means they employ to pursue this goal. Most of these means are nonviolent, such as charities and political parties. Some are violent—militias and terrorist networks, for example.[39] In the case of the former, Islamist political movements are active throughout the Muslim world. In Jordan, Islamic parties won the largest bloc of seats in Parliament without violence. Meanwhile, in the 1990s Islamic parties gained ground in Turkey—a fiercely secular state in which the military has intervened repeatedly to prevent religious expression in politics—and a former Islamist leader has been prime minister since 2003.

Since Islamist movements seek changes primarily in domestic policies, why do they matter for IR? Islamist politics may lead to a change in foreign policies, but the more important answer is that Islamist movements have become a transnational force shaping world order and global North-South relations in important ways.

In several countries, Islamic fundamentalists reject Western-oriented secular states in favour of governments more explicitly oriented to Islamic values.[40] These movements reflect long-standing *anti-Western* sentiment in these countries—against the old European

Islam/Muslims A broad and diverse world religion whose divergent populations include Sunni Muslims, Shi'ite Muslims and many smaller branches and sects; practised by Muslims from Nigeria to Indonesia, and centred in the Middle East.

---

[38] Mark Juergensmeyer, *The New Cold War? Religious Nationalism Confronts the Secular State* (Berkeley: U California P, 1993). Kevin Phillips, *American Theocracy: The Peril and Politics of Radical Religion, Oil, and Borrowed Money in the 21st Century* (New York: Viking, 2006).

[39] Mir Zohair Husain, *Global Islamic Politics*, 2nd ed. (NY: Longman, 2003). John L. Esposito, *Unholy War: Terror in the Name of Islam* (Oxford, 2002). Bernard Lewis, *The Crisis of Islam: Holy War and Unholy Terror* (NY: Modern Library Edition, 2003).

[40] James Turner Johnson and John Kelsay, *Cross, Crescent, and Sword: The Justification and Limitation of War in Western and Islamic Tradition* (NY: Greenwood, 1990). James Piscatori, *Islam in a World of Nation-States* (NY: Cambridge UP, 1984). Scott W. Hibbard and David Little, *Islamic Activism and U.S. Foreign Policy* (Washington, DC: U.S. Institute of Peace, 1997). Leonard Binder, *Islamic Liberalism: A Critique of Development Ideologies* (Chicago: U Chicago P, 1988).

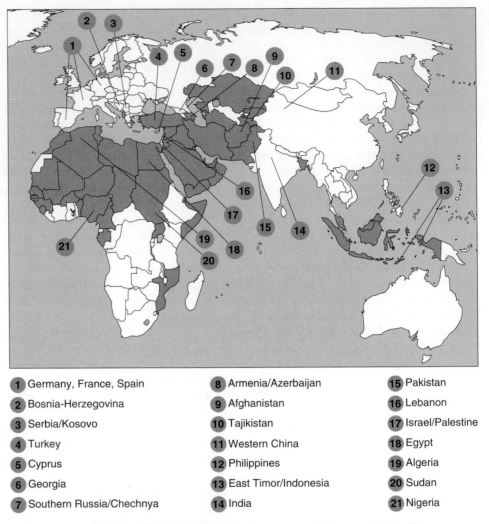

1 Germany, France, Spain	8 Armenia/Azerbaijan	15 Pakistan
2 Bosnia-Herzegovina	9 Afghanistan	16 Lebanon
3 Serbia/Kosovo	10 Tajikistan	17 Israel/Palestine
4 Turkey	11 Western China	18 Egypt
5 Cyprus	12 Philippines	19 Algeria
6 Georgia	13 East Timor/Indonesia	20 Sudan
7 Southern Russia/Chechnya	14 India	21 Nigeria

Figure 6.3 Members of the Islamic Conference and Areas of Conflict

Shaded countries are members of the conference; numbered regions are areas of conflict between Muslims and non-Muslims or secular authorities.

colonizers who were Christian—and are in some ways *nationalist* movements expressed through religious channels. In some Middle Eastern countries with authoritarian govern-ments, religious institutions (mosques) have been the only available avenue for political opposition. Religion has therefore become a means for expressing opposition to the status quo in both politics and culture.

Public opinion in Muslim and non-Muslim countries shows some misconceptions and differences in opinion. Support for Islamist radicals varies greatly, from a majority in Jordan to 13 percent in Turkey and Morocco. In five Western industrialized countries, 40 to 80 percent thought Muslims were "fanatical" and 60 to 80 percent said they did not respect women. In three of five Muslim countries, more than 60 percent thought non-Muslims were "fanatical" and in four of those five countries a majority thought non-Muslims did not respect women.

Since 2003, the Iraq War has greatly inflamed anti-American and anti-Western feeling and helped radicalize politics across the Muslim world, especially in Arab countries that saw the U.S. invasion as a humiliation to Arab dignity and a parallel to Israel's occupation of Arab land. In 2003, Turkey's parliament refused to let U.S. troops move through Turkey (a NATO ally) en route to Iraq and U.S. forces had to make do without a northern front. Anti-Western sentiment in Islamic countries reached a head in 2006 after a Danish newspaper published offensive cartoons depicting the prophet Mohammed. Across the world, Muslims protested, rioted (with dozens of deaths resulting) and boycotted Danish goods.

Anti-Western sentiment in predominantly Islamic countries has accelerated the growth of violent Islamist groups. Although the minority, they have disproportionate effects on IR and receive a great deal of public attention. Armed Islamic groups vary tremendously from one another, and in some cases violently disagree. In particular, divisions between the Sunni and Shi'ite factions of Islam have led to violence, especially in and around Iraq—a Shi'ite-majority country ruled by Sunnis under Saddam Hussein. Iraq's war against Shi'ite Iran killed a million people, and Saddam's repression of a Shi'ite uprising after the 1991 Gulf War killed an estimated tens of thousands. Under the U.S. occupation of Iraq, Shi'ite parties took power in 2003 and Shi'ite militias exacted revenge, while some Sunnis waged a relentless and brutal insurgency. In 2006, after the bombing of a revered Shi'ite mosque in Iraq, a wave of sectarian killings led to the death of tens of thousands of Iraqis and pushed the country into a low-level civil war with the potential to escalate—and even to spark a regional Sunni-Shi'ite war.

In the worldwide picture, Islamist groups divide into Sunni and Shi'ite factions which do not generally cooperate. On the Shi'ite side, the most important groups are Iran's revolutionary guards, the Mahdi Army in southern Iraq (and other Shi'ite militias there) and Hezbollah (or Hizbollah) in southern Lebanon. These groups are all relatively successful—in Iran the religious leadership controls the state, and in both southern Iraq and southern Lebanon Shi'ite Islamist militias control a territory and hold seats in the national legislature.

In Iran, a popular uprising in 1979 overthrew the U.S.-backed shah and installed an Islamic government which allowed the top religious leaders (ayatollahs) to overturn the laws passed by the parliament. Following the war with Iraq, Iran's very large young population rebelled against the ayatollahs in both cultural and political spheres. Public opinion was relatively pro-Western. A reformer was elected president of Iran, but he was unable to deliver the reforms his supporters expected, given the lack of power in his position. An Islamist supporter of the ayatollahs, Mahmoud Ahmadinejad, was elected president in 2005, again putting all of Iran's government firmly in Islamists' hands. Defying the UN Security Council, Iran is currently developing nuclear technology that could produce nuclear weapons within a decade.

Iran strongly supports—with money, arms and training—the Hezbollah party in Lebanon. Hezbollah runs hundreds of schools, hospitals and other charities, but is also included on the Canadian list of terrorist organizations. Hezbollah claimed that its attacks propelled Israel to withdraw from southern Lebanon in 2000. Then in 2006, Hezbollah proved itself to be a competent military force, putting up a stiff fight in a brief but destructive conflict with Israel. Hezbollah's success in "standing up to Israel" won it popular support throughout the Arab world, including among Sunnis. However, it raised old divisions within Lebanon, creating another source of political instability in the Middle East in 2007.

On the Sunni side, the major radical Islamist groups adhere to some version of Wahhabism, a fundamentalist interpretation of Islamic law with roots in Saudi Arabia. Currently, the most important centre of this fundamentalist movement is in Afghanistan and neighbouring areas of western Pakistan.

Focus on Canadian Scholarship

Numerous scholars pursue questions of international conflict at Canadian universities. At the University of Toronto, **Janice Gross Stein** has examined issues of security in the Middle East. Also at the University of Toronto, **Thomas Homer-Dixon** has explored links between demographic and environmental change and violence as well as the social psychology of group identities and ethnocentrism. **Brian Job** at the University of British Columbia examines international security studies and the evolving security order of the Asia Pacific, and his colleague Allen Sens is interested in UN peacekeeping, European security and NATO. At Kingston's Royal Military College, **Walter Dorn** examines security sector reform as well as international interventions and genocide. **William Moul,** at the University of Waterloo, is interested in interstate conflict and the causes of war. At the University of Victoria, **Scott Watson** examines the construction of Kurdish security and identity. At Simon Fraser University, **Douglas Ross** examines security and arms control in the North Pacific and Canadian-U.S. aerospace defence relations. Rob Huebert of the University of Calgary researches questions concerning the law of the sea and Arctic sovereignty. At the University of Saskatchewan, **Bohdan Kordan** has explored questions of war, ethnicity and the Canadian state during World War II. **Ken Bush** at St. Paul's University examines intra-group dynamics in ethnic conflicts and his colleague **Jean François Rioux** is interested

in the history of conflict, resolution and peacebuilding. At the University of Windsor, **Timothy Donais** researches peacebuilding in Bosnia. **Pierre Lizée** of Brock University focuses on reconfigurations of international security and governance, with a focus on Southeast Asia. At Carleton's Norman Paterson School of International Affairs, **David Carment** examines ethnic conflict and interstate crises. **Charles Pentland** at Queen's University examines the security implications of European Union enlargement. At the University of Sherbrooke, **Danny Deschênes** examines Canadian security and defence policy, and at the University of Waterloo, **Ashok Kapur** examines issues of regional security in the Asia-Pacific region. Also at Waterloo, **William Moul** focuses on interstate conflict and the causes of war, especially between great powers. **Nergis Canefe** of York University examines crimes against humanity and ethno-religious conflicts in the Balkans and **Nicola Short** studies the political economy of the peacebuilding process in Guatemala. At McGill University, **T.V. Paul** focuses on the India-Pakistan conflict as well as more general questions about the changing national security state and his colleague, **Rex Brynen,** examines peacebuilding and post-conflict reconstruction. Also at McGill, **Stephen Saideman** examines ethnic politics and international conflict. At the University of Ottawa, **Roland Paris** examines questions of post-conflict peace-building.

An Islamic government was established in Afghanistan in 1992 after a civil war (and following a decade of ill-fated Soviet occupation). Rival Islamic factions then continued the war with even greater intensity for several years. By 1997 a faction called the Taliban had taken control of most of Afghanistan and imposed an extreme interpretation of Islamic law. Through beatings and executions, the regime forced women to wear head-to-toe coverings, girls to stay out of school and men to grow beards, among other repressive policies. By the late 1990s, the war in Afghanistan had become the world's most destructive war and threatened to fuel conflicts in Russia, China and other nearby countries where various forms of Muslim nationalism are at odds with state governments. As noted earlier, Afghanistan is the world's primary source of opium for narcotics.

The incendiary mixture in Afghanistan in the 1990s—unending war, grinding poverty, religious fundamentalism and an ideologically driven repressive government—did not spread to neighbouring countries. It did, however, jump oceans to hit the United States in September 2001. The Taliban's allies and counterparts from other countries used Afghanistan as a base for terrorist operations, culminating in the 2001 attacks. In response, the U.S. exerted its power to remove the Taliban from rule in Afghanistan and disrupt the al Qaeda terrorist network's headquarters. However, the Taliban and other forces opposed to Western occupation remain strong in Afghanistan, and continue to engage NATO forces, including members of the Canadian Forces, in daily attacks.

In Palestine, the radical Islamist faction Hamas is another important Sunni Islamist militia, not closely connected with al Qaeda or the Taliban. Centred in the Gaza Strip, Hamas sent suicide bombers to kill hundreds of Israelis after 2000, then won free parliamentary elections in 2006 because it was seen as less corrupt than the dominant secular Fatah party. However, the Palestinian presidency remains in Fatah control, and rival security organizations have fought increasingly violent street battles, with Hamas wresting control of the Gaza Strip in mid 2007.

The Changing World Order

Religious and Ethnic Difference in World Order

When the Cold War between the United States and the Soviet Union unravelled in the late 1980s, there was much speculation about the shape of future conflict. Some realist commentators suggested that we would all soon miss the Cold War because tensions between the two superpowers had kept a lid on other sources of conflict; for example, those deriving from ethnic or religious differences. Some suggested that we would see a clash of civilizations between "the West" and "the rest" and others predicted a "coming anarchy."

From this perspective, the Cold War provided something of a bipolar balance between the U.S. and the Soviet Union. This did not mean conflict would never occur during the Cold War, but rather that there were some things that could be anticipated, given the balance of power, such as *who* to be concerned about (if you lived in the West, then the Soviet Union; if you lived in the communist bloc, then the United States), *what* to be concerned about (nuclear weapons) and *how* to address the threat (nuclear deterrence). The fact that a war between the Soviet Union and United States had never taken place, and that nuclear weapons had never been used in such a conflict, was seen as evidence in support of the idea of this balance. With the collapse of the Cold War, all the certainties of the Cold War rivalry were gone, and the world became a more dangerous and unpredictable place.

Other commentators, informed by a liberal-pluralist approach, anticipated instead the possibility of a peace dividend at the end of the Cold War. By this view, the vast expenditures on military armaments that had taken place to maintain nuclear weapons and the infrastructure that sustained them during the Cold War could be redirected into social spending: housing, education and health care. By this view, too, there would be more room for international institutions. While Cold War rivalries had made organizations like the United Nations largely ineffective, this institution would now be able to fulfill its most important goal: to protect future generations from the scourge of war.

Critical theorists challenged the realist and liberal predictions. Critical theorists noted that the Cold War had not been a period of peace and stability for most people in the world. Living under the threat of nuclear annihilation was not actually a situation of peace. More importantly, while it was true that a third world war had not broken out between the Soviet Union and the United States, Cold War rivalry nonetheless had played out in violent conflicts throughout the world, usually in the global South, resulting in millions of casualties. Critical theorists were also skeptical about the prospects for either a peace dividend or a larger role for institutions like the UN. By this view, a hegemonic power like the United States would soon go in search of new legitimations for its hegemony and continued military spending—hence, for critical theorists, the current interest in terrorists, religious fundamentalism and ethnic conflict.

Events of the last decade have neither confirmed nor refuted any of these perspectives. Rising conflicts in the global South attributed to ethnic or religious differences appear to confirm the realist view, as do the terrorist attacks against the United States in September 2001. The exponential increase of UN missions around the world appears to confirm what the liberal pluralists had anticipated: a much larger role for international institutions. The new so-called war on terror, which targets Muslims and Arab peoples, seems to confirm the critical view.

Which of these views do you find most persuasive? Are any of them reflective of a new world order?

FROM FAITH TO FRENZY
Religious intolerance can exacerbate tensions between groups, sometimes crossing the line into violence, with international implications. The bombing of this revered Shi'ite mosque in Samarra, Iraq, in 2006 set off sectarian violence between Sunnis and Shi'ites that pushed Iraq to the brink of civil war and threatened to undo U.S. efforts to build a new, viable Iraqi state.

Sunni countries Pakistan and Sudan adopted Islamic laws without a revolution, as did the northern province of Nigeria. In Sudan and Nigeria, however, the adoption of Islamic law in one region heightened tensions with other regions that are not predominantly Muslim.

The predominantly Sunni Muslim republic of Chechnya, one of the republics of Russia (the Russian Federation), tried to split away from Russia in the early 1990s after the Soviet Union collapsed. In 1994–1995, Russia sent in a huge military force that destroyed the Chechen capital, but faced fierce resistance from Chechen nationalist guerrillas and withdrew in defeat. In 1999–2000, another destructive Russian campaign won a tentative grip on power in the province. Today, Chechen guerrillas continue to fight Russian control and have taken their fight into Russian territory through means such as airline hijackings, hostage takings and suicide bombings. In 2004, hundreds of children died after Chechen terrorists took students of a school hostage. In 2005, Russian forces killed the Chechen separatist leader responsible.

From the perspective of some outsiders, the religious conflicts boiling and simmering at the edges of the Islamic world look like an expansionist threat to be contained. The view from within looks more like being surrounded and repressed from several directions—a view reinforced by massacres of Muslims in Bosnia, Chechnya and India in the 1990s and by the invasion of Iraq in 2003. Overall, conflicts involving Islamist movements are more complex than most religious conflicts; they concern power, economic relations, ethnic chauvinism and historical empires in addition to religion.

Ideological Conflict

To a large extent, ideology is like religion: it symbolizes and intensifies conflicts between groups and states more than it causes them. Ideologies have a somewhat weaker hold on core values and absolute truth than religions do, so they pose somewhat fewer problems for the international system.

For realists, ideological differences among states do not matter much, because all members of the international system pursue their national interests in the context of relatively fluid alliances. For example, during the Cold War there was a global ideological struggle between capitalist democracy and communism, but the alliances and military competitions in that struggle were fairly detached from ideological factors. The two communist giants—the Soviet

Union and China—did not stay aligned very long. Even the two great rival superpowers managed to live within the rules of the international system for the most part (both remained UN members, for example).

Over the long run, even countries that experience revolutions based on strong ideologies tend to lose their ideological fervour—be it Iran's Islamic fundamentalism in 1979, China's Maoist communism in 1949, Russia's Leninist communism in 1917 or U.S. democracy in 1776. In each case, the revolutionaries expected that their assumption of power would dramatically alter their state's foreign policy, because in each case their ideology had profound international implications.

Yet, within a few decades, each of these revolutionary governments turned to the pursuit of national interests above ideological ones. The Soviet Union soon became in many ways just another great power on the European scene—strengthening its armed forces, expanding its territory at the expense of Poland and making alliances with former enemies. Likewise, China's Chairman Mao wanted to spread a "prairie fire" of revolution through the global South to liberate it from U.S. imperialism, but within a few decades Mao was welcoming the very embodiment of U.S. imperialism, President Nixon, to pursue mutual national interests.

Sometimes even self-proclaimed ideological struggles are not really ideological. In Angola in the 1980s, the United States backed a rebel army called UNITA against a Soviet-aligned government—supposedly a struggle of democracy against Marxism. In truth, the ideological differences were quite arbitrary. The government mouthed Marxist rhetoric to convince the Soviet Union to donate aid (a policy that was reversed as soon as Soviet aid dried up). Meanwhile, the "democratic" rebels adopted democratic rhetoric to get U.S. support but practised nothing of the sort. In fact, they had earlier received Chinese support and had mouthed Maoist rhetoric. When UN-sponsored elections were won by the government, the "democratic" UNITA refused to accept the results and resumed fighting. This conflict, which finally ended in 2002, really had nothing to do with ideology.

In the short term, revolutions *do* change international relations—they make wars more likely—but not because of ideology. Rather, the sudden change of governments can alter alliances and change the balance of power. With calculations of power being revised by all parties, it is easy to miscalculate or to exaggerate threats on both sides. Ideology itself plays a small role in this post-revolutionary propensity for wars: revolutions are seldom exported to other states.[41]

LET A HUNDRED FLOWERS BLOOM
Ideology plays only a limited role in most international conflicts. After revolutions, such as China's in 1949, ideologies such as Maoism may affect foreign policy. Over the next 10 or 20 years, however, such countries typically revert to a foreign policy based more on national interests (for China, territorial integrity and trade-based prosperity) than ideology (communism). Nonetheless, the clashing cultures of Western-style democracy and Chinese-style communism still are a source of conflict. Here, students demonstrate for democracy in Tiananmen Square, Beijing, 1989. The violent repression of those demonstrations cast a shadow over Chinese relations with numerous countries of the West, including Canada.

---

[41] Stephen M. Walt, *Revolution and War* (Ithaca, NY: Cornell UP, 1996).

We should not assume, however, that ideology and political philosophies do not play any role in international politics. Ideologies can help to *mobilize* national populations to support a state in its international dealings, such as war. Fascism (the Nazi ideology) inflamed German nationalism before World War II, legitimizing German aggression by placing it in an ideological framework. And ideology can sharpen and intensify a conflict between two rivals, as happened to the superpowers during the Cold War. In some proxy wars of that era—for instance, in Vietnam in the 1960s and Nicaragua in the 1980s—rebels and governments had real ideological differences that resonated with the Cold War rivalry.

Political democracy is also an ideology, and it may be the exception to the rule that ideology does not have much effect in IR. Democracy has become a global-level force in world politics, transcending the interests of particular states. A commitment to democracy does not yet outweigh a commitment to national interest in states' foreign policies, and perhaps never will, but global democracy is slowly emerging as a norm that states are increasingly pursuing in their dealings with other states. Democracies and nondemocracies may more often find themselves in conflict with each other if this trend continues. Because democracies almost never fight wars with one another (although they still have conflicts), the spread of democratic ideology may have great implications for future prospects for peace. At the same time, some international interventions (most recently the 2003 Iraq War) have been carried out in the name of promoting democracy—a rationale that critical theorists, and other observers of global politics, find deeply suspect.

If conflicts of ideas can be intractable because of psychological and emotional factors, conflicts about material interests are somewhat easier to settle based on the reciprocity principle. In theory, given enough positive leverage—a payment in some form—any state would agree to another state's terms on a disputed issue. This also means that any states or actors unable to deliver a "payment" have less bargaining power and manoeuvrability in global politics.

Just as there are many possible outcomes of conflict, many types of war and varied propensities for violence among different states, so too is there great diversity in how force is used if conflict leads to violence. States develop a wide array of military forces, which vary tremendously in their purposes and capabilities—having in common only that they are instruments used to apply violence in some form. We will now turn our focus to these military forces.

Thinking Critically

1. Suppose that you were the mediator in negotiations between two states, each claiming the same piece of land. What principles could you follow in developing a mutually acceptable plan for ownership of the territory? What means could you use to convince the two states to accept your plan?

2. How many of the six types of international conflict discussed in this chapter can you connect with the phenomenon of nationalism discussed on pp. 28–30 in Chapter 1? What are the connections in each case?

3. European textbooks were revised after World War II to reduce ethnic and national stereotypes and to give a fairer portrayal of Europe's various nations. What about the textbooks you used to learn your country's history? Did they give an accurate picture, or did they overstate the virtues of your own ethnic group or nation at the expense of others? How?

4. The rise of fundamentalism among the world's major religions challenges traditional notions of state sovereignty. How might this trend strengthen, or weaken, the United Nations and other attempts to create supranational authority (which also challenge state sovereignty)?

5. Given the definition of war provided on p. 159, name three current international situations that clearly fit this definition and three that are ambiguous "quasi-wars" (almost but not quite fitting the definition). Which do you think are more serious, the wars or the quasi-wars? Do they involve different types of actors? Different kinds of conflicts? Different capabilities?

Chapter Summary

- War and other forms of international violence are used as leverage to try to improve the terms of settlement of conflicts.

- When violent means are used as leverage in international conflicts, varied kinds of war result. They differ greatly in size and character, from guerrilla wars and raids to hegemonic war for leadership of the international system. Given this spectrum of violence, the exact definition of war is uncertain.

- Many theories have been offered as general explanations about when different forms of leverage come into play—the causes of war. Contradictory theories have been proposed at each level of analysis and, with two exceptions, none has strong empirical support. Thus, political scientists cannot reliably predict the outbreak of war.

- States come into conflict with each other and with nonstate actors for a variety of reasons. For realists, conflicts will always exist among international actors.

- Territorial disputes are among the most serious international conflicts because states place great value on territorial integrity. With a few exceptions, however, almost all of the world's borders are now firmly fixed and internationally recognized.

- Conflicts over the control of entire states (through control of governments) are also serious and are relatively likely to lead to the use of force.

- From the perspective of economic liberals, economic conflicts lead to violence much less often because positive gains from economic activities are more important inducements than negative threats of violence. Critical theorists, by contrast, would argue that economic relations of inequality are at the root of most conflicts.

- Trafficking in gems, minerals, timber and drugs creates several kinds of conflict that attract both state and nonstate actors. Conflicts over resources such as minerals, timber, oil and water are viewed by some as the most likely source of future international conflicts. Trafficking in persons, to serve as combatants, prostitutes or forced labourers, can exacerbate conflicts.

- Ethnic conflicts, especially when linked with territorial disputes, are very difficult to resolve because of psychological biases. It is hard to explain why people's loyalties are sometimes to their ethnic group and sometimes to a multiethnic nation.

- Fundamentalist religious movements of all kinds pose a broad challenge to the rules of the international system in general and state sovereignty in particular.

- Ideologies are not of significant importance in international relations. State leaders tend to use ideologies to justify whatever actions are in their interests.

Key Terms

hegemonic war   159
total war   159
limited war   159
civil war   159
guerrilla war   160
counterinsurgency   160
conflict   161
settlement   161
irredentism   166
ethnic cleansing   168

territorial waters   171
airspace   172
lateral pressure   174
ethnic groups   178
ethnocentrism   181
dehumanization   182
truth commissions   182
secular (state)   184
Islam/Muslims   185

Research Navigator Question

Research
Navigator.com
RESOURCES FOR COLLEGE RESEARCH ASSIGNMENTS

Use the Link Library for History—World History on Research Navigator™ and explore several of the sites that focus on the Arab-Israeli conflict. Construct a timeline of the conflict. Does the timeline help you discern the causes of this conflict and its prospects for resolution?

Weblinks

The following links are a sampling of research centres or NGOs that focus on different aspects of international conflict and security:

Canadian Consortium on Asia Pacific Security:
http://www.cancaps.ca

The Canadian Peacebuilding Coordinating Committee:
http://www.peacebuild.ca

Canadian Security Intelligence Service:
http://www.csis-scrs.gc.ca

International Peace Academy:
http://www.ipacademy.org

York Centre for International and Security Studies:
http://www.yorku.ca/yciss

Militaries and the Use of Force

Fighters In Sierra Leone, 2000.

THE USE OF FORCE

A state leader or other decision-maker in a conflict situation can apply various kinds of leverage to reach a favourable outcome (see Figure 7.1 on p. 196). One set of levers represents nonviolent means of influencing other states, such as foreign aid, economic sanctions, personal diplomacy and so forth (less tangible means include use of norms, morality and other ideas). A second set of levers—the subject of this chapter—represents violent actions. These levers threaten to set armies marching, bombs exploding or missiles flying. They tend to be costly to both the attacker and the attacked. The use of force is usually a last resort, and there is evidence that the utility of military force relative to nonmilitary means of resolving conflict is slowly declining over time.

However, most states still devote vast resources to military capabilities as compared with other means of influence. For example, a country like the United States has about 20 000 diplomatic personnel but 2 million soldiers; it spends about US$10 billion a year on foreign aid compared with about US$400 billion on military forces. Though the numbers are smaller in a country like Canada, the ratios are similar: about 7000 diplomatic personnel work for Foreign Affairs and International Trade Canada, but 87 244 military personnel and a further 20 000 public servants are employed by the Department of National Defence. The Canadian government spent approximately $14.5 billion on defence in 2006. In the same year, the Canadian International

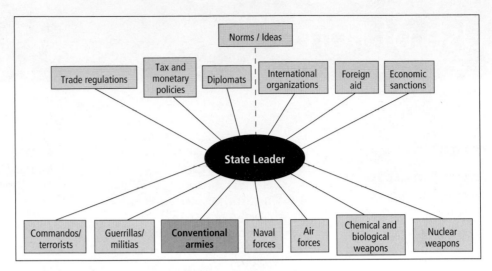

Figure 7.1 Military and Nonmilitary Means of Leverage

Conventional armed force is the most commonly used military form of leverage.

Development Agency, which administers 80 percent of Canada's foreign assistance, had a budget of some $2.5 billion.[1]

Beyond defending their territories, states develop military capabilities for several other purposes. They often hope to *deter* attack by having the means to retaliate. They may also hope to *compel* other states to behave in certain ways, by threatening an attack if the state does not comply, for example. The sizes and types of military forces can make threats credible.

States are increasingly using military forces for purposes other than fighting (or threatening) wars. These purposes include humanitarian assistance after disasters, surveillance of drug trafficking and repression of domestic political dissent, among others. Peacekeeping operations (see pp. 262–267) are a specialization of certain military forces, especially that of Canada, and a focus of NATO's Partnership for Peace program (see p. 249).

Great powers continue to dominate the composition of world military forces. Table 7.1 summarizes the estimated military capabilities of the great powers. Together, they account for almost two-thirds of world military spending, a third of the world's soldiers, about 50 percent of the weapons, 99 percent of nuclear weapons and 85 percent of arms exports. (The table also indicates the sizeable military forces maintained by Germany and Japan despite their nontraditional roles in international security affairs since World War II.)

CONVENTIONAL FORCES

Military capabilities are generally divided into three types—conventional forces, irregular forces (terrorism, militias) and weapons of mass destruction (nuclear, chemical and biological weapons). Conventional forces are most important—they are active in all 12 wars currently being fought.

---

[1] Statistics Canada, "Remembrance Day . . . By the Numbers," 6 Nov. 2006, available at http://www42. statcan.ca/smr08/smr08_064_e.htm. "What does Canada's foreign aid buy? That's private," CBC News Online, available at http://www.cbc.ca/canada/ottawa/story/2006/09/21/foreign-aid-privacy.html.

Table 7.1 Estimated Great-Power Military Capabilities, 2001–2003

| | Military Expenditures[b] (Billions of US $) | Soldiers[c] (Millions) | Heavy Weapons[a] | | | Nuclear Weapons[d] | Arms Exported[e] (Billions of US $) |
			Tanks	Carriers/ Warships/ Submarines	Combat Airplanes		
United States	460	1.4	10,000	11 / 112 / 74	3,600	10,000*	14
Russia	10–20*	1.5	20,000*	1 / 40 / 69	1,800	20,000*	4
China	35	2.8	10,000	0 / 29 / 6	2,100*	410	1
France	35	0.3	1,000	0 / 19 / 12	300	350	1
Britain	40	0.2	1,000	0 / 35 / 16	300	185	5
Germany	30	0.2	3,000	0 / 14 / 0	400	0	1
Japan	50	0.2	1,000	0 / 39 / 20	300	0	0
Approximate % of world total	70%	30%	25%	100 / 60 / 50%	40%	99%	85%

Notes: Data are for 2003 unless otherwise noted, and are in 2004 dollars. In the 1990s, the military forces of many of these states—Russia above all—were profoundly restructured. Numbers of weapons or soldiers do not indicate quality (levels of technology) or predict how armed forces would actually perform in combat. Russian forces are disorganized and in disrepair, with rampant desertion, nonoperational equipment, and low morale. Chinese forces are lower-tech than the others. Expenditure data are notoriously unreliable for Russia and China.

Data on soldiers exclude reserves. Tanks include only main battle tanks. Warships are major surface combat ships over 3,000 tons. Nuclear warheads include both strategic and tactical weapons. Arms exports are deliveries, not orders, for 2003.

*Problematic data: Russian military expenditure estimates vary. Many Chinese aircraft and Russian tanks are old and of limited military use. U.S. and Russian nuclear warheads include deployed strategic weapons (6,000 U.S., 6,000 Russian) with the remainder held in reserve or retired (awaiting destruction).

Sources: Author's estimates based on data provided by the Institute for Defense and Disarmament Studies (IDDS). Cambridge, MA.[a] Main sources are: 2001 data from IDDS World Arms Database 2001 (www.idds.org).[b] SIPRI Yearbook 2003. Not adjusted for purchasing power parity.[c] Institute for International and Strategic Studies. *The Military Balance 2001–2002; 299–304.*[d] Carnegie Endowment for International Peace (www.ceip.org).[e] Richard F. Grimmett. *Conventional Arms Transfers to Developing Nations. 1993–2003* (Washington, DC: Congressional Research Service, 2004).

Types of Forces

Whatever their ultimate causes and objectives, most wars involve a struggle to *control territory*. Territory holds a central place in warfare because of its importance in the international system, and vice versa. Borders define where a state's own military forces and rival states' military forces are free to move. Military logistics make territoriality even more important because of the need to control territories connecting military forces with each other. An army's supplies must flow from home territory along *supply lines* to the field. Thus the most fundamental purpose of conventional forces is to take, hold or defend territory.

Armies *Armies* are adapted to this purpose. Infantry soldiers armed with automatic rifles can generally control a local piece of territory. Military forces with such a presence are said to *occupy* a territory militarily. Although inhabitants may make soldiers' lives unhappy through violent or nonviolent resistance, generally only another organized, armed military force can displace occupiers.

infantry Foot soldiers who use assault rifles and other light weaponry (mines, machine guns and the like).

Foot soldiers are called **infantry.** They use assault rifles and other light weapons (such as mines and machine guns) as well as heavy artillery of various types. Artillery is extremely destructive and not very discriminating: it usually causes the most damage and casualties in wars. *Armour* refers to tanks and armoured vehicles. In open terrain, such as desert, mechanized ground forces typically combine armour, artillery and infantry. In close terrain, such as jungles and cities, however, foot soldiers are more effective.

For this reason, the armies of industrialized states have an advantage over poor armies in open conventional warfare, such as in the Kuwaiti desert. In jungle, mountain or urban warfare, however—as in Afghanistan or Iraq—this advantage is lost, and a cheaper and more lightly armed force of motivated foot soldiers or guerrillas may ultimately prevail over an expensive conventional army.

The superiority of conventional armed forces to irregular forces in open battle was demonstrated in Somalia at the end of 2006. An Islamist militia had taken control of most of the country and the capital, leaving a transitional government near Ethiopia's border, backed by Ethiopia's large conventional military. The militia closed schools and sent teenagers with rifles in pickup trucks to attack the provisional government. They were no match for the Ethiopian army, which succeeded in ousting them from the entire country within two weeks. The militia, like most irregular forces, then had to rely on guerrilla attacks rather than taking and holding territory.

counterinsurgency
Counterinsurgency warfare often includes programs that try to "win the hearts and minds" of populations so that they stop sheltering guerrillas. While battling armed factions of an insurgency, a government must essentially conduct a public relations campaign to convince the population to abandon the movement, while providing public services (such as education and welfare programs) to show their responsiveness to the population.

Counterinsurgency has received growing attention in recent years because of Iraq, but is in fact central to all 12 wars currently in progress worldwide. Counterinsurgency warfare often includes programs that try to "win the hearts and minds" of populations so that they stop sheltering guerrillas.

In some ways, because counterinsurgency warfare is as much about political gains as it is military strategy, it is the most complex type of warfare. While battling armed factions of an insurgency, a government must essentially conduct a public relations campaign to convince the population to abandon the movement, while providing public services (such as education and welfare programs) to show their responsiveness to the population. A government must be strong militarily, but cannot be too brutal in the application of force, lest more of the population begin to support insurgent guerrilla forces.

landmines Concealed explosive devices that kill or maim civilians after war's end. Such mines number more than 100 million, primarily in Angola, Bosnia, Afghanistan and Cambodia. A movement to ban landmines is underway, and nearly 100 states have agreed to do so.

A common tool of guerrillas, insurgents and the governments fighting them are **landmines,** which are simple, small and cheap containers of explosives that are trigger-activated by contacts or sensors. These mines were a particular focus of public attention in the 1990s, because in places such as Angola, Afghanistan, Cambodia and Bosnia they were used extensively by irregular military forces and never disarmed. Anti-personnel landmines are triggered by a person stepping on them or picking them up, whereas anti-tank landmines are aimed at tanks and usually require a heavier load to be triggered. Long after a war ends, landmines continue to maim and kill civilians attempting to re-establish their lives in former war zones. As many as 100 million landmines remain from recent wars. They injure about 25 000 people a year (a third of whom are children), and although they are cheap to deploy, the cost of finding and disarming them is about $1000 per mine.

Public opinion and NGOs have pressured governments to restrict the future use of landmines, and in particular anti-personnel mines (Chapter 8). After the 1997 death of Britain's Princess Diana, who had actively supported the campaign, a treaty to ban anti-personnel landmines was signed by more than 100 countries at a conference that year organized by Canada's then minister of Foreign Affairs, Lloyd Axworthy. Russia and Japan signed on shortly afterward, but the United States and China refused to sign. The U.S. government argued that landmines were essential for defending South Korea if the massed troops of North Korea tried to invade the demilitarized zone. The United States is also a large producer of landmines. By 2005, 40 million landmines had been destroyed under the treaty, with 69 countries eliminating their stockpiles.

Navies *Navies* are adapted primarily to control passage through the seas and to attack land near coastlines.[2] Unlike armies, navies are not tied to territory because the oceans beyond coastal waters are not owned by any state. Controlling the seas in wartime allows states to move their own goods and military forces while preventing enemies from doing so.

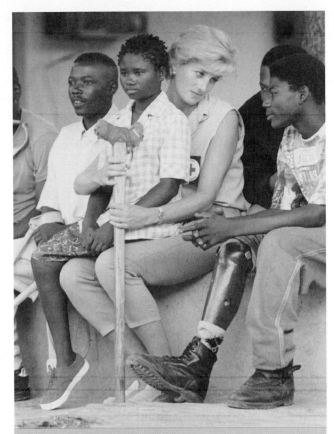

INVISIBLE KILLERS
Landmines continue to kill and maim civilians long after war's end. A movement to ban landmines culminated in a 1997 treaty signed in Ottawa by over 100 countries (not including the United States or China). Britain's Princess Diana, shown here with Angolan mine victims in 1997, was a major supporter of the movement, and her death in 1997 helped galvanize support for the treaty.

Aircraft carriers—mobile platforms for attack aircraft—are instruments of **power projection** that can exert negative leverage against virtually any state in the world. Merely sending an aircraft carrier to the vicinity of an international conflict implies a threat to use force—a modern version of what was known in the nineteenth century as "gunboat diplomacy."

power projection The ability to use military force in areas far from a country's region or sphere of influence.

Aircraft carriers are extremely expensive, and typically require 20 to 25 supporting ships for protection and supply. Few states can afford even one. Only the United States currently operates large carriers (12 in total, at a cost of more than $5 billion each). Eight other countries (France, India, Russia, Spain, Brazil, Italy, Thailand and the United Kingdom) maintain smaller carriers to launch helicopters or small airplanes.

---

[2] John Keegan, *The Price of Admiralty: The Evolution of Naval Warfare* (NY: Viking, 1988).

Canada had a number of aircraft carriers during World War II, but has since focused on smaller surface vessels and several submarines.

Surface ships, which account for the majority of warships, rely increasingly on guided missiles for use in conflict and are as such vulnerable to attack by enemy missiles (fired from ships, planes, submarines or land). Since the range of small missiles can reach dozens or hundreds of kilometres, naval warfare emphasizes detection at great distances while escaping detection oneself—a cat-and-mouse game of radar surveillance and electronic countermeasures.

Marines (part of the navy in the United States, Britain and Russia) travel to battle on ships but fight on land—amphibious warfare. Marines are useful for great-power intervention in distant conflicts where they can insert themselves quickly and establish local control. In the 1992–1993 intervention in Somalia, U.S. marines were waiting offshore while the UN Security Council debated whether to authorize the use of force.

Air Forces *Air forces* serve several distinct purposes—strategic bombing of land or sea targets, "close air support" (battlefield bombing), interception of other aircraft, reconnaissance and airlift of supplies, weapons and troops.

Traditionally, and still to a large extent, aerial bombing resembles artillery shelling in that it causes great destruction with little discrimination. This has begun to change with the evolution of "smart bombs," which improve accuracy. For instance, laser-guided bombs follow a sensor pointed at a target from the air. Television viewers during the 1991 Gulf War watched video images of bombs scoring direct hits (though not all were accurate). For many critics, these images desensitize viewers to the death and destruction being caused by directing attention instead to "fascinating" new technologies. Most of the bombing in that war was high-altitude saturation bombing using large numbers of "dumb bombs," with which pilots can fulfill their missions without seeing or experiencing the effects of their actions on the ground.

In other more typical wars, such as Russia's repression of Chechnya in 1995 and the invasion of Iraq in 2003, bombing of cities causes high civilian casualties, no matter how "smart" the technology. In cases of low-intensity conflicts and guerrilla wars, especially where forces intermingle with civilians in closed terrain such as Vietnamese jungles or Somali cities, bombing is of limited utility. Air forces are also vulnerable to missile fire. In the 2003 Iraq War, the threat of shoulder-fired missiles kept the Baghdad airport closed to all commercial traffic and most military traffic for months after the invasion began.

PROJECTING POWER
Different types of military forces are adapted for different purposes. Naval forces are used to project power in distant regions. Special forces soldiers, like this member of Canada's Joint Task Force 2 (JTF2), work in covert and commando operations.

Even more than ships, aircraft rely heavily on electronics, especially radar. The best-equipped air forces have specialized AWACS (Airborne Warning and Control System) airplanes to survey large areas with radar and coordinate the movements of dozens of aircraft. The increasing sophistication of electronic equipment and high performance requirements of attack aircraft make air forces expensive—and totally out of reach for some states.

Logistics and Intelligence All military operations rely heavily on logistical support such as food, fuel and ordnance (weapons and ammunition). Military logistics are a huge operation, and in most armed forces the majority of soldiers are not combat troops. Before the Gulf War, the United States moved an army of half a million people and a vast quantity of supplies to Saudi Arabia in a six-month effort that was the largest military logistical operation in such a time frame in history.

Global reach capabilities combine long-distance logistical support with various power projection forces.[3] These capabilities allow a great power to project military power to distant corners of the world and to maintain a military presence in most of the world's regions simultaneously. Today, only the United States fully possesses such a capability—with worldwide military alliances, air and naval bases, troops stationed overseas and aircraft carriers plying the world's oceans (refer to Table 7.1 on page 197). Britain and France are in second place, able to mount occasional distant operations of only modest size, such as in the Falkland/Malvinas Islands War. Russia is preoccupied with internal conflicts and its CIS neighbours, and China's military forces are oriented toward regional conflicts and are not global in scope.

Space forces are military forces designed to attack in or from outer space.[4] Ballistic missiles, which briefly travel through space, are not generally included in this category. Only the United States and Russia have substantial military capabilities in space. China put an astronaut into orbit in 2003, but has far fewer space capabilities overall. The development of space weapons has been constrained by the technical challenges and expense of space operations, and by norms against militarizing space. In 2001, U.S. policy-makers announced a plan to begin testing space-based lasers (for intercepting ballistic missiles) several years down the road.

Satellites are used extensively for military purposes, but these purposes thus far do not include attack. Satellites perform military surveillance and mapping, communications, weather assessment and early warning of ballistic missile launches. Satellites also provide navigational information to army units, ships, planes and even guided missiles in flight. Analysts pore over masses of satellite reconnaissance data every day. Poorer states can buy satellite photos on the commercial market—including high-resolution pictures from Russia in exchange for hard currency.

Locations can be calculated to within about 15 metres by small receivers, which pick up beacons transmitted from a network of 18 U.S. satellites known as a *Global Positioning System (GPS)*. Handheld receivers are available commercially, so the military forces of non-superpowers can use these satellite navigation beacons for free.

---

[3] Robert E. Harkavy, *Bases Abroad: The Global Foreign Military Presence* (NY: Oxford, 1989).

[4] Bob Preston, ed., *Space Weapons: Earth Wars* (Santa Monica, CA: Rand, 2002). Bhupendra Jasani, ed., *Space Weapons and International Security* (Oxford: Oxford UP, 1987). Stephen Kirby and Gordon Robson, eds., *The Militarisation of Space* (Boulder, CO: Rienner, 1987).

Intelligence gathering relies on various other means, such as electronic monitoring of telephone lines and other communications, reports from embassies and information in the open press. Some information is obtained by sending agents into foreign countries as spies, who use ingenuity (plus money and technology) to penetrate walls of secrecy that foreign governments have constructed around their plans and capabilities.

Evolving Technologies

Through the centuries, the lethalness of weapons has increased steadily—from swords to muskets, machine guns to missiles. Technological developments have changed the nature of military force in several ways. First, the resort to force in international conflicts now has more profound costs and consequences than it did at the outset of the international system several centuries ago. Great powers in particular can no longer use force to settle disputes without risking massive destruction and economic ruin.

A second long-term effect of technological change is that military engagements now occur across greater standoff distances between opposing forces. Missiles of all types are accelerating this trend. Its effect is to undermine the territorial basis of war and of the state itself. The state once had a hard shell of militarily protected borders, but today the protection offered by borders is diminishing.[5] For example, Israel's successful defence of its borders could not stop Iraqi Scud missiles from hitting its cities during the Gulf War.

SMALL BUT DEADLY
The information revolution is making smaller weapons more potent. The U.S.-made Stinger anti-aircraft missile—portable and shoulder-launched—helped turn the tide against the Soviet Union in the war in Afghanistan in the 1980s, with far-reaching consequences. Iraqi insurgents, like those shown here in late 2003, kept the Baghdad airport closed. The missiles pose a threat to commercial aviation worldwide.

---

[5] John H. Herz, *International Politics in the Atomic Age* (NY: Columbia UP, 1959).

In recent decades, the technological revolution in electronics has profoundly affected military forces, especially their command and control. **Electronic warfare** (now broadened to *information warfare*) refers to the uses of the electromagnetic spectrum (radio waves, radar, infrared, etc.) in war—employing electromagnetic signals for one's own benefit while denying their use to an enemy. Electromagnetic signals are used for sensing beyond the normal visual range, through radar, infrared and imaging equipment, to see in darkness, through fog or at great distances. These and other technologies have illuminated the battlefield such that forces cannot be easily hidden.

Electronic countermeasures are technologies designed to counteract enemy electronic systems such as radar and radio communications. **Stealth technology** uses special radar-absorbent materials and unusual shapes in the design of aircraft, missiles and ships to scatter enemy radar. However, stealth technology is extremely expensive (the B-2 stealth bomber costs about US$2 billion per plane, or about three times its weight in gold) and is prone to technical problems. Electronics are changing the costs and relative capabilities of weapons across the board. Computer chips in guided missiles have made them a formidable weapon on land, sea and air. The miniaturization of such weaponry is making smaller and cheaper military forces more powerful than ever. An infantry soldier can now use a shoulder-fired missile that costs $10 000 to destroy a main battle tank that costs $1 million. Similarly, a small boat firing an anti-ship missile that costs $250 000 can potentially destroy a major warship at the cost of hundreds of millions of dollars.

Technological developments are in some ways increasing the advantages of great powers over less-powerful states, while in other ways undermining those advantages. For example, China's military has developed radar systems to detect stealth technology, and land-based missiles could destroy expensive U.S. aircraft carriers.

U.S. forces in turn are developing new battlefield tactics calling for smaller, more mobile weapons and troop units along with more unmanned systems linked by intensive communications networks. Unmanned drones in Afghanistan in 2001 were retrofitted with remote-controlled missiles and monitored Taliban movements from the air. Within the decade, the U.S. military may begin deploying a new generation of laser weapons that will fire from planes at targets on the ground.

Strategies for *cyberwar*—disrupting enemy computer networks to degrade command-and-control, or even hacking into bank accounts electronically—were developed by NATO forces during the 1999 Kosovo war (though for the most part were not implemented) and will probably figure in future wars. Some experts fear that terrorist attacks might also target computer networks.[6]

electronic warfare The use of the electromagnetic spectrum (radio waves, radar, infrared, etc.) in war; employing electromagnetic signals for one's own benefit while denying their use to an enemy.

stealth technology The use of special radar-absorbent materials and unusual shapes in the design of aircraft, missiles and ships to scatter enemy radar.

TERRORISM

The Canadian Department of Public Safety lists some 40 terrorist organizations around the world. Since September 2001, governments and ordinary people in the West have paid much more attention to terrorism than ever before. However, terrorism itself is not new; it is essentially another step along the spectrum of violent leverage, from total war to guerrilla war. Indeed, terrorism and guerrilla war often occur together.

Terrorism differs from other kinds of wars. *Terrorism* refers to political violence that deliberately and indiscriminately targets civilians. Other criteria can be applied beyond

---

[6] Gregory J. Rattray, *Strategic Warfare in Cyberspace* (Cambridge, MA: MIT P, 2001). Neil Munro, *The Quick and the Dead: Electronic Combat and Modern Warfare* (NY: St. Martin's, 1991).

this basic definition, but the definitions become politically motivated. One person's freedom fighter is another's terrorist. More than guerrilla warfare, terrorism is a shadowy world of faceless enemies and irregular tactics marked by extreme brutality.[7]

In Canada, the 1970 kidnapping of British trade commissioner James Cross and the kidnapping and murder of Québec minister of labour Pierre Laporte by the Front de Libération du Québec (FLQ) constituted one of the only terrorist acts committed on Canadian soil. The Liberal government of Pierre Elliott Trudeau invoked the War Measures Act, declared martial law, suspended civil liberties throughout the country and deployed Canadian Forces to Québec, marking the first time that Canada had invoked the War Measures Act during peacetime. Some observers felt the federal government's reaction was an appropriate response to a perceived insurrection, while many others argued it was an overreaction in its overestimation of the nature of the threat posed by the FLQ—with its suspension of the civil liberties of all Canadians and the arbitrary arrest of any Canadian thought to have communist or FLQ sympathies. The suspension of civil liberties and arbitrary arrests are common tactics employed by states in the face of terrorism, as seen most recently since the attacks on the United States in 2001.

Another terrorist incident in which Canada was involved occurred in 1985 with the bombing of Air India Flight 182, killing 329 people, some 280 of them Canadian. Two British Columbia men faced murder charges for the explosion and were alleged to have planted the bomb in luggage checked at the Vancouver airport and then transferred to the Air India flight in Toronto, but both were acquitted in 2005 after a 19-month trial. In a related bomb explosion, two luggage handlers were killed at Japan's Narita airport on the same day as the Air India flight, and one man, Inderjit Singh Reyat, a British citizen, was convicted in 1991 and sentenced to 10 years for his role in building that bomb. Reyat later pleaded guilty to one count of manslaughter and bomb-making for his role in the Air India flight and was sentenced to a further five years in 2003.

Much controversy surrounds the Air India bombing and the subsequent investigations, which after more than 20 years have resulted in only one conviction. Evidence at trial indicated that some agencies within the Canadian government were working at odds with one another—a Canadian Security Intelligence Service (CSIS) agent, for example, admitted to destroying hundreds of hours of taped interviews with Sikh informants rather than turn them over to the RCMP. He was concerned that the RCMP would not protect the identities of his informants (see Chapter 5, p. 139 on the clash between agencies and departments within governments). In 2006 the Canadian government announced a commission of inquiry into the Investigation of the Bombing of Air India Flight 182 after much pressure from victims' families. Government departments continued to clash at the Inquiry, with CSIS and the RCMP submitting documents that had been entirely "blacked out" and as such were unusable by the commission. By early 2007, the inquiry had heard evidence that suggested Canadian authorities had been forewarned of the planned attack but had failed to respond adequately, and likewise had not responded after the bombing to arrest known suspects. The inquiry's final report was scheduled to be delivered in the summer of 2007.[8]

---

[7] Annamarie Oliverio, *The State of Terror* (Albany: SUNY P, 1998). Adrian Guelke, *The Age of Terrorism and the International Political System* (NY: Tauris/St. Martin's, 1995). Edward S. Herman and Gerry O'Sullivan, *The "Terrorism" Industry: The Experts and Institutions That Shape Our View of Terror* (NY: Random/Pantheon, 1991). Walter Reich, ed., *Origins of Terrorism: Psychologies, Ideologies, Theologies, States of Mind* (NY: Cambridge UP, 1990). David C. Rapoport, ed., *Inside Terrorist Organizations* (NY: Columbia UP, 1988).

[8] Zuhair Kashmeri, "Sabotage Feared as 329 Die in Jet," *The Globe and Mail* 4 Aug. 1986. Robert Matas, "Air-India Trial Puts Focus on Lax Security," *The Globe and Mail* 13 May 2003: A1. "Air India in Depth," CBC News Online, available at http://www.cbc.ca/news/airindia.

Despite these events, most terrorist incidents in the past have occurred in the Middle East, Europe and South Asia. In an interdependent world, Canada can no longer keep global problems such as terrorism at a distance. In the years before the 2001 attacks, the al Qaeda terrorist organization had thousands of members operating in dozens of countries, including Canada. Canada's border with the United States has been raised as a source of concern for authorities in both countries, particularly after the arrest at the British Columbia border of a suspected terrorist with plans to attack the Seattle Space Needle during millennium celebrations.[9]

Generally, the purpose of terrorism is to demoralize a civilian population in order to use its discontent as leverage on national governments or other parties in a conflict. Related to this is the aim of creating drama in order to gain media attention for a cause. When the IRA planted bombs in London, it hoped to make life miserable enough for Londoners that they would insist their government settle the Northern Ireland issue; the bombing also sought to keep the troubles in Northern Ireland in the news. The British government would then be pressured to concede terms more favourable to the IRA than would otherwise be the case. Terrorism is seldom without purpose; it is usually a calculated use of violence as leverage. However, motives and means of terrorism vary widely, having in common only that one actor is using violence to send a message to other actors.

The primary effect of terrorism is psychological. In part, the effectiveness of terrorism in capturing attention is due to the dramatic nature of incidents, especially as shown on television news. Terrorism also gains attention because its victims are generally random. Though only a few dozen people might be injured by a bomb left in a market, millions of people realize "it could have been me," because they, too, shop in markets. Attacks on airplanes augment this fear because many people already fear flying. Terrorism thus amplifies a small amount of power through its psychological effect on large populations, which is why it is usually a tool of the powerless.

In the attack on the World Trade Center in the United States, tangible damage was far greater than in previous terrorist attacks—reaching the thousands in lives lost and tens of billions of dollars. The psychological impact was even stronger than the physical damage—changing the U.S. political and cultural landscape instantly. In contrast to historical instances of terrorism, real costs began to loom large. The terrorist network responsible was reportedly trying to obtain nuclear weapons with which to kill not thousands but tens of thousands of Americans. Similarly, although the mailed anthrax attacks in the fall of 2001 killed only a few people, they had a far more psychological than physical effect. The door had been opened to a new bioterrorism that also could kill tens of thousands. That same kind of widespread fear occurred in Japan in 1995 when a religious cult released Sarin gas in a Tokyo subway, killing 12 and injuring nearly 6000 people.

ASYMMETRICAL CONFLICT
Terrorist attacks often reflect the weakness of the perpetrators and their lack of access to other means of leverage. Terror can sometimes amplify a small group's power and affect outcomes. Al Qaeda's September 11 attacks, staged by a relatively small nonstate actor, ultimately led to the withdrawal of U.S. troops from Saudi Arabia, drew the United States into a counterinsurgency war in Iraq and attracted a surge of recruits to al Qaeda itself.

---

[9] James Fergusson, "National Missile Defense, Homeland Defense, and Outer Space: Policy Dilemmas in the Canada-US Relationship," *Canada among Nations 2001: The Axworthy Legacy,* ed. Fen Osler Hampson, Norman Hillmer and Maureen Appel Molot (NY: Oxford UP, 2001).

Generally, terrorism has failed to accomplish its perpetrators' goals. The September 2001 attacks presumably aimed to weaken the United States, to change U.S. policy on two issues—support for Israel and the stationing of troops in Saudi Arabia—and to mobilize Muslims against the West, strengthening Islamic radicals including al Qaeda. Instead, in the immediate aftermath of the attack, the U.S. became more united domestically (e.g., national will, solidarity) and found widespread support internationally (e.g., alliances, moral support, use of military bases). The attacks had a large economic cost, especially given the pre-existing recession, but not enough to permanently weaken the country. U.S. determination to support Israel and keep troops in Saudi Arabia remained unchanged. The 2005 public transit bombings in London, which killed 52 and injured over 700, did little to alter Britain's foreign policy or its commitment to supporting the U.S. in Iraq. The attacks did show, however, that even democratic countries like the United States and Britain will not hesitate to suspend civil liberties or employ tactics like racial profiling when confronted by a terrorist threat.

By contrast, terrorist attacks on Spain in 2004, in reaction to Spain's involvement in the war against Iraq, had an almost immediate impact on Spanish foreign policy. The Spanish public had been overwhelmingly opposed to Spain sending troops to Iraq, and three days after the bombing of commuter trains in Madrid, a general election resulted in a change of government, one committed to withdrawing from Iraq.

Classic cases of terrorism—from the 1970s to the present—are those in which a *nonstate* actor has used attacks against *civilians* by secret *nonuniformed* forces, operating *across international borders*, as a leverage against *state* actors. Radical political factions or separatist groups have hijacked or blown up airplanes, or planted bombs in cafés, clubs or other crowded places. For example, a Palestinian faction held hostage and then killed Israeli athletes at the 1972 Olympic Games in Munich. In 2004, Chechen insurgents seized a school in Beslan, a small city in the Caucasus, and for three days, nearly 1200 children, parents and teachers were held without food or water. When Russian troops stormed the school, they detonated many traps set by the terrorists, setting off explosions. In the end, more than 300 people died, including 172 children. Such tactics create spectacular incidents that draw attention to the terrorists' cause. Typically, the message is, "We won't go away; we will make you unhappy until you deal with us."

States themselves carry out acts designed to terrorize their own populations or those of other states, and use many of the same techniques, including assassinations and bombings. Scholars do not agree on whether to use the label "terrorism" for such acts. Realists and liberals reject the label when states resort to such tactics, preferring to call it repression or war. Russia's indiscriminate attacks in Chechnya in 1995 are an example. By contrast, Chechen radicals' bombings of Moscow apartment buildings, the seizing of a Moscow theatre in 2002, the assassination of the Chechen president in 2004 and the Beslan school massacre can only be described as terrorism. Critical theorists insist that it is the act of violence, and not who commits it, that should be the defining characteristic of terrorism. From this perspective, states are the biggest and most frequent terrorists.[10] Of course, because war itself is hard to define, so too is terrorism; warring parties often call each other terrorists. In the Central American civil wars of the 1980s, both the states and the guerrillas employed tactics that, if employed in peacetime, would easily qualify as terrorism.

---

[10] Noam Chomsky, "Who Are the Global Terrorists?" *Worlds in Collision: Terror and the Future of Global Order,* eds. Ken Booth and Tim Dunne (London: Palgrave Macmillan, 2002). James Der Derian, "The Terrorist Discourse: Signs, States and Systems of Global Political Violence," *Antidiplomacy: Spies, Terror, Speed, and War* (Cambridge: Blackwell, 1992).

The narrowest definition of terrorism would exclude acts either by or against *uniformed military forces* rather than civilians. It would also exclude the killing of 243 U.S. marines by a car bomb in Lebanon in 1983, and the 2001 attack on the Pentagon, because both acts were directed at military targets. A narrow definition would also exclude the bombing of German cities in World War II, although its purpose was to terrorize civilians. In today's world of undeclared war, guerrilla war, civil war and ethnic violence, a large grey zone exists around clear cases of terrorism. Disagreements about whether a definition of terrorism should include Palestinian attacks on Israel or Pakistani attacks in Kashmir scuttled efforts to pass a UN treaty on terrorism in late 2001.

State-sponsored terrorism refers to the use of terrorist groups by states—usually under control of a state's intelligence agency—to achieve political aims.[11] In 1988, a bomb scattered pieces of Pan Am Flight 103 over the Scottish countryside. Combing the fields for debris, investigators found fragments of a tape recorder that had contained a sophisticated plastic-explosive bomb. A tiny strand of wire from the triggering device was discovered to be a rare variety, through which the investigators traced the origins of the bomb. The U.S. and British governments identified two Libyan intelligence agents who had smuggled the tape recorder onto Flight 103 in Frankfurt. In 1992, backed by the UN Security Council, they demanded that Libya turn over the two agents for trial. When Libya refused, the UN imposed sanctions, including a ban on international flights to or from Libya. In 1999, Libya relinquished the suspects for trial—two received life in prison while a third was acquitted—and the sanctions were lifted. In 2003, Libya formally took responsibility for the bombing and struck a multibillion-dollar compensation deal with the victims' families in an effort to secure a place of some legitimacy in the international community.

state-sponsored terrorism
The use of terrorist groups by states, usually under control of a state's intelligence agency, to achieve political aims.

As of 2007, the United States accuses five states of supporting international terrorism: North Korea, Iran, Syria, Sudan and Cuba. Iraq and Libya have recently been removed from this list. In 1996, the United States barred U.S. companies from doing business with those states. However, these kinds of sanctions are of limited effect since most industrialized states do not share U.S. views about one or more of these target states. Cuba does business with Canada and Iran with Russia. The U.S. position was also undermined when it carved an exception in its rule to allow a U.S. oil company to bid on a lucrative pipeline project in Sudan.

Often, state involvement in terrorism is very difficult to trace. Indeed, had the bomb on Flight 103 exploded as scheduled over the Atlantic Ocean, instead of prematurely, the clues would not have been found. Counterterrorism has become a sophisticated operation as well as a big business—a trend that accelerated after September 2001. International agencies, notably the *Interpol* police agency (and in Europe, *Europol*), coordinate the actions of states in tracking and apprehending suspected terrorists (as well as drug traffickers and other criminals). National governments have investigative agencies, such as the RCMP and CSIS in Canada or the FBI and CIA in the United States, to try to break through the wall of secrecy around terrorist operations. Lately, many private companies have expanded the business of providing security services, including antiterrorist equipment and forces, to companies and individuals doing business internationally. These companies have been very busy since September 2001, as governments, companies and individuals worldwide adapt to the new security environment that evolves after a global terrorist threat.

---

[11] Walter Laqueur, *A History of Terrorism* (Piscataway, NJ: Transaction, 2001). Paul R. Pilar, *Terrorism and U.S. Foreign Policy* (Washington, DC: Brookings, 2001). Jessica Stern, *The Ultimate Terrorist* (Cambridge, MA: Harvard UP, 2000). Rosemary H. T. O'Kane, *Terror, Force, and States: The Path from Modernity* (Aldershot, UK: Elgar, 1996). Michael Stohl and George A. Lopez, eds., *Terrible Beyond Endurance? The Foreign Policy of State Terrorism* (Westport, CT: Greenwood, 1988).

WEAPONS OF MASS DESTRUCTION

The term **weapons of mass destruction** includes three general types of weapons: nuclear, chemical and biological. They are distinguished from conventional weapons by their enormous potential lethality, given their small size, and by their relative lack of discrimination in whom they kill. These differences offer state leaders types of leverage that differ from conventional military forces. When deployed on ballistic missiles, they can potentially be fired from the home territory of one state and wreak great destruction on the home territory of another.

To date, such an event has not happened, but its mere threat undermines the territorial integrity and security of states in the international system. Thus scholars pay special attention to weapons of mass destruction and the missiles that can deliver them. Of central concern today are the potentials for proliferation—the possession of weapons of mass destruction by an increasing number of states.

Weapons of mass destruction serve different purposes than do conventional weapons. With a few exceptions, their purpose is to deter attack (especially by other weapons of mass destruction) by giving state leaders the means to inflict great pain against a would-be conqueror or destroyer. For middle powers, these weapons also provide destructive capabilities more in line with the great powers, serving as symbolic equalizers. For terrorists, potentially, the purpose of these weapons is to kill a great many people.

Nuclear Weapons

Nuclear weapons are, in sheer explosive power, the world's most destructive weapons. A single weapon the size of a refrigerator can destroy a city. Defending against nuclear attack is extremely difficult, at best.

To understand the potential for nuclear proliferation, one has to know something about how nuclear weapons work. There are two types. *Fission* weapons (atomic bombs or A-bombs) are simpler and less expensive than **fusion weapons** (also called thermonuclear bombs, hydrogen bombs or H-bombs). The term *bomb* refers to a warhead that can be delivered by missile, bomb, artillery shell or other means.

When a fission weapon explodes, one type of atom (element) is split or "fissioned" into new types with less total mass. The lost mass is transformed into energy according to Albert Einstein's famous formula, $E = mc^2$, which shows that a little bit of mass is equivalent to a great deal of energy. In fact, the fission bomb that U.S. forces used to destroy Nagasaki, Japan, in 1945 converted to energy of roughly the amount of mass in a single penny. Two elements can be split in this way, and each has been used to make fission weapons. These elements—known as **fissionable material**—are uranium-235 (or U-235) and plutonium.

Fission weapons work by taking subcritical masses of fissionable material—amounts not dense enough to start a chain reaction—and compressing them into a critical mass, which explodes. In the simplest design, one piece of uranium is propelled down a tube (by conventional explosives) into another piece of uranium. A more efficient but technically demanding design precisely arranges high explosives around a hollow sphere of plutonium so as to implode the sphere and create a critical mass. Enhanced designs add an outer sphere of neutron-reflecting material to increase the number of speeding neutrons released during the explosion.

Although these designs require sophisticated engineering, they are well within the capabilities of many states and some private groups. The only obstacle is in obtaining fissionable material. Only 4.5 to 45 kilograms are required for each bomb, but even these

The Revolution in Military Affairs

Military historians refer to a period of rapid change in the conduct of war as a "revolution in military affairs." These periods usually combine innovative applications of new technology with changes in military doctrine, organization or operations. Such revolutions may arise from innovations in organization, as when revolutionary France first mobilized an entire nation into a war machine two centuries ago. Or they may arise from new military doctrine, as when Germany used the "blitzkrieg" to overwhelm Poland and France at the outset of World War II. They might also arise from technology alone, as with the invention of nuclear weapons.

Many military analysts consider the present period, starting with the 1991 Gulf War, to be a revolution in military affairs. Current technologies allow armed forces to cut through Clausewitz's famous "fog of war" (see p. 232), the confusion and uncertainty that greatly reduces the effectiveness of armies in battle. Stealth airplanes, laser-guided weapons and so-called smart bombs dropped by high-flying aircraft are all elements of the revolution in military affairs.

From a realist perspective, critics worry that the revolution has brought an unrealistic expectation of low casualties in war, which may make political leaders unduly cautious in applying military force. For example, in Afghanistan, terrorist leaders including Osama bin Laden slipped away as the United States relied on local warlords to hunt them, when larger numbers of U.S. troops might have captured them (but with U.S. casualties).

Others are concerned that the revolution in military affairs "sanitizes" the conduct of war. Images of bomber pilots who take off from an airbase, drop their "payload" on targets halfway around the world and are home in time to have breakfast with their kids normalize militarism and make bombing raids (which wreak violent death and destruction) appear no different from any other "day at the office."

Still others have pointed out that state militaries do not hold a monopoly on the revolution in military affairs. The people involved in the September 2001 attacks against the U.S. used information technology, such as encrypted internet communications, to coordinate forces while keeping authorities in the dark. They carried out precision strikes over long distances with very small, dispersed units. As a result, 19 attackers killed more than 3000 people, and an expenditure of under $1 million caused tens of *billions* of dollars in damage.

amounts are not easily obtained. U-235, which can be used in the simplest bomb designs, is especially difficult to obtain. Natural uranium (mined in various countries) has less than 1 percent U-235 mixed with nonfissionable uranium. Extracting the fissionable U-235, referred to as enriching the uranium up to weapons grade (or high grade), is slow, expensive and technically complex—a major obstacle to proliferation. However, North Korea, Iran, Iraq and Libya have all built the infrastructure to do so in recent years. North Korea was still actively pursuing this route in 2007 in parallel with its testing of a plutonium bomb in 2006. In 2004, Iran agreed to suspend its uranium enrichment program, but later broke the deal, resumed enrichment and was rebuked by the UN Security Council in 2006. (Diplomacy continued in 2007.) After the U.S. invasion of Iraq, American inspectors discovered that Iraq had shelved its nuclear program years earlier, as UN inspectors had argued prior to the invasion.

Plutonium is more easily produced from low-grade uranium in nuclear power reactors—although extracting plutonium requires a separation plant. A plutonium bomb is more difficult to build than a uranium one—another obstacle to proliferation. Plutonium is also used in commercial breeder reactors (reactors that create more fissionable material than they consume), which Japan has built recently—another source of fissionable material. In the 1990s, Japan shipped tons of plutonium home from separation plants in Europe by sea—creating a possible temptation for theft and a weapons-capable stockpile for Japan. (Thus, if it decided to do so in the future, Japan could build a formidable nuclear arsenal fairly quickly.)

Fission weapons were invented 60 years ago by scientists in a secret World War II project in the U.S. known as the *Manhattan Project*. In 1945, one uranium bomb and one plutonium bomb were used to destroy Hiroshima and Nagasaki, killing 100 000 civilians in each city and inducing Japan to surrender unconditionally. By today's standards, those bombs were crude, low-yield weapons, but they are akin to a nuclear weapon that might be built by a relatively poor state or a nonstate actor.

Fusion weapons are extremely expensive and technically demanding. They provide leverage for only the richest, largest, most technologically capable states. In fusion weapons, two small atoms (variants of hydrogen) fuse into a larger atom, releasing energy. This reaction occurs only at very high temperatures (the sun "burns" hydrogen through fusion). Weapons designers use fission weapons to create these high energies and trigger an explosive fusion reaction. The explosive power of most fission weapons is between one and 200 kilotonnes (each kilotonne is the equivalent of 1000 tonnes of conventional explosive). The power of fusion weapons is typically one to 20 megatonnes (a megatonne is 1000 kilotonnes). In the post–Cold War era, fusion weapons have become less important.

The effects of nuclear weapons include not only the blast of the explosion, but also heat and radiation. Heat can potentially create a self-sustaining firestorm in a city. Radiation creates radiation sickness, which at high doses kills people in a few days and at

LIVING WITH NUKES
Nuclear weapons were invented during World War II. Tens of thousands of nuclear weapons have been built; eight or nine countries possess at least a few. Obtaining fissionable material is the main difficulty in making nuclear weapons. The worldwide nuclear industry—ranging from commercial plants to weapons facilities—has become a key security concern since September 2001. Here a Florida sheriff guards a nuclear power plant, 2001.

low doses creates long-term health problems, especially cancers. Radiation is most intense in the local vicinity of (and downwind from) a nuclear explosion, but is carried up into the atmosphere and falls in more distant locations as nuclear fallout. Nuclear weapons create an electromagnetic pulse (EMP) that can disrupt and destroy electronic equipment (some weapons are designed to maximize this effect). Using many nuclear weapons at once (as in a war) would also have substantial effects on global climate—possibly a nuclear winter in which years of colder and darker conditions would trigger an environmental catastrophe.

Ballistic Missiles and Other Delivery Systems

The *delivery systems* for getting nuclear weapons to their targets—much more than the weapons themselves—are the basis of states' nuclear arsenals and strategies (discussed shortly). Inasmuch as nuclear warheads can be made quite small—weighing a few hundred kilograms or even less—they are adaptable to a wide variety of delivery systems.

During the Cold War, nuclear delivery systems were divided into two categories. *Strategic* weapons were those that could hit an enemy's homeland, usually at long range (for instance, Moscow from Nebraska). Once carried on long-range bombers, they are now primarily carried on missiles. *Tactical* nuclear weapons were those designed for battlefield use in a theatre of military engagement. In the Cold War years, both superpowers integrated tactical nuclear weapons into their conventional air, sea and land forces using a variety of delivery systems—gravity bombs, artillery shells, short-range missiles, landmines, depth charges and so forth. Once integrated, however, the tens of thousands of nuclear warheads posed dangers such as theft or accident. Their actual use would have entailed grave risks of escalation to strategic nuclear war, putting home cities at risk. Thus, the superpowers phased out tactical nuclear weapons almost entirely when the Cold War ended. The tactical weapons deployed in the former Soviet republics were shipped back to Russia for storage and eventual disassembly.

The main strategic delivery vehicles are **ballistic missiles.** Unlike airplanes, they are extremely difficult to defend against. Ballistic missiles carry a warhead up along a trajectory and let it drop on a target. A trajectory typically rises out of the atmosphere—at least 80 kilometres high—before descending. A powerful rocket is needed, and a guidance system adjusts the trajectory so that the warhead drops closer to the target. Various ballistic missiles differ in their range, accuracy and throw weight (how heavy a warhead they can carry). In addition, some missiles fire from fixed sites, whereas others are mobile (making them hard to target).

ballistic missiles The major strategic delivery vehicles for nuclear weapons; they carry a warhead along a trajectory (typically rising at least 80 kilometres high) and let it drop on a target.

The longest-range missiles are **intercontinental ballistic missiles (ICBMs)** with ranges of over 8000 kilometres (the distance from Chicago to Moscow). Some carry up to 10 warheads for use in hitting different targets. Most ICBMs are owned by the United States and Russia; a few are owned by China. Intermediate- and medium-range missiles have ranges of about 1600 to 5000 kilometres. They can be land-based but also include most submarine-launched ballistic missiles. The U.S. and Soviet intermediate nuclear weapons deployed in Europe were eliminated under the 1987 Intermediate Nuclear Forces (INF) Treaty.

intercontinental ballistic missiles (ICBMs) The longest-range ballistic missiles, able to travel 8000 kilometres.

Of special interest today are short-range ballistic missiles (SRBMs) with ranges of well under 1600 kilometres. The modified Scud missiles fired by Iraq at Saudi Arabia and Israel during the Gulf War were (conventionally armed) SRBMs. In regional conflicts, the long range of more powerful missiles may not be necessary. The cities of

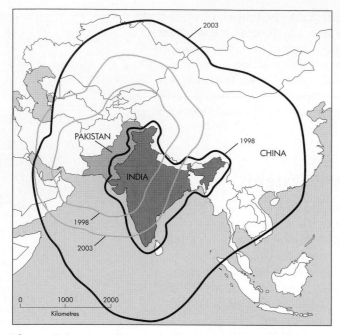

Figure 7.2 Expanding Ranges of Indian and Pakistani Missiles, 1998–2003

Source: Washington Post 29 May 1999: A32, Table 6.3.

cruise missile A small, winged missile that can navigate across thousands of kilometres of previously mapped terrain to reach a particular target; it can carry either a nuclear or a conventional warhead.

Syria and Israel have a mere 214 kilometres between them, and the capital cities of Iraq and Iran are less than 800 kilometres apart, as are those of India and Pakistan, as shown in Figure 7.2. All of these states own ballistic missiles. Short-range and some medium-range ballistic missiles are cheap enough to be obtained and even home-produced by small middle-income states. Table 7.2 lists the capabilities of the 29 states with ballistic missiles.

Many short-range ballistic missiles, including those used by Iraq during the Gulf War, are highly inaccurate but still very difficult to defend against.[12] With conventional warheads, they have more psychological than military utility (demoralizing an enemy population by attacking cities indiscriminately). Equipped with nuclear, chemical or biological warheads, however, these missiles could be deadlier. A number of states now possess short-range ballistic missiles armed with weapons of mass destruction, but none has ever been used.

Great powers, especially the United States, have greater accuracy in delivery systems of all ranges. After travelling thousands of kilometres, the best U.S. missiles can land within 15 metres of a target 50 percent of the time. The trend in the U.S. nuclear arsenal has been toward flexibility, using less-powerful warheads but more accurate missiles.

The newest capable class of delivery system is the **cruise missile,** a small, winged missile that can navigate across thousands of kilometres of previously mapped terrain to reach a particular target. Cruise missiles can be launched from ships, submarines, airplanes or land. As a nuclear-weapon vehicle, cruise missiles are owned only by the United States and Russia, and several states have developed conventionally armed versions. Argentina hit a British warship with a French-made cruise missile in the 1982 Falklands/Malvinas War. U.S. leaders have discovered that conventionally armed cruise missiles can attack distant targets without risking American lives—a politically safe strategy used increasingly in recent years. In 1993, President Bill Clinton attacked the Iraqi intelligence headquarters with dozens of cruise missiles fired from hundreds of kilometres away—the first all-cruise-missile attack in history. The United States used cruise missiles extensively against Serbian forces in Bosnia in 1995, and against Serbia in 1999, Iraq in 2003 and for smaller-scale strikes such as against terrorist bases in Afghanistan in 1998.

In all nuclear arsenals, delivery systems include special provisions for command and control.[13] Because the weapons are so dangerous, control is highly centralized. In the United States and Russia, presidents are accompanied everywhere by military officers

---

[12] Theodore A. Postol, "Lessons of the Gulf War Experience with Patriot," *International Security* 16.3 (1991–92): 119–71.

[13] Scott D. Sagan, *The Limits of Safety: Organizations, Accidents, and Nuclear Weapons* (Princeton, NJ: Princeton UP, 1993). Janne E. Nolan, *Guardians of the Arsenal: The Politics of Nuclear Strategy* (NY: Basic, 1989). C. Kenneth Allard, *Command, Control, and the Common Defense* (New Haven, CT: Yale UP, 1990).

Table 7.2 Ballistic Missile Capabilities, 2006

Country	Range (Miles)	Potential Targets
United States[a]	13,000	(World)
Russia[a]	13,000	(World)
China[a]	13,000	(World)
Britain[a]	4,600	(World; submarine-launched)
France[a]	3,700 [4,600]	(World; submarine-launched)
North Korea[a]	800 [3,500]	South Korea, Russia, China [All Asia]
Iran[b,c]	900 [3,500]	Iraq, Kuwait, Afghanistan, Israel [Europe to Asia]
Israel[a,c]	900 [3,500]	Syria, Iraq, Saudi Arabia, Egypt [Iran]
India[a,c]	1,500 [2,000]	Pakistan, China, Afghanistan, Iran, Turkey
Pakistan[a]	800 [2,000]	India [Russia, Turkey, Israel]
Saudi Arabia	1,700	Iran, Iraq, Syria, Israel, Turkey, Yemen, Egypt, Libya, Sudan
Syria	300 [400]	Israel, Jordan, Iraq, Turkey
Egypt	400	Libya, Sudan, Israel
Libya	200	Egypt, Tunisia, Algeria
Yemen	200	Saudi Arabia
United Arab Emirates	200	Saudi Arabia, Iran
Afghanistan	200	Pakistan, Tajikistan, Uzbekistan
Kazakhstan	200	Uzbekistan, Tajikistan, Kyrgyzstan, Russia
Turkmenistan	200	Iran, Afghanistan, Uzbekistan, Tajikistan
Armenia	200	Azerbaijan
Belarus	200	Russia, Ukraine, Poland
Ukraine	200	Russia, Belarus, Poland, Hungary, Romania
South Korea	200	North Korea
Vietnam	200	China, Cambodia
Taiwan	80 [200]	China
Greece	100	Turkey
Turkey	100	Greece
Bahrain	100	Saudi Arabia, Qatar
Slovakia	80	Czech Rep., Hungary, Poland
Japan[c]	—	

Number of states with ballistic missiles: 29

[a]States that have nuclear weapons.

[b]States believed to be trying to build nuclear weapons.

[c]States developing space-launch missiles adaptable as long-range ballistic missiles.

Notes: Bracketed range numbers indicate missiles under development. List of potential targets includes both hostile and friendly states, and is suggestive rather than comprehensive. Missile ranges increase with smaller payloads. 200-mile ranges (scud-B) and 300-mile ranges (scud Mod-C) are approximate for a 3/4-ton payload. Saudi range is for a two-ton payload; South Korean range is for a half-ton payload.

Source: Carnegie Endowment for International Peace.

Focus on Canadian Scholarship

Scholars at Canadian universities who examine questions of militaries, defence and the use of force include **Richard Price** at the University of British Columbia, who has researched the chemical weapons taboo. His colleague at UBC, **Michael Wallace,** is interested in arms races and accidental or inadvertent war. At the University of Toronto in the department of history, **Wesley Wark** focuses on terrorism, intelligence and national security. At York University, **David Mutimer** has examined weapons proliferation as a reconfigured security concern. **Gavin Cameron** at the University of Calgary is interested in nuclear terrorism and negotiations between states and terrorist organizations. At Carleton's Norman Paterson School of International Affairs, **David Mendeloff** is interested in proliferation, preventive war and post-conflict peacebuilding. At the University of Saskatchewan, **Ron Wheeler** focuses on political terrorism and international conflict, and at the University of Manitoba, **James Ferguson** is interested in ballistic missile defence and Canadian force structure requirements. **Laure Paquette** at Laurentian University has explored issues of strategy and counter-terrorism and counter-insurgency. **Peter Nyers**

of McMaster University has explored the construction of states of emergency, especially via refugees and citizenship. At Queen's University, **Joel Sokolsky** is interested in Canadian defence policy, NATO and seapower in the nuclear age. **Michael Dartnell** at the University of New Brunswick St. John examines terrorism and new forms of conflict, including cyber activism and violence. At the Royal Military College, **David Last** is interested in third-party intervention and protracted conflict and has focused also on conflict de-escalation in peacekeeping operations. His colleague, **John David Young,** currently researches regional security institutions and intervention regimes in support of peace operations. At the Canadian Forces College, **Chris Madsen** is interested in maritime strategy and history and his colleague **Craig Stone** focuses on defence economics. **Michael Lipson** at Concordia University examines peacekeeping and transgovernmental networks and nonproliferation. **Jean-François Thibault** at the University of Moncton has examined the ethics of humanitarian intervention. At the University of Northern British Columbia, **Don Munton** is interested in nuclear weapons, arms control and disarmament.

carrying briefcases with the secret codes required to order such an attack. So far, at least, control procedures have succeeded in preventing any accidental or unauthorized use of nuclear weapons, but there have been four recorded "false alarms"—in 1979, 1980, 1983 and 1995—in which either U.S. or Soviet/Russian forces were given preliminary launch warnings.[14]

Missile Technology Control Regime A set of agreements through which industrialized states try to limit the flow of missile-relevant technology to states of the global South.

The proliferation of ballistic missiles is difficult to control.[15] There is a **Missile Technology Control Regime** through which industrialized states try to limit the flow of missile-relevant technology to states of the global South. One success was the interruption of an Egyptian-Argentinean-Iraqi partnership to develop a medium-range missile in the 1980s. West German companies were induced to stop secretly selling technology to the project. However, in general, the regime has been less than successful. Short- and medium-range missiles (with ranges up to about 3200 kilometres) are apparently being developed by Iran, Israel, Saudi Arabia, Pakistan, India, North Korea and possibly Argentina and Brazil. Russian-made short-range ballistic missiles are owned by a number of states in the global South. China has sold missiles and technology to some countries of

[14] Bulletin of the Atomic Scientists, "5 Minutes to Midnight—Board Statement" 17 Jan. 2007, available at http://www.thebulletin.org/minutes-to-midnight/board-statements.html.

[15] Aaron Karp, *Ballistic Missile Proliferation: The Politics and Technics* (NY: Oxford UP/SIPRI, 1996). Steve Fetter, "Ballistic Missiles and Weapons of Mass Destruction: What Is the Threat? What Should Be Done?" *International Security* 16.1 (1991): 5–42. Janne E. Nolan, *Trappings of Power: Ballistic Missiles in the Third World* (Washington, DC: Brookings, 1991).

the South (bringing lower prices to buyers and hard currency to China)—a sore point in relations with the West.[16]

Small states or substate groups that may acquire nuclear weapons in the future could deliver them through innovative means. Because nuclear weapons are small, one could be smuggled into a target state by car, by speedboat or in diplomatic pouches, and then detonated like any terrorist bomb. An advantage of such methods would be the ease of concealing the identity of the perpetrator.

Since the 2001 attacks on the United States, there has been increasing attention devoted to container security initiatives aimed at preventing weapons of mass destruction from reaching North America in shipping containers. However, doing so without impeding the flow of international trade is a daunting challenge. Canada's Border Services Agency works with U.S. Customs through the "Container Security Initiative" to accomplish precisely this goal: securing containerized shipping while allowing legitimate cargo containers to move quickly and efficiently across borders. This is not unlike other "Smart Border" initiatives aimed at allowing frequent (and especially business) travellers to avoid delays at borders. Liberals and realists argue that this is an appropriate response and an important effort in balancing the trade-off between security and liberty (see Chapter 5, p. 155). Critical theorists, however, point to the ways the supposed trade-off legitimizes subjecting "citizens" to increasingly sophisticated forms of surveillance and control and aims at identifying (dangerous) noncitizens—who, not coincidentally, are usually racialized "others."[17]

Chemical and Biological Weapons

A *chemical weapon* releases chemicals that disable and kill people.[18] Chemicals used might be lethal, such as nerve gas, or merely irritating, such as tear gas. Chemicals can interfere with the nervous system, blood, breathing or other body functions. Some can be absorbed through the skin, others must be inhaled. Some persist in the target area long after their use, others disperse quickly.

It is possible to defend against most chemical weapons by dressing troops in protective clothing and gas masks and following elaborate procedures to decontaminate equipment. Protective suits are hot, however, and antichemical measures reduce the efficiency of armies. Civilians are much less likely to have protection against chemicals than are military forces (the well-prepared Israeli civilians were an exception). Chemical weapons are by nature indiscriminate about whom they kill. On several occasions, chemical weapons have been deliberately used against civilians (most recently by the Iraqi government against Iraqi Kurds in the 1980s).

Use of chemical weapons in war has been rare. Mustard gas, which produces skin blisters and lung damage, was widely used (in artillery shells) in World War I. After the horrors of that war, the use of chemical weapons was banned in the 1925 Geneva protocol, a treaty that is still in effect. In World War II, both sides were armed with chemical weapons but neither used them, for fear of retaliation. Since then (with possibly a few

[16] Richard A. Bitzinger, "Arms to Go: Chinese Arms Sales to the Third World," *International Security* 17.2 (1992): 84–111.

[17] Colleen Bell, "Surveillance Strategies and Populations at Risk: Biopolitical Governance in Canada's National Security Policy," *Security Dialogue* 37.2 (2006): 147–65.

[18] Richard M. Price, *The Chemical Weapons Taboo* (Ithaca, NY: Cornell UP, 1997). Valerie Adams, *Chemical Warfare, Chemical Disarmament* (Bloomington: Indiana UP, 1990). Trevor Findlay, ed., *Chemical Weapons and Missile Proliferation: With Implications for the Asia/Pacific Region* (Boulder, CO: Rienner, 1991).

unclear exceptions), only Iraq has violated the treaty—against Iran in the 1980s. Unfortunately, Iraq's actions not only breached a psychological barrier against using chemical weapons, but also showed such weapons to be cheap and effective against human waves of attacking soldiers without protective gear. This example stimulated more states to begin acquiring chemical weapons. Dozens now have them. During the Gulf War, Iraq deployed but apparently did not use chemical weapons. However, the bombing of an Iraqi chemical weapons depot exposed thousands of U.S. troops to chemicals, with a link to Gulf War Syndrome (mysterious illnesses affecting veterans of the war) suspected but not proven. In the 2003 Iraq War, Iraq did not use chemical weapons, and nor were stockpiles of chemical weapons discovered.

Chemical weapons are a cheap way for states to gain weapons of mass destruction as potential leverage in international conflicts. Chemical weapons can be produced using processes and facilities similar to those used for pesticides, pharmaceuticals and other civilian products. It is difficult to locate chemical weapons facilities in suspect countries, or to deny those states access to the needed chemicals and equipment. In 1998, a U.S. cruise missile attack destroyed a suspected weapons facility in Sudan that was later revealed to be a pharmaceutical factory.

Chemical Weapons Convention (1992) Treaty banning the production and possession of chemical weapons, which includes strict verification provisions and the threat of sanctions against violators, including nonparticipants in the treaty.

The 1925 treaty did not ban the production or possession of chemical weapons, and several dozen states built stockpiles of them. The United States and the Soviet Union maintained large arsenals of chemical weapons during the Cold War but have reduced them greatly in the past decade. In 1992, a new **Chemical Weapons Convention** to ban the production and possession of chemical weapons was concluded after years of negotiation, and has been signed by most of the world's states (with the exclusion of Egypt, Syria

VULNERABLE
Civilians are more vulnerable to chemical weapons than soldiers. A 1992 treaty aims to ban chemical weapons worldwide. Here, Israeli kindergarteners prepare against a chemical warfare threat from Iraqi Scud missiles during the Gulf War, 1991.

and North Korea). The new treaty includes strict verification provisions and the threat of sanctions against violators, including those who are nonparticipants in the treaty (an important extension). It went into effect in 1997. Opponents argued that the treaty would be ineffective, but within months several states (including India, China, South Korea, France and Britain) admitted to having secret chemical weapons programs, which are being dismantled under international observation. Russia still faces very costly and long-term work to destroy a 40 000-tonne arsenal of chemical weapons built during the Cold War. From 1997 to 2002, the treaty organization oversaw the elimination of about one-sixth of the world's chemical weapons.

Biological weapons resemble chemical ones, except that instead of chemicals they use micro-organisms or biologically derived toxins. Some use viruses or bacteria that cause fatal diseases, such as smallpox, bubonic plague and anthrax. Others cause nonfatal but incapacitating diseases or diseases that kill livestock. Theoretically, a single weapon could spark an epidemic in an entire population, but this is considered too dangerous and use of less-contagious micro-organisms is preferred. Biological weapons have virtually never been used in war (Japan tried some on a few Chinese villages in World War II). Their potential strikes many political leaders as a Pandora's box that could let loose uncontrollable forces if opened.

For this reason, the development, production and possession of biological weapons are banned under the 1972 **Biological Weapons Convention,** signed by more than 100 countries including the great powers. The superpowers destroyed their stocks of biological weapons and had to restrict their biological weapons complexes to defensive research rather than the development of weapons. However, because the treaty makes no provision for inspection and because biological weapons programs are, like chemical ones, relatively easy to hide, several states—including Libya and Syria—remain under suspicion of having biological weapons. Evidence surfaced after the collapse of the Soviet Union that a secret biological weapons program had been underway there. UN inspections of Iraq in the mid-1990s uncovered an active biological weapons program. However, the invasion of Iraq in 2003 discovered no weapons of mass destruction. In 2001, the United States pulled out of talks to strengthen the 1972 treaty, declaring the proposed modifications unworkable.

Anthrax spores were one of the main biological weapons produced by the secret Soviet program, and they were also produced by the U.S. military. In 1997, the U.S. military began to vaccinate all 2.4 million U.S. soldiers against anthrax, and other countries such as Canada stockpiled vaccines. In 2001, soon after the September terrorist attacks against the United States, small amounts of anthrax spores were sent through the U.S. mail to high government and media offices, killing several people and massively disrupting mail distribution. As of early 2007 the attack remains unsolved, but reportedly originated from anthrax stolen from the U.S. military rather than foreign terrorists. However, the episode showed that deadly biological weapons are a real threat and not a futuristic worry.

Today the United States and perhaps a dozen other countries maintain biological weapons research (not banned by the treaty). Researchers try to ascertain the military implications of advances in biotechnology and prepare defences against the use of biological weapons. Most states doing such research claim that they are doing so only to deter another state from developing biological weapons.[19]

Biological Weapons Convention (1972) Treaty that prohibits the development, production and possession of biological weapons, but makes no provision for inspections.

---

[19] Joshua Lederberg, ed., *Biological Weapons: Limiting the Threat* (Cambridge, MA: MIT P, 1999). Jonathan B. Tucker, ed., *Toxic Terror: Assessing Terrorist Use of Chemical and Biological Weapons* (Cambridge, MA: MIT P, 2000). Ken Alibek with Stephen Handelman, *Biohazard: The Chilling True Story of the Largest Covert Biological Weapons Program in the World—Told from Inside by the Man Who Ran It* (NY: Random House, 1999). Andrew T. Price-Smith, ed., *Plagues and Politics: Infectious Diseases and International Policy* (NY: Palgrave, 2001). Andrew T. Price-Smith, *The Health of Nations* (Cambridge, MA: MIT P, 2001).

Proliferation

Proliferation is the spread of weapons of mass destruction—nuclear weapons, ballistic missiles and chemical or biological weapons—into the hands of more actors. The implications of proliferation for international relations are difficult to predict but evidently profound. Ballistic missiles with weapons of mass destruction remove the territorial protection offered by state borders and make each state vulnerable to others. Some realists, who believe in the basic rationality of state actions, are not so upset by this prospect, and some even welcome it. They reason that in a world where the use of military force could lead to mutual annihilation, there would be fewer wars—just as during the superpower arms race of the Cold War. Other IR scholars who put less faith in the rationality of state leaders are much more alarmed by proliferation. They fear that with more and more nuclear (or chemical/biological) actors, miscalculation or accident—or terrorism—could lead to the use of weapons of mass destruction on a scale not seen since 1945.[20] Some suggest that "rogue" states cannot be counted on to act rationally. Critics of this latter view often point out that only one state has ever actually used nuclear weapons on civilian targets—the United States, which is not normally characterized as a "rogue."

For liberals and realists, there is also a widespread fear that these weapons may fall into the hands of terrorists or other nonstate actors who would be immune to threats of retaliation (with no territory or cities to defend). Evidence captured during the 2001 war in Afghanistan showed that the al Qaeda organization was trying to obtain weapons of mass destruction and would be willing to use them. Lax security at the vast, far-flung former Soviet nuclear complex in the 1990s has increased fears that fissionable materials could reach terrorists.[21]

Critical scholarship on proliferation has pointed to the ways in which a relatively coherent discourse on weapons proliferation emerged in the early 1990s and continued through the 2000s. This discourse, it is argued, tended to focus on the "technologies" of weapons rather than the human political, economic and institutional determinants of their spread, leading in turn to technological solutions to proliferation (better surveillance and monitoring) rather than political ones. A technological approach to proliferation, in which weapons are depicted as spreading almost "naturally," also directs our attention away from the political economy of arms production and the various interests involved in producing and exporting weapons of all kinds.[22]

States that sell technology with proliferation potential can make a great deal of money. For example, in the mid-1990s the United States pressured both Russia and China to stop selling nuclear technology to Iran (which the United States said was trying to

---

[20] Devin T. Hagerty, *The Consequences of Nuclear Proliferation: Lessons from South Asia* (Cambridge, MA: MIT P, 1998). T. V. Paul, Richard J. Harknett and James J. Wirtz, eds., *The Absolute Weapon Revisited* (Ann Arbor: U Michigan P, 1998). David Mutimer, *The Weapons State: Proliferation and the Framing of Security* (Boulder, CO: Rienner, 1999). Leonard S. Spector, Gregory P. Webb and Mark G. McDonough, *Tracking Nuclear Proliferation: A Guide in Maps and Charts, 1998* (Washington, DC: Brookings/Carnegie Endowment for International Peace, 1998).

[21] Peter Finn, "Experts Discuss Chances of Nuclear Terrorism," *Washington Post* 3 Nov. 2001: A19. Steven Erlanger, "Lax Nuclear Security in Russia Is Cited as Way for bin Laden to Get Arms," *New York Times* 12 Nov. 2001: B1. Nadine Gur and Benjamin Cole, *The New Face of Terrorism: Threats from Weapons of Mass Destruction* (NY: Tauris, 2000). Richard A. Falkenrath, Robert D. Newman and Bradley A. Thayer, *America's Achilles' Heel: Nuclear, Biological, and Chemical Terrorism and Covert Attack* (Cambridge, MA: MIT P, 1998).

[22] David Mutimer, *The Weapons State: Proliferation and the Framing of Security* (Boulder: Lynne Rienner Publishers, 2000).

build nuclear weapons). Russia and China were being asked to give up hundreds of millions of dollars in sales in doing so. Though not directly implicated in the proliferation of nuclear weapons, the U.S. is one of the largest weapons manufacturers in the world. Industrialized states have competed to sell technology and have simultaneously worked to restrain such sales by other states. This is another international collective-goods problem (see p. 82), in which states pursuing their individual interests end up collectively worse off.

Nuclear proliferation could also occur simply by a state or nonstate actor's buying (or stealing) one or more nuclear weapons or the components to build one. The means to prevent this act range from covert intelligence to tight security measures to safeguards preventing a stolen weapon from being used. The economic crisis in Russia in the 1990s left hundreds of tonnes of Russian fissile materials in the control of underpaid civilian workers and military officers at poorly funded facilities with lax security and recurrent corruption. In 2002, the G8 countries pledged US$20 billion to address the problem, but a 2003 study by 21 research groups found that little had been spent and problems remained rampant. The study focused on 100 insecure research reactors with weapons-grade uranium in 40 countries.

A more lasting form of nuclear proliferation is the development by states of nuclear complexes to produce their own nuclear weapons on an ongoing basis.[23] Here larger numbers of weapons are involved, and there are strong potentials for arms races in regional conflicts and rivalries. The relevant regional conflicts are those between Israel and the Arab states, Iran and its neighbours, India and Pakistan,[24] the two Koreas and possibly Taiwan and China. India and Pakistan have both exploded nuclear devices underground, and are moving forward to build arsenals and the missiles to deliver them. North Korea conducted its first nuclear test in 2006, of a plutonium bomb, and produced a low-yield fission explosion. In early 2007, North Korea pledged to shut down its nuclear testing in return for a resumption of humanitarian and food aid, which had been suspended after the North Korean test.[25] In addition, South Africa reported after the fact that it had built several nuclear weapons but then dismantled them in the 1980s (while still under white minority rule).

Israel has never test-exploded nuclear weapons or admitted to having them, but is widely believed to have a hundred or more nuclear warheads on combat airplanes and medium-range missiles. (In 2006, Israeli prime minister Ehud Olmert let slip publicly the open secret that Israel has nuclear weapons.) Israel wants these capabilities to use as a last resort if it were about to be conquered by its neighbours.[26] By implicitly threatening such action, Israeli leaders hope to convince Arab leaders that a military conquest of Israel is impossible. However, by keeping its weapons secret, Israel tried to minimize the possibility of provoking its neighbours to develop their own nuclear weapons. To prevent Iraq from doing so, Israel carried out a bombing raid on the main facility of the Iraqi nuclear

---

[23] Itty Abraham, *The Making of the Indian Atomic Bomb: Science, Secrecy, and the Post-Colonial State* (NY: Zed/St. Martin's, 1998). George Perkovich, *India's Nuclear Bomb: The Impact on Global Proliferation* (Berkeley: U California P, 1999). John Wilson Lewis and Xus Litai, *China Builds the Bomb* (Palo Alto, CA: Stanford UP, 1988).

[24] David Albright and Mark Hibbs, "India's Silent Bomb," *Bulletin of the Atomic Scientists* 48.7 (1992): 27–31. David Albright and Mark Hibbs, "Pakistan's Bomb: Out of the Closet," *Bulletin of the Atomic Scientists* 48.6 (1992): 38–43.

[25] "North Korea willing to abandon nuclear weapons: Senior official," CBC News Online 1 March 2007, available at http://www.cbc.ca/world/story/2007/03/01/koreanukes.html.

[26] Avner Cohen, *Israel and the Bomb* (NY: Columbia UP, 1998).

complex in 1981. Without this raid, Iraq probably would have had nuclear weapons by the time of the 1991 Gulf War.

The **Non-Proliferation Treaty (NPT)** of 1968 created a framework for controlling the spread of nuclear materials and expertise.[27] The International Atomic Energy Agency (IAEA), a UN agency based in Vienna, is charged with inspecting the nuclear power industry in member states to prevent secret military diversions of nuclear materials. However, a number of potential nuclear states (such as Israel) have not signed the NPT, and even those states that have signed may sneak around its provisions by keeping some facilities secret (as Iraq did). Under the terms of the Gulf War ceasefire, Iraq's nuclear program was uncovered and dismantled by the IAEA.[28]

North Korea withdrew from the IAEA in 1993, then bargained with Western leaders to get economic assistance, including safer reactors, in exchange for freezing its nuclear program. North Korea's leader died months later, but the compromise held up. Despite fears that its leaders were just playing for time and aid to prop up a failed regime, North Korea allowed inspection of a disputed underground complex in 1999 and agreed to suspend missile tests in exchange for aid and partial lifting of U.S. trade sanctions.[29]

This hopeful picture was shattered in 2002, however, when the United States confronted North Korea with evidence of a secret nuclear enrichment program, which the North Koreans confirmed. As relations deteriorated, North Korea pulled out of the agreement and of the IAEA, restarted its nuclear reactor and threatened to turn existing plutonium into half a dozen bombs within months. U.S. monitoring detected certain molecules indicative of plutonium reprocessing, and North Korea then announced it had finished. In 2006, North Korea tested a bomb, and although it produced only a small-yield explosion, it confirmed its place as the world's ninth nuclear-weapons power.

Nonetheless, nuclear proliferation has been less widespread than was feared decades ago. The five permanent members of the Security Council, which all had nuclear weapons by 1964, have continued to make up the nuclear club of states with large, openly acknowledged arsenals. A number of middle powers and two great powers (Japan and Germany) have the potential to make nuclear weapons but have chosen not to do so. The reasons for deciding against "going nuclear" include norms against using nuclear weapons, fears of retaliation and practical constraints, including cost. At present, declared nuclear states are the "big five," India and Pakistan (with dozens of warheads each, and growing) and North Korea (with perhaps half a dozen). Israel is an undeclared nuclear power with perhaps a hundred warheads.

Despite denials, Iran appears to be working to develop nuclear weapons, as it had begun to do under the Shah in the 1970s. In the years since 2003, Iran agreed to suspend its uranium enrichment program and allow surprise IAEA inspections, then restarted enrichment, suspended it again, then restarted it once more. In 2005, European efforts to offer Iran economic incentives to dismantle its program, and Russian efforts to enrich Iran's uranium on Russian soil with safeguards, both broke down. In 2006, the IAEA

Non-Proliferation Treaty (NPT) (1968) Treaty that created a framework for controlling the spread of nuclear materials and expertise, including the International Atomic Energy Agency (IAEA), a UN agency based in Vienna that is charged with inspecting the nuclear power industry in NPT member states to prevent secret military diversions of nuclear materials.

---

[27] Richard Kokoski, *Technology and the Proliferation of Nuclear Weapons* (NY: Oxford UP/SIPRI, 1996). Ian Bellany, Coit D. Blacker and Joseph Gallacher, eds., *The Nuclear Non-Proliferation Treaty* (Totowa, NJ: F. Cass, 1985).

[28] David Albright and Mark Hibbs, "Iraq's Nuclear Hide-and-Seek," *Bulletin of the Atomic Scientists* 47.7 (1991): 14–23.

[29] Leon V. Sigal, *Disarming Strangers: Nuclear Diplomacy with North Korea* (Princeton, NJ: Princeton UP, 1999).

referred the issue to the UN Security Council, which condemned Iran's actions and imposed fairly mild sanctions. Iran insisted on its sovereign right to enrich uranium for what it called peaceful purposes. The standoff continued in 2007.[30]

In 2004, after years of resistance, Brazil gave IAEA inspectors access to a controversial uranium enrichment plant (not part of a nuclear weapons program, evidently).

In 1995, the NPT came up for a 25-year review. In that period, the nonnuclear states that were supposed to stay nonnuclear had largely done so, with the exception of Israel, India and Pakistan, which had never signed the treaty. The nuclear states were supposed to have undertaken serious nuclear disarmament; they had largely failed to do so. A 2005 review conference ended in failure as the United States and other countries disagreed over Iran's program and loopholes in the treaty. In 2006, a deal to share nuclear technology between the United States and India led many states to question the treaty, since those benefits were supposedly reserved for signatories of the NPT.

In early 2007, the *Bulletin of the Atomic Scientists* moved the hands on the Doomsday

HOT STUFF

The most important hurdle in making nuclear weapons is access to fissionable materials (plutonium and uranium). In 2003, North Korea restarted its plutonium-producing reactor at Yongbyon, which had been shut down since 1994, and apparently produced half a dozen bombs, becoming the world's ninth nuclear-armed state. This 1996 photo, released in 2003, shows nuclear fuel rods in a cooling pond at Yongbyon.

Clock two minutes closer to midnight to reflect its concern that humanity is edging closer to catastrophic destruction. At the end of the Cold War in 1991, the hands were moved to "17 minutes to midnight," the furthest they had been from midnight (and the end of the world) since the inception of the clock in 1947. Since then, the hands moved slowly forward, and in 2007 the *Bulletin* expressed concerns about a second nuclear age resulting from the failure of the NPT, problems of unsecured fission materials, North Korea's nuclear test and Iran's nuclear aspirations, along with the continued failure of the world's two largest nuclear powers to make significant strides toward complete disarmament. The U.S. and Russia possess 26 000 of the world's 27 000 nuclear weapons, and since 2002 the U.S. has declared through its Nuclear Posture Review that nuclear weapons remain an important military option. The *Bulletin* is considered to represent largely liberal pluralist views, but these same concerns were expressed by a group of prominent realist thinkers in early 2007, including Henry Kissinger, who called also for drastic reductions of remaining nuclear arsenals and a move away from the operational readiness of nuclear weapons.[31]

---

[30] Paul L. Leventhal and Sharon Tanzer, eds., *Averting a Latin American Nuclear Arms Race: New Prospects and Challenges for Argentine-Brazil Nuclear Cooperation* (NY: St. Martin's, 1992).

[31] Bulletin of the Atomic Scientists, "5 Minutes to Midnight—Board Statement," see footnote 14 above. George P. Shultz, William J. Perry, Henry A. Kissinger and Sam Nunn, "A World Free of Nuclear Weapons," *The Wall Street Journal* 4 Jan. 2007, available at http://online.wsj.com/article/SB116787515251566636.html. Rebecca Johnson, "The Realist Message: Abolish Nuclear Weapons," *Disarmament Diplomacy* 83 (Winter 2006), available at http://www.acronym.org.uk/dd/dd83/83rej.htm.

Nuclear Strategy

The term *nuclear strategy* refers to decisions about how many nuclear weapons to deploy, what delivery systems to use and what policies to adopt regarding the circumstances in which they would be employed.[32]

The reason for possessing nuclear weapons is almost always to deter another state from a nuclear or conventional attack by threatening ruinous retaliation. The strategy should work if state leaders are rational actors wanting to avoid the huge costs of a nuclear attack. However, it will work only if other states believe that a state's threat to use nuclear weapons is credible. The search for a credible deterrent by two or more hostile states tends to lead to an ever-growing arsenal of nuclear weapons. Following this logic, look at Pakistan's deployment of its first nuclear missile aimed at India (the example also works with the countries reversed). India would not attack—that is, unless it could prevent Pakistan from using its missile. India could do this by building offensive forces capable of

THE RACE IS ON
India and Pakistan are building arsenals of nuclear-tipped missiles that could devastate each other's big cities. Their current arms race follows that of the superpowers during the Cold War. Superpower arms control agreements helped develop norms and expectations about the role of nuclear weapons, but did not stop a buildup of tens of thousands of nuclear weapons. Here, India shows off its new intermediate-range ballistic missile, 2002.

---

[32] Charles L. Glaser, *Analyzing Strategic Nuclear Policy* (Princeton, NJ: Princeton UP, 1990). Scott D. Sagan, *Moving Targets: Nuclear Strategy and National Security* (Princeton, NJ: Princeton UP, 1989). Joseph S. Nye, Graham T. Allison and Albert Carnesdale, eds., *Fateful Visions: Avoiding Nuclear Catastrophe* (Cambridge, MA: Ballinger, 1988). Edward Rhodes, *Power and Madness: The Logic of Nuclear Coercion* (NY: Columbia UP, 1989). Robert Jervis, *The Meaning of the Nuclear Revolution: Statecraft and the Prospect of Armageddon* (Ithaca, NY: Cornell UP, 1989). Steven Kull, *Minds at War* (NY: Basic, 1988). Strobe Talbott, *The Master of the Game: Paul Nitze and the Nuclear Peace* (NY: Knopf, 1988).

wiping out the Pakistani missile (probably using nuclear weapons, but that is not the key point here). The Pakistani missile, rather than deterring India, would merely spur it to destroy the missile before any other attack. An attack intended to destroy—largely or entirely—a state's nuclear weapons before they can be used is called a *first strike*.

Pakistan could make its missile survivable (probably by making it mobile). It could also build more nuclear missiles so that even if some were destroyed in an Indian first strike, there would some left with which to retaliate. Weapons that can take a first strike and still strike back give a state *second-strike* capabilities. A state that deploys the fewest nuclear forces needed for an assured second-strike capability (between tens and hundreds) has a minimum deterrent. Possession of second-strike capabilities by both sides is called **mutually assured destruction (MAD)** because neither side can prevent the other from destroying it. The term implies that the strategy, though reflecting "rationality," is actually insane (mad) because deviations from rationality could destroy both sides.

If India could not assuredly *destroy* Pakistan's missile, it would undoubtedly deploy its own nuclear missile(s) to *deter* Pakistan from using its own. India, too, could achieve a second-strike capability. Now the question of credibility becomes important. In theory, India could launch a nonnuclear attack on Pakistan, knowing that rational Pakistani leaders would rather lose such a war than use their nuclear weapons and bring on an Indian nuclear response. The nuclear missiles in effect cancel each other out.

During the Cold War, the same problem was faced by U.S. war planners trying to deter a Soviet conventional attack on Western Europe. They could threaten to use nuclear weapons in response, but rational Soviet leaders would know that rational U.S. leaders would never act on such a threat and risk escalation to global nuclear war. Better to lose West Germany, according to this line of thinking, than lose both West Germany and New York. U.S. planners thus tried to convince the Soviets that such an attack would be too risky by integrating thousands of tactical nuclear weapons into conventional forces so that the escalation to nuclear war might happen more or less automatically in the event of conventional war. This was the equivalent of "throwing away the steering wheel" in a game of chicken (see p. 60). China currently uses a similar form of "rational irrationality" in its relations with Taiwan, trying to make credible the threat of war (which would be disastrous for China as well as Taiwan) if Taiwan declares independence (see p. 71).

Nuclear *warfighting*, or *counterforce*, specifically targets another state's forces. Without such a capability, a state's only available lever is to blow up another state's cities—a countervalue capability (targeting something of value to the other side). The trouble with nuclear warfighting forces, however, is that they must be very accurate, powerful and massive in order to successfully knock out the other side's nuclear weapons. This makes them effective first-strike weapons—very threatening to the other state and likely to provoke further buildup of the other state's weapons in response. Most first-strike weapons are considered inherently unstable in a crisis because they are so threatening that the other side would be tempted to make a first strike of its own—a "use 'em or lose 'em" problem (this is less true of SLBMs, which can serve as first-strike weapons, but because they are deployed on submarines and difficult to detect, they are less vulnerable).[33]

The problem is accentuated by the use of multiple warheads on a single missile (multiple independently targeted re-entry vehicles, or MIRVs). The more warheads on a missile, the more tempting a target it makes for the other side. (One successful strike

mutually assured destruction (MAD) The possession of second-strike nuclear capabilities by two adversaries, which ensures that neither could prevent the other from destroying it in an all-out war. See also *deterrence*.

---

[33] R. Harrison Wagner, "Nuclear Deterrence, Counterforce Strategies, and the Incentive to Strike First," *American Political Science Review* 85.3 (1991): 727–50.

can prevent multiple enemy strikes.) Thus, fixed land-based MIRVed missiles are considered destabilizing weapons. In the 1992 START II treaty (ratified in 2000), the United States and Russia agreed to phase them out.

Some of the language associated with nuclear weaponry is discussed by IR theorists. Particularly for critical theorists, referring to strikes against cities and people as "counter value" attacks (versus the "counterforce" targeting of military installations) or describing unintended strikes against civilian targets as "collateral damage" are ways of sanitizing the impact of a nuclear attack. The use of even one nuclear weapon would be catastrophic; it would involve the incineration of tens of thousands of people and untold long-term suffering. Some critical theorists argue that the language used by strategic thinkers (and theorists) makes it easy to think about the possibility of nuclear war without really considering its actual consequences.[34]

Strategic Defense Initiative (SDI) A U.S. effort, also known as "star wars," to develop defences that could shoot down incoming ballistic missiles, spurred by President Ronald Reagan in 1983. Critics call it an expensive failure that would violate the ABM Treaty. See also *Anti-Ballistic Missile (ABM) Treaty.*

Defence has played little role in nuclear strategy because no effective defence against missile attack has been devised. However, the United States is spending billions of dollars a year to try to develop defences that could shoot down incoming ballistic missiles. The program is called the **Strategic Defense Initiative (SDI)**, "star wars" or "Ballistic Missile Defense" (BMD). It originated in President Ronald Reagan's 1983 call for a comprehensive shield that would make nuclear missiles obsolete.[35] However, the mission soon shifted to a (slightly) more realistic one of defending U.S. missiles in a massive Soviet attack. After the Cold War, the mission shifted to one of protecting U.S. territory from a very limited missile attack (at most a few missiles), such as might occur in an unauthorized launch, accident or attack by a small state.

Current plans call for the deployment of ground-based, nonnuclear missiles to try to intercept incoming warheads. To proceed with this system, the Bush administration formally signalled in late 2001 that it would withdraw from the Anti-Ballistic Missile Treaty with Russia (see p. 275), which it did in 2002. Allies such as Canada have expressed mixed support for the U.S. project (also called National Missile Defense or NMD). The Liberal government under Paul Martin initially signalled an interest in supporting the U.S. in missile defence, but later declined to participate. The Conservative government is in principle more amenable to the project, but as of mid-2007 had yet to take a position on the plan. Prime Minister Stephen Harper said shortly after the 2006 election that if asked directly by the U.S., he would submit the question to a free vote in Parliament. Some observers noted that the U.S. would not make such a direct request until the Conservatives had secured a majority government in Ottawa.[36]

Japan plans to spend $1 billion a year to build a U.S.-designed land-and-sea missile defence system by 2007. In 2004, the United States began deploying a prototype missile

---

[34] Carol Cohn, "Sex and Death in the Rational World of Defense Intellectuals," *Signs: Journal of Women in Culture and Society* 12.4 (Summer 1987): 687–718.

[35] James M. Lindsay and Michael O'Hanlon, *Defending America: The Case for Limited National Missile Defense* (Washington, DC: Brookings, 2001). James Chace and Caleb Carr, *America Invulnerable: The Quest for Absolute Security from 1812 to Star Wars* (NY: Summit, 1988). David B. H. Denoon, *Ballistic Missile Defense in the Post–Cold War Era* (Boulder, CO: Westview, 1995).

[36] David Rudd, "Muddling through on Missile Defence: The Politics of Indecision," *Policy Options* (May 2005): 30–34. Julian Schofield and Ara Karaboghossian, "National Missile Defence: A Wise Decision for the Moment," *Policy Options* (May 2005): 51–56. John Siebert, "Canada under a New Government," *The Ploughshares Monitor* 27.1 (Spring 2006), available at http://www.ploughshares.ca/libraries/monitor/monm06b.pdf. David S. McDonough, "BMD and US Strategic Doctrine: Canadian Strategic Interests in the Debate on Missile Defence," *Journal of Military and Strategic Studies* 9.3 (Spring 2006/07), available at http://www.jmss.org/2007/2007spring/articles/mcdonough.pdf.

intercept system based in Alaska and a destroyer in the Sea of Japan, off the coast of North Korea, that could possibly shoot down a North Korean missile in its boost phase after launch (when their engines make them easy to detect, and warheads and decoys have not yet deployed). It also moved to put in place—against strong Chinese opposition—a missile-defence collaboration in Asia that would include Japan, Australia, possibly India and Taiwan. Four Japanese destroyers are to join the U.S. one, and Patriot missiles based in Japan would try to shoot down incoming missiles. Several tests of the U.S. system failed in 2004.

Other technologies are also being tested, including lasers fired from either space or ships to disable ballistic missiles in the boost phase. Overall, no reliable defence against ballistic missiles exists, and experts disagree on whether such a defence is close or many years away.

In addition to the technical challenges of stopping incoming ballistic missile warheads, a true strategic defence should also stop cruise missiles and airplanes, if not more innovative delivery systems. This problem has yet to be solved.

All weapons of mass destruction are relatively difficult and expensive to build, and provide only specialized capabilities that are rarely if ever actually used. As a result, a number of states have decided that such weapons are not worth acquiring, though it would be technically possible to do so. Such cost-benefit thinking also applies more broadly to states' decisions about the acquisition of all kinds of military forces.

STATES AND MILITARIES

Given the range of military capabilities available to states (at various costs), how should state leaders choose which to acquire?

Military Economics

Choices about military forces depend on the connection between a state's military spending and its economic health. Not long ago, it was widely believed in some countries that "war is good for the economy" (seemingly, military spending helped end the Great Depression in the late 1930s). If this were true, state leaders would not face difficult choices in setting military budgets. High military spending would provide both military capabilities for use in international conflicts *and* economic growth for domestic needs (buying popular and political support in various ways).

Unfortunately for state leaders, the economics of military spending is not so favourable. Over the long run, military spending tends to compete with other economic needs, such as investment in civilian industry or government projects. Over time, allocating economic resources for military purposes deprives the rest of the economy and reduces its growth. High-technology military development (using engineers, scientists and technicians) tends to starve civilian sectors of talent and technology. Fewer jobs are created in the military than in education, housing, construction and similar areas (military spending is more capital-intensive and less labour-intensive). Conversely, reductions in military spending tend to free up economic resources for more productive purposes and strengthen the growth of the economy in the long term.

Thus, over the long term, state leaders face a trade-off between increasing available military leverage and increasing overall economic health. This trade-off explains in part why, during the Cold War, the great power with the highest military spending—the

Soviet Union, at perhaps 20 percent of GDP—had the worst economic performance, whereas the great power with the lowest military spending (Japan, with around 1 percent of GDP) had the best economic performance.[37]

From a global perspective, the amount of world military spending decreased substantially in the post–Cold War era, by about one-third overall in the 1990s, although it began to increase again after 1998. World military spending makes up close to 2 percent of the total goods and services in the world economy—about US$1.2 trillion every year, or roughly $1 million every 30 seconds. Most is spent by a few big states; nearly half by the United States alone. World military spending is a vast flow of money that could, if redirected to other purposes, change the world profoundly and improve major world problems.[38] Of course, "the world" does not spend this money or choose how to direct it; states do.

When the Cold War ended, U.S. leaders promised to cut military spending to reap a peace dividend—more money for cities, education, the environment and so forth.[39] The savings in the next decade, estimated at more than US$100 billion, may not have changed problems in those areas but did help reduce the U.S. budget deficit. And, while nuclear arsenals were reduced, high-tech investment in projects such as the National Missile Defense program tend to offset any savings. The U.S. also began to demand that prosperous allies in Europe and Japan pay more for maintaining U.S. military forces in those countries—a concept known as *burden sharing*. The U.S. has pressured countries like Canada to devote more resources to maintaining their militaries.

Unfortunately, the short-term effects of military spending (or reductions in spending) tend to run counter to the long-term effects. The immediate effect of a sharp reduction in military spending (as at the end of a war) often throws people out of work and disrupts economic growth. Conversely, the effect of increased military spending in the short term can pick up the slack in a national economy operating below capacity (as the United States and Canada were in the 1930s, for example). Because of these short-term effects, U.S. military spending cuts after the Cold War deepened their recession in the early 1990s. Only later in the decade did the United States enjoy unprecedented prosperity.

At the same time, Russia and the other former Soviet republics drastically curtailed military spending, which their tattered economies could not support. Russia's cuts in military spending did little to stop its economic free fall. There and throughout the former Soviet Union—and somewhat less desperately in the West—political leaders scrambled to develop plans for **economic conversion**—use of former military facilities and industries for new civilian production.[40]

economic conversion The use of former military facilities and industries for new civilian production.

---

[37] Alex Mintz and Steve Chan, *Defense, Welfare and Growth: Perspectives and Evidence* (NY: Routledge, 1992). Richard J. Samuels, *Rich Nation, Strong Army: National Security and the Technological Transformation of Japan* (Ithaca, NY: Cornell UP, 1994).

[38] Randall Forsberg, Robert Elias and Matthew Goodman, "Peace Issues and Strategies," Institute for Defense and Disarmament Studies *Peace Resource Book 1986* (Cambridge, MA: Ballinger, 1985) 5–13.

[39] Michael D. Ward and David R. Davis, "Sizing Up the Peace Dividend: Economic Growth and Military Spending in the United States, 1948–1996," *American Political Science Review* 86.3 (1992): 748–58. Alex Mintz, ed., *The Political Economy of Military Spending in the United States* (NY: Routledge, 1992). William W. Kaufmann, *Glasnost, Perestroika, and U.S. Defense Spending* (Washington, DC: Brookings, 1990).

[40] Ian Anthony, *The Future of the Defense Industries in Central and Eastern Europe* (NY: Oxford UP, 1994). Lawrence R. Klein, Fu-chen Lo and Warwick J. McKibbin, eds., *Arms Reduction: Economic Implications in the Post–Cold War Era* (NY: UN UP, 1995). Bonn International Center for Conversion, *Conversion Survey 1997: Global Disarmament and the Disposal of Surplus Weapons* (NY: Oxford UP, 1997). Lloyd J. Dumas and Marek Thee, eds., *Making Peace Possible: The Promise of Economic Conversion* (NY: Pergamon, 1989).

Canada was quick to take advantage of its comparative advantage in peacekeeping at the end of the Cold War. Not only were Canadian forces deployed on more missions during the 1990s, but Canada also became actively involved in training peacekeepers, both its own and those from other countries. Training was delivered either on Canadian military bases or at the Pearson Peacekeeping Centre in Cornwallis, Nova Scotia.[41] In the 2000s, Canada shifted to more combat-oriented missions and away from traditional peacekeeping. As of 2006, the Conservative government pledged to increase military spending by an additional $5.3 billion over five years. Critics noted that this was a good start but insufficient. As of 2007, and based on 2005 data, Canada was ranked 131st overall in terms of its military expenditures as a percentage of GDP, far behind countries such as Burundi, Swaziland, Botswana and even the Solomon Islands. However, in real dollars, Canada is the seventh highest military spender among all NATO members, a commitment that critics of overspending claim comes at the expense of Canada's support for development and overseas assistance.[42]

Both the long- and short-term effects of military spending are magnified by actual warfare. War not only stimulates high military spending; it destroys capital (people, cities, farms and factories in battle areas) and causes inflation (reducing the supply of various goods while increasing demand for them). Governments must pay for war goods by borrowing money (increasing government debt), printing more currency (fuelling inflation) or raising taxes (reducing spending and investment). U.S. revolutionary Thomas Paine warned in 1787 that "war . . . has but one thing certain, and that is to increase taxes."[43]

Nonetheless, war and high military spending can have certain economic benefits, which is seen as particularly important by liberal pluralists. The short-term stimulation resulting from a boost in military spending has been mentioned. Another potential benefit, important from the perspective of realism, is the acquisition of territory (containing resources and capital). One more potential economic benefit of war is to stir up a population's patriotism so that it will work harder for less pay. Overall, however, the benefits of war rarely equal the economic costs.

State leaders, then, face complex choices in setting overall levels of military spending. Over the long term, low military spending is economically preferable, but in

THE WAR IS OVER
U.S. and Russian nuclear forces were greatly reduced in the 1990s. Here, U.S. B-52 bombers are being chopped up, under the eye of Russian satellites, to bring force levels down.

[41] Jocelyn Coulon, *Soldiers of Diplomacy: The United Nations, Peacekeeping, and the New World Order* (Toronto: U Toronto P, 1998). Joseph T. Jockel, *Canada and International Peacekeeping* (Washington: Center for Strategic and International Studies, 1994).

[42] CIA, "Rank Order Military Expenditures—Percent of GDP," *The World Factbook*, available at https://www.cia.gov/cia/publications/factbook/rankorder/2034rank.html. Steven Staples and Bill Robinson, "It's Never Enough: Canada's Alarming Rise in Military Spending" 25 Oct. 2005 (Ottawa: The Polaris Institute).

[43] Thomas Paine, *The Writings of Thomas Paine*, vol. 2 (NY: Knickerbocker, 1894).

the short term, higher military spending can stimulate the economy. Sudden changes in military spending, up or down, are usually disruptive to economic health and stability. Such sudden changes usually reflect the beginnings or ends of wars, which entail even more complex trade-offs of costs and benefits (economic *and* political) for state leaders.

The Choice of Capabilities

Despite the complexity of trade-offs, state leaders must adopt military budgets, choose particular military capabilities to obtain and often structure other economic activities to support those choices (for instance, nurturing the military-industrial complex). Leaders try to assess the threats to their state from other states' military capabilities and develop affordable strategies to reduce those threats accordingly.

The most basic choice facing state leaders is how much to spend on military capabilities. This varies widely, from Costa Rica, with virtually no military spending at all, to states such as North Korea, which devotes 20 percent or more of all economic activity to military purposes. If military budgets are too low, states may be unprepared to meet a security threat; in the worst case, they may be overrun and conquered militarily. If leaders set military budgets too high, they will overburden the national economy in the long run. (So far, Costa Rica has not been attacked despite recent wars in neighbouring Nicaragua and Panama, whereas North Korea is virtually bankrupt.)

In recent years, U.S. leaders have been rethinking military capabilities. Given the tremendous U.S. lead over other great powers, how much U.S. superiority is enough? And, at the same time, does the configuration of the U.S. military allow it to fight in war zones such as the Gulf in the early 1990s and Baghdad in the early 2000s? In Canada, by contrast, the concern has been that reductions in military spending during the 1980s and 1990s have so reduced the quality of infrastructure and equipment that members of the Canadian Forces are at risk. After 2006 the Conservative government pledged to devote greater resources to military spending. However, whether Canada could actually defend itself against an attack, given the size of the Canadian military, is a question that is raised regularly.

Other states have been making similar assessments—most dramatically in Russia and the other republics of the former Soviet Union. Although military spending was reduced as quickly as possible, there were no jobs available for laid-off soldiers and military-industrial workers and no housing for troops brought home from Eastern Europe. For the next few years at least, military forces in Russia and most of the other former Soviet republics appear destined to struggle in a much reduced and weakened condition.

The cutbacks are less dramatic in Western Europe, where NATO members spend several percent of GDP on military forces. In Japan, where military spending was already only 1 percent of GDP, dramatic cutbacks are not planned. In China, military spending does not greatly affect economic growth because the army is largely self-supporting (it runs its own farms, factories, etc.)—which also makes Chinese military spending hard to calculate. Chinese military forces underwent a substantial reduction with modernization in the 1980s and 1990s. Because it lags in technology, however, China's army remains the weakest of the great-power militaries, with the possible exception of Russia.

Middle powers like Canada, the Netherlands and Australia remained heavily committed to peacekeeping missions in the immediate post–Cold War period of the 1990s. These missions do not require the same capital expenditure or acquisition of arms as

⊕ Thinking Theoretically

During the Cold War, the superpowers poured money into military budgets at rates ranging from 5 to 10 percent of GDP for the United States and perhaps 20 percent for the Soviet Union. What theories can explain the superpowers' military spending levels, as well as the sharp decreases in military spending in the 1990s?

One approach is based on reciprocity (see pp. 81–82). Each superpower responds to the other's military spending by raising or lowering its own military budget in the next time period. From this perspective, the superpower arms race may fit the model of a repeated Prisoner's Dilemma—as seen in laboratory experiments in which university students play PD repeatedly, and both sides eventually learn to get out of the cycle of mutual defection (the spiralling arms race) and lock into stable cooperation. This pattern could explain the recent sharp decrease in military spending.

An alternative model has each superpower's military spending domestically driven. This would follow from ideas such as the organizational process model of foreign policy (see pp. 139–140) or, from a critical theory perspective, the power of the military-industrial complex (see pp. 152–153). Hundreds of research studies have tried to test these models against the empirical evidence provided by 40 years of military budgets. Typically they use a mathematical model of the arms race, and then employ quantitative data on arms spending to statistically test whether the model explains the data well. The test shows how well, on average, a country's military spending correlates with the other country's previous spending.

So which theory is supported by these tests? The answer is that none can be evaluated with much confidence because the quantitative data on military spending are unreliable. Not only did both superpowers conceal military spending (and even military activity from which spending levels might be inferred), but comparing the two was problematic. Costs of weapons and salaries were very different in the two countries; the soldiers and equipment were not of comparable quality; rubles were not convertible into dollars; and macroeconomic indicators such as GDP were not compatible across communist and capitalist economies. As a result, no one could say for certain if Soviet military spending was up or down in a given year, or whether it was greater or less than U.S. spending. Thus, military spending can be explained by at least three good theories—good in the sense that they can explain the outcome in terms of a general model with implications for other cases—and that neither model can be ruled out by empirical evidence.

other configurations of forces. The policies of some middle powers began to shift dramatically during the 2000s, however. Australia supported the U.S. in the Iraq War, and Canada's largest military deployment in 2007 was in Afghanistan as part of the NATO-led (and UN-sanctioned) International Assistance Force. Some 2500 of the total 2673 Canadian Forces deployed abroad in early 2007 were stationed in Afghanistan. In a few short years, a country that had been described as the world's peacekeeper *"par excellence"* had fewer than 200 military personnel actually deployed on peacekeeping missions.

In the global South, military spending varies greatly from one country to another, depending in part on the government in power (military or civilian).[44] Spending also depends heavily on available hard currency, from exports of oil or other products, to pay for arms purchases.

Weapons imports by states of the global South make up two-thirds of all arms sales. About half of the South's arms imports are in the Middle East, where oil exports

---

[44] Norman A. Graham, ed., *Seeking Security and Development: The Impact of Military Spending and Arms Transfers* (Boulder, CO: Rienner, 1994). Ravinder Pal Singh, ed., *Arms Procurement Decision-Making Processes: China, India, Israel, Japan, and South Korea* (NY: Oxford UP/SIPRI, 1997). Bates Gill and J. N. Mak, eds., *Arms Trade, Transparency, and Security in South-East Asia* (NY: Oxford UP/SIPRI, 1997).

create a ready source of funding. The remaining arms purchases are spread across Latin America, South Asia, East Asia and Africa. Of all international arms exports, a third come from the United States, with Russia and Britain ranked next. Worldwide, these three countries and France together account for three-quarters of international arms sales.[45]

In recent years, activists have called attention to the sale of small arms, especially assault rifles, to unstable conflict zones where regular and irregular armies commit brutalities. In 2003 (the last year for which data is available), the largest exporters of small arms, by value, were the Russian Federation, the United States, Italy, Germany, Brazil and China. The largest importers (importing a value of at least US$100 million) were the United States, Cyprus and Germany. Of the US$3 to $4 billion in small arms and ammunition exported in 2003, Russian exports accounted for over $430 million, followed by the U.S. with $370 million, Italy with $347 million and Germany with $201 million (all in U.S. dollars). Canada is also a significant exporter of small arms, at $57 million.[46]

In 2001, 140 states agreed to a voluntary pact to curb small-arms sales to conflict zones. Canada is a strong supporter of limiting small-arms sales, but countries like the United States have blocked proposals to restrict sales of military weapons to rebel movements and civilians. The U.S. favours export licensing by individual exporters over multilateral efforts to address small arms. In December 2006 the UN General Assembly voted to begin work on an arms trade treaty, although the United States is in opposition and its success is far from assured.[47] One problem with licensing or with other agreements as suggested by the U.S. is that they may not address the "cascade" effect of re-selling arms and ammunition—what is called trade in "surplus stock." This accounts for a large portion of annual small-arms sales, with wealthy states selling older or outdated arms usually to poorer southern states. The Geneva-based *Small Arms Survey* estimates a large increase in sales of surplus stock over the next 10 to 15 years, as the world's largest importers launch major procurement programs.[48]

Beyond considerations about the size of military forces, the question of configuration also presents difficult choices. Should Canada, for example, emphasize its navy or its air force? Should the army have more soldiers or more tanks? Which bases should be closed in periods of military cutbacks? Should Japan build nuclear weapons? Should Syria buy medium-range missiles?

Different missions require different forces. During the Cold War, about half of all military spending in the U.S.—and of world military spending—was directed toward the capitalist-communist conflict in Europe. Now other missions, such as intervention in

---

[45] Richard F. Grimmett, *Conventional Arms Transfers to Developing Nations, 1993–2000* (Washington, DC: Congressional Research Service, 2001). Randall Forsberg, ed., *The Arms Production Dilemma: Contraction and Restraint in the World Combat Aircraft Industry* (Cambridge, MA: MIT P, 1994). Edward A. Kolodziej, *Making and Marketing Arms: The French Experience and Its Implications for the International System* (Princeton, NJ: Princeton, 1987).

[46] Small Arms Survey, *Small Arms Survey 2006: Profiling the Problem* (Oxford: Oxford UP, 2006). Ken Epps, "Canada and Small Arms Exports," Project Ploughshares *Working Paper*, 06-02, March 2006.

[47] See http://www.controlarms.org. Jeffrey Boutwell and Michael T. Klare, *Light Weapons and Civil Conflict: Controlling the Tools of Violence* (Lanham, MD: Rowman & Littlefield, 1999). "Small Arms, Big Business," *Washington Post* 8 July 2001: A19.

[48] *Small Arms Survey 2006*, see note 46 above.

regional conflicts, are more important. Some scholars think that North-South threats are replacing capitalist-communist ones.[49] Other new missions for military forces include humanitarian assistance, drug interdiction, disaster assistance at home (such as the 1997 Manitoba flood and the 1998 ice storm in eastern Ontario and Québec) and aid to other nations in building roads and schools.

Decisions about a state's military role give direction to its entire economy. During the Cold War, U.S. scientific research and industrial innovation were concentrated in the military sector. By contrast, Japan's research and development in those years focused on commercial products, contributing to Japan's prosperity.

Whatever configuration of military forces a state maintains, the leaders of the state face ongoing decisions about when and how to use those forces.

CONTROL OF MILITARY FORCES

The first issue of concern to a state leader in pulling a lever to exert influence is whether the lever is attached to anything. That is, how are the decisions of leaders translated into actual actions in distant locations?

Command

The use of military force generally requires coordinating the efforts of thousands, sometimes millions, of individuals performing many different functions in many locations. Such coordination is what is meant by *command*. One cannot take for granted the ability of a state leader to make military forces take desired actions. At best, military forces are large and complex institutions, operating in especially difficult conditions during wartime. At worst, military forces have a mind of their own (see pp. 234–237). Sometimes a state leader appears to exert incomplete control over the military.

UNDER CONTROL

Through a hierarchical chain of command, states control the actions of millions of individual soldiers, creating effective leverage in the hands of state leaders. Here, Chinese women soldiers march in a military parade, Guangzhou, 1991.

---

[49] John D. Steinbruner, *Principles of Global Security* (Washington, DC: Brookings, 2000). Richard N. Haass, *Intervention: The Use of American Military Force in the Post–Cold War World*, rev. ed. (Washington, DC: Brookings Institution, 1999). Murray J. Douglas and Paul R. Viotti, eds., *The Defense Policies of Nations: A Comparative Study*, 3rd ed. (Baltimore: Johns Hopkins UP, 1994). Ken Booth, ed., *New Thinking about Strategy and International Security* (Boston: Unwin Hyman, 1991). Bjørn Møller, *The Dictionary of Alternative Defence* (Boulder, CO: Rienner, 1992).

States control military forces through a *chain of command* running from the highest authority through a hierarchy down to low-level soldiers. The highest authority, or commander in chief, is usually the top political leader—the Canadian prime minister, U.S. president, Russian president and so forth. A military hierarchy consists of levels of officers and soldiers.

In actual conditions of battle, controlling armed forces is especially difficult because of complex operations, rapid change and the fog of war created by the gap between battlefield activity and command-level information. Participants are pumped up with adrenaline, deafened by noise and confused by a mass of activity that—from the centre of things—may seem to make no sense. They are called on to perform actions that run against basic instincts as well as moral norms—killing people and risking death. It is difficult to coordinate forces effectively in order to carry out overall plans of action.

These factors reduce the effectiveness of military forces as instruments of state power, but several means for counteracting these problems have been developed. The principle of military discipline states that orders given from higher levels of a hierarchy must be obeyed by the lower levels—whether or not those at the lower level agree. Failure to do so is referred to as insubordination, or a mutiny if a whole group is involved. Leaving one's unit is called deserting. These are serious offences punishable by prison or death.

Members of most contemporary armed forces are trained as to the highly structured lines of authority that make up the chain of command from the moment they arrive as new recruits. Basic training and other initiation exercises aim to enforce obedience and promote an intense bonding among soldiers. No one, at any level, is allowed to deviate from the chain of command, and soldiers learn that their chances of survival in battle are enhanced if they respond to orders instantly and without question.[50]

Discipline depends not only on punishment but also on patriotism and professionalism on the part of soldiers. Officers play to nationalist sentiments, reminding soldiers that they fight for their nation and family. Whatever the motivation of soldiers, they require training in order to function as instruments of state power. Military training includes both technical training and training in the habit of obeying commands—a central purpose of basic training in every military force. Soldiers are deliberately stripped of their individuality—hairstyles, clothes, habits and mannerisms—to become part of a group. This action has both good and bad effects on individuals, but it works for the purposes of the military. Soldiers practise exercises repeatedly until certain operations become second nature.

To maintain control of forces in battle, military units also rely on soldiers' sense of group solidarity. Soldiers risk their lives because their "buddies" depend on them.[51] Abstractions such as nationalism, patriotism or religious fervour are important, but loyalty to the immediate group (along with a survival instinct) is a more effective motivator.

---

[50] Deborah Harrison and Lucie Laliberté, *No Life Like It: Military Wives in Canada* (Toronto: Lorimer, 1994).

[51] Joanna Bourke, *An Intimate History of Killing: Face-to-Face Killing in Twentieth-Century Warfare* (NY: Basic, 1999). Dave Grossman, *On Killing: The Psychological Cost of Learning to Kill in War and Society* (Boston: Little, Brown, 1995). Richard Holmes, *Acts of War: The Behavior of Men in Battle* (NY: Free Press, 1985). Anthony Kellett, "The Soldier in Battle: Motivational and Behavioral Aspects of the Combat Experience," *Psychological Dimensions of War*, ed. Betty Glad (Newbury Park, CA: Sage, 1990) 215–35. Paul Fussell, *Wartime: Understanding and Behavior in the Second World War* (NY: Oxford UP, 1989). J. Glenn Gray, *The Warriors: Reflections on Men in Battle* (1959; NY: Harper & Row, 1967).

Unfortunately, some of the means by which soldiers learn to bond with one another and to submit to military authority are accomplished through denigrating anyone who is seen as "the enemy"—which might include ethnic minorities, women, homosexuals and people of colour. Some analysts have suggested that indoctrinating soldiers in this way can influence how they treat the people in countries to which they are deployed. In some of the most extreme cases, this has resulted in soldiers dehumanizing, torturing and even killing local peoples. Canada was witness to such an incident when members of the Canadian Airborne Regiment tortured and murdered Somali teenager Shidane Arone in the early 1990s.[52] In 2004 in Iraq, U.S. soldiers were photographed humiliating and torturing Iraqi prisoners.

Troops operating in the field also rely on logistical support in order to function effectively. For states to use military leverage, they cannot simply push armies around on a map like chess pieces. Rather, they must support those armies with large quantities of supplies. More than a century ago, leaders in Prussia (Germany) used well-oiled logistics based on railroads to defeat both Austria and France, which were using rapid offensives.

A further difficulty that states must overcome in the effective use of military forces is providing accurate information about what is going on in the field—intelligence—to top officers and political leaders so that they might make good decisions.[53] They also need

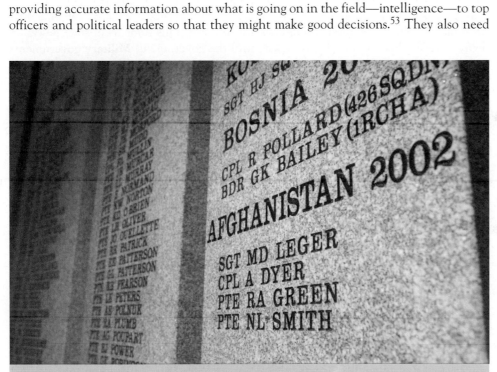

MILITARY MEMORIAL
The name of the four Princess Patricia's Canadian Light Infantry soldiers killed by friendly fire in Afghanistan are seen engraved along with other Canadian military dead at a memorial in Calgary, June 19, 2003.

---

[52] Sandra Whitworth, *Men, Militarism and UN Peacekeeping: A Gendered Analysis* (Boulder, CO: Rienner, 2004). Alfred W. McCoy, "'Same Banana': Hazing and Honor at the Philippine Military Academy," *The Journal of Asian Studies* 54.3 (August 1995): 689–726.

[53] Mark M. Lowenthal, *Intelligence: From Secrets to Policy* (Washington, DC: CQ, 2000). Jeffery T. Richelson, *A Century of Spies: Intelligence in the Twentieth Century* (NY: Oxford UP, 1995).

extensive communications networks, including the ability to use codes to ensure secrecy. Such functions are known as "command and control," or sometimes C3I—for command, control, communications and intelligence. During the Cold War, it was assumed that C3I capabilities would be the first targets in a nuclear war. The information aspect of controlling military forces has become increasingly important. In the Gulf War, a top U.S. priority was to target Iraqi communications facilities so as to disable Iraq's command and control.

The number of so-called friendly fire deaths in the Gulf War and in Afghanistan suggest that command and communications lines are not always effective. In Afghanistan, four Canadian soldiers were killed and eight were wounded in 2002 when American pilots dropped a 227-kilogram bomb. The pilots mistook flashes from the Canadian soldiers' live ammunition exercise on the ground as anti-aircraft fire and assumed they were under attack. The incident occurred despite the fact that the Canadians had informed U.S. command of their planned exercises. The information did not reach the pilots in time to avert tragedy.

States and Militaries Overcoming chaos and complexity is only part of the task for state leaders seeking to control military forces. Sometimes they must also overcome their own military officers. Although militaries are considered instruments of state power, in many states, military forces themselves control the government. **Military governments** are most common in countries of the global South, where the military may be the only large modern institution in the country.

Military leaders are able to exercise political control because the same violent forms of leverage that work internationally also work domestically. In fact, there may be little or no counter-leverage to the use of military force at the domestic level. Military officers thus have an inherent power advantage over civilian political leaders. Ironically, the disciplined central command of military forces, which makes them effective as tools of state influence, also allows the state to lose control to military officers. Soldiers are trained to follow the orders of their commanding officers, not to think about politics.

A **coup d'état** (French for "blow against the state") is the seizure of political power by domestic military forces—a change of political power outside the state's constitutional order.[54] Thailand and Fiji, both functioning democracies, had coups in 2006. Senior officers sometimes mount coups to overthrow politicians who, in the officers' view, have taken the country on a wrong track. Other times, coups are mounted by ambitious junior officers against top generals. Officers who break the chain of command can take along with them those sections of the military hierarchy that fall below them. Coup leaders move quickly to seize centres of power—official state buildings as well as television stations and transmitters—before other units of the military can put down the coup attempt or unleash a civil war. Civilian politicians in power and uncooperative military officers are arrested or killed. Coup leaders try to create a sense of inevitability around the change in government and hope that fellow officers throughout the military defect to their side. In some cases, as in Haiti in 2004, it is former (and not current) members of the military who launch a coup.

---

military governments States in which military forces control the government; more common in countries of the global South, where the military may be the only large modern institution.

coup d'état French for "blow against the state"; the seizure of political power by domestic military forces—that is, a change of political power outside the state's constitutional order.

[54] Peter D. Feaver and Richard D. Kohn, eds., *Soldiers and Civilians* (Cambridge, MA: MIT P, 2001). Steven R. David, *Third World Coups d'État and International Security* (Baltimore: Johns Hopkins UP, 1987). Talukder Maniruzzaman, "Arms Transfers, Military Coups, and Military Rule in Developing States," *Journal of Conflict Resolution* 36.4 (1992): 733–55. William J. Foltz and Henry S. Bienen, eds., *Arms and the African: Military Influences on Africa's International Relations* (New Haven, CT: Yale UP, 1985). Robert S. Jackman, Rosemary H. T. O'Kane, Thomas H. Johnson, Pat McGowan and Robert O. Slater, "Explaining African Coups d'État," *American Political Science Review* 80.1 (1986): 225–50.

The outcome of a coup is hard to predict. If most or all of the military go along with a coup, civilian leaders are generally helpless to stop it. If most military officers follow the existing chain of command, the coup is doomed. In the Philippines in the late 1980s, the top general, Fidel Ramos, remained loyal to the civilian president, Corazón Aquino, in seven coup attempts by subordinate officers. In each case, the bulk of the Philippine military forces stayed loyal to Ramos, and the coups failed. In 1992, Ramos himself was elected president with the backing of a grateful Aquino.

Coups may be put down by an outside military force. A government threatened with a coup may call on foreign friends for military assistance. However, because coups are largely considered an internal affair—and because they are over so quickly—direct foreign intervention is relatively rare. One exception to this rule occurred in 1996, when Paraguay's larger neighbours—Brazil and Argentina—heavily pressured a general to cease an attempted coup against Paraguay's president.

Military governments often have difficulty gaining popular legitimacy for their rule because their power is clearly based on force rather than popular mandate, although the public may support the new regime if the old one was especially bad. To stay in power, both military and civilian governments require at least passive acceptance by their people. In relatively new democracies, support from key elite groups such as business leaders and military officers is especially important.

Even in nonmilitary governments, interaction between civilian and military leaders—called civil-military relations—is an important factor in how states use force.

HIGHLY IRREGULAR
A coup is a change of government carried out by domestic military forces operating outside the state's constitution. The number of military governments in the world is declining, but dozens remain. Pakistan's military government took power in a 1999 coup and became a key ally in fighting Taliban-ruled Afghanistan in 2001. Here soldiers deploy to the provincial legislature in Lahore after the coup.

Military leaders may undermine the authority of civilian leaders in carrying out foreign policies, or they may even threaten a coup if certain actions are taken in international conflicts.

NATO forces operate under strong civilian control. At times, however, military desires run counter to civilian decisions. After the Vietnam War, top U.S. military officers became more reluctant to send U.S. forces into combat. The Pentagon now generally supports using military force only when there is a clear goal that can be achieved militarily, when the public supports the action and when military forces can be used massively for a quick victory. Panama in 1989, Kuwait in 1991 and Afghanistan in 2001 fit these conditions. Members of the U.S. military were divided on the invasion of Iraq, with some suggesting that none of these conditions held.

Military officers also want autonomy of decision once force is committed, in order to avoid the problems created in Vietnam when President Johnson sat in the White House situation room daily picking targets for bombing raids. In NATO's 1999 bombing of Serbia, specific targets had to be approved by politicians in multiple countries.

Covert operations are the dagger part of the "cloak and dagger" spy business. Several thousand such operations were mounted during the Cold War, when the CIA in the U.S. and the Soviet Union's KGB waged an ongoing worldwide secret war. CIA covert operations in the 1950s overthrew unfriendly foreign governments—in Iran and Guatemala—by organizing coups against them. The CIA-organized Bay of Pigs invasion in Cuba in 1961 was its first big failure, followed by other failed efforts against the Castro government (including eight assassination attempts). CIA covert activities were sharply scaled back after congressional hearings in the 1970s revealed scandals. Such covert operations now must be reported to special congressional *oversight* committees through an elaborate set of procedures. After September 2001, the executive branch enjoyed greater authority in conducting covert operations without congressional scrutiny, although the limits of executive authority remain uncertain, especially after Democrats won the U.S. Congress in 2006 and promised stronger oversight.

The Canadian Security Intelligence Service (CSIS) was established in 1984 and is mandated to provide advance warning to government departments about any activities that may constitute a threat to Canadian security. Prior to 1984, the Royal Canadian Mounted Police (RCMP) provided security intelligence within Canada, but a number of scandals led the Canadian government to decide that a civilian body would be better suited to this role. During the last few years of the Cold War, CSIS was involved primarily in countering the espionage activities of foreign governments. Like the CIA in the United States, it now focuses on counterterrorism but also investigates economic espionage. CSIS does not have quite the "cloak and dagger" reputation of the CIA, but in its early years it was subject to considerable domestic criticism for spying on its own citizens. CSIS is not permitted to take direct action against any perceived threats; instead, responses to security threats are left to the police and military.

Another factor in controlling military forces is the increasing reliance on private companies to provide services that militaries themselves used to provide, such as logistical support, base maintenance and even bodyguards and virtual private armies that operate in war zones.[55] In the U.S. operation in Iraq, a very large contract with the company Halliburton came under criticism, and investigators found financial problems with the partnership.

The traditions of civil-military relations in a state do not necessarily reflect the extent of its democracy. Even some states with long histories of democracy have had trouble

---

[55] Deborah Avant, *The Market for Force: The Consequences of Privatizing Security* (Cambridge UP, 2005).

controlling the military, notably in Latin America. And states with strong traditions of civilian control over military forces include some authoritarian states, such as the former Soviet Union (where the Communist Party controlled the military). The tradition of civilian (Communist Party) control of the military in China is more ambiguous. Regional military leaders coordinate their activities through the Central Military Commission under direction of the party, but during the cultural revolution in the 1960s, and again in the Tiananmen protests in 1989, military forces essentially held power at times of internal strife.

Overall, states face complex choices regarding the configuration of their military forces in the post–Cold War era. Not only have immediate contingencies and threats changed drastically, but the nature of threats in the new era is unknown. Perhaps most important, world order itself is evolving along with military technologies. The next chapter discusses the evolving structures and norms governing international political relations and how they are changing the nature of world order.

Thinking Critically

1. If you were the leader of, say, Vietnam, what size and kinds of military forces would you want your country to have? What kinds of threats would prompt the use of specific capabilities?

2. Suppose it was discovered that Iran had obtained three tactical nuclear warheads from the former Soviet arsenal and had been keeping them in unknown locations. What, if anything, should the great powers do about this? What consequences might follow from their actions?

3. Imagine a world in which most of the states, as opposed to just a few, had nuclear weapons and long-range ballistic missiles. Would it be more peaceful or more war-prone? Why?

4. Most of the great powers are reconfiguring their military forces in the post–Cold War era. What kinds of capabilities do you think your own country needs in this period? Are there other priorities, beyond military capabilities, for which you would want to advocate?

5. World military spending is around US$1.2 trillion annually. If you could redirect these funds, how would you use them? Would such uses be better or worse for the states involved? Do you think there is a realistic chance of redirecting military spending in the way you suggest?

Chapter Summary

- Military forces provide states with means of leverage beyond the various nonmilitary means of influence widely used in international bargaining.

- Political leaders face difficult choices in configuring and paying for military forces. Military spending tends to stimulate economic growth in the short term but reduce growth over the long term.

- Control of territory is fundamental to state sovereignty and is accomplished primarily with ground forces.

- Air war, using precision-guided bombs against battlefield targets, proved extremely effective in the U.S. campaigns in Iraq in 1991, Serbia in 1999 and Afghanistan in 2001.

- Small missiles and electronic warfare are increasingly important, especially for naval and air forces. The role of satellites is expanding in communications, navigation and reconnaissance.

- Terrorism is effective if it damages morale in a population and gains media exposure for the cause.

- The September 2001 attacks differed from earlier terrorism in terms of both scale of destruction and the long reach of the global al Qaeda terrorist network. The attacks forced dramatic changes in U.S. and worldwide security arrangements, and sparked U.S. military intervention in Afghanistan to overthrow the Taliban regime and destroy al Qaeda bases.

- Weapons of mass destruction—nuclear, chemical and biological—have been used only a handful of times in war.

- The production of nuclear weapons is technically within the means of many states and some nonstate actors, but the necessary fissionable material (uranium-235 or plutonium) is very difficult to obtain.

- Most industrialized states, as well as many poor ones, have voluntarily refrained from acquiring nuclear weapons. These states include two great powers, Germany and Japan.

- More states are acquiring ballistic missiles capable of striking other states from hundreds of kilometres away (or farther, depending on the missile's range). However, no state has ever attacked another with weapons of mass destruction mounted on ballistic missiles.

- Chemical weapons are cheaper to build than nuclear weapons, have similar threat value and their production is harder to detect. More middle powers have chemical weapons than nuclear ones. A 1992 treaty bans the possession and use of chemical weapons.

- Several states conduct research into biological warfare, but by treaty the possession of such weapons is banned.

- Slowing the proliferation of ballistic missiles and weapons of mass destruction in the global South is a central concern of the great powers.

- The United States is testing systems to defend against ballistic missile attack, although none has proven feasible, and it withdrew from the ABM treaty with Russia to pursue this program.

- The United States and Russia have arsenals of thousands of nuclear weapons; China, Britain and France have hundreds. Israel, India, Pakistan and North Korea each have scores. Weapons deployments are guided by nuclear strategy based on the concept of deterrence.

- In the 1990s, military forces and expenditures of the great powers—especially Russia—were reduced and restructured.

- Military forces include a wide variety of capabilities suited to different purposes. Conventional warfare requires different kinds of forces than those needed to threaten the use of nuclear, chemical or biological weapons.

- Except in time of civil war, state leaders—whether civilian or military—control military forces through a single hierarchical chain of command.

- Military forces can threaten the domestic power of state leaders, who are vulnerable to being overthrown by coups d'état.

Key Terms

infantry   198

counterinsurgency   198

landmines   198

power projection   199

electronic warfare   203

stealth technology   203

state-sponsored terrorism   207

weapons of mass destruction   208

fusion weapons   208

fissionable material   208

ballistic missiles   211

intercontinental ballistic missiles
   (ICBMs)   211

cruise missile   212

Missile Technology Control
   Regime   214

Chemical Weapons Convention   216

Biological Weapons Convention   217

proliferation   218

Non-Proliferation Treaty (NPT)   220

mutually assured destruction
   (MAD)   223

Strategic Defense Initiative (SDI)   224

economic conversion   226

military governments   234

coup d'état   234

Research Navigator Question

Log on to Research Navigator and use Content Search under the Political Science database to find recent articles on the changed nature of Canada's military deployments, from an emphasis on peacekeeping to a more combat-oriented posture with the mission to Afghanistan. What information can you find about the reasons for this reorientation? Is there any discussion of the pressures that this orientation puts on the Canadian Forces? Or is it viewed as advantageous? Do any of the articles discuss the change in Canadian identity away from the notion of Canada as a peacekeeper *par excellence*?

Weblinks

The following links are a sampling of government departments, research centres or advocacy groups that focus on different aspects of militaries and military force:

Canadian Defence and Foreign Affairs Institute:
http://www.cdfai.org

Canadian Department of National Defence:
http://www.dnd.ca

NATO:
http://www.nato.int

Nuclear Files.org:
http://www.nuclearfiles.org

Pearson Peacekeeping Centre:
http://www.peaceoperations.org

Public Safety Canada:
http://www.ps-sp.gc.ca/index-en.asp

Project on Defense Alternatives:
http://www.comw.org/pda

Small Arms Survey (Geneva):
http://www.smallarmssurvey.org

International Law and Organization

Greece's foreign minister addresses the UN Security Council, 2006.

WORLD ORDER

According to liberal pluralists (and even many realists), most international conflicts are not settled by military force. Despite the realist vision of an anarchic international system based on state sovereignty, the security dilemma does not usually lead to a breakdown in basic cooperation among states. States generally refrain from taking maximum short-term advantage of each other (such as by invading and conquering). States work *with* other states for mutual gain and take advantage of each other only "at the margin." Unfortunately the day-to-day cooperative activities of states often are less newsworthy than when states use force.

States work together by following rules they develop to govern their interactions. Over time, the rules become more firmly established and institutions grow up around them. States then develop a habit of working through those institutions and within the rules. They may do so because of self-interest: given the regulation of international interactions through institutions and rules, they can realize great gains, thereby avoiding the costly outcomes associated with a breakdown of cooperation (see pp. 82–84).

International anarchy thus does not mean a lack of order, structure and rules. In many ways, actors in international society now work together as cooperatively as actors in domestic society—and sometimes even more so. Today, most wars are civil, not interstate, a change that reflects the general success of international norms, organizations and laws—in addition to the balance of power—in maintaining peace among states.

The Evolution of World Order

Over centuries, international institutions and rules have grown stronger, more complex and more important. For liberals, this means that while international order started out based largely on raw power, it has evolved to be based more on legitimacy and habit. *Domestic law*, too, was once enforced only by the most powerful for the most powerful. The first states and civilizations were largely military dictatorships. Law was what the top ruler decreed. International law and organization likewise began as terms imposed by powerful winners on losers after wars.

The international institutions and rules that operate today took shape predominantly during periods of hegemony (see "Hegemony" on pp. 69–70), when one state dominated in international power following a hegemonic war among the great powers. For realists, in fact, international organizations or alliances operate largely at the behest of the interests of powerful states, and when those states no longer find such institutions useful, they will be abandoned. The international organizations and agreements that today form the institutional framework for international interactions—such as the UN, NATO, the Organization of American States and the World Bank—were created after World War II under U.S. leadership.

Rules of international behaviour have been established as norms over time and are often codified as international law. This is a more incremental process than the creation of institutions; it goes on between and during periods of war and of hegemony. Still, the most powerful states, especially hegemons, have great influence on the rules and values that become embedded over time in international law.

For example, the principle of free passage on the open seas is now formally established in international law.[1] At one time, however, warships from one state did not hesitate to seize the ships of other states and ransack their cargoes. This practice was profitable to the state that pulled off such raids, but of course their own shipping could be raided in return. Such behaviour made long-distance trade more dangerous, less predictable and less profitable. Trading states could benefit more by doing away with the practice, and over time a norm was established around the concept of freedom of navigation on the high seas. It became one of the first areas of international law developed by the Dutch legal scholar *Hugo Grotius* in the mid-1600s—a time when the Dutch dominated world trade and could benefit most from free navigation.

Dutch power, then, provided the backbone for the international legal concept of freedom of the seas. Later, when Britain was dominant, it enforced the principle of free seas through the cannons of its warships. As the world's main trading state, Britain benefited from a worldwide norm of free shipping and trade. And with the world's most powerful navy, it was in a position to define and enforce those rules.

Likewise, twentieth-century world order depended heavily on the power of the United States (and, for a few decades, on the division of power between the United States and the Soviet Union). The U.S. has been instrumental in maintaining global norms around trade and security issues, but its enormous power and foreign policy agendas have also disrupted previously accepted norms. Some observers note that this has been true recently in emerging debates about torture, secret arrests and detentions. Despite long-standing moral and legal prohibitions against torture, and long-standing judicial expectations about due process when making arrests in most Western countries, a "new normal" has emerged in which discussions of torture have been resurrected as a necessary if unfortunate part of the war against terror, and by which rules of due process

---

[1] Ken Booth, *Law, Force and Diplomacy at Sea* (Winchester, MA: Allen & Unwin, 1985).

are being diluted in the case of suspected terrorists.[2] That numerous states are practising these changes is cause for concern for many human rights advocates (discussed later in this chapter).

These observations suggest a Gramscian vision of hegemony, which points to the way order is established through a combination of coercion and consent. Hegemony is "working," by the Gramscian view, when the relations of power that maintain any given system are understood to be the natural order of things. From this more critical perspective, international law and organization are means through which those relations of power, and a particular world order, are maintained. This critical view thus does not see international law and organization in the benign or straightforwardly positive way that liberals do, but neither does it see international institutions working simply at the behest of strong states, because the relations of power that sustain any world order are more complex than state interests (and can include, for example, the class interests associated with globalizing capitalism).[3]

International Norms

international norms The expectations held by participants about normal relations among states.

The rules that govern most interactions in IR are rooted in norms. **International norms** are the expectations held by state leaders about normal international relations. For some observers of IR, the decisions of state leaders should have some basis in ethical or moral norms.[4] Iraq's 1990 invasion of Kuwait was not only illegal, but widely viewed as immoral—beyond the acceptable range of behaviour of states (that is, beyond the normal amount of cheating generally permissible). Political leaders in Canada and around the world drew on moral norms to generate support for a collective response to Iraq.

These norms, however, are often disputed. International morality is supposed to differ somewhat from state morality, which is strongly influenced by the particular culture and traditions of a given state. By contrast, international morality is presumed to be a more universal set of moral standards and rules applicable to the interactions of states themselves.

In practice, however, this is seldom the case. There is often no consensus about specific violations of international norms. While there may have been some broad agreement regarding Iraq's invasion of Kuwait, it was not shared by all states (the leaders of Jordan and Yemen, for example, strongly disagreed). There was even less agreement about the U.S.-led invasion of Iraq in 2003 (with which many of the United States' allies did not agree), or NATO's bombing of the former Yugoslavia in 1999 or how to handle the Rwandan genocide in 1994. Sometimes a consensus emerges "after the fact" (particularly evident in the case of the Rwandan genocide), but that consensus is often very difficult to discern before or during an event or crisis.

The attempt to define universal norms nonetheless follows a centuries-long philosophical tradition. Philosophers such as Kant (see Chapter 3, pp. 79) argued that it was natural for autonomous individuals (or states) to cooperate for mutual benefit because they

---

[2] Louise Arbour, "In Our Name and on Our Behalf," *International and Comparative Law Quarterly* 55 (July 2006): 511–526. Rosemary Foot, "Torture: The Struggle over a Peremptory Norm in a Counter-Terrorist Era," *International Relations* 20.2 (2006): 131–151.

[3] Robert W. Cox, "Multilateralism and World Order," *Approaches to World Order*, R. W. Cox and T. Sinclair, eds. (NY: Cambridge UP, 1996).

[4] Rosalind Irwin, ed., *Ethics and Security in Canadian Foreign Policy* (Vancouver: UBC P, 2001).

could see that pursuing their narrow individual interests would end up hurting all. Sovereign states could work together through structures and organizations (like Kant's proposed world federation) that would respect each member's autonomy and not create a world government. In the nineteenth century, such ideas were embodied in practical organizations in which states participated to manage specific issues such as the international postal service and control of traffic on European rivers.

Agreed norms of behaviour, institutionalized through such organizations, become *habitual* over time and gain *legitimacy*. State leaders become used to behaving in a normal way and stop calculating, for each action, whether violating norms would pay off. For instance, the U.S. president does not spend time calculating whether the costs of invading and plundering Canada would outweigh the benefits. The willingness to maintain normal

CRITICAL INTERVENTION
International norms are evolving in such areas as humanitarian intervention versus national sovereignty, which help define the roles of international organizations (IOs). Here, in 2006, protesters at the UN compound in Ivory Coast object to foreign mediators' decision to dissolve parliament as part of a postwar settlement, which the protesters call an infringement of sovereignty.

behaviour has psychological roots in "satisficing" and in aversion to risk (see "Individual Decision-Makers" on pp. 133–137). Legitimacy and habit explain why international norms can be effective even when they are not codified and enforced, or when they are not universally held.

The end of the Cold War put basic expectations up for grabs to an even greater degree. One problem with rapid change is that nobody knows what to expect; whatever prevailing norms exist break down because leaders do not have common expectations. Through a long process of coping with a series of incidents, international leaders build up new understandings of the rules of the game.

Norms today remain unsettled. New expectations appeared to be emerging in areas of human rights, UN peacekeeping and **humanitarian intervention** in the immediate post–Cold War period—though these too are sometimes contested, particularly by those who argue that there are real problems in the assumption that the only response to contemporary conflicts is a militarized response.[5] The terrorist attacks against the U.S. in 2001, Spain in 2004 and the U.K. in 2005 shifted international norms, bringing about greater cooperation among states for a time, but also greater attention to the trade-offs between liberty and security (see Chapter 5, p. 155).

humanitarian intervention
Armed intrusion into a state, without its consent, to prevent or alleviate widespread or severe human rights violations.

---

[5] Nicholas J. Wheeler, *Saving Strangers: Humanitarian Intervention in International Society* (NY: Oxford UP, 2001). Alan J. Kuperman, *The Limits of Humanitarian Intervention* (Washington, DC: Brookings, 2001). Thomas G. Weiss, *Military-Civilian Interactions: Intervening in Humanitarian Crises* (Lanham, MD: Rowman & Littlefield, 1999).

The Information Revolution
Consolidating Norms

The post–Cold War era has created uncertainty about international norms (the shared expectations about how states should behave). New rules are still being written and tested. One unsettled aspect of international norms is the changing view of when outsiders can interfere in states' internal affairs. Will technological change tear down walls and force states to accept international norms in such areas as human rights, nonproliferation and environmental protection?

To explore this question, go to www.pearsoned.ca/goldstein.

international organizations (IOs)
Institutions including intergovernmental organizations (IGOs) such as the UN and nongovernmental organizations (NGOs) such as Médecins Sans Frontières or Amnesty International.

Roles of International Organizations

Especially in times of change, when shared norms and habits may not contribute to solving international dilemmas or achieving mutual cooperation, institutions play a key role. They are concrete, tangible structures with specific functions and missions. These institutions have proliferated rapidly in recent decades, and continue to play an increasing role in international affairs. **International organizations (IOs)** include *intergovernmental organizations (IGOs)* such as the UN, and *nongovernmental organizations (NGOs)* such as Médecins Sans Frontières (Doctors Without Borders) or Amnesty International.

The number of IOs has grown more than fivefold since 1945, with close to 400 independent IGOs and tens of thousands of NGOs (depending somewhat on definitions). New NGOs are created daily around the world. Figure 8.1 illustrates this growth. This weaving together of people across national boundaries through specialized groups reflects world interdependence (see "Interdependence" on pp. 316–318).[6]

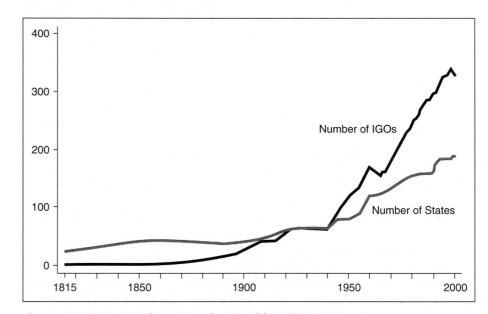

Figure 8.1 States and IGOs in the World, 1815–2000

---

[6] John Boli and George M. Thomas, eds., *Constructing World Culture: International Nongovernmental Organizations since 1875* (Palo Alto, CA: Stanford UP, 1999). David Armstrong, Lorna Lloyd and John Redmond, *From Versailles to Maastricht: International Organization in the Twentieth Century* (NY: St. Martin's, 1996). Craig Murphy, *International Organization and Industrial Change: Global Governance since 1850* (NY: Oxford UP, 1994).

Some IGOs are global in scope, others are regional or just bilateral (having only two states as members). Some are general in their purpose, others have specific functional objectives. Overall, the success of IGOs has been mixed. Regional groups have had more success than global ones, and groups with specific functional or technical purposes have worked better than those with broad goals (see pp. 13–14). IGOs hold together not because of vague ideals, but because they promote the national interests (or enhance the leverage) of their member states.

The European Union is among the most important *regional* IGOs (see Chapter 11), but it is not the only example. Others include the Association of South East Asian Nations (ASEAN), the Southern Cone Common Market (MERCOSUR) and the African Union. The functional roles of IOs are important to their overall effect on international relations, but those roles will be discussed in the section on international integration in Chapter 11. Here, we will rely on the more general theoretical discussion of international institutions begun in Chapter 3.

Global IGOs (aside from the UN) usually have functional purposes involving coordinating the actions of some set of states. The IGO called Intelsat, for example, is a consortium of governments and private businesses that operates communications satellites. Members of the Organization of Petroleum Exporting Countries (OPEC) are major oil producers who meet periodically in Vienna to set production quotas for members in an effort to keep world oil prices high and stable. The North Atlantic Treaty Organization (NATO) (discussed on pp. 247–249) is an IGO created from a military alliance. Note that while the key members of IGOs are states, NGOs, businesses or individuals can have important advisory and consulting roles.

NGOs tend to be more specialized in function than IGOs. For instance, someone wanting to meet political scientists from other countries can join the International Political Science Association. Many NGOs have economic or business-related functions. The International Air Transport Association coordinates the work of airline companies. Other NGOs have global political purposes—Amnesty International for human rights, Planned Parenthood for reproductive rights and family planning or the Women's International League for Peace and Freedom for issues of women in conflict and peace. Still other NGOs have cultural purposes—for example, the International Olympic Committee.

Religious groups are among the largest NGOs—their memberships often span many countries. In today's world and historically, sects of Christianity, Islam, Buddhism, Judaism, Hinduism and other world religions have organized across state borders, often in the face of hostility from one or more national governments. Missionaries have deliberately built and nurtured these transnational links. The Catholic Church historically held a special position in the European international system, especially before the seventeenth century. NGOs with broad purposes and geographical scope often maintain observer status in the UN so that they can participate in meetings about issues of concern. For example, Greenpeace attends UN meetings about global environment issues.

A web of international organizations and agreements of various sizes and types now connects people in all countries. The rapid growth of this network, and the increasingly intense communications and interactions that occur within it, are indicative of rising international interdependence. These organizations or agreements in turn provide the institutional mesh to hold together some kind of world order even when leaders and contexts come and go, and even when norms are undermined by sudden changes in power relations. Some agreements involve military coalitions between two or more states, called alliances.

ALLIANCES

An *alliance* is a coalition of states that coordinate their actions to accomplish some end. Some alliances are *formalized* in written treaties, concern a *common threat* and related issues of international security, *endure* across a range of issues and a period of time and are institutionalized in an IGO. If actors' purposes in banding together are short-term, less formal or issue-specific (such as the current efforts to stop international terrorism), the association is usually called a *coalition* rather than an alliance. Informal but enduring strategic *alignments* in a region are discussed shortly. These terms are somewhat ambiguous. Two countries may have a formal alliance and yet be bitter enemies, such as the Soviet Union and China in the 1960s or NATO members Greece and Turkey today. Or, two countries may create the practical equivalent of an alliance without a formal treaty.

Purpose of Alliances

Alliances generally have the purpose of augmenting their members' power relative to other states. By pooling their power capabilities, two or more states can exert greater leverage in bargaining with other states. For smaller states, alliances can be their most important power element, and for great powers the structure of alliances shapes the configuration of power in the system. Of all the elements of power, none can change as quickly and decisively as alliances.

Most alliances form in response to a perceived threat. When a state's power grows and threatens to surpass that of its rivals, the latter often form an alliance to limit that power. Thucydides attributed the outbreak of the Peloponnesian Wars more than 2000 years ago to the growing power of Athens and the fear it caused in Sparta. Sparta turned to its neighbours in the Peloponnesian League, and that alliance managed to defeat Athens.

Alliances are an important component of the balance of power for realists. Except in the rare circumstance of hegemony, every state is weaker than some combination of other states. If states overstep norms of international conduct, they may face a powerful alliance of opposing states. This happened to Iraq after its invasion of Kuwait in 1990, as it had to Hitler's Germany in the 1940s and to Napoleon's France in the 1800s.

Realists emphasize the fluidity of alliances. Because of the autonomy of states, alliances can be made or broken fairly easily. Alliances are not marriages of love, they are marriages of convenience. Alliances, for realists, are based on national interests, and can shift as national interests change. This fluidity helps the balance-of-power process to operate effectively.

As critics of realism point out, it is not simple or costless to break an alliance: one's reputation may suffer and future alliances may be harder to establish. There is an important norm that written treaties should be honoured—in Latin, *pacta sunt servanda*—so states often adhere to alliance terms even when it is not in their short-term interest to do so. Nonetheless, because of the nature of international anarchy, there is no mechanism to enforce contracts in IR, so the possibility of turning against a friend always exists. Realists would agree with British statesman Lord Palmerston, who told Parliament in 1848 that "We have no eternal allies and we have no perpetual enemies. Our interests are perpetual and eternal and those interests it is our duty to follow."[7]

Examples of fluid alliances are many. Anticommunist U.S. president Richard Nixon cooperated with communist Mao Zedong in 1972. Joseph Stalin signed a nonaggression pact with a fascist, Adolf Hitler, and then cooperated with the capitalist West against him.

---

[7] Remarks in the British House of Commons, March 1, 1848.

The United States backed Islamic militants in Afghanistan against the Soviet Union in the 1980s, then attacked them in 2001. Every time history brings another such reversal in international alignments, many people are surprised or even shocked. Realists are not so surprised.

The fluidity of alliances deepens the security dilemma in a world of multiple actors. Recall that the dilemma occurs when one state's efforts to ensure its own security (building up military capabilities) reduces the security of another state. With only two states, each could match capabilities so that both have adequate defence but are unable to attack successfully. But if a third state is free to ally with either side, then each state must build adequate defences against the potential alliance of its enemy with the third state. The threat is greater and the security dilemma is harder to escape.

Alliance cohesion is the ease with which members hold together an alliance.[8] Cohesion tends to be high when national interests converge and when cooperation within the alliance becomes institutionalized and habitual. When states with divergent interests form an alliance against a common enemy, the alliance may come apart if the threat subsides (as with the U.S.-Soviet alliance in World War II, for instance). Even when alliance cohesion is high, as in NATO during the Cold War, conflicts may arise over who bears the costs of the alliance (**burden sharing**).[9]

Great powers often form alliances with smaller states, sometimes called client states.[10] In the Cold War, each superpower extended a security umbrella over its allies. The issue of credibility in such an alliance is whether (and under what circumstances) the great power will assist its clients in a war. Extended deterrence refers to a strong state's use of threats to deter attacks on weaker clients—such as the U.S. threat to attack the Soviet Union if it invaded Western Europe.

Great powers face a real danger of being dragged into wars with one another over relatively unimportant regional issues if their respective clients go to war. If great powers do not come to their clients' protection, they may lose credibility with other clients. If they do, they may end up fighting a costly war.[11] The Soviet Union worried that its commitments to China in the 1950s, Cuba in the 1960s and Syria and Egypt in the 1970s (among others) could result in a disastrous war with the United States.

NATO

By far the most powerful formal military alliance today (although with a somewhat uncertain future in the post–Cold War era) is the **North Atlantic Treaty Organization (NATO)**, which encompasses Western Europe and North America. Using GDP as a measure of power, the 26 NATO members possess nearly half the world total (roughly twice the power of the United States alone). Members are the United States, Canada, Britain, France, Germany, Italy, Belgium, the Netherlands, Luxembourg, Denmark,

alliance cohesion The ease with which members hold together an alliance; it tends to be high when national interests converge and when cooperation among allies becomes institutionalized.

burden sharing The distribution of the costs of an alliance among members; the term also refers to the conflicts that may arise over such distribution.

North Atlantic Treaty Organization (NATO) A U.S.-led military alliance, formed in 1949 with mainly West European members, to oppose and deter Soviet power in Europe. It has recently expanded into the former Soviet bloc. See also *Warsaw Pact*.

---

[8] Charles W. Kegley and Gregory A. Raymond, *When Trust Breaks Down: Alliance Norms and World Politics* (Columbia: U South Carolina P, 1990).

[9] John R. Oneal, "The Theory of Collective Action and Burden Sharing in NATO," *International Organization* 44.3 (1990): 379–402. Glenn Palmer, "Corralling the Free Rider: Deterrence and the Western Alliance," *International Studies Quarterly* 34.2 (1990): 147–64.

[10] Steven R. David, *Choosing Sides: Alignment and Realignment in the Third World* (Baltimore: Johns Hopkins UP, 1991).

[11] Glenn H. Snyder, *Alliance Politics* (Ithaca, NY: Cornell UP, 1997). Randolph M. Siverson and Michael R. Tennefoss, "Power, Alliance, and the Escalation of International Conflict, 1815–1965," *American Political Science Review* 78.4 (1984): 1057–69.

Norway, Iceland, Spain, Portugal, Greece, Turkey, Poland, the Czech Republic, Hungary, Bulgaria, Estonia, Latvia, Lithuania, Romania, Slovakia and Slovenia. At NATO headquarters in Brussels, Belgium, military staffs from member countries coordinate plans and periodically direct exercises in the field. In NATO, each state contributes its own military units—with its own national culture, language and equipment specifications.

Warsaw Pact A Soviet-led Eastern European military alliance founded in 1955 and disbanded in 1991. It opposed the NATO alliance. See also *North Atlantic Treaty Organization (NATO).*

NATO was founded in 1949 to oppose and deter Soviet power in Europe. Its counterpart in Eastern Europe during the Cold War, the Soviet-led **Warsaw Pact,** was founded in 1955 and disbanded in 1991. During the Cold War, the United States maintained more than 300 000 troops in Europe, with advanced planes, tanks and other equipment. After the Cold War ended, these forces were cut to about 100 000. NATO stayed together because its members believed it provided useful stability even though its mission was unclear.[12] Article V, considered the heart of NATO, asks members to come to the defence of a fellow member under attack. It was envisioned as a U.S. commitment to help defend Western Europe against the Soviet Union, but was instead invoked for the first time when Europe came to the defence of the United States after the terrorist attacks in 2001.

The first actual use of force by NATO was in Bosnia in 1994, in support of a UN mission. A "dual key" arrangement gave the UN control of NATO's actions in Bosnia, and the UN feared retaliation against its lightly armed peacekeepers if NATO attacked Serbian forces to protect Bosnian civilians. As a result, NATO made threats, underlined by symbolic air strikes, then backed down after UN qualms. This waffling undermined NATO credibility. More extensive NATO air strikes in 1995 alarmed Russian leaders, who were already concerned by NATO's expansion plans. These problems, along with tensions between the American and European NATO members over Bosnian policy, dogged the first major NATO mission of the post–Cold War era. Later NATO actions in the Balkans (the air war for Kosovo in 1999 and peacekeeping in Macedonia in 2001) went more smoothly in terms of alliance cohesion. Currently, NATO forces from a number of member countries, including Canada, are fighting in Afghanistan.

The European Union formed its own rapid deployment force outside NATO. The decision grew in part from European military weaknesses demonstrated in the 1999 Kosovo war, in which the United States contributed by far the most power. Although Eurocorps generally works *with* NATO in future operations, it also gives Europe a level of independence from the United States. In 2003, the European Union sent military forces as peacekeepers to Democratic Congo—the first multinational European military operation to occur outside NATO. In 2004, NATO and U.S. forces withdrew from Bosnia after nine years, turning over peacekeeping duties to the European Union (as they had in Macedonia). NATO forces remain next door in Kosovo.

The biggest issue for NATO is eastward expansion beyond the East-West Cold War dividing line. In 1999, former Soviet-bloc countries Poland, the Czech Republic and Hungary joined the alliance. Bulgaria, Estonia, Latvia, Lithuania, Romania, Slovakia and Slovenia joined in 2004. This was the fifth and largest round of enlargement in NATO's history. Making new members' militaries compatible with NATO is a major undertaking, requiring increased military spending by existing and new NATO members. Arms industries look forward to new sales as Eastern European countries restructure their military forces to meet NATO requirements.

---

12 David S. Yost, *NATO Transformed: The Alliance's New Roles in International Security* (Washington, DC: U.S. Institute of Peace Press, 1999). George W. Grayson, *Strange Bedfellows: NATO Marches East* (Lanham, MD: UP America, 1999). James M. Goldgeier, *Not Whether But When: The Decision to Enlarge NATO* (Washington, DC: Brookings, 1999).

NATO expansion was justified by liberals as a way to solidify new democracies while keeping Europe peaceful, and by conservatives as protection against possible future Russian aggression. NATO forces have participated in the war in Afghanistan, but Russian leaders oppose NATO's expansion into Eastern Europe, viewing it as aggressive and anti-Russian. They see NATO expansion as reasserting dividing lines closer to Russia's borders on the map of Europe. These fears strengthen nationalist and anti-Western political forces in Russia. To mitigate the problems, NATO created a category of symbolic membership—the Partnership for Peace—which was joined by almost all Eastern European and former Soviet states, including Russia. However, the 1999 NATO bombing of Serbia heightened Russian fears regarding eastward expansion.

NORAD

The **North American Aerospace Defense Command (NORAD)** was established in 1958 through an agreement (not a formal treaty) between Canada and the United States. Both countries agreed to work together to monitor and defend North American airspace. The commander in chief of NORAD is appointed by and responsible to the prime minister of Canada and the president of the United States. Normally, the commander of NORAD is appointed from the U.S. Air Force and the deputy commander from the Canadian Forces (these roles are reversed in Canada, where the deputy commander of the Canadian NORAD region is appointed from the U.S. while the commander of the Canadian region is Canadian). The U.S. NORAD headquarters is located in Colorado, with its command and control centre buried deep in Cheyenne Mountain. Canada's NORAD headquarters is located in Winnipeg, with its command and control centre located in North Bay. The NORAD agreement has been renewed nine times since 1958, and its most recent renewal, for the first time ever, did not indicate an expiry date.[13] Some analysts have noted that with its most recent renewal in May 2006, revisions to the agreement entrenched Canada's participation in ballistic missile defence. Thus, the debate about whether Canada should or should not join in national missile defence, according to this argument, has been rendered moot (and outside of wider public discussion) as it is now a requisite element of the NORAD agreement.[14]

North American Aerospace Defense Command (NORAD) A binational military organization established in 1958 by Canada and the U.S. to monitor and defend North American airspace.

The Former Soviet Republics

The 12 members of the *Commonwealth of Independent States (CIS)* include the former Soviet republics with the exception of the Baltic states (Estonia, Latvia and Lithuania). Russia is the leading member and Ukraine the second largest. Officially, CIS headquarters is in the city of Minsk, Belarus, but in practice there is no strong centre and meeting locations rotate. Russia controls the former Soviet Union's nuclear weapons, and the other former Soviet republics agreed to become nonnuclear states. Although some

---

[13] Joseph T. Jockel and Joel J. Sokolsky, "Renewing NORAD—Now if not Forever," *Policy Options* (July–August 2006): 53–58.

[14] Ann Denholm Crosby, "The New Conservative Government and Missile Defence: Is Canadian Participation Back on the Agenda, or Was It Ever Off?" in Andrew F. Cooper and Dane Rowlands (eds.), *Canada Among Nations 2006: Minorities and Priorities*, (Kingston and Montreal: Queen's UP 2006), 164–183.

military coordination takes place through the CIS, initial plans for a joint military force instead of 12 independent armies did not succeed. Among the largest CIS members, Kazakhstan and Belarus are the most closely aligned with Russia, while Ukraine is the most independent. For the years leading up to 1997, Russia and Ukraine debated ownership of the Black Sea fleet, whose port was in Ukraine but whose history was distinctly Russian. (The fleet will be split and Russia's basing rights maintained for 20 years.)

It is to the CIS's credit that in the post-Soviet chaos no major war erupted between major CIS member states. Substantial conflict did occur between some of the smaller members (notably Armenia and Azerbaijan); there was civil violence in several other CIS states (Russia, Georgia, Moldova and Tajikistan); CIS forces were drawn into a few small clashes. The large members, however, were not drawn into major wars. The outcome could have been much worse.

The most important relationship within the CIS is between its two largest members, Russia and Ukraine. They distrust each other somewhat but have managed to cooperate fairly effectively since gaining independence. Disputes over issues such as ownership of the Black Sea fleet have been negotiated step by step, often painfully but productively.

Regional Alignments

Beyond the three alliances just discussed and the regional IGOs mentioned earlier, most international alignments and coalitions are not formalized in alliances. Among the great powers, a close working relationship (through the UN) developed among the United States, Western European powers, Japan and Russia after the Cold War. By the mid-1990s, new strains had appeared in great-power relations, including economic conflicts among the former Western allies, differences over policy in Bosnia and Kosovo and Western alarm at Russia's war in the secession-minded Chechnya province. Of the great powers, China continues to be the most independent, but prudently avoids conflict unless its immediate security interests are at stake.

nonaligned movement
Movement of states, largely from the global South, led by India and the former Yugoslavia, that attempted to stand apart from the U.S.-Soviet rivalry during the Cold War.

Many states of the global South (and some states from other regions of the world) joined a **nonaligned movement** during the Cold War, standing apart from the U.S.-Soviet rivalry. This movement, led by India and the former Yugoslavia, was undermined by the membership of states such as Cuba that were clearly clients of one superpower. In 1992, the nonaligned movement agreed to stay in business, though its future is unclear.

One vestige of past centuries is the Commonwealth—a group of countries with historical ties to Britain (including Canada and Australia) working together for mutual economic and cultural benefit. France also maintains ties (including regular summit meetings) with its former colonies in Africa. France had troops stationed in six African countries in the late 1990s, but began to reduce its African ties and in 1997 did not intervene when friendly governments were overthrown.

At the turn of the century, the 53-member Organization of African Unity, an IGO with few powers, reformed as the **African Union (AU)**, a stronger organization with a continent-wide parliament, central bank and court. The African Union's first real test came with allegations of genocide in the Darfur region of Sudan in 2004. In response, the AU deployed 3000 troops, but their effectiveness remained limited as of early 2007.

In Asia, China has long been loosely aligned with Pakistan in opposition to India. The United States has 35 000 troops stationed in South Korea under terms of a formal bilateral alliance dating from the Korean War, and has some 50 000 troops stationed in Japan via the U.S.-Japanese Security Treaty of 1951 (which also pledges the U.S. to defend Japan if attacked). In late 2005, the first East Asia Summit included 16 states from

India to Russia and New Zealand. With China and Japan still squabbling about World War II, the unity of this new grouping appeared doubtful.

In the Middle East, the Arab-Israeli conflict created a general anti-Israel alignment of Arab countries for decades, but that alignment broke down as Egypt, in 1978, and the Palestine Liberation Organization (PLO) and Jordan, in 1993–1994, made peace with Israel. As the Israeli-Palestinian peace process moves forward and backward year by year, Arab countries continue to express varying degrees of solidarity with one another and varying degrees of opposition to Israel. The latest trough in Israeli-Arab relations came in 2006 when Israel fought a month-long war with Hezbollah guerrillas in southern Lebanon and, simultaneously, fought Hamas militants in Palestinian-administered areas. Meanwhile, Israel and Turkey formed a close military relationship that amplifies Israeli power and provides a link to the oil-rich Caspian Sea region.

It is unclear what new international alignments may emerge in the years to come. The fluidity of alliances makes them a wild card for scholars to understand and for policy-makers to anticipate. The web of connections that bind states together today includes far more than military alliances; it also includes international institutions, the most important of which is the United Nations.

THE UNITED NATIONS

The UN and other international organizations have both strengths and weaknesses in the anarchic international system. State sovereignty creates a real need for such organizations on a practical level, because no central world government performs the function of coordinating the actions of states for mutual benefit. However, state sovereignty also severely limits the power of the UN and other IOs, because governments reserve power for themselves and are stingy in delegating it to the UN or anyone else. The UN has had a mixed record with these strengths and weaknesses—in some ways providing remarkable global-level management and in other ways appearing helpless against the sovereignty of even modest-sized states (not to mention great powers).

The UN System

At just over 60 years old, the UN is a relatively new institution. And although it has played a more prominent role in international security affairs in the years since the end of the Cold War, the UN's main purposes are the same now as when it was founded after World War II.[15]

Purposes of the UN   The UN is the closest thing to a world government that has ever existed, but it is not a world government. Its members are sovereign states that have not empowered the UN to enforce its will within state territories without the consent of state governments. Thus, although the UN strengthens world order, its design acknowledges the realities of international anarchy and the unwillingness of states to surrender sovereignty. Within these limits, the basic purpose of the UN is to provide a global institutional structure through which states can sometimes settle conflicts without reliance on the use of force.

---

[15] Evan Luard and Derek Heater, *The United Nations: How It Works and What It Does*, 2nd ed. (NY: St. Martin's, 1994). Chadwick F. Alger, Gene M. Lyons and John E. Trent, eds., *The United Nations System: The Policies of Member States* (NY: United Nations UP, 1995).

UN Charter The founding document of the United Nations; it is based on the principles that states are equal, have sovereignty over their own affairs, enjoy independence and territorial integrity and must fulfill international obligations. The Charter also lays out the structure and methods of the UN.

The **UN Charter** is based on the principles that states are *equal* under international law; that they have full *sovereignty* over their own affairs; that they should have full *independence* and *territorial integrity*; and that they should carry out their international *obligations*—such as respecting diplomatic privileges, refraining from committing aggression and observing the terms of treaties they sign. The Charter also lays out the structure of the UN and the methods by which it operates.

The UN does not exist because it has power to force its will on the world's states; it exists because states have created it to serve their needs. A state's membership in the UN is essentially a form of indirect leverage. States gain leverage by using the UN to seek more beneficial outcomes in conflicts (especially on general multilateral issues where a global forum brings all parties together). The cost of this leverage is modest: UN dues and the expenses of diplomatic representatives, in addition to the agreement to behave in accordance with the Charter (most of the time).

States get several benefits from the UN. Foremost is the international stability (especially in security affairs) that the UN tries to safeguard; this allows states to realize gains from trade and other forms of exchange (see Chapter 9). The UN is a *symbol* of international order and even of global identity. It is also a *forum* where states promote their views and bring disputes, and it is a *mechanism* for *conflict resolution* in international security affairs. The UN also promotes and coordinates development assistance (see Chapter 13) and other programs of *economic* and *social development* in countries of the global South. These programs reflect the belief that economic and social problems—above all, poverty—are an important source of international conflict and war. Finally, the UN is a coordinating system for *information* and planning by hundreds of internal and external agencies and programs, and for the publication of international data.

Despite its heavy tasks, the UN is a small and fragile institution. Every year, the world spends about $1.2 trillion on the military, and less than $2 billion on the UN regular budget. The combined budget of UN operations, peacekeeping, programs and agencies is under $20 billion, or less than 2 percent of world military spending.

Sometimes the UN succeeds and sometimes it fails. The UN deals with perhaps *the* most difficult issues in the world. If groups of states could easily solve problems such as ethnic conflicts, human rights, refugees and world hunger among themselves, they most likely would have done so. Instead, states turn many of these difficult problems over to the UN and hope they will be resolved.

UN General Assembly Comprising representatives of all states, it allocates UN funds, passes nonbinding resolutions and coordinates development programs and various autonomous agencies through the Economic and Social Council (ECOSOC).

UN Security Council A body of five great powers (which can veto resolutions) and 10 rotating member states; it makes decisions about international peace and security, including the dispatch of UN peacekeeping forces.

UN Secretariat The UN's executive branch, led by the secretary-general.

Structure of the UN The UN's structure, shown in Figure 8.2, centres around the **UN General Assembly,** where representatives of all states gather in a huge room, listen to speeches and pass resolutions. The General Assembly coordinates a variety of development programs and other autonomous agencies through the *Economic and Social Council (ECOSOC)*. Parallel to the General Assembly is the **UN Security Council,** in which five permanent and 10 rotating member states make decisions about international peace and security. The Security Council is responsible for dispatching peacekeeping forces to trouble spots. The administration of the UN takes place through the **UN Secretariat** (executive branch), led by the secretary-general of the UN. The *World Court* (International Court of Justice), which is discussed later in the chapter, is a judicial arm of the UN. (A *Trusteeship Council* oversaw the transition of a handful of former colonial territories to full independence. With the last trust territory's independence in 1994, the Council suspended operations.)

National delegations to the UN, headed by ambassadors from each member state, work and meet together at UN headquarters in New York City. They have diplomatic status in the United States, which as host country also assumes certain other obligations

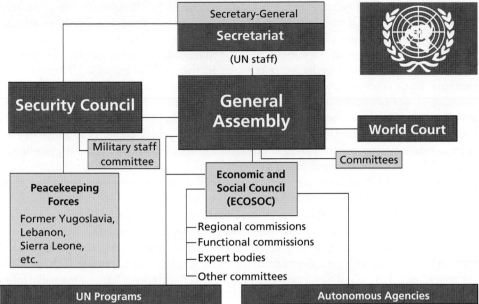

Secretary-General

Secretariat

(UN staff)

Security Council

General Assembly

World Court

Military staff committee

Committees

Peacekeeping Forces

Former Yugoslavia, Lebanon, Sierra Leone, etc.

Economic and Social Council (ECOSOC)

Regional commissions
Functional commissions
Expert bodies
Other committees

UN Programs	
UNEP	UN Environment Programme
UNICEF	UN Children's Fund
UNDRO	Office of the UN Disaster Relief Coordinator
UNHCR	Office of the UN High Commissioner for Refugees
UNRWA*	UN Relief Works Agency [for Palestinian Refugees]
UNDP	UN Development Programme
UNITAR*	UN Institute for Training and Research
UNIFEM	UN Development Fund for Women
INSTRAW	UN International Research and Training Institute [for women]
UNCTAD	UN Conference on Trade and Development
WFP	World Food Programme
WFC	World Food Council
UNCHS	Human Settlements (Habitat)
UNFPA	UN Population Fund
UNU	UN University
UNDCP	Drug Control Programme
ITC	International Trade Center

*Does not report to ECOSOC.

Autonomous Agencies	
IAEA*	International Atomic Energy Agency (Vienna)
WHO	World Health Organization (Geneva)
FAO	Food and Agriculture Organization (Rome)
IFAD	International Fund for Agricultural Development (Rome)
ILO	International Labour Organization (Geneva)
UNESCO	UN Educational, Scientific, and Cultural Organization (Paris)
UNIDO	UN Industrial Development Organization (Vienna)
ITU	International Telecommunications Union (Geneva)
IPU	International Postal Union (Berne)
ICAO	International Civil Aviation Organization (Montreal)
IMO	International Maritime Organization (London)
WIPO	World Intellectual Property Organization (Geneva)
WMO	World Meteorological Association (Geneva)
MIGA	Multilateral Investment Guarantee Agency
IMF	International Monetary Fund (Washington)
IBRD	International Bank for Reconstruction and Development [World Bank] (Washington)
IDA	International Development Association (Washington)
IFC	International Finance Corporation (Washington)
WTO*	World Trade Organization (Geneva)

*Does not report to ECOSOC.

Figure 8.2 The United Nations

to facilitate the UN's functioning. For example, the U.S. government has permitted people such as Fidel Castro—normally barred from entry to the United States—to visit New York long enough to address the UN.

A major strength of the UN structure is the *universality of its membership*. There were 192 members in 2007. Virtually every territory in the world is either a UN member or formally a province or colony of a UN member. Switzerland, which traditionally maintains strict neutrality in the international system, joined only in 2002. Timor-Leste joined in the same year, and the UN's newest member, Montenegro, joined in 2006. Formal agreement on the Charter, even if sometimes breached, commits all states to a set of basic rules governing their relations. The old League of Nations, by contrast, was flawed by the absence of several important actors.

One way the UN induced all the great powers to join was to reassure them that their participation in the UN would not harm their national interests. Recognizing the role of power in world order, the UN Charter gave each of the permanent members, the five great powers, a veto over substantive decisions of the Security Council.

The UN Charter establishes a mechanism for *collective security*—the banding together of the world's states to stop an aggressor. Chapter 7 of the Charter explicitly authorizes the Security Council to use military force against aggression if the nonviolent means called for in Chapter 6 have failed. However, because of the great-power veto, the UN cannot effectively stop aggression by (or supported by) a great power. In 2006, Iran's president asked the General Assembly, "If the governments of the United States or the United Kingdom commit atrocities or violate international law, which of the organizations in the United Nations can take them to account?" (Of course, the answer is none of them.)

Thus Chapter 7 was used only once during the Cold War—in the Korean War when the Soviet delegation unwisely boycotted proceedings (and when China's seat was held by the nationalists on Taiwan). It was under Chapter 7 of the Charter that the UN authorized the use of force to reverse Iraqi aggression against Kuwait in 1990 and to respond to the humanitarian disaster in Somalia in the early 1990s.

History of the UN The UN was founded in 1945 in San Francisco when representatives from 50 states, including Canada, attended the United Nations Conference on International Organization.[16] It was the successor to the League of Nations, which had failed to effectively counter aggression in

ASSEMBLY OF EQUALS
The universal membership of the United Nations is one of its strengths. All member states have a voice and a vote in the General Assembly, where state leaders rotate each autumn. Here, U.S. president George W. Bush takes his turn, 2004.

---

[16] Denis Stairs, "Founding the United Nations: Canada at San Francisco, 1945," *Policy Options* (September 2005): 15–20.

the 1930s—Japan simply quit when the League condemned Japanese aggression against China. Like the League, the UN was founded to increase international order and the rule of law to prevent another world war.

There has long been a certain tension between the UN and the United States. The United States had not joined the League, and it was partly to assure U.S. interest that the UN headquarters was located in New York. The UN in some ways constrains the United States by creating a coalition that can rival U.S. power—that of all the states. A certain isolationist streak in U.S. foreign policy runs counter to the UN concept. At the same time, however, the UN can *amplify* U.S. power because the United States leads the global UN coalition. The U.S. has regularly refused to pay its dues to the UN, often in reaction to criticism, particularly from countries in the global South. At one point, the U.S. stood in arrears of more than $1 billion; at the end of 2003, its arrears totalled $762 million. When it does pay its dues, however, the U.S. is the largest single contributor state to the United Nations. The United States is not rich or strong enough to keep order in the world by itself. And, as a great trading nation, the United States benefits from the stability and order that the UN helps to create.

Canada has long supported the United Nations. It was enthusiastically involved in its founding and has been an active participant ever since. For years, Canadian foreign policy has viewed activity in multilateral organizations like the UN as a central element of achieving foreign policy goals, not least because multilateral efforts offset any lack of influence resulting from its middle power status in international relations. Canadian foreign policy has also been informed by a liberal internationalist impulse and a real faith that international organizations are the most effective means of managing global-level politics. Canada's long commitment to the United Nations has earned it high regard within UN and other IO circles. At the UN, for example, Canada's status is reflected in the number of times it has served as one of the 10 rotating members on the Security Council—with six terms, it is one of the highest "repeater" countries among the nonpermanent members.[17]

In the 1950s and 1960s, the UN's membership more than doubled as colonies in Asia and Africa won independence. This expansion changed the character of the General

MAKING THE CASE
Collective security rests with the UN Security Council, which has authorized such military interventions as the Gulf War and the 2001 campaign in Afghanistan. Military actions not approved by the Council—such as the 1999 bombing of Serbia and the 2003 U.S.-British invasion of Iraq—tend to be controversial. Here, U.S. secretary of state Colin Powell tries, unsuccessfully, to convince the Security Council to authorize military action against Iraq to eliminate Iraq's weapons of mass destruction, February 2003. Powell holds a vial representing enough anthrax spores (a substance Iraq had produced) to kill thousands of people.

---

[17] Michael Pearson, "Humanizing the UN Security Council," *Canada among Nations 2001: The Axworthy Legacy*, ed. Fen Osler Hampson, Norman Hillmer and Maureen Appel Molot (Toronto: Oxford UP, 2001).

Assembly, where each state has one vote regardless of size. The new members had different concerns from those of the Western industrialized countries and in many cases resented having been colonized by Westerners. The General Assembly is one of the few international bodies in which countries from the global South hold a majority of seats and have the largest voice. Many new members (and a few of the original members) believed that the United States enjoyed too much power in the UN, and noticed that the UN is usually effective in international security affairs only when the United States leads the effort (which happens primarily when U.S. interests are at stake).

The growth in membership thus affected voting patterns. During the UN's first two decades, the Assembly regularly sided with the United States, and the Soviet Union was the main power using its veto in the Security Council to counterbalance that tendency. As newly independent states began to dominate, the United States found itself in the minority on many issues, and by the 1970s and 1980s it had become the main user of the veto.[18]

Until 1971, China's seat on the Security Council (and in the General Assembly) was occupied by the nationalist government on the island of Taiwan, which had lost power in mainland China in 1949. The exclusion of communist China was an exception to the UN principle of universal membership, and in 1971 the Chinese seat was taken from the nationalists and given to the communist government. Today, the government of Taiwan—which functions autonomously in many international matters despite its formal status as a Chinese province—is not a member of the UN.

Throughout the Cold War, the UN had few successes in international security because the U.S.-Soviet conflict prevented consensus. The UN appeared somewhat irrelevant in a world order structured by two opposing alliance blocs. There were a few notable exceptions, such as agreements to station peacekeeping forces in the Middle East, but generally the UN did not play a central role in solving international conflicts during this time. The General Assembly concentrated on the economic and social problems of poor countries, which became the main work of the UN.

After the Cold War, the bipolar world order gave way to one in which multilateral action was more important. The great powers could finally agree on measures regarding international security. Also, states of the global South could not hope to play the super-powers against each other, so they cautiously avoided alienating the United States. In this context, the UN moved to centre stage in international security affairs.[19]

The UN had several major successes in bringing to an end violent regional conflicts (in Central America and in the Iran-Iraq War) in the late 1980s. Ceasefires were negotiated under UN auspices, and peacekeeping forces were dispatched to monitor the situation. In Namibia (Africa), a UN force oversaw independence from South Africa and the nation's first free elections. By the 1990s, the UN had emerged as the world's most important tool for settling international conflicts. Between 1987 and 1993, Security Council resolutions increased from 15 to 78, peacekeeping missions from five to 17, peacekeepers from 12 000 to 78 000 and countries sending troops from 26 to 76.

---

[18] Robert W. Gregg, *About Face: The United States and the United Nations* (Boulder, CO: Rienner, 1993). Jack E. Vincent, *Support Patterns at the United Nations* (Lanham, MD: UP America, 1991).

[19] Thomas G. Weiss, ed., *The United Nations and Civil Wars* (Boulder, CO: Rienner, 1995). G. R. Berridge, ed., *Return to the U.N.: U.N. Diplomacy in Regional Conflicts* (NY: St. Martin's, 1991). Peter R. Baehr and Leon Gordenker, *The United Nations at the End of the 1990s*, 3rd ed. (NY: St. Martin's, 1999). Paul Taylor and A. J. R. Groom, eds., *Global Issues in the United Nations Framework* (NY: St. Martin's, 1989).

THE UN TARGETED
The UN headquarters in Iraq was targeted by suicide bombers in August 2003, killing and injuring many people. The UN formally withdrew from Iraq after the attack.

The new missions ran into serious problems, however. Inadequate funding and management problems undermined peacekeeping efforts in Angola, Somalia and Cambodia. In the former Yugoslavia in 1993–1995, the UN undertook a large peacekeeping mission before a ceasefire was in place—"peacekeeping where there is no peace to keep." In response to these problems (and to the unpaid U.S. dues), the UN scaled back peacekeeping operations in 1995–1997 (from 78 000 to 19 000 troops) and carried out reductions and reforms in the UN Secretariat and UN programs.

For years the United States failed to pay its bills, even though the UN shrank budgets and jobs as demanded by the U.S. The U.S. Congress first refused to allocate funds, then attached abortion-related riders that triggered presidential vetoes. The United States also fell behind in payments to other international organizations, including the World Bank and the Food and Agriculture Organization. This U.S. free-riding shows that support of intergovernmental organizations presents a difficult collective goods problem (see p. 82).

However, a vigorous 1999 lobbying campaign by American UN supporters noted that "Great nations pay their bills." Close U.S. allies became outspoken in criticizing U.S. failure to honour its international commitments. Finally, a compromise was hammered out and the United States agreed to pay up, but not the entire outstanding amounts. The U.S. continues to pay its dues late (usually by about a year). In December 2005, then-U.S. ambassador to the UN John Bolton convinced other member states to impose a spending cap on the UN unless reforms were implemented within six months. By June 2006, the UN very nearly ceased operations until a compromise was reached. As the largest contributor to the UN, the U.S. wants more oversight in the use of its dues, but critics say that U.S. tactics make it impossible to actually implement the UN reforms it demands.

The 2001 terrorist attacks increased U.S. participation in the UN, where a decisive coalition of member states supported U.S. positions on terrorism. In 2003, however, the Security Council refused to support the U.S. plan to invade Iraq in search of weapons of mass destruction. The U.S. ignored UN efforts to prevent the invasion and attacked Iraq with what it called a "coalition of the willing." Canada, among other allies, did not join the U.S.-led coalition, in part because of its long-standing commitment to the United Nations, and in part because it opposed an invasion that appeared to be aimed primarily at regime change.

For some observers, the fact that the U.S. ignored the Security Council on such an important matter signalled the death knell for the UN and underlined its irrelevance. Many people in the United States, political leaders and average citizens alike, were angered at the UN's lack of support. The U.S. action seemed to lend some credence to the realist account of international organizations: useful when they support the foreign policy agendas of powerful states but disregarded when they do not.

Liberal commentators argued instead that the UN would have been proven irrelevant had it simply supported the U.S. position. It is true that the UN does not have the resources or enforcement capabilities to prevent an invasion by a powerful state such as the United States. However, according to liberals, the UN's divergence from the U.S. on Iraq signalled that neither does it act simply at the behest of powerful states. Instead, the UN charts an independent course based on a global calculation of international norms, rather than a state-based calculation of national interest.[20] The UN was also called upon immediately after the formal war had ended to help in the rebuilding of Iraq, and its Baghdad headquarters was targeted in a bomb attack in August 2003. The UN sustained significant casualties, which included a number of Canadian UN workers as well as the loss of the UN's chief of mission, Sergio Vieira de Mello. The UN formally withdrew from Iraq after the attack.

To further aggravate U.S.-UN tensions, documents recovered during the Iraq War showed that high-ranking UN, French, Chinese and Russian officials (and American oil companies) illegally profited from the UN's $64 billion oil-for-food program for Iraq, which was supposed to ease the civilian suffering caused by economic sanctions in the 1990s. A Swiss company under investigation for suspected fraud in the Iraq program turned out to be paying UN Secretary-General Kofi Annan's son thousands of dollars a month, creating what Annan admitted was a "perception problem." In 2005, an independent investigation cleared Annan of personal wrongdoing, but found the program corrupt and heavily criticized the UN for mismanagement and poor oversight.[21]

Currently, the UN follows a principle of "three pillars"—security, economic development and human rights—which are considered mutually necessary for any of them to succeed. At the end of 2006, the outgoing and incoming secretary-generals both referred to this principle. Particularly in a postwar conflict situation, security, economic and human rights situations reinforce one another.

The Security Council

The Security Council is responsible for maintaining international peace and security, and for restoring peace when it breaks down. Its decisions are *binding* on all UN member states. The Security Council has tremendous power to *define* the existence and

---

[20] W. Andy Knight, "Don't Write off the UN Just Yet," *Japan Times* 24 March 2003.

[21] James Traub, *The Best Intentions: Kofi Annan and the UN in the Era of American World Power* (Farrar, Straus & Giroux, 2006).

nature of a security threat, to *structure* the response to such a threat and to *enforce* its decisions through mandatory directives to UN members (such as by halting trade with an aggressor).

In six decades, the Council has passed more than 1700 resolutions, with new ones added by the week. In periods of crisis, they may be added by the day. These resolutions represent the great powers' blueprints for resolving the world's various security disputes, especially in regional conflicts. (Because of the veto system, the Council avoids conflicts among great powers themselves, such as on arms control.) The resolutions reflect what the great powers can all agree upon. This means that resolutions are sometimes criticized for being rather vague and imprecise. Resolutions with clear wording, or bold statements about an issue or event, reflect considerable consensus within the Security Council.

The five *permanent members* of the Council—the United States, Britain, France, Russia and China—are the most important. The Council also has 10 *nonpermanent members* who rotate for two-year terms. As noted above, Canada has served as a nonpermanent member on the Security Council six times since the UN was founded. Nonpermanent members are elected (five each year) by the General Assembly from a list prepared by informal regional caucuses. Usually there is a mix of regions and country sizes, though not by any strict formula. The Council's *chairperson* rotates among the members monthly. Sometimes this matters: in 1990, the United States pushed for action against Iraq before the chair passed from the United States to Yemen, which opposed the U.S. position.

Substantive Security Council resolutions require *nine* votes from among the 15 members. A "no" vote by any permanent member defeats the resolution—referred to as the *veto* power. Many resolutions have been vetoed by the permanent members, and many more have never been proposed because they would have faced certain veto. During the Cold War, the United States and the Soviet Union used their vetoes most often, followed in distant third place by Britain. However, since 1991, the use of the veto has dropped abruptly to just 18 vetoes in the last 16 years—13 of them by the United States, three by Russia and two by China.

Members can *abstain* on resolutions, an option that some permanent members use to register misgivings about a resolution without vetoing. China abstains with regularity because it generally reserves its veto for matters directly affecting Chinese security. Its 1997 veto of a resolution on Guatemala (a country with strong ties to Taiwan) was its first veto in nearly 25 years. As a power with more regional than global interests, China avoids alienating other great powers by blocking their actions in distant parts of the world. (If the Security Council tried to condemn China, no such restraint would apply.) The United States has abstained several times on resolutions critical of Israel.

The Security Council meets in the UN's New York headquarters upon request of a UN member—often a state with a grievance regarding another state's actions. When Kuwait was invaded and when Bosnia was being overrun, the victims called on the Security Council—a kind of 911 phone number for the world (but one without a standing police force). Because international security continues to be troublesome in many regions, and because these troubles often drag on for months or years, meetings of the Council are frequent.

The Security Council's *power is limited* in two major ways; both reflect the strength of state sovereignty in the international system. First, the Council's decisions depend entirely on the interests of its member states. Ambassadors who represent those states cannot change a Council resolution without authorization from their governments. Second, although Security Council resolutions in theory bind all UN members, member states in practice often try to evade or soften their effect. For instance, trade sanctions are difficult to enforce because it is tempting and relatively easy to cheat. A Security Council resolution can be enforced in practice only if enough powerful states care about it.

The Security Council has a formal mechanism for coordinating multilateral military action in response to aggression, called the *Military Staff Committee*. It is composed of military officers from the permanent Council member states. However, the United States opposes placing its forces under non-U.S. commanders, and the committee has never been used.

Instead, military forces responding to aggression under the auspices of Security Council resolutions have remained under national command. For example, U.S. forces in the Gulf War had the mission of enforcing UN resolutions but did not display UN insignia or flags, nor did U.S. soldiers sent to Somalia in late 1992 to restore humanitarian relief efforts disrupted by civil war. Similarly, NATO forces in the former Yugoslavia, the Australian-led force in East Timor and the British-led force in Afghanistan all operate under a national flag but were authorized by UN resolution.

In most *peacekeeping* operations, by contrast, UN forces operate under UN command, wear UN insignia (including blue helmets or berets), travel in UN-marked vehicles and so forth.

Even when the Security Council cannot agree on means of enforcement, its resolutions shape the way disputes are seen and ultimately how they are resolved. Security Council Resolution 242 after the Arab-Israeli war of 1967 laid out the principles for a just peace in that conflict—primarily the right of all states in the region to live within secure and well-defined borders and the return by Israel of territories captured in the 1967 war. (The parties are still arguing about whether "territories to be returned by Israel" means "all" territories.) Reaffirmed in Resolution 338 after the 1973 war, these resolutions helped shape the 1978 Camp David agreement and later formed the basis for the peace negotiations between Israel and its Arab neighbours that began in 1991.

The Security Council can also signal through its resolutions the kinds of concerns it wants UN personnel to be aware of, as well as the general issues it wants to address through its work. For example, in October 2000 the Security Council adopted Resolution 1325 on Women, Peace and Security, noting the differential impact of armed conflict on women and men and calling for the greater presence of women on peacekeeping missions and in peace negotiations. In April 2004, the Security Council adopted resolution 1539 on Children and Armed Conflict, in which it condemned the use of child soldiers and indicated it might resort to trade sanctions against any state that continued to recruit children into armed forces. It also acknowledged the sexual exploitation children can be subjected to during conflicts, in some cases even by the humanitarian workers and peacekeepers who have ostensibly come to assist them.

Proposed Changes   The structure of the Security Council is not without problems. Japan and Germany are great powers that contribute substantial UN dues (based on economic size) and make large contributions to UN programs and peacekeeping operations. Yet they have exactly the same formal representation in the UN as tiny states with less than one-hundredth of their population—one vote in the General Assembly and the chance to rotate onto the Security Council (in practice they rotate on more often than the tiny states). As global trading powers, Japan and Germany have huge stakes in the ground rules for international *security* affairs and would like seats at the table.[22]

---

[22] David M. Malone, "UN Reform: A Sisyphean Task," *Canada Among Nations 2006: Minorities and Priorities*, ed. Andrew F. Cooper and Dane Rowlands (Kingston and Montreal: McGill-Queen's University Press, 2006). Adam Chapnick, "UN Security Council Reform and Canadian Foreign Policy: Then and Now," *Canadian Foreign Policy* 13.1 (2008): 81–96.

Including Japan and Germany as permanent Council members would not be simple. If Germany joined, three of the seven permanent members would be European, giving that region unfair weight (especially from the viewpoint of former European colonies in the global South). The three European seats could be combined into one (a rotating seat or one representing the European Union), but this would water down the power of Britain and France, which can veto any such change in the Charter. Japan's bid for a seat faces Chinese opposition. Also, if Japan or Germany were given a seat, then what about India, with 20 percent of the world's population? And what about an Islamic country such as Indonesia? Finally, what about Latin America and Africa? Possible new members could include Japan, Germany, India, Brazil, Egypt and either Nigeria or South Africa.

None of these plans have made much progress. Any overhaul of the Security Council would require a change in the UN Charter, and a change in membership would reduce the power of the current five permanent members, any one of which could veto the reform, making change very difficult. In late 2004, an expert panel appointed by then-Secretary-General Kofi Annan recommended expanding the Security Council to 24 members under one of two formulas, neither of which would change veto powers. These proposals were debated in 2005 but no agreement was reached and the issue was put on hold. During the debate, 42 million people in China and 40 other countries signed a petition against Japan's getting a Council seat until it recognizes and sincerely apologizes for its war crimes in World War II.

Table 8.1 shows the recent rotations of members onto the Security Council. The system of nomination by regional caucuses has worked to keep regional balance on

Table 8.1 Regional Representation on the UN Security Council

Region	Permanent Members[a]	Nonpermanent Members[b]			Possible Contenders for New Permanent Seats[c]
		2006	2005	2004	
North America	United States				
W. Europe	Britain France	Denmark Greece	Denmark Greece	Germany Spain	Germany
Japan/Pacific		Japan	Japan		Japan
Russia & E. Europe	Russia	Slovakia	Romania	Romania	
China	China				
Middle East		Qatar	Algeria	Algeria	Egypt?
Latin America		Peru Argentina	Brazil Argentina	Brazil Chile	Brazil, Mexico?
South Asia				Pakistan Philippines	India, Indonesia?
			Philippines		
Africa		Tanzania Ghana Congo Republic	Tanzania Benin	Angola Benin	Nigeria? South Africa?

[a]The five permanent members hold veto power.

[b]Nonpermanent members are elected for two-year terms by the General Assembly, based on nominations by regional caucuses.

[c]Possible new permanent seats might have fewer if any veto powers.

the Council fairly constant as individual states come and go. Major regional actors, including those mentioned as candidates for possible new permanent seats (shown at right in the table), tend to rotate onto the Council more often than less important states.

Peacekeeping Forces

Peacekeeping forces are not mentioned in the UN Charter. Secretary-General Dag Hammarskjöld in the 1960s joked that they were allowed under "Chapter Six and a Half"—somewhere between the nonviolent dispute resolution called for in Chapter 6 of the Charter and the authorization of force provided for in Chapter 7. The Charter requires member states to place military forces at the disposal of the UN, but such forces were envisioned as being used in response to aggression (under collective security). In practice, when the UN has authorized force to reverse aggression—as in the Gulf War in 1990—the forces involved have been *national* forces not under UN command.

The UN's *own* forces—borrowed from armies of member states but under the flag and command of the UN—have been *peacekeeping* forces to calm regional conflicts, playing a neutral role between warring forces.[23] The first UN peacekeeping mission was established in the Suez in 1956 after Britain, France and Israel invaded Egypt when the Nasser government nationalized the Suez Canal Company. That peacekeeping mission was aimed as much at allowing Britain and France—two Security Council members—to withdraw without losing face as it was at bringing the conflict to an end. The plan for the mission, United Nations Emergency Force I (UNEF I), was developed by Canada's then ambassador to the UN, Lester B. Pearson, who would win a Nobel Peace Prize for his efforts. UN troops acted as a buffer between Israeli and Egyptian forces until 1967, and in large part, UNEF I was considered a success. It also set the principles that served as the basis of all subsequent peacekeeping missions: the importance of securing the consent of the parties to the dispute; the non-use of force, except in self-defence; and impartiality.[24]

Throughout the Cold War, it was normally small or middle powers that contributed troops to peacekeeping missions, such as Ireland, India, Pakistan, Canada, Fiji, Indonesia, the Netherlands, Italy and the Nordic countries. Large powers tended to make financial contributions but only rarely contributed troops. Though more large powers have begun to deploy troops on peace missions, peacekeeping remains largely a preserve of smaller and middle powers. Canada was not only actively involved in the creation of peacekeeping, it was until recently an active participant in most peacekeeping missions and is described by some observers as the peacekeeping country "par excellence."[25] This role has changed

---

[23] Michael W. Doyle, Ian Johnstone and Robert C. Orr, eds., *Keeping the Peace: Multidimensional UN Operations in Cambodia and El Salvador* (NY: Cambridge UP, 1997). James Mayall, ed., *The New Interventionism, 1991–1994: United Nations Experience in Cambodia, Former Yugoslavia, and Somalia* (NY: Cambridge UP, 1996). William J. Durch, ed., *The Evolution of UN Peacekeeping: Case Studies and Comparative Analysis* (NY: St. Martin's, 1993). Steven R. Ratner, *The New UN Peacekeeping: Building Peace in Lands of Conflict after the Cold War* (NY: St. Martin's, 1995).

[24] Jocelyn Coulon, *Soldiers of Diplomacy: The United Nations, Peacekeeping, and the New World Order* (U Toronto P, 1998). A. B. Fetherston, *Towards a Theory of United Nations Peacekeeping* (Basingstoke, UK: Macmillan, 1994).

[25] Joseph T. Jockel, *Canada and International Peacekeeping* (Washington, DC: Center for Strategic and International Studies, 1994).

recently, with Canada now deploying far more troops to Afghanistan's NATO-led mission than on any peacekeeping duties. By 2004, most of the largest troop-contributing countries were small and middle powers of the global South: Bangladesh, Ethiopia, Ghana, India, Jordan, Kenya, Nepal, Nigeria, Pakistan, Senegal and Uruguay. UN forces themselves won the Nobel Peace Prize in 1988 in recognition of their growing importance and success.

Peacekeeping Missions The secretary-general assembles a peacekeeping force for each mission, usually from a few states totally uninvolved in the conflict, united under a single commander. The soldiers are commonly called **blue helmets** or blue berets. Peacekeeping forces serve at the invitation of a host government and must leave if that government orders them out (as Egypt did in 1967).

    Authority for peacekeeping forces is granted by the Security Council, usually for a period of three to six months, which may be renewed—in some cases for decades. In the Suez crisis in 1956, the General Assembly authorized forces under the "Uniting for Peace" resolution, allowing the Assembly to take up security matters when the Security Council was deadlocked (because of France and Britain's involvement in the conflict). In the Congo in 1960 it was the secretary-general who took the initiative. Today the Security Council controls peacekeeping operations, and they are authorized by Security Council resolutions.

blue helmets UN peacekeeping forces, so called because they wear helmets or berets in the UN colour, blue, with UN insignia.

KEEPING THE PEACE
UN peacekeeping forces operate under authority of the Security Council with troops contributed voluntarily by an assortment of states. Peacekeeping grew rapidly in the early 1990s, declined in the late 1990s after several problem-plagued missions and has grown again in recent years. Here, peacekeeping troops from Nepal patrol southern Lebanon, 1978.

Funds must be voted by the General Assembly, and lack of funds is the single greatest constraint on the use of peacekeeping forces today. Special assessments against member states pay for peacekeeping operations. With the expansion of peacekeeping in 1988–1994, the expenses of these forces (about $5 billion in 2006) are several times larger than the regular UN budget. Total unpaid contributions to peacekeeping, in mid-2004, were US$1.19 billion, what many observers described as amounting to a financial crisis within the UN. (See Global Policy Forum, http://www.globalpolicy.org.)

Recent Missions In mid-2007, the UN maintained 83 271 troops, civilian police and military observers from 115 countries in 15 separate peacekeeping or observing missions spanning five world regions (see Table 8.2). (Missions change from year to year.)

The largest peacekeeping mission was in Democratic Congo in early 2007, where 17 500 peacekeepers monitored a ceasefire and protected civilians after a civil war. In 2005, the Security Council approved a 10 000-troop peacekeeping force for the Darfur region in Sudan at a cost of nearly $1 billion, but Sudan refused to allow it, and smaller, ineffective African Union forces remained the only peacekeepers there as violence escalated in 2006 and 2007. Other large-scale UN peacekeeping operations were in Liberia (maintaining a ceasefire after a civil war), Ivory Coast and Burundi (stabilizing peace agreements), Lebanon (following the 2006 Israeli-Hezbollah war) and Haiti (trying to maintain stability after a military coup). The largest recent missions reflect the resurgence of UN peacekeeping after the shakeout of the mid-1990s. UN leaders expect a surge of well over 100 000 peacekeepers and $6 billion in 2007.

Table 8.2 UN Peacekeeping Missions as of April 2006

Location	Region	Size	Annual Cost (million $)	Role	Since
Democratic Congo	Africa	17,500	$1,150	Observe ceasefire; protect civilians	1999
Liberia	Africa	17,000	760	Assist transitional govt.	2003
Sudan	Africa	8,800	970	Support agreement; monitor war	2005
Ivory Coast	Africa	8,000	440	Help implement peace agreement	2004
Burundi	Africa	5,000	310	Help implement peace agreement	2004
Ethiopia/Eritrea	Africa	3,500	185	Monitor post-war border	2000
Western Sahara	Africa	350	50	Organize referendum in territory	1991
India/Pakistan	South Asia	80	8	Observe India-Pakistan ceasefire	1949
Kosovo	Russia/E. Eur.	3,100	250	Civil administration; relief	1999
Georgia	Russia/E. Eur.	250	40	Observe ceasefire in civil war	1993
Lebanon	Middle East	2,100	100	Monitor ceasefire on Israeli border	1978
Syria (Golan Heights)	Middle East	1,200	45	Monitor Israel-Syria ceasefire	1974
Cyprus	Middle East	1,000	50	Monitor Greek-Turkish ceasefire	1964
Israel	Middle East	300	30	Observe Arab-Israeli truce	1948
Haiti	Latin America	9,900	540	Assist transitional govt.	2004
Total		77,980	4,928		

Note: Size indicates total international personnel (mostly troops but some civilian administrators and police).

NATO-led forces largely replaced UN peacekeepers in Bosnia in the late 1990s (and, later, took military control of Kosovo). UN operations in these countries focus on civilian governmental functions, leaving security matters largely to UN-authorized but independently commanded international forces. The same approach was used in East Timor with an Australian-led force.

At its peak in the early 1990s, the UN ran several other large peacekeeping operations in addition to those in the former Yugoslavia and in Lebanon. One of the most important was in *Cambodia*, called the United Nations Transitional Authority in Cambodia, or UNTAC. There, more than 15 000 peacekeepers were coupled with a large force of UN administrators, police and volunteers to take substantial control of the Cambodian government under a fragile pact that ended (for the most part) a long and devastating civil war. Despite difficulty in obtaining the cooperation of the Khmer Rouge faction (which refused to disarm as it had agreed), the UN pressed forward to hold elections in 1993 that chose a Cambodian government (though not a stable one).[26]

However, UNTAC also illustrated some of the other problems associated with large-scale peacekeeping missions. The arrival of over 20 000 UN troops and civilian personnel had an enormous social impact on Cambodia: prostitution increased exponentially, as did cases of HIV/AIDS and reports of sexual assaults against local women. The presence of these foreign personnel (most of whom earned more money in a single day than the average Cambodian earned in a year) also had disruptive economic effects, causing rampant inflation such that the cost of basic goods, food and housing skyrocketed.[27]

Some of the lessons learned in Cambodia helped the UN accomplish a similar mission more easily in *Mozambique*. A peace agreement ended a long and devastating civil war there, setting up mechanisms for disarmament, the integration of military forces and the holding of internationally supervised elections for a new government. However, reports of sexual exploitation of local women and children plagued that mission as well, and similar charges emerged in 2004 regarding UN personnel on the peacekeeping mission to the Democratic Republic of the Congo. Secretary-General Annan called the reported behaviour of UN troops from several countries serving in Democratic Congo "shameful." Investigators there found hundreds of cases of sexual crimes by UN personnel.[28]

In an effort to provide longer-term support after wars, the UN created a Peacebuilding Commission in 2005 to coordinate reconstruction, institution-building and economic recovery efforts in postwar societies after peacekeeping missions end. The accomplishments of peacekeeping missions are quite mixed: sometimes they have made important contributions to keeping the peace, but they do not always achieve their goals, and sometimes the negative social impact on the country in which the mission has been deployed can be quite serious.

---

[26] Michael W. Doyle, *UN Peacekeeping in Cambodia: UNTAC's Civilian Mandate* (Boulder, CO: Rienner, 1995).

[27] Peter Utting, ed., *Between Hope and Insecurity: The Social Consequences of the Cambodian Peace Process* (Geneva: United Nations Research Institute for Social Development, 1994). Sandra Whitworth, *Men, Militarism and UN Peacekeeping: A Gendered Analysis* (Boulder, CO: Rienner, 2004).

[28] Graça Machel, "The Impact of Armed Conflict on Children Report of the Expert of the Secretary-General, Ms. Graça Machel, Submitted Pursuant to General Assembly Resolution 48/157," United Nations General Assembly, A/51/306 (26 Aug. 1996). Kate Holt and Sarah Hughes, "SA soldiers fingered in DRC abuse scandal," *Pretoria News* 12 July 2004: 1.

Observing and Peacekeeping "Peacekeepers" perform two different functions—observing and peacekeeping. *Observers* are unarmed military officers sent to a conflict area in small numbers simply to watch what happens and report back to the UN. With the UN watching, the parties to a conflict are often less likely to break a ceasefire. Observers can *monitor* various aspects of a country's situation—ceasefires, elections, respect for human rights and other areas. (Such monitoring—such as certifying whether an election is fair—is often organized by IGOs and NGOs outside the UN.) This kind of monitoring was useful in the transitions from war to democracy in Nicaragua and El Salvador in the 1990s.

The function of *peacekeeping* is carried out by lightly armed soldiers (in armoured vehicles with automatic rifles but without artillery, tanks and other heavy weapons). Such forces play several roles. They can *interpose* themselves physically between warring parties to keep them apart (more accurately, to force them to attack the UN forces in order to get to their enemy). UN peacekeepers often try to *negotiate* with military officers on both sides. This channel of communication can bring about tactical actions and understandings that support a ceasefire. UN forces in a war zone cannot easily get from one side's positions to those of the other to conduct negotiations.

Peacekeeping is much more difficult if one side sees the UN forces as being *biased* toward the other. Israel feels this way about UN forces in southern Lebanon, for example. On occasion, Israeli forces have broken through UN lines to attack enemies, and they have allegedly targeted UN outposts on occasion. In Cambodia and the former Yugoslavia in the early 1990s, one party deliberately attacked UN forces many times, causing a number of deaths. In general, when ceasefires break down, UN troops are caught in the middle. Over 2300 have been killed over the years—the majority in the Congo (Zaire) in 1960–1964, in Cyprus since 1964, in southern Lebanon since 1978 and in the former Yugoslavia in the 1990s. Canada has lost 114 peacekeeping personnel serving on UN missions. In some conflicts, peacekeepers organized outside the UN framework have been used instead of UN-commanded forces; CIS troops have occasionally played this role in the former Soviet Union, and U.S. forces have acted as peacekeepers in Egypt's Sinai desert since the 1970s.

Peacemaking In the past, peacekeeping forces have generally been unable to make peace, only to keep it. To go into a shooting war and suppress hostilities requires military forces far beyond those of past UN peacekeeping missions. Thus, peacekeepers are usually not sent until a ceasefire has been arranged, has taken effect and has held up for some time. Often dozens of ceasefires are broken before one sticks—wars may simmer along for years, taking a terrible toll, before the UN gets its chance.

To address this problem, in 1992, the secretary-general proposed the creation of UN *peacemaking* (or *peace enforcement*) units that would not only monitor a ceasefire but enforce it if it broke down. The secretary-general called for member states to make available, on a rapid deployment basis, 1000 soldiers each—specially trained volunteers—to create a standby UN army that could respond quickly to crises.[29] Not only did the member states refuse the request for soldiers, they shot down the idea of peacemaking altogether. Since then the UN has authorized member states to provide real military forces, not peacekeepers, when fighting may be required. In an exception that may or may not indicate a trend, the Security Council broadened the mandate of UN

---

[29] Boutros Boutros-Ghali, *An Agenda for Peace: Preventive Diplomacy, Peacemaking and Peace-keeping* (NY: United Nations, 1992). Tom Woodhouse, Robert Bruce and Malcolm Dando, eds., *Peacekeeping and Peacemaking: Towards Effective Intervention in Post–Cold War Conflicts* (NY: St. Martin's, 1998).

peacekeepers in Democratic Congo to allow them to protect civilians. In 2005, Pakistani peacekeepers there killed 50 militia fighters after nine peacekeepers from Bangladesh were killed in an ambush.

Peacekeeping missions themselves were scaled back drastically in the mid-1990s. In some cases, great powers turned down the secretary-general's urgent requests for peacekeeping missions to head off impending disasters—for example, in Burundi in 1995, when the same Hutu-Tutsi conflict as in Rwanda threatened to erupt into another genocide.

In the late 1990s, as peacekeeping again expanded, seven countries—Denmark, Norway, Sweden, Poland, the Netherlands, Austria and Canada—formed a 4000-troop Multinational Stand-By High Readiness Brigade for United Nations Operations (SHIRBRIG). Headquartered in Denmark and available to deploy to conflict areas in two to four weeks rather than months, the brigade is controlled by the Security Council. As of 2007, it had participated in four peacekeeping missions, and 16 countries are now members.

UN Secretary-General, Ban Ki-moon, at the United Nations headquarters in 2006.

The secretary-general is *nominated* by the Security Council—requiring the consent of all five permanent members—and must be *approved* by the General Assembly. The term of office is five years and may be renewed. Past secretary-generals have come from various regions of the world but never from a great power. They are Trygve Lie (from Norway, 1946–1952), Dag Hammarskjöld (Sweden, 1953–1961), U Thant (Burma, 1961–1971), Kurt Waldheim (Austria, 1972–1981), Javier Perez de Cuellar (Peru, 1982–1991), Boutros Boutros-Ghali (Egypt, 1992–1996) and Kofi Annan (Ghana, 1997–2006). The current secretary-general is Ban Ki-Moon, who began his term in 2007. Secretary-generals who lose the support of one or more members of the Security Council will not be renewed (as was the case in 1981 when China vetoed a third term for Kurt Waldheim and in 1996 when Boutros Boutros-Ghali did not receive support from the U.S. for a second term).

Kofi Annan, the UN's first secretary-general from sub-Saharan Africa, served two full terms from 1997 to 2006 and focused on reinvigorating and streamlining the UN. He won the 100th-anniversary Nobel Peace Prize in 2001 and enjoyed strong support from the U.S. for much of his tenure (with critics saying he was far too close to the U.S.). However, in his final years he was increasingly critical of U.S. policies and was often criticized in turn by the U.S. for the slow pace of UN reform. The 2004 oil-for-food scandal in which Annan himself was cleared but his son Kojo was implicated also tarnished his reputation (see p. 258). Ban Ki-Moon is a former foreign minister of South Korea and is focused on UN reform, economic development, human rights, terrorism, proliferation, environmental problems and HIV/AIDS.

The Secretariat

The secretary-general of the UN is the closest thing to a "president or prime minister of the world" that exists, but the secretary-general represents member states—especially the five permanent Security Council members—and not the world's six billion people. A past secretary-general, Boutros Boutros-Ghali, was fond of calling himself the "humble servant" of member states. When the great powers do not have consensus, it is in fact hard for the secretary-general to be anything more than a humble servant.

The Secretariat of the UN is its executive branch, headed by the secretary-general. It is a bureaucracy for administering UN policy and programs, just as Foreign Affairs and International Trade Canada is a bureaucracy for Canadian foreign policy. In security matters, the secretary-general personally works with the Security Council; development programs are coordinated by a second-in-command—the director-general for Development and International Economic Co-operation. The Secretariat is divided into functional areas, with undersecretaries-general and assistant secretaries-general.

The *UN staff* in these areas includes administrative personnel as well as technical experts and economic advisers working on various programs and projects in member countries. The staff numbers about 15 000 people, and the total number of employees in the UN system is just over 60 000. There is a concentration of UN-related agency offices in Geneva, Switzerland. Geneva is a frequent site of international negotiations and is seen by some as more neutral than New York. A few development programs are headquartered in cities of the global South.

One purpose of the UN Secretariat is to develop an *international civil service* of diplomats and bureaucrats whose loyalties lie at the global level, and not with their states of origin. The UN Charter sets the secretary-general and staff apart from the authority of national governments and calls on member states to respect the staff's "exclusively international character." The UN has been fairly successful in this regard; the secretary-general is usually seen as an independent diplomat thinking about the whole world's interests, not a pawn of any state. Enthusiastic support by any one member of the Security Council can call a secretary-general's independence into question.

The secretary-general, however, is more than a bureaucratic manager. He (it has not yet been a she) is a visible public figure whose personal attention to a regional conflict can move it toward resolution. The Charter allows the secretary-general to use the UN's "good offices" to serve as a neutral mediator in international conflicts—to bring hostile parties together in negotiations. For example, Boutros-Ghali was personally involved in trying to mediate conflicts in Somalia and the former Yugoslavia. Annan tried to talk Iraq into compliance with UN inspections in 1997, to which Iraq did not respond until 2003. In 2001, Annan used his position to try to galvanize a stronger (and better funded) international program against AIDS (see p. 533).

The secretary-general also works to bring together the great-power consensus on which Security Council action depends—a much harder job than mere bureaucratic management. The secretary-general has the power under the Charter to bring to the Security Council any matter that might threaten international peace and security, and thus plays a major role in setting the UN's agenda in international security affairs. Just as the Canadian prime minister can have tensions with cabinet over foreign policy, the secretary-general sometimes has tensions with the Security Council. However, the secretary-general is chosen by the Security Council and has less autonomy than the Canadian prime minister. When the secretary-general asks for authority for a peacekeeping mission for six months, the Security Council is likely to say "three months." If the secretary-general asks for $10 million, he might get $5 million. Thus the secretary-general remains, like the entire UN system, constrained by state sovereignty.

The General Assembly

The General Assembly is made up of all 192 member states of the UN, each with one vote. It usually meets every year, from late September through January, in *plenary session*. State leaders or foreign ministers, including the Canadian prime minister, generally address the assemblage one-by-one. The Assembly sessions, like most UN deliberations, are simultaneously translated into dozens of languages so that delegates from around the world can carry on a single conversation. This global town hall is a unique institution and provides a powerful medium for states to put forward their ideas and arguments. Presiding over it is a president elected by the Assembly—a post without much power.

The Assembly convenes for *special sessions* every few years on general topics such as economic cooperation. The UN special session on disarmament in June 1982 provided the occasion for the largest political rally in U.S. history—a peace demonstration of a million people in New York. The Assembly has met in *emergency session* in the past to deal with an immediate threat to international peace and security, but this has happened only nine times and has now become uncommon.

The General Assembly has the power to accredit national delegations as members of the UN (through its Credentials Committee). For instance, in 1971 the delegation of the People's Republic of China was given China's seat in the UN (including on the Security Council) in place of the nationalists in Taiwan. For decades, neither North nor South Korea were members of the UN (because both claimed the whole of Korea), but finally took seats as separate delegations in 1991. Some political entities that fall short of state status send *permanent observer missions* to the UN. These missions participate without a vote in the General Assembly. They include the Vatican (Holy See) and the Palestine Liberation Organization (PLO).

The General Assembly's main power lies in its *control of finances* for UN programs and operations, including peacekeeping. It also can *pass resolutions* on various matters, but these are purely advisory and not binding on member states. The Assembly also *elects members* of certain UN agencies and programs. Finally, the Assembly coordinates UN programs and agencies through its own system of committees, commissions, councils and so forth.

The Assembly coordinates UN programs and agencies through the Economic and Social Council (ECOSOC), which has 54 member states elected by the General Assembly for three-year terms. ECOSOC manages the overlapping work of a large number of programs and agencies. Its *regional commissions* look at how UN programs work together in a particular region; its *functional commissions* deal with global topics such as population growth, narcotics trafficking, human rights and the status of women; its *expert bodies* work on technical subjects that cut across various UN programs in areas such as crime prevention and public finances. Outside of ECOSOC, the General Assembly operates many *other specialized committees*. Standing committees ease the work of the Assembly in issues such as decolonization, legal matters or disarmament.

Many of the activities associated with the UN do not take place under tight control of either the General Assembly or the Security Council. They occur in functional agencies and programs with varying degrees of autonomy from UN control.

UN Programs

Through the Economic and Social Council, the General Assembly oversees more than a dozen major programs to advance economic development and social stability in poor states of the global South. Through its programs, the UN helps to manage global North-South relations: it organizes a flow of resources and skills from the richer parts of the world to support development in the poorer parts.

The programs are *funded* partly by General Assembly allocations and partly by contributions raised directly from member states, businesses or private charitable contributors. The degree of General Assembly funding, and of operational autonomy from the Assembly, vary from one program to another. Each UN program has a staff, a headquarters and various operations in the field, where it works with host governments in member states.

Several of these programs are of growing importance. The *UN Environment Program (UNEP)* became prominent in the 1990s as the economic development of the global South and the growing economies of the industrialized world took a toll on the environment (see Chapter 14). UNEP grapples with global environmental strategies, guided by principles adopted at the Earth Summit (the UN Conference on Environment and Development) in Brazil in 1992. UNEP provides technical assistance to member states, monitors environmental conditions globally, develops standards and recommends alternative energy sources.

UNICEF is the UN Children's Fund, which gives technical and financial assistance to developing countries for programs benefiting children. It is also involved in research—in areas such as the use of child soldiers, for example. Unfortunately, the needs of children in many countries are urgent, and UNICEF is kept busy. Financed by voluntary contributions, UNICEF has, for decades, organized U.S. and Canadian children in an annual Halloween fund drive on behalf of their counterparts in poorer countries.

The *Office of the UN High Commissioner for Refugees (UNHCR)* has also been kept busy in recent

HELPING WHERE NEEDED
An array of UN programs, operating under the General Assembly, aim to help countries in the global South overcome social and economic problems. These programs played a crucial role in the massive international assistance effort that followed the December 2004 Indian Ocean tsunami, and are involved in the long-term development of devastated regions. This helicopter from the UN refugee agency, on loan from the Swiss government, delivers supplies in Indonesia, January 2005.

years. UNHCR coordinates efforts to protect, assist and eventually repatriate the many refugees who flee across international borders each year to escape war and political violence. (The longer-standing problem of Palestinian refugees is handled by a different program, the *UN Relief Works Agency*, or *UNRWA*.)

The *UN Development Program (UNDP)*, funded by voluntary contributions, coordinates all UN efforts related to development in the global South. With about 5000 projects operating simultaneously around the world, UNDP is the world's largest international agency for technical development assistance. The UN also runs several development-related agencies for training and for promoting women's roles in development.

Many developing countries depend on export revenues to finance economic development, making those countries vulnerable to fluctuations in commodity prices and other problems involved in international trade. The **UN Conference on Trade and Development (UNCTAD)** seeks to negotiate international trade agreements to stabilize commodity prices and promote development. Because countries of the global South do not have much power in the international economy, however, UNCTAD has little leverage with which to promote their interests in trade (see p. 485).

Other UN programs manage problems such as disaster relief, food aid, housing and population issues. In poorer countries, the UN maintains an active presence in economic and social affairs.

UN Conference on Trade and Development (UNCTAD) A structure established in 1964 to promote development in the global South through various trade proposals.

Autonomous Agencies

In addition to its own programs, the UN General Assembly maintains formal ties with about 20 autonomous international agencies not under its control. Most are specialized technical organizations through which states pool their efforts to address problems such as health care and labour conditions.

The only such agency in international security affairs is the *International Atomic Energy Agency (IAEA)*, headquartered in Vienna, Austria. It was established under the UN but is formally autonomous. Although the IAEA has an economic role in helping to develop civilian nuclear power plants, it mainly works to prevent nuclear proliferation (see p. 218). The IAEA was responsible for inspections in Iraq in 2002–2003, which found no evidence of a secret nuclear weapons program. It is involved in monitoring Iran's nuclear program to the extent Iran allows. The IAEA won the 2005 Nobel Peace Prize.

In the area of health care, the **World Health Organization (WHO),** based in Geneva, provides technical assistance to improve conditions in the global South and conducts major immunization campaigns in poor countries. In the 1960s and 1970s, the WHO led one of the great public health victories of all time—the worldwide eradication of smallpox. Today, the WHO is a leading player in the worldwide fight to control AIDS (see pp. 533–535). In 2003, Canadians became directly aware of the WHO's work when it issued a travel advisory against Toronto due to the outbreak of Severe Acute Respiratory Syndrome (SARS).

In agriculture, the Food and Agriculture Organization (FAO) is the lead agency. For labour standards, it is the International Labor Organization (ILO). UNESCO—the UN Educational, Scientific, and Cultural Organization—facilitates international communication and scientific collaboration. The UN Industrial Development Organization (UNIDO) promotes industrialization in the global South.

World Health Organization (WHO) Based in Geneva, an IO that provides technical assistance to improve health conditions primarily in the global South (but can address health concerns anywhere around the world) and conducts major immunization campaigns.

The longest-established IOs, with some of the most successful records, are specialized agencies dealing with technical aspects of international coordination, such as aviation and postal exchange. For instance, the *International Telecommunications Union (ITU)* allocates radio frequencies. The *Universal Postal Union (UPU)* sets standards for international mail. The *International Civil Aviation Organization (ICAO)* sets binding standards for international air traffic. The *International Maritime Organization (IMO)* facilitates international cooperation on shipping at sea. The *World Intellectual Property Organization (WIPO)* seeks world compliance with copyrights and patents, and promotes development and technology transfer within a legal framework that protects such intellectual property (see p. 525). Finally, the *World Meteorological Association (WMO)* oversees a world weather watch and promotes the exchange of weather information.

The major coordinating agencies of the world economy (discussed in Chapters 9, 10 and 13) are also UN-affiliated. The World Bank and the International Monetary Fund (IMF) give loans, grants and technical assistance for economic development (and the IMF manages international balance-of-payments accounting). The World Trade Organization (WTO) sets rules for international trade.

Overall, the density of connections across national borders, both within the UN system and through other IOs, increases each year. In a less tangible way, people are connecting across international borders through the meshing of ideas, including norms and rules. Gradually, those rules are becoming international law.

INTERNATIONAL LAW

International law, unlike national law, derives not from actions of a legislative branch or other central authority but from tradition and agreements signed by states. It also differs in the difficulty of enforcement, which depends not on the power and authority of central government but on reciprocity, collective action and international norms.[30]

Sources of International Law

Laws within states come from central authorities—legislatures or dictators. Because states are sovereign and recognize no central authority, international law differs greatly. The declarations of the UN General Assembly are not laws, and most do not bind members. The Security Council can compel certain actions by states, but these are commands rather than laws: they are specific to a situation. No body of international law has been passed by a legislative body. Where, then, does international law come from? Four sources of international law are recognized: treaties, customs, general principles of law (such as equity) and legal scholarship (including past judicial decisions).

---

[30] Michael Byers, ed., *The Role of Law in International Politics* (NY: Oxford UP, 2000). Malcolm N. Shaw, *International Law*, 4th ed. (Cambridge: Cambridge UP, 1998). Anthony D'Amato, *International Law: Process and Prospect,* 2nd ed. (Ardsley, NY: Transnational, 1995). Rosalyn Higgins, *Problems and Process: International Law and How We Use It* (NY: Oxford UP, 1994). Thomas M. Franck, *Fairness in International Law and Institutions* (NY: Oxford UP, 1995).

Treaties and other written conventions signed by states are the most important source.[31] International treaties now fill more than a thousand thick volumes with tens of thousands of individual agreements. A principle in international law states that once signed and ratified, treaties must be observed (*pacta sunt servanda*). States violate the terms of treaties they have signed only if a matter is very important or if the penalties for such a violation seem very small. In Canada, treaties are ratified by Cabinet. Implementing the treaty (if it requires changes to existing Canadian legislation or the creation of new legislation) is charged to Parliament or, if appropriate, provincial legislatures.

Treaties and other international obligations such as debts are *binding on successor governments*, whether a new government takes power through an election, coup or revolution. After the revolutions in Eastern Europe around 1990, newly democratic governments were held responsible for debts incurred by their communist predecessors. Even when the Soviet Union broke up, Russia as the successor state had to guarantee that Soviet debts would be paid and Soviet treaties honoured. Although revolution does not free a state from its obligations, some treaties have built-in escape clauses that let states legally withdraw, after giving due notice, without violating international law. As discussed below, in 2001 the United States invoked the six-month opt-out provision of the ABM treaty.

Because of the universal commitment for all states to respect certain basic principles of international law, the UN Charter is one of the world's most important treaties. Its implications are broad and far-reaching, in contrast to more specific treaties, such as a fishery management agreement. Specialized agreements are usually easier to interpret and more enforceable than broad treaties such as the Charter.

Custom is the second major source of international law. If states behave a certain way toward each other for long enough, their behaviour may become generally accepted practice with the status of law. Western international law (though not Islamic law) tends to be *positivist* in this regard—it draws on actual customs, the practical realities of self-interest and the need for consent rather than on an abstract concept of divine or natural law.

General principles of law also serve as a source of international law. Actions recognized in most national legal systems as crimes, such as theft and assault, tend to have the same meaning in an international context. Iraq's invasion of Kuwait was illegal under treaties signed by Iraq (including the UN Charter and that of the Arab League) and illegal under the custom Iraq and Kuwait had established of living in peace as sovereign states. Beyond treaty or custom, the invasion violated international law because of the general principle that one state may not overrun its neighbour's territory and annex it by force. (Of course, a state may still think it can get away with such a violation of international law.)

The fourth source of international law, recognized by the World Court as subsidiary to the others, is *legal scholarship*—the written arguments of judges and lawyers around the world on the issues in question. Only the writings of the most highly qualified and respected legal figures can be taken into account, and then only to resolve issues not settled by the first three sources of international law.

Often, international law lags behind changes in norms; law is quite tradition-bound. Certain activities, such as espionage, are technically illegal but are so widely condoned that they cannot be said to violate international norms. Other activities are still legal but have come to be frowned upon and seen as abnormal. For example, China's shooting of student demonstrators in 1989 violated international norms but not international law.

---

[31] Paul Reuter, *Introduction to the Law of Treaties* (London: Pinter, 1992).

The Place of International Law

World orders encompass not only power relationships, but the rules and norms that shape behaviour on the international stage. International law provides an important and detailed guide to such behaviour, which generally—though not perfectly—is obeyed by states. In particular, great powers usually follow the laws of war (though less so in counter-guerrilla warfare, such as in Vietnam in the 1960s, Afghanistan in the 1980s or Chechnya in the 1990s).

A prominent feature of world order in the decade before 2001 was the increasing strength of international law. The UN convened tribunals to hear war-crimes cases from the former Yugoslavia and Rwanda, and many states worked to craft a new permanent International Criminal Court with powers to try such cases from anywhere in the world. International law began extending into new areas, such as human rights and humanitarian intervention. UN Secretary-General Kofi Annan said after the 1999 Kosovo war that nations must not use the UN Charter as cover to commit genocide, and that human rights took "precedence over concerns of state sovereignty." However, he added, these norms were "evolving" and did not negate the continuing importance of sovereignty.

Clearly, terrorist attacks violate the laws of war, which concentrate heavily on maintaining a distinction between armed combatants and civilians. Combatants are to wear uniforms and insignia to identify themselves and are to direct their attacks at other combatants and avoid, to the extent militarily feasible, attacking civilians. Violation of these principles earned Serbia's leader Slobodan Milosevic a trial for war crimes before a UN tribunal in 2002.

Will the war on terrorism deepen the trend toward stronger international law that characterized the evolving post–Cold War era before September 11? Or will it reverse that trend and reassert the primacy of raw power over the niceties of conventions and norms?

Early reference points for this question were the U.S. treatment of suspected al Qaeda and Taliban fighters captured in battle in Afghanistan in 2001–2002, and the treatment of Iraqi prisoners after the U.S. invasion in 2003. In Afghanistan, the United States took hundreds of prisoners to a detention centre on the U.S. military base at Guantanamo Bay, Cuba. (Since the communist revolution in Cuba, the United States has maintained a military base on a corner of Cuba, separated from Cuban

Abu Ghraib Prison, Iraq, 2003–2004.

society.) By holding the prisoners outside U.S. territory, the government avoided restrictions that apply under U.S. law. The United States announced its intention to try the suspects in secret military tribunals, and initially claimed that the Geneva Conventions did not apply.

The 1949 Geneva Conventions extend special protections to prisoners of war (POWs) belonging to uniformed armies. These provisions reflect states' mutual interest in protecting their own soldiers if captured. They do not cover irregular forces who, by operating out of uniform, violate the laws of war and blur the distinction between combatants and civilians. Thus, in World War II, Allied soldiers were held as POWs by Germany, but French resistance fighters were often summarily executed upon capture.

In 2002, under prodding from the State Department and international opinion, President Bush agreed to deal with the Guantanamo Bay "detainees" (this term avoids the word "prisoner") according to provisions of the Conventions, but not as POWs. (While POWs must provide only name, rank and serial number, the terrorist suspects were interrogated and military tribunals proceeded.)

Questions arose again in Iraq when, in 2004, photographs emerged from the Abu Ghraib prison of systematic mistreatment of Iraqi prisoners. Photographs showed prisoners subjected to physical and sexual torture and humiliation. Some observers suggested that the interrogation techniques the U.S. had developed for suspected al Qaeda operatives at Guantanamo Bay were being employed in Iraq. While the U.S may have been able to make the case that they were not bound by the Geneva Conventions when dealing with suspected terrorists, it was harder to make this claim about prisoners captured in a more traditional war zone.*

What do these events tell us about international law? Is the argument that the U.S. government has a moral right and duty to do whatever it takes to destroy terrorists and protect the U.S. homeland from catastrophic attack a persuasive one? Even if it means dispensing with international law?

* Peter Yost, "Geneva Code Too 'Quaint,' Bush Was Told," *Ottawa Citizen* 17 May 2004: A7. Seymour Hersh, "The Gray Zone: How a Secret Pentagon Program Came to Abu Ghraib," *The New Yorker* 24 May 2004: 38–44.

Treaties: The Case of Arms Control Agreements

Treaties are a source of international law, and in questions of international security, arms control agreements are one of the most important types of treaty. During the Cold War, the superpowers' nuclear forces grew and technologies developed. These evolving force structures were codified (more than constrained) by a series of arms control agreements. *Arms control* is an effort by two or more states to regulate by formal agreement their acquisition of weapons.[32] Arms control involves more than just nuclear weapons—for instance, after World War I the great powers negotiated limits on sizes of navies—but in recent decades nuclear weapons have been the main focus. Arms control agreements typically require long, formal negotiations with many technical discussions, culminating in a treaty. Some arms control treaties are multilateral, but during the Cold War most were bilateral (U.S.-Soviet). Some stay in effect indefinitely; others have a limited term.

In the 1960s, the U.S. and the Soviet Union began to use arms control agreements to regulate their relations. They gained confidence that they could do business with each other from these agreements and that they would not let the arms race lead them into a nuclear war—fear of which had increased after the Cuban Missile Crisis of 1962. Nuclear arms control talks and agreements did not stop either superpower from developing any weapon it wanted, but did *manage* the arms race and bring about a convergence of expectations about its structure.

For example, the first agreements, in the 1960s, banned activities that both sides could easily live without—testing nuclear weapons in the atmosphere and putting nuclear weapons in space. The Non-Proliferation Treaty (1968) built on the superpowers' common fears of China and other potential new nuclear states. Other confidence-building measures were directed at the management of potential crises. The hot-line agreement connected U.S. and Soviet heads of state by telephone. A later agreement on incidents at sea provided for efforts to control escalation after a hostile encounter or accident on the high seas. Eventually, the superpowers developed centres and systems for the exchange of information in a crisis.

Several treaties in the 1970s locked in the superpowers' basic parity in nuclear capabilities under MAD. The 1972 **Anti-Ballistic Missile (ABM) Treaty** prevented either side from using a ballistic missile defence as a shield from which to launch a first strike. However, as more states acquired ballistic missiles (see p. 211), the United States decided to try to develop a defensive system against them. To allow full-scale testing of missile-defence technologies, the United States withdrew from the ABM Treaty with six months' notice (as provided for in the treaty itself), effective mid-2002. President Bush called the treaty a relic of the Cold War, but critics called U.S. missile defence a costly blunder that could induce China to greatly enlarge its minimal nuclear arsenal (which in turn could accelerate India's nuclear weapons production, and thus Pakistan's as well).

Anti-Ballistic Missile (ABM) Treaty (1972) Treaty that prohibited the United States and the Soviet Union from using a ballistic missile defence as a shield, a tactic that would have undermined mutually assured destruction and the basis of deterrence. See also *mutually assured destruction (MAD)* and *Strategic Defense Initiative (SDI)*.

---

[32] Emanuel Adler, ed., *The International Practice of Arms Control* (Baltimore: Johns Hopkins UP, 1992).

Strategic Arms Limitation Treaties (SALT) SALT I (1972) and SALT II (1979) put formal ceilings on the growth of U.S. and Soviet strategic weapons. SALT II was never ratified by the U.S. Senate (due to the subsequent Soviet invasion of Afghanistan).

Intermediate Nuclear Forces (INF) Treaty (1987) Treaty that banned an entire class of missiles that both the Soviet Union and the United States had deployed in Europe.

Strategic Arms Reduction Treaties (START) START I (1991) called for a reduction in the superpowers' strategic arsenals by about 30 percent. START II (1992) proposes to cut the remaining weapons by more than half in the next decade. START III is under discussion.

Comprehensive Test Ban Treaty (CTBT) (1996) Treaty that bans all nuclear weapons testing, thereby broadening the ban on atmospheric testing negotiated in 1963.

The **Strategic Arms Limitation Treaties (SALT)** put formal ceilings on the growth of both sides' strategic weapons. SALT I was signed in 1972 and SALT II in 1979—but SALT II was never ratified by the U.S. Senate (due to the subsequent Soviet invasion of Afghanistan). The U.S. arsenal peaked in the 1960s at more than 30 000 warheads; the Soviet arsenal peaked in the 1980s at more than 40 000.

More recent arms control agreements regulated a substantial reduction of nuclear forces after the end of the Cold War.[33] The **Intermediate Nuclear Forces (INF) Treaty** of 1987 banned an entire class of missiles that the superpowers had deployed in Europe—for the first time actually reducing nuclear forces instead of just limiting their growth. The 1991 **Strategic Arms Reduction Treaty (START I),** which took a decade to negotiate, called for a reduction in the superpowers' strategic arsenals by about 30 percent.[34] The final START I milestone was reached in 2001 as both sides reduced strategic nuclear weapons to below 6000. In 2002 they agreed on future cuts. Meanwhile, the 1992 START II treaty was negotiated in less than a year, but not ratified by Russia's parliament until eight years later. Under the U.S.-Russian Strategic Offensive Reductions Treaty, each side is to reduce deployed warheads from about 6000 to 2200 within a decade. (These reductions are in addition to the elimination of most tactical nuclear weapons.) The INF and START treaties provide for strict verification, including on-site inspection of facilities in the other side's nuclear complex. When coupled with satellite reconnaissance, these agreements create considerable transparency in nuclear matters.

A **Comprehensive Test Ban Treaty (CTBT)** to halt all nuclear test explosions was signed in 1996 after decades of stalemate. It aims to impede the development of new types of nuclear weapons. Technological advances—in the design of weapons (without needing to actually explode one) and in verifying that no tests are occurring—overcame the previous reluctance of the great powers to undertake this step. However, the treaty does not take effect until signed and ratified by all 44 states believed capable of building at least a crude nuclear weapon. India did not sign the CTBT, and defied it in 1998 with five nuclear tests. Pakistan followed suit with its own tests. The U.S. Senate voted in 1999 against ratifying the CTBT, and the Bush administration opposes it. Russia ratified it in 2000.

Nuclear arsenals may be further reduced in the coming years. Perhaps Russia and the United States will find they need no more than the several hundred nuclear weapons in the arsenals of other great powers—Britain, France and China. These arsenals provide a credible second-strike capability. Whether nuclear weapons can be eliminated altogether is a more difficult question, because in a nuclear-free world a handful of weapons of mass destruction might become all-powerful.

Another convention aimed at the elimination of weapons of mass destruction is the Convention on the Prohibition of the Development, Production and Stockpiling of Bacteriological (Biological) and Toxin Weapons and on Their Destruction, signed in 1972, which came into effect in 1975. Signatories to the Convention undertake never to develop, produce, stockpile or otherwise acquire or retain biological or chemical weapons. Canada was an early signatory to the convention and has been actively involved in

---

[33] Bennett Ramberg, ed., *Arms Control without Negotiation: From the Cold War to the New World Order* (Boulder, CO: Rienner, 1993). Michele A. Flournoy, ed., *Nuclear Weapons after the Cold War: Guidelines for U.S. Policy* (NY: HarperCollins, 1993). Charles L. Glaser, "Nuclear Policy without an Adversary: U.S. Planning for the Post-Soviet Era," *International Security* 16.4 (1992): 34–78.

[34] Spec. issue on START, *Bulletin of the Atomic Scientists* 47.9 (1991): 12–40. Brian Frederking, *Resolving Security Dilemmas: A Constructivist Explanation of the INF Treaty* (Burlington, VT: Ashgate, 2000).

attempting to strengthen its effectiveness, in one small part by producing a website devoted to disseminating official information about the Convention to the widest possible audience (http://www.opbw.org).

Arms control efforts outside the area of nuclear weapons have had mixed success. For decades, NATO and Warsaw Pact countries carried out Mutual and Balanced Force Reduction (MBFR) talks aimed at limiting conventional military forces in Europe. The **Conventional Forces in Europe (CFE) Treaty** was not signed until the last years of the Cold War, and within two years it was virtually obsolete. The signatories have kept the treaty in effect as a guard against any future arms buildup in Europe, but have relaxed limits on Russian forces deployed near southern Russia, a new conflict zone.

Efforts to control the conventional arms trade through arms control treaties have been largely unsuccessful. After the Gulf War, the five permanent Security Council members tried to negotiate limits on the supply of weapons to the Middle East. The five participants account for most of the weapons sold in the Middle East, but no participant wanted to give up its own lucrative arms sales in the region, which each naturally saw as justified. At this point, no formal treaty has been developed to control the arms trade, but numerous countries have participated in the UN Programme of Action to Prevent, Combat and Eradicate the Illicit Trade in Small Arms and Light Weapons in All Its Aspects.

The Convention on Prohibitions or Restrictions on the Use of Certain Conventional Weapons Which May Be Deemed to Be Excessively Injurious or to Have Indiscriminate Effects, also known as the Certain Conventional Weapons Convention (CCW) or the Inhumane Weapons Convention, was signed in 1980 and came into effect in 1983. It involves weapons that leave undetectable fragments in the human body, mines, booby-traps, incendiary weapons, blinding laser weapons and explosive remnants of war. As of 2004, only 94 states, including Canada, were parties to the convention.

As discussed in Chapter 5, Canada was the lead state in achieving a Convention to Ban Anti-Personnel Landmines, signed in 1997. The Anti-Personnel Landmines Ban imparts a stronger set of restrictions for weapons previously covered in the CCW, and is aimed at eliminating the use, stockpiling, production and transfer of anti-personnel landmines.

Many of the disarmament treaties noted above are "deposited" with the United Nations, which means that the secretary-general is charged with overseeing new signatories, ratifications and implementation. The UN also usually organizes or helps to organize review conferences and meetings for each convention. The Department of Disarmament Affairs is the body within the United Nations most involved in this work.

Conventional Forces in Europe (CFE) Treaty (1990) A U.S.-Soviet agreement that provided for asymmetrical reductions in Soviet forces in Europe and limited the forces of both sides.

Enforcement of International Law

Although the sources of international law distinguish it from national law, an even greater difference exists as to the *enforcement* of the two types of law. International law is much more difficult to enforce. There is no world police force. Enforcement of international law depends on the power of states themselves, individually or collectively, to punish transgressors.

Enforcement of international law depends heavily on practical reciprocity (see pp. 81–82). States follow international law most of the time because they want other states to do so. The reason no chemical weapons were used in World War II was not because anyone could *enforce* the treaty banning use of such weapons. It was because the other side would probably respond by using chemical weapons, too, and the costs would be high to both sides. International law recognizes in certain circumstances the legitimacy of *reprisals*: actions that would have been illegal under international law may sometimes be legal if taken in response to the illegal actions of another state.

States also follow international law because of the general or long-term costs that could result from disregarding it (rather than just immediate retaliation). If a state fails to pay its debts, it will not be able to borrow money on world markets. If it cheats on the terms of treaties it signs, other states will not sign future treaties with it. The resulting isolation could be very costly.

A state that breaks international law may also face a collective response by a group of states, such as the imposition of *sanctions*—agreements among other states to stop trading with the violator or to stop some particular commodity trade (most often military goods) as punishment for its violation. Over time, a sanctioned state can become a *pariah* in a community of nations, cut off from normal relations with others. This is very costly in today's world, when economic well-being everywhere depends on trade and economic exchange in world markets. Libya, for example, suffered from its isolated status in the international community for decades, and decided in late 2003 to make a clean break and regain normal status. Libya admitted responsibility for past terrorism, began to compensate victims and agreed to disclose and dismantle its nuclear, chemical and biological weapons programs.

Even the world's superpower constrains its behaviour, at least some of the time, to adhere to international law. For example, in late 2002 a North Korean freighter was caught en route to Yemen with a hidden load of 15 Scud missiles. The United States had an evident national interest in preventing such proliferation, and had the power to prevent it, but when U.S. government lawyers determined that the shipment did not violate international law, the United States backed off and let the delivery continue.

International law enforcement through reciprocity and collective response has one great weakness—it depends entirely on national power. Reciprocity works only if the aggrieved state has the power to inflict costs on the violator. Collective response works only if the collective cares enough about an issue to respond. Thus, it is relatively easy to cheat on small issues (or to get away with major violations if one has enough power).

If international law extends only as far as power reaches, what good is it? The answer lies in the uncertainties of power (see Chapter 2). Without common expectations regarding the rules of the game and adherence to those rules most of the time by most actors, power alone would create great instability in the anarchic international system. International law, even without perfect enforcement, creates expectations about what constitutes legal behaviour by states. Because violations or divergences from those expectations stand out, it is easier to identify and punish states that deviate from accepted rules. When states agree to the rules by signing treaties (such as the UN Charter), violations become more visible and clearly illegitimate. In most cases, although power continues to reside in states, international law establishes workable rules for those states to follow. The resulting stability is so beneficial that usually the costs of breaking the rules outweigh the short-term benefits that could be gained from such violations.

The World Court

World Court (International Court of Justice) The judicial arm of the UN; located in The Hague, it hears only cases between states.

As international law has developed, a general world legal framework in which states can pursue grievances against each other has begun to take shape. The rudiments of such a system now exist in the **World Court** (formally called the **International Court of Justice**), although its jurisdiction is limited and its caseload is light.[35] The World Court is a branch of the UN.

---

[35] Richard Falk, *Reviving the World Court* (Charlottesville: U Virginia P, 1986). Keith Highet, "The Peace Palace Heats Up: The World Court in Business Again?" *American Journal of International Law* 85.4 (1991): 646–54.

Only states, not individuals or businesses, can sue or be sued in the World Court. When one state has a grievance against another, it can take the case to the World Court for an impartial hearing. The Security Council or General Assembly may also request advisory court opinions on matters of international law.

The World Court is a panel of 15 judges elected for nine-year terms (five judges every three years) by a majority of both the Security Council and General Assembly. The court meets in The Hague, Netherlands. It is customary for permanent members of the Security Council to have one of their nationals as a judge at all times. Ad hoc judges may be added to the 15 if a party to a case does not have one of its nationals as a judge.

ALL RISE
The World Court hears international disputes but has little power to enforce judgments. Here, in 2004, judges rule in favour of Mexico's complaint that the U.S. death penalty against Mexican citizens violated a 1963 treaty.

The great *weakness* of the World Court is that states have not comprehensively agreed to subject themselves to its jurisdiction or to obey its decisions. Almost all states have signed the treaty creating the court, but only about a third have signed the *optional clause* in the treaty agreeing to give the court jurisdiction in certain cases—and many of those signatories have added their own stipulations reserving their rights and limiting the degree to which the court can infringe on national sovereignty. The United States withdrew from the optional clause when it was sued by Nicaragua in 1986 (over the CIA's mining of Nicaraguan harbours).[36] Similarly, Iran refused to acknowledge the jurisdiction of the court when sued by the United States in 1979 over its seizure of the U.S. embassy in Iran. In such a case, the court may hear the case anyway, and usually rules in favour of the participating side—but has no means to enforce the ruling. Justice can move slowly: in 2006, the court began hearing Bosnia's case accusing Serbia of genocide, after some 13 years of preliminary manoeuvring.

In one of its most notable successes, the World Court settled a complex border dispute between El Salvador and Honduras in 1992. By mutual agreement in 1986, the two states had asked the court to settle territorial disputes along six stretches of border, three islands and territorial waters. The disputes dated from 1861 and had led to a war in 1969. The World Court drew borders that gave about two-thirds of the total land to Honduras and split the territorial waters between both countries and Nicaragua. Both countries abided by the decision. In 2002, the World Court settled a long-standing and sometimes violent dispute over an oil-rich peninsula on the Cameroon-Nigeria border, giving ownership to Cameroon, and Nigeria (which is more powerful) pulled troops out in 2006. In 2004, the World Court ruled that Israel's 700-kilometre-long security barrier in

[36] David P. Forsythe, *The Politics of International Law: U.S. Foreign Policy Reconsidered* (Boulder, CO: Rienner, 1990).

the West Bank was a violation of international law and that parts of it should be torn down. Israel quickly declared that it would disregard the ruling.

Today an important use of the World Court is to arbitrate issues of secondary importance between countries with friendly overall relations. The court has settled commercial disputes between Canada and the U.S., for example. Because security interests are not at stake, and because the overall friendly relations are more important than the particular issue, states have been willing to submit to the court's jurisdiction in these kinds of decisions.

There are other international forums for the arbitration of grievances (by mutual consent). Some regional courts, notably in Europe, resemble the World Court in function. Various bodies are capable of conducting arbitration—as when Israel and Egypt submitted their dispute about the tiny territory of Taba to binding arbitration after failing to reach a settlement. Arbitration can remove domestic political pressures from state leaders by taking decisions out of their hands. But for major disputes involving issues of great importance to states, there is still little effective international legal apparatus.

Because of the difficulty of winning enforceable agreements on major conflicts through the World Court, states have used the court infrequently over the years: between 1947 and 2007 only 136 cases were entered into its general case list and 24 advisory opinions sought. In mid-2007, 12 cases were pending and two were in the process of being heard.

International Cases in National Courts

Most legal cases concerning international matters—whether brought by governments or private individuals or companies—remain entirely within the legal systems of one or more states. National courts hear cases brought under national laws and can enforce judgments by collecting damages (in civil suits) or imposing punishments (in criminal ones).

A party with a dispute that crosses national boundaries gains several advantages by pursuing the matter through the national courts of one or more of the relevant states, rather than through international channels. First, judgments are enforceable. The party that wins a lawsuit in a national court can collect from the other party's assets within the state. Second, individuals and companies can pursue legal complaints through national courts (as can subnational governmental bodies), whereas in most areas of international law, states must themselves bring suits on behalf of their citizens. (In truth, even national governments pursue most of their legal actions against each other through national courts.)

Third, there is often a choice of more than one state within which a case could legally be heard; one can pick the legal system most favourable to one's case. It is up to each state's court system to decide whether it has *jurisdiction* in a case (the right to hear it), and courts tend to extend their own authority with a broad interpretation. Traditionally, a national court may hear cases concerning any activity on its national territory, any actions of its own citizens anywhere in the world and actions taken toward its citizens elsewhere in the world. Noncitizens can use the national courts to enforce damages against citizens, because the national court has authority to impose fines and, if necessary, seize bank accounts and property.

The United States is a favourite jurisdiction within which to bring cases for two reasons. First, U.S. juries have a reputation of awarding bigger settlements in lawsuits than juries elsewhere in the world (likely because the United States is a rich country). Second, because many people and governments do business in the United States, it is often possible to collect damages awarded by a U.S. court. For these reasons, in recent years U.S. courts have ruled on human-rights cases brought by Chinese dissidents over the 1989 Tiananmen massacre, Cuban exiles against the Cuban government and a Paraguayan doctor suing a Paraguayan police official for torturing the doctor's son. Human rights activists have used U.S. laws against companies dealing with repressive governments, as when they sued U.S. oil companies Exxon Mobil and Unocal for aiding abusive regimes. The rapid extension of U.S. legal jurisdiction may bring a reciprocal response from European (and other) states, which may seek on occasion to extend their national laws to U.S. shores.[37]

Belgium's national courts have also become a favourite venue for international human rights cases, as a result of a 1993 law that gives Belgian courts jurisdiction over any violation of the Geneva Convention. In 2001, four people accused of war crimes in Rwanda in 1994 were sent to prison by a Belgian jury. Canada has also laid charges against an individual suspected of involvement in the Rwandan genocide. Under Canada's new Crimes Against Humanity and War Crimes Act, Canadian authorities arrested Desire Munyaneza and laid seven indictments, including charges of genocide, war crimes and crimes against humanity. As of October 2007 his Canadian trial was ongoing.

There are important limits to the use of national courts to resolve international disputes, however. Most important is that the authority of national courts stops at a state's borders, where sovereignty ends. A court in Zambia cannot compel a resident of Thailand to testify; it cannot authorize the seizure of a British bank account to pay damages; it cannot arrest a criminal suspect (Zambian or foreigner) except on Zambian soil. To take such actions beyond national borders, states must persuade other states to cooperate.

To bring a person outside a state's territory to trial, that state's government must ask a second government to arrest the person on the second state's territory and hand him or her over for trial. *Extradition* is a matter of international law because it is a legal treaty arrangement *between* states. If no such treaty exists, the individual generally remains immune from a state's courts by staying off its territory. Canada does not usually extradite suspects to countries in which they would face the death penalty, such as the United States (but will do so if agreement can be secured that the death penalty will not be imposed in a finding of guilt).

In one high-profile debate about extradition, the former Chilean military dictator Augusto Pinochet was arrested in England in 1999 on a Spanish warrant, based on crimes committed against Spanish citizens in Chile during his rule. His supporters claimed he should have immunity for acts taken as head of state, but since he was not an accredited diplomat in England (where he had gone to seek medical treatment), and was no longer head of state, British courts held him on Spain's request to extradite him for trial. Once on British soil without current diplomatic immunity, Pinochet was subject to British law, including its extradition treaties. However, the British government eventually let him return to Chile, citing his medical condition, and a Chilean court suspended his case on health grounds. He died in 2006 without standing trial.

There are many grey areas in the jurisdiction of national courts over foreigners. If a government can lure a suspect onto the high seas, it can nab the person without violating another country's territoriality. More troublesome are cases in which a government obtains a foreign citizen from a foreign country for trial without going through extradition procedures. In a famous case in the 1980s, a Mexican doctor was wanted by U.S. authorities for allegedly participating in the torture and murder of a U.S. drug agent in Mexico. The U.S. government paid a group of bounty hunters to kidnap the doctor in Mexico, carry him forcibly across the border and deliver him to the custody of U.S. courts. The U.S. Supreme Court gave U.S. courts jurisdiction in the case despite the kidnapping. The doctor himself

---

[37] William Glaberson, "U.S. Courts Become Arbiters of Global Rights and Wrongs around the World, *New York Times* 21 June 2001: A1.

eventually returned home after the case was thrown out for lack of evidence. In late 2004, Colombia arranged the abduction of a leading Colombian rebel living in Venezuela, provoking Venezuelan protests about the violation of sovereignty.

Since 2001, the war on terrorism has expanded international legal and law-enforcement cooperation, but with sometimes quite controversial results. The 2002 Maher Arar case in which a dual (Canadian-Syrian) citizen was arrested while travelling through the U.S. and deported to Syria where he was subject to torture has brought attention to this issue in Canada (see Chapter 5, p. 155). Arar was cleared in Canada, and awarded damages in 2006 as a result of Canada's role in supplying inaccurate intelligence information to U.S. authorities, information that had precipitated his arrest and deportation to Syria. However, the U.S. continued to include Arar on a travel watch list in 2007, barring his travel to the U.S.

immigration law National laws that establish the conditions under which foreigners may travel within a state's territory, work within the state and become citizens of the state (naturalization).

The principle of territoriality also governs **immigration law.** When a person crosses a border into a new country, the decision about whether he or she can remain there, and under what conditions, is up to the new state. The state of origin cannot compel his or her return. National laws establish conditions by which foreigners can travel within a state's territory, work within the state and become citizens of the state (*naturalization*). Many other legal issues are raised by people travelling or living outside their own country—passports and visas, babies born in foreign countries, marriages to foreign nationals, bank accounts, businesses, taxes and so forth. Practices vary from country to country, but the general principle is that *national laws prevail on the territory of a state*.

Despite the continued importance of national court systems in international legal affairs and the lack of enforcement powers of the World Court, it would be wrong to conclude that state sovereignty is supreme and international law impotent. Rather, there is a balance of sovereignty and law in international interactions.

LAW AND SOVEREIGNTY

The remainder of this chapter discusses specific areas of international law, from the most firmly rooted and widely respected to newer and less-established areas. In each area, the influence of law and norms runs counter to the unimpeded exercise of state sovereignty. This struggle becomes more intense as one shifts focus from long-standing traditions of diplomatic law to recent norms governing human rights.

Laws of Diplomacy

diplomatic recognition The process by which the status of embassies and that of an ambassador as an official state representative are explicitly defined.

The status of embassies and of an ambassador as an official state representative is explicitly defined in the process of **diplomatic recognition.** Diplomats are *accredited* to each other's governments (they present "credentials"), and thereafter the individuals so defined enjoy certain rights and protections as foreign diplomats in the host country.

Diplomats have the right to occupy an *embassy* in the host country as though it were their own state's territory. On the grounds of the Canadian embassy in Kuwait, for instance, the laws of Canada, and not those of Kuwait, apply. Members of the Canadian Forces, RCMP or military police occupy the embassy compound as though it were Canadian territory, and those of Kuwait may not enter without permission. This principle of international law explains why, when Iraq invaded Kuwait in 1990, it did not set foot inside most foreign embassy compounds even though it could have overrun them easily. Despite Iraq's claim that since Kuwait no longer existed, its embassies no longer enjoyed diplomatic status, it was not willing to press the point.

A flagrant violation of the sanctity of embassies occurred in Iran after Islamic revolutionaries took power in 1979. Iranian students seized and occupied the U.S. embassy compound, holding U.S. diplomats hostage for more than a year. The Iranian government did not directly commit this act but did condone it and refused to force the students out of the embassy. (Host countries are expected, if necessary, to use force against their own citizens to protect a foreign embassy.) Six American embassy staff escaped the compound as it was being seized and were hidden at the Canadian embassy by Ambassador Ken Taylor until fake passports could be obtained to spirit the Americans safely out of Iran.

Diplomats enjoy **diplomatic immunity** even when they leave the embassy grounds. The right to travel varies from one country to another; diplomats may be restricted to one city or free to roam about the countryside. Diplomats stand apart from all foreign nationals in that they are beyond the jurisdiction of the host country's

AGAINST THE LAW
International law prohibits attacks on diplomats. This fundamental principle, like others in international law, can ultimately be enforced only by applying the power of other states (through such leverage as imposing economic sanctions, freezing relations or threatening military force). Pictured here are U.S. diplomats on their first day as hostages in the U.S. embassy in Tehran, Iran, 1979.

national courts. If they commit crimes, from jaywalking to murder, they may not be arrested and tried. The host country's only recourse is to take away a diplomat's accreditation and *expel* the person from the host country. However, strong countries can sometimes pressure weaker ones to lift immunity so that a diplomat may face trial for a crime. This happened twice in 1997, when the United States and France were allowed to prosecute diplomats from Georgia and Zaire, respectively, for reckless driving that killed children. By contrast, a Russian diplomat, allegedly driving drunk, struck two pedestrians in Ottawa in 2001, killing one of them. Despite local and national outrage over the incident, the diplomat quickly invoked his diplomatic immunity and returned to Russia, where he was tried in a Russian court.

U.S. commitments as host country to the UN include extending diplomatic immunity to diplomats accredited to the UN. UN delegates thus cannot be prosecuted under U.S. law. Given this immunity, delegates simply tear up thousands of parking tickets each year, for example. Occasionally, UN representatives are accused of more serious crimes (murder, in one case in the 1980s), but they cannot be brought to trial in the United States unless they or their country of origin agree to waive their diplomatic immunity.

Because of diplomatic immunity, it is common to conduct espionage activities out of an embassy through the diplomatic corps. Spies are often posted to low-level positions in embassies, such as cultural attaché, press liaison or military attaché. If the host country catches them spying, it cannot prosecute them, so it merely expels

diplomatic immunity Refers to diplomats' activity being outside the jurisdiction of the host country's national courts.

them. Diplomatic norms (though not law) call for politeness when expelling spies; the standard reason given is "for activities not consistent with his/her diplomatic status." If a spy operates under cover of being a businessperson or tourist, then no immunity applies: the person can be arrested and prosecuted under the host country's laws.

A *diplomatic pouch* is a package sent between an embassy and its home country. As the name implies, diplomatic pouches began historically as small and occasional shipments, but today there is a large and steady volume of such shipments all over the world. Diplomatic pouches, too, enjoy the status of home country territoriality: they cannot be opened, searched or confiscated by a host country. Although we do not know how much mischief goes on in diplomatic pouches (due to their secrecy), it is safe to assume that illicit goods such as guns and drugs regularly find their way across borders in this way.

To *break diplomatic relations* means to withdraw one's diplomats from a foreign state and expel foreign diplomats from one's home state. This tactic is used to show displeasure with another government; it is a refusal to do business as usual. When a revolutionary government comes into power, some countries may withdraw recognition—as the U.S. did after the Cuban revolution of 1959. Canada, by contrast, maintained diplomatic relations with Cuba and continues to do so. Most activity regarding diplomatic recognition today occurs when small states recognize Taiwan diplomatically, are subsequently pressured by China and occasionally withdraw recognition.

When two countries lack diplomatic relations, they often do business through a third country willing to represent a country's interests formally through its own embassy. This is called an *interests section* in the third country's embassy. Thus, the practical needs of diplomacy can overcome a formal lack of relations between states. For instance, U.S. interests are represented by the Swiss embassy in Cuba, and Cuban interests are represented by the Swiss embassy in the United States. In practice, these interests sections are located in the U.S. and Cuban embassies and staffed with U.S. and Cuban diplomats.

States register lower levels of displeasure by *recalling their ambassadors* home for some period of time; diplomatic norms call for a trip home "for consultations" even when everyone knows the purpose is to signal annoyance. Milder still is the expression of displeasure by a *formal complaint*. Usually the complaining government does so in its own capital city, to the other's ambassador.

The law of diplomacy is repeatedly violated in one context—terrorism (see pp. 203–207). Because the sanctity of diplomats is so important to states, diplomats make a tempting target for terrorists, and because terrorist groups do not enjoy the benefits of diplomatic law (as states do), they are willing to break diplomatic norms and laws. An attack on diplomats or embassies is an attack on the territory of the state itself—yet can be carried out far from the state's home territory. Being a diplomat has become a dangerous occupation, and many have been killed in recent decades. In 1998, the U.S. embassies in Kenya and Tanzania were bombed, killing more than 200 people, most of whom were local employees of the embassies. Individuals and groups may stage demonstrations in front of embassies to protest that state's policies. These demonstrations can be peaceful but can also become quite violent. In 2003 demonstrators at Thailand's embassy in Cambodia set the embassy ablaze in response to disputes over Cambodia's Angkor Wat temples. Also in 2003, four individuals set themselves on fire on the steps of the French embassy in London to protest the arrests of 150 members of an Iranian opposition group in Paris.

Just War Doctrine

After the law of diplomacy, international law regarding war is one of the most developed areas of international law. Laws concerning war are divided into two areas— *jus ad bellum*, laws *of* war (when is war permissible) and *jus in bello*, laws *in* war (how wars are fought).[38]

International law distinguishes **just wars** (which are legal) from wars of aggression (which are illegal). This area of law grows out of centuries-old religious writings about just wars (which once could be enforced by threats to excommunicate individuals from the church). Today, the legality of war is defined by the UN Charter, which outlaws aggression. Above and beyond the legal standing of the just war doctrine, it has become a strong international norm; not one followed by all states but an important part of the modern intellectual tradition governing matters of war and peace that evolved in Europe.[39]

The idea of aggression, around which the doctrine of just war evolved, is based on a violation of the sovereignty and territorial integrity of states. It assumes recognized borders that are legally inviolable. *Aggression* refers to a state's use of force, or the imminent threat to do so, against another state's territory or sovereignty—unless the use of force is in response to aggression. Tanks swarming across a border constitute aggression, but so do tanks massing at a border if their state has threatened to invade. The lines are somewhat fuzzy, but for a threat to constitute aggression (and justify the use of force in response) it must be a clear threat of using force, not just a hostile policy or general rivalry.

States have the right to respond to aggression in the only manner thought to be reliable— military force. Just war doctrine is not based on nonviolence. Responses can include both the *repelling* of the attack itself and the *punishment* of the aggressor. Responses may come from the victim of aggression or from other states not directly affected—as a way of maintaining the norm of nonaggression in the international system. The collective actions of UN members against Iraq after its 1990 invasion of Kuwait are a classic case of such a response.

Response to aggression is the only allowable use of military force according to just war doctrine. The just war approach thus explicitly rules out war as an instrument to change another state's government or policies, or in ethnic and religious conflicts. In fact, the UN Charter makes no provision for "war" but rather for "international police actions" against aggressors. The analogy is with law and order in a national society, enforced by police when necessary. Because only aggression justifies military force, if all states obeyed the law against aggression there would be no international war.

Just war doctrine has been undermined, even more seriously than have laws of war crimes, by the changing nature of warfare.[40] In civil wars and low-intensity conflicts, belligerents range from poorly organized militias to national armies, and the battleground is often a patchwork of enclaves and positions with no clear front lines (much less borders). It is harder to identify an aggressor in such situations than in traditional warfare, and harder to balance the relative merits of peace and justice.

just war doctrine A branch of international law and political theory that defines when wars can be justly started (*jus ad bellum*) and how they can be justly fought (*jus in bello*). See also *war crimes*.

---

[38] Michael Howard, George J. Andreopoulos and Mark R. Shulman, eds., *The Laws of War: Constraints on Warfare in the Western World* (New Haven, CT: Yale UP, 1994). Geoffrey Best, *War and Law since 1945* (NY: Oxford UP, 1994).

[39] Michael Walzer, *Just and Unjust Wars: A Moral Argument with Historical Illustrations*, 2nd ed. (NY: Basic, 1992). *Twenty Years of Just and Unjust Wars* [symposium with articles by Michael Joseph Smith, David C. Hendrickson, Theodore J. Koontz and Joseph Boyle], *Ethics & International Affairs* 11 (1997): 3–104.

[40] James Turner Johnson, *Can Modern War Be Just?* (New Haven, CT: Yale UP, 1984). Another change in the nature of warfare is the development of nuclear weapons. It is generally recognized that nuclear war could not be an adequate response to aggression. Thus, the use of nuclear weapons could never be just in the view of most scholars of the subject. Some scholars of just war theory argue that it is not just even to possess such weapons.

For a war to be *morally* just, it must be more than a response to aggression; it must be waged for the *purpose* of responding to aggression. The *intent* must be just. A state may not take advantage of another's aggression to wage a war that is essentially aggressive. Although the U.S.-led war effort to oust Iraq from Kuwait in 1990 was certainly a response to aggression, critics found the justness of the war to be compromised by U.S. interest in obtaining cheap oil from the Middle East—not an allowable reason for waging war.

War Crimes

war crimes Violations of the law governing the conduct of warfare, such as mistreating prisoners of war or unnecessarily targeting civilians. See also *just war doctrine*.

Laws *of* war focus on whether a war is justified, but tell us little about what goes on during the conduct of the war itself, which is the domain of laws *in* war or *jus in bello*. Large-scale abuses of human rights regularly occur during the conduct of war. Serious violations of this kind are considered **war crimes.** The Roman politician Cicero once said, "Laws are silent in time of war."[41] However, this is no longer true. In wartime, international law is especially difficult to enforce, but there are extensive norms of legal conduct that are widely followed. After a war, losers can be punished for violations of the laws of war (war crimes).

Laws concerning crimes committed during the conduct of war date back to the Nuremberg trials. Beyond the war crimes committed by German officers were their acts of *genocide* (attempts to exterminate a whole people) in which close to ten million civilians were killed in death camps. Clearly this ranked among the most terrible crimes ever committed, yet it did not violate either international law or German law. The solution was to create a new category of legal offences— **crimes against humanity**—under which those responsible were punished.

crimes against humanity A category of legal offences created at the Nuremberg trials after World War II to encompass genocide and other acts committed by the political and military leaders of the Third Reich (Nazi Germany). See also *dehumanization* and *genocide*.

In the 1990s, for the first time since World War II, the UN Security Council authorized an international war crimes tribunal, directed against war crimes in the former Yugoslavia. Similar tribunals were later established for genocide in Rwanda and Sierra Leone.[42] The tribunal on the former Yugoslavia, headquartered in The Hague, Netherlands, issued indictments against the top Bosnian Serb leaders and other Serbian and Croatian officers, and in 1999 against Serbian leader Slobodan Milosevic during the expulsion of Albanians from Kosovo. The tribunal was hampered by lack of funding and by its lack of power to arrest suspects who enjoyed the protection of Serbia and Croatia. In 1999, a newly elected Croatian government began to cooperate with the tribunal, and after Milosevic lost power in Serbia, the new Serbian government turned him over to the tribunal in 2001. He died in custody in 2006. In late 2004 and early 2005, six suspects from all sides of the conflict surrendered to the Hague tribunal for trial.

Following the civil war in Sierra Leone, that country's government has run a war crimes tribunal jointly with the UN. In 2003, it indicted the sitting state leader in neighbouring Liberia, Charles Taylor, for his role in the war's extreme brutality. He fled for Nigeria shortly afterward but was captured and turned over to the tribunal for trial in 2006.

International Criminal Court (ICC) Permanent tribunal for war crimes and crimes against humanity.

Following the UN tribunals on former Yugoslavia and Rwanda, 120 of the world's states signed the Rome Statute in 1998 to create a permanent **International Criminal Court (ICC).** This is the first treaty-based court ever established, and it will hear cases of genocide, war crimes and crimes against humanity from anywhere in the world. The statute called for the establishment of the court upon ratification by 60 signatory states,

---

[41] Pro Milone Cicero, *The Speeches of Cicero,* ed. and trans. N. H. Watts (Cambridge, MA: Harvard UP, 1931). See also Richard Falk, Irene Gendzier and Robert Jay Lifton, eds., *Crimes of War: Iraq* (NY: Nation, 2006).

[42] Gary Jonathan Bass, *Stay the Hand of Vengeance: The Politics of War Crimes Tribunals* (Princeton, NJ: Princeton UP, 2000).

which occurred in 2002. The court is in The Hague in the Netherlands, and is currently functional with 18 judges from around the world.

Canada played a pivotal role in the creation of the ICC, having chaired a coalition of states involved in motivating ratification of the Rome Statute and providing funding for state representatives from poorer states, along with NGO representatives, to participate in the ICC process. The current president of the court is also a Canadian, Judge Philippe Kirsch. Some countries, like the United States, have not ratified the Rome Statute and are opposed to the court primarily because it infringes on sovereignty. The United States has also expressed opposition because the ICC might someday prosecute U.S. soldiers. The ICC issued its first arrest warrants in 2005, arising from the long civil war in Uganda,

⊕ Thinking Theoretically

The United Nations Security Council can invoke Chapter 7 of the UN Charter to launch a peace enforcement mission in situations deemed to be a threat to international peace and security. Chapter 7 missions were launched only once during the Cold War (in Korea). Since 1989, the Security Council has interpreted "threats to the peace" quite broadly, and has authorized missions under Chapter 7 in the 1991 Gulf War, and to Somalia, Rwanda, Haiti, East Timor, Democratic Republic of the Congo, Sierra Leone and Côte d'Ivoire. What might account for the dramatic increase in Chapter 7 missions?

A realist interpretation would likely focus on tensions between the Soviet Union and the United States during the Cold War, which played out in the Security Council. Both used their vetoes to prevent any mission seen to impact on their interests. Thus the Security Council was held hostage to a great-power conflict, but once that conflict dissipated the Security Council was able to do its work. For realists, state representatives to the Security Council will act based on a calculation of their own national interest before any global interest. Members of the Security Council can now agree to deploy Chapter 7 missions because they do not, at this time, see those missions as threatening their own national interests. This means that if tensions emerge in future between any of the permanent members, or if any single member decides that supporting the UN is not in its interests, the Security Council's work could once again be slowed or effectively stopped.

A liberal might focus instead on the emergence of new international norms concerning human rights and humanitarian intervention. By this view, human rights advocates have, until recently, been limited to strategies of persuasion or the "shaming" of human rights abusers. Increasingly, states, individuals, human rights NGOs and international organizations such as the UN have demanded that more be done, especially in the face of systematic atrocities. The Security Council's greater willingness to use Chapter 7, by this view, reflects a greater willingness to use force to prevent genocide, slaughter and crimes against humanity. For some liberals, this represents a new era in human rights, in which military enforcement, alongside the use of judicial entities such as the International Criminal Court, will strengthen and give more meaning to the human rights regime. The more habitual such activities become, the greater legitimacy they will have and the harder it will be for states to ignore them.

For critical theorists, it is worth investigating the arguments used to authorize any intervention, including the current proliferation of Chapter 7 missions. By this view, imperialism was justified in part through the narratives told about "backward third world peoples" desperately in need of the civilizing missions of colonialism. Colonizers were depicted as superior, indigenous people as barely human. Once understood in this way, the military, economic, cultural and social domination of colonized lands and peoples was seen as justified. Critical theorists would argue that many of the same narratives are being deployed to justify current interventions: the international community is understood as the heroic saviour coming to the rescue of poor helpless victims trapped in conflict-prone third world countries. Salvation comes in the form of Western systems of governance, free market capitalism and militarized responses to conflict. For critical theorists, these narratives had tragic consequences when used to justify imperialism, and could have similarly tragic consequences today.*

* Anne Orford, *Rereading Humanitarian Intervention: Human Rights and the Use of Force in International Law* (Cambridge: Cambridge UP, 2003).

and in 2006 Congolese militia leader Lubanga Dyilo was the first individual arrested and surrendered to the court. War crimes in Darfur, Sudan—which a UN commission found grave but short of "genocide"—have also been referred to the ICC.[43]

What makes the ICC different (and controversial) is the idea of *universal jurisdiction*— that the court has the ability to prosecute individuals of any nation. This differentiates the ICC from the World Court, which has only states as complainants and defendants. Under the ICC, individuals can be prosecuted for their roles in violations of human rights. Three mechanisms can trigger an ICC trial. First, a state may agree to turn over an individual for trial. Second, against the wishes of a state, a special prosecutor at the ICC can begin a trial if the crimes occurred in the territory of a signatory to the ICC. Third, the UN Security Council can begin proceedings against individuals from nonsignatory states.

As with most international law, the enforcement of laws of war occurs mostly through practical reciprocity and group response, reinforced by habit and legitimacy. A state that violates laws of war can find itself isolated without allies and subject to reprisals.

The most important principle of the laws of war is the effort to limit warfare to the combatants and to protect civilians when possible. It is illegal to target civilians in a war unless there is a compelling military utility in doing so. Even then, the amount of force used must be *proportional* to military gain, and only the *necessary* amount of force may be employed.

IN THE DOCK

War crimes include unnecessary targeting of civilians and mistreatment of prisoners of war (POWs), among others. A special court set up by the UN hears cases from the war in Sierra Leone, where mutilation, rape and the use of child soldiers were common. The former president of neighbouring Liberia, Charles Taylor, was charged with war crimes and crimes against humanity for his role in the war. Arrested in Nigeria where he had been living in exile, Taylor (second from right) appears before the court in 2006. His trial will likely take place in the Netherlands to avoid a possible destabilizing effect on West Africa.

---

[43] Adrian L. Jones, "Continental Divide and the Politics of Complex Sovereignty: Canada, the United States and the International Criminal Court," *Canadian Journal of Political Science* 39.2 (June 2006): 227–48.

To help separate combatants from civilians, soldiers must wear uniforms and insignia; for example, Canadian armed forces typically have a shoulder patch with a Canadian flag. This provision is frequently violated in guerrilla warfare, making it particularly brutal and destructive of civilian life. If one cannot tell the difference between a bystander and a combatant, one is likely to kill both when in doubt (and in the "fog of war," soldiers are frequently in doubt). By contrast, in a large-scale conventional war, it is much easier to distinguish civilians from soldiers, although the effort is never completely successful, and so-called friendly-fire casualties are numerous.[44]

Soldiers who are captured or surrender their status as combatants become **prisoners of war (POWs).** POWs are provided protections under the laws of war, and may not be killed, tortured, mistreated or forced to disclose information beyond their name, rank and serial number. The law of POWs is enforced through practical reciprocity. Once, late in World War II, German forces executed 80 POWs from French partisan forces (whom Germany did not recognize as legitimate belligerents). The partisans responded by executing 80 German POWs.

The laws of war reserve a special role for the **International Committee of the Red Cross (ICRC).** The ICRC provides practical support—such as medical care, food and letters from home—to civilians caught in wars and to POWs. The ICRC works with national societies of the Red Cross or Red Crescent from 178 countries. Exchanges of POWs are usually negotiated through the ICRC. Armed forces must respect the neutrality of the ICRC, and most of the time they do so (again, guerrilla war is problematic). In the current war on terrorism, the United States does not consider the "enemy combatants" it detains to be POWs, but has granted the ICRC access to most (though not all) of them. More controversial is the U.S. policy called "extraordinary rendition," which lets terrorist suspects captured overseas be transferred to other countries—including some that use torture—for questioning.

The laws of war impose moral responsibility on individuals in wartime, as well as on states. The Nuremberg Tribunal after World War II established that participants can be held accountable for committing war crimes. German officers defended their actions as "just following orders," but this defence was rejected; the officers were punished, with some even executed for their war crimes.

Not all Nuremberg defendants were found guilty, however. For example, laws of war limit the use of force against civilians to that which is necessary and proportional to military objectives. That can translate to a high limit in a total war. In World War II, the German army besieged the Russian city of Leningrad (St. Petersburg) for two years, and civilians in the city were starving. Sieges of this kind are permitted under international law if an army cannot easily capture a city. The impact of the use of nuclear weapons on civilian casualties is horrific, and it has always been understood that nuclear weapons will result in massive "collateral damage." Nonetheless, nuclear weapons remain a legitimate weapon of war.

Changing Context The laws of war have been undermined by the changing nature of war. Conventional wars by defined armed forces on defined battlegrounds are giving way to irregular and "low-intensity" wars fought by guerrillas and death squads in cities or jungles. The lines between civilians and soldiers blur in these situations, and war crimes become more commonplace. In the Vietnam War, one of the largest problems faced by the United States was that the enemy seemed to be everywhere and nowhere. This led frustrated U.S. forces to attack civilian villages that were seen as supporting the guerrillas. In one infamous case, a U.S. officer was court-martialled for ordering his soldiers to massacre hundreds of unarmed

prisoners of war (POWs)
Soldiers who are captured or have surrendered (and who thereby receive special status under the laws of war).

International Committee of the Red Cross (ICRC) An organization based in Geneva, Switzerland, that provides practical support, such as medical care, food and letters from home, to civilians caught in wars and to prisoners of war (POWs). The ICRC works with national societies of the Red Cross or Red Crescent. Exchanges of POWs are usually negotiated through the ICRC.

---

[44] Nicholas G. Fotion, "The Gulf War: Cleanly Fought," *Bulletin of the Atomic Scientists* 47.7 (1991): 24–29. George A. Lopez, "The Gulf War: Not So Clean," *Bulletin of the Atomic Scientists* 47.7 (1991): 30–35.

civilians in the village of My Lai in 1968 (he was convicted but given a light sentence). In today's irregular warfare, the laws of war are increasingly difficult to uphold.

Another factor undermining laws of war is that states now rarely issue a *declaration of war* setting out whom they are warring against and the cause of their action. This practice, common until about 50 years ago, helped distinguish belligerents from bystanders, protecting neutral countries and invoking the rights and responsibilities of the warring states. Today, such declarations are seldom used because they bring little benefit to the state declaring war and incur obligations under international law. States now fight wars without declaring them. In many cases, such as with revolutionary and counterrevolutionary civil wars in the global South, a declaration would not even be appropriate, because wars are declared only against states, not internal groups. In undeclared wars, the distinctions between participants and nonparticipants are challenged (along with the protection of the latter). The Bush administration called the 2001 terrorist attacks acts of war, and the response a war on terrorism, but Congress did not formally declare war (just as it had not during the Vietnam War). Likewise, the U.S. government also claimed that suspected Taliban and al Qaeda prisoners taken from Afghanistan to Guantanamo Bay were not prisoners of war, and therefore not subject to protection under the Geneva Convention (to much criticism by the ICRC and human rights organizations such as Amnesty International).

The laws of war have never been aimed at outlawing war, but rather at signalling the conditions under which a war may be conducted. Critics of the laws of war have thus noted the ways they actually facilitate war, setting the terms under which war is made possible. Anomalies can therefore occur, especially when determining whether an act was committed as part of armed conflict or outside of it. For example, recent clarifications about rape as a war crime effectively distinguish rape perpetrated as an act of war (which would therefore be prohibited under the laws of war) versus rape perpetrated under other circumstances (which would not be prohibited under the laws of war, though would presumably fall under other local legal standards).[45]

HUMAN RIGHTS

human rights Rights of all persons to be free from abuses such as torture or imprisonment for their political beliefs (political and civil rights), and to enjoy certain minimum economic and social protections (economic and social rights).

One of the newest and least developed areas of international law concerns **human rights**—the universal rights of all human beings against certain abuses from their *own* governments.[46]

Individual Rights versus Sovereignty

The very idea of human rights flies in the face of the sovereignty and territorial integrity of states. In its strictest sense, sovereignty means that states can do what they want within their own territory, including violating the rights of their own citizens. Efforts to promote human rights are routinely criticized by governments with poor human rights records as "interference in our internal affairs."

---

[45] Liz Philipose, "The Laws of War and Women's Human Rights," *Hypatia* 11.4 (1996): 46–62. Judith G. Gardam and Michelle J. Jarvis, *Women, Armed Conflict and International Law* (The Hague: Kluwer, 2001).

[46] Richard A. Falk, *Human Rights Horizons* (NY: Routledge, 2000). Daniel Thomas, *The Helsinki Effect: International Norms, Human Rights, and the Demise of Communism* (Princeton, NJ: Princeton UP, 2001). Thomas Risse, Stephen C. Ropp and Kathryn Sikkink, eds., *The Power of Human Rights: International Norms and Domestic Change* (NY: Cambridge UP, 1999). Cynthia Price Cohen, ed., *Human Rights of Indigenous Peoples* (Ardsley, NY: Transnational, 1998). Michael Perry, *The Idea of Human Rights: Four Inquiries* (NY: Oxford UP, 1998). Henry J. Steiner and Philip Alston, *International Human Rights in Context: Law, Politics, Morals* (Oxford: Clarendon, 1996).

The concept of human rights arises from at least three sources.[47] The first is religion. Nearly every major world religion has at its foundation the idea that humans were created in an image of a higher power and that therefore all humans are to be afforded a certain dignity and respect. Second, for centuries, Western political and legal philosophy has discussed the idea of natural law and natural rights. From Aristotle to John Locke to Immanuel Kant to Jean-Jacques Rousseau, political philosophers have developed the idea that a natural law exists that grants all humans the right to life, liberty, property and happiness.[48] Finally, political revolutions in the eighteenth century, such as the French and American revolutions, translated the theory of natural law and natural rights into practice. In France, for example, the Declaration of the Rights of Man and Citizen created laws that solidified the idea that humans have certain rights no state or other individuals can take away.

Of course, criticisms of these ideas of human rights exist on both a theoretical and a practical level. There are several ways of thinking about human rights. One approach argues that rights are *universal*. No matter where a person resides, no matter their ethnic nationality and no matter their local religious, ethnic or clan traditions, that person has certain rights that must be respected. The other approach to human rights is often labelled *relativism*. According to this idea, local traditions and histories should be given due respect, even if it means limiting rights that others outside that local context find important. Theoretically, relativists point out that much of the origin and development of the human rights ideas in widest circulation today (at least two of the three sources discussed) are Western in origin. Non-Western societies have different philosophical traditions and may choose to emphasize group or family rights, for example, over individual ones. At a practical level, many (especially non-Western) critics are quick to point out that even after the eighteenth-century revolutions in Europe and America, rights were still not universal. Women, children and often non-white males were not assumed to enjoy the same rights as land-holding white males, making the very idea of universal rights misleading.

Partly because of this controversy, there are no globally agreed-upon definitions of essential human rights. Rights are often

HUMAN RIGHTS AND SOVEREIGNTY
International norms concerning human rights conflict with state sovereignty, causing friction in relationships such as Burma/Myanmar's with Japan. Here, Burmese residents in Japan hold pictures of their leader, Aung San Suu Kyi, and protest against Burma/Myanmar's military government for its human rights abuses. (Those opposed to the military regime also reject the name Myanmar, which was adopted by the military government in 1989, and use Burma instead. The United Nations and some other national governments, in deference to state sovereignty, use Myanmar.)

---

[47] Paul Gordon Lauren, *The Evolution of International Human Rights: Visions Seen* (Philadelphia, PA: U Pennsylvania P, 2003).

[48] Patrick Hayden, ed., *The Philosophy of Human Rights.* (St. Paul: Paragon House, 2001).

divided into three broad types. First-generation rights usually refer to civil-political rights, sometimes also referred to as "negative rights." These include what are considered traditional Western rights such as freedom of speech, freedom of religion, equal protection under the law and freedom from arbitrary imprisonment. They are "negative" insofar as they are acknowledged in the breach; they are invoked when they are violated. Second-generation rights are economic-social rights and are sometimes referred to as "positive rights." These include rights to good living conditions, food, health care, social security and education. They are "positive" insofar as they require some socially provided good or service to be fulfilled (the provision of basic housing, of food and the like). Third-generation rights are described as "peoples' rights," and were embodied in the 1981 African Charter of Human Rights and Peoples Rights. The rights of a people can arguably be positive and negative. Peoples' rights refer to the rights of a "people" to self-determination and may involve the protection of distinct ethnic or cultural practices, languages and so on. Peoples' rights are the least articulated of the three broad types of rights.[49]

No state has a perfect record on any type of human rights, and states differ as to which areas they respect or violate. When the United States criticizes China for prohibiting free speech, using prison labour and torturing political dissidents (civil-political rights), China notes that the United States has 40 million poor people, the highest ratio of prison inmates in the world and a history of racism and violence (economic-social rights).[50] During the Cold War, the United States consistently criticized the Soviet Union and China for violations of civil-political rights, yet refused to endorse treaties championing economic-social rights. Likewise, communist states encouraged the development of the latter rights while ignoring calls for the former. Canada has regularly been criticized by human rights bodies for its treatment of its native populations, historically through the residential schools system and currently because of the deplorable state of many native reserves.

Historically, a significant global shift in human rights occurred at the end of World War II. Horrified by Nazi Germany's attempt to exterminate the Jewish population, along with Gypsies, homosexuals, labour union activists and others, and by Japanese abuses of Chinese citizens, many scholars and practitioners began to suggest there were limits to state sovereignty. States could not claim to be sovereign and above interference if they attempted to massacre their own people. It was in the aftermath of World War II and during the creation of the United Nations that some of the most significant international attempts to codify and enforce human rights began. In the next section, we examine some of these agreements and institutions.

Human Rights Institutions

Declaration of Human Rights (UDHR) Adopted by the UN General Assembly in 1948, the UNDHR is considered the core international document concerning human rights.

In 1948, the UN General Assembly adopted what is considered the core international document concerning human rights: the **Universal Declaration of Human Rights (UDHR).** The UDHR does not have the force of international law, but sets forth (hoped-for) international norms regarding behaviour by governments toward their own citizens and foreigners alike. The declaration is rooted in the principle that violations of human rights upset international order (causing outrage, sparking rebellion, etc.) and in the fact that the UN Charter commits states to respect fundamental freedoms. The declaration

---

[49] Jack Donnelly, *International Human Rights* (Boulder, CO: Westview, 1993).

[50] People's Republic of China, State Council, "America's 'Abominable' Human Rights Conditions," *Washington Post* 16 Feb. 1997: C3.

Focus on Canadian Scholarship

Scholars at Canadian universities who are interested in questions of international norms, human rights, treaties, international organizations and international law (see also Chapter 3) include **W. Andy Knight** at the University of Alberta, who focuses on the United Nations. **Michael Byers** of the University of British Columbia examines international law, human rights and armed conflict. At the University of Victoria, **Claire Cutler** is interested in developing critical theory in international law and focuses currently on institutions and processes for dispute resolution within international law. **James F. Keeley** at the University of Calgary is interested in international law and organizations, particularly international regimes and nuclear non-proliferation. **Shreesh Juyal** at the University of Regina has focused on the United Nations system. **Reeta Chowdhari Tremblay** at Memorial University in Newfoundland focuses on human rights in comparative perspective. **Susan Henders**, at York University, focuses on international human rights in multiethnic and religious societies. At the Canadian Forces College, **Barbara J. Falk** is interested in transitional justice in post-conflict and regime-change settings, and her colleague, **Adam Chapnick,** has written on Canada and the founding of the United Nations. At Carleton University's Norman Paterson School of International Affairs, **Trevor Findlay** is interested in issues of treaty compliance around questions of arms control, disarmament and non-proliferation issues, and his colleague **Christopher Kenneth Penny** focuses on the international legal regulation of the use of force and international criminal law. Also at the Norman Paterson School, **James Ron** examines human rights activism and conflict. **Joanna Quinn** at the University of Western Ontario is interested in human rights and truth commissions. At Acadia University, **Marshall William Conley** is interested in human rights education. At McMaster University, **Stefania Miller** examines human rights and post-communist political systems in Eastern Europe, and her colleague, **Lana Wylie,** examines state responses to American pressure over the International Criminal Court. **Karen Knop** of the University of Toronto is interested in public international law and self-determination and feminism and international law. **Alistair Edgar** at Wilfred Laurier University has focused on sovereignty and humanitarian intervention as competing norms in global governance, and his colleague **Paul Heinbecker** at Laurier's Centre for Global Relations focuses on the United Nations. At Concordia University, **Elizabeth Bloodgood** is interested in NGOs and has examined the activities of Greenpeace, the International Campaign to Ban Landmines and Friends of the Earth.

proclaims that "all human beings are born free and equal" without regard to race, sex, language, religion, political affiliation or the status of the territory in which they were born. It promotes norms in a wide variety of areas, from banning torture to guaranteeing religious and political freedom to the right of economic well-being.

Since the adoption of the UDHR, the UN has opened a number of treaties for state signature to further define protections of human rights. Unlike the UDHR, these treaties are legally binding contracts signed by states. Of course, international law is only as good as the enforcement mechanisms behind it, yet these treaties are important in outlining the basic protections for individuals expected by the international community.

Two key treaties are the *International Covenant on Civil and Political Rights* and the *International Covenant on Economic, Social, and Cultural Rights*. These treaties, both of which entered into force in 1976, codify the promises of the UDHR while dividing the list of rights in the UDHR into civil-political and economic-social rights, respectively. These two covenants along with the UDHR are often referred to as the International Bill of Human Rights.

The remaining treaties each deal with a particular group that the international community considers vulnerable. The International Convention on the Elimination of All Forms of Racial Discrimination (ICERD) entered into force in 1969 and bans discrimination against individuals based on race, ethnicity, religion or national origin. The ICERD did not include language concerning gender discrimination. The

Convention on the Elimination of All Forms of Discrimination Against Women (CEDAW), however, fills this void. CEDAW entered into force in 1981.

The Convention Against Torture (CAT) entered into effect in 1987 and bans dehumanizing, degrading and inhumane treatment of individuals even in times of war. The Convention on the Rights of the Child (CRC) entered into force in 1990 and affords special protection to children to promote their health, education and physical well-being. Finally, the most recent treaty is the International Convention on the Protection of the Rights of All Migrant Workers and Members of their Families, which was brought into force in 2003. The CMW attempts to protect the political, labour and social rights of the nearly 100 million migrant workers around the globe.

In addition to these seven treaties, two further treaties have been approved by the UN General Assembly but have not yet entered into force. These are the International Convention for the Protection of All Persons from Enforced Disappearance and the Convention on the Rights of Persons with Disabilities, both adopted by the UN General Assembly in late 2006.

Human rights conventions must first be signed by state parties, then ratified by their governments. Ratification indicates that the state agrees to be bound by the terms of the convention and usually entails submitting reports to the relevant UN body outlining progress toward meeting commitments under the convention. To enter into force, a convention must normally receive a certain prescribed number of ratifications (determined when the convention is approved by the General Assembly). The Convention for the Protection of All Persons from Enforced Disappearance, for example, will enter into force 30 days after it has been ratified by 20 states.

Some states will sign a treaty, but not ratify it. The United States, for example, has regularly expressed support for the principle of human rights protections by signing a convention, but then signalling its reluctance to be bound by an international human rights instrument by refusing to ratify. This was the case with the Convention on the Elimination of Discrimination Against Women. In other cases, the U.S. expresses its resistance to certain types of rights by not signing: for example, the U.S. has signed and ratified the Covenant on Civil and Political Rights, but has refused to sign the Covenant on Economic, Social, and Cultural Rights (because it disagrees that economic rights are human rights). Canada, by contrast, regularly signs and ratifies and is a state party to all major human rights conventions currently in force. Though it had not yet signed the Convention on Enforced Disappearance as of mid-2007, the Canadian minister of Foreign Affairs indicated on the first day it was open for signature that Canada would also immediately sign the Convention Protecting Persons with Disabilities.

There are two main types of bodies within the UN that oversee human rights protection: Charter bodies and Treaty bodies. Treaty bodies are small expert panels that review every state's compliance under the human rights treaties described above. So, for example, there is a Committee on Torture, a Committee on the Elimination of Discrimination Against Women, a Committee on the Rights of the Child, and so on. States that have signed and ratified any of the treaties must submit regular reports to the associated treaty body, outlining their efforts to fulfill their obligations under the treaty, and in turn, states receive reports back from respective committees assessing their compliance.[51]

The main UN Charter body is the newly created Human Rights Council, established in 2006 to replace the Human Rights Commission. The Council comprises 47 members

---

[51] "Human Rights Bodies," Office of the High Commissioner for Human Rights, available at http://www.ohchr.org/english/bodies/index.htm.

elected by the General Assembly in a secret ballot and representing a geographic distribution, with 13 members from the African group, 13 from the Asian group, six from the Eastern European group, seven from the Latin American and Caribbean group and seven from the Western European and Other States group. Members of the Council serve three-year terms. The new Human Rights Council is scheduled to meet more regularly than the former Commission (which met only once annually for a six-week session). It issues declarations or reports, often around thematic areas, and also investigates human rights abuses by particular member states.

The Council was also created in part to address concerns that the former Human Rights Commission had become a human rights "abusers club" with the appointment of many members with questionable human rights records. Members of the Commission were rarely sanctioned for human rights abuses despite their actual human rights record. Members also protected friends and allies, regularly voting for "no action" motions and bringing deliberations to a halt. The Commission became known for a record of selectivity and double standards.[52] Full balloting to elect members to the Council (rather than the previous appointment process) was intended to address some of these concerns, but in one of the first elections in early 2006, human rights groups warned that the Council was replicating old patterns. Egypt, Qatar and Angola gained seats despite problematic human rights records. Egypt gained its seat despite protests from a dozen human rights groups. At the same time, Belarus was denied a place on the Council, which some observers saw as a victory. Louise Fréchette, a Canadian and former UN deputy secretary-general, noted that the problem was not one of the UN or the new Council but of the voting by members of the General Assembly, and signalled that a strong global consensus on human rights still did not exist.[53]

The UN also has an office of the High Commissioner for Human Rights, which is a department of the Secretariat and is independently mandated to protect and promote human rights. This office is led by the High Commissioner for Human Rights (whose powers do not, of course, include making states do anything, but do include publicizing their abuses). That position is currently held by a Canadian, Louise Arbour, who reports directly to the UN secretary-general and is involved in promoting human rights issues and in coordinating the human rights work done by various agencies within the UN.

Besides UN-related human rights bodies, several regional IOs have also promoted the protection of human rights. Nowhere is this truer than in Europe, where the European Union, the Council of Europe and the European Court of Human Rights all work to ensure that human rights are respected by all states in the region (see Chapter 11). In Latin America, the *Inter-American Court of Human Rights* has had some success in promoting human rights, yet has been limited by state refusal to abide by its decisions. Finally, the African Union helps to support the African Human Rights Commission, but has been hampered by its lack of monetary and political support from African states.

Today, NGOs play a key role in efforts to win basic political rights in authoritarian countries—including a halt to the torture, execution and imprisonment of those expressing political or religious beliefs. The leading organization pressing this struggle is **Amnesty International,** an NGO that operates globally to monitor and try to rectify glaring abuses of human rights. Amnesty International has a reputation for impartiality and has criticized abuses in many countries, including Canada. Other groups, such as

Amnesty International An influential nongovernmental organization that operates globally to monitor and try to rectify glaring abuses of political (not economic or social) human rights.

---

[52] Ladan Rahmani-Ocora, "Giving the Emperor Real Clothes: The UN Human Rights Council," *Global Governance* 12 (2006): 15–20.

[53] Olivia Ward, "Despite Abuse, Egypt Joins Rights Council: History of Torture in African Nation Makes Mockery of UN, Critics Say," *The Toronto Star* 18 May 2007, available at http://www.thestar.com/article/215319.

Human Rights Watch, work in a similar way but often with a more regional or national focus. NGOs often provide information and advocacy for the UN and other regional organizations that attempt to promote human rights. They essentially serve as a bridge between global or regional organizations and efforts to promote human rights "on the ground."[54]

Enforcement of norms of human rights is difficult, because it involves interference in a state's internal affairs. Cutting off trade or contact with a government that violates human rights tends to hurt the citizens whose rights are being violated by further isolating them. The most effective method of enforcement seems to be a combination of *publicity* and *pressure*. Publicity entails digging up information about human rights abuses, as Amnesty International does. Pressure from other governments, as well as from private individuals and businesses, consists of threats to punish the offender in some way through nonviolent means. For instance, in Canada, proponents of human rights both inside government and externally have argued that the terms of Canadian trade with China should be linked to China's human rights record. But inasmuch as most governments seek to maintain normal relations with one another, this kind of intrusive punishment by one government of another's human rights violations is rare—and not reliably successful.

Also rare are humanitarian interventions using military force to overcome armed resistance by local authorities or warlords and bring help to civilian victims of wars and disasters.[55] Three such interventions in the 1990s were in Kurdish areas of Iraq, in Somalia and in Kosovo (Serbia). In September 2000, the International Commission on Intervention and State Sovereignty (ICISS) was formed under the sponsorship of the Canadian government. Its goal was to develop a set of global principles about the conditions under which the international community should respond to emerging crises involving widespread crimes against humanity. *The Responsibility to Protect* report concluded that states are responsible for the protection of their own citizens, and that "where a population is suffering serious harm, as a result of internal war, insurgency, repression or state failure, and the state in question is unwilling or unable to halt or avert it," it becomes the responsibility of the international community to intervene for protection purposes. The UN has followed up with further elaborations of what has been called the **"Responsibility to Protect (R2P),"** which is focused primarily on establishing the parameters around which states will be urged to take action (as opposed to binding agreements or treaties).[56]

Despite many limitations, concern about human rights is a force to be reckoned with in international relations. There are now widely held norms about how governments *should* behave, and someday governments may adhere to all those norms as they have already begun to do in select areas, such as the abolition of legal slavery. With the downfall of many authoritarian and military governments in the former Soviet Union, Eastern Europe, Latin America and Africa, a growing emphasis on human rights seems likely.

The concern of states for the human rights of individuals living in other states is a far cry from the realist concerns that have dominated the theory and practice of IR in the

Responsibility to Protect (R2P) A report issued by the International Commission on Intervention and State Sovereignty and formed under the sponsorship of the Canadian government. It focuses on the responsibilities states have to protect populations suffering serious harm or human rights abuses as a result of conflict.

---

[54] Amnesty International, *Amnesty International Report* (London, annual). Ann Marie Clark, *Diplomacy of Conscience: Amnesty International and Changing Human Rights Norms* (Princeton, NJ: Princeton UP, 2000). Stephen Hopgood, *Keepers of the Flame: Understanding Amnesty International* (Cornell UP, 2006).

[55] Thomas G. Weiss, *Military-Civilian Interactions: Humanitarian Crises and the Responsibility to Protect*, 2nd ed. (Lanham, MD: Rowman & Littlefield, 2005). Jennifer M. Welsh, ed., *Humanitarian Intervention and International Relations* (Oxford UP, 2004).

[56] See "Responsibility to Protect: Engaging Civil Society" at http://www.responsibilitytoprotect.org/index.php.

past. Indeed, the entire discipline of international law and organization runs counter to fundamental realist assertions about international anarchy. The remaining chapters of this book move away from two other aspects of realism—its emphasis on military force above other forms of leverage and its pessimism about the potentials for international cooperation as an outcome of bargaining.

Careers in International Relations
Jobs in Government and IGOs

Summary

Jobs in government and diplomacy offer team players the chance to affect policy, but require patience with large bureaucracies.

Benefits and Costs Governments and intergovernmental organizations (IGOs) play key roles in international relations and employ millions of people with interests and training in IR.

Despite differences between careers in IGOs and governments, there are numerous similarities. Both are hierarchical organizations, with competitive and highly regulated work environments. In the case of the Canadian bureaucracy or the UN, entrance into and promotion in these organizations is regulated by exams, performance evaluations and tenure with the organization.

Another similarity lies in the challenges of being pulled in many directions concerning policies. Governments face competing pressures of public opinion, constituencies and interests groups—each with distinct policy opinions. IGOs also deal with interest groups (such as NGOs, see Chapter 12, p. 448), but the IGOs' constituents are states, which in many cases disagree among themselves.

Many employees of IGOs or governments thrive on making decisions that influence policies. Both work environments attract employees with deep interests in international affairs, and the resulting networks of contacts can bring professional and intellectual rewards. Finally, jobs in governments or IGOs may involve travel or living abroad, which many people enjoy.

However, promotion in these fields can be slow and frustrating. Usually, only individuals with advanced degrees or technical specializations achieve non-entry level positions. It can take years to climb the ladder of such an organization, and the process may involve working in departments far from your original interests. In addition, IGOs and governments are bureaucracies with formal rules and procedures, requiring great patience.

Employees often express frustration that initiative and "thinking outside the box" are not rewarded.

Skills to Hone The key to working in IGOs or government is to get your foot in the door. Be flexible and willing to take entry positions that are not exactly in your area of interest. For example, the Department of Foreign Affairs and International Trade is only one of many parts of the Canadian state that deal with IR. Do not assume that to work in foreign affairs, one must be a diplomat.

Foreign language training is important, especially for work in large IGOs with many field offices. The ability to work well in groups and to network within and across organizations is also an important asset. People who can strengthen lines of communication can gain support from many places in an organization.

Resources

Linda Fasulo. *An Insider's Guide to the UN.* New Haven: Yale University Press, 2005.

http://jobs.un.org

www.worldbank.org/careers

http://www.international.gc.ca/department/service/menu-en.asp

http://url.url.org

http://www.jobs-emplois.gc.ca/menu/home_e.htm

Thinking Critically

1. Suppose you were asked to recommend changes in the structure of the UN Security Council (especially in permanent membership and the veto). What changes would you recommend, if any? Based on what logic?

2. A former UN secretary-general, Boutros-Ghali, proposed (without success) the creation of a standby army of peacemaking forces loaned by member states (see p. 266). This would reduce state sovereignty and increase supranational authority. Canada strongly supported this idea. Discuss this plan's merits and drawbacks.

3. Collective security against aggression depends on states' willingness to bear the costs of fighting wars to repel and punish aggressors. Sometimes states have been willing to bear such costs; at other times they have not. What considerations do you think should guide such decisions? Give examples of situations (actual or potential) that would and would not merit the intervention of foreign states to reverse aggression.

4. Given the difficulty of enforcing international law, how might the role of the World Court be strengthened in the future? What obstacles might such plans encounter? How would they change the court's role if successful? Does the creation of an International Criminal Court strengthen the prospects for international law?

5. Although international norms concerning human rights are becoming stronger, many states continue to consider them an internal affair over which the state has sovereignty within its territory. Do you think human rights are a legitimate subject for one state to discuss with another? If so, how do you reconcile the tensions between state autonomy and universal rights? What practical steps could be taken to convince sovereign states to acknowledge universal human rights?

Chapter Summary

- International anarchy is balanced by world order—rules and institutions through which states cooperate for mutual benefit.

- World order has always been grounded in power, but order mediates raw power by establishing norms and habits that govern interactions among states.

- States follow the rules—both moral norms and formal international laws—much more often than not.

- International rules operate through agreements, such as military alliances and institutions (IOs) like the UN.

- States form alliances to increase their effective power relative to another state or alliance.

- Alliances can shift rapidly, with major effects on power relations.

- The world's main alliances, including NATO, NORAD and the CIS, face uncertain roles in a changing world order.

- The UN embodies a tension between state sovereignty and supranational authority. In its Charter and history, the UN has made sovereignty the more important principle. This has limited the UN's power.

- The UN defers particularly to the sovereignty of great powers, five of whom, as permanent Security Council members, can block any security-related resolution binding UN member states.

- In part because of its deference to state sovereignty, the UN has attracted virtually universal membership of the world's states, including all the great powers.

- Each of the 192 UN member states has one vote in the General Assembly, which serves mainly as a world forum and an umbrella organization for social and economic development efforts.

- The Security Council has 10 rotating member states and five permanent members: the United States, Russia, China, Britain and France. Canada has been one of the highest "repeater" countries among the nonpermanent members, at six terms.

- The UN is administered by international civil servants in the Secretariat, headed by the secretary-general.

- The regular UN budget plus all peacekeeping missions together amount to a fraction of what the world spends on military forces.

- Voting patterns and coalitions in the UN have changed over the years with expanding membership and changing conditions. Some countries, including the U.S., have refused to pay their dues to the UN.

- UN peacekeeping forces are deployed in regional conflicts around the world. Their main role is to monitor compliance with agreements such as ceasefires, disarmament plans and fair election rules.

- UN peacekeepers operate under UN command and flag. Sometimes national troops operate under their own flag and command to carry out UN resolutions.

- IOs include UN programs (mostly on economic and social issues), autonomous UN agencies and organizations with no formal tie to the UN. This institutional network helps to strengthen and stabilize the rules of IR.

- International law, the formal body of rules for state relations, is derived from treaties (most importantly), customs, general principles and legal scholarship—not from legislation passed by any government.

- Arms control agreements are a particularly important type of treaty in issues of international security.

- International law is difficult to enforce and is enforced in practice by national power, international coalitions and the practice of reciprocity.

- The World Court hears grievances of one state against another but cannot infringe on state sovereignty in most cases. It is an increasingly useful avenue for arbitrating relatively minor conflicts.

- Most cases involving international relations are tried in national courts, where a state can enforce judgments within its own territory.

- A permanent International Criminal Court (ICC) was ratified and came into operation in 2002. Taking over from two UN tribunals, it hears cases of genocide, war crimes and crimes against humanity.

- In international law, the rights of diplomats have long held special status. Embassies are considered to be the territory of their home country.

- Laws of war are long-standing and well-established. They distinguish combatants from civilians, giving each certain rights and responsibilities. Guerrilla wars and ethnic conflicts have blurred these distinctions.

- Wars of aggression violate norms in a just war—one waged only to repel or punish aggression. It is sometimes (but not always) difficult to identify the aggressor in a violent international conflict.

- International norms concerning human rights are becoming stronger and more widely accepted. However, human rights law is problematic because it entails interference by one state in another's internal affairs.

Key Terms

international norms   242
humanitarian intervention   243
international organizations (IOs)   244
alliance cohesion   247
burden sharing   247
North Atlantic Treaty Organization
    (NATO)   247
Warsaw Pact   248
North American Aerospace Defense
    Command (NORAD)   249
nonaligned movement   250
UN Charter   252
UN General Assembly   252
UN Security Council   252
UN Secretariat   252
blue helmets   263
UN Conference on Trade and
    Development (UNCTAD)   271
World Health Organization (WHO)   271
Anti-Ballistic Missile (ABM) Treaty   275
Strategic Arms Limitation Treaties
    (SALT)   276
Intermediate Nuclear Forces (INF)
    Treaty   276

Strategic Arms Reduction Treaties
    (START)   276
Comprehensive Test Ban Treaty
    (CTBT)   276
Conventional Forces in Europe (CFE)
    Treaty   277
World Court (International Court
    of Justice)   278
immigration law   282
diplomatic recognition   282
diplomatic immunity   283
just war doctrine   285
war crimes   286
crimes against humanity   286
International Criminal Court
    (ICC)   286
prisoners of war (POWs)   289
International Committee of the Red
    Cross (ICRC)   289
human rights   290
Universal Declaration of Human
    Rights   292
Amnesty International   295
Responsibility to Protect (R2P)   296

Research Navigator Question

Research
Navigator.com
RESOURCES FOR COLLEGE RESEARCH ASSIGNMENTS

Use the *New York Times* database on Research Navigator to find two or three articles that describe recent work of the United Nations. In a small group, compare the articles you found with those found by other students. What, in your group's view, are the greatest strengths and weaknesses of the UN, based on these articles? Try to summarize your overall impressions, and present them as though you are preparing the newly appointed Canadian ambassador to the United Nations. What information does he or she most need to know in preparation for this position?

Weblinks

There are innumerable UN and other international organization websites, as well as NGO sites. Here is a small sampling:

Amnesty International:
http://www.amnesty.org

International Criminal Court:
http://www.icc-cpi.int

The United Nations:
http://www.un.org

United Nations Department of Peacekeeping Operations:
http://www.un.org/Depts/dpko/dpko/index.asp

United Nations Office of the High Commissioner for Human Rights:
http://www.unhchr.ch/html/menu2/2/chr.htm

International Alert:
http://www.international-alert.org

International Committee of the Red Cross:
http://www.icrc.org/eng

Rights and Democracy (Montreal):
http://www.ichrdd.ca/frame00e.html

Women's International League for Peace and Freedom:
http://www.peacewomen.org

Trade

9

Port in Valpairaiso, Chile, 2005.

FROM SECURITY TO POLITICAL ECONOMY

We will now shift our focus from security and international institutions to political economy. Scholars of *international political economy (IPE)* are generally dissatisfied with the way much of the literature in international relations has emphasized questions of "high politics" and security. In the minds of IPE scholars, not enough thought is given to the relationship between domestic and international politics in IR, and there exists an inappropriate and usually untenable separation of "politics" and "economics."

International political economists approach their work in a variety of ways. Some look to different actors (adding firms, international organizations and social movements to the usual consideration of state behaviour). Others focus instead on the addition of new issues, arguing that trade, monetary and international development are as important in their own right as military and strategic issues. Still others examine the array of social forces that sustain particular versions of world order, specifically capitalist world order.[1]

This and the following chapters will examine some of the most frequently studied issues raised in IPE: trade, monetary relations, multinational corporations and North-South relations (see this chapter and Chapters 10, 12 and 13). Two topics of special interest in recent years are the economic integration of Europe and other regions (Chapter 11) and the international politics of the global environment (Chapter 14).

---

[1] Richard Stubbs and Geoffrey R. D. Underhill, *Political Economy and the Changing Global Order*, 3rd ed. (Toronto: Oxford UP, 2006). Stephen Gill and David Law, *The Global Political Economy: Perspectives, Problems and Policies* (Baltimore: Johns Hopkins UP, 1988).

The review of theoretical approaches to international relations (discussed in Chapters 2, 3 and 4) noted that the different perspectives had applications to questions of international political economy. This chapter will review the mercantilist and economic liberal approaches to IPE.

Economic Liberalism and Mercantilism

On a key assumption of realism—international anarchy—two major approaches within IPE differ.[2] One approach, called mercantilism (see p. 74), generally shares with realism the belief that each state must protect its own interests at the expense of others—not relying on international organizations to create a framework for mutual gains. Mercantilists therefore emphasize relative power (as do realists): what matters is not so much a state's absolute amount of well-being as its position relative to rival states.[3]

Economic liberalism (see p. 101) argues that states are only one of many actors in the global political economy, which also includes individuals, households and firms. It holds that by building international organizations, institutions and norms, and by conducting relations through the unfettered operations of a market, states can mutually benefit from economic exchanges. It matters little to liberals whether one state gains more or less than another—just whether the state's wealth is increasing in *absolute* terms. This concept parallels the idea that IOs allow states to relax their narrow, short-term pursuit of self-interest in order to realize longer-term mutual interests. (See pp. 241–242.)

Economic liberalism and mercantilism are theories of political economy, but they also inform the position taken by some states when developing policy. One of critical theory's most "developed" approaches to economics is Marxism. Marxist approaches are attuned to economic exploitation as a force in shaping political relations (see Chapter 4 and Chapter 13).

In IPE, contrary to questions of international security, economic liberalism is the dominant tradition of scholarship and mercantilism is a very distant second. In truth, most international economic exchanges (as well as security relationships) contain some element of mutual interest—joint gains that can be realized through cooperation—and some element of conflicting interests. Game theorists call this a "mixed interest" game. For example, in the game of Chicken (see p. 60), two drivers share an interest in avoiding a head-on collision, yet their interests diverge in that one can be a hero only if the other is a chicken. In international trade, economic liberals argue that when two states trade, both benefit (a shared interest), though one or the other will benefit more depending on the price of the transaction (a conflicting interest).

Liberalism puts emphasis on the shared interests of economic exchanges, whereas mercantilism emphasizes conflicting interests. Liberals see the most important goal of economic policy as the maximum creation of total wealth through achieving optimal *efficiency* (maximizing output, minimizing waste). Mercantilists see the most important goal as the creation of the most favourable possible *distribution* of wealth for particular states.

economic liberalism
An approach to IPE that emphasizes the gains made through trade and that, in practice, is committed to free trade, free capital flows and an "open" world economy. See also *mercantilism* and *neoliberalism*.

---

[2] George T. Crane and Abla M. Amawi, eds., *The Theoretical Evolution of International Political Economy: A Reader*, 2nd ed. (NY: Oxford UP, 1997).

[3] Robert Gilpin, *Global Political Economy: Understanding the International Economic Order* (Princeton, NJ: Princeton, 2001). Joseph Grieco and John Ikenberry, *State Power and World Markets: The International Political Economy* (NY: Norton, 2002). Gregory P. Nowell, *Mercantile States and the World Oil Cartel, 1900–1939* (Ithaca, NY: Cornell UP, 1994). John A. Conybeare, *Trade Wars: The Theory and Practice of International Commercial Rivalry* (NY: Columbia UP, 1987). Brian M. Pollins, "Does Trade Still Follow the Flag?" *American Political Science Review* 83.2 (1989): 465–80.

Economic liberals would argue that in practice, great gains have been realized from free trade. In any economic exchange that is not coerced by negative leverage, both parties gain because they place different values on the items being exchanged. Each party attributes less value on the item it starts with than the other party does. For instance, when a supermarket sells a head of cabbage, the consumer values the cabbage more than the cash they use to pay for it, and the supermarket values the cash more than the cabbage. This simple principle is the basis for economic exchange.

Even though both parties gain in an exchange, they may not gain equally: the distribution of benefits from trade may not be divided equally among participating states. One party may benefit greatly from an exchange, whereas the other party benefits only slightly. Economic liberals are interested in maximizing the overall (joint) benefits from exchange—a condition called *Pareto-optimal* (after an economist named Pareto). They have little to say about how total benefits are distributed among parties. Rather, the distribution of benefits is a matter of implicit or explicit bargaining, and hence a matter for politics and the use of leverage to influence outcomes.[4] States as participants in the international economy try to realize the greatest overall gains for all states while simultaneously bargaining to maximize their own share of those gains. Power does matter in such bargaining, but the most relevant forms of leverage are positive (the prospect of gains by striking a deal) rather than negative. Because the exchange process creates wealth, there is much room for bargaining over the distribution of that wealth.

Economic liberalism sees individual households and firms as the key actors in the economy and views government's most useful role as one of non-interference, except for the regulation of markets in order to help them function efficiently (and to create infrastructure, such as roads, that also helps the economy function efficiently). Politics, in this view, should serve the interests of economic efficiency. With the hand of government removed from markets, the "invisible hand" of supply and demand can determine the most efficient patterns of production, exchange and consumption (through the mechanism of prices). Because of the benefits of free trade, liberals disdain realists' obsession with international borders, because borders constrain the maximum efficiency of exchange.

For mercantilists, by contrast, economics should serve politics: the creation of wealth underlies state power. Because power is relative, trade is desirable only when the distribution of benefits favours one's own state over rivals. The terms of exchange shape the relative rates at which states accumulate power and thus shape the way power distributions in the international system change over time. As Japan and Germany achieved great prosperity, for instance, mercantilists saw them potentially overtaking the United States. Liberals, by contrast, thought Japanese and German wealth boosted the entire world economy and ultimately benefited all nations, including the United States.

Mercantilism achieved prominence several hundred years ago, and Britain used trade to rise in relative power in the international system around the eighteenth century. At that time mercantilism meant specifically the creation of a trade surplus (see "Balance of Trade" later in this chapter) in order to stockpile money in the form of precious metal (gold and silver), which could then be used to buy military capabilities (mercenary armies and weapons) in time of war.

---

[4] Joseph M. Grieco, *Cooperation among Nations: Europe, America, and Non-Tariff Barriers to Trade* (Ithaca, NY: Cornell UP, 1990). Joanne Gowa, *Allies, Adversaries, and International Trade* (Princeton, NJ: Princeton UP, 1993). S. Sideri, *Trade and Power* (Rotterdam: Rotterdam UP, 1970). Albert O. Hirschman, *National Power and the Structure of Foreign Trade* (Berkeley: U California P, 1945).

Mercantilism declined in the nineteenth century as Britain decided it had more to gain from free trade than from protectionism. It returned as a major approach in the period between World Wars I and II, when liberal global trading relations broke down. In recent years, with the weakening of the liberal international economic order created after World War II, mercantilism has begun to re-emerge.[5]

The distinction between liberalism and mercantilism is reflected in the difference between hegemonies and empires. Under hegemony (see p. 69), a dominant state creates an international order that facilitates free trade but does not try to control economic transactions by itself. An empire, by contrast, centrally controls economic transactions in its area. Historically, empires have a poor record of economic performance, whereas hegemony has been much more successful in achieving economic growth and prosperity.[6] Of course, under hegemony, rival states also share (with the hegemon) overall growth and prosperity, which can ultimately erode the hegemon's relative power and end its hegemony.

Globalization

The ascendance of liberal over mercantilist economics in recent decades forms one strand of a complex mosaic of changes in the world political economy—changes that together are called **globalization**. This term refers to the increasing importance of the world level of analysis in economics as the scope of economic activities expands worldwide.

Globalization encompasses many aspects, including expanded international trade, telecommunications, monetary coordination, multinational corporations, technical and scientific cooperation, cultural exchanges of new types and scales, migration and refugee flows and relations between the world's rich and poor countries. The coming chapters address this broad range of topics, each affected by globalization.[7]

Although globalization clearly is very important, it is rather vaguely defined and not well explained by any one theory. One popular conception of globalization is as "the widening, deepening and speeding up of worldwide interconnectedness in all aspects of contemporary social life. . . . "[8] At least three different conceptions of this process compete, however.

One view, informed by economic liberalism, sees globalization as the fruition of liberal economic principles. A global marketplace has brought growth and prosperity (not to all countries but to those most integrated in the global market). This economic process has made traditional states obsolete as economic units. States are thus losing authority to supranational institutions such as the IMF and EU, and to transnational actors such as MNCs and NGOs. The values of technocrats and elite educated citizens in liberal democracies are becoming global values, reflecting an emerging global civilization. The old North-South division is seen as less important, since the global South is moving in divergent directions depending on countries' and regions' integration with world markets.

globalization The increasing integration of the world in terms of communications, culture and economics; may also refer to changing subjective experiences of space and time that accompany this process.

---

[5] David J. Sylvan, "The Newest Mercantilism," *International Organization* 35.2 (1981): 375–81.

[6] Richard Rosencrance, *The Rise of the Virtual State: Wealth and Power in the Coming Century* (NY: Basic, 2000).

[7] David Held, Anthony McGrew, David Goldblatt and Jonathan Perraton, *Global Transformations: Politics, Economics and Culture* (Palo Alto, CA: Stanford UP, 1999). Anthony Giddens, *Runaway World: How Globalization Is Reshaping Our Lives* (London: Profile, 1999). John J. Kirton, Joseph P. Daniels and Andreas Freytag, eds., *Guiding Global Order: G8 Governance in the Twenty-first Century* (Burlington, VT: Ashgate, 2001). Thomas L. Friedman, *The Lexus and the Olive Tree* (NY: Farrar Straus & Giroux, 1999). Jan Aart Scholte, *Globalization: A Critical Introduction* (UK: Palgrave, 2000).

[8] Held et al. (see footnote 7 above) 2.

THINK GLOBALLY
As the world economy becomes more integrated, markets and production are likewise becoming global in scope. This volunteer in London in 2004 offers fair-trade coffee, which guarantees a decent price to producers in the global South.

A second perspective, informed by critical theorists, is skeptical of liberal claims about globalization. These observers doubt that regional and geographic distinctions such as the North-South divide are disappearing in favour of a single global market. Rather, they see the North-South gap as increasing with globalization, and they believe globalization is a process with long historical origins, not a recent phenomenon as economic liberals regularly suggest. This perspective is also concerned about the extent to which the idea of a "global civilization" is really a civilization based on norms associated with the West and the spread of a neoliberal market ideology around the world. This increasing homogeneity is in part offset by small, local moments of resistance in which people try to identify along lines of language, religion and other cultural factors.

A third school of thought, informed by mercantilism, sees globalization as quite profound, but is uncertain of its positive connotations—for different reasons than those outlined by critical theorists. Mercantilists see state sovereignty as being eroded by the EU, WTO and other new institutions, so that sovereignty is no longer an absolute but just one part of a spectrum of bargaining leverages held by states. Bargaining itself increasingly involves nonstate actors and nonterritorial organizations. Thus globalization diffuses authority. Whether or not state power is strengthened or weakened by globalization remains to be seen. It may be that state power will be transformed to operate in new contexts with new tools. However, the concern from this perspective is that states will be eclipsed by new, and more powerful, global actors.

While scholars discuss concepts of globalization, popular debates focus on the growing power of large global corporations, the disruptive costs associated with joining world markets (e.g., job loss and environmental impacts), the perception of growing disparities between the rich and the poor and the collusion of national governments in these wrongs through their participation in IOs such as the WTO and IMF.[9]

Policies to expand free trade are a central focus of "antiglobalization" protesters (see "Resistance to Trade," pp. 335–337). At the 1999 Seattle WTO meeting (see p. 334), thousands of demonstrators from labour unions and environmental groups—often on opposite sides in the past—joined in street protests to demand that future trade agreements address their concerns. Anarchists "trashed" downtown Seattle to vent their anger with big corporations, while police blanketed the area with tear gas.

Street protests also turned host cities into besieged fortresses in Washington, DC (2000 IMF and World Bank meetings), Québec (2001 summit working toward a Free Trade

---

[9] Walden Bello, *Deglobalization: Ideas for a New World Economy* (Blackwood, NS: Fernwood, 2002). Robin Broad, *Citizen Backlash to Economic Globalization* (Lanham, MD: Rowman & Littlefield, 2002). Jagdish Bhagwati, *The Wind of the Hundred Days: How Washington Mismanaged Globalization* (Cambridge, MA: MIT P, 2001). Brian Milani, *Designing the Green Economy: The Post-Industrial Alternative to Corporate Globalization* (Lanham, MD: Rowman & Littlefield, 2000).

Area of the Americas) and Genoa, Italy (2001 G8 summit), where protesters and police engaged in battles that killed one person. The key 2001 WTO meeting to launch a new trade round was held in Qatar, where protesters had little access. The Canadian government followed suit and held the 2002 G8 Summit in Kananaskis, Alberta. Protesters could only get as close as Calgary, about 100 kilometres from the site. Hosts of some subsequent summits have tried to find equally inaccessible locations to keep protesters at bay, as the U.S. did in 2004 by holding the annual G8 meeting on Sea Island, Georgia.

Just as scholars disagree on concepts of globalization, so do protesters on their goals and tactics. Union members from the global North want to stop globalization from shipping their jobs south. Workers in impoverished countries in the global South, however, may desperately want those jobs as a first step toward decent wages and working conditions (relative to other options in their countries). Violence perpetrated by protesters or police can steal media attention from some of the goals of activists. Thus, neither globalization nor the backlash against it is simple. However you view the positive and negative effects of globalization, it is important to understand the interrelated processes that make up today's world political economy—trade, money, business, integration, communication, environmental management and the economic development of poor countries. Trade is central to this list.

MARKETS

International exchanges of goods and services now occur in *global markets*. Liberal economics supports the use of market processes, relatively unhindered by political elements; mercantilism favours greater political control over markets and exchanges; and critical theorists examine the inequalities inherent in market relations. The stakes in this debate are high because of the growing volume and importance of international trade.

Global Patterns of Trade

International trade amounts to a sixth of the total economic activity in the world. More than $10 trillion worth of trade crosses international borders each year.[10] This is a very large figure, nearly 10 times the world's military spending, for example. This great volume of international trade reflects the fact that trade is profitable.

The role of trade in the economy varies somewhat from one region to another, but it is at least as important overall in the developing regions of the global South as in the industrialized regions of the world. Nonetheless, in the world economy as a whole, the global South accounts for a relatively small part of all trade, because its economic activity is only 40 percent of the world's total (see pp. 414–415). This creates an asymmetrical dependence in North-South trade (see Chapters 12 and 13).

Overall, most political activity related to trade is concentrated in the industrialized West (North America, Western Europe and Japan/Pacific), which accounts for about two-thirds of all international trade. Trade between these areas and the global South, although less in volume, is also a topic of interest to IPE scholars (see Chapter 12).[11] Of significance today are trade issues in the former communist transitional economies of

---

[10] Data in this chapter are calculated from World Trade Organization, *International Trade Statistics 2005* (Geneva: WTO, 2005).

[11] Timothy J. McKeown, "A Liberal Trade Order? The Long-Run Pattern of Imports to the Advanced Capitalist States," *International Studies Quarterly* 35.2 (1991): 151–72.

Russia and Eastern Europe, which face formidable challenges as they try to join the capitalist world economy.

Two contradictory trends are at work in current global trading patterns. One is toward the integration of industrialized regions with each other in a truly global market. The World Trade Organization (discussed later in this chapter) is especially important to this global integration process. The second trend is the emerging potential division of the industrialized West into three competing trading blocs, each internally integrated but not very open to the other two blocs. Regional free trade areas in Europe and North America, and perhaps in Asia in the future, raise the possibility of trading zones practising liberalism inwardly and mercantilism outwardly. However, as information technologies link the world across space, the integrating trend seems to have the upper hand and a more global vision of free trade is shaping the agenda.

comparative advantage
The principle that states should specialize in trading those goods that they produce with the greatest relative efficiency and at the lowest relative cost (relative, that is, to other goods produced by the same state).

Comparative Advantage

For economic liberals, the overall success of market economies is due to the substantial gains that can be realized through trade.[12] These gains result from the **comparative advantage** that different states enjoy in producing different goods (a concept pioneered by economists Adam Smith and David Ricardo 200 years ago). States vary in their abilities to produce certain goods because of differences in natural resources, labour force characteristics and other such factors. In order to maximize the overall creation of wealth, by this view, each state should specialize in producing the goods for which it has a comparative advantage and then trade for goods that another state is better at producing. Of course, the costs of transportation and of processing information in the trade (called *transaction costs*) must be included in the costs of production. Frequently these costs are low relative to the differences in the cost of producing items in different locations.

A state need not have an absolute advantage over others in producing one kind of good in order to make specialization pay. It need only specialize in producing goods that are lower in cost than other goods relative to world market prices. Imagine that Japan discovered a way to produce synthetic oil using the same mix of labour and capital that it now uses to produce cars, and that this synthetic oil could be produced a bit more cheaply than what it costs Saudi Arabia to produce oil, but that Japan could still produce cars *much* more cheaply than could Saudi Arabia. From a strictly economic point of view, Japan should keep producing cars

The Information Revolution
Decentralizing Markets

Markets are said to be more efficient when participants have more information about each other. Information systems underlie the rapid growth of international trade. In a world where small producers and consumers meet in cyberspace instead of at the village marketplace, how will the character of international trade change? Two commodities of great importance in the world are oil and cars. It is much cheaper to produce oil (or another energy source) in Saudi Arabia than in Japan, and much cheaper to produce cars in Japan than in Saudi Arabia. Japan needs oil to run its industry (including its car industry), and Saudi Arabia needs cars to travel its vast territory (including reaching its remote oil wells). Even with shipping and transaction costs, huge amounts of money are saved by shipping Japanese cars to Saudi Arabia and Saudi oil to Japan, compared with the costs if each were self-sufficient.

To explore this question, go to www.pearsoned.ca/goldstein.

---

[12] David A. Lake, ed., *The International Political Economy of Trade* (Brookfield, VT: Elgar, 1993). John S. Odell and Thomas D. Willett, eds., *International Trade Policies: Gains from Exchange between Economics and Political Science* (Ann Arbor: U Michigan P, 1990). Benjamin J. Cohen, "The Political Economy of International Trade," [review article] *International Organization* 44.2 (1990): 261–78.

(its comparative advantage) and not divert capital and labour to make synthetic oil (where it had only a slight advantage). The extra profits Japan would make from exporting more cars would more than compensate for the slightly higher price it would pay to import oil.

Thus, international trade generally expands the joint benefits for both Japan and Saudi by increasing the overall efficiency of production. Free trade allocates global resources to states that have the greatest comparative advantage in producing each kind of commodity. As a result, prices are lower overall and more consistent worldwide. Increasingly, production is oriented to the world market.

The Changing World Order
Trade versus Security?

World orders encompass rules and patterns of international political economy as well as security relationships. Historically, periods of hegemony have seen increasing trade, interdependence and prosperity. The first post–Cold War decade of the 1990s fit that pattern. Corporations operated more globally, producing components in scattered locations and bringing them together into final products at the last minute ("just-in-time" inventory). By taking redundancies out of the global production system and facilitating the flow of goods and services across borders, these technical and managerial changes helped bring about a decade of unparalleled prosperity for much of the industrialized West and parts of the global South.

The 2001 terrorist attacks on the United States exposed the "soft underbelly of globalization"—the vulnerability of a world without borders.* In the aftermath of September 11, tighter security slowed the movement of goods, services and people across borders. Canadian truckers, for example, waited for hours—and in some cases days—at U.S. border crossings. Air traffic and business travel around the world became more difficult. Corporations waited for delayed materials coming from foreign sources, and governments worried that a terrorist attack could shut down an entire country.

Millions of shipping containers travel from port to port and disperse over road and rail networks throughout industrialized countries. Very few are searched, and to do so would be prohibitively costly—a drag on trade-based prosperity. Authorities worry that weapons of mass destruction could enter countries through ports, and that finding them would be like "finding a needle in a haystack." Customs agents now routinely wear radiation-detecting Geiger counters that sound an alarm if nuclear

New York, late 2003.

material is nearby (and not sufficiently shielded to pass undetected).

Economic liberals would argue that any impediments to the free flow of trade—including security measures—should be as minimal as possible, but mercantilists argue that greater security measures are necessary in the post-9/11 world order, and that states should reduce their dependence on trade and aim for greater self-reliance.

In a world of heightened vulnerability, is it better for countries to rely more on their own resources and abilities at a cost of slower economic growth and lower living standards? Or should they continue the openness of the 1990s, with increasing trade, economic growth and interdependence, at the cost of higher military spending and the risk of devastating attacks?

* William Booth, "Where Sea Meets Shore, Scenarios for Terrorists," *Washington Post* 3 Jan. 2002: A1.

Trade is not without drawbacks, however, when seen from a political rather than purely economic vantage point (see "Resistance to Trade" at the end of this chapter). One drawback is familiar from the previous discussions of international security—for liberals, long-term benefits may incur short-term costs. When a state begins to import goods it had previously been producing domestically, there may be disruptions to its economy: workers may be fired or need to retrain and find new jobs, and capital may not be easy to convert to new uses.

Another problem is that the benefits and costs of trade tend not to be evenly distributed *within* a state. Some industries or communities may benefit at the expense of others. For example, if a Canadian manufacturing company moves its factory to Mexico to take advantage of cheaper labour, and exports its goods back to Canada, the workers at the old Canadian factory lose their jobs, but Canadian consumers enjoy cheaper goods. The costs of such a move fall heavily on a few workers, while the benefits are spread thinly across many consumers.

Mercantilists might suggest the use of protectionist measures to try to save jobs lost due to globalization, with the argument that the loss of jobs (and greater dependence on foreign suppliers) potentially weakens the state. For liberals, protectionist measures benefit a few people greatly, and cost many people a bit. By one estimate, a 20 percent steel tariff contemplated by the Bush administration in 2002 would have cost consumers US$7 billion and saved 7300 U.S. jobs—a pricey US$326 000 per job.[13] Yet those 7300 workers (and their unions and companies) would have benefited greatly, whereas the roughly $20 cost per U.S. citizen would go unnoticed. This kind of unequal distribution of costs and benefits often creates political problems for free trade even when the *overall* economic benefits outweigh costs.

Between states (as well as within each state), the distribution of benefits from trade can also be unequal. New wealth created by international trade can be divided in any manner between participants. For instance, it would be worthwhile for Saudi Arabia to import cars even at a price much higher than what it cost Japan to produce them, as long as the price was less than what it would cost Saudi Arabia to produce cars itself (or to buy them elsewhere). Similarly, Saudi Arabia would profit from selling oil even at a price just a bit above what the oil costs to produce (or what it can sell the oil for elsewhere). With so much added value from the exchange process, there is a great deal of room for bargaining over the distribution of benefits.

If there were only two states in the world, bargaining over prices (that is, over the distribution of benefits from trade) would essentially be a political process entailing the use of leverage, possibly including military force. In a world of many states (and even more substate economic actors, such as companies and households), this is less true. Prices are set instead by market competition. If Japan's cars are too expensive, Saudi Arabia can buy German cars; if Saudi oil is too expensive, Japan can buy Alaskan oil.

Prices and Markets

The *terms* of an exchange are defined by the price at which goods are traded. Often, the *bargaining space*—defined by the difference between the lowest price a seller would accept and the highest price a buyer would pay—is quite large. For example, Saudi Arabia would be willing to sell a barrel of oil (if it had no better option) for as little as, say, $10 a barrel,

---

[13] Joseph Kahn, "U.S. Trade Panel Backs Putting Hefty Duties on Imported Steel," *New York Times* 8 Dec. 2001: C1, C3.

and industrialized countries are willing to pay as much as $75 a barrel for the oil. (In practice, oil prices have fluctuated in this broad range in recent decades.) How are prices determined? That is, how do the participants decide on the distribution of benefits from the exchange?

When there are multiple buyers and sellers of a good (or equivalent goods that it can be substituted for), prices are determined by market competition.[14] In terms of the above bargaining framework, sellers bargain for a high price, using as leverage the threat to sell to another buyer. Meanwhile buyers bargain for a low price, with the leverage being a threat to buy from another seller. In practice, free markets are supposed to (and sometimes do) produce stable patterns of buying and selling at fairly uniform prices. At *market price*, sellers know that an effort to raise the price would drive the buyer to seek another seller, and buyers know that an effort to lower the price would drive the seller to seek another buyer. Because of this stability, the process of bargaining is greatly simplified and most economic exchanges take place in a fairly routine manner.

Buyers vary in the value they place on an item (like a barrel of oil). If the price rises, fewer people are willing to buy it, and if the price drops, more people are willing to buy. This is called the *demand curve* for the item. Sellers also vary in the value they place on the item. If the price rises, more sellers are willing to supply the item to buyers; if the price drops, fewer sellers are willing to supply it. This is called the *supply curve*.

In a free market, the price at which the supply and demand curves intersect is the *equilibrium price*. At this price, sellers are willing to supply the same number of units that buyers are willing to purchase. (In practice, prices reflect *expectations* about supply and demand in the near future.) In a trade of Saudi oil for Japanese cars, for example, prices would be determined by the world demand for, and supply of, oil and cars.

Thus, in liberal economics, *bilateral* relations between states are less important than they are in security affairs. The existence of world markets reduces the leverage that one state can exert over another in economic affairs (because the second state can simply find other partners). Imagine Japan trying to exert power by refusing to sell cars to Saudi Arabia. It would only hurt itself—Saudi Arabia would buy cars elsewhere. In IPE, then, power is more diffuse and involves more actors at once than in international security.

The currency used to express world prices is somewhat arbitrary. Prices were once pegged to the value of gold or silver, but are now expressed in national currencies—most prominently the U.S. dollar, Japanese yen and European euro. In practice, the conversion of money among national currencies is complex (see Chapter 10), but for the sake of simplicity we will proceed as if there were a common currency.

A major alternative to a market economy is a **centrally planned** (or **command**) **economy,** in which political authorities set prices and decide on quotas for production and consumption of each commodity according to a long-term plan. For decades, this type of economy was standard in the communist states of the former Soviet Union, Eastern Europe, China and several smaller countries—and is still in place in Cuba and North Korea. Proponents of central planning claim it makes economies both more rational and more just. Instead, communist economics has, in recent years, been discredited as hopelessly inefficient and discarded in whole or in part by virtually all of its former followers.

The economies of Russia and Eastern Europe stagnated throughout the Cold War while environmental damage and military spending took an increasing economic toll. Now, the former Soviet republics and Eastern Europe are almost all **transitional economies,**

centrally planned (command) economy An economy in which political authorities set prices and decide on quotas for production and consumption of each commodity according to a long-term plan.

transitional economies Countries in Russia and Eastern Europe that are trying to convert from communism to capitalism, with varying degrees of success.

---

[14] Charles E. Lindblom, *The Market System: What It Is, How It Works, and What to Make of It* (New Haven, CT: Yale UP, 2001).

DUSTBIN OF HISTORY
The unreliable, polluting East German Trabant car reflected the inefficiency of production in the centrally planned economies of the communist countries during the Cold War era. All those countries are now making transitions—by various routes and with varying degrees of success—toward market-based economies. This Trabant in East Berlin was discarded as Germany unified, 1990.

attempting to make a *transition* to a market-based economy connected to the world capitalist economy.[15] This transition has proved very difficult. In the first half of the 1990s, the total GDP of the region *shrank* by about *35 percent*—a great depression worse than the one Canada experienced in the early 1930s (see p. 31). Living standards dropped dramatically for most citizens, and remained low for the rest of the decade. A program of *shock therapy*—a radical, sudden shift to market principles—seemed to work in Poland despite short-term dislocation, but a similar program in Russia stalled after being effectively blocked by old-time communist officials. President Putin (2000–present) brought new energy to economic reform and progress in some areas, but his centralization of power could choke off capitalist growth, and the overall path of Russia's transition remains uncertain.

China, whose government continues to follow a Marxist *political* line (central control by the Communist party), has shifted substantially toward a market *economy*. This transition dramatically increased China's economic growth in the 1980s, reaching a sustained annual rate of about 10 percent throughout the 1990s and slowing to more sustainable rates with the global recession of 2001 (see "The Chinese Experience" on pp. 458–462). Perhaps because China is not yet industrialized (and hence is more flexible about how to profitably invest capital), the introduction of market principles in China's economy has been less painful than in the "developed" (but actually poorly developed) economies of Russia and Eastern Europe.

Politics of Markets

A free and efficient market requires a fairly large number of buyers looking for an item and a large number of sellers supplying it. It also requires that participants have fairly complete information about the other participants and transactions in the market. The willingness of participants to deal with one another should not be distorted by personal (or political) preferences but should be governed only by price and quality considerations. Failures to meet these various conditions are called *market imperfections*: they

---

[15] Thane Gustafson, *Capitalism Russian-Style* (NY: Cambridge UP, 1999). Anders Aslund, *How Russia Became a Market Economy* (Washington, DC: Brookings, 1995). Leah A. Haus, *Globalizing the GATT: The Soviet Union's Successor States, Eastern Europe, and the International Trading System* (Washington, DC: Brookings, 1992).

PLAY BALL

Economic sanctions, such as U.S. restrictions on trade with Cuba, are among the most obvious ways that politics interferes in markets. Sanctions are hard to enforce, especially when not all countries participate, because doing business is profitable. The U.S. government tried to exclude Cuba from the World Baseball Classic in 2006 but backed down after strong complaints from other countries that do not apply sanctions to Cuba. Here, Japan's Ichiro Suzuki and Cuban players celebrate after Japan beat Cuba in the championship game in San Diego.

reduce efficiency (to the dismay of liberal economists). Most political intrusions into economic transactions are market imperfections.

International trade occurs more often at world market prices than does *domestic* economic exchange. No world government owns industries, provides subsidies or regulates prices. Nonetheless, world markets are often affected by politics. When states are the principal actors in international economic affairs, the number of participants is often small. When there is just one supplier of an item—a *monopoly*—the supplier can set the price quite high. For example, the South African company De Beers produces half the world supply and controls two-thirds of the world market for uncut diamonds. An *oligopoly* is a monopoly shared by just a few large sellers—often allowing for tacit or explicit coordination to force prices up. For example, members of the Organization of Petroleum Exporting Countries (OPEC) agree to limit oil production to keep prices up. To the extent that companies band together along national lines, monopolies and oligopolies are more likely.

Governments can use antitrust policies to break up monopolies and keep markets competitive. Home governments (states where a monopoly company's headquarters are located) often *benefit* from the ability to distort international markets and gain revenue (whether they are state-owned or taxed by the state). *Foreign* governments have little power to break up such monopolies.

Another common market imperfection in international trade is *corruption*; individuals may receive payoffs to trade at nonmarket prices. The government or company involved may lose some of the benefits being distributed, but the individual government official or company negotiator gets increased benefits (see pp. 473–475).

One difficulty in transitioning from centrally planned to market economies (as occurred in Russia and Eastern Europe) involves market imperfections, which can cause (and can be caused by) political corruption. For example, to become competitive internationally, states sell their state-owned industries to private citizens, who allow markets to determine the prices of their goods in international markets (which are higher than were set under the old system). These industries, however, continue to receive supplies domestically at fixed prices (set under the old system). The result is that the private citizens make high profits turning subsidized raw materials into highly priced goods for the international market. This partial reform brings some short-term gains, but concentrates abnormally large profits into the hands of a powerful few.[16] In Russia, President Putin jailed a leading oil tycoon who became politically outspoken, a move widely interpreted as a warning to Russia's new capitalist elite.

Politics provides a *legal framework* for markets—assuring that participants keep commitments, that contracts are binding, that buyers pay for goods they purchase, that counterfeit money is not used and so forth. In the international economy, which lacks a central government authority, rules are less easily enforced. As in security affairs, such rules can be codified in international treaties, but enforcement depends on practical reciprocity (see pp. 81–82).

Taxation is another political influence on markets. Taxes are used both to generate revenue for the government and to regulate economic activity by incentives. For instance, a government may keep taxes on foreign companies low in hopes of attracting them to locate and invest in the country. Taxes applied to international trade itself, called tariffs, are a frequent source of international conflict (see "Protectionism," pp. 319–323).

Political interference in free markets is most explicit when governments apply *sanctions* against economic interactions of certain kinds or between certain actors. Political power then prohibits an economic exchange that would have otherwise been mutually beneficial.

Enforcing sanctions is always a difficult task because there is a financial incentive to break them through parallel economies or other means.[17] For instance, despite UN sanctions against trading with Serbia in the early 1990s, many people and companies took risks to smuggle goods across Serbia's borders, because doing so was profitable. Without broad multilateral support for international sanctions, they generally fail. When the United States tried to punish the Soviet Union in the 1970s by applying trade sanctions against a Soviet oil pipeline to Western Europe, it did not stop the pipeline. It just took profitable business away from a U.S. company (Caterpillar) and allowed European companies to profit instead (because European states did not join in the sanctions). By contrast, when more states became involved in sanctions against apartheid-era South Africa, the impact is thought to have contributed to the transformation of that society from white minority rule in the early 1990s.

The difficulty of applying sanctions reflects a general point made earlier—that power in IPE is more diffused among states than it is in security affairs. Canada rarely

---

[16] Joel S. Hellman, "Winners Take All: The Politics of Partial Reform in Postcommunist Transitions," *World Politics* 50.2 (1998): 203–34.

[17] Daniel W. Drezner, *The Sanctions Paradox: Economic Statecraft and International Relations* (NY: Cambridge UP, 1999). Richard N. Haass and Meghan L. O'Sullivan, eds., *Honey and Vinegar: Incentives, Sanctions, and Foreign Policy* (Washington, DC: Brookings, 2000). George E. Shambaugh, *States, Firms, and Power: Successful Sanctions in United States Foreign Policy* (Albany: SUNY P, 2000). George A. Lopez and David Cortwright, *The Sanctions Decade: Assessing UN Strategies in the 1990s* (Boulder, CO: Rienner, 2000). Lisa L. Martin, *Coercive Cooperation: Explaining Multilateral Economic Sanctions* (Princeton, NJ: Princeton UP, 1992).

imposes economic sanctions unilaterally, and instead (through federal legislation called the United Nations Act) imposes them when the United Nations Security Council calls for members of the UN to do so. Canada can choose to impose sanctions in the absence of a Security Council Resolution (through the Special Economic Measures Regulations or the Export and Import Permits Act), but again, tends to do so only if called for by an international organization or if there is a perceived threat to international peace and security.

If one state tries to use economic means of leverage to influence another, other states can profitably take over. Refusing to participate in mutually profitable economic trade often harms oneself more than the target of one's actions, unless nearly all other states follow suit. This is one of the reasons Canada prefers to engage (when it engages in sanctions at all) in multilateral efforts.

Balance of Trade

Mercantilists favour political control of trade so that trade relations serve a state's political interests—even at the cost of wealth that might be created by free markets. Their preferred means of accomplishing this end is to create a favourable balance of trade. The **balance of trade** is the value of a state's imports relative to its exports.

A state that exports more than it imports has a *positive balance of trade*, or *trade surplus*. Japan has run a trade surplus in recent years: it gets more money for cars and other goods it exports than it pays for oil and other imported goods. A state that imports more than it exports has a *negative balance of trade* (*trade deficit*). A trade deficit is different from a budget deficit in government spending. Canada has run an overall trade surplus for a number of years as a result of trade with the United States. Canada consistently runs a trade deficit with almost all of its other trading partners.

The balance of trade must ultimately be reconciled, one way or another. It is tracked financially through a system of national accounts (see pp. 352–354). In the short term, a state can trade for a few years at a deficit followed by a few years at a surplus. The imbalances are carried on the national accounts as a kind of loan. However, a trade deficit that persists for years becomes a problem. As noted above, Canada has in recent years run a trade surplus overall (and in Canada-U.S. bilateral trade), while the United States has run a deficit. To balance trade, the United States then "exports" currency (dollars) to Canada, which can use the dollars to buy shares of U.S. companies, U.S. Treasury bills or U.S. real estate. In essence (though oversimplified), a state with a chronic trade deficit must export part of its standing wealth (real estate, companies, bank accounts, etc.) by giving ownership of such wealth to foreigners.

This is one reason why mercantilists favour national economic policies to create a trade surplus. The state can then "own" parts of other states, gaining power over them. Rather than being indebted to others, the state holds IOUs. Rather than being unable to find the money it might need to cope with a crisis or fight a war, the state sits on a pile of money representing potential power. Historically, mercantilism literally meant stockpiling gold (gained from running a trade surplus) as a fungible form of power (see Figure 9.1).

balance of trade The value of a state's exports relative to its imports.

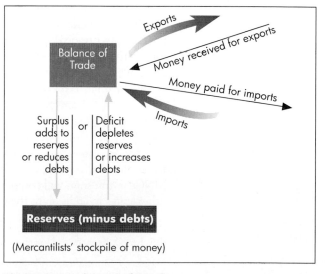

Figure 9.1 Balance of Trade

Such a strategy is attuned to realism's emphasis on relative power. For one state to have a trade surplus, another must have a deficit.

There is a price for mercantilist-derived power. Often a trade surplus lowers the short-term standard of living. For instance, if Canadians cashed in their trade surplus each year for imported goods, they could enjoy those goods now instead of piling up money for the future. Mercantilists are willing to pay such short-term costs because they are more concerned with power than with standards of living.

Interdependence

interdependence A political and economic situation in which two or more states are simultaneously dependent on one another for their well-being. Degrees of interdependence are sometimes designated in terms of "sensitivity" or "vulnerability."

When the well-being of a state depends on the cooperation of a second state, the first state is *dependent* on the second. When two or more states are simultaneously dependent on one another, they are *interdependent*. **Interdependence** is both a political and economic phenomenon. Economic liberals tend to see interdependence as mutually beneficial over the long term. Mercantilists are concerned about the risks to state power associated with interdependence. Critical theorists would say that interdependence is rarely a neutral condition, and usually involves relations of inequality.

Trading states become mutually dependent on each other's *political* cooperation in order to realize economic gains. In IPE, interdependence refers less to a bilateral mutual dependence than to a multilateral dependence in which each state depends on the political cooperation of most or all of the others to keep world markets operating efficiently. Most states depend on the world market, and not on specific trading partners (though for large industrialized states, each bilateral trade relationship is also important).

The mutual dependence of two or more states does not mean that their degree of dependence is equal or symmetrical. Often one is more dependent than another. This is especially true because world markets vary in their openness and efficiency from one commodity and region to another. Saudi Arabia, for instance, has more power over the price of oil than Japan has over the price of cars.

The degree of a state's *short-term* dependence on another may differ from its *long-term* dependence. The short-term dislocation caused by disrupting exchange with another country is the *sensitivity* of supply. When oil prices rose sharply in the early 1970s, Japan and other industrialized states did not have policies to cope with the increases: they were *sensitive* to the disruption, and long lines formed at gas stations. Over the long term, states may be able to change their policies to take advantage of alternatives that could substitute for disrupted trade. Japan expanded nuclear power in response to oil price increases—a long-term strategy. A state that *cannot* adjust its policies to cope with disrupted trade, even over the long run, suffers from *vulnerability* of supply.[18]

Over time, as the world economy develops and technology advances, states are becoming *increasingly interdependent*. Some IR scholars point out that this is not entirely new. The great powers were very interdependent before World War I; for instance, international trade was about the same percentage of GDP then as now. But several other dimensions of interdependence show dramatic change. One is the extent to which individual *firms*, which used to be nationally based, are now international in their holdings and interests (becoming MNCs or transnational corporations—TNCs), and are thus dependent on the well-being of other states in addition to their home state (making them tend to favour free trade).[19]

---

[18] Robert O. Keohane and Joseph S. Nye, *Power and Interdependence*, 3rd ed. (NY: Longman, 2001).

[19] Helen V. Milner, *Resisting Protectionism: Global Industries and the Politics of International Trade* (Princeton, NJ: Princeton UP, 1988).

Another key aspect of interdependence is the tight integration of world markets through the ever-expanding flow of *information* and communication worldwide (see pp. 397–400). This facilitates the free competition of goods and services in global markets as well as expanding the volume of money (capital) that moves around the world every day. Yet another dimension of change is the expansion of *scope* in the global economy, from one based in Europe to a more diffuse network encompassing the world. Asian economic expansion and the integration of Russia and Eastern Europe into the world market economy are accelerating this trend.

Whether based on a specific bilateral trading relationship, an integrated global (or regional) market or the international nature of corporate holdings, interdependence arises from comparative advantage—that is, from the greater absolute wealth that two or more states can produce by collaborating. This wealth depends on international political cooperation, which is therefore in the interests of all participants. Furthermore, violence is usually not an effective leverage in bringing about such cooperation. Thus, many liberal IR scholars argue that *interdependence inherently promotes peace*.[20] It alters the cost-benefit calculations of national leaders so as to make military leverage less attractive. (Some IR scholars saw similar trends in international interdependence just before World War I, but war occurred anyway.)

Despite the added wealth that states enjoy as a result of trade and the power that such wealth creates, interdependence does have drawbacks. The more a state gains from trade cooperation, the more its own well-being depends on other states, which therefore have power over it. In situations of asymmetrical interdependence in particular, the economic benefits of cooperation may be accompanied by inherent vulnerabilities. The potential for those vulnerabilities to be taken advantage of would be the kind of thing a mercantilist would caution against. For example, it is cheaper for Japan to import energy than to produce it domestically, but dependence on energy imports has historically put Japan at a disadvantage in power. In the 1930s, the United States cut off its oil exports to Japan to protest Japanese militarism. Exports and imports can create dependence (on those who buy the product); UN sanctions against Iraq's oil exports have deprived Iraq of revenue.

Interdependence thus ties the well-being of a state's population and society to policies and conditions in other states outside its control. The price of trade-generated wealth (and the power it brings) is a loss of state autonomy and sovereignty. These problems are intensifying as world markets become more closely interwoven, especially with regional integration in places like Europe (see Chapter 10).

UNSETTLING CHANGES
Growing trade makes states more interdependent. This may make them more peaceful, but can also introduce new insecurities and sources of conflict. Free trade creates winners and losers. Backlash against free trade agreements led to a spectacular failure at the WTO summit meeting in Seattle in 1999. As environmentalists and labour unions led protests in the streets, the assembled states could not agree on an agenda for a new round of trade talks.

---

[20] Edward D. Mansfield, *Power, Trade, and War* (Princeton, NJ: Princeton UP, 1994).

As states become more interdependent, power becomes more rather than less important in IR. The intensification of linkages among states multiplies the number of issues affecting their relations and the avenues of influence by which outcomes are shaped. It is true that because power operates on multiple complex dimensions in a highly interdependent world, the importance of one dimension—military power—is gradually diminishing relative to other means of influence (diplomatic, economic, cultural, etc.). The overall importance of international power on all dimensions combined is increasing as the world becomes more interdependent.

TRADE STRATEGIES

To manage the trade-offs of gains and losses in power and wealth, states develop economic strategies—trade strategies in particular—in order to maximize their own wealth while minimizing their vulnerability and dependence on others. Some strategies can be implemented by single states; most involve participation in some broader framework.

Autarky

autarky (self-reliance)
A policy of avoiding or minimizing trade and trying to produce everything one needs (or the most vital things) by oneself.

An obvious way to avoid becoming dependent on other states, especially for a weak state whose trading partners tend to be more powerful, is to avoid trading and instead to try to produce everything it needs by itself. Such a strategy is called *self-reliance* or **autarky.** As the theory of comparative advantage suggests, autarky is ineffective. A self-reliant state pays a very high cost to produce goods for which it does not have a comparative advantage. As other states cooperate among themselves to maximize their joint creation of wealth, the relative power of the autarkic state in the international system tends to fall.

In practice, when states have relied on a policy of autarky they have indeed lagged behind others. A classic case in recent decades was the small state of Albania, next to the former Yugoslavia. A communist state that split from the Soviet Union and China, Albania did not participate in world markets for decades but relied on a centrally planned economy designed for self-sufficiency. Few foreigners were allowed to visit, little trade took place and Albania pursued autarky to prevent outsiders from gaining power over it. When this curtain of isolation finally fell in 1991, Albania was as poor as decades earlier. Little additional wealth had been generated; little economic development had taken place. This contributed to Albania's political instability, which affected conflicts in Kosovo and Macedonia that precipitated NATO military intervention.

China's experience also illustrates autarky's ineffectiveness. China's economic isolation in the 1950s and 1960s, resulting from an economic embargo imposed by the United States and its allies, was deepened during its own Cultural Revolution in the late 1960s when it broke ties with the Soviet Union. In that period, all things foreign were rejected. For instance, Chinese computer programmers were not allowed to use foreign software, such as Assembler language and Fortran—standards in the rest of the world. Instead they were forced to create all software from scratch. As a result, the computer industry lagged far behind, "reinventing the wheel" as the world's computer revolution unfolded.

When China opened up to the world economy in the 1980s, the pattern was reversed. The rapid expansion of trade, along with market-oriented reforms in its domestic economy, resulted in rapid economic growth that has continued into the new century. By contrast, North Korea maintained a policy of self-reliance and isolation even after the Cold War. This policy (along with high military spending and other problems) led to mass starvation in the 1990s.

Protectionism

Although few states pursue strategies of autarky, many states try to manipulate international trade in order to strengthen one or more domestic industries and shelter them from world markets. Such policies are broadly known as **protectionism**—protection of domestic industries from international competition. Although this term encompasses a range of trade policies arising from various motivations, all are contrary to liberalism in that they seek to distort free markets to gain an advantage for the state (or for substate actors within it), generally by discouraging imports of competing goods or services.[21]

Government policies discouraging imports can help domestic industries or communities avoid the costs inherent in full participation in world markets. Such costs often fall disproportionately on a small segment of the population and lead that group to pressure the government for protection. The benefits of greater global efficiency, by contrast, are spread more broadly across the population and do not create similar domestic pressures (see p. 303).

A state's *motivation* to protect domestic industry can arise from several sources. Often governments simply cater to the political demands of important domestic industries and interests, regardless of overall national interest. An industry may lobby or give campaign contributions in order to win special tax breaks, subsidies or restrictions on competing imports (see "Industries and Interest Groups" later in this chapter).

States often attempt to protect an *infant industry* during its initial start-up, until it reaches a point where it can compete in world markets. For instance, when South Korea first developed an automobile industry, it was not yet competitive with imports, so the government gave consumers incentives to buy Korean cars. Eventually the industry grew and could compete with foreign producers and even export cars profitably. In a number of poor states, the *textile* trade has been a favoured infant industry (adding value without heavy capital requirements) protected by governments.[22] Protection of infant industry is considered a relatively legitimate reason for (temporary) protectionism. Britain became a strong advocate of free trade by the eighteenth and nineteenth centuries, but mercantilists argued that it did so only after its own industries became strong enough to withstand foreign competition. This is one reason why mercantilists, as well as critical theorists, argue that free trade is a policy of the already rich and powerful.

Another motivation for protectionism is to give a domestic industry breathing room when market conditions shift or new competitors surface. Sometimes domestic industry requires time to adapt and can emerge a few years later in a healthy condition. When gas prices jumped in the 1970s, U.S. auto producers were slow to shift to smaller cars, and smaller Japanese cars gained a great advantage in the U.S. market. The U.S. government used a variety of measures, including import quotas and loan guarantees, to help the U.S. industry through this transition.

Yet another motivation is the safeguarding of industry considered vital to national security. In the 1980s U.S. officials sought to protect the U.S. electronics and computer industries against being driven out of business by Japanese competitors, because those industries were considered crucial to military production. A government-sponsored consortium of U.S. computer-chip companies called Sematech was formed to promote the U.S. capability to produce chips cheaply (ordinarily the U.S. government would

protectionism The protection of domestic industries against international competition by trade tariffs and other means.

---

[21] Dominick Salvatore, ed., *Protectionism and World Welfare* (NY: Cambridge UP, 1993). Judith Goldstein, "The Political Economy of Trade: Institutions of Protection," *American Political Science Review* 801 (1986): 161–84.

[22] Vinod K. Aggarwal, *Liberal Protectionism: The International Politics of Organized Textile Trade* (Berkeley: U California P, 1985).

discourage such a consortium as an antitrust violation). To ensure self-sufficiency for military goods, states are often willing to sacrifice some economic efficiency. Thus, in the event of war, the state will be less vulnerable.

In Canada, a common motivation for protectionism has been to guard industries considered vital to maintaining Canadian cultural diversity. Foreign content, and in particular U.S. content, of Canadian radio, television, books, magazines and feature films has long been considered a threat to the preservation of Canadian cultural industries. The government has sought a variety of ways to promote the development of Canadian culture, by funding such institutions as the Canadian Broadcasting Corporation (the CBC), arts councils and the National Film Board; by providing tax incentives to domestically produced cultural products; and by regulating, through agencies such as the Canadian Radio-television and Telecommunications Commission (the CRTC), access to radio, television and cable broadcasting.[23]

Any government support for cultural industries can be seen as providing an unfair trade advantage. In some cases, the Canadian government simply attempts to block foreign-owned cultural products. In 1994, for example, the CRTC revoked the broadcast licence of Country Music Television (CMT), a U.S.-owned country music station, in order to facilitate a Canadian country music station, Canada's New Country Network. The CRTC has regularly denied licences (or as in this case, revoked them) to foreign-owned companies that were in direct competition with Canadian-owned ones. In this case, the U.S. threatened retaliatory trade sanctions, but in the end CMT bought a portion of Canada's New Country Network and renamed it CMT Canada, retaining access to the Canadian market. The most recent round of World Trade negotiations (the Doha Round, see below) is attempting to address, among other issues, intellectual property rights, which may have a significant impact on the ability of states to protect cultural industries.[24]

Finally, protection may be motivated by a defensive effort to ward off predatory practices by foreign companies or states. *Predatory* generally refers to efforts to unfairly capture a large share of world markets, or even a near-monopoly, so that eventually the predator can raise prices without fearing competition. Most often these efforts entail **dumping** products in foreign markets at prices below the minimum level necessary to make a profit. The reason a state would want its companies to dump products is that money lost in the short term could lead to dominance of a market, which eventually lets the state's companies raise prices enough to recoup their losses and to profit more. In the 1980s and 1990s, the Canadian government sought to protect the domestic footwear industry, sometimes by claiming that foreign producers like Brazil and China were dumping low-priced shoes in the Canadian market. Critics argued that the Canadian government was inappropriately applying anti-dumping protections: the shoes were simply produced more cheaply by foreign producers, and were not being dumped. This is one of the concerns that generally arise in cases of dumping: Is the product being intentionally undervalued by exporters seeking unfair access to a market (with the intention of establishing a monopoly over time), or has its price simply dropped by virtue of more efficient production techniques?

In a domestic economy, the government can use antitrust laws to break up an impending monopoly, but because no such mechanism exists in IR, governments try to

dumping The sale of products in foreign markets at prices below the minimum level necessary to make a profit (or below cost).

---

[23] Steven Shrybman, *A Citizen's Guide to the World Trade Organization* (Toronto: Canadian Centre for Policy Alternatives and Lorimer, 1999).

[24] Daniel Drache and Marc D. Froese, "Globalisation, World Trade and the Cultural Commons: Identity, Citizenship and Pluralism," *New Political Economy* 11.3 (Sept. 2006): 361–82.

COMPETITION AND PROTECTIONISM

Protectionism uses various means to keep foreign imports from competing with domestic products. U.S. tariffs on imported lumber from Canada were ruled illegal by the WTO and NAFTA.

restrict imports in such situations to protect their state's industries. Up to the late 1980s, industrialized countries such as Australia, Canada, the U.S. and members of the EU accounted for most anti-dumping cases, but by the mid-1990s, countries of the global South such as Argentina, Brazil, India, Mexico, South Korea and South Africa began to use anti-dumping laws to protect themselves against predatory trade practices.[25] These conflicts now generally are resolved through the WTO (see pp. 332–335).

Just as there are several motivations for protectionism, governments use several methods to restrict imports. The simplest is a **tariff** (or *duty*)—a tax imposed on certain types of imported goods, usually as a percentage of their value, as they enter the country. Tariffs not only restrict imports but can also be an important source of state revenues. If a state is going to engage in protectionism, international norms favour tariffs as the preferred method of protection because they are clear and straightforward (see pp. 382–384). Most states maintain long and complex schedules of tariffs based on thousands of categories and subcategories of goods organized by industry.

Other means of discouraging imports are **nontariff barriers** to trade. Imports can be limited by a *quota*. Quotas are ceilings on how many goods of a certain kind can be imported; they are imposed to restrict the growth of such imports. The extreme version is a flat prohibition against importing a certain type of good (or goods from a certain country). The softwood lumber agreement of 1996 between Canada and the United

tariff A duty or tax levied on certain types of imports (usually as a percentage of their value) as they enter a country.

nontariff barriers Forms of restricting imports other than tariffs, such as quotas (ceilings on how many goods of a certain kind can be imported).

---

[25] Thomas J. Prusa, "On the Spread and Impact of Antidumping," National Bureau of Economic Research Working Paper 7404, Cambridge.

Focus on Canadian Scholarship

Scholars who work on questions of international trade include **Marjorie Griffin Cohen** at Simon Fraser University, who focuses on issues of free trade and women's work. At Brock University, **Daniel Madar** focuses on international trade issues in the world's steel industry. At Carleton University, **Michael Dolan** focuses on international negotiations around a variety of political economy areas, including trade. **Michael Hart**, at Carleton's Norman Paterson School of International Affairs, studies the laws and institutions of international trade with a particular focus on Canadian trade policy, and his colleague **Yanling Wang** focuses on trade and technology diffusion. **Gilbert Gagné** of Bishop's University concentrates on international trade rules and NAFTA. At Dalhousie University, **Gilbert Winham** conducts research on international trade policy. At York University, **Leah Vosko** focuses on global labour and trade regulations and the impact on precarious work, and her colleague **Daniel Drache** examines WTO trade negotiations, NAFTA, trade blocs and employment policies. **Mark Brawley** at McGill University looks at power and trade and the rise of the trading state, and his colleague, **Mark Manger,** focuses on regional trade agreements with particular emphasis on Asia. At McMaster University,

Robert O'Brien studies global social movements and international financial institutions, including the WTO. At the University of Prince Edward Island, **David Cook** researches regional and multilateral trade negotiations and the WTO. **Patricia Goff** of Wilfrid Laurier University focuses on trade and cultural policies. **Louis Bélanger** at the University of Laval examines NAFTA. At the University of Guelph, **Brian Woodrow** researches trade in telecommunications and insurance services, and his colleague **Ken Woodside** examines the impact of NAFTA on Canadian domestic policies. **Xu Yi-Chong** of St. Francis Xavier University focuses on international civil servants and the GATT/WTO. At the University of Québec at Montréal, **Christian Deblock** studies free trade areas with a particular focus on NAFTA. At the University of Ottawa, **Marie-Josée Massicotte** is interested in trade and economic integration in the Americas. **Sylvia Ostry** at the University of Toronto examines the multilateral trading system, and her colleague **Carla Norrlöf** focuses on the relationship between the WTO and other trade agreements. Also at the University of Toronto, **Alan Alexandroff** studies China and the WTO. **Anna Lanoszka** of the University of Windsor researches the WTO and new trade issues.

States set quotas on Canadian exports of softwood lumber to the U.S. Any exports above the quota were subject to steep tariffs. The agreement expired in March 2001, and since that time, Canada and the U.S. have been engaged in ongoing disputes about softwood lumber exports. The U.S. argues that Canadian lumber exporters are receiving unfair subsidies from the Canadian government and dumping softwood lumber on the U.S. market at below-market prices.[26] In 2004, the WTO and a North American Free Trade Agreement (NAFTA) panel found that the U.S. claims were flawed.

Related to the example above, a third way to protect domestic industry is by providing *subsidies* to a domestic industry, which allows it to lower its prices without losing money. Subsidies can be funnelled to industries in a variety of ways. A state can give *tax breaks* to an industry struggling to get established or facing strong foreign competition. It can make *loans* (or guarantee private loans) on favourable terms to companies in a threatened industry. Sometimes governments buy goods from domestic producers at high *guaranteed prices* and resell them on world markets at lower prices; the European Community does this with agricultural products—to the dismay of U.S. farmers, as does the United States—to the dismay of European farmers. Under WTO regulations

---

[26] Gilbert Gagné, "The Canada-US Softwood Lumber Dispute," *International Journal* 58.3 (Summer 2003): 335–68. Greg Anderson, "Can Someone Please Settle This Dispute? Canadian Softwood Lumber and the Dispute Settlement Mechanisms of the NAFTA and the WTO," *World Economy* 29.5 (2006): 585–610.

(see below), states may be allowed to use countervailing duties against goods that receive subsidies or other forms of support deemed unfair under global trading rules.

Fourth, imports can be limited by *restrictions* and *regulations*, or sometimes simply different language requirements that make it hard to distribute and market a product even when it can be imported. In Canada, for example, products that are produced in a foreign country must conform to the requirement to display both official languages, French and English. States that have different hygienic production regulations can block imports that do not meet those same standards. The discovery of disease in agricultural exports—hoof and mouth disease in Britain in 2001, for example, and mad cow disease in British cattle in 1986 and in some Canadian cattle starting in 2003 (by 2006 there were eight confirmed Canadian cases)—led to restrictions on beef exports from both these countries.[27]

Protectionism has positive and negative effects on an economy, most often helping producers but hurting consumers. For instance, although the U.S. lumber industry has been aided somewhat by the restrictions imposed on Canadian imports, U.S. lumber consumers paid more as a result. By some U.S. estimates, for example, the cost of a new home in the United States was between US$800 and US$1300 higher than it would have been without trade restrictions.[28] As liberals argue, the cost of lumber to consumers may be greater than the benefits to its producers; but those costs are spread among millions of households, whereas the benefits are concentrated on a few firms. This means that the firms most affected will be highly motivated to try to influence governments to act in their favour, more so than the many individuals and households who bear the costs of protectionism. For economic liberals, another problem with protectionism is that domestic industry may use protection to avoid needed improvements and may therefore remain inefficient and uncompetitive—especially if protection continues over many years.

Industries and Interest Groups

Industries and other domestic political actors often seek to influence a state's foreign economic policies (see "Interest Groups," pp. 146–148).[29] These pressures do not always favour protectionism. In the lumber example above, it was Home Builders Associations in the United States that used estimates of increased new house prices to lobby the U.S. government to abandon restrictions on Canadian softwood lumber. From that industry's perspective, opening up free trade to Canadian softwood lumber would reduce the price its members pay for necessary inputs into home building. They did not want to pay the higher prices demanded by domestic producers.

Industries that are advanced and competitive in world markets often try to influence their governments to adopt free trade policies. This strategy promotes a global free trade

---

[27] Michael J. Broadway, "'Mad Cow' and the Neighbours: Canada's Beef with the US Border Closure," *Canadian Foreign Policy* 12.3 (2005/2006): 105–17.

[28] Cato Institute, "Nailing the Homeowner? Assessing the Impact of Trade Restrictions on Softwood Lumber," Cato Institute Policy Forum, October 26, 2000.

[29] John M. Rothgeb, *U.S. Trade Policy: Balancing Economic Dreams and Political Realities* (Washington, DC: CQ Press, 2001). Beth A. Simmons, *Who Adjusts? Domestic Sources of Foreign Economic Policy during the Interwar Years* (Princeton, NJ: Princeton UP, 1994). I. M. Destler, *American Trade Politics*, 2nd ed. (Washington, DC: Institute for International Economics, 1992). G. John Ikenberry, David A. Lake and Michael Mastanduno, eds., *The State and American Foreign Economic Policy*, spec. issue of *International Organization* 42.1 (1988). Daniel Verdier, *Democracy and International Trade: Britain, France, and the United States, 1860–1990* (Princeton, NJ: Princeton UP, 1994).

system in which such industries can prosper. By contrast, industries that lag behind their global competitors tend to seek government restrictions on imports or other forms of protection.

Means to influence foreign economic policy include lobbying; forming coalitions, organizations or agencies; paying bribes; or even encouraging coups. Actors include industry-sponsored groups, companies, labour unions and individuals. Within an industry, such efforts usually work in a common direction because, despite competition among companies and between management and labour, all share common interests regarding trade policies. However, a different industry may be pushing in a different direction. For instance, some Canadian industries supported the North American Free Trade Agreement (NAFTA); others opposed it.

A good example of how competing domestic interests can pull state trade policy in opposite directions has to do with U.S. tobacco exports. U.S. companies have a global comparative advantage in producing cigarettes. As the U.S. market for cigarettes shrank in the 1980s (because of education about the dangers of smoking), manufacturers more aggressively marketed U.S. cigarettes overseas. They challenged regulations in foreign countries restricting cigarette advertising, claiming the regulations were protectionist measures aimed at excluding a U.S. product from lucrative markets. In the late 1980s, the U.S. government sided with the tobacco companies and pressed foreign states to open their markets to U.S. cigarettes, threatening retaliatory trade measures if they refused. In 2001, U.S. pressure stopped South Korea from imposing tariffs on imported cigarettes. In 2002, Turkey met a U.S.-backed IMF demand to privatize the state tobacco monopoly, allowing foreign companies like Philip Morris to greatly expand their market in Turkey.

Health groups like the American Cancer Society opposed such U.S. policies, which they viewed as unethical. With the U.S. government's help, tobacco companies racked up high profits from rapidly growing sales in new foreign markets. The U.S. government was criticized for putting up obstacles to the negotiation of an international tobacco-control agreement in 2001–2003.

In many countries, government not only responds to industry influence, but works actively with them to promote their growth and tailor trade policy to their needs.[30] Such **industrial policy** is especially common in states where one or two industries are crucial to the entire economy (and of course where states own industries directly), and is also becoming a major issue in economic relations among great powers.[31] In Japan, the government coordinates industrial policy through the powerful Ministry of International Trade and Industry (MITI), which plans an overall strategy to take best advantage of Japan's strengths by directing capital and technology into promising areas. In Canada, the federal department Industry Canada focuses more on supporting innovation and investment and finding ways to enhance the global trading opportunities for Canadian companies than it does directing overall industrial decisions.

Interest groups not organized along industry lines also have particular interests in state trade policies. Canadian environmentalists, for example, do not want Canadian or U.S. companies to use the North American Free Trade Agreement (NAFTA) to avoid pollution controls by relocating to Mexico (where environmental laws are less strict). Canadian labour unions do not want companies to use NAFTA to avoid paying high wages.

industrial policy The strategies by which a government works actively with industries to promote their growth and tailor trade policy to their needs.

---

[30] Susan Strange, *States and Markets: An Introduction to International Political Economy*, 2nd ed. (NY: St. Martin's, 1994).

[31] Lars S. Skalnes, *Politics, Markets, and Grand Strategy: Foreign Economic Policies as Strategic Instruments* (Ann Arbor: U Michigan P, 2000).

Several industries are particularly important in current trade negotiations. First is agriculture, which has traditionally been protected from foreign competition on grounds that self-sufficiency in food reduces national vulnerability (especially in time of war). Although such security concerns have somewhat faded, farmers are well-organized and powerful domestic political actors in Japan, Europe, Canada, the United States and other countries. In Japan, farmers are a key constituency in the Liberal Democratic Party (LDP), which governed for decades. Farmers argue that Japan's rice-centred culture demands self-sufficiency in rice production. In France, farmers enjoy wide political support and have a huge stake in the trade policies of the European Union. Subsidies to farmers in France (and elsewhere in Europe) protect them against competition from U.S. farmers. During WTO negotiations in Doha, Qatar, in 2001, France bitterly resisted proposals to phase down the EU farm subsidies (compromise wording put the issue off).

Intellectual property rights are a second contentious area of trade negotiations. Intellectual property rights are the rights of creators of books, films, computer software and similar products to receive royalties when their products are sold. The United States has had major conflicts with states such as China, Taiwan, India, Thailand and Russia over piracy of computer software, music, films and other creative works—products in which the United States has a strong global comparative advantage. Infringement of intellectual property rights is widespread in many countries, on products ranging from videotaped movies to prescription drugs. In response, the international community has developed the World Intellectual Property Organization (WIPO), an extensive IGO with 178 member states, which tries to regularize patent and copyright law across borders. Most states signed an important 1994 patent treaty and a 1996 copyright treaty.

CRUSHING POLICY
Intellectual property rights have been an important focus of recent trade negotiations. In many countries, pirated copies of videos, music and software sell on the street with no royalty payments. Occasionally, governments collect and destroy pirated material, as here in Brazil in 2003, but generally fail to put much of a dent in the problem.

The 2001 WTO meeting raised serious disputes about drug patents—especially expensive HIV/AIDS medications produced under patent in the West but available from India and Brazil in cheap generic versions (which ignore the patent). Canada's Stephen Lewis, serving as UN Special Envoy for HIV/AIDS, has called on Western countries to ease up on drug patent restrictions that make access to life-saving drugs practically impossible for most countries of the global South to afford. Patented HIV/AIDS medication, for example, costs on average $10 000 a year per patient, while the same drugs produced by generic manufacturers cost approximately $300. Canada is home to both generic drug manufacturers and brand-name companies. The Canadian government has sought changes to the patent act that would permit generic producers greater freedom to export drugs (to combat not only HIV/AIDS, but also tuberculosis

intellectual property rights The legal protection of the original works of inventors, authors, creators and performers under patent, copyright and trademark law. Such rights became a contentious area of trade negotiations in the 1990s.

and malaria), and at the same time maintain domestic restrictions to protect the interests of the brand-name producers.[32]

Another key trade issue is the openness of countries to trade in the **service sector** of the economy. This sector includes many services, especially those concerning information, but the key focus in international trade negotiations is on banking, insurance and related financial services. U.S. companies, and some in Asia, enjoy a comparative advantage in these areas because of their information-processing technologies and experience in financial management. The North American Free Trade Agreement (NAFTA) allows U.S. and Canadian banks and insurance companies to operate in Mexico. In general, as telecommunications become cheaper and more pervasive, services offered by companies in one country can be efficiently used by consumers in other countries. Canadian consumers phoning customer service at Canadian companies may not realize that the person at the other end is in Barbados, India or another country of the global South—a long-distance trade in services.

Another especially important industry in international trade is the arms trade, which operates largely outside the framework of normal commercial transactions because of its national security implications.[33] Governments in industrialized countries want to protect their domestic arms industries rather than rely on imports to meet their weapons needs. Domestic arms industries become stronger and more economically viable by exporting their products (as well as supplying their own governments). Governments usually actively participate in the military-industrial sector of the economy (see "The Military-Industrial Complex" on pp. 152–153). Even when arms-exporting countries agree in principle to try to limit arms exports to a region, they have found it extremely difficult to give up the power and profits that such exports bring.

Illicit Trade A different problem is presented by the "industry" of illicit trade, or *smuggling*. No matter what restrictions governments put on trading certain goods, someone is usually willing to risk punishment to make a profit in such trade. Smuggling exists because it is profitable to sell fake Taiwanese copies of MS-DOS in Germany, for example, or Colombian cocaine in Canada, even though these products are illegal in those countries. Even with legal goods, profits can be increased by evading tariffs (by moving goods secretly, mislabelling them or bribing customs officials), as might happen with smuggling U.S. cigarettes into Canada, for example.

Illegal goods, and legal goods imported illegally, often are sold in parallel markets—sometimes called secreted markets or black markets. Parallel markets are widespread and flourish particularly in economies heavily regulated by government, such as centrally planned economies. In many countries of the global South, and in most of the transitional economies such as Russia, parallel markets are a substantial though hard-to-measure fraction of the total economic activity and deprive the government of significant revenue. Parallel markets also exist for foreign currency exchange (see Chapter 10).

The extent of illicit trade varies from one country and industry to another, depending on profitability and enforcement. Drugs and weapons are most profitable, and worldwide illegal trade networks exist for both. International illegal markets for weapons trade, beyond government controls, are notorious. A state with enough money can buy—at premium prices—most kinds of weapons.

---

[32] Heather Scoffield and Steven Chase, "Ottawa Heeds Call on AIDS," *The Globe and Mail* 26 Sept. 2003.

[33] Robert E. Harkavy and Stephanie G. Neuman, eds., *The Arms Trade: Problems and Prospects in the Post–Cold War World*, Annals of the American Academy of Political and Social Science, vol. 535 (Thousand Oaks, CA: Sage, 1994).

service sector The part of an economy that concerns services (as opposed to the production of tangible goods); the key focus of this sector in international trade negotiations is on banking, insurance and related financial services.

Different states have different interests in enforcing political control over illicit trade. With illegal arms exports, the exporting state may gain economically from the trade while the importing state gains access to weapons; the losers are the other exporters that neither got the export revenue nor kept the weapons out of the hands of the importer (not to mention the people who then must live in highly weaponized societies). Thus, illicit trade often creates conflicts of interest among states and leads to complex political bargaining among governments, each looking after its own interests.

Cooperation in Trade

Successful trade strategies are those that achieve mutual gains from cooperation with other states. A global system of free trade is a

THE MEDIUM IS THE MESSAGE
Agriculture and trade in services are two issues high on the agenda of international trade negotiations. This British farmer combines a little of each: when an outbreak of mad cow disease halted exports of British beef in 1996, the farmer decided to use his location near a busy freeway to sell advertising space to a U.S. company—in effect, an export of services.

collective good, according to economic liberals. Given the lack of world government, the benefits of trade depend on international cooperation—to enforce contracts, prevent monopolies and discourage protectionism. A single state can profitably subsidize its own state-owned industries, create its own monopolies or erect barriers to competitive imports as long as not too many other states do the same. If other states also break the rules of free trade, the benefits of free exchange slip away from all parties involved.

As with international law generally, economic agreements between states depend strongly on reciprocity for enforcement (see pp. 72–74, 277–278). If one state protects its industries, puts tariffs on the goods of other states or violates the copyright on works produced in other countries, the main response from other states is to apply similar measures against the offending state. The use of reciprocity to enforce equal terms of exchange is especially important in international trade, where states often negotiate complex agreements—commodity by commodity, industry by industry—based on reciprocity.[34]

Enforcement of fair trade is complicated by differing interpretations of what is fair. States generally decide what practices of other states they consider unfair (often prodded by affected domestic industries) and then take (or threaten) retaliatory actions to punish those practices. A disadvantage of reciprocity is that it can lead to a downward spiral of non-cooperation, popularly called a trade war (the economic equivalent of the arms race discussed on p. 74). To prevent this, states often negotiate agreements regarding what practices they consider unfair. In some cases, third-party arbitration can be used to

---

[34] Thomas O. Bayard, Kimberly Ann Elliott, Amelia Porges and Charles Iceland, *Reciprocity and Retaliation in U.S. Trade Policy* (Washington, DC: Institute for International Economics, 1994). Carolyn Rhodes, "Reciprocity in Trade: The Utility of a Bargaining Strategy," *International Organization* 43.2 (1989): 273–300.

Thinking Theoretically

In 1957, newly elected prime minister John Diefenbaker returned from a meeting of Commonwealth heads of government and announced that in order to strengthen Commonwealth trade ties, he wanted to shift 15 percent of Canadian trade away from the United States to Britain. Analyses by his civil service indicated that in order to reach this goal, Britain would have to buy twice as many Canadian exports as they were purchasing at the time, and likewise, British exports to Canada would have to double. Critics pointed out that Canadian consumers would suffer, not only by paying more for some goods, but also because the range and quality of goods available would become more limited. Would British cars be able to start on cold winter mornings, for example?*

Diefenbaker's desire to shift trade in response to a political goal (closer ties with the Commonwealth) reflects a mercantilist orientation. What are some of the arguments in support of that position? Economic liberals, by contrast, would argue that trade does not (easily) respond to political imperatives and has negative consequences both for consumers and overall growth. What might critical theorists say about Diefenbaker's plan?

*Michael Hart, "Lessons from Canada's History as a Trading Nation," *International Journal* 58.1 (Winter 2002–2003): 25–42.

resolve trade disputes. Currently, the World Trade Organization (see pp. 332–335) hears complaints and sets levels of acceptable retaliation.

Retaliation for unfair trade practices is usually based on an attempt to match the violation in type and extent. Under WTO rules, a state may impose retaliatory tariffs equivalent to the losses caused by another state's unfair trade practices (as determined by WTO hearings). In 2000, for example, the WTO permitted Canada to impose retaliatory trade sanctions of up to $344.2 million per year against Brazil as a result of Brazilian subsidies to its aircraft industry.

Trade disputes and retaliatory measures are common. States keep close track of the exact terms of trade. Large bureaucracies monitor international economic transactions (prices relative to world market levels, tariffs, etc.) and develop detailed policies to reciprocate any other state's deviations from cooperation.

Trade cooperation is easier to achieve under hegemony (see "Hegemony" on p. 69, and "Hegemonic Stability" on pp. 84–86). The efficient operation of markets depends on a stable political framework, something hegemony can provide. Political power can protect economic exchange from the distorting influences of violent leverage, unfair or fraudulent trade practices and uncertainties of international currency rates. A hegemon can provide a world currency in which value can be universally calculated. It can punish the use of violence and can enforce norms of fair trade. Because its economy is so large and dominating, the hegemon has a potent leverage in the threat to break off trade ties, even without resorting to military force. For example, to be denied access to U.S. markets today would be a serious punishment for export industries in many states, Canada in particular.

U.S. hegemony helped create the major norms and institutions of international trade in the post-1945 era. Now that it seems to be giving way to a more multipolar world—especially in economic affairs among the great powers—institutions are even more important for the success of the world trading system. The remainder of this chapter addresses the role and operation of major trade regimes and institutions.

TRADE REGIMES

Trade regimes are common expectations held by governments about the rules for international trade. A range of partially overlapping regimes concerned with international trade has developed, mostly since World War II. The most central of these are bilateral and regional arrangements and the World Trade Organization.

Bilateral and Regional Agreements

Most international trade is governed by specific international political agreements. These are of two general types: bilateral trade agreements and regional free trade areas.

Bilateral Agreements Bilateral treaties regarding trade are reciprocal arrangements to lower barriers to trade between two states and are usually fairly specific. For instance, one country may reduce its prohibition on imports of product X (which the second country exports at competitive prices) while the second country lowers its tariff on product Y (which the first country exports).

Part of the idea behind the General Agreements on Tariffs and Trade (GATT) and the World Trade Organization (WTO) (discussed below) was to strip away the maze of bilateral agreements on trade and simplify the system of tariffs and preferences. This effort has only partially succeeded. Bilateral trade agreements continue to play an important role.[35] They have the advantage of reducing the collective goods problem inherent in multilateral negotiations and facilitating reciprocity as a means of achieving cooperation. When multilateral negotiations have bogged down, some state leaders will find bilateral agreements are more achievable than global agreements. Inasmuch as most states have only a few top trading partners, bilateral agreements can go a long way in structuring a state's trade relations.

Free Trade Areas Regional free trade areas are also important in the structure of world trade. In such areas, groups of neighbouring states agree to remove the entire structure of trade barriers (or most of it) within their area. Trade with outside countries continues to be governed by bilateral treaties and the multilateral framework. (A free trade area resembles a "common market" or "customs union"; see p. 383.) The creation of a regional free trade area allows a group of states to cooperate in increasing their wealth without waiting for the rest of the world. In fact, from an economic nationalist perspective, a free trade area can enhance a region's power at the expense of other areas of the world.

The most important free trade area is in Europe; it is connected with the European Union but has a somewhat larger membership. Because Europe contains a number of small industrialized states living close together, the creation of a single integrated market allows these states to gain the economic advantages that come inherently to larger states. The European free trade experiment has been seen by many observers as a great success overall, contributing to Europe's accumulation of wealth since World War II (see Chapter 11).

The United States and Canada signed the Free Trade Agreement (FTA) in 1988 (which came into effect in January 1989) and followed this with the **North American Free Trade Agreement (NAFTA)** in 1994 between Canada, the U.S. and Mexico.[36] In Canada's early history, industrial development was based on efforts such as Sir John A. Macdonald's 1879 National Policy, which included high tariffs. After the end of World

North American Free Trade Agreement (NAFTA) A free trade zone encompassing the United States, Canada and Mexico established in 1994.

---

[35] Beth V. Yarbrough and Robert M. Yarbrough, *Cooperation and Governance in International Trade: The Strategic Organizational Approach* (Princeton, NJ: Princeton UP, 1992). Kenneth A. Oye, *Economic Discrimination and Political Exchange: World Political Economy in the 1930s and 1980s* (Princeton, NJ: Princeton UP, 1992).

[36] Delal M. Baer and Sidney Weintraub, eds., *The NAFTA Debate: Grappling with Unconventional Trade Issues* (Boulder, CO: Rienner, 1994).

CHEAP LABOUR

Labour, environmental and human rights organizations have all criticized unrestricted free trade. They argue that free trade agreements encourage MNCs to produce goods under unfair and unhealthy conditions, including the use of child labour. This boy in India makes soccer balls, 2002.

War II, however, Canada began an increasingly open trading relationship with the United States. Different federal governments attempted to diversify Canada's trading markets, but by the 1980s the United States was firmly, and still remains, Canada's most important trading partner. The FTA and NAFTA were adopted by Canada for primarily defensive reasons. The FTA was an effort to ensure continued access to the American market in the face of global competition from other countries as well as rising protectionist pressures within the United States, and Canada agreed to the NAFTA primarily to retain gains made under FTA.[37]

Opponents of the FTA and NAFTA included labour unions and environmental groups, who feared job losses, low wages and declining labour standards. Some have noted that at the very least, the enormous gains that proponents of the two agreements predicted never materialized: manufacturing wages remain stagnant, new investment has shifted outside of Canada and unemployment levels remain largely unchanged. Free trade has not, however, resulted in a massive movement of industry out of Canada, with the exception of a wave of plant closures in the early years of the FTA.[38] Environmentalists criticized Mexico's lax environmental laws (relative to those of the United States and Canada) and saw NAFTA as giving U.S. and Canadian corporations licence to pollute by moving into Mexico (see pp. 517–519).

Most of the same criticisms directed at the WTO (see pp. 332–335) are raised by critics about NAFTA. This should come as no surprise: as some observers have remarked, NAFTA served as the template for more global elements of the trade regime, such as the World Trade Organization.[39]

In the 1990s, many politicians in North and South America spoke of creating a single free trade area in the Western hemisphere, from Alaska to Argentina—the *Free Trade Area of the Americas (FTAA)*. Proponents of the FTAA included Canada and a number of South American countries, but it was a goal that increasingly lost favour in the United

[37] Laura Macdonald, "Going Global: The Politics of Canada's Foreign Economic Relations," *Understanding Canada: Building on the New Canadian Political Economy*, ed. Wallace Clement (McGill-Queen's UP, 1997) 172–96.

[38] Andrew Jackson, "The Free Trade Agreement—A Decade Later," *Studies in Political Economy* 58 (Spring 1999): 141–60.

[39] John N. McDougall, "National Differences and the NAFTA," *International Journal* 55.2 (Spring 2000): 281–91.

States. In late 2005, trade talks failed at a summit meeting in Argentina, where one participant, Venezuelan president Hugo Chavez, led a 25 000-person anti-American rally in the streets. In early 2007 the FTAA talks remained in near-hibernation, and the weight of trade negotiations fell to the WTO. Canada had also been interested in establishing more open relations between the countries of NAFTA and the European Union, but here, too, U.S. support is lukewarm and progress unlikely.[40]

Efforts to create a free trade area, or even a semi-free trade area, in Asia began in the late 1980s but moved slowly. Malaysia was the leading country promoting such an arrangement, which it hoped would boost its economic development (though economists expected Japan would benefit most). Unlike the European and North American arrangements, an Asian bloc would include very different kinds of states—rich ones such as Japan, poor ones like the Philippines; democracies, dictatorships and communist states. It is unclear how well such a diverse collection could coordinate their common interests, especially because their existing trade patterns are not focused on each other but are spread out among other states, including the United States and Canada (again in contrast to trade patterns existing before the creation of the European and North American free trade areas). Despite these problems, the 10 ASEAN countries met with China, Japan, India, Australia and New Zealand to begin negotiating an East Asian free trade area in 2007. The group, unlike some other Asia-Pacific IGOs, does not include the United States, but does include half the world's population and some of its most dynamic economies. If the concept succeeds, it will form a third great regional trading bloc after the European Union and the North American free trade area.

During the Cold War, the Soviet bloc maintained its own trading bloc, the Council for Mutual Economic Assistance (CMEA), also known as COMECON. After the Soviet Union collapsed, members scrambled to join up with the world economy, from which they had been largely cut off. The Commonwealth of Independent States (CIS), formed by 12 former Soviet republics, may become an economic coordinating body and quite possibly a free trade area. The existing patterns of trade favour a CIS free trade area because the CIS was previously a free trade zone by virtue of being part of a single state, using transportation, communication and other infrastructure links.

Other efforts to create free trade areas have had mixed results. The Southern Cone Common Market (Mercosur) tripled trade among its members—Brazil, Argentina, Uruguay and Paraguay—in its first four years in the early 1990s. In the late 1990s, Chile and Bolivia joined as associate members, and in 2001 Mercosur was negotiating a free trade agreement with the Andean countries. Nonetheless, Mercosur members trade twice as much with the United States as with each other. A Caribbean common market (CARICOM) was created in 1973, but the area is neither large nor rich enough to make regional free trade a very important accelerator of economic growth. Eleven countries created a Latin American Free Trade Association (LAFTA) in 1960 (changed in 1980 to the Latin American Integration Association), but the effort was held back by the different levels of poverty and wealth among members and their existing patterns of trade (as in the Asian group previously mentioned). Venezuela, Colombia, Ecuador, Peru and Bolivia created the Andean Common Market in 1969; it had modest successes but not dramatic results because trade within the bloc was not important enough. (Venezuela left when it recently joined Mercosur, and Chile is attempting to rejoin in 2007 after a 30-year absence).

---

[40] Donald Barry, "Pursuing Free Trade: Canada, the Western Hemisphere, and the European Union," *International Journal* 55.2 (Spring 2000): 292–300.

The World Trade Organization

World Trade Organization (WTO) An organization begun in 1995 that expanded the GATT's traditional focus on manufactured goods and created monitoring and enforcement mechanisms.

General Agreement on Tariffs and Trade (GATT) A world organization established in 1947 to work for freer trade on a multilateral basis; the GATT has been more of a negotiating framework than an administrative institution. It became the World Trade Organization (WTO) in 1995.

The single most important international institution in the global trading regime is the **World Trade Organization (WTO).** The WTO is a global, multilateral IGO that promotes, monitors and adjudicates international trade. Together with the regional and bilateral arrangements described above, the WTO is central to the overall expectations and practices of states with regard to international trade.[41] The WTO is the successor organization to the **General Agreement on Tariffs and Trade (GATT),** which was created in 1947 to facilitate freer trade on a multilateral basis. The GATT was more of a negotiating framework than an administrative institution. It did not actually regulate trade. Although the GATT was a regime with little institutional infrastructure until the mid-1990s, it did have a small secretariat with headquarters in Geneva, Switzerland. In addition to its main role as a negotiating forum, the GATT helped to arbitrate trade disputes, clarifying rules and helping states observe them.

In 1995, the GATT became the WTO. The GATT agreements on manufactured goods were subsumed into the WTO framework and then extended to include trade in services and intellectual property. The WTO has some powers of enforcement and an international bureaucracy (more than 500 people from 60 countries), which monitors trade policies and practices in each member state and adjudicates disputes among

MAKING MAGIC
Rounds of trade negotiations, such as the Doha Round begun in 2001, last for years as members negotiate complex deals that must be approved by consensus of all 149 member states. A conference of trade ministers in December 2005 tried to regain momentum for the stalled Doha Round, with mixed success. Here, WTO head Pascal Lamy opens the conference with the tool he hopes will bring success—a magic wand.

---

[41] Bernard Hoekman and Michel Kostecki, *The Political Economy of the World Trading System: From GATT to WTO,* 2nd ed. (NY: Oxford UP, 1999).

members. It is unclear how much power the WTO will eventually be able to wield over states in practice. A growing public backlash against free trade (see below) reflects uneasiness about the potential power of a foreign and secretive organization to force changes in democratically enacted national laws. However, the WTO is the central international institution governing trade and therefore one that almost all countries want to participate in and develop.

By 2007, 150 countries—almost all the world's major trading states except Russia— had joined the WTO. In 2006, Russia and the United States reached an agreement expected to lead to Russia's admission in the coming years. Vietnam joined in 2007. More than 25 states are seeking admission, the most important of which are Ukraine, Iran and Iraq. After more than a decade of negotiations, China joined in December 2001. Chinese Taipei (Taiwan) joined the following January. Members of the WTO demand, as a condition of membership, liberalization of the trading practices of would-be members.

The WTO framework is based on the principles of reciprocity—that one state's lowering of trade barriers to another should be matched in return—and of nondiscrimination. The latter principle is embodied in the **most-favoured nation (MFN) concept,** which says that trade restrictions imposed by a WTO member on its most-favoured trading partner must be applied equally to all WTO members. If Australia applies a 20 percent tariff on auto parts imported from France, it should not apply a 40 percent tariff on auto parts imported from Canada. Thus, the WTO does not do away with barriers to trade altogether but equalizes them in a global framework to create a level playing field for all member states. States are not prevented from protecting their own industries but cannot play favourites among their trading partners. States may also extend MFN status to others that are not WTO members.

An exception to the MFN system is the **Generalized System of Preferences (GSP),** dating from the 1970s, by which industrialized states give trade concessions to states of the global South to help the latter's economic development. Preferences amount to a promise by rich states to allow imports from poor ones under lower tariffs than those imposed under MFN.[42]

The WTO continues the GATT's role as a negotiating forum for multilateral trade agreements that lower trade barriers on a fair and reciprocal basis. These detailed and complex agreements specify the commitments of various states and regions to lower certain trade barriers by certain amounts on fixed schedules. Almost every commitment entails domestic political costs because domestic industries lose protection against foreign competition. Even when other states agree to make similar commitments in other areas, the lowering of trade barriers is often hard for national governments.

As a result, negotiations on these multilateral agreements are long and difficult. Typically, they stretch on for several years or more in a *round of negotiations;* once completed, members begin a new round. Among the five rounds of GATT negotiations from 1947 to 1995, the Kennedy Round in the 1960s—so called because it started during the Kennedy administration—paid special attention to the growing role of the (increasingly integrated) European Economic Community (EEC). The Tokyo Round (begun in Tokyo) in the 1970s had to adjust rules to new conditions of world interdependence as, for instance, OPEC raised oil prices and Japan began to dominate the automobile export business.

most-favoured nation (MFN) concept The principle that one state, by granting another state MFN status, promises to give it the same treatment given to the first state's most-favoured trading partner.

Generalized System of Preferences (GSP) A mechanism by which some industrialized states began to give tariff concessions to global South states on certain imports in the 1970s; an exception to the most-favoured nation (MFN) principle.

---

[42] Akira Hirata and Ippei Yamazawa, eds., *Trade Policies towards Developing Countries* (NY: St. Martin's, 1993). David J. Glover and Diana Tussie, eds., *The Developing Countries in World Trade: Policies and Bargaining Strategies* (Boulder, CO: Rienner, 1993). Jock A. Finlayson and Mark W. Zacher, *Managing International Markets: Developing Countries and the Commodity Trade Regime* (NY: Columbia UP, 1988).

Uruguay Round A series of negotiations under the General Agreement on Tariffs and Trade (GATT) that began in Uruguay in 1986, and concluded in 1994 with agreement to create the World Trade Organization. The Uruguay Round followed earlier GATT negotiations such as the Kennedy Round and the Tokyo Round. See also *World Trade Organization (WTO)*.

The **Uruguay Round** began in 1986 in Uruguay. The Kennedy and Tokyo Rounds had been very successful in reducing tariff barriers on manufactured goods. The Uruguay Round tried to lower tariffs further, but also began to tackle the more difficult, and more politically sensitive, issues of nontariff barriers and agricultural trade. Although the rough outlines of a new GATT agreement emerged after a few years, closure eluded five successive G7 summit meetings from 1990 to 1994. As the round dragged on year after year, participants said the GATT should be renamed the "general agreement to talk and talk." A successful conclusion to the round would add more than US$100 billion to the world economy annually—money that was to be a collective good, enjoyed both by states that made concessions in the final negotiations and by states that did not. Agreement was finally reached in late 1994.

From 1947, the GATT had concentrated on manufactured goods and succeeded in substantially reducing the average tariffs from 40 percent of the goods' value decades ago to 3 percent by 2002 (under the Uruguay Round agreement). Tariff rates in the global South are much higher—around 30 percent (reflecting the greater protection that industry in the developing world sees itself as needing).

Agricultural trade, more politically sensitive than trade in manufactured goods, was seriously addressed only in the Uruguay Round when in 1986 a group of medium-sized agricultural exporting states created what is called the Cairns Group. Composed of 17 states from the North and South, the Cairns Group arose from concerns that its members' interests would be overlooked by larger agricultural exporters such as the U.S. and EU. Its membership is diverse and includes countries such as Canada, New Zealand and Australia as well as Chile, Brazil, Argentina, Fiji, Indonesia, Malaysia and others. Its focus is on liberalizing agricultural trade, but it is also an important bridge-building coalition between countries from North and South.[43]

Trade in services such as banking and insurance is currently another major focus of the WTO. Such trade approached one-quarter of the total value of world trade in the 1990s. Trade in telecommunications is a related area of interest. In 1997, 70 states (negotiating through the WTO) agreed on a treaty to allow telecommunications companies to enter each other's markets.

The problems in expanding into these and other sensitive areas became obvious in 1999. First, a North-South divide in the WTO emerged when the WTO could not agree on a new leader and split the five-year term between a New Zealander supported mostly by the North and a Thai politician supported mainly by the South (and particularly Asia).

Then the 1999 Seattle WTO conference, where trade ministers had hoped to launch a new round of trade negotiations, turned into a fiasco. Most industrialized countries wanted to include provisions in areas such as environmental protection and labour laws on the negotiating agenda for the round, areas that poorer countries considered an attack on their sovereignty and a way to maintain the North's advantage in trade. The North's main advantage is technology, whereas the South's is cheap labour and natural resources. Economic liberals argue that these differences in comparative advantage are "givens," while critical theorists (and to some extent mercantilists) would suggest that the world's trading system has both created and reinforced these unequal differences.

Representatives of poorer countries argued that they needed trade to raise incomes, and could not meet the standards of industrialized countries (which had allowed low wages, harsh working conditions and environmental destruction when *they* began industrializing). Environmental and labour activists, joined by anarchists, students and citizen

---

[43] William P. Avery, ed., *World Agriculture and the GATT* (Boulder, CO: Rienner, 1992). Ian Taylor, "The Cairns Group and the Commonwealth," *The Round Table* 355 (2000): 375–86.

groups, staged street protests that delayed the conference opening. Trade ministers could not agree on a new agenda for trade talks, and the meeting ended in failure.

Recovering from Seattle, trade ministers meeting in Doha, Qatar, in 2001 agreed to launch a new round of trade negotiations, which began in 2003. The agenda includes agriculture, services, industrial products, intellectual property, WTO rules (including how to handle antidumping cases), dispute settlement and some trade and environmental questions. The Doha Round was slated to conclude by January 2005, but the deadline was then extended to July 2007. At the 2003 meeting in Cancun, Mexico, states from the global South walked out after the industrialized countries would not agree to eliminate agricultural subsidies, which effectively shut out agricultural exports from the South. At the 2005 Hong Kong meeting, wealthy states agreed to end export subsidies, but tough negotiations continued over tariffs on manufactured goods, protection of intellectual property and opening financial sectors. WTO members faced much work to conclude the Doha Round before the 2007 deadline and by May 2007 most commentators saw little hope that the differences between states from the global North and South could be bridged.

In general, states continue to participate in the WTO because they consider the benefits in terms of global wealth creation to outweigh the costs in terms of harm to domestic industries or painful adjustments in national economies. States try to change the rules in their favour during the rounds of negotiations (never with complete success), and between rounds they try to evade the rules in minor ways. The overall benefits are seen as too great to jeopardize by nonparticipation or by allowing frequent trade wars to occur.

Resistance to Trade

The globalization of the world economy, which includes growing trade and other aspects (see Chapters 10–14), has created a backlash in many parts of the world, including Canada. Global-level integration has fuelled a countercurrent of growing nationalism in several world regions where people believe their identities and communities are threatened by the penetration of foreign influences. Even more fundamental to the backlash are the material dislocations caused by globalization, which directly affect the self-interests and sometimes the well-being of certain segments of a population.

Workers in industrialized countries in industries that face increasing competition from low-wage countries in the global South—from steel and automobiles to electronics and clothing—are among the most adversely affected by free trade. Inevitably, the competition from low-wage countries holds down wages in those same sectors in industrialized countries. It also creates pressures to relax standards of labour regulation, such as those protecting worker safety, and it can lead to job losses if manufacturers close down plants in high-wage countries and move operations to the global South. Not surprisingly, labour unions have been among the strongest political opponents of unfettered trade expansion.

Human rights NGOs, international organizations and social movement activists have joined labour unions in pushing for trade agreements to include requirements for the improvement of working conditions in low-wage countries; these could include laws regarding a minimum wage, child labour and worker safety. In June 2000, Canada ratified the International Labour Organization convention on Child Labour. Meanwhile, clothing manufacturers such as Nike and Reebok, stung by criticism of "sweatshop" conditions in their Asian factories, adopted a voluntary program to end the worst abuses. Critics claim it will make little difference, however, as much of the production for companies like

Nike and Reebok has been "sourced" out to other manufacturers that continue to operate under the same unacceptable working conditions.[44] About 250 million children under age 14 are working in the global South, according to the UN-affiliated International Labour Organization—about 20 percent of 10- to 14-year-olds in Latin America and Asia and 40 percent in Africa. In Côte d'Ivoire, the world's largest exporter of cocoa (for chocolate consumed in the global North), tens of thousands of children work for low wages, or even as slaves, on cocoa plantations.

Environmental groups have also actively opposed the unrestricted expansion of trade, which they see as undermining environmental laws in industrialized countries and promoting environmentally harmful practices worldwide (see p. 503). For example, U.S. regulations require commercial shrimp boats to use devices that prevent endangered species of sea turtles from drowning in shrimp nets. Indonesia, India, Malaysia, Thailand and Pakistan, whose shrimp exports to the United States were blocked because they do not require use of such devices, filed a complaint with the World Trade Organization, arguing that the U.S. regulation unfairly discriminated against them. In 1998, the United States lost the WTO ruling and appeal. Sea turtles became a symbol of environmentalist opposition to the WTO. (In 2001, the WTO ruled the U.S. law acceptable after changes had made application of the law more even-handed.)

In 1997, Canada tried to limit shipments of gasoline containing the additive MMT. The Canadian federal government argued that MMT impaired onboard diagnostic systems designed to detect the emission of pollutants and therefore was a potential health hazard. A U.S. producer of MMT, Ethyl Corporation, filed a complaint against the regulations through the North American Free Trade Agreement (NAFTA). NAFTA ruled in Ethyl Corporation's favour and imposed $19 million in damages, and eventually the Canadian government, under additional pressure from provincial producers of MMT, also repealed the legislation attempting to limit MMT shipments.[45]

In general, unrestricted trade tends to force countries to harmonize their regulations in a variety of areas not limited to labour and environmental rules, and there is concern that harmonization will always be directed toward more lax, rather than more stringent, standards. For example, the WTO ruled in 1997 that Europeans' fears about the use of growth hormones in beef were not scientifically warranted, and therefore EU regulations could not be used to exclude U.S. beef containing hormones. When the European Union persisted, the United States was allowed to impose trade restrictions on European exports worth approximately US$117 million a year. Similarly, in 2006 the WTO ruled that European restrictions on imports of genetically modified food from the United States violated trade rules. Meanwhile, U.S. consumers harbour fears about pesticide-laced produce grown in Mexico, but at the same time the U.S. has consistently blocked progress toward ratifying the Cartagena "Biosafety Protocol," part of the UN Convention on Biological Diversity aimed at governing trade in genetically modified food and organisms. Efforts to achieve a protocol became all the more important, according to environmental groups like Greenpeace, when genetic contamination was discovered in maize in Mexico in late 2001.

Canadians have mobilized against free trade out of concern that it adversely impacts Canadian cultural industries (as discussed on pp. 320–323). In an attempt to promote the Canadian magazine industry, the federal government subsidized domestically produced

---

[44] Naomi Klein, *No Logo: Taking Aim at the Brand Bullies* (Toronto: Knopf Canada, 2000).

[45] Chris Kukucha, "Domestic Politics and Canadian Foreign Trade Policy: Intrusive Interdependence, the WTO and NAFTA," *Canadian Foreign Policy* 10.2 (2003): 59–86.

magazines in the 1990s through tax exemptions and a postal subsidy. U.S.-based Time Warner sought the same kinds of support for what are called "split-run" magazines: editions that retain the primarily U.S. content of a magazine but solicit Canadian advertisers and usually offer a few pages devoted to local stories. The Canadian government lost its case at the WTO, which ruled that both the made-in-Canada magazines and the U.S. split-run editions had to receive the same level of national treatment.[46]

These examples illustrate the variety of sources of backlash against free trade agreements. Labour, environmental, nationalist and consumer groups all portray the WTO and other elements of the trading regime, such as NAFTA, as secretive bureaucracies outside democratic control that serve the interests of big corporations at the expense of ordinary people in both the global North and South. Critics object to organizations like the WTO holding all major deliberations behind closed doors. More fundamentally, these critics distrust the corporate-driven "globalization" (see pp. 305–307) of which the WTO and NAFTA are a part. Street protests have become a regular feature of any major international meeting concerning economic policies.

Protests against free trade have made visible some of the arguments against trade liberalization. Prior to Seattle, few people knew about organizations like the WTO and most people probably did not think it was an organization that affected their lives. Few thought about what free trade or free trade agreements like NAFTA might mean, unless they were directly affected by job losses. Whether or not one agrees with antiglobalization protesters, their activism has opened up public debate about the costs and benefits of free trade.

States have often found it worthwhile to expand trade steadily, using a range of regimes and institutions to do so—the WTO, free trade areas and bilateral agreements. Stable political rules governing trade allow states to realize the great economic gains that can result from international exchange. This can come with a price, however, in terms of job losses and some of the problems associated with harmonization of culture, services and environmental and health standards. The kinds of political stability that are thought to be advantageous in trading relations are also important, especially for economic liberals, in international monetary and business relations. And, as with trade, much debate exists about some of the costs associated with that stability. Monetary and business relations are the subject of Chapter 10.

Thinking Critically

1. Suppose your state had a chance to reach a major trade agreement by making substantial concessions. The agreement would produce $5 billion in new wealth for your state as well as $10 billion for each of the other states involved (which are political allies but economic rivals). What advice would a mercantilist give your state's leader about making such a deal? What arguments would support the advice? How would liberal advice and arguments differ? How would a critical theorist respond?

2. China seems to be making a successful transition to a market economy and is growing rapidly, emerging as the world's second-largest economy. Do you think this is good or bad for your state? Does your reasoning reflect mercantilist, critical or liberal assumptions?

---

[46] John Schofield, "Back to Square One: Washington Wins a Hotly Contested Trade Fight," *Maclean's* 14 July 1997: 36.

3. Before reading this chapter, to what extent did you have a preference for buying products made in your own country? Has reading this chapter changed your views on that subject? How?

4. NAFTA, the free trade agreement between Canada, Mexico and the United States, is 10 years old. Given that wages are lower in Mexico and technology less developed than in Canada, which Canadian industries do you imagine supported NAFTA? Specifically, do you think labour-intensive or high-technology industries were more supportive of the deal? Who was opposed? Why?

Chapter Summary

- Most international exchanges entail some conflicting interests and some mutual interests on the part of the states involved. Deals can be made because both sides benefit, but conflict over specific outcomes necessitates bargaining.

- Globalization is perceived differently by various scholars, but generally refers to the growing scope, speed and intensity of connectedness worldwide. The process may be weakening, strengthening or transforming the power of states. Antiglobalization activists oppose growing corporate power but disagree on goals and tactics.

- The volume of world trade is very large—about 15 percent of global economic activity—and is concentrated heavily in the states of the industrialized West (Western Europe, North America and Japan/Pacific).

- Trade creates wealth, according to economic liberals, by allowing states to specialize in producing goods and services for which they have a comparative advantage (and to import other needed goods).

- The distribution of benefits from an exchange is determined by the price of the goods exchanged. Prices are generally determined by market equilibrium (supply and demand).

- Communist states operated centrally planned economies during the Cold War in which national governments set prices and allocated resources. Almost all of these states are now in transition toward market-based economies, which seem to be more efficient in generating wealth. The transition has been very painful in Russia and Eastern Europe, but less so in China.

- Politics intrude on international markets in many ways, including the use of economic sanctions as political leverage on a target state. However, sanctions are difficult to enforce unless all major economic actors agree to abide by them.

- Mercantilists favour trade policies that produce a trade surplus for their own state. Such a positive trade balance generates money that can be used to enhance state power.

- States are becoming increasingly interdependent in that the well-being of states depends on mutual cooperation. Economic liberal scholars have long argued that rising interdependence makes military force a less useful form of leverage in international bargaining.

- States that have reduced their dependence on others by pursuing self-sufficient autarky have failed to generate new wealth to increase their well-being. Self-reliance, like central planning, has been largely discredited as a viable economic strategy.

- Through protectionist policies, many states try to protect certain domestic industries from international competition. Such policies tend to slow down the global creation of wealth but do help the protected industry.

- Protectionism can be pursued through various means, including import tariffs, quotas, subsidies and other nontariff barriers.

- Industries often lobby their own governments for protection. Governments in many states develop industrial policies to guide their efforts to strengthen domestic industries in the context of global markets.

- Certain products—especially food, intellectual property, services and military goods—tend to deviate more than others from market principles. Political conflicts among states concerning trade in these products are frequent.

- According to economic liberals, a world market based on free trade is a collective good (available to all members regardless of their individual contribution) inasmuch as states benefit from access to foreign markets whether or not they have opened their own markets to foreign products.

- Because there is no world government to enforce rules of trade, such enforcement depends on reciprocity and state power. In particular, states reciprocate each other's cooperation in opening markets (or punish each other's refusal to let in foreign products). Although it occasionally leads to trade wars, reciprocity has achieved substantial cooperation in trade.

- Over time, the rules embodied in trade regimes (and other issue areas in IR) become the basis for permanent institutions, whose administrative functions provide yet further stability and efficiency in global trade.

- Regional free trade areas (with few if any tariff or nontariff barriers) have been created in Europe, North America and several other areas. NAFTA includes Canada, Mexico and the United States.

- Free trade agreements have led to a backlash from politically active interest groups adversely affected by globalization; these include labour unions, environmental and human rights NGOs and certain consumers.

- The World Trade Organization, formerly the GATT, is the most important multilateral global trade agreement. In successive rounds of GATT negotiations over nearly 50 years, states have lowered overall tariff rates (especially on manufactured goods).

- The Uruguay Round of the GATT, completed in 1994, focused on agricultural trade and nontariff barriers to trade. The Doha Round of the WTO began in 2003.

- The GATT was institutionalized in 1995 with the creation of the World Trade Organization (WTO), which expanded considerably the focus of free trade discussions.

- Although the WTO provides a global framework, states continue to operate under thousands of bilateral trade agreements specifying the rules for trade in specific products between specific countries.

Key Terms

economic liberalism   303
globalization   305
comparative advantage   308
centrally planned (command)
    economy   311

transitional economies   311
balance of trade   315
interdependence   316
autarky (self-reliance)   318
protectionism   319

Research Navigator Question

Log on to Research Navigator and use Content Search under the Political Science database to find a recent article on the WTO and agriculture from a journal such as *Review of International Political Economy* or *Journal of Third World Studies* or a magazine such as *Canadian Dimension*. Read the article and answer the following questions: What does the author(s) say about agricultural trade and the WTO? What are the largest impediments to liberalizing trade in agriculture? *Should* states attempt to liberalize agricultural trade? Why or why not?

Weblinks

The following are links to a sampling of research centres, government departments and international organizations focused on trade:

Centre for Research on Globalization:
http://globalresearch.ca

Foreign Affairs and International Trade Canada:
http://www.itcan-cican.gc.ca/menu-en.asp

The Council of Canadians:
http://www.canadians.org

NAFTA Secretariat:
http://www.nafta-sec-alena.org/DefaultSite/index.html

World Trade Organization:
http://www.wto.org/index.htm

Money and Business

International currencies.

ABOUT MONEY

This chapter summarizes the politics of the world monetary system and discusses the role of private companies as nonstate actors in the world economy. The monetary system is just one aspect of the political environment created by governments—an environment that shapes the rules for international business and the context for the actions of multinational corporations (MNCs).

Imagine a world *without* money. In order to conduct economic exchange, goods would have to be brought together in one place and traded in quantities reflecting their relative values. This kind of trade, involving no money, is called *barter*. It sometimes still occurs when monetary systems do not operate well. For example, during the Chinese-Soviet hostility of the 1960s and 1970s, Soviet money was worthless in China, and vice versa, so traders brought goods to the border, agreed on their value (expressed nominally in Swiss francs) and traded the appropriate quantities.

The unit of currency used in an economy is arbitrary, but must have roughly the same value for different people. With money, goods can move directly from sellers to buyers without having to be brought together in a central place. In a world economy, goods can flow freely among many states—the exchange of money keeps track of who owes whom for what. Money provides a single medium against which all goods can be valued. Different buyers and sellers place different values on goods, but all buyers and sellers place about the same value on money, so it serves as a standard against which other values can be measured.

Money itself has little or no inherent value. What gives it value is the widespread belief that it has value—that it can be exchanged for goods. Because it depends on the willingness of people to honour and use it, money's value rests on trust. Governments have the job of creating money and of maintaining public confidence in its value. For money to have stable value, the political environment must be stable. Political instability erodes public confidence that money today will be exchangeable for needed goods tomorrow. The result of this lack of confidence is inflation (discussed later in this chapter).

The international economy is based on national currencies, rather than a world currency, because of the nature of state sovereignty. One of the main powers of a national government is to create its own currency as the sole legal tender in the territory it controls. A national currency is of no inherent value in a foreign country, but can be exchanged one for another.[1] How can the value of goods or currencies be judged in a world lacking a central government and a world unit of money?

Traditionally, the European state system used *precious metals* as a global currency, valued in all countries. *Gold* was most important, and *silver* second. These metals had inherent value because they looked pretty and were easily moulded into jewellery or similar objects. They were relatively rare, and the mining of new gold and silver was relatively slow. Precious metals lasted a long time and were difficult to dilute or counterfeit.

Over time, gold and silver became valuable *because* they were a world currency—because other people around the world trusted that they could be exchanged for future goods—which overshadowed any inherent functional value of gold or silver. Bars of gold and silver were held by states in a kind of bank account of international currency. These piles of gold (literal and figurative) were the object of mercantilist trade policies in past centuries (see Chapters 2 and 9). Gold has long been a key power resource with which states could buy armies or other means of leverage.

In recent years, the world has not used the **gold standard** but has developed an international monetary system divorced from any tangible medium such as precious metal. Until recently, and even still to some extent, private investors have bought stocks of gold or silver at times of political instability as a haven that would have a reliable future value. However, gold and silver have now for the most part become like other commodities with unpredictable fluctuations in price, and their role as private havens is diminishing. The change from bars of gold to purely abstract money in the world economy makes international economics more efficient; the only drawback is that without tangible backing in gold, currencies may seem less worthy of people's confidence.

gold standard A system in international monetary relations, prominent for a century before the 1970s, in which the value of national currencies was pegged to the value of gold or other precious metals.

THE CURRENCY SYSTEM

Today, national currencies are valued against one another rather than against gold or silver. Each state's currency can be exchanged for a different state's currency according to an **exchange rate**—defining, for instance, how many Canadian dollars are equivalent to one U.S. dollar. Exchange rates are important because they affect almost every international economic transaction—trade, investment, tourism and so forth.[2] We will consider the mechanics by which exchange rates are set and adjusted, then the factors influencing the longer-term movements of exchange rates and finally the banking institutions that manage these issues.

Most exchange rates are expressed in terms of the world's most important currencies—the U.S. dollar, the Japanese yen and the EU's euro. Thus, the rate for exchanging Danish

exchange rate The rate at which one state's currency can be exchanged for the currency of another state. Since 1973, the international monetary system has depended mainly on flexible (or floating) rather than fixed exchange rates. See also *convertibility fixed exchange rates; Exchange Rate Mechanism (ERM);* and *managed float.*

---

[1] Eric Helleiner, *The Making of National Money: Territorial Currencies in Historical Perspective* (Ithaca: Cornell UP, 2003).

[2] Robert Z. Aliber, *The International Money Game*, 5th ed. (NY: Basic, 1987).

kroner for Brazilian reals depends on the value of each relative to these world currencies. Exchange rates that most affect the world economy are those of the G7 states—U.S. dollars, euros, yen, British pounds and Canadian dollars.

The relative values of currencies at a given point in time are arbitrary; only the *changes* in values over time are meaningful. For instance, in 2007, a Canadian dollar would trade for nearly 0.7 of a euro, but if traded for the Japanese currency, a single dollar would buy over 110 yen. In itself this disparity says nothing about the desirability of these currencies or the financial positions of their states. However, when the value of yen rises (or falls) *relative* to dollars, because yen are considered more (or less) valuable than before, the yen is said to be strong (or weak).

Some states do not have **convertible currencies.** The holder of such money has no guarantee of being able to trade it for another currency, which is often the case in states cut off from the world capitalist economy, such as the former Soviet Union. In practice, even nonconvertible currency can often be sold—in parallel markets or by dealing directly with the government issuing the currency—but the price may be extremely low. Some currencies are practically nonconvertible because they are inflating so rapidly that holding them for even a short period means losing money. Nobody wants to hold currency that is rapidly inflating—losing value relative to goods and services. Inflation reduces a currency's value relative to more stable (more slowly inflating) currencies.

The industrialized West has kept inflation relatively low—mostly below 5 percent annually—since 1980. (The 1970s saw inflation of more than 10 percent per year in many industrialized economies, including Canada.) Inflation in the global South is lower than a decade ago (see Table 10.1). Latin America has brought inflation from 750 percent to less than 15 percent, while China and South Asia have lowered inflation rates to below 10 percent. Most dramatically, in Russia and other former Soviet republics, inflation rates of more than 1000 percent have been lowered to less than 10 percent.

Extremely high uncontrolled inflation—more than 50 percent per month, or 13 000 percent per year—is called **hyperinflation.** The 10-billion-dinar notes printed by Serbia in 1993 were worth only pennies after hyperinflation reached 100 trillion percent per year. Even at less extreme levels, currencies can lose 95 percent of their

convertible currency The guarantee that the holder of a particular currency can exchange it for another currency. Some states' currencies are nonconvertible. See also *hard currency*.

hyperinflation An extremely rapid, uncontrolled rise in prices, such as occurred in Germany in the 1920s and some global South countries more recently.

Table 10.1 Inflation Rates by Region, 1993–2005

Region	Inflation Rate (percent per year)		
	1993	1996	2005[a]
Industrialized West	3	2	2
Russia and Eastern Europe	1,400	48	11
China	15	8	4
Middle East	27	34	4
Latin America	750	19	6
South Asia	6	6	7
Africa	112	37	10

[a]Data are estimates based on partial data for 2005.

Note: Regions are not identical to those used elsewhere in this book.

Source: Adapted from United Nations. *World Economic Situation and Prospects 2006.* New York: United Nations, 2006, pp. 133–4.

value in a year. In such conditions, money loses 5 percent of its value every week, and it becomes hard to conduct business domestically, let alone internationally.

In contrast to nonconvertible currency, **hard currency** is money that can be readily converted to leading world currencies (which now have relatively low inflation). For example, a Russian oil producer can export oil and receive payment in euros or another hard currency, which can then be used to pay for imported goods. However, a Russian sausage producer selling products within Russia would be paid in rubles, which could not be used easily outside the country (despite the removal of currency restrictions in Russia in 2006).

States maintain **reserves** of hard currency. Reserves are the equivalent of the stockpiles of gold in centuries past. National currencies today are backed by hard-currency reserves, although some states continue to maintain gold reserves. Industrialized countries have financial reserves roughly in proportion to the size of their economies.

One form of currency exchange uses **fixed exchange rates.** Here governments decide, individually or jointly, to establish official rates of exchange for their currencies. For example, the Canadian and U.S. dollars were fixed in value for two periods (1939 to 1950 and 1962 to 1970) and a rate of 1-to-1 was maintained (this is no longer true). States have various means for trying to maintain, or modify, such fixed rates in the face of changing economic conditions (see "Why Currencies Rise or Fall" later in this chapter).

Floating exchange rates are now commonly used for the world's major currencies. Rates are determined by global currency markets and are used by private investors and governments alike to buy and sell currencies. There is a supply and demand for each state's currency, with prices constantly adjusting in response to market conditions. Just as investors might buy shares of General Motors stock if they expected its value to rise, so too would they buy a pile of Japanese yen if they expected that currency's value to rise in the future. Through short-term speculative trading in international currencies, exchange rates adjust to changes in the long-term supply and demand for currencies.

There are major international currency markets in a handful of cities—the most important being New York, London, Zurich, Tokyo and Hong Kong—linked together by instantaneous computerized communications. These markets are driven in the short term by one question: What will a state's currency be worth in the future relative to its worth today? International currency markets involve huge amounts of money—a trillion dollars moving around the world every day (in actuality, only the computerized information moves). These are private markets and are not as strongly regulated by governments as stock markets.[3]

National governments periodically *intervene* in financial markets, buying and selling currencies in order to manipulate their value. (These interventions may also involve changing interest rates paid

hard currency Money that can be readily converted to leading world currencies. See also *convertible currency.*

reserves Hard-currency stockpiles kept by states.

fixed exchange rates The official rates of exchange for currencies set by governments; not a dominant mechanism in the international monetary system since 1973.

floating exchange rates The rates determined by global currency markets; used by private investors and governments alike to buy and sell currencies.

IT'S JUST MONEY
Money has value only because people trust its worth. Inflation erodes a currency's value if governments print too much money or if political instability erodes public confidence in the government. Brazil initially survived a loss of confidence in emerging markets that resulted from the 1997 Asian financial crisis. The next year, however, Brazil had to devalue its currency. This trader reacts to a stock market crash in 1998, after domestic politics threatened a $41 billion IMF agreement and shook investors' confidence in Brazil's economy.

---

[3] Richard O'Brien, "Who Rules the World's Financial Markets?" *Harvard Business Review* 73.2 (1995): 144–51.

by the government; see pp. 348–349.) Government intervention to manage the otherwise free-floating currency rates is called a **managed float** system. The leading industrialized states often work together in such interventions, but not always. If the price of the Canadian dollar, for instance, falls too much relative to other important currencies (a political judgment), governments and private investors will step in and buy Canadian dollars. With a higher demand for Canadian dollars, the price may then stabilize and perhaps rise again. (If the price got too high, governments would step in to sell dollars, increasing supply and driving the price down.) Such interventions happen quickly, usually in one day, but may be repeated several times within a few weeks in order to have the desired effect.[4]

In their interventions in international currency markets, governments are at a disadvantage because, even acting together, they control only a fraction of the money being moved; most of it is privately owned. Governments do have the advantage that they can work together to have enough impact to make at least modest changes in price. Governments can also operate in secret, keeping private investors in the dark regarding how much currency governments may eventually buy or sell, and at what price. The public is not aware of any coordinated multinational intervention until after its conclusion. (If speculators knew in advance, they could make money at the government's expense.)

Those interventions are often conducted by the world's major industrialized countries, or the **Group of 7 (G7).** The G7 consists of France, the United States, Britain, Germany, Japan, Italy and Canada. Since 1998, the G7 has also included Russia in its annual summits of government leaders, and in this capacity operates as the G8. On some economic issues, particularly monetary and financial issues in which Russia is at a disadvantage because its currency is not yet convertible, the group still operates as the G7. In 2006, Russia hosted the G8 summit for the first time, symbolically becoming a full member (despite its currency issues), and in 2007 Germany was the scheduled host state.

A successful intervention can make money for governments at the expense of private speculators. If, for example, the G7 governments step in to raise the price of dollars by buying them around the world (selling other hard currencies), and if they succeed, they can then sell again and pocket a profit. However, if the intervention fails and the price of dollars keeps falling, governments will *lose* money and may have to keep buying and buying in order to stop the slide. In fact, governments might run out of money before then and have to absorb a huge loss. Thus governments have to be realistic about the limited effects they can have on currency prices.

These limits were illustrated spectacularly in the 2001 Argentine financial collapse. In the 1990s, Argentina pegged the value of its currency at a fixed rate to the U.S. dollar—a wonderfully effective way to stop runaway inflation that had recently wreaked devastation on Argentina's economy.

Tying the peso to the dollar, however, represented a loss of sovereignty over monetary policy, one of the key levers to controlling an economy. Argentina and the United States had different needs in the late 1990s. As a historic U.S. expansion brought unprecedented prosperity (allowing interest rates to be kept relatively high), Argentina suffered four years of recession, but could not lower interest rates to stimulate growth. Argentina accumulated well over US$100 billion in foreign loans, and could not service its debts. IMF assistance in restructuring debt was contingent on a tight financial policy of tax increases and spending cuts—a mistake during a major multiyear recession, according to critics. In 2001, as the United States and IMF stood by, Argentina's economy collapsed, two presidents resigned

managed float A system of occasional multinational government interventions in currency markets to manage otherwise free-floating currency rates.

Group of 7 (G7) The world's seven largest industrial market economies: the United States, Japan, Germany, France, Britain, Italy and Canada. The leaders of G7 countries meet in annual summits, and G7 finance ministers meet several times a year. When the group includes Russia, as it has done at summits since 1998, it is called the G8. On some issues, particularly monetary matters, the G7 acts without Russia (primarily because Russia's currency is not yet fully convertible).

---

[4] Randall D. Germain, *The International Organization of Credit: States and Global Finance in the World Economy* (Cambridge: Cambridge UP, 1997). Jonathan Kirshner, *Currency and Coercion: The Political Economy of International Monetary Power* (Princeton NJ: Princeton UP, 1997).

in short order and a populist took power, who defaulted on foreign debts and devalued the peso to create jobs—an embarrassing chapter for the IMF and a painful one for Argentina. In 2003, Argentina defaulted on a US$3 billion payment to the IMF, the largest default in IMF history. Its economy eventually turned around and Argentina was able to pay the IMF in 2006, though negotiations with foreign government creditors continued.

Currently, pressures are building in a vastly more important case—China's currency. The current policy of pegging China's currency to the dollar does not adjust to different economic conditions in China and the United States. China runs a big trade surplus while the United States runs a big trade deficit—more than $200 billion with China alone in 2006 and $800 billion in total. Because of underlying U.S. economic problems, the value of the U.S. dollar dropped by about one-quarter against the euro in 2001–2004. The same underlying trends would have pushed the dollar lower against the Chinese yuan, too, if rates floated freely. Instead, the dollar-yuan ratio was held artificially high, which made China's exports to the United States cheaper and contributed to the trade imbalance and the loss of U.S. manufacturing jobs—an issue in U.S. domestic politics. In 2006 China let its currency begin rising incrementally, but not enough to satisfy U.S. critics.

In 2006, China, Japan and South Korea announced plans to work toward coordinating their currency policies. Along with the ASEAN countries, they are considering the creation of an Asian currency unit that would track the aggregate value of the region's currencies. Both measures are possible early steps toward the eventual creation of an Asian currency like the euro (see Chapter 11).

Why Currencies Rise or Fall

In the short term, exchange rates depend on speculation about the future value of currencies. Over the long term, however, the value of a state's currency tends to rise or fall relative to others because of changes in the long-term supply and demand for the currency. *Supply* is determined by the amount of money a government prints. Printing money is a quick way to generate revenue for the government, but the more money printed, the lower its price. Domestically, printing too much money creates inflation because the amount of goods in the economy is unchanged but more money with which to buy them is circulating. *Demand* for a currency depends on a state's economic health and political stability. People do not want to own the currency of an unstable country, because political instability leads to the breakdown of economic efficiency and of trust in currency. Conversely, political stability boosts a currency's value. In 2001, when a new Indonesian president took office after a period of political and economic turmoil, the Indonesian currency jumped 13 percent in two days on expectations of greater stability.

A *strong* currency is one that increases in value relative to other currencies—not just in day-to-day fluctuations on currency markets, but in a longer-term perspective. A *weak* currency is the opposite. The strength of a state's currency tends to reflect that state's monetary policy and economic growth rate. Investors seek a currency that will not be watered down by inflation and that can be profitably invested in a growing economy.

To some extent, states have *common* interests—opposed to those of private investors—in maintaining stable currency exchange rates. This is hard to achieve. In 1990, the Canadian dollar traded for 134 Japanese yen, but by 1995 it had dropped to 61 yen. Canadian goods in Japan became cheaper and Japanese goods imported into Canada became more expensive. The Canadian trade deficit with Japan shrank. By 1997, the dollar rose to 86 yen, so the trade deficit once again widened. By 1998 the dollar jumped to 92 yen, then down to 73 in 2000, and up to 113 in 2007.

PRICES SUBJECT TO CHANGE
Changes in exchange rates directly affect the prices of imported goods like these Apple computers for sale in Japan, 1992.

Instability in exchange rates disrupts business in trade-oriented sectors since companies might face sudden and unpredictable changes in their plans for income and expenses. States have a shared interest in currency stability because instability tends to be profitable for speculators at the expense of central banks—a direct cost to the governments involved. Most states also share an interest in the integrity of their currencies against counterfeiting, but some states may feel otherwise. In 2006, the Unites States accused North Korea of passing off tens of millions of dollars in extremely realistic counterfeit $100 bills—a direct gain for the North Korean regime at the expense of the U.S. Treasury.

Despite shared interests in currency stability, states also experience *conflicts* over currency exchanges. States often prefer a *low* value for their own currency relative to others because a low value promotes exports and helps turn trade deficits into surpluses—as mercantilists especially favour (see "Balance of Trade" on pp. 315–316).

To some extent, exchange rates and trade surpluses or deficits tend to adjust automatically toward equilibrium (the preferred outcome for liberals). An *overvalued* currency is one whose exchange rate is too high, resulting in a chronic trade deficit. The deficit can be covered by printing more money, which in turn dilutes the currency's value and brings down the exchange rate (assuming it is allowed to float freely).

Because they see adjustments as harmless, liberals are not bothered by exchange rate changes such as the fall of the dollar relative to the yen. These are viewed as mechanisms for allowing the world economy to work out inefficiencies and maximize overall growth.

A unilateral move to reduce the value of one's own currency by changing a fixed or official exchange rate is called a **devaluation.** Generally, devaluation is a quick fix for financial problems in the short term, but it can create new problems over the long run. It causes losses to foreigners in possession of that currency (which is suddenly worth less). Such losses reduce the trust people place in the currency—that it will be worth as much in

devaluation A unilateral move to reduce the value of a currency by changing a fixed or official exchange rate. See also *exchange rate.*

the future as today. As a result, demand for the currency drops, even at the new lower rate. Investors become wary of future devaluations, and indeed such devaluations often follow one after another in unstable economies. A currency may be devalued by allowing it to float freely, often bringing a single sharp drop in values.

The weakening of a currency, while encouraging exports, carries dangers. For example, the Mexican peso dropped 20 percent in one day (50 percent over several months) when allowed to float freely at the end of 1994. With imported goods shooting up in price, inflation jumped to a 45 percent annualized rate and standards of living fell. And with U.S. dollar-denominated loans suddenly becoming more expensive to service, corporate profits dropped. The Bank of Mexico had to offer 50 percent interest rates to attract capital. The resulting economic dislocations were a big setback to Mexico's economic growth and development, although the country eventually stabilized and paid back its loans in 1997. In general, any sharp or artificial change in exchange rates tends to disrupt smooth international trade and hence interfere with the creation of wealth.

Central Banks

Governments control the printing of money. In some states, the politicians or generals who control the government directly control the amounts of money printed. It is not surprising that inflation tends to be high in those states, because political problems can often be solved by printing more money to use for various purposes. In most industrialized countries, however, politicians know they cannot trust themselves with day-to-day decisions about printing money. To enforce self-discipline and enhance public trust in the value of money, these decisions are turned over to a **central bank.**

central bank An institution common in industrialized countries whose major tasks are to maintain the value of a state's currency and to control inflation.

The economists and technical experts who run a state's central bank seek to maintain the value of the state's currency by limiting the amount of money printed and preventing high inflation. Politicians appoint the people who run the bank, generally for long terms that do not coincide with those of the politicians. The term for the governor of the Bank of Canada, for example, is seven years. Thus, central bank managers try to run the bank in the national interest, a step removed from partisan politics. If a state leader orders a military intervention, state generals obey, but if the leader orders an intervention in currency markets, the central bank does not have to comply. In practice, the autonomy of central banks varies; the head of Thailand's central bank was fired by the prime minister in a dispute over interest rates in 2001.

In Canada, the central bank is the *Bank of Canada*. The Bank of Canada can affect the economy by releasing or hoarding its money. Internationally, it does this by intervening in currency markets (as described earlier). Multilateral interventions are usually coordinated by the heads of central banks and finance (treasury) ministries in leading countries. The long-term, relatively nonpartisan perspective of central bankers makes it easier for states to achieve the collective good of a stable world monetary system.

discount rate The interest rate charged by governments when they lend money to private banks. The discount rate (called the bank rate in Canada) is set by countries' central banks.

Domestically, the Bank of Canada exercises its power mainly by setting the **discount rate,** called the *bank rate*—the interest rate the government charges when it loans money to private banks. (Central banks have only private banks, not individuals and corporations, as their customers.) In effect, this rate controls how quickly money is injected into the economy. If the Bank of Canada sets the bank rate too low, too much money will go into circulation and inflation will result. If the rate is set too high, too little money will circulate and consumers and businesses will find it hard to borrow as much or as cheaply from private banks; economic growth will be depressed. Again, a

Focus on Canadian Scholarship

Scholarship at Canadian universities that focuses on international financial institutions, monetary issues and multinational corporations includes the work of **Eric Helleiner** at the University of Waterloo, who examines prospects for a North American monetary union and the history of global finance. At the University of Victoria, **Michael Webb** focuses on the impact of globalization on corporate taxation policies and transfer prices. **Jacqueline Best** of the University of Ottawa examines transparency in international finance and the moral politics of IMF reforms. At Simon Fraser University, **Stephen McBride** researches the impact of globalization on the state. **Randall Germain** at Carleton University examines the international organization of credit, and **Teddy Samy** of Carleton's Norman Paterson School of International Affairs focuses on international finance and economic development. At the University of British Columbia, **Angela O'Mahony** studies the impact of international integration on domestic policies, with a particular focus on exchange rates, and her colleague **Yves Tiberghien** examines globalization and comparative corporate restructuring in France, Japan and South Korea. At York University, **Isabella Bakker** has studied neo-liberal governance structures and their impact on gender. **Rob Aitken** of the University of Alberta is interested in the globalization of finance and the culture of everyday economic spaces. At the University of Québec at Montréal, **Michèle Rioux** examines global regulation in the telecommunications industry. At the University of Western Ontario, **Adam Harmes** has conducted research on mutual funds and global political economy. **Nilgun Onder** of the University of Regina is interested in the globalization of financial markets and governance issues in global finance. **Tony Porter** at McMaster University examines globalization and finance and the private governance of international industries. At St. Mary's University, **Marc Doucet** is interested in globalization and social movements.

state leader cannot order the central bank to lower the discount rate and inject more money into the economy, but can only ask for such action. Central bankers will inject money only if they are convinced that it will not be too inflationary.

Central bank decisions about the discount rate have important international consequences. If interest rates are higher in one state than another, foreign capital tends to be attracted to the state with the higher rate. And if economic growth is high in a foreign country, more goods can be exported to it. Thus, states care about other states' monetary policies. Any resulting international conflicts can only be resolved politically (such as at G8 summit meetings), and not technically, because each central bank, although removed from domestic politics, still looks out for its own state's interests.

For example, in the unfolding of the global recession of 2001, the U.S. Federal Reserve (the central bank in the United States, also sometimes called "the Fed") worried more about slow economic growth than about inflation, so it repeatedly lowered interest rates. The European Central Bank, which controls the euro, was more worried about inflation than about slow growth. Therefore, Europeans waited longer to lower their lending rates.

Although central banks control sizeable reserves of currency, they are constrained by the limited share of world money they own. Most wealth is controlled by private banks and corporations. As economic actors, states do not drive the direction of the world economy; in many ways they follow it, at least over the long run. However, states still have key advantages as actors in the international economy. Most important, they control the legal use of force (violent leverage) against which even a large amount of wealth usually cannot stand—leaders can jail corporate executives who do not follow their state's rules. Ultimately, then, political power is the state's trump card as an economic actor.

The World Bank and the IMF

Because of the importance of international cooperation for a stable world monetary system and because of the need to overcome collective goods problems, international regimes and institutions have developed around norms of behaviour in monetary relations. Just as the UN institutionally supports regimes based on norms of behaviour in international security affairs (see Chapter 7), the same is true for world monetary regimes.

Paralleling security affairs, the main international economic institutions were created near the end of World War II. The **Bretton Woods system** was adopted at a conference of the winning states in 1944 (at Bretton Woods, New Hampshire). It established the *International Bank for Reconstruction and Development (IBRD)*, more commonly called the **World Bank,** as a source of loans for the reconstruction of Western European economies after the war and to help states through future financial difficulties. (Later, the main borrowers were countries of the global South and, in the 1990s, Eastern European states.) Closely linked with the World Bank, the **International Monetary Fund (IMF)** coordinates international currency exchange, the balance of international payments and national accounts (discussed shortly). The World Bank and the IMF continue to be the pillars of the international financial system. (The roles of the World Bank and the IMF in development of the global South are discussed in Chapter 13.)

Bretton Woods set a regime of stable monetary exchange, based on the U.S. dollar and backed by gold, that lasted from 1944 until 1971.[5] During this period, the dollar had a fixed value equal to a thirty-fifth of an ounce of gold, and the U.S. government guaranteed that dollars could be bought for gold at this rate (from a Fort Knox, Kentucky, stockpile). Other states' currencies were exchanged at fixed rates relative to the dollar, set by the IMF based on the long-term equilibrium level that could be sustained for each currency (rather than short-term political considerations). International currency markets operated within a narrow range around the fixed rate. If a country's currency fell more than 1 percent from the fixed rate, the country had to use its hard-currency reserves to buy its own currency back and thus shore up the price. (Or, if the price rose more than 1 percent, it had to sell its currency to drive the price down.)

The dollar standard was abandoned in 1971—an event sometimes called the "collapse of Bretton Woods." The term is not quite accurate: the institutions survived, and even the monetary regime underwent more of an adjustment than a collapse. The U.S. economy no longer held the overwhelming dominance it had in 1944—mostly because of European and Japanese recovery from World War II—but also because of U.S. overspending on the Vietnam War and other programs. Throughout the 1950s and 1960s, the U.S. spent dollars abroad to stimulate world economic growth and fight the Cold War, but the money spent far exceeded the diminishing stocks of gold held by the Federal Reserve (called the dollar overhang: a situation in which there were more dollars in circulation than could be backed by gold). So successful were the efforts to reinvigorate the economies of Japan and Europe that the United States suffered a relative decline in its trade position.

As a result, the U.S. dollar became seriously overvalued. By 1971, it was no longer worth one thirty-fifth of an ounce of gold, and the United States had to abandon its fixed exchange rate. Without consulting any of the other signatories to the Bretton Woods

Bretton Woods system
A post–World War II arrangement for managing the world economy, established at a meeting in Bretton Woods, New Hampshire, in 1944. Its main institutional components are the World Bank and the International Monetary Fund (IMF).

World Bank Formally the International Bank for Reconstruction and Development (IBRD), it was established in 1944 as a source of loans to help reconstruct the European economies. Later, the main borrowers were countries of the global South and, in the 1990s, Eastern European states.

International Monetary Fund (IMF) An intergovernmental organization (IGO) that coordinates international currency exchange, the balance of international payments and national accounts. Along with the World Bank, it is a pillar of the international financial system. See also *IMF conditionality*.

[5] Eric Helleiner, "The Evolution of the International Monetary and Financial System," *Global Political Economy*, ed. J. Ravenhill (Oxford: Oxford UP, 2005). Harold James, *International Monetary Cooperation since Bretton Woods* (NY: Oxford UP, 1996). Barry Eichengreen, *Globalizing Capital: A History of the International Monetary System* (Princeton, NJ: Princeton UP, 1996).

🌐 Thinking Theoretically

Monetary systems often entail a trade-off between international monetary stability and domestic political autonomy. When exchange rates are fixed either to gold or to the dollar, these systems provide considerable international monetary stability: states, firms and individuals can be assured that exchange rates between currencies will remain the same from day to day, week to week, and often year to year. This is in contrast to a floating exchange rate system, in which exchange rates can fluctuate wildly, sometimes changing hourly or even every few minutes.

The stability of fixed rates usually comes at a price: the loss of some domestic political autonomy. This is because exchange rates do not stay "fixed" just because legislators order them to do so. Currencies are constantly traded against one another and their prices rise and fall accordingly. They are subject, like the trade of goods, to the rules of the market. To keep the market price of a currency in line with its fixed price, domestic monetary managers sometimes have to try to manipulate the market by adjusting the supply or demand of their currency (for example, by buying or selling reserves or adjusting domestic interest rates). When currencies were pegged to gold, millions of dollars' worth of gold could flow from a country's reserves in order to bring the market value of a currency back in line with its fixed price.

For economic liberals, this is simply the price a state pays for the advantages that come with international monetary stability, for the certainty of knowing that the value between currencies will remain stable over time. For mercantilists, the loss of domestic political autonomy is too high a price: stores of wealth in the form of gold or other currencies might be needed for other domestic political goals, such as building up a military or investing in industry. Certainly, as a critical theorist might suggest, a fixed rate system is based on the assumption that a country will have massive reserves of gold (in the case of the gold standard) or other convertible currencies available simply for the purpose of maintaining an exchange rate. It is a system, in other words, based on the assumption that a state is already enormously rich.*

*Robert Gilpin, *The Political Economy of International Relations* (Princeton, NJ: Princeton UP, 1987).

Agreements, President Nixon announced in August 1971 that the U.S. would no longer convert gold for dollars. The dollar was allowed to float freely, and it soon fell to a fraction of its former value relative to gold.

The abandonment of Bretton Woods was good for the United States but bad for Canada, Japan and Europe, where leaders expressed shock at the unilateral U.S. actions. The interdependence of the world capitalist economy, which had produced record economic growth for all Western countries after World War II, had also created conditions for new international conflicts.

The IMF created a new world currency, the **Special Drawing Right (SDR),** in the late 1960s. After the dollar standard was abandoned in 1971, the SDR was put to greater use to replace both gold and the U.S. dollar as a world standard. The SDR has been called "paper gold" because it is created in limited amounts by the IMF, is held as a hard-currency reserve by states' central banks and can be exchanged for various international currencies. The SDR is today the closest thing to a world currency that exists, but it cannot buy goods— only currencies. It is owned only by states (central banks), not by individuals or companies.

In the early 1970s, the value of the U.S. dollar was pegged to the SDR rather than to gold, at a fixed exchange rate (but one that the IMF periodically adjusted to reflect the dollar's strength or weakness). SDRs are linked in value to a basket of several key international currencies. When one currency rises and another falls, the SDR does not change much in value; but if all currencies rise (worldwide inflation), the SDR rises with them.

Since the early 1970s, major national currencies have been governed by a managed float system. Transition from the dollar regime to a managed float regime was difficult. The United States was no longer dominant enough to single-handedly provide stability to

Special Drawing Right (SDR) A world currency created by the International Monetary Fund (IMF) to replace gold as a world standard. Valued by a "basket" of national currencies, the SDR has been called "paper gold."

IT'S ALL RELATIVE
Gold historically served as a world currency but has now been largely replaced by the World Bank's SDR ("paper gold"). Thus currencies are valued only against each other, and not against an external standard like gold. Here, currency is traded in São Paulo, Brazil, 2006.

the world monetary system. States had to bargain politically over the targets for currency exchange rates in the meetings now known as G7 summits.

The technical mechanisms of the IMF are based on each member state's deposit of financial reserves with the IMF. Upon joining the IMF, a state is assigned a *quota* for such deposits, partly of hard currency and partly of the state's own currency (this quota is not related to the concept of trade quotas, which are import restrictions). The quota is based on the size and strength of a state's economy. A state can then borrow against its quota (even exceeding it somewhat) to stabilize its economy in difficult times, and repay the IMF in subsequent years.

Unlike the UN General Assembly or the Security Council, the IMF and the World Bank use a *weighted voting* system—each state has a vote equal to its quota. Thus the G7 states control the IMF, even though nearly all the world's states are members. The United States has the single largest vote, and its capital city hosts the headquarters for both the IMF and the World Bank.

Since 1944, the IMF and the World Bank have tried to accomplish three major missions. First, they sought to provide stability and access to capital for states ravaged by World War II, especially Japan and the states of Western Europe. This mission was a great success, leading to growth and prosperity. Second, especially in the 1970s and 1980s but still continuing today, the Bank and the IMF have tried to promote economic development in countries of the global South. That mission has been far less successful—as seen in the lingering (and even deepening) poverty in much of the global South (see Chapter 12). The third mission, in the 1990s, was the integration of Eastern Europe and Russia into the world capitalist economy. This effort posted a mixed record and the long-term outlook remains uncertain.

STATE FINANCIAL POSITIONS

As currency rates change and state economies grow, the overall positions of states relative to each other shift.

National Accounts

balance of payments
A summary of all the flows of money into and out of a country. It includes three types of international transactions: the current account (including the merchandise trade balance), flows of capital and changes in reserves.

The IMF maintains a system of *national accounts* statistics to keep track of the overall monetary position of each state. A state's **balance of payments** is like the financial statement of a company: it summarizes all the flows of money into and out of the country. The system itself is technical, but it has important political implications. Essentially, three types of international transactions go into the balance of payments: the current account, flows of capital and changes in reserves (see Table 10.2).

Table 10.2 Balance of Payments Accounts, 2001
   In Billions of 2001 US Dollars

	United States	Germany	Japan	Canada
Current Account				
Exports (goods and services)	998	658	448	304
− Imports (goods and services)	−1,356	−620	−442	−268
= Trade balance	−358	38	26	36
+ Government transactions and remittances	−35	−35	−8	−17
= Current account balance	−393	−3	88	19
Capital Flows (net money received)				
+ Foreign investment and loans received	398	−8	−150	−17
Changes in Reserves				
= Changes in reserves	+5	−5	−62	−2

Source: Data adapted from World Bank country data, Sept. 2003.

The *current account* is basically the balance of trade discussed in Chapter 9. Money flows out of a state to pay for imports and flows into the state to pay for exports. Goods imported or exported include merchandise and services. For instance, money spent by a British tourist on Prince Edward Island is equivalent to money spent by a British consumer buying PEI lobsters in a London market; in both cases, money flows into the Canadian current account. The current account includes two other items. *Government transactions* are military and foreign aid grants, as well as salaries and pensions paid to government employees abroad. *Remittances* are funds sent home by companies or individuals outside a country. For example, a Bombardier subsidiary in Britain may send profits back to Bombardier in Montreal. Conversely, a British citizen working in Québec City may send money to her parents in London.

A second category in the accounts is *capital flows*, which are foreign investments in, and by, a country.[6] Capital flows are measured in *net* terms—the total investments and loans foreigners make *in* a country minus the investments and loans that country's companies, citizens and government invest in *other* countries. Most of such investment is private, although some is by (or in) government agencies and state-owned industries. Capital flows are divided into **foreign direct investment** (or *direct foreign investment*)—such as building a factory, owning a company or buying real estate in a foreign country—and indirect *portfolio investment*, such as buying stocks and bonds or making loans to a foreign company. The various kinds of capital flows have somewhat different political consequences (see "International Debt" and "Foreign Direct Investment" later in this chapter), but are basically equivalent in the overall national accounts picture.

The third category, *changes in foreign exchange reserves*, balances the payments in national accounts. Any difference between the inflows and outflows of money (in the current account and capital flows combined) is made up by an equal but opposite change

foreign direct investment
The acquisition by residents of one country of control over a new or existing business in another country. Also called *direct foreign investment*.

[6] Charles P. Kindleberger, *International Capital Movements* (NY: Cambridge UP, 1987).

in reserves. These changes consist of the state's purchases and sales of SDRs, gold and hard currencies other than its own, and changes in its deposits with the IMF. If a state has more money flowing out than in, it takes that money from its reserves. If it has more money flowing in than out, it adds the money to its reserves.

Thus, national accounts always balance. Or at least, they almost balance; there is a residual category—errors and omissions—because even the most efficient and honest government (many governments are neither) cannot keep track of every bit of money crossing its borders.

An important issue raised by some political observers is that systems of national accounts determine value based exclusively on transactions that pass through a market. This means that any productive activity that does not pass through the market does not appear in national accounts measures: including, for example, anything produced for subsistence (growing or preparing food for one's own consumption), and unpaid child care or elder care. Feminists and other critical theorists suggest that this omission makes the work of much of the world's women invisible. This has an impact on people's lives: political and economic agendas flow from the kinds of statistics kept in the system of national accounts. Anyone who does not "appear" in those statistics will not see their interests and concerns represented in political and economic agendas.

These same critics point out further anomalies in a system that values only that which passes through a market. Other things that remain invisible are elements of the natural world: trees and forests, plant species, animals and insects. If someone does not want to buy or sell a particular tree or animal or insect, then it has no value. Yet many people today would argue that animal, plant and insect species have an inherent value (see Chapter 14). An important implication of the system of national accounts is that if plant or animal species do not have value, then their disappearance through extinction is not reflected in a loss or a debit in the national accounts.[7]

International Debt

In one sense, an economy is constantly in motion, as money moves through the processes of production, trade and consumption. Economies also contain *standing wealth*. The hard-currency reserves owned by governments are one form of standing wealth, but not the most important. Most standing wealth is in the form of homes and cars, farms and factories, ports and railroads. In particular, *capital* goods (such as factories) are products that can be used as inputs for further production. Nothing lasts forever, but standing wealth lasts for enough years to be treated differently from goods that are quickly consumed. The main difference is that capital can be used to create more wealth: factories produce goods, railroads support commerce and so forth. Standing wealth creates new wealth, so the economy tends to grow over time. As it grows, more standing wealth is created. In a capitalist economy, money makes more money.

Interest rates reflect this inherent growth dynamic. *Real* interest rates are the rates for borrowing money above and beyond the rate of inflation (for instance, if money is loaned at an annual interest rate of 8 percent but inflation is 3 percent, the real interest rate is 5 percent). Businesses and households borrow money because they think they can use it to create new wealth faster than the rate of interest on the loan.

Borrowing and lending are like any other economic exchange; both parties must see them as beneficial. The borrower values the money now more than the promise of more money in

---

[7] Marilyn Waring, *Counting for Nothing: What Men Value and What Women Are Worth*, 2nd ed. (Toronto: U Toronto P, 1999).

the future, whereas the lender values the promise of more money in the future more than the money now. The distribution of benefits from an exchange is, of course, subject to bargaining. Imagine that a profitable business can use a loan to generate 10 percent annual profit (above the inflation rate). At one extreme, the business could pay 1 percent real interest and keep 9 percent for itself; at the other, it could pay 9 percent interest and keep 1 percent.

The actual split, reflected in prevailing interest rates, is determined by the market for money. Lenders seek out businesses profitable enough to pay high interest; businesses seek out lenders with enough idle cash to lend it at low interest rates. In an imperfect but workable way, the supply and demand for money determine interest rates.

Now imagine that the business borrowing the money is an entire state—including a government, companies and households. If the state's economy is healthy, it can borrow money from foreign governments, banks or companies and create enough new wealth to repay the debts a few years later. However, states, like businesses, sometimes operate at a loss, and their debts mount up. In a vicious circle, more and more of the income generated might go to paying interest, and more money must be borrowed to keep the state in operation. If its fortunes reverse, a state or business can create wealth again and over time pay back the principal on its debts to climb out of the hole. If not, it will have to begin selling part of its standing wealth (buildings, airplanes, factories and the like). The *net worth* of the state or business (all its assets minus all its liabilities) will decrease.

When a state's debts accumulate, its standing wealth is diminished as assets are sold off to pay the debts. Failure to repay debts makes it hard to borrow in the future, a huge impediment to economic growth. In the 1970s and 1980s, debts accumulated in some countries of the global South to the point of virtual national bankruptcy. The debts became unpayable, and the lenders (banks and governments) were forced to write them off the books or settle them at a fraction of their official value. In 2001, Argentina defaulted on over $100 billion of debt accumulated over the prior decade—undergoing street riots and two changes of president within a week in the process.[8] (All amounts in this section are in U.S. dollars.)

Industrialized states, by contrast, have enough standing wealth that even in their most indebted times they have substantial net worth. Still, rising debts are encumbrances against the future creation of wealth, and foreign lenders come to own a greater share of a state's total standing wealth. Naturally, such a situation horrifies mercantilists. To them, national debt represents a loss of power. It is the opposite of what they desire: a pile of reserves.[9]

Why do states go into debt? One major reason is a trade deficit. In the balance of payments, a trade deficit must somehow be made up, and it is common to borrow money to do so. A second reason is the income and consumption patterns of households and businesses. If people and firms spend more than they take in, they must borrow to pay their bills. The credit card they use may be from a local bank, but that bank may be getting the money it lends to them from foreign lenders. As will be discussed in more detail in Chapter 13, consideration of the massive amounts of private debt accumulated by developing countries, especially during the 1980s, must also take into account the aggressive lending policies of northern banks.[10]

---

[8] William R. Cline, *International Debt Reexamined* (Washington, DC: Institute for International Economics, 1994).

[9] Ethan B. Kapstein, *Governing the Global Economy: International Finance and the State* (Cambridge, MA: Harvard UP, 1994). Eric Helleiner, *States and the Reemergence of Global Finance: From Bretton Woods to the 1990s* (Ithaca, NY: Cornell UP, 1994).

[10] Susan George, *A Fate Worse than Debt* (NY: Grove Press 1988).

Keynesian economics
The principles articulated by British economist John Maynard Keynes, which were used successfully in the Great Depression of the 1930s and include the view that governments should sometimes use deficit spending to stimulate economic growth.

fiscal policy A government's decisions about spending and taxation, and one of the two major tools of macroeconomic policy-making (the other being monetary policy).

monetary policy A government's decisions about printing and circulating money, and one of the two major tools of macroeconomic policy-making (the other being fiscal policy).

Another reason for national debt is government spending relative to taxation. Under the principles of **Keynesian economics** (named for economist John Maynard Keynes), governments sometimes spend more than they take in— *deficit spending*—to stimulate economic growth. If the strategy works, increased economic growth eventually generates higher tax revenues to make up the deficit. The government lends money to the nation and recovers it later from a healthier economy. Where does the government get this money? It could print more money, but this step would be inflationary, so central banks try to prevent it. Instead, the government often borrows money from domestic and foreign sources.

Government decisions about spending and taxation are called **fiscal policy**; decisions about printing and circulating money are called **monetary policy**.[11] These are the two main tools available for government to use in managing an economy. There is no such thing as a free lunch: high taxation chokes off economic growth, printing excess money causes inflation and borrowing to cover a deficit puts a mortgage on a state's standing wealth. Thus, for all the complexities of governmental economic policies and international economic transactions, a state's wealth and power ultimately depend more than anything on the underlying health of its economy—the education and training of its labour force, the amount and modernity of its capital goods, the morale of its population and the skill of its managers. In the long run, international debt reflects these underlying realities.

The Position of the United States

The United States is an extraordinarily wealthy and powerful state. Its most *unique* strengths may be in the area of international security—as the world's only superpower— but its economic strengths are also striking. It is not only the world's largest economy but also the most technologically advanced in such growth sectors as computers, telecommunications, aviation and aerospace and biotechnology. The U.S. position in the fields of scientific research and higher education is unparalleled in the world.

The U.S. position in the international economy, however, has shifted. U.S. hegemony peaked after World War II, then gradually eroded as competitors gained relative ground (especially in Western Europe and Asia). In the early 1950s, the U.S. economy (GDP) was about twice the size of the next six advanced industrial states *combined*. By the 1980s, its relative share of world GDP had dropped by almost half. In 1950, the United States held half of the world's financial reserves; by 1980 it held less than 10 percent. This long-term decline after the extraordinary post–1945 U.S. hegemony was natural and probably unavoidable.

In the early 1980s, the trade deficit (exports minus imports) grew from near zero to $200 billion in just a few years. The trade deficit shrank, but then grew to $500 billion a year by 2003. Meanwhile, the budget deficit jumped to $300 billion per year in the early 1980s, then closed in the 1990s and became a large surplus, only to return to $500 billion by 2004 as a result of war spending, tax cuts and recession. These trends have caused alarm regarding U.S. international economic leadership.[12]

---

[11] Jeffry A. Frieden, "Invested Interests: The Politics of National Economic Policies in a World of Global Finance," *International Organization* 45.4 (1991): 425–52.

[12] Kenneth W. Dam, *The Rules of the Global Game: A New Look at U.S. International Economic Policy Making* (Chicago: U Chicago P, 2001). Paul A. Volcker and Toyoo Gyohten, *Changing Fortunes: The World's Money and the Threat to American Leadership* (NY: Random House, 1992).

The U.S. economy showed remarkable resiliency in the mid- to late-1990s, as those of other industrialized countries (notably Japan) stumbled. Technological change and restructuring created strong growth of productivity, especially with the advent of computer networks. The United States ended the 1990s with all-time low unemployment, low inflation, robust growth and stock market gains. The budget deficit became a surplus. Despite these successes, the U.S. expansion eventually ran out of steam, the bubble of internet investment burst and the United States was again in recession by 2001—this time joined by all the world's major economies. This was painfully hammered home by the economic disruptions that followed the September 2001 attacks.

While growth has resumed, the accumulated debt from 20 years of deficit spending remains. The U.S. government's **national debt** grew from close to $1 trillion at the beginning of the 1980s to $3 trillion by the end of that decade, and to $8 trillion today. The interest payments were equivalent to what would otherwise be a healthy rate of economic growth. Not long ago, the United States was the world's leading lender state; now it is the world's leading debtor.

national debt The amount a government owes in debt as a result of deficit spending.

U.S. financial trends have profound implications for the global political economy. They first undermined (in the 1980s) and then reconstructed (in the 1990s) and then undermined again (since 2000) the leading U.S. role in stabilizing international trade and monetary relations, in assuring the provision of collective goods and in providing capital for the economic development of other world regions. In a more decentralized, more privatized world economy with an uncertain U.S. role, collective goods problems would be harder to solve and free trade harder to achieve.

The Position of Canada

Canada is considered a "middle power" on questions of security, and in some ways its position reflects a similarly mixed position economically. On the one hand, Canada is a member of the G7, a reflection of its status as one of the world's most important economies. Canada was also a strong supporter of the establishment of the **Group of 20 (G20)** in 1999, which is composed of the G7, Australia, Argentina, Brazil, China, India, Indonesia, Mexico, Korea, Russia, Saudi Arabia, South Africa and Turkey, along with the European Union, International Monetary Fund and the World Bank. Members of the G7 had realized that even acting together, they were not sufficient in number to manage world financial markets. G20 finance ministers and central bank governors meet annually.

Group of 20 (G20) The G20 is composed of the G7 states, plus Australia, Argentina, Brazil, China, India, Indonesia, Mexico, Korea, Russia, Saudi Arabia, South Africa and Turkey, along with the European Union, International Monetary Fund and World Bank. Members of the G7 realized that even acting together, they were not sufficient in number to manage world financial markets.

On the other hand, despite Canada's role in the G7 and G20, its economic trends do not have the same impact on the rest of the world as does the U.S. economy. In general terms, the Canadian economy tends to follow trends in the rest of the world (most particularly in the U.S.) rather than lead them. The Canadian dollar floats (or more accurately, is a managed float), and its value is usually given in relation to the U.S. dollar. Canada's enormous trade surplus (see Chapter 9) with the United States—which grew from approximately $17 billion in 1994 to $96.5 billion in 2006—was largely the result of the strong economic performance of the U.S. over that period (and therefore rising demand for Canadian exports). Over some of this period, Canada's declining exchange rate relative to the U.S. dollar made Canadian exports more attractive to U.S. consumers, but as of 2007, its rising exchange rate resulted in the first decline of merchandise exports to the U.S. since 2004.[13]

---

[13] Statistics Canada, "Canadian International Merchandise Trade," *The Daily* 13 Feb. 2007, available at http://www.statcan.ca/Daily/English/070213/d070213a.htm.

Canada's position as a country that follows the global political economy more than it leads it explains its enthusiasm for formal and informal multilateral efforts, such as the G7 and G20. Canada can exert more influence through these kinds of initiatives than its economy can alone.

The Position of Russia and Eastern Europe

At the end of World War II, the United States provided considerable capital and aid to stimulate new growth in Western Europe and Japan, but did not repeat those efforts to help get the Russian and Eastern European region on its feet after the Cold War.

Instead, states in this region face daunting challenges as they try to convert from centrally planned to capitalist economies and to join the world capitalist economy. These challenges include integration into the world trading system (membership in the WTO, bilateral trade agreements and so forth) and attracting foreign investment. Among the most difficult tasks are the attempts of states in this region to join the international monetary system. Having a stable and convertible currency is a key element in attracting foreign business and expanding international trade.

Most of the states of the former Soviet bloc became members of the IMF and were assigned financial reserves quotas, but the IMF and World Bank would not make loans freely available until their governments took strong action to curb inflation, balance government budgets and assure economic stability. Such stability would have been easier to achieve with foreign loans, however, creating a chicken-and-egg problem.

The economies of the region experienced a deep depression (shrinking GDP) from 1989 to 1991. By 1992, only Poland had resumed economic growth—a 1 to 4 percent annual growth of GDP following a 20 percent shrinkage in 1990–1991. The rest of the economies in Eastern Europe (except Bulgaria and Slovakia) stopped shrinking by 1994, but the states of the former Soviet Union continued downward, until by 1996 the total economic activity of those states had been cut by half over seven years (see Table 10.3).

Table 10.3 Economic Collapse in Russia and Eastern Europe

Country	Cumulative (10-Year) Change in GDP, 1990–1999
Former Soviet Republics[a]	−50%
Former Yugoslavia	−35%
Estonia, Latvia and Lithuania	−29%
Bulgaria	−29%
Romania	−28%
Albania	−12%
Czech Republic	−11%
Slovakia	−1%
Hungary	−1%
Poland	+21%

[a]Russia, Ukraine and 10 other CIS members

Source: Author's estimates based on United Nations, *World Economics and Social Survey 1999* (New York: United Nations, 1999) 263.

In general, the Eastern European countries have stabilized their economies more effectively than have the former Soviet republics. Among the latter, Russia was better off than some of the others; it had inherited much of the Soviet Union's economic infrastructure and natural resources and was large enough to gain the attention of the West. However, internal power struggles created political instability in Russia, discouraging foreign investment. The costs of wars in Chechnya made matters worse. Inflation reached 1500 percent in 1992 but was brought down to less than 10 percent by 2006. Growth returned—over 6 percent a year from 2000 to 2005—and a new flat tax on income boosted tax collections. Changes in currency regulations in 2006 were a step toward making the ruble fully convertible. In 2006, Russia struck a deal to join the WTO at some point in the following few years.

Ukraine had even more severe economic woes, as did some other former Soviet republics. Some states printed their own currency while others kept using the Russian ruble (through the framework of the CIS). In other former Soviet republics—Azerbaijan, Armenia, Georgia and Tajikistan—devastating wars wrecked economies and further fuelled inflation.

Soaring inflation and general economic collapse throughout the region made it much harder to resolve these problems and arrive at a stable political and economic environment in which IMF and World Bank assistance would be useful and not just wasted. In any case, the amounts of money available for such assistance were limited because of the economic recession of the early 1990s in the world's leading economies. Nonetheless, the former Soviet republics joined the IMF after negotiating reform plans. In 1996, creditor states renegotiated (to a longer-term basis) $40 billion in previous Russian debts; this reduced interest payments but did not address the underlying causes of the debts.

Organized crime emerged as a major problem in the 1990s. For example, in 1996 a U.S. entrepreneur was killed gangland-style in Moscow (which did not encourage foreign investment), and the chairman of Russia's central bank had his apartment windows shot out. "Plutocrats" seized formerly state-owned companies and drained their wealth into private bank accounts. The chaos of transition also provided fertile ground for corruption among government officials. In 2004, Russia's largest oil company (Yukos) was shut down by President Vladimir Putin due to nonpayment of a $10 billion tax bill, only to have its assets purchased by a state-owned business. (Yukos's owner was an opponent of Putin.)

The economic and financial problems of the region were compounded by security problems—ethnic and national conflicts along the southern rim of the former Soviet Union—which disrupted trade and monetary relations. For example, rail traffic from Russia was disrupted by separatists in Georgia, and Azerbaijan cut off energy supplies to Armenia. The main oil pipeline from Azerbaijan went right through the bombed-out capital of Chechnya, and was shut down for years.

Since its financial crisis in 1998, Russia has registered strong economic growth and reduced runaway inflation to below 10 percent per year. Recently, high oil prices have helped Russia (an oil exporter) to pay off debts and build large foreign reserves. Incomes are rising and poverty shrinking. Russia reached a breakthrough agreement with the United States in 2006 that should lead to Russia's WTO membership. However, structural obstacles remain, including corruption, weak rule of law and political uncertainty as President Putin centralizes power and reasserts state control over business and the press. It appears that Russia faces continuing struggles to find the economic and political stability to fully integrate into the world capitalist economy, with a stable convertible currency, expanded trade and increased foreign investment, but it has made progress in that direction.

The Position of Asia

Financial positions in the leading economies of Asia were in some ways the reverse of the Canadian and U.S. path in the 1980s and 1990s. Whereas Canadian and U.S. positions deteriorated in the 1980s and early 1990s but strengthened in the late 1990s, the main Asian economies enjoyed a tremendous boom in the 1980s and early 1990s but serious financial deterioration in the late 1990s (with the exception of China). Only in the 2001 recession did Asia and North America find synchrony, along with Europe.

Japan has led Asia through highs and lows. Following decades of robust growth after the devastation of World War II, Japan by the 1980s seemed to be emerging as a possible rival to the United States as the world's leading industrial power. Japanese auto manufacturers gained ground on U.S. rivals when smaller cars became popular after the oil-price shocks of the 1970s. In electronics and other fields, Japanese products began to dominate world markets, and Japanese capital became a major economic force in nearby developing economies (such as China and Thailand) and even in the United States, where Japanese creditors financed much of the growing U.S. national debt.

These successes masked serious problems. The go-go economic growth of the 1980s drove prices of stocks and real estate to unrealistic levels based on speculation rather than inherent value. When prices collapsed at the end of the 1980s, many banks were left with bad loans backed by deflated stocks and real estate. These losses were covered up, and the underlying problems—lax banking regulation, political cronyism and outright corruption and fraud—persisted through the 1990s. A reform-oriented prime minister (Junichiro Koizumi) took office in 2001, but Japan faced a worldwide recession that is expected to depress exports.

BITTER FRUITS

Inflation and unemployment in Russia and other former Soviet republics in the 1990s cut the GDP approximately in half and created political turmoil. These women in Moscow try to make ends meet by selling pickled vegetables grown in their yards, 1999.

Despite the example of Japan's financial system, these mistakes were repeated almost exactly in the 1990s by the newly industrializing countries (NICs, see pp. 455–461) of East and Southeast Asia. Real estate and stocks became overvalued as rapid economic growth led to speculation and ever-rising expectations. Banks made massive bad loans based on overvalued assets and got away with it because of political corruption and cronyism. In 1997, these economies suffered a serious financial crisis, which jumped across international borders and sent shockwaves around the globe that reverberated for two years.

The *1997 Asian financial crisis* began when currency speculators began selling off the currencies of Southeast Asian countries. Thailand, the Philippines, Malaysia and Indonesia were forced to let their currencies be devalued. Such pressure on currencies creates pressure on prospects for economic growth—because governments will have to cut back money supplies (and raise interest rates) in response. Reduced prospects for economic growth in turn put pressure on stock prices, since companies will be less profitable. Also, currency devaluation reduces foreign investment (because investors lose confidence) and makes foreign loans harder to repay (since more local currency is needed to repay each unit of foreign currency). Thus, the currency problems of Asian countries led to several stock market crashes. Other so-called *emerging markets* around the world—notably Brazil—suffered as investors generalized the problems in Asia.

The Philippines addressed the problem in a manner preferred by international agencies and foreign investors. After losing $1 billion unsuccessfully defending its currency's value, the Philippines let its currency float and then asked the IMF for a $1 billion stabilization loan, which was approved in a week. In return for the IMF loan, the government of the Philippines agreed to keep interest rates high and budget deficits low (to reduce inflation), to pass a tax reform law and to tighten control of banks that had made bad real estate loans. These kinds of tough measures create political problems, especially when banks are politically connected or when governments are corrupt. The Philippines, by addressing such problems, won international approval.

Thailand promised, in return for a $16 billion IMF bailout, to close dozens of indebted banks, raise taxes, cut government deficits and lower economic growth rates by more than half. The government of Thailand, a shaky coalition based on political patronage, soon collapsed as street protests vented anger at the economic downturn. A reform-minded prime minister was appointed and the situation stabilized.

Other Asian countries did not act decisively. In Malaysia, the prime minister annoyed foreign investors by accusing currency speculators, including George Soros (see p. 486), of political motives in undermining Asian economies, because of racism and differences regarding human rights. He said that currency speculation should be illegal. (Soros has in fact used his wealth to support programs in transitional countries to foster an "open society," but there is no reason to doubt that the speculators' motive in Malaysia was to make money.) Malaysian controls on capital and currency were successful in this case.

The currency speculators, meanwhile, moved on to attack Indonesia, which had to let its currency fall, raised interest rates and let its stock market drop. Within months, Indonesia, too, sought tens of billions of dollars in IMF loans, with the usual conditions attached. Indonesia resisted implementing the promised reforms, however, and its economy continued to slide (as did its political stability) in 1998. Riots and student protests eventually forced Indonesia's president Suharto to resign after 30 years of dictatorship. Megawati Sukarnoputra, the daughter of Suharto's arch-rival, became president in 2001.

Overall, in Thailand, Malaysia and Indonesia, stock markets lost about half their value and currencies about a quarter of their value in the first nine months of 1997. Observers declared the "Asian economic miracle" to be at an end. The impact on people's lives was devastating, with massive job losses and increased costs for basic goods and services.

IS MY MONEY SAFE?
The Asian financial crisis of 1997 led to currency devaluations, bank failures and stock market crashes in a number of fast-growing Asian economies. Ordinary people faced hardships as a result, and financial analysts worried that the effects could seriously impact international financial markets. Here, depositors gather outside a Hong Kong bank after a rumour of a run on the bank during the 1997 crisis.

Despite a healthy resurgence in many of these economies since 1997, the go-go years appear to be gone for good.

China escaped harm in the 1997 crisis for several reasons: its economic growth had been less speculative (although rapid), its currency was not freely convertible, it held massive reserves of hard currency and its government had shown the discipline necessary to bring inflation under control. Lowering the economic growth rate from 14 to 10 percent annually, the government reduced inflation from 20 percent to less than 4 percent from 1995 to 1997. The engineer of this tight-money policy, Zhu Rongji, became the Chinese prime minister in 1998, just as successful inflation-fighters became presidents of Brazil and Argentina in the 1990s. China then rode out the Asian crisis without devaluing its currency by further lowering growth to 7 percent by 1999, still a very strong pace.

Hong Kong, like China, did not devalue in 1997. Just months after coming under Chinese control, Hong Kong became the central target of currency speculators. To maintain the Hong Kong dollar, which was (and remains) pegged at a fixed rate per the U.S. dollar, the Hong Kong government had to raise interest rates drastically and watch the stock market lose a third of its value in weeks. The Hong Kong stock crash triggered a huge global sell-off, but its government remained firm in maintaining its currency's value—which it saw as critical to foreign investors' long-term confidence—despite the costs of financial collapse and economic slowdown. In the first test of China's "one country, two systems" formula, the Chinese government allowed the Hong Kong administration to manage the crisis.

When South Korea caught the "Asian flu," however, the stakes increased. South Korea is the largest of the NICs, an economic power in the region ranking behind only Japan and China. Yet by the end of 1997, South Korea's currency was down 20 percent, its stock markets collapsing and its banks saddled with $50 billion in bad loans. The IMF stepped in with a $60 billion international bailout—the largest ever—and the Korean government adopted stringent austerity measures. Some nationalist South Koreans called signing the IMF agreement a "Day of National Humiliation," but Koreans elected a new reformist president, Kim Dae Jong—a former political prisoner. He convinced South Koreans that foreign investment was positive; they accepted the IMF and even started using it as a face-saving way to reduce the costs of extravagant status-oriented weddings and funerals.[14] Thus in South Korea, as in Thailand and Indonesia, the financial crisis brought about democratization and reform as well as pain.

The Asian crisis suddenly dried up huge sums of capital that had been pouring into Southeast Asia, doubling every two years and reaching nearly $100 billion annually. In 1997 and 1998, about $10 billion per year moved *out* of Southeast Asia. The capital flight also hit other so-called emerging markets in other regions. Brazil in particular was the recurrent target

---

[14] Sandra. A Sugawara, "'Xenophobic' Nation Is Sold on Aid from Foreigners," *Washington Post* 24 Feb 1998: A15.

of currency speculators because Brazil found it hard to pass legislation to stem a $50 billion government deficit. Every time the Brazilian political system stumbled in making promised reforms, Brazil's stock market fell and its currency came under attack. It devalued in 1999.

The Asian financial crisis of 1997 illustrates the importance of currency exchange rates in overall economic stability and growth. Governments face a dilemma in that politically desirable policies—from stimulating growth and keeping taxes low to supporting banks and businesses owned by friends and relatives—tend to undermine currency stability. If allowed to continue, such policies may lead to an economic collapse and the loss of foreign investment, but tough policies to maintain currency stability may cause a government to lose power.

Overall, troubling signs of economic instability have shadowed the past decade—in the turbulent, recession-plagued years that followed the end of the Cold War, in the financial collapses in Asia and Russia in the late 1990s, in Japan's decade-long stagnation, in the U.S. technology sector's bursting stock bubble and in the synchronized global recession of 2001–2002.

In the regions just discussed—North America, Asia and especially Russia and Eastern Europe—the role of private business is expanding relative to that of the state. Throughout the world, private business plays a role in the economy that exceeds that of the state. The remainder of this chapter considers the international political issues related to the operation of private businesses across state borders.

The Information Revolution
Liquid Capital

Technology has allowed electronic transfer of money around the world. As a result, more than $1 trillion crosses borders daily in international currency exchanges, and international investment capital can quickly bail out of emerging markets in crises. Currency speculators can drive foreign governments and economies into ruin, but in so doing may stimulate needed reforms. Will the liquidity of international capital ultimately prove destabilizing to the global economy?

In theory, the instant free flow of capital around the world—a result of global communications technologies and an important feature of globalization—should stabilize economies. Investors can shift money quickly, and thus incrementally, as conditions indicate shifting strengths and weaknesses of different currencies and economies. Instead of waiting for governments to devalue or revalue currencies when problems are far along, markets can gradually adjust values day by day. In practice, however, the global liquidity of capital has also shown a destabilizing tendency, as small events can be amplified and reverberate in distant locations. Thus the problems of Thailand became an Asian crisis and then an emerging-markets crisis, as liquid capital fled for cover at the speed of light.

To explore this question, go to www.pearsoned.ca/goldstein.

MULTINATIONAL BUSINESS

Although states are the primary rule makers for currency exchange and other international economic transactions, those transactions are carried out mainly by private firms and individuals, not governments. Most important among these private actors are multinational corporations.

Multinational Corporations

Multinational corporations (MNCs) are companies based in one state with affiliated branches or subsidiaries operating in other states. There is no exact definition, but the clearest case of an MNC is a large corporation that operates globally in many countries simultaneously, with fixed facilities and employees in each. With no exact definition, there is also no exact count of the total number of MNCs, but most estimates are in the tens of thousands worldwide.

multinational corporations (MNCs) Companies based in one state with affiliated branches or subsidiaries operating in other states. See also *home country* and *host country*.

Most important are *industrial corporations*, which make goods in factories in various countries and sell them to businesses and consumers around the world. The automobile, oil and electronics industries have the largest MNCs. Almost all of the largest MNCs are based in G7 states, and the largest of all, based on revenues, are American or Japanese.

Financial corporations (the most important being banks) also operate multinationally—although often with more restrictions than industrial MNCs. Canada's six major domestic banks operate internationally in the United States and various countries of Latin America, the Caribbean and Asia. Approximately one-third of their revenues is derived from international operations, but none figure among the top financial institutions in the world. For a long time, the U.S. did not hold a leading position among the world's largest commercial banks—reflecting the traditional U.S. antitrust policy that limits banks' geographic expansion and restricts them from certain financial services (such as stock brokerage and insurance). With legislative changes in 1999, however, U.S. banks expanded globally and took up two of the top 10 positions, which include banks from Japan, Germany, Switzerland, the U.K. and France.

The growing international integration of financial markets was illustrated spectacularly in 1995, when a single 28-year-old trader in Singapore lost $1 billion speculating on Japanese stock and bond markets, bankrupting his employer, a 200-year-old British investment bank. The 1997 stock market crash in Hong Kong created a wave of sell-offs across international time zones as markets opened in Europe and North America. Money moves across borders at the rate of $1.5 trillion per day. In this context, financial corporations are becoming more internationalized.

Some MNCs sell *services*.[15] McDonald's fast-food chain and Nortel are good examples. So are the international airlines, which sell tickets in dozens of states (and currencies) for travel all over the world.

The role of MNCs in international political relations is complex and is the subject of some dispute.[16] Some scholars see MNCs virtually as agents of their home national governments. This view resonates with mercantilism, in which economic activity ultimately serves political authorities; thus MNCs have clear national identities and act as members of their national society under state authority. A variant of this theme (from a more critical world view) considers national governments as agents of their MNCs; state interventions (economic and military) serve private, monied interests. MNCs are, by this view, contemporary agents of imperialism.

Others see MNCs as citizens of the world beholden to no government, a view congruent with economic liberalism. The head of Dow Chemical once said he dreamed of buying an island beyond any state's territory and putting Dow's world headquarters there. In such a view, MNCs act globally in the interests of their (international) stockholders and owe loyalty to no state. In any case, MNCs are motivated by the need to maximize profits, and managers who fail to do so are likely to be fired. Only in the case of state-owned MNCs—an important exception but a small minority of the total companies worldwide—do MNC actions reflect state interests. Even then, managers have won greater autonomy to pursue

---

[15] Jonathan D. Aronson, "The Service Industries: Growth, Trade, and Development Prospects," *Growth, Exports and Jobs in a Changing World Economy: Agenda 1988*, ed. John W. Sewell and Stuart K. Tucker (New Brunswick, NJ: Transaction [for the Overseas Development Council], 1988).

[16] Paul N. Doremus, William W. Keller, Louis W. Pauly and Simon Reich, *The Myth of the Global Corporation* (Princeton, NJ: Princeton UP, 1998). David J. Saari, *Global Corporations and Sovereign Nations: Collision or Cooperation?* (Westport, CT: Quorum/Greenwood, 1999). Razeen Sally, *States and Firms: Multinational Enterprises in Institutional Competition* (NY: Routledge, 1995). Robert Gilpin, *U.S. Power and the Multinational Corporation* (NY: Basic, 1975).

profit in recent years (as part of economic reforms instituted in many countries), and in many cases state-owned enterprises are being sold off (privatized).

As independent actors in the international arena, MNCs are increasingly powerful. Dozens of industrial MNCs have annual sales of tens of billions of dollars (hundreds of billions for top corporations, such as Wal-Mart, GM and Exxon Mobil). Only 35 states have more economic activity per year (GDP) than did the largest MNC in 2006, Exxon Mobil. However, the *largest* government (the United States) has government revenues of $2 trillion—nearly eight times larger than Exxon Mobil. Canadian government revenues are closer to that of Exxon, at just under $225 billion in 2006; but Canada's gross domestic product is $1.2 trillion. Thus the power of MNCs does not rival that of the largest states but exceeds that of many poorer states, which affects MNC operations in the global South (see pp. 475–477).

Giant MNCs contribute to global interdependence. They are so deeply entwined in so many states that they have a profound interest in the stable operation of the international system—in security affairs as well as in trade and monetary relations. MNCs prosper in a stable international atmosphere that permits freedom of trade, movement and capital flows (investments)—all governed by market forces with minimal government interference. Thus MNCs are, overall, a strong force for economic liberalism in the world economy, despite the fact that MNCs in particular industries push for certain mercantilist policies to protect their own interests.

Most MNCs have a world management system based on *subsidiaries* in each state in which they operate. The operations within a given state are subject to the legal authority of that state's government. Foreign subsidiaries are owned (in whole or in substantial part) by the parent MNC in the home country. The parent MNC hires and fires the top managers of its foreign subsidiaries.

Corporations that do business internationally and the states that host them have created a global *infrastructure* of facilities, services, communication links and the like that facilitate the conduct of business. Business infrastructure is a key aspect of *transnational relations*—linkages among people and groups across national borders.

In addition to the direct connections among members of a single MNC, the operations of MNCs support a global business infrastructure connecting a transnational community of businesspeople. A Canadian manager arriving in Seoul, South Korea, for instance, does not find a bewildering scene of unfamiliar languages, locations and customs. Rather, she or he moves through a familiar sequence of airport lounges, telephone calls and faxes, international hotels, business conference rooms and CNN broadcasts—most likely hearing English spoken throughout.

Foreign Direct Investment

MNCs do not just operate in foreign countries, they also own capital (standing wealth) there—buildings, factories, cars and so forth. For instance, Canadian and German MNCs own some capital in Japan, and Japanese MNCs own capital located in Canada and Germany. *Investment* means exchanging money for ownership of capital (for the purpose of producing a stream of income that will, over time, more than compensate for the money invested). Investments in foreign countries are among the most important, and politically sensitive, activities of MNCs.

Unlike portfolio investment (on paper), *foreign direct investment* involves tangible goods such as factories and office buildings (including ownership of a sizeable fraction of a company's total stock, as opposed to a portfolio with little bits of many companies). Paper can be traded on a global market relatively freely, but direct investments cannot be freely moved from one state to another when conditions change. Direct investment is long term, and it is more visible than portfolio investment. Investments in the manufacturing sector usually entail the greatest investment in fixed facilities, which are difficult to move, and in training workers and managers. Investments in the extraction of minerals or fuels are less expensive, but even less moveable. Investments in the service sector tend to be less expensive and easier to walk away from if conditions change.

Mercantilists tend to view foreign investments in their own country with suspicion. In countries of the global South, foreign direct investment often causes concerns about a loss of sovereignty, because governments may be less powerful than the MNCs that invest in their country. These fears also reflect the historical fact that most foreign investment in the global South used to come from colonizers. Furthermore, although such investments create jobs, they also bring dislocations of traditional ways of life and cultures. For example, in 2001, villagers in Thailand tried to block a planned $500 million gas pipeline in their area, fearful that it would destroy their way of life and attract problems ranging from industrial pollution to AIDS.[17]

Because many poor and transitional states are in desperate need of capital from any source to stimulate economic growth, foreign direct investment is generally welcomed and encouraged despite the fears of economic nationalists.[18] (North-South investment is discussed further in Chapter 12, pp. 429–435.) Most foreign direct investment (like most portfolio investment) is not in the developing world, however, but in industrialized countries.

Economic nationalists in industrialized countries also worry about losing power and sovereignty due to foreign investment. In Canada, for instance, mercantilists are alarmed that U.S. firms own more than half of Canada's manufacturing industry and more than two-thirds of their oil and gas industry. Canada is much smaller than the United States, and it depends heavily on U.S. trade. In this asymmetrical situation, some Canadians worry that they are being turned into an annex of the United States—economically, culturally and ultimately politically—losing their own national culture and control of their economy.

Meanwhile, U.S. economic nationalists have similar concerns over foreign direct investment in the United States. Partly this reflects alarm over the accumulation of U.S. debts. Mercantilists see a loss of power when foreign investors buy up companies and real estate in a debtor country. Such concerns seem to be stronger when a foreign MNC buys an existing company or building than when it builds a new factory or other facility. For example, when Japanese investors bought Columbia movie studios in Los Angeles and (temporarily) Rockefeller Center in New York, many Americans saw these properties as somehow representative of the American spirit, and their sale was seen as a U.S. loss. When Honda built a new car factory in Ohio, adding jobs and facilities to the U.S. economy, no such loss was perceived.

Critical theorists share some of the concerns raised by mercantilists, and would claim also that MNCs pull wealth out of countries rather than bring it in. They do this through various mechanisms, such as transfer prices and licensing agreements. This is particularly true, critical theorists argue, when MNCs set up in countries of the global South. Their arguments will be explored in more detail in Chapter 12.

---

[17] Wayne Arnold, "A Gas Pipeline to World Outside," *New York Times* 26 Oct. 2001: C1.

[18] Ben Gomes-Casseres and David B. Yoffie, eds., *The International Political Economy of Direct Foreign Investment* (Brookfield, VT: Elgar, 1993). Thomas J. Biersteker, *Distortion or Development? Contending Perspectives on the Multinational Corporation* (Cambridge, MA: MIT, 1978). Margaret M. Pearson, *Joint Ventures in the People's Republic of China: The Control of Foreign Direct Investment under Socialism* (Princeton, NJ: Princeton UP, 1992).

IT'S A JOB
Foreign direct investment is often sought by host governments because it stimulates employment and economic growth, though at wage levels that home countries would not tolerate. Here, Muslim women in Indonesia assemble Barbies at a Mattel factory. Note that along with investment, a host country imports certain cultural trappings of the MNC's activity—such as Mattel's rendition of femininity in its doll. (This is a literal case of what postmodern feminists call the social construction of gender roles.)

Liberals do not agree with such arguments. Economic liberals emphasize that global efficiency and the increased generation of wealth result from the ability of MNCs to invest freely across international borders. Investment decisions should be made solely on economic grounds, not nationalist ones. By this view, U.S. investments in Canadian manufacturing or resource extraction generate economic growth: they create employment and benefit Canadian consumers. While some profits may be sent to the home country of the MNC, much of it is reinvested locally. Liberals also point out a glaring inconsistency in the U.S. public's preoccupation with Japanese investment in the United States in the late 1980s: more than half of all foreign investment in the United States was from Western Europe, and only a third as much was from Japan, yet there was little outcry about a loss of U.S. sovereignty to Europe. Presumably this disparity reflects either racism or a lingering shadow of World War II in the U.S. public's perceptions. The tables were turned in the late 1990s when financial crises in Japan made Americans worry that Japanese investors would pull out of the United States, and that no more would come in.

Host and Home Government Relations

A state in which a foreign MNC operates is called a **host country,** and the state where the MNC has its headquarters is called its **home country.** MNC operations create a variety of problems and opportunities for both the host and home countries' governments. Conflicts between the host government and the MNC may spill over to become an interstate

host country A state in which a foreign multinational corporation (MNC) operates.

home country The state where a multinational corporation (MNC) has its headquarters.

conflict between the host and home governments. For example, if a host government takes an MNC's property without compensation or arrests its executives, the home government may step in to help the MNC.[19]

Because host governments can regulate activities in their own territories, in general an MNC cannot operate in a state against the wishes of its government. Conversely, because MNCs have many states to choose from, a host government cannot generally force an MNC to do business against its wishes. At least in theory, MNCs operate in host countries only when it is in the interests of both the MNC and the host government. Common interests result from the creation of wealth in the host country by the MNC. Both the MNC and the host government benefit—the MNC from profits, the government directly by taxation and indirectly through economic growth (generating future taxes and political support).

However, there are also conflicts in the relationship. An obvious one concerns the distribution of new wealth between the MNC and host government. This distribution depends on the rate at which MNC activities or profits are taxed, as well as on the ground rules for MNC operations. Before an MNC invests or opens a subsidiary in a host country, it negotiates such issues with the government. Threats of violent leverage are largely irrelevant. Rather, the government's main leverage is to promise a favourable climate for doing business and making money; the MNC's main leverage is the threat of taking its capital elsewhere. In an increasingly globalized economy, this threat is more frequently invoked.

Governments can offer MNCs a variety of incentives to invest. Special terms of taxation and regulation are common. In cases of resource extraction, negotiations may revolve around the rates the government will charge to lease land and mineral rights to the MNC. National and local governments may offer to provide business infrastructure—such as roads, airports or phone lines—at the government's expense. (An MNC could also offer to build such infrastructure if allowed to operate on favourable terms in the country.) Over time, certain locations may develop a strong business infrastructure and gain a comparative advantage in luring MNCs to establish there. This has been particularly true in Export Processing Zones, which are established specifically to attract MNCs. Critics point out, however, that the concessions by host country governments are often so large that little direct benefit flows to the host state.

These issues all concern the distribution of the new wealth that will be created by MNC operations. MNCs seek host governments that will let them keep more of that wealth; governments seek MNCs that will let the government keep more. With many MNCs and quite a few governments involved in such negotiations, there is a market process at work in the worldwide investment decisions of MNCs.

In addition to questions of distribution, MNC relations with host governments entail several other sources of potential conflict. One is the potential for governments to break their agreements with MNCs and change the terms of taxes, regulations or other conditions. The extreme case is nationalization, in which a host government takes ownership of MNC facilities and assets in the host country (with or without compensation). Once an MNC has invested in fixed facilities, it loses much of its leverage over the government because it cannot move to another country without incurring huge expenses. However, governments hesitate to break their word with MNCs because to do so might discourage other MNCs from investing in the future. Nationalization of foreign assets is now rare. It is more common for MNCs to break their agreements, pull up stakes and move out.

---

[19] Kenneth A. Rodman, *Sanctity versus Sovereignty: U.S. Policy toward the Nationalization of Natural Resource Investments in the Third World* (NY: Columbia UP, 1988).

Another source of conflict is the trade policies of the host government. Government restrictions on trade seldom help foreign MNCs; more often they help the host country's own industries—which often directly compete with foreign MNCs. Ironically, although they favour global free trade, MNCs may funnel direct investment to states that restrict imports, because MNCs can avoid the import restrictions by producing goods in the host country (rather than exporting from the home country). Trade restrictions are thus another form of leverage that states have in luring foreign direct investment.

Trade regulations often seek to create as many jobs and as much taxable income as possible within a host country. If Toyota assembles cars at a factory in Canada (perhaps to avoid Canadian import restrictions), the Canadian government tends to pressure Toyota to use more Canadian parts in building the cars (such "domestic content" rules were part of the 1992 North American Free Trade Agreement). MNCs generally want the freedom to assemble goods anyplace they want from parts made anywhere; governments by contrast want to maximize the amount of wealth created on their own territories. With parts and supplies from many countries now routinely converging to go into a product completed in one country, it is very difficult to say exactly where the product was made. The question is complex and entails long negotiations between MNCs and host governments.

Monetary policy also leads to conflicts between MNCs and host governments. When a state's currency is devalued, imports suddenly become more expensive. A foreign MNC selling an imported product (or a product assembled from imported parts) in the host country can be devastated by such a change. For example, if the Canadian dollar falls relative to the yen, Toyota Canada may have to charge more Canadian dollars for its cars in order to pay for the parts imports from Japan. Therefore, an MNC making a long-term investment in a host country wants the country's currency to be reasonably stable.

Finally, MNCs may conflict with host governments on issues of international security as well as domestic political stability. When an MNC invests in a country, it puts much effort into political **risk assessment** before making international investments. It wants to determine the probability that political conditions in future years (during which the investments will be paid back) will change so radically that the flow of income is disrupted. If a war or revolution takes away an MNC's facility, the company loses not just income but capital—the standing wealth embodied in that facility. In 2001, Exxon Mobil suspended operations in gas fields in Aceh province of Indonesia for three months until the Indonesian government—which earns $1 billion a year from the operation—brought in military forces to suppress armed separatists who had been attacking Exxon Mobil.

MNCs thus depend on host country governments to provide domestic security for business operations. If Toyota builds a factory in Italy, it wants the Italian government to apprehend criminals who kidnap Toyota executives or steal Toyota payrolls, not to mention terrorists who might plant bombs to protest Toyota's presence. Many corporations have their own security personnel, and independent companies provide security services to businesses. However, such capabilities do not compare with those of the armed forces maintained by states, so MNCs ultimately rely on host and sometimes their home governments to provide a secure environment for business.

In negotiating over various sources of conflict, MNCs use a variety of means to influence host governments. These generally follow the same patterns as those used by domestic corporations (see "Interest Groups" on pp. 146–148, and "Industries and Interest Groups" on pp. 323–326). MNCs hire lobbyists, use advertisements to influence public opinion and offer incentives to host-country politicians (such as locating facilities in their districts). Such activities are politically sensitive because host country citizens and politicians may resent being influenced by foreigners. If Toyota

risk assessment The pre-investment efforts by corporations (especially banks) to determine how likely it is that future political conditions in a target country will change so radically as to disrupt the flow of income.

The Changing World Order

Corporate Social Responsibility

Concerns about corporate social responsibility have been widely raised in recent years, not least around issues of sweatshop labour conditions in apparel and shoe manufacturing. Anti-globalization activists have focused on problems of international trade and monetary relations as well as the conduct of MNCs around the world. In the view of many activists, these activities will be altered only through dramatic social and political transformation. Others, however, have focused their efforts on global corporate social responsibility—finding the means for corporations to voluntarily adjust their behaviour and practices. In 1999, then UN Secretary-General Kofi Annan called for the Global Compact—an initiative that would bring companies together with UN agencies, labour unions and civil society organizations in order to support the pursuit of universal environmental and social principles. The Global Compact focuses on four areas: human rights, labour, the environment and anti-corruption.

Mining is a sector in which some work has been done as part of these initiatives. The Global Mining Initiative (which would later be renamed the International Council on Mining and Metals) is a voluntary organization of mining companies, NGOs and other associations that focus on issues of mining, including the ways that mining practices can contribute to instability and can fuel violent conflict as well as promote environmental and developmentally unsustainable practices. Two Canadian mining companies, Placer Dome and Noranda (now Barricks and Falconbridge), were important founding members of the initiative.*

Scholars of international relations have explored the extent to which corporate social responsibility initiatives are motivated by an authentic concern about problematic business and industrial practices versus a more calculated corporate assessment of the economic and political fallout that results from bad PR. Explore the Global Compact and International Council on Mining and Metals websites listed at the end of this chapter and review their efforts. What is your view of the motivations of—and prospects for—global corporate social responsibility initiatives?

* Hevina S. Dashwood, "Canadian Mining Companies and the Shaping of Global Norms of Corporate Social Responsibility," *International Journal* 61.4 (2005): 977–97. Bonnie Campbell, "Peace and Security in Africa and the Role of Canadian Mining Interests: New Challenges for Canadian Foreign Policy," *Labour, Capital and Society* 37 (2004): 98–129.

Canada ran television ads supporting a Canadian prime ministerial candidate who supported free trade, Canadian voters might react negatively to this foreign intrusion into Canadian politics.

Domestic political stability also means that MNCs regularly resist trade union activity within their subsidiary operations, and often seek support from host country governments in limiting, or eliminating, trade union activism. In some of the most egregious examples of MNC interference in host countries' political affairs, MNCs have actively used their home country governments to assist in the overthrow of political candidates. This occurred in Chile in 1973, when democratically elected Salvador Allende was overthrown in a military coup after he planned to nationalize the U.S.-based International Telegraph and Telegraph's local subsidiary. In 1995, the Nigerian government executed poet and political activist Ken Saro-Wiwa because of his protests against the environmental and human costs of Shell Oil activities in southern Nigeria. Though Royal Dutch Shell did not have a direct hand in the execution, it was accused of contributing to the repressive activities of the Nigerian government by ignoring the economic and environmental impact of its operations.[20]

Canadian companies have not been immune to these kinds of accusations. A number of Canadian mining companies have been associated with the repression of local protests

---

[20] Thomas D. Lairson and David Skidmore, *International Political Economy: The Struggle for Power and Wealth*, 3rd ed. (Florence, KY: Wadsworth, 2003).

WHICH WAY OUT?
International business prospers in stable political environments in host countries, but the relationship of a host country to an investing MNC can be complex. Foreign investors are wary of putting money into business environments marked by inflation, crime, corruption and especially armed violence that could hit their facilities and employees. Oil companies have had trouble finding politically stable countries through which to export Caspian Sea oil. This pipeline, under construction in 2003, runs from Azerbaijan to Georgia to Turkey, bypassing Chechnya.

against mining operations, for example in Suriname in 1995 and in Chile in 1996. A question that arises in these cases is whether a firm is directly involved in quashing local protests (usually it is not) or whether its presence increases the repressive activities of domestic regimes eager to attract foreign investment. The Canadian oil company Talisman Energy has also faced these kinds of accusations as a result of its activities in Sudan, where UN and Amnesty International reports indicate that police and military forces violently displaced civilian populations to clear a 100-kilometre area around Talisman's oilfields and that roads constructed for the company were also used by the military to launch attacks against civilians.[21]

Corruption is another means of influence over host governments that cannot be overlooked. Nobody knows the full extent to which MNCs use payoffs, kickbacks, gifts and similar methods to win the approval of individual government officials for policies favourable to the MNC. Certainly this is a frequent occurrence with host governments in the global South (where government officials may be more desperate for income), but corruption also regularly occurs in rich, industrialized countries. For example, in the early

---

[21] Craig Forcese, "'Militarized Commerce' in Sudan's Oilfields: Lessons for Canadian Foreign Policy," *Canadian Foreign Policy* 8.3 (Spring 2001): 37–56. Liisa North, Timothy Clark and Viviana Patroni, *Community Rights and Corporate Responsibility: Canadian Mining and Oil Companies in Latin America* (Toronto: Between the Lines, 2006).

1990s the Bank of Commerce and Credit International (BCCI) was found to have operated a vast, illegal, worldwide network of money laundering, fraud and corruption.[22]

As criticism toward MNCs has emerged, a variety of responses have been generated. If activities are clearly illegal, MNCs can be prosecuted. In some cases, MNCs have agreed to adopt a voluntary code of conduct (though compliance is difficult to determine). In other cases, sanctions can be imposed or, as in the Talisman case, activists have lobbied for shareholders to divest themselves of questionable stocks. Home country governments usually do little to rein in their own companies, out of concern that it will result in financial (and employment) losses for a domestic firm.

MNCs also have a range of conflicts with home governments (where their headquarters are located), just as they do with host states.[23] Because MNCs are not citizens in their home states, they have somewhat more freedom of action in influencing their home governments than they do in influencing host governments. For instance, U.S. MNCs routinely contribute to U.S. politicians' campaigns in hopes that they will support policies favourable to the MNCs' global operations. In Canada, strict limitations came into effect in 2004 to limit the amount of campaign contributions corporations (and trade unions) can make to politicians in any given year.

Some MNC conflicts with home governments resemble conflicts with host governments. Taxation is an important issue. Trade policies are another. A recurrent complaint of MNCs against home governments is that policies adopted to punish political adversaries—economic sanctions and less extreme restrictions—end up harming the home-country MNCs more than the intended target. Usually, a competing MNC from another country is able to step into the gap when a government restricts its own MNCs. Unless ordered to do so, MNCs tend to go on doing business wherever it is profitable, with little regard for the political preferences of their governments. True to the wealth-maximizing principles of liberalism, MNCs generally prefer to keep politics from interfering with business.

For example, the U.S.-based oil company Unocal described the 1996 capture of Afghanistan's capital by the fundamentalist Taliban faction as "positive," while U.S. Secretary of State Albright called the Taliban's treatment of women "despicable." The oil company hoped that any faction, of whatever political or religious beliefs, could capture all of Afghanistan and end a civil war, so that a multibillion dollar natural gas pipeline crossing Afghanistan could be built.

The location of an MNC's headquarters determines its home nationality. The shareholders and top executives of an MNC are usually from its home country. However, as the world economy becomes more integrated, this is becoming less true. Just as MNCs are increasingly doing business all over the world and assembling products from parts made in many countries, so are shareholders and managers becoming more international.

We do not yet live in a world without national borders—not by a long shot—but the international activities of MNCs are moving us in that direction. Chapter 10 explores some of the ways in which people, companies and ideas are becoming globally integrated across states.

---

[22] James Ring Adams and Douglas Frantz, *A Full Service Bank: How BCCI Stole Billions around the World* (NY: Pocket, 1992).

[23] Louis W. Pauly, *Who Elected the Bankers? Surveillance and Control in the World Economy* (Ithaca, NY: Cornell UP, 1997). Benjamin J. Cohen, *In Whose Interest? International Banking and American Foreign Policy* (New Haven, CT: Yale UP, 1986).

Jobs in International Business

Summary

Jobs in international business offer high pay, interesting work and demanding hours for those with language and cultural skills.

Benefits and Costs As the pace and scope of globalization have accelerated, opportunities to work in international business have blossomed. For many large companies, the domestic/global distinction has ceased to exist. This new context provides opportunities and challenges for potential employees.

Careers in international business offer many advantages. Business jobs can pay substantially more than those in governments or NGOs and can open opportunities to travel extensively and network globally. Foreign-based jobs mean relocation to another country to work and immersing oneself in another culture.

However, such a career choice also has potential costs. Many jobs require extensive hours, gruelling travel and frequent relocation. As with any job, promotion and advancement may fall victim to external circumstances such as global business cycles. These jobs can also be especially hard on families.

International opportunities arise in many business sectors. The fields of banking, marketing (public relations), sales and computing/telecommunications have seen tremendous growth in recent years. These jobs fall into three broad categories: (1) those located domestically, yet involving significant interactions with firms abroad; (2) domestic jobs with foreign-based companies; and (3) those that are based abroad, with foreign or domestic firms.

Skills to Hone A key to landing in the international business world is to develop two families of skills: those related to international relations and those related to business operations. Traditional MBA (Masters in Business Administration) and business school programs will be helpful for all three types of jobs, yet for jobs based abroad, employers often also look for a broader set of skills taught in economics, political science and communications. Thus, language and cultural skills are essential in addition to traditional business skills. Employers look for candidates who have knowledge of a country's human and economic geography as well as culture. Experience with study abroad, and especially working abroad, can help show an ability to adapt and function well in other cultures. Strong analytical and writing abilities also matter greatly to employers.

Research helps in landing a job. Employers often look for knowledge of a particular industry or company in order to make the best use of an employee's language and cultural skills. Of course, while experience in non-international business never hurts, be mindful that the practices, customs and models of business in one country may not apply well abroad. Cross-cultural skills combined with substantive business knowledge in order to translate the operational needs of companies from the business world to the global realm are highly valued.

Resources

Edward J. Halloran, *Careers in International Business,* 2nd ed. NY: McGraw-Hill, 2003.

Deborah Penrith, ed., *The Directory of Jobs and Careers Abroad,* 12th ed. Oxford, UK: Vacation Work Publications, 2005.

http://www.rileyguide.com/internat.html

http://www.jobsabroad.com/search.cfm

http://www.transitionsabroad.com/listings/work/careers/index.shtml

http://www.dfait-maeci.gc.ca/123go/menu-en.asp

Thinking Critically

1. Find a recent newspaper article about a change in currency exchange rates (usually located in the business section). Analyze the various influences that may have been at work in the change of currency values and that affect investors' confidence in a currency—monetary policies, the underlying state of national economies, the actions of central banks (separately or in coordination) and factors such as political uncertainty.

2. Many scholars and politicians think private international investment is the best hope for the economies of Russia and Eastern Europe. Given the current economic and political disarray in that region, what kinds of investors from the industrialized West might be willing to invest there? What actions could the governments of Western states take to encourage such investment? What pitfalls would governments and investors have to watch out for?

3. If you were representing an MNC such as Toyota in negotiations over building an automobile factory in a foreign country, what kinds of concessions would you ask the host government for? What would you offer as incentives? In your report to Toyota's top management regarding the deal, what points would you emphasize as most important? If instead you were representing the host state in the negotiations and reporting to top state leaders, what would be your negotiating goals and the focus of your report?

4. If you were representing a trade union or human rights organization over allegations that a foreign-owned MNC had acted improperly within your country, what kinds of arguments do you think would be most effective? Who do you want to speak to most? Governments? The public in your country? The public in the MNC's home country? What kinds of networks might be usefully employed to get your message out?

Chapter Summary

- Each state uses its own currency. These currencies have no inherent value but depend on people's belief that they can be traded for future goods and services.

- Gold and silver were once used as world currencies that had value in different countries. Today's system is more abstract: national currencies are valued against each other through exchange rates.

- The most important currencies—against which most other states' currencies are compared—are the U.S. dollar, EU euro and Japanese yen.

- Inflation, most often resulting from printing currency faster than new goods and services can be created, causes the value of a currency to fall relative to other currencies. Inflation rates vary widely but are generally much higher in the global South and former Soviet bloc than in the industrialized West.

- States maintain reserves of hard currency and gold. These reserves back a national currency and cover short-term imbalances in international financial flows.

- Fixed exchange rates can be used to set the relative value of currencies, but more often states use floating exchange rates driven by supply and demand on world currency markets.

- Governments cooperate to manage the fluctuations of (floating) exchange rates but are limited in this effort by the fact that most money traded on world markets is privately owned.

- Over the long term, the relative values of national currencies are determined by the underlying health of national economies and by the monetary policies of governments (how much money they print).

- Governments often prefer a low (weak) value for their own currency, as it promotes exports and discourages imports, and hence improves the state's balance of trade. However, a sudden unilateral devaluation of a currency is a risky strategy because it undermines confidence.

- To ensure discipline in printing money—and to avoid inflation—industrialized states turn monetary policy over to semi-autonomous central banks, such as the Bank of Canada. By adjusting interest rates on government money loaned to private banks, a central bank can control the supply of money in a national economy.

- The World Bank and the International Monetary Fund (IMF) work with states' central banks to maintain stable international monetary relations. From 1945 to 1971, this was done by pegging state currencies to the U.S. dollar and the dollar in turn to gold (backed by gold reserves held by the U.S. government). Since then, the system has used Special Drawing Rights (SDRs)—a kind of world currency controlled by the IMF—in place of gold.

- The IMF operates a system of national accounts to keep track of the flow of money into and out of states. The balance of trade (exports minus imports) must be balanced by capital flows (investments and loans) and changes in reserves.

- International debt results from a protracted imbalance in capital flows—a state borrowing more than it lends—in order to cover a chronic trade deficit or government budget deficit. The result is that the net worth of the debtor state is reduced and wealth generated is diverted to pay interest (with the creditor state's wealth increasing accordingly).

- The U.S. financial position declined naturally from an extraordinary dominance immediately after World War II. The fall of the dollar-gold standard in 1971 reflects this decline.

- In the 1980s, the U.S. position worsened dramatically. A chronic budget deficit and trade deficit expanded the country's debt burden. Economic growth in the mid-1990s helped bring the budget deficit back down.

- Canada's position in the global political economy is somewhat mixed. On one hand, it is a member of the G7, and therefore is considered one of the seven strongest industrialized economies in the world. At the same time, Canada's economy is more affected by economic conditions in the rest of the world than it affects those conditions; in particular, the Canadian economy is affected by the U.S. economy.

- The positions of Russia and the other states of the former Soviet bloc have declined drastically in the past decade as they have tried to make the difficult transition from communism to capitalism. Though the uncontrolled inflation of the early 1990s has subsided, the economies of the former Soviet republics are about half their former size. Western states have not extended massive economic assistance to Russia and Eastern Europe.

- Multinational corporations (MNCs) do business in more than one state simultaneously. The largest are based in the leading industrialized states, and most are privately owned. MNCs are increasingly powerful in international economic affairs.

- MNCs contribute to international interdependence in various ways. States depend on MNCs to create new wealth, and MNCs depend on states to maintain international stability conducive to doing business globally.

- MNCs try to negotiate favourable terms and look for states with stable currencies and political environments in which to make direct investments. Governments seek such foreign investments in their territories so as to benefit from the future stream of income.

- MNCs try to influence the international political policies of both their home state and the other states in which they operate. Generally MNCs promote policies favourable to business—low taxes, light regulation, stable currencies and free trade. They also support stable international security relations, because war generally disrupts business.

Key Terms

gold standard   342
exchange rate   342
convertible currency   343
hyperinflation   343
hard currency   344
reserves   344
fixed exchange rates   344
floating exchange rates   344
managed float   345
Group of 7 (G7)   345
devaluation   347
central bank   348
discount rate   348
Bretton Woods system   350
World Bank   350

International Monetary
    Fund (IMF)   350
Special Drawing Right (SDR)   351
balance of payments   352
foreign direct investment   353
Keynesian economics   356
fiscal policy   356
monetary policy   356
national debt   357
Group of 20 (G20)   357
multinational corporations
    (MNCs)   363
host country   367
home country   367
risk assessment   369

Research Navigator Question

Research Navigator.com
RESOURCES FOR COLLEGE RESEARCH ASSIGNMENTS

Use the Link Library for History—World History on Research Navigator and explore several of the sites that focus on the coup in Guatemala in 1954. What kind of picture emerges from these sites concerning the behaviour of MNCs in the global South? Do you think corporations continue to act as the United Fruit Company did in Latin America during the 1950s and 1960s?

Weblinks

The following links are a sampling of research centres, government departments and international organizations focused on money and business:

Bretton Woods Project:
http://www.brettonwoodsproject.org/index.shtml

Department of Finance Canada:
http://www.fin.gc.ca/fin-eng.html

The Global Compact:
http://www.unglobalcompact.org

The Globalization Website:
http://www.emory.edu/SOC/globalization/index.html

G8 Information Centre at the University of Toronto:
http://www.g7.utoronto.ca

International Council on Mining & Metals:
http://www.icmm.com/index.php

International Monetary Fund:
http://www.imf.org

The World Bank:
http://www.worldbank.org

Integration

11

Blogger in Bahrain, 2005.

SUPRANATIONALISM

This chapter and the next continue to develop a theme that arose in the discussion of MNCs—that of nonstate actors in interaction with state actors. Although MNCs are *substate* actors in the formation of state foreign policy (see pp. 145–148), they are also *transnational* actors bridging national borders and creating new avenues of interdependence among states.[1] This chapter discusses transnational and international nonstate actors whose roles and influences are **supranational**—they subsume a number of states within a larger whole.

The UN, as we have seen, has some supranational aspects, though they are limited by the UN Charter, which is based on state sovereignty. On a regional level, the European Union (EU) is a somewhat more supranational entity than the UN; other regional organizations have tried to follow Europe's path, but with only limited success. These IOs face a struggle between the contradictory forces of *nationalism* and *supranationalism*—between state sovereignty and the higher authority (in level but not yet in power or legitimacy) of supranational structures.

Formal IGOs such as the UN and EU are not the only way that supranationalism is developing. Even more far-reaching in many ways are the effects of information technologies that operate globally and regionally across state boundaries without formal political structures. Here, too, supranational influences compete for influence with sovereign states.

supranationalism The subordination of state authority or national identity to larger institutions and groupings, such as the European Union.

---

[1] Joseph S. Nye, Jr., and Robert O. Keohane, eds., *Transnational Relations and World Politics* (Cambridge, MA: Harvard UP, 1972).

This chapter considers the various supranational influences on international politics, from the formal structures of the EU to the globalizing effects of information.

INTEGRATION THEORY

international integration
The process by which supranational institutions come to replace national ones; the gradual shifting upward of sovereignty from the state to regional or global structures.

The theory of international integration can help to explain these developments, which challenge once again the foundations of realism (state sovereignty and territorial integrity). **International integration** refers to the process by which supranational institutions replace national ones—the gradual shifting upward of sovereignty from state to regional or global structures. The ultimate expression of integration would be the merger of several (or many) states into a single state—or ultimately into a single world government. Such a shift in sovereignty to the supranational level would likely entail some version of federalism, in which states or other political units recognize the sovereignty of a central government while retaining certain powers for themselves. This is the form of government adopted in Canada through the BNA Act.

Today one might hear calls for a "United States of Europe"—or even of the world—but in practice, the process of integration has never gone beyond a partial and uneasy sharing of power between state and supranational levels. States have been unwilling to give up their exclusive claim to sovereignty and have severely limited the power and authority of supranational institutions. The UN, certainly, falls far short of a federal model (see Chapter 7). It represents only a step in the direction of international integration. Other modest examples of the integration process have been discussed in previous chapters—for example, NAFTA and the WTO. Monetary regimes and MNCs are also examples.

The most successful example of the process of integration by far—though even that success is only partial—is the European Union. Although we can observe aspects of international integration at work elsewhere in the world, these processes have gone much further in Europe than anywhere else. Western Europe's current trend of regional coordination is a new historical phenomenon achieved in the years since World War II.[2]

Until 50 years ago, the European continent was the embodiment of national sovereignty, state rivalry and war. For 500 years until 1945, the states of Europe

TEAR DOWN THE WALLS
Integration processes in Europe and elsewhere are making state borders more permeable to people, goods and ideas—increasing interdependence. The European Union is deepening economic integration while contemplating eastward expansion. Here, the opening of the Berlin Wall makes integration very tangible, 1989.

---

[2] Andrew Moravcsik, *The Choice for Europe: Social Purpose and State Power from Messina to Maastricht* (Ithaca, NY: Cornell UP, 1998). Robert O. Keohane and Stanley Hoffman, eds., *The New European Community: Decisionmaking and Institutional Change* (Boulder, CO: Westview, 1991). Miles Kahler, *International Institutions and the Political Economy of Integration* (Washington, DC: Brookings, 1995).

were locked in chronic intermittent warfare; indeed, it was in Europe that the idea (and practice) of the Westphalian state system was born. In the twentieth century alone, two world wars left the continent in ruins. European states have historical and present-day religious, ethnic and cultural differences. The 27 members of the EU in 2007 speak 23 different official languages. If ever there were a candidate for the failure of integration, Europe would appear to fill the role. Even more surprising, European integration began with the cooperation of Europe's two bitterest enemies over the past 100 years, France and Germany—enemies in three major wars since 1870. (References to "Germany" refer to West Germany from 1944 to 1990 and unified Germany since.)

That Western European states began forming supranational institutions and creating an economic community to promote free trade and coordinate economic policies caught the attention of IR scholars, who used the term *integration* to describe what they observed. Seemingly, integration challenged the assumption of realism that states were strictly autonomous and would never yield power or sovereignty.

IR scholars proposed that European moves toward integration could be explained by *functionalism*—growth of specialized technical organizations that cross national borders.[3] According to functionalists, technological and economic development leads to an increase in supranational structures as states seek practical means to fulfill necessary *functions*, such as delivering mail from one country to another or coordinating the use of rivers that cross borders. Some IR scholars tried to measure the extent of functional connections in Europe; for instance, by counting flows of mail and other communications between countries.[4] As the connections became denser and the flows faster, functionalism predicted that states would be drawn together into stronger international economic structures.

The European experience, however, went beyond the creation of specialized agencies to include the development of more general, more political supranational bodies, such as the European Parliament. **Neofunctionalism** is a modification of functional theory by IR scholars to explain these developments. Neofunctionalists argue that economic integration (functionalism) generates a *political* dynamic that drives integration further. Closer economic ties require more political coordination in order to operate effectively and eventually lead to political integration as well—a process called *spillover*.

Some scholars focused on the less-tangible *sense of community* ("we" feeling) that began to develop alongside nationalist feelings among Europeans. The low expectation of violence in the states of Western Europe created a **security community** in which these feelings could grow.[5] The emergence of a European identity was also assisted by efforts such as the textbook revision project (see p. 182).

Elsewhere in the world, economies were becoming more interdependent at both regional and global levels. The Andean Common Market, begun in 1969, promoted a limited degree of regional integration in its member states of Venezuela, Colombia,

neofunctionalism The theory that holds that economic integration (functionalism) generates a "spillover" effect, resulting in increased political integration.

security community A situation in which low expectations of interstate violence permit a high degree of political cooperation.

---

[3] David Mitrany, *The Functional Theory of Politics* (London: London School of Economics/Robertson, 1975). Ernst B. Haas, *Beyond the Nation-State: Functionalism and International Organization* (Palo Alto, CA: Stanford UP, 1964). Ernst B. Haas, *When Knowledge Is Power: Three Models of Change in International Organizations* (Berkeley: U California P, 1989). Eugene B. Skolnikoff, *The Elusive Transformation: Science, Technology, and the Evolution of International Politics* (Princeton, NJ: Princeton UP, 1994).

[4] Claudio Cioffi-Revilla, Richard L. Merritt and Dina A. Zinnes, eds., *Communication and Interaction in Global Politics* (Newbury Park, CA: Sage, 1987).

[5] Emanuel Adler and Michael Barnett, eds., *Security Communities* (Cambridge: Cambridge UP, 1998). Karl W. Deutsch, *Political Community and the North Atlantic Area: International Organization in the Light of Historical Experience* (Princeton, NJ: Princeton UP, 1957). Richard H. Ullman, *Securing Europe* (Princeton, NJ: Princeton UP, 1991).

Ecuador, Peru and Bolivia. In Asia, the Association of South East Asian Nations (ASEAN) chalked up some successes in promoting regional economic coordination over several decades.[6] Most recently, the countries of Africa formed the African Union in 2002, an ambitious plan to coordinate economic and foreign policies, elect an African parliament and create a stronger infrastructure than its predecessor, the Organization of African Union (OAU). None of these organizations have experienced the success of the EU, but their aims are often similar.

Costs of Integration The new wave of integration in Europe and elsewhere is encountering limits and setbacks just as scholars are reinvigorating the theory of integration. Integration reduces states' ability to shield themselves and their citizens from the world's many problems and conflicts. For example, in the early 1990s Venezuela found that its open border with Colombia allowed in large shipments of cocaine bound for the United States.

Integration can mean greater centralization at a time when individuals, local groups and national populations demand more say over their own affairs. The centralization of political authority, information and culture as a result of integration can threaten individual and group freedom. Ethnic groups want to safeguard their cultures, languages and institutions against the bland homogeneity that a global or regional melting pot would create. As a result, many states and citizens, in Europe and elsewhere, have responded to the new wave of integration with resurgent nationalism over the past decade.

Indeed these forces have set in motion a wave of *disintegration* of states that runs counter to (though simultaneous with) integrating tendencies in today's world. The wave of disintegration in some ways began with the decolonization of former European empires in Africa, Asia and the Middle East after World War II. After the Cold War, disintegration was most pronounced in Russia and Eastern Europe—especially in the former Soviet Union and former Yugoslavia. States in other regions—for example Somalia and Democratic Republic of the Congo—appear to be in danger of breaking into pieces, at least in practice if not formally.

A common thread of tension between nationalism and supranational loyalties (regionalism or globalism) can be seen in both successful and unsuccessful attempts at integration. In less-successful attempts, nationalism stays virtually unchallenged, and even in the most successful cases nationalism remains a potent force locked in continual struggle with supranationalism. This struggle is a central theme in even the most successful case of integration—the European Union.

THE EUROPEAN UNION

Like the UN, the **European Union (EU)** was created after World War II. Whereas the UN structure has changed little since the Charter was adopted, the EU has gone through several waves of expansion in its scope, membership and mission over the past 50 years.[7] The EU currently has nearly 500 million citizens and nearly equals the U.S. economy in GDP.

European Union (EU)
The official term for the European Community (formerly the European Economic Community) and associated treaty organizations. The EU has 27 member states and is negotiating with other states that have applied for membership. See also *Maastricht Treaty.*

---

[6] Walter Mattli, *The Logic of Regional Integration: Europe and Beyond* (NY: Cambridge UP, 1999). Kenneth P. Thomas and Mary Ann Tétrault, eds., *Racing to Regionalize: Democracy, Capitalism, and Regional Political Economy* (Boulder, CO: Rienner, 1999). Gordon Mace and Louis Belanger, eds., *The Americas in Transition: The Contours of Regionalism* (Boulder, CO: Rienner, 1999).

[7] Dusan Sidjanski, *The Federal Future of Europe: From the European Community to the European Union* (Ann Arbor: U Michigan P, 2000). James A. Caporaso, *The European Union: Dilemmas of Regional Integration* (Boulder, CO: Westview, 2000). Stanley Henig, *The Uniting of Europe: From Discord to Concord* (NY: Routledge, 1997). Desmond Dinan, ed., *Encyclopedia of the European Union* (Boulder, CO: Rienner, 1998). Brent F. Nelsen and Alexander C. Stubb, eds., *The European Union: Readings on the Theory and Practice of European Integration* (Boulder, CO: Rienner, 1994).

The Vision of a United Europe

Europe had been decimated by war by 1945. Most of the next decade was spent recovering, with help from the United States through the Marshall Plan. Two French leaders, Jean Monnet and Robert Schuman, were already developing a plan to implement the idea of functionalism in Europe—that Europe could be saved from future wars by creating economic linkages that would eventually bind states together politically.

Schuman, a French foreign minister, proposed a modest first step in 1950—the merger of French and German steel (iron) and coal industries into a single framework that could most efficiently use the two states' coal resources and steel mills. Coal and steel were key to European recovery and growth. The Schuman plan gave birth to the *European Coal and Steel Community (ECSC)* in 1952, in which France and Germany were joined by Italy (the third largest industrial country of continental Europe) and by three smaller countries—Belgium, Netherlands and Luxembourg (together called the Benelux countries). These six states worked through the ECSC to reduce trade barriers in coal and steel and to coordinate their coal and steel policies. The ECSC also established a High Authority that to some extent could bypass governments to deal directly with companies, labour unions and individuals.

Functionalists focused on issues that were largely matters for engineers and technical experts, and did not threaten politicians. Since 1952, technical experts have served as the leaders of the integration process in other aspects of European life as well as outside Europe. Of course, coal and steel were not randomly chosen for integration, since both were essential to make war, but functionalists emphasized the technical (as opposed to the political) parameters of the issue. As mentioned in Chapter 8, technical IOs such as the Universal Postal Union were established before political ones such as the UN.

International scientific communities deserve special mention in this regard. German and French steel experts may have had more in common than German and French politicians, but this is even truer of scientists. Today the European scientific community is one of the most internationally integrated areas of society. For example, the EU operates the European Space Agency and the European Molecular Biology Laboratory.

Although technical cooperation succeeded in 1952, political and military cooperation proved much more difficult. In line with the vision of a united Europe, the six ECSC states signed a second treaty in 1952 to create a European Defence Community to work toward integrating Europe's military forces under one budget and command. The French Parliament failed to ratify the treaty, however, and the United Kingdom refused to join (the U.K. had also failed to join the ECSC). The ECSC states also discussed formation of a European Political Community in 1953, but could not agree on its terms. Thus, the supranational institutions succeeded in economic cooperation, but in political and military affairs state sovereignty prevailed.

The Treaty of Rome

Treaty of Rome (1957)
The founding document of the European Economic Community (EEC) or Common Market, now subsumed by the European Union.

Euratom An organization created in the Treaty of Rome in 1957 to coordinate nuclear power development by pooling research, investment and management.

In the 1957's **Treaty of Rome,** the same six states (France, Germany, Italy, Belgium, Netherlands and Luxembourg) created two new organizations. One extended the coal-and-steel idea into a new realm, atomic energy. **Euratom,** the European Atomic Energy Community, was formed to coordinate nuclear power development by pooling research, investment and management. It continues to operate today with an expanded membership. The second organization was the *European Economic Community (EEC),* later renamed the *European Community (EC).* After its founding in 1957, the EEC was often called simply the *Common Market.* In fact, a common market was not immediately created but was established as a goal, which has since largely been realized.

As discussed briefly in Chapter 9, there are important differences between *free trade areas*, *customs unions* and *common markets*. Creating a **free trade area** means lifting tariffs and restrictions on the movement of goods across (EEC) borders, as was done shortly after 1957. Today the *European Free Trade Association (EFTA)* is an extended free trade area associated with the EU; its members are Norway, Iceland, Liechtenstein and Switzerland. (All but Switzerland, along with the EU, became the European Economic Area, participating in the "Europe 1992" single market described below.)

A **customs union** means that participating states adopt a unified set of tariffs with regard to goods coming in from outside a free trade area. Without this, any good could be imported into the state with the lowest tariff and then re-exported (tariff-free) to other states in the free trade area, which would be inefficient. The Treaty of Rome committed the six states to creating a customs union by 1969. A customs union creates free and open trade among its member states, bringing great economic benefits. Thus, the customs union remains at the heart of the EU and the one aspect widely copied elsewhere in the world.

The existence of a **common market** means that in addition to a customs union, member states allow labour and capital (as well as goods) to flow freely across borders. For instance, a Belgian financier can invest in Germany on the same terms as a German investor. Although the Treaty of Rome adopted the goal of a common market, even today it has been only partially achieved.

A key aspect of a common market was achieved, at least in theory, in the 1960s when the EU (then the EC) adopted a **Common Agricultural Policy (CAP)**. In practice, the CAP has led to recurrent conflicts among member states and tensions between nationalism and regionalism. Recall that agriculture has been one of the most difficult sectors of the world economy in which to achieve free trade (see pp. 323–326). To promote national self-sufficiency in food, many governments give subsidies to farmers. The CAP was based on the principle that a subsidy extended to farmers in any EC country should be extended to farmers in all EC countries. That way, no EC government would be forced to alienate politically powerful farmers by removing subsidies, yet the overall policy would be equalized throughout the community in line with the common-market principle. As a result, subsidies to farmers today account for as much as two-thirds of the total EU budget and are the single greatest source of trade friction between Europe and the rest of the world (see pp. 388–390).

The fourth step in the plan for European integration (after a free trade area, customs union and common market) was an *economic and monetary union (EMU)*, in which the overall economic policies of member states would be coordinated to achieve the greatest efficiency and stability. In this step, a single currency would replace separate national currencies (see "Monetary Union," pp. 390–391). A future fifth step would be the supranational coordination of economic policies such as budgets and taxes.

To reduce state leaders' fears of losing sovereignty, the Treaty of Rome provides that changes in its provisions must be approved by all member states. For example, France vetoed the United Kingdom's applications for membership in the EEC in 1963 and 1967. The U.K. finally joined in 1973, however, along with Ireland and Denmark. This action expanded the organization's membership to nine, including the largest and richest countries in the region.

In 1981, Greece was admitted, and Portugal and Spain joined in 1986. In May 2004, 10 new members joined, including Poland, the Czech Republic, Slovakia, Hungary, Latvia, Lithuania, Estonia, Malta, Slovenia and Cyprus. Romania and Bulgaria joined in 2007 and discussions continue with other states about EU membership. Inclusion of poorer countries with less industry and lower standards of living has created difficulties in effectively integrating Europe's economies. Richer European states give substantial aid to

free trade area A zone in which there are no tariffs or other restrictions on the movement of goods and services across borders.

customs union A common external tariff adopted by members of a free trade area; that is, participating states adopt a unified set of tariffs with regard to goods coming in from outside.

common market A zone in which labour and capital (as well as goods) flow freely across borders.

Common Agricultural Policy (CAP) A European Union policy based on the principle that a subsidy extended to farmers in any member country should be extended to farmers in all member countries.

POLITICS AND MARKETS
Under the free-trade area first created by the 1957 Treaty of Rome, goods can move freely across European borders to reach consumers in any member country. In agriculture, creating an integrated free market in Europe has not been easy; the EC adopted a Common Agricultural Policy in the 1960s to address the problem. Prices in this French marketplace are affected by subsidies to French farmers, 1991.

Focus on Canadian Scholarship

Scholars who work on questions of integration, the European Union and technology in Canadian universities include **Amy Verdun** at the University of Victoria, who examines the political economy of European integration and the impact of EU enlargement, and her colleague **Oliver Schmidtke,** who focuses on international migration and transnational citizenship issues in Europe. At the University of Toronto, **Ronald Deibert** researches communication technologies and international relations, global civil society and media theory. **Richard Stubbs** of McMaster University focuses on regional economic integration in Asia. At the University of Saskatchewan, **Hans J. Michelmann** explores agriculture and trade policies in the EU. **Axel Huelsemeyer** at Concordia University examines regional economic integration schemes, primarily in Europe and the Western hemisphere. **Feyzi Baban** of Trent University explores issues of Turkey and postnational Europe. At the University of Western Ontario, **John**

McDougall is interested in both European and North American integration. **Barbara Haskel** at McGill University studies the political economy of the European Union. At McMaster University, **Martin Hering** focuses on European integration and welfare states. At Memorial University of Newfoundland, **Osvaldo Croci** has conducted research on EU enlargement. At York University, **Willem Maas** explores questions of citizenship and European expansion, and his colleague **Edelgard Mahant** is interested in the relationship between Canada and the EU. **Diane Ethier** at the University of Montréal explores interests of states to participate in EU enlargement, and her colleague **Frédéric Merand** is interested in EU security and defence policy. At Dalhousie University, **Finn Laursen** has focused on European integration and the role played by the EU in the global system. **Toivo Koivukoski** of Nippissing University examines globalization, technology and philosophy.

poorer ones in the hopes of strengthening weak links. Richer states expect new EU members to undergo rapid liberalization of their economies, which some critics argue will have negative effects, especially on social programs and prices for basic goods and services. Popular reaction to expansion has been mixed, with alarming expressions of xenophobia alongside celebrations welcoming the new members, many of which were under communist rule little more than a decade before.[8]

Structure of the European Union

The structure of the EU reflects its roots in technical and economic cooperation. Coal and steel experts have been joined by specialists in trade, agriculture and finance at the heart of the community. The EU headquarters and staff have a reputation of being colourless bureaucrats—sometimes called *Eurocrats*—who care more about technical problem-solving than about politics. Supranational bureaucrats are balanced in the EU structure by provisions that uphold the power of states and state leaders.

Although the rule of Eurocrats follows the functionalist plan, they have created problems as the EU has progressed. Politicians in member states have qualms about losing power to the Eurocrats. Citizens have become more uncomfortable in recent years with the growing power of faceless Eurocrats over their lives. Citizens can throw their own political leaders out of office in national elections, but Eurocrats seem less accountable.

The EU's structure is illustrated in Figure 11.1. Eurocrats are a staff of some 24 000, organized under the **European Commission** at EU headquarters in Brussels, Belgium. The commission has 27 individual members—one from each member state—who are chosen for four-year renewable terms. Their role is to identify problems and propose solutions to

European Commission
A European Union body whose members, while appointed by states, are supposed to represent EU interests. Supported by a multinational civil service in Brussels, the commission's role is to identify problems and propose solutions to the Council of the European Union.

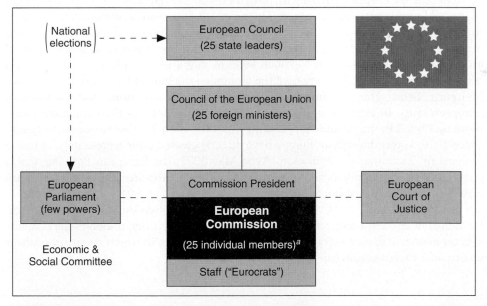

Figure 11.1 Structure of the European Union (EU)

[a] The commission will have 30 members until November 2004, then a maximum of 26, with one per country.

___
[8] Ed Vulliamy, "In from the Cold," *Guardian Unlimited* 11 April 2004.

the Council of the European Union. The Commission selects one of its members as president. Commission members are supposed to represent the interests of Europe as a whole (supranational interests), and not those of their own states, but this goal has been only imperfectly met.

The European Commission lacks formal autonomous power except for day-to-day EU operations. Formally, the commission reports to, and implements policies of, the **Council of the European Union** (formerly known as the *Council of Ministers*). The council is the main legislative and decision-making body in the EU and is composed of relevant ministers from the 27 member countries. Agenda items for workshop meetings of the council dictate which ministers will attend (foreign, economic, agriculture, finance, etc.). When policy decisions must be made, the council includes elected leaders such as presidents or prime ministers. This structure means that the individuals making up the council vary from one meeting to the next, and that technical issues tend to receive priority over political ones.

In theory, the Council of the European Union has a weighted voting system based on each state's population, but in practice it operates by consensus on major policy issues (all 27 members must agree). On other issues, decisions might be made by qualified majorities, overriding national sovereignty. The council's presidency rotates every six months and has limited power. The Council of the European Union must approve the policies of the European Commission and give it general direction.[9]

In the 1970s, state leaders (prime ministers or presidents) created a special place for themselves in the EC, in order to provide input into the direction of the community. The *European Council* refers to the regular meetings of the 27 heads of state or of the governments of all EU members. The European Council meets at least twice a year with the European Commission president.

There is a **European Parliament,** which falls somewhat short of a true legislature that would pass laws for all of Europe. The proposed European constitution would have strengthened it. At present it operates partly as a watchdog over the Commission, but maintains some power to legislate.[10] The parliament shares power with the Council under a "codecision procedure" in such areas as migration, employment, health and consumer protection. It must approve the Commission's budget but cannot exert item-by-item control. The parliament also serves as a debating forum and a symbol of European unity. In 1999, an independent commission created by the parliament found waste and fraud in the commission, leading all of the then 20 commissioners to resign. Since 1979, voters throughout Europe have directly elected their representatives to the parliament, according to population. As of May 2007, the European Parliament was composed of 785 members representing 492 million citizens. Political parties are organized across national lines.

An *Economic and Social Committee* discusses continent-wide issues that affect particular industries or constituencies. This committee is purely advisory; it lobbies the commission on matters it deems important. It is designed as a forum in which companies, labour unions and interest groups can bargain transnationally.

Council of the European Union (formerly known as the Council of Ministers)
The main legislative and decision-making body in the European Union, composed of relevant ministers (foreign, economic, agriculture, finance, etc.) from the 27 member countries. When a meeting takes place, it is called the "European Council."

European Parliament
The quasi-legislative body of the European Union that operates mainly as a watchdog over the European Commission and has little real legislative power.

[9] Emil Joseph Kirchner, *Decision Making in the European Community: The Council Presidency and European Integration* (Manchester, UK: Manchester UP, 1992).

[10] Richard Corbett, *The European Parliament's Role in Closer EU Integration* (NY: Palgrave, 2001). Julie Smith, *Voice of the People: The European Parliament in the 1990s* (Washington, DC: Brookings, 1995). David Judge and David Earnshaw, *The European Parliament* (NY: Palgrave, 2003). Neill Nugent, *The Government and Politics of the European Union*, 5th ed. (Durham, NC: Duke UP, 2003.)

A **European Court of Justice** in Luxembourg adjudicates disputes in matters covered by the Treaty of Rome—which encompasses many issues. Unlike the World Court (see pp. 278–280), the European Court has actively established its jurisdiction and does not merely serve as a mechanism of international mediation. The court can overrule national law when it is in conflict with EU law—giving it unique powers among international courts. It hears cases brought by individuals, not just governments. In hundreds of cases, the court has ruled on matters ranging from discrimination in the workplace to the pensions of commission staff members.

European Court of Justice
A judicial arm of the European Union, based in Luxembourg. The court has actively established its jurisdiction and the right to overrule national law when it conflicts with EU law.

The Single European Act

European integration has progressed in a step-by-step process that produces tangible successes, reduces politicians' fears of losing sovereignty and creates pressure to continue. Often major steps forward are followed by periods of stagnation or even reversals in integration. The first major revision of the Treaty of Rome—the 1985 **Single European Act**—began a new phase of accelerated integration. The EU set a target of the end of 1992 for the creation of a true common market in Europe.[11] This comprehensive set of changes was nicknamed *Europe 1992*.

Single European Act (1985)
A revision of the Treaty of Rome that set a target of the end of 1992 for the creation of a true common market (free cross-border movement of goods, capital, people and services) in the European Community (EC).

The 1992 process focused on close to 300 directives from the European Commission, aimed at eliminating nontariff barriers to free trade in goods, services, labour and capital within the EC. The issues tended to be complex and technical. For instance, professionals licensed in one state should be free to practise in another; but Spain's licensing requirements for, say, physical therapists may have differed from those of the United Kingdom. Commission bureaucrats worked to smooth out such inconsistencies and create a uniform set of standards. Each national government had to pass laws to implement these measures.

For example, a dispute raged for decades over the definition of chocolate. Belgium—famous for its chocolates—requires the exclusive use of cocoa butter for a product to be called chocolate; the United Kingdom and other countries use a cheaper process that partially substitutes other vegetable oils. With deepening integration and seamless trade, Belgium worried that it would lose its competitive advantage in the US$30 billion worldwide chocolate market (half of which came from Europe). The United Kingdom and six other EU countries that had joined the EU since 1973 won an exemption from the all–cocoa butter rule. Under the pressure of integration, however, the EU is moving to unify standards like food regulations. The chocolate wars illustrate that the seemingly simple concept of economic integration sets in motion forces of change that reach into every corner of society and affect the daily lives of millions of people.

The Single European Act gave a new push to the creation of a European Central Bank (in Frankfurt, Germany), and a single currency and monetary system—long-standing goals that have now been accomplished for many EU members. As long as the economies of EU members were tied to separate states (with separate central banks), efforts to maintain fixed exchange rates were difficult. For example, British politicians were reluctant to deepen a recession in order to save German politicians from inflation in 1992.

The 1992 process moved economic integration into more political and controversial areas, eroding sovereignty more visibly than before. It also deepened a trend toward the EU's dealing directly with provinces rather than the states they belong to—thus

---

[11] Andrew Moravcsik, "Negotiating the Single European Act: National Interests and Conventional Statecraft in the European Community," *International Organization* 45.1 (1991): 19–56.

beginning to "hollow out" the state from below (stronger provincial governments) as well as above (stronger Europe-wide government). However, Europe 1992 continued to put aside the difficult problems of political and military integration.

The Maastricht Treaty

Maastricht Treaty Signed in the Dutch city of Maastricht in 1992, this treaty committed the European Union to monetary union (a single currency and European central bank) and to a common foreign policy. See also *European Union (EU)*.

The **Maastricht Treaty,** signed in the Dutch city of Maastricht in 1992, renamed the EC as the EU and committed it to further progress in three main areas. Monetary union (discussed shortly) would abolish existing national currencies and replace them with a single European currency. A second set of changes, regarding justice and home affairs, created a European police agency and responded to the new reality that borders were open to immigrants, criminals, sex traffickers and contraband. It also expanded the idea of citizenship so that, for example, a French citizen living in Germany can vote in local elections. A third goal of Maastricht is even more controversial—political and military integration. The treaty commits European states to work toward a common foreign policy with a goal of eventually establishing a joint military force. These areas of change all infringe on state sovereignty.

The Maastricht Treaty encountered problems soon after its signing. One issue was the fractious response of EU members to the war in former Yugoslavia—next door on the European continent. Efforts by the EU to mediate the conflict failed repeatedly as the war spread and the humanitarian and refugee crises worsened. In 1992, French president Mitterrand secretly flew straight from an EU summit meeting to the embattled Bosnian capital, Sarajevo; this unilateral initiative reflected the EU's inability to act in unison. Members of the EU also diverged sharply over support for the U.S.-led invasion of Iraq, with the U.K. one of its strongest supporters and France one of its strongest opponents.

Closer to home, some citizens of Europe began to react strongly against the loss of national identity and sovereignty implicit in Maastricht.[12] Through the years of European integration, public opinion has been largely supportive. In recent polls, a strong majority of European citizens favour greater political and military integration, and expansion of the powers of the European Parliament—although support for political union is weak in Denmark and the United Kingdom. Perhaps Eurocrats took public support too much for granted, for a substantial and growing minority are having second thoughts—much like the backlash against free trade discussed at the end of Chapter 9.

As an amendment to the Treaty of Rome, Maastricht had to be ratified by all (then 12) members. The ratification process stirred strong public feelings against a closer European union in several countries. British politicians had already received assurances that allowed the United Kingdom to stay outside a monetary union and a unified European social policy, if it so chose. In other EU states, however, political leaders and citizens had not fully anticipated public reaction to Maastricht before signing. Suddenly, citizens and leaders in several countries seemed to realize that the faceless Eurocrats in Brussels were stripping away their national sovereignty.

When the EU implemented the Maastricht Treaty, it did so more slowly and with fewer participating countries than originally hoped. Nonetheless, economic and

---

[12] Sieglende Gstohl, *Reluctant Europeans: Norway, Sweden, and Switzerland and the Process of Integration* (Boulder, CO: Rienner, 2002). Carl Lankowski, ed., *Europe's Emerging Identity: Opposition Movements vs. Regional Integration in the European Community* (Boulder, CO: Rienner, 1993).

technical integration, including the monetary union of 12 members, has maintained momentum.

Europe's economic integration has begun to reshape the political economy at a global level. The EU now sets the rules for access to one of the world's largest markets, for a vast production and technology network and for the world's strongest currency. Canada was impacted early: when Britain joined the EU in 1973, it resulted in the demise of the Commonwealth preferential treatment system from which Canada had benefited in its trading relationship with the U.K.[13] Europe's newest powers are illustrated in its environmental initiatives. The U.S. chemical industry has operated under U.S. regulations that exempt 80 percent of chemicals. The EU is adopting stricter chemical regulations, requiring tests of health effects of all

INTEGRATION MARCHES ON
The Maastricht Treaty called for a monetary union with a common currency. In 2002, the euro came into effect smoothly in 12 countries, and after a year of weakness, gained strength and emerged as a world currency that rivals the U.S. dollar. This Italian chef celebrated the new currency by making a pizza decorated with the euro symbol (f).

chemicals used in products and mandating efforts to substitute for toxic chemicals in everyday products. Similarly, several major U.S. cosmetics companies are reformulating their products to comply with new EU cosmetics regulations calling for removal of unhealthy substances. And Japanese car manufacturers are adapting production processes to meet the EU's requirement that new cars consist of 85 percent recyclable components by 2006 (and 95 percent by 2015).[14]

Political and military integration have been much more problematic. In 1999, the EU decided to develop a 60 000-troop military force (see p. 248), which is still under development, but NATO will continue to be more important and may even subsume the new force in practice.[15] The struggle between nationalism and supranationalism seems precariously balanced between the two; the transition to supranationalism has not yet

[13] Marie Bernard-Meunier, "Did You Say Europe? How Canada Ignores Europe and Why That Is Wrong," in *Canada Among Nations 2006: Minorities and Priorities*, ed. Andrew F. Cooper and Dane Rowlands (Kingston and Montreal: McGill-Queen's University Press, 2006) 109–124.

[14] Mark Schapiro, "New Power for 'Old Europe,'" *The Nation* 27 Dec. 2004.

[15] Simon Duke, *The Elusive Quest for European Security: From EDC to CFSP* (NY: St. Martin's, 2000). Sophie Vanhoonacker, *The Bush Administration and the Development of a European Security Identity* (Brookfield, VT: Ashgate, 2001). Brian White, *Understanding European Foreign Policy* (NY: Palgrave, 2001).

been accomplished regarding sovereignty and foreign and military policy. Even after 50 years of preparation, spillover is elusive.

Monetary Union

euro Also called the ECU (European Currency Unit), the euro is a single European currency used by 12 members of the European Union (EU).

A European currency, the **euro,** has replaced national currencies in 12 of the 27 EU member states, as mandated in the Maastricht process. After several years as an abstract unit like the IMF's SDR (see p. 351), used by national governments and for international exchange, the euro came into full circulation in 2002 and national currencies for those 12 states ceased to exist. A European central bank took over the functions of state central banks.[16]

Monetary union is difficult for both economic and political reasons. In participating states, fundamental economic and financial conditions must be equalized. One state cannot stimulate its economy with low interest rates (because of a recession, for example) while another cools inflation with high interest rates (because of high economic growth). For example, in 2005 the unemployment rate was 18 percent in Poland but 5 percent in the Netherlands. In an integrated economy that is also politically centralized, the central government can reallocate resources, as the Canadian federal government might do if British Columbia was booming and New Brunswick was in recession, but the EU does not have centralized powers of taxation or control of national budgets. This split of fiscal and monetary policy is unusual and makes monetary union more difficult.

One solution is to work toward equalizing Europe's economies. For example, to reduce the disparity between rich and poor EU states, the Maastricht Treaty increased the EU budget by US$25 billion annually to provide economic assistance to poorer members. Richer EU members pay the cost for this aid, however, and it is insufficient to truly equalize rich and poor countries.

The main solution adopted at Maastricht was to restrict membership in the monetary union, at least in the first round, to only those countries with enough financial stability not to jeopardize the union. To join the unified currency, a state had to achieve certain benchmarks: a budget deficit less than 3 percent of GDP, a national debt less than 60 percent of GDP, an inflation rate no more than 1.5 percentage points above the average of the three lowest-inflation EU members and stable interest rates and national currency values.

These targets proved difficult for many EU members to meet. There was talk of loosening the standards for admission, but EU leaders believed this to be a dangerous course that could undermine the ultimate stability of the euro. Instead, the leaders of states wanting to participate agreed to buckle down and try to meet the standards. This meant hard choices by governments in France, Spain, Italy and other countries to cut budgets and benefits and to make other politically unpopular moves. French workers responded on several occasions with massive strikes. Governments fell to opposition parties in several countries, but new leaders generally kept to the same course. As a result

---

[16] Paul Grauwe, *The Economics of Monetary Integration,* 4th ed. (NY: Oxford UP, 2000). Randall Henning and Pier Carlo Padon, *Transatlantic Perspectives on the Euro* (Washington, DC: Brookings, 2000). Barry Eichengreen and Jeffry Frieden, *The Political Economy of European Monetary Unification* (Boulder, CO: Westview, 2000). Kenneth Dyson and Kevin Featherstone, *The Road to Maastricht: Negotiating Economic and Monetary Union* (NY: Oxford UP, 1999). Steven Weber, *Globalization and the European Political Economy* (NY: Columbia UP, 2001).

of their newfound fiscal discipline, all 12 EU members that wanted to participate in the euro ultimately qualified. The United Kingdom, Denmark and Sweden opted to retain their national currencies.

Germany's participation was central because its currency, the mark, was the strongest currency in Europe. In a sense, the euro replaced the mark and other countries tagged along. (This is why the European central bank is in Frankfurt, where the German central bank was located.) Proponents of monetary union hope that Germany's sacrifice of its own respected currency will help reassure Europe that German reunification (see pp. 427–248) does not threaten other European countries.

Money is more political than steel tariffs or chocolate ingredients. A monetary union infringes on a core prerogative of states—the right to print currency. Because citizens use money every day, a unified European currency could deepen citizens' sense of identification with Europe—a victory for supranationalism over nationalism. When the euro went into circulation in 2002, people could for the first time "put Europe in their pocket." However, precisely for this reason, some state leaders and citizens resisted the idea of giving up the symbolic value of their national currencies. These problems were reflected in the task of designing euro banknotes and coins. How could any country's leaders or monuments become Europe-wide symbols? The solution was to put generic architectural elements (not identifiable by country) on the front of the banknotes and a map of Europe on the back. Coins come in various member-state designs (all valid throughout the euro zone).

The EU met its timetable to launch the euro in 2002. Production of euro banknotes and coins began in 1998. Currency exchange rates were frozen in 1999, and a transition to European Central Bank control began. International currency markets began trading the euro instead of the national currencies. Cash registers across Europe were reprogrammed, and prices were displayed in both euros and national currencies for the transition years. The circulation of euros as legal tender, and the cancellation of national currencies, came in 2002. On E-day, January 1, 2002, 300 million Europeans met with US$600 billion in freshly printed money in a surprisingly smooth process. In 2003, however, Germany and France ran budget deficits higher than allowed under euro rules, raising conflicts within the euro zone. In 2004, the European Commission sued the EU members for voting to let France and Germany break the rules, but after the European Court of Justice told both sides to work harder at resolving the dispute, the Commission suspended its threats (although it continued to apply serious pressure on Germany in 2006). Meanwhile, Greece admitted it had falsified its economic data in order to be admitted. And Latvia's government lost power within six months of the country's joining the EU, under pressure of unpopular budget cuts needed to meet the euro rules within four years. Before the euro even went into circulation, its value slumped as investor confidence in the experiment initially proved shaky. Having survived its birth, however, the euro gained back its value, standing at $1.47 (Canadian) in early 2007. The creation of a European currency is arguably the largest financial overhaul ever attempted in history, and in its first five years it was largely successful.

Expanding the European Union

Despite the resistance encountered in the Maastricht process, the EU has been successful enough to attract neighbouring states to want to join. In fact, the larger and more integrated the EU becomes, the less attractive is the prospect of remaining outside it for any state in the vicinity of Europe. The EU has expanded from 15 members to 27 since

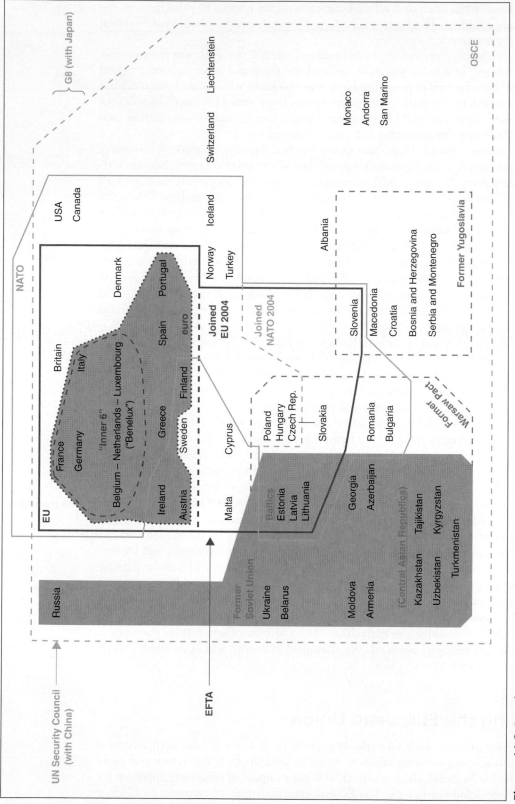

Figure 11.2 Overlapping Memberships of European States

2004, with potentially far-reaching changes in how the EU operates. The two most recent members (Romania and Bulgaria) joined on 1 January 2007, but unlike previous members, Britain and Ireland imposed work restrictions on the citizens of the new members.

Turkey continues to seek membership. Although it rebuffed Turkey in 2002, the EU later agreed to begin formal entry negotiations in 2005—the start of a years-long process. The EU has not reached a consensus on admitting Turkey as a full member. Proponents note that Turkey has made major economic and political changes, including abolishing the death penalty and improving human rights, to try to win EU membership. Granting full membership would reward these changes, keeping an implicit promise to reciprocate Turkey's actions. At current growth rates, Turkey would eventually contribute nearly 10 billion euros a year to the EU by 2020. And Turkish workers could help alleviate a labour shortage in Western Europe. Supporters also argue that as an EU member, Turkey would serve as a bridge between Europe and the important Middle East region, providing an example of secular democracy to other Middle Eastern countries.

Opponents note that Turkey would be the only Muslim country in the EU, yet would be the second most populous EU member after Germany. With two million Turks already living in Germany, opponents argue that EU membership would open the floodgates for immigration from a large, poor country, overwhelming smaller and richer

🌐 Thinking Theoretically

Over the years, the membership of the European Union has expanded from six members to 27. Further expansion is planned, and it is likely the EU will have at least 30 members within the decade. According to collective goods theory (see p. 82), the expansion should make it easier to free-ride on the community's larger, richer members without being as visible and without disrupting the overall provision of collective goods by the community. This approach could help explain the difficulties faced by the EU in the years since the 1992 Maastricht Treaty—popular resistance and razor-thin referendum margins, disunity over foreign affairs such as in Bosnia, the United Kingdom's shunning of the euro, squabbles over future directions and so forth.

However, other theories could also explain these outcomes. A realist could simply point to differences in national interests as creating a natural barrier to integration beyond a certain point. In this view, it was the gradual infringement of national sovereignty (hitting some natural limit) rather than the expansion of membership that explains the problems of EU integration in the 1990s. Critical theorists might argue that support for integration (which in the EU was shared not only by business elites, but by many trade unionists and social democrats as well) will decline as social classes recalculate the costs associated with EU membership as it expands.

We can judge these theories in part by how well they predict the effects of EU expansion in the next few years. The number-of-actors theory would predict increasing difficulties in holding the EU together as the number of actors keeps growing. Institutional structures and rules would have to change as a result. In particular, the unanimity rule, giving each member state a veto, would have to be much more narrowly restricted. Eventually, a smaller core group might emerge—perhaps even a German-French duopoly or German hegemony—to dictate policy and enforce cooperation in order to overcome collective goods problems.

If public protests and riots increase as EU membership expands, it might be a sign that critical theorists are correct. By contrast, realism should predict little effect from the expansion in membership, since the problem is the level of infringement on sovereignty (which does not change when more members are added). Indeed, by one logic, the expansion of membership is slowing down the deepening of ties among today's EU members. In that case, expansion would actually smooth out the EU's problems by slowing the assault on national sovereignty.

Theories play different roles, but one important function of a theory is the ability to improve projections of future possibilities. By watching the effects of EU expansion in the coming years, we will be able to see which theory best explained the outcome.

EU members. In France, opposition to Turkey's admission, and to immigration generally, created a backlash that helped derail the proposed EU constitution in 2005.[17] In economic terms, Turkey would be the poorest member, even poorer than the EU's new Eastern European members (see Figure 11.2). Costs to subsidize Turkish farmers and expand social programs could reach tens of billions of euros. Turkey also carries a large debt-to-income ratio, twice as high as any current member. Finally, opponents want Turkey to remove its military forces from Cyprus, where a Greek-Turkish partition has endured for decades.

As new members joined the EU in 2004 and 2007, the ability of the EU to reach decisions by consensus became more complicated. The working time required by the Council of Ministers to make decisions expanded, with potential conflicts and alliances on a particular issue ensuing among 27 rather than 15 members.

Furthermore, by Western European standards, the new members are relatively poor. Existing EU members are wary of being dragged down by these economies, most of which are still embroiled in the painful transition from socialism to capitalism and sometimes lack stable currencies. Their prospects for joining a European monetary union will not surface for some years in the future at best. The tensions between nationalism and supranationalism might intensify with more states pulling in more directions at once.

Discussions about expansion usually hinge on a choice between deepening the community through a monetary union and other measures envisioned by Maastricht or broadening it by adding members. States that favour deepening the EU—France especially—argue that an enlarged membership would prove unwieldy and would endanger any gains the EU has made. Those that favour broadening (such as the United Kingdom) argue that the ideal of a united Europe requires the EU to take in those who want to join, even though progress toward economic integration would be slowed down. The United Kingdom is less eager to deepen the European Union and favours expansion partly because it would slow down such deepening.

Perhaps as a result of these pressures, the EU has shown signs of dividing into "inner" and "outer" layers in the last decades—with states such as France and Germany joining a currency union and deepening their integration, and the U.K. and perhaps the new members operating at the edges of the EU with more autonomy. This division was illustrated in 1995, when seven countries from Portugal to Germany established what has been called the Schengen area (after the town in Luxembourg where the agreement was originally signed in 1985). The Schengen area abolished border controls and the need for passports but in turn tightened border controls between themselves and the eight other EU members that did not join the free-movement zone (though most joined later). Suddenly, Germans who crossed into Denmark (a nonparticipant) on Sunday mornings to buy bread (because German bakeries were closed on Sundays) began to need identification at the border; formerly they had just waved their bags of bread at the border guards as they crossed back into Germany.

To grapple with the implications of an expanding EU, the (then) 25 leaders signed an EU constitution in late 2004 and the European Parliament gave it a strong vote of support in 2005. To take effect, it had to be ratified by all 25 states, including several requiring referendums. The constitution's purpose was to establish a stronger president of the EU and a foreign minister to represent Europe as a global superpower in world affairs. It was to

---

[17] Seyla Benhabib and Türküler Isiksel, "Ancient Battles, New Prejudices, and Future Perspectives: Turkey and the EU," *Constellations* 13.2 (2006): 218–33.

WE'RE IN!
The European Union added 10 members, mostly from Eastern Europe, in 2004. Here, Latvia's president and prime minister sign the treaty of accession, 2003.

replace the requirement for consensus in EU decision making with majority voting in more cases, and it was to guarantee fundamental rights to all EU citizens. After long debate, one contentious issue was dropped: the document did not refer to Christianity as a core European value. Voters in France and the Netherlands rejected the constitution and the process halted, with EU leaders entering a period of self-described "reflection" on Europe's future. For many observers, the wide margin by which the new EU constitution failed in 2005 is an important reminder that many Europeans feel cautious about giving up national sovereignty.[18]

Beyond the EU itself, Europe is a patchwork of overlapping structures with varying memberships. Despite the Single European Act, there are still many Europes. Around the edges are EFTA states, participating in the European Economic Area. NATO membership overlaps partly with the EU. More distantly, a number of countries seek closer ties to the EU, including Canada. The European Union is Canada's second-largest trade and investment partner, and Canada signed a Framework Agreement for Commercial and Economic Cooperation with the (then) European Community in 1976, following that up with an Action Plan in 1996, both intended to enhance Canada-EU commercial, trade and investment relations.

One truly universal intergovernmental organization exists in Europe—the *Organization for Security and Cooperation in Europe (OSCE)*. Operating by consensus, with a large and expanding universal membership of 55 states, the OSCE has little actual

---

[18] Kathryn M. E. Dominguez, "The European Central Bank, the Euro, and Global Financial Markets," *Journal of Economic Perspectives* 20.4 (Fall 2006): 67–88. Philip R. Lane, "The Real Effects of European Monetary Union," *Journal of Economic Perspectives* 20.4 (Fall 2006) 47–66.

power except to act as a forum for multilateral discussions of security issues. (The name was upgraded in 1994 from "Conference" to "Organization"—CSCE to OSCE.) In the late 1990s, the OSCE shifted tasks to include running elections and helping political parties in Bosnia and Kosovo, as well as providing various forms of monitoring and assistance in half a dozen Eastern European countries.

A NORTH AMERICAN MONETARY UNION?

North American Monetary Union (NAMU) A proposed currency union between Canada and the U.S. The NAMU has become a regular feature in some policy discussions but has never been endorsed by a federal political party.

With increasing economic integration between Canada and the United States through the FTA and NAFTA, it was natural that there would be some consideration given to creating a **North American Monetary Union (NAMU).** Since 1999, the idea of a currency union has become a regular feature in some policy discussions, especially in the media and conservative think-tanks such as the Vancouver-based Fraser Institute. No federal political party, however, has officially endorsed the idea of a monetary union.

Some of the discussions about NAMU have proposed the creation of a new single currency, not unlike the euro. Most advocates realize that such a scenario is unlikely, given U.S. reluctance to give up sovereignty to a supranational institution such as a North American central bank (which would be needed, as it is in Europe, to manage the new currency). Thus most discussions have instead focused on the adoption of the U.S. dollar within Canada, or what is also called "dollarization."

Those who favour NAMU suggest that it is practically inevitable, especially given the integrative measures already undertaken with NAFTA. They argue that a monetary union would increase efficiency between the U.S. and Canada, result in price stability and stabilize wages. The idea has also received support from sovereigntists in Québec, who partly support it for the symbolic value associated with abandoning the Canadian dollar, but also as an obvious choice for a province that trades more with the United States than it does with the rest of Canada.

A number of observers, however, point to a series of problems presented by the idea of a monetary union. One, and perhaps the most difficult from a political perspective, is a surprising lack of support from financial and business elites in Canada. Unlike the EU, where support was relatively strong among business classes, there is no such consensus in Canada. Canadian business associations, such as the Conference Board of Canada and the Canadian Chamber of Commerce, have indicated support for the existing currency system, and some of the strongest opposition to NAMU comes from Canadian banks. The C.D. Howe Institute, another conservative think-tank in Canada, was originally a supporter of NAMU but published a study in 2000 arguing against it. Opponents from the business and financial communities are joined by trade union members, social movement activists and social democrats in their stance against a currency union.

Some of those opposed to NAMU argue that it would accomplish little and cost a lot: Canadian business transactions are often already conducted using the U.S. dollar by this view, and there is little need to formalize it by creating new structures and institutions. Others insist that maintaining a separate monetary system provides Canadian monetary authorities with greater flexibility (and sovereignty) to adjust to economic disruptions that may result from fluctuations in the U.S. economy. Some note that Canadian and U.S. economies are far too different to be integrated successfully through a monetary union, and that manufacturing growth in Canada since the late 1990s has been facilitated in part by an undervalued Canadian dollar (making our exports cheaper for foreign buyers). Abandoning that difference, in other words, would result in job losses, not economic gains.

A North American Monetary Union is not as inevitable as its proponents like to suggest, but neither has it been completely dismissed. Discussion and debate about NAMU will undoubtedly continue for years to come.[19]

These examples of integration illustrate that it is not a matter of a single group or organization, but more a mosaic of structures tying states together. The various structures of the European political system, centred by the EU, are IGOs composed of states. Such would be the case if a North American Monetary Union was ever created. As was mentioned at the outset of this chapter, a more diffuse, less tangible aspect of integration also deserves attention—the sense of identity that develops over time as economic (and other functional) ties bring people closer together across borders. Supranational identity, culture and communication are also aspects of international integration. The remainder of this chapter considers how information technologies are bypassing states and bringing about this kind of global integration.

THE POWER OF INFORMATION

Global telecommunications are profoundly changing how information and culture function in international relations.[20] Technological advances, at the centre of globalization, are bringing the identity principle to the fore as communities interact across distances and borders. Newly empowered individuals and groups are creating transnational networks worldwide, bypassing states.

Wiring the World

New international political possibilities arise from technological developments.[21] The media over which information travels—telephones, television, films, magazines, the internet and so forth—shape the way ideas take form and spread from one place to another. The media with the strongest political impact are radio, television and the internet. There are nearly two billion television sets and three billion radio receivers in the world. The power of these media lies in their ability to take a single source of information and reproduce it many times in many locations. Radio, and increasingly television, reach

---

[19] This material is drawn from Jim Stanford, "Future for the Loonie? Introduction to Forum on North American Monetary Integration"; Eric Helleiner, "The Strange Politics of Canada's NAMU Debate"; and Mario Seccareccia, "Is Dollarization a Desirable Alternative to the Monetary Status Quo? A Critical Evaluation of Competing Currency Arrangements for Canada," in the "Forum on Dollarization," *Studies in Political Economy* 71/72 (Autumn 2003/Winter 2004): 59–108. See also Eric Helleiner, *Towards North American Monetary Union? A Political History of Canada's Exchange Rate Regime* (Montreal: McGill-Queen's University Press, 2006); H. Grubel, *The Case for the Amero: The Economics and Politics of a North American Monetary Union* (Vancouver: Fraser Institute, 1999); and D. Laidler and F. Poschmann, *Leaving Well Enough Alone: Canada's Monetary Order in a Changing International Environment* (Toronto: C.D. Howe Institute, 2000).

[20] Juliann E. Allison, ed., *Technology, Development, and Democracy: International Conflict and Cooperation in the Information Age* (NY: SUNY, 2002). Edward A. Comor, ed., *The Global Political Economy of Communication: Hegemony, Telecommunication and the Information Economy* (NY: St. Martin's, 1994). Cees J. Hamelink, *The Politics of World Communication* (Thousand Oaks, CA: Sage, 1994). Howard H. Frederick, *Global Communication and International Relations* (Belmont, CA: Wadsworth, 1993).

[21] Craig Warkentin, *Reshaping World Politics: NGOs, the Internet, and Global Civil Society* (Lanham, MD: Rowman & Littlefield, 2001). Ithiel de Sola Pool, *Technologies without Boundaries: On Telecommunications in a Global Age*, ed. Eli M. Noam (Cambridge, MA: Harvard UP, 1990). William J. Drake, ed., *The New Information Infrastructure: Strategies for U.S. Policy* (Washington, DC: Brookings, 1995).

even the poorest rural areas of the global South. Peasants who cannot read can understand radio. Shortwave radio—typically stations such as the Canadian Broadcasting Corporation (CBC), the British Broadcasting Corporation (BBC) and Radio Moscow—is very popular in remote locations.

Television is especially powerful. The combination of pictures and sounds affects viewers emotionally and intellectually. Viewers can fully experience distant events. As technology develops, viewers may be provided with an even wider range of channels and information—from a local city council meeting to simultaneous translation of news broadcasts from around the world. Independent television news channels have attracted large audiences in India, Pakistan and Nepal.

Ordinary over-the-air television and radio signals are radio waves carried on specific frequencies. Frequencies are a limited resource in high demand, which governments regulate and allocate to users. Because radio waves do not respect national borders, the allocation of frequencies is a subject of interstate bargaining. International regimes have grown up around the regulation of international communications technologies.[22]

Satellite transmissions bypass the normal over-the-air radio spectrum and transmit signals over a huge area to dish-shaped antennas. This capability, bypassing states' control, fortifies transnational or supranational identity politics by allowing, for example, all Arabs in the world to see Arab satellite television coverage. The Qatar-based all-news satellite television network, Al Jazeera, which began broadcasting in 1996, has become a force in Middle East politics. It reaches an influential audience across the region and world. In a 2006 poll in six Arab countries, citizens listed Al Jazeera as their main source of international news by a large margin over any other satellite television network.[23] Criticized by Western governments for airing Osama bin Laden videos and anti-American propaganda, Al Jazeera also occasionally broadcasts interviews with top U.S. and other Western officials. The only foreign network allowed to report regularly from Taliban-ruled Afghanistan during the 2001 U.S. bombing, its office there was destroyed by a U.S. missile. When photographs emerged of U.S. physical and sexual abuse against Iraqi prisoners in the Abu Ghraib prison facility in 2004, Al Jazeera quickly broadcast the photos to audiences in the Middle East. When President George W. Bush delivered his televised apology to the Iraqi people for the abuse, he intentionally chose to make his address on a U.S.-supported network in Iraq rather than Al Jazeera. Though the idea that Al Jazeera only inflamed local sentiment by broadcasting the Abu Ghraib photographs likely informed President Bush's decision to snub the network, the credibility of his apology may have been enhanced had he chosen to be interviewed by Al Jazeera.

Images and sounds are being recorded, reproduced and viewed in new ways through audio- and videotapes. Videocassette recorders (VCRs) and DVDs have proliferated in many countries in recent years. Audio- and videotapes can be played repeatedly and passed from person to person, giving the listener and viewer control. Video and cell phone cameras are empowering ordinary citizens to create their own visual records, such as videos of political demonstrations in one country that might end up on the television news in another. In 2007, these capabilities were dramatically demonstrated when a cell phone video of Saddam Hussein's execution (showing him being taunted by Shi'ite guards) spread instantly on the internet and provoked outrage among Sunni Iraqis.

---

[22] Marcus Franda, *Governing the Internet: The Emergence of an International Regime* (Boulder, CO: Rienner, 2001).

[23] Sadat Chair, University of Maryland, "Arab Attitudes toward Political and Social Issues, Foreign Policy and the Media," available at http://www.bsos.umd.edu/SADAT/PUB/Arab-attitudes-2005.htm.

Even more empowering to ordinary citizens are telephones and the internet. Unlike television and radio, phones are a two-way medium through which users interact without any centralized information source. Phones are becoming more powerful with the advent of fibre-optic cables, communication satellites, cellular phones, satellite phones, fax machines and modems. The minutes of international phone traffic worldwide quadrupled from 1991 to 2004, a clear indicator of globalization. Growth of phones and internet use worldwide has been explosive in the past decade, with cell phones leading this upsurge of connectivity. Nearly three billion people had cell phones in 2007, and a billion were internet users—in each case representing a 25-fold increase over the last decade.

In Africa, cheap cell phones with cheap prepaid calling cards have let millions of relatively poor individuals bypass the lack of infrastructure previously needed to communicate. Sub-Saharan Africa has fewer phone lines in total than Manhattan alone. In less than a decade, however, sub-Saharan Africa has seen cell phone subscribers increase from near zero to over 100 million.

Examined independently, the growth of phone and internet capabilities in poor countries is impressive. When compared with rich regions, a growing gap becomes evident. A person living in the global North is four times more likely than a person in the global South to have a land line or cell phone, and eight times more likely to use the internet. This gap, along with the gap in access to information technologies *within* countries, is known as the **digital divide.**[24]

digital divide The gap in access to information technologies between and within countries.

As the internet wires parts of the world into a tight network centred in the United States, Europe and East Asia—where more than 90 percent of web users live—other regions are largely left out. Poor countries and poor people cannot afford computers, which are the equivalent of years of wages for a typical person in a poor country. Users of the World Wide Web in 2006 included nearly 70 percent of the population in the United States and Canada, 16 percent in Russia and 2 percent in South Asia, the Middle East and Africa. In Canada, 73 percent of Canadian adults have internet access from at least one location.[25] The explosive growth of internet use is occurring mainly among the richest strata of the world's people.

World regions have their own digital divides. In Africa, three-quarters of the land lines in 2004 were in just six countries. In the EU, older members have nearly three times the internet use per capita of new Eastern European members, and eight times that of Russia and the other former Soviet republics.[26]

Some activists hope that the internet can transform poor villages in the global South, in part by allowing them to produce traditional goods locally and market them globally. In a successful experiment in India in recent years, a businessman put computer screens with pointing and clicking devices and high-speed internet access in walls and kiosks in very poor slums. In each location, neighbourhood kids quickly gathered, taught themselves to browse the internet and even invented their own terminology to describe the unfamiliar cursor and icons on the screen. This small-scale "hole in the wall experiment" shows that simple methods can go far to span the digital divide between the world's rich and poor.

A model project in Cambodia in 2001 helped revive a village silk-weaving industry by marketing locally made scarves on a village website. However, critics noted that the project was feasible only because a satellite company owned by the Thai prime minister donated $18 000 per year of link time. A U.S. aid organization provided the computers, training,

---

[24] Pippa Norris, *Digital Divide: Civic Engagement, Information Poverty, and the Internet Worldwide* (Cambridge UP, 2001).

[25] Ispos-Reid data (2003).

[26] Data on information access are from the International Telecommunication Union (ITU) unless otherwise noted.

website design and credit card processing required to sell scarves from the village. The reality is that most poor villages cannot afford the internet, cannot read the language of most websites and cannot maintain computers and websites without extensive training.[27]

Information as a Tool of Governments

With more information travelling around the world than ever before, it has become an important instrument of governments' power (domestic and interstate).[28] Above all, governments want *access to information*. In 1992, U.S. secretary of state James Baker made his first visit to the newly independent Asian republics of the former Soviet Union (the poorest and most remote CIS members). At each stop, one of the first questions Baker was asked by state leaders was, "How do I get CNN?"[29] CNN, state leaders hoped, would tie them directly to the Western world and symbolize their independence from Russia.

U.S. military leaders recognized the importance of playing to a global audience when, during the bombing of Bosnian Serb forces in 1995, they designated an ammunition dump close to Sarajevo as the "CNN site" because they knew the explosion would make good footage for Sarajevo-based television cameras. During the Gulf War, the U.S. military fed television networks pictures of precision weapons striking targets, hoping to "sanitize" the bombing campaign.

Governments spend large amounts of money and effort trying to gain information about what is happening inside and outside their territories. They keep files on citizens ranging from social security records to secret police files. They compile economic statistics to chart their own economic health and make estimates of the economic health of other states. Most operate intelligence-gathering agencies.

With today's information technologies, it is easier for governments to gather, organize and store huge amounts of information. In this respect, the information revolution empowers governments more than ever. In the past, a wanted criminal, drug lord or terrorist could slip over a border and take refuge in a foreign country. The terrorists who attacked the United States in 2001 demonstrated how easy this was. Today, however, it is just as likely that a routine traffic ticket in a foreign country could trigger an instant directive for arrest. Information technologies give repressive governments more power to keep tabs on citizens, spy on dissidents and manipulate public opinion. Those technologies are now also being mobilized in force to strengthen international counterterrorism, in sometimes equally repressive ways.

Just as citizens and terrorists find it harder to hide from governments, so are state governments finding it harder to hide information from one another. The military importance of satellite reconnaissance has been cited (see p. 201). An influential state such as the United States can increase its power through information technologies. It can and does monitor phone calls, faxes, data transmissions and radio conversations in foreign countries.

As the cost of information technology decreases, it comes within reach of more states. The great powers have always been able to maintain a worldwide presence and gather information globally, and now small states can gain a few of the same capabilities electronically. Even sophisticated information is becoming cheaper and more accessible—

---

[27] Rajiv Chandrasekaran, "Cambodian Village Wired to Future," *The Washington Post* 13 May 2001: A1.

[28] Karl W. Deutsch, *The Nerves of Government: Models of Political Communication and Control* (NY: Free Press, 1969).

[29] *New York Times* 2 Feb. 1992: A10.

The Changing World Order

Big Brother Is Watching

One outcome of the Cold War was the victory of "free" countries over those whose governments tried to know about and control all aspects of their citizens' lives. In communist societies like East Germany, the ruthless secret police kept files on everyone, had informers on every block and monitored the streets with video cameras. George Orwell's futuristic novel, *1984*, published in 1948, envisioned a totalitarian state so powerful that it watched everything and everyone through two-way televisions in every room. Signs proclaimed, "Big Brother Is Watching You!" to intimidate citizens. However, the year 1984 passed, and such extreme totalitarian societies did not develop. Instead, the Soviet Union and China (in different ways) relaxed their control over personal spaces. With right-wing totalitarianism having been defeated in World War II, it seemed that free societies were the rule. See-all-and-know-all government was a thing of the past.

Yet the information revolution delivered tremendous new power into the hands of governments to extend the reach of their surveillance horizontally (to every square metre of distant countries) and vertically (peering into what had previously been private in citizens' lives).

The changes in world order since September 11, 2001, have changed this balance between the state's responsibility to provide security and individuals' rights to not have the government constantly looking over their shoulders. In response to the threat of terrorism, law-enforcement agencies around the world began to expand and network their surveillance systems.

Privacy and human rights advocates argue that governmental intrusions into traditionally private areas of life undermine the very values that Western democracies were founded on. We live in an age when authorities employ video cameras and face recognition software in public locations, listen to volumes of phone calls and emails, peer behind walls with infrared detectors, examine bodily fluids by using drug tests, scan carry-on luggage with X-rays and require fingerprint identification for international travel. Since September 11, governments have used these powers more freely, and citizens have largely acquiesced.

How should privacy rights change in a time of terrorism? Do you think governments should be free to use new technologies to monitor all aspects of social life in hopes of finding terrorists? Or should government powers be limited? Where would you draw the line?

high-resolution satellite photos are now available commercially within the price range of most states. These images can be used for military purposes or natural-resource management—finding out what states (including one's own) have resources such as minerals, forests and farmland, and the rate at which they are being used.

The very nature of interstate interactions is affected by changes in information technology. The risks of surprise in IR are reduced by the information revolution. The security dilemma is less severe as a result (states do not need to arm against unknown potential threats since they know what the "real" threats are). Similarly, the ability to monitor performance of agreements makes collective goods problems easier to resolve. (Collective goods are more easily maintained when cheaters and free riders can be identified; see p. 82.)

The ability of governments to bargain effectively with one another and to reach mutually beneficial outcomes is enhanced by the availability of instant communications channels. The "hot line" connecting Washington with Moscow is an early classic example.

Governments use information as a power capability by disseminating it internationally and domestically. In today's information-intensive world, television transmitters may be more powerful than tanks. Even in war itself, propaganda plays a key role. For instance, in the Gulf War, pamphlets and loudspeakers were used to appeal to Iraqi soldiers, which

HOT OFF THE PRESS
Governments and their opponents struggle over control of information. Here, a staff member of Kenya's daily newspaper surveys the damage after police—responding to unfavourable coverage of the president—stormed its offices and burned tens of thousands of copies, 2006.

probably contributed to their mass surrenders. Dropping leaflets and pamphlets can also backfire, however. The United Nations mission to Somalia in the early 1990s used written leaflets to explain their goals to Somalis, even though the Somali people are an overwhelmingly oral culture. To make matters worse, due to a translation error, the first leaflets announced that "slave nations have come to help you."[30]

Information disseminated by a government often crosses international borders, intentionally and otherwise. The government of Jordan, for example, is well aware that its Arabic programs are received by Arab citizens of Israel and that its English programs are watched by Israeli Jews. When Jordanian television broadcasts, say, a Canadian documentary about social activism in the West (with Arabic subtitles), the message influences Israeli-Palestinian relations across the border.

Most governments create explicit channels of information dissemination to influence domestic and international audiences. Stations such as Radio Moscow broadcast radio programs in dozens of languages aimed at all the world's regions. The United States operates the Voice of America (VOA) shortwave radio network, which is picked up in many regions of the global South—where it may be one of the few outside information sources. The United States also beams specialized programming into Cuba (TV/Radio Marti) and China (Radio Free Asia, which includes programs in the minority Tibetan and Uighur languages), among others. During the 2001 U.S.-Chinese crisis regarding a U.S.

---

[30] Tamara Duffey, "Cultural Issues in Contemporary Peacekeeping," *International Peacekeeping* 7.1 (Spring 2000): 142–68.

LET'S TALK
Information, which easily crosses state borders, has become a major factor in international and domestic politics and may even be laying technological foundations for a global identity. Telecommunications could change the path of development in poor countries, possibly bypassing traditional infrastructure like phone lines and leapfrogging to a wireless networked economy. Cheap phones and prepaid calling cards are putting cell phones in reach of a growing segment of Africa's population. This shop does a brisk business in Abidjan, Ivory Coast, 2001.

reconnaissance plane that crash-landed in China, the Chinese government heavily jammed broadcasts of VOA and Radio Free Asia into China.

Governments sometimes spread false information as a means of international influence. This is called *disinformation*. In the 1930s, the Nazis discovered that the "big lie," if repeated often enough, would be accepted as truth by most people. It is harder to fool international audiences these days, but domestic ones may still respond to propagandistic misinformation. Anyone who follows international events should remember that even stories reported in the Western news as fact are sometimes disinformation.

Most governments own and operate at least one main television station (in Canada, the CBC), and many hold a monopoly on television stations. Thus television signals often rank with military equipment and currency as capabilities so important to a government that it must control them itself. Indeed, in a military coup d'état, usually one of the first and most important targets seized are television broadcasting facilities. When power is up for grabs in a state, it is now as likely that fighting will occur in government television studios or at a transmitting antenna as at the legislature or presidential offices. As the Soviet Union broke up in the early 1990s, television towers were the scene of confrontations in several republics. In Lithuania, a crowd of nationalists surrounded the television tower, and Soviet troops killed a dozen people shooting their way in.

Information as a Tool against Governments

Information can also be used against governments, by foreign governments or by domestic political opponents.[31] Some governments fear the free flow of information, for good reason. When they are allowed to circulate among a population, ideas become a powerful force that can sweep governments aside. New information technologies have become powerful tools of domestic opposition movements and their allies in foreign governments. Television coverage feeds popular discontent regarding the U.S. war in Iraq today, just as it did regarding Vietnam in the 1960s and 1970s and the Russian war in Chechnya in 1995. Television and film coverage of antiglobalization activists have made some of their critiques of neoliberalism available to people not active in the movement.

In Iran, millions of people use the internet, uncensored, to talk about taboo topics such as sex, fashion and politics. Stores sell prepaid internet cards good for 10 hours of access. Similarly, in China, people have increasing access to service providers and an estimated hundred million Chinese use the internet. The Chinese government, however, has been accused of monitoring internet use and shutting down controversial sites. Both Iran and China want the economic benefits of accessing the internet, but still attempt to control information. An important new area of research in IR explores government surveillance of internet use (see Citizen Lab under Weblinks at the end of this chapter).

In the Philippines in 2001, huge protests that swept a president from office were organized through text messages on cell phones (sent to entire lists at a time). The harsh military government in Burma (Myanmar) faced the power of shortwave radio broadcasts by the opposition movement, made using a transmitter owned by the government of Norway. In Ghana, very popular talk shows on private FM radio stations—allowed after 1995—gave voice to ordinary people who then threw out the ruling party in 2000. Organizers of the global antiwar demonstrations preceding the invasion of Iraq in 2003 used information technology to turn out millions of people

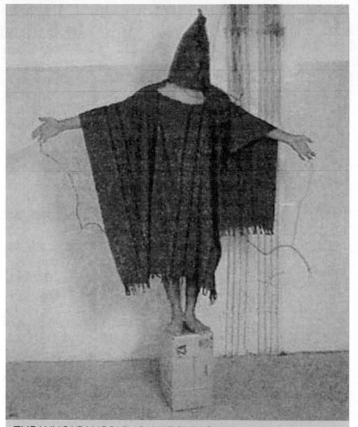

THE WHOLE WORLD IS WATCHING

States do not control the global flow of information, which has become a potent force in world politics. State leaders are joining other sets of players in a worldwide competition to reach audiences and markets and to "spin" stories a certain way. For example, U.S. actions in Iraq since 2003 play out regionally and globally in the media, making the Iraq issue a high priority even for citizens of Arab countries not materially affected by the conflict. This photo and others showing Iraqi prisoners being abused and humiliated by U.S. soldiers were reprinted widely throughout the Arab world and elsewhere in 2004, deepening anti-American sentiment and setting back U.S. efforts to win allies and support for its foreign policy goals.

---

[31] Adam Jones, "Wired World: Communications Technology, Governance, and the Democratic Uprising," *The Global Political Economy of Communication: Hegemony, Telecommunication and the Information Economy*, ed. Edward A. Comor (NY: St. Martin's, 1994).

in dozens of countries on short notice. One U.S. group (MoveOn.org) used a website to schedule protesters' phone calls to their Congressional representatives every minute of the day, the kind of coordinated action that would have required a large staff and budget in the past (MoveOn.org had a staff of four).[32]

To counteract such uses of information, governments throughout the world try to limit the flow of unfavourable information—especially information from foreign sources. For example, China and several other developing countries have channelled all access to the internet (and the World Wide Web) through a few state-controlled service providers. This system lets the government monitor and control who can have access to the mass of information available through the internet.[33] During and after the 1989 Tiananmen protests, before the internet was a factor, the Chinese government tried desperately to suppress the flow of information into and out of China. It stationed police at every fax machine in the country to screen incoming faxes after foreigners in Hong Kong, North America and Europe began sending reports of the shooting of hundreds of protesters in Beijing. In 2004, the Chinese government began filtering the hundreds of billions of instant text messages exchanged annually among 300 million Chinese cell phone subscribers. The U.S. company Google, complying with Chinese law but angering U.S. critics, blocks politically sensitive words from its Chinese search engine.

In an extreme case, the Soviet Union had only 16 international long-distance circuits in and out of the country during the Cold War, all routed through Moscow. This helped the government to reduce the influence of foreign ideas and to closely monitor foreigners—but at a huge cost to economic efficiency. When the Soviet Union broke up there were still only 91 circuits. A decade later Russia had 50 000.[34]

Efforts by one government to project power through media broadcasts often bring counterefforts by other governments to block them. The VOA, the BBC and other foreign media were routinely jammed by the Soviet Union during the Cold War, but Soviet efforts to control information did not prevent the collapse of that society. To the contrary, the effort to run a modern economy without photocopy machines, international phone lines, computers and other information technologies clearly contributed to the economic stagnation of the country.

All in all, the tide of technology seems to be running against governments (though not all scholars would agree). Information gets through, and no political power seems capable of holding it back for long. As more and more communication channels carry more information to more places, governments become just another player in a crowded field.

As the information revolution continues to unfold, it will further increase international interdependence, making actions in one state reverberate in other states more strongly than they would have in the past. Information is thus slowly undermining the assumptions of state sovereignty and territorial integrity held dear by realists. At the same time, by empowering substate and transnational actors, information technology is undermining the centrality of states themselves in world affairs.

---

[32] Fathi Nazila and Erik Eckholm, "Taboo Surfing: Click Here for Iran . . . and Click Here for China," *New York Times* 4 Aug. 2002. Philip Shenon, "Mobile Phones Primed, Affluent Thais Join Fray," *New York Times* 20 May 1992: A10. Uli Schmetzer, "Cellphones Spurred Filipinos' Coup," *Chicago Tribune* 22 Jan. 2001. Barbara Crossette, "Burmese Opposition Gets Oslo Radio Service," *New York Times* 19 July 1992: A11. Thomas L. Friedman, "Low-Tech Democracy," *New York Times* 1 May 2001: A27.

[33] Ron Deibert, "Dark Guests and Great Firewalls: Chinese Internet Security Policy," *Journal of Social Issues*. 58.1 (2001): 143–58.

[34] Anthony Ramirez, "Dial Direct to Moscow and Beyond," *New York Times* 20 May 1992: D1. United States, CIA *World Factbook*, 2001.

TELECOMMUNICATIONS AND GLOBAL CULTURE

The information revolution greatly increases *transparency* in international relations. Moreover, the ability of governments to bargain effectively with one another and to reach mutually beneficial outcomes is enhanced by the availability of instant communications channels.

Telecommunications, with its ability to connect communities beyond geographic space, is also strengthening the ability of individuals and groups to organize around and express particular identities that often transcend national borders. Not only can people in one part of the world communicate with those elsewhere, they can also find common interests. Riding the telecommunications revolution, a **global culture** is beginning to develop, notwithstanding the great divisions remaining in culture and perspective (especially between the rich and poor regions of the world; see Chapter 12). In the global village, distance and borders matter less and less. Across dozens of countries, people are tuned in to the same news, the same music, the same sports events. Along with international politics, these activities now take place on a world stage with a world audience. The process might be seen as a form of cultural integration, similar to economic and technical integration.

Although a global culture is both nascent and, in some ways, problematic, people have begun to participate in specific communities that bridge national boundaries. International journalists, for example, are members of such a community. They work with colleagues from various countries and travel from state to state together. Though a journalist's identity as a journalist rarely takes precedence over his or her national identity, the existence of the transnational community of journalists creates a new form of international interdependence. Part of that interdependence results from their shared vulnerability covering news stories that states or other groups or organizations do not wish to become public. In some cases journalists risk imprisonment, persecution and death in the course of their work. In Canada, the Canadian Journalists for Free Expression presents annual awards to journalists from around the world who have faced such persecution, and also lobbies on behalf of imprisoned journalists.

Like journalists, scientists and church members work in communities spanning national borders. So do members of transnational movements, such as those linking women, environmentalists or human rights activists from various countries. Again, their effect is to undermine the state's role as the primary actor in international affairs. More important, the links forged in such transnational communities may create a new functionalism that could encourage international integration on a global scale.

International sports competition is one of the broadest-based transnational communities, particularly at the regional level. Millions of fans watch their teams compete with teams from other countries. Of course, international sports competition can stir up animosities between neighbours, as when English soccer hooligans rampage in other European countries after their team loses a game. Sports also create a sense of participation in a supranational community. This is especially true of world-level sports events in which a global athletic community participates. The Olympic Games (sponsored by the International Olympic Committee, an NGO) are a global event broadcast to a worldwide audience.[35] Some people, in particular liberal pluralists, view sports as a force for peace. Sports events bring people from different countries together in shared activities. Citizens of different states share their admiration of sports stars, who become international celebrities.

global culture Worldwide cultural integration based on a massive increase in satellite television, radio and internet communication.

---

[35] Christopher R. Hill, *Olympic Politics* (Manchester, UK: Manchester UP, 1992). Lincoln Allison, *The Changing Politics of Sports* (NY: St. Martin's, 1993). John Bale and Joseph McGuire, eds., *The Global Sports Arena: Athletic Talent Migration in an Interdependent World* (Ilford, UK: Cass, 1994). Hugh Dauncey and Geoff Hare, eds., *France and the 1998 World Cup: The National Impact of a World Sporting Event* (Ilford, UK: Cass, 1999).

Above all, the emerging global culture is dominated by the world's superpower, the United States; this dominance has been referred to as **cultural imperialism.**[38] U.S. cultural influence is at least as strong as U.S. military influence. If there is a world language, it is English. If there is a "president of the world," it is more likely the U.S. president than the UN secretary-general.

U.S. films and television shows dominate world markets. For instance, U.S. movies dominate in countries from Europe to Asia to Latin America (although top music titles, and most top television shows, tend to be national, not American).[39] Culture may be just another economic product, to be produced in the place of greatest comparative advantage, but it also is central to national identity and politics. France, for example, held up the GATT agreement in 1994 until it could protect its film industry from U.S. competition.

Industrialized countries have responded to U.S. cultural dominance in various ways. As discussed in Chapter 9, Canada has long resisted American cultural influence, but critics worry that it is more inundated than ever by American magazines, books, films and television broadcasts. In English Canada, the most popular television shows and music are generally from the U.S. In some ways, Québec's efforts to maintain its cultural heritage vis-à-vis the rest of Canada, coupled with the difference in language, has permitted it more leverage to insulate itself from an overwhelming U.S. cultural influence. Québec television viewers are more likely to tune in to Radio-Canada for French-language programming than they are an American broadcast, and popular music fans regularly hear Québécois performers on local radio stations. By contrast, France has been especially wary of U.S. influence; commissions periodically try to weed English expressions out of the French language (not an easy task). However, Japan seemingly incorporated whole segments of U.S. culture after World War II—from baseball to hamburgers—yet also retained distinctively Japanese cultural practices.

Global culture and cultural imperialism shape the news that is reported by television, radio and print media. To an increasing extent, everyone in the world follows the same storyline of world news from day to day. There is now a single drama unfolding at the global level, and the day's top international story on CNN is likely to be reported by Canadian television networks, the national television news in France, Japan, Russia and most other states, and the world's radio and print media. The fact that everyone is following the same story reflects the globalizing influence of world communications. Cultural imperialism is reflected in the fact that the story often revolves around U.S. actions, reflects U.S. values or is reported by U.S. reporters and news organizations. The 1991 attack on Iraq illustrates in the extreme how the whole world watches one story—a story shaped by U.S. perspectives. When the bombing of Baghdad began, Saddam Hussein reportedly sat in his bunker watching the war unfold on CNN.

cultural imperialism
A critical term for Western (especially U.S.) dominance of the emerging global culture.

The Information Revolution
World Wide Web

The internet-based World Wide Web grew explosively in the late 1990s, becoming a ubiquitous element in corporate and cultural life, as well as increasingly a business venue. Will the web create new transnational communities and interest groups that redraw international politics by empowering nonstate actors?

To explore this question, go to www.pearsoned.ca/goldstein.

---

[38] Richard Maxwell, *Culture Works: The Political Economy of Culture* (Minneapolis: U Minnesota P, 2001). Karin Gwinn Wilkins, *Redeveloping Communication for Social Change: Theory, Practice, Power* (Lanham, MD: Rowman & Littlefield, 2000). Thomas L. Friedman, *The Lexus and the Olive Tree* (NY: Farrar Straus & Giroux, 1999). Benjamin R. Barber, *Jihad vs. McWorld* (NY: Times Books, 1995). John Tomlinson, *Cultural Imperialism: A Critical Introduction* (Baltimore, MD: Johns Hopkins UP, 1991).

[39] Philip Shenon, "Indonesian Films Squeezed Out by U.S. Giant," *New York Times* 29 Oct. 1992: A17. "The Media Business: What Is Playing in the Global Village?" *New York Times* 26 May 1997: D4–D5.

Even the architecture of cyberspace assumes the United States as the default for domain names such as ".gov" (U.S. government) and ".mil" (U.S. military) and ".edu" (U.S. universities). At the UN-sponsored World Summit on the Information Society in 2005, a number of countries tried unsuccessfully to break the monopoly held by a U.S. consortium over the registration of domain names—including country-code domains such as ".ca" (Canada), ".uk" (Britain) and ".cn" (China)—that states want to control as a matter of national sovereignty.

Supranational cultural influences are still in their infancy. Over the coming years and decades, their shape will become clearer and scholars will be able to determine more accurately how they are influencing world politics and state sovereignty. We need not wait as long to see the effects of a different kind of supranational influence, however. Issues of North-South development transcend national borders and lead to activism and the development of policies that are necessarily supranational. These issues are discussed in Chapter 12.

Thinking Critically

1. Functional economic ties among European states have contributed to the emergence of a supranational political structure, the EU, which has considerable though not unlimited power. Do you think the same thing could happen in North America? Could the U.S.-Canadian-Mexican NAFTA develop into a future North American union like the EU? What problems would it be likely to face?

2. Suppose you happen to be chatting with the president of the European Commission, who is complaining about the public reaction in European states against the growing power of the commission's Eurocrats. What advice would you give? What steps could the commission take to calm such fears without reversing the process of integration? How would your suggestions address the resentment that many European citizens or governments feel against Brussels?

3. Suppose the government of Turkey hired you as a consultant to help it develop a presentation to the EU about why Turkey should be admitted as a member. What arguments would you propose using? What kinds of rebuttals might you expect from the present EU members? How would you recommend responding?

4. Information technologies are strengthening transnational and supranational communications and identity. However, they are also providing states with new instruments of power and control. Which aspect do you find predominant now? Are these new capabilities helpful or harmful to state governments? Why? Do you expect your answer will change in the future, as technology continues to develop?

5. In your opinion, what are the good and bad effects of the emergence of global communications and culture? Should we be cheering or lamenting the possibility of one world culture? Does the answer depend on where one lives in the world? Give concrete examples of the effects you discuss.

Chapter Summary

- Supranational processes bring states together in larger structures and identities. These processes generally lead to an ongoing struggle between nationalism and supranationalism.

- International integration—the partial shifting of sovereignty from state to supranational institutions—is considered an outgrowth of international cooperation in functional (technical and economic) issue areas.

- Integration theorists thought that functional cooperation would spill over into political integration in foreign policy and military issue areas. Instead, powerful forces of disintegration are tearing apart previously existing states in some regions (especially in the former Soviet Union and Yugoslavia).

- The European Union (EU) is the most advanced example of integration. Its 27 member states have given it considerable power in economic decision making and 12 have adopted a common currency, the euro. However, national power still outweighs supranational power, even in the EU.

- Since the founding of the European Coal and Steel Community (ECSC) in 1952, the mission and membership of what is now the EU have expanded continually.

- The most important and most successful element of the EU is its customs union (and the associated free trade area). Goods can freely cross borders of member states, and members adopt unified tariffs with regard to goods entering from outside the EU.

- Under the EU's Common Agricultural Policy (CAP), subsidies to farmers are made uniform within the community. Carrying out the CAP consumes two-thirds of the EU's budget. EU agricultural subsidies are a major source of trade conflict with the United States.

- The EU has a new monetary union with a single European currency (the euro) in 12 of the 27 EU states. It is the biggest experiment with money in history. Such a union requires roughly comparable inflation rates and financial stability in participating states.

- In structure, the EU revolves around a permanent staff of "Eurocrats" under the European Commission. The commission's president, individual members and staff serve Europe as a whole—a supranational role. However, the Council of the European Union (also called by its former name, the Council of Ministers) representing member states (in national roles) has power over the commission.

- The European Parliament has members directly elected by citizens in EU states, but has few powers and cannot legislate the rules for the community. The European Court of Justice also has limited powers, but has extended its jurisdiction more successfully than any other international court and can overrule national laws.

- The Single European Act, or "Europe 1992," created a common market throughout the EU, with uniform standards, open borders and freedom of goods, services, labour and capital within the EU.

- The 1992 Maastricht Treaty on closer European integration (monetary union and political-military coordination) provoked a public backlash in several countries. Some citizens began to resent the power of EU bureaucrats over national culture and daily life. The treaty was ratified despite these difficulties, however.

- The EU took in three new members in 1995—Austria, Finland and Sweden—but Norwegians voted not to join. Ten others, mostly in Eastern Europe, joined in 2004. The EU faces challenges in deciding how far to expand its membership. To some extent the broadening of membership conflicts with the deepening of ties among existing members.

- In addition to the EU and the associated European Free Trade Association (EFTA), there are a variety of overlapping groupings, formal and informal, that reflect the process of integration in Europe.

- There has been some discussion in Canada about a currency union with the United States, called a North American Monetary Union; such a union is much debated in

Canada, and though its proponents describe it as inevitable, no political party has officially endorsed the idea.

- A different type of international integration can be seen in the growing role of communication and information operating across national borders. Supranational relationships and identities are being fostered by new information technologies—especially mass media such as television, radio and the internet—although the process is still in an early stage.

- Greater access to information increases government power domestically and internationally. Governments use the dissemination of information across borders as a means of influencing other states. Thus information technologies can serve national and not just supranational purposes.

- Government access to information increases the stability of international relationships. The security dilemma and other collective goods problems are made less difficult in a transparent world where governments have information about each other's actions.

- The greater and freer flow of information around the world can also undermine the authority and power of governments. It is now extremely difficult for authoritarian governments to limit the flow of information into and out of their states. Information technologies can empower ordinary citizens and contribute to transnational and supranational structures that bypass the state.

- Telecommunications are contributing to the development of global cultural integration. This process may hold the potential for the establishment of a single world culture. However, some people worry about cultural imperialism—that such a culture would be too strongly dominated by the United States.

- Transnational communities are developing in areas such as sports, music and tourism, but these too are problematic. Sports, for example, is a multibillion-dollar industry with strong corporate ties.

Key Terms

supranationalism   378
international integration   379
neofunctionalism   380
security community   380
European Union (EU)   381
Treaty of Rome   382
Euratom   382
free trade area   383
customs union   383
common market   383
Common Agricultural Policy
    (CAP)   383

European Commission   385
Council of the European Union   386
European Parliament   386
European Court of Justice   387
Single European Act   387
Maastricht Treaty   388
euro   390
North American Monetary Union
    (NAMU)   396
digital divide   399
global culture   406
cultural imperialism   409

Research Navigator Question

Log on to Research Navigator and, using the Finance and Economics database, find an article about monetary union in Europe. Read the article and consider whether the arguments (either for or against) can be applied to the prospect of a North American Monetary Union. What is similar and what is different about the cases of Europe and a possible North American union?

Weblinks

The following links are a sampling of some of the world's regional organizations and research centres involved in media, specifically the internet and world politics:

African Union:
http://www.africa-union.org

Association of Southeast Asian Nations (ASEAN):
http://www.aseansec.org/home.htm

Citizen Lab, at the Munk Centre for International Studies, University of Toronto:
http://www.citizenlab.org

The Economic Community of West African States (ECOWAS):
http://www.ecowas.int

The European Union (EU):
http://europa.eu.int

Organization of American States (OAS):
http://www.oas.org

North-South

Ethiopian refugees, 2000.

THE STATE OF THE SOUTH

This and the following chapter concern the world's poor regions—the global South—where most people live. States in these regions are called various names: third world countries, less-developed countries (LDCs), *underdeveloped countries* (UDCs) or **developing countries**.[1] This chapter discusses the gap in wealth between the world's industrialized regions, which are predominantly in the North, and the global South. Chapter 13 discusses international aspects of economic development in the South.

Poverty can be viewed from several theoretical perspectives. IR scholars do not all agree on the causes or implications of poverty, or on solutions (if any) to the problem. Thus, they also disagree about the nature of relations between rich and poor states (North-South relations). Everyone agrees, however, that much of the global South is extremely poor.

In all, about a billion people live in abject poverty, without access to basic nutrition or health care. They are concentrated in Africa, where income levels have lagged for decades.[2] Twenty years ago the concentration was as strong in South Asia, but that area's economic growth has greatly reduced its extreme poverty. Still, the average income per

developing countries States in the global South, the poorest regions of the world—also called *third world countries, less-developed countries* and *underdeveloped countries.*

---

[1] Larry A. Swatuk and Timothy M. Shaw, eds., *The South at the End of the Twentieth Century: Rethinking the Political Economy of Foreign Policy in Africa, Asia, the Caribbean and Latin America* (NY: St. Martin's, 1994). Manochehr Dorraj, ed., *The Changing Political Economy of the Third World* (Boulder, CO: Rienner, 1995).

[2] Deryke Belshaw and Ian Livingstone, *Renewing Development in Sub-Saharan Africa: Policy, Performance and Prospects* (NY: Routledge, 2002).

person in South Asia—home to two billion people—is only $3500 per year, and in Africa it is $2500 (even after adjusting for the lower costs of living in these regions compared with richer ones). Although billions of people are rising out of poverty, because of population growth there nonetheless remains about the same number of very poor people.[3]

The bottom line is that every six seconds, somewhere in the world, a child dies as a result of malnutrition. That is 600 every hour, 14 000 every day, 5 million every year. The world produces enough food to nourish these children and enough income to afford to nourish them, but their own families or states do not have access to that income. They die, ultimately, from poverty. Meanwhile, in that same six seconds the world spends $220 000 on military forces, a thousandth of which could save a child's life. Likewise, people lack water, shelter, health care and other necessities because they cannot afford them. The widespread, grinding poverty of people who cannot afford necessities is more important than the dramatic examples of starvation triggered by war or drought, because chronic poverty affects many more people.

In 2000, the UN adopted the **Millennium Development Goals,** which set targets for basic needs measures to be achieved by 2015 and compared against 1990 data. The first of the eight goals is to cut in half the proportion of the world's population living in "extreme poverty," defined as income below $1 per day (in 1990 dollars, or about $1.60 in 2007 dollars). For the global South as a whole, that proportion fell from 28 to 19 percent between 1990 and 2002. China's rate has already fallen by half (33 to 14 percent), but Africa's has hardly changed at 44 percent.[4]

Millennium Development Goals Targets established by the UN in 2000 for meeting basic human needs around the world by 2015. The first of the eight goals is to cut in half the proportion of the world's population living in "extreme poverty," defined as income below $1 per day.

The five regions of the global South differ not only in poverty reduction, but in income level and growth. The regions experiencing the fastest growth—China and South Asia—are neither the highest nor lowest income regions. The Middle East is about as developed as China in terms of GDP per capita, but growing at only half the rate. Chapter 13 will explore the reasons for these differences, but here we note simply that the world's regions vary in income and growth, with no correlation between the two dimensions.

There is disagreement about the extent to which poverty and inequality have decreased, with some arguing that poverty has been halved through rapid economic growth and that the global distribution of income is shifting from having rich and poor extremes to having a bell curve distribution with a large population at middle incomes—an emerging global middle class. The World Bank describes progress as slower.[5] Between 1990 and 2005, income per person (adjusted for inflation, in today's dollars) in the global South as a whole rose from about $3000 to about $5000. In the global North it rose from close to $20 000 to about $28 000. Does this indicate a slow closing of the gap because the ratio fell from around 6.6 to 5.6 as a result of a higher rate of growth in the South? Or does it indicate a widening of the gap between a person in the North and one in the South because in absolute terms it increased from $17 000 to $23 000? Each has some truth.

In the postcolonial era, some states of the global South have made progress toward accumulation; others have not. Some (though not all) are caught in a cycle of abject poverty. Until incomes rise, the population will not move through the demographic transition (see pp. 529–530); population growth will remain high and incomes low.

---

[3] World Bank, *World Development Indicators 2006* (Washington: World Bank, 2006).

[4] United Nations, *The Millennium Development Goals Report 2006* (NY: UN, 2006).

[5] Sala-i-Martin, "The World Distribution of Income (Estimated from Individual Country Distributions)," *NBER Working Paper* No. 8933 (Washington, DC: National Bureau of Economic Research, 2002). Surjit S. Bhalla, *Imagine There's No Country: Poverty Inequality and Growth in the Era of Globalization* (Washington, DC: Institute for International Economics, 2002).

DIRT POOR

Nearly a billion people in the global South—most of them in Africa and South Asia—live in abject poverty. The majority lack such basic needs as safe water, housing, food and the ability to read. Natural disasters, droughts, wars or other events that displace subsistence farmers from their land can quickly put large numbers of lives at risk. These earthquake survivors isolated in the mountains of Pakistan try to get through the winter in makeshift shelters and tents, 2006.

Basic Human Needs

basic human needs
The fundamental needs of people for adequate food, shelter, health care, sanitation and education. Meeting such needs may be thought of as both a moral imperative and a form of investment in the "human capital" essential for economic growth.

In order to put accumulation on a firm foundation, and to move through the demographic transition, the **basic human needs** of most of the population must be met.[6] People need food, shelter and other necessities of daily life in order to feel secure.

Children are central to meeting a population's basic needs. In particular, education allows a new generation to meet other basic needs and move through the demographic transition.[7] Literacy—which UNESCO defines as the ability to read and write a simple sentence—is the key component of education. A person who can read and write can obtain a wealth of information about farming, health care, birth control and so forth. Some countries of the global South have raised literacy rates substantially; others lag behind. Nearly half the adults in South Asia, Africa and the Middle East are illiterate, compared with fewer than 10 percent in some middle-income developing countries and fewer than 5 percent in the industrialized West.

---

[6] Paul Streeten et al., *First Things First: Meeting Basic Human Needs in the Development Countries* (NY: Oxford UP, 1981). Joshua S. Goldstein, "Basic Human Needs: The Plateau Curve," *World Development* 13 (1985): 595–609.

[7] Abdun Noor, *Education and Basic Human Needs* (Washington, DC: World Bank, 1981).

DO THE MATH
Children are a main focus of efforts to provide basic human needs in the global South. Education is critical to both economic development and the demographic transition. Worldwide, girls receive less education than boys, and in Afghanistan under the Taliban, they were banned from schools altogether. This math class in Kandahar, Afghanistan, in 2002, followed the Taliban's fall.

There is also great variation in schooling. Primary school attendance in 2003–2004 was above 90 percent in most world regions, though only 64 percent in Africa. Secondary education—middle and high school—is another matter. In the North, about 90 percent attend, but in most of the South, fewer than half are enrolled. University is available to only a small fraction of the population.

In 2004, in the global South, one in six children suffered severe hunger, one in seven lacked access to health care and one in five had no safe drinking water, according to UNICEF. The AIDS epidemic is undoing progress made over decades in reducing child mortality and increasing education.[8]

Effective health care in poor countries is not expensive—just $4 per person per year for primary care. UNICEF has promoted four inexpensive methods that together are credited with saving the lives of millions of children each year. One method is growth monitoring. It is estimated that regular weighing and advice could prevent half of all cases of malnutrition. A second method is oral rehydration therapy (ORT), which stops diarrhea in children before they die from dehydration. A facility that produces 300 packets per day of the simple sugar-salt remedy, at a cost of 1.5 cents each, was built in Guatemala for just $550. Child deaths from diarrhea were cut in half in one year. The third method is immunization against six common deadly diseases: measles, polio,

---

[8] Carol Bellamy, *The State of the World's Children 2005: Childhood under Threat* (NY: UNICEF, 2004).

tuberculosis, tetanus, whooping cough and diphtheria. In the past 25 years, the number of children immunized in countries of the global South has risen from 5 percent to more than 50 percent.

The fourth method is the promotion of breast-feeding rather than the use of infant formula. Many mothers consider baby formula more modern and better for a baby—a view promoted at times by unethical MNCs eager to market formula to large populations of the global South. In the worst cases, salespeople dressed as nurses gave out free samples to new mothers. Once mothers started using the samples, their own milk dried up and they had to continue with the costly formula, which is inferior to breast milk and can be dangerous when water supplies are unsafe and means of sterilization and refrigeration are lacking. After a consumer boycott of a well-known MNC (Nestlé), formula producers agreed in the 1980s to abide by WHO guidelines for selling formula in poor countries.

Since 1990, despite the daunting problems of war and the HIV/AIDS epidemic, public health in the global South registered some important gains. Infant tetanus deaths were halved and access to safe water was extended to a billion more people. Polio was nearly eliminated, but resistance to vaccination in parts of Nigeria caused the disease to spread again, with four countries having indigenous virus populations as of 2006. In eight African countries in 2006, following successful trials in several other countries, authorities combined the distribution of insecticide-treated mosquito nets for malaria with measles and polio vaccines, deworming pills, Vitamin A supplements and educational materials—a combined approach proven to work. In Cambodia, the government turned over basic health care to NGOs after a World Bank study found them more effective than the government.[9]

Globally, the disparities in access to health care are striking. The 75 percent of the world's people living in the South have about 30 percent of the world's doctors and nurses. In medical research, less than 5 percent of world expenditures are directed at problems in developing countries, according to the WHO. The biggest killers are acute respiratory infections, diarrhea, TB, malaria and hepatitis. More than 600 million people are infected with tropical diseases—400 to 500 million with malaria alone. Yet, because the people with such diseases are poor, there is often not a large enough market for drug companies (MNCs) in the industrialized world to invest in medicines for them. And when poor countries need medicines developed for rich markets, the drugs may be prohibitively expensive—as with the AIDS drugs discussed in Chapter 14 (see pp. 533–535).

In one case, the U.S. Army created a lotion that can protect against infection by snail-borne worms that carry schistosomiasis, which the WHO considers the second-worst public health problem in the world. Soldiers who serve in tropical areas can now be protected, but the drug company that produces the lotion has no plans to make it available to ordinary people because the market cannot afford the product. In another case, a drug used against "river blindness" disease was profitably marketed by a drug company as a veterinary medicine in the North but was not profitable as a human medicine in the South. After the company began donating the drug, an international campaign gave it annually to 25 million people and largely eliminated river blindness in West Africa.[10]

Safe water is another essential element of meeting basic human needs. In many rural locations, people (usually women and girls) must walk kilometres every day to fetch water.

---

[9] Milton J. Esman and Ronald J. Herring, eds., *Carrots, Sticks and Ethnic Conflict: Rethinking Development Assistance* (Ann Arbor, MI: U Michigan P, 2001). World Health Organization, "Polio Endemic Countries Hit All-Time Low of Four" [News Release]. Geneva: 1 Feb. 2006. Celia W. Dugger, "A Cure That Really Works: Cambodia Tries the Nonprofit Path to Health Care," *The New York Times* 8 Jan. 2006: 8.

[10] *Science* 246 (8 Dec. 1989): 1242. David Brown, "Blindness Prevention Expanded in Africa," *Washington Post* 15 Dec. 2001: A24.

Access to water does not mean running water in every house, but a clean well or faucet for a village. In 2004 (the last year for which data are available), one in six people worldwide, the great majority of them in rural areas, lacked access to safe drinking water. Even among those with access, many lack sanitation facilities (such as sewers and sanitary latrines). Forty percent of the world's population does not have access to sanitation, and as a result suffers from recurrent epidemics and widespread diarrhea, which kill millions of children each year.

Shelter is another key basic need. Of the world's 6.5 billion people, about one in six lives in substandard housing or is homeless altogether. Using indicator after indicator, about a billion people are found to be left behind with nothing. Different indicators do not overlap perfectly, but basically the bottom billion of humanity, mostly living in rural areas, is in desperate poverty.

In theory, providing for basic needs should give poor people hope of progress and should ensure political stability. However, this is not always the result. In Sri Lanka, a progressive-minded government implemented one of the world's most successful basic needs strategies, addressing nutrition, health care and literacy. The policy showed that even a very poor country could meet basic needs at low levels of per capita income. Then a civil war broke out. The war became more and more brutal—with death squads and indiscriminate reprisals on civilians—and consumed any progress Sri Lanka had made.

War in the global South—both international and civil—is a leading obstacle to the provision of basic needs and political stability.[11] War causes much greater damage to society than merely the direct deaths and injuries it inflicts. In war zones, economic infrastructure such as transportation is disrupted, as are government services such as health care and education. Wars drastically reduce the confidence in economic and political stability on which investment and trade depend.

There appears to be a relationship between recent or present warfare and a lack of basic needs (in turn correlated with income level). If the correlation is true, then what really causes what? Does being at war keep a society poor and prevent it from meeting its population's basic needs? Or does being poor, with unmet basic needs, make a society more war prone? Probably both are true. War is often part of a vicious cycle for states unable to rise out of poverty.

The fragility of life in poor, developing countries was demonstrated all too starkly in December 2004, when a major underwater earthquake caused a deadly tsunami that struck Indonesia, Sri Lanka, India, Thailand and other states in the region. The human cost of the natural disaster was horrific, as officials estimated that more than 160 000 were killed. Some coastal villages lost nearly 70 percent of their populations. The tsunami destroyed hundreds of coastal villages in the region, decimated fishing industries and exacerbated poverty in the area.

The tsunami's effect on coastal areas was described by then U.S. secretary of state Colin Powell as "similar to a nuclear weapon." The loss of villages, ports and ships will mean dependence by tens of thousands on outside assistance. The already overburdened health infrastructure had to deal with immediate tsunami-related injuries as well as long-term threats of typhoid, cholera and malaria due to contaminated water supplies, destruction of sanitation facilities and the destruction of shelters to guard against insects. In addition, tourism income will suffer. These factors led the Asian Development Bank to predict that more than two million people will be thrown into poverty by the tsunami.

---

[11] William J. Dixon and Bruce E. Moon, "Domestic Political Conflict and Basic Needs Outcomes: An Empirical Assessment," *Comparative Political Studies* 22.2 (1989): 178–98.

The disaster also affected political violence in Sri Lanka and Indonesia, where victims were caught between their governments, rebel groups and international aid organizations, which all brought different agendas to the relief effort. Although natural disasters are costly no matter where they occur, disasters in the developing world can make a difficult situation even worse—in the case of the tsunami, in a matter of hours. The international community began work on a tsunami warning system for the Indian Ocean similar to one already operating in the Pacific.

World Hunger

malnutrition A lack of needed foods, including protein and vitamins; about 10 million children die each year from malnutrition-related causes.

undernourishment A lack of needed foods; a lack of calories.

Of all the basic needs of people in the global South, the most central is *food*. **Malnutrition** (or malnourishment) refers to a lack of needed foods, including protein and vitamins. The term *hunger* refers broadly to malnutrition or outright **undernourishment**—a lack of calories. Hunger does not usually kill people through outright starvation, but weakens them and leaves them susceptible to infectious diseases that would not ordinarily be fatal.[12]

Some 820 million people—about one in eight worldwide—are chronically undernourished (see Table 12.1). Their potential contribution to economic accumulation is wasted because they cannot do even light work. They cannot forgo short-term consumption for long-term investment. And they are a potential source of political instability—including international instability—as long as they stay hungry. At a World Food Summit in 1996, world leaders adopted a goal to cut hunger in half by 2015. By 1999, with the number of undernourished people falling by only eight million a year and only in selected countries, the FAO stated that "there is no hope of meeting that goal."[13] In 2006, UNICEF reported that China had made great progress in reducing child malnutrition, but

Table 12.1 Who's Hungry?
Chronically Undernourished People by Region, c. 2002

Region	Number (millions)	Percentage of Population	10 Years Earlier
S. Asia	380	16%	20%
China	140	11%	16%
Africa	200	33%	36%
Latin America	50	10%	13%
Middle East	40	10%	8%
Russia/E. Europe	30	7%	6%
Industrialized Countries	10	n.a.	n.a.
Total World	850	13%	16%

Notes: Data are from 2000–2002 and 1990–1992. Chronic undernourishment means failing to consume enough food on average over a year to maintain body weight and support light activity.

Source: Based on Food and Agriculture Organization. *The State of Food Insecurity in the World 2004.* Rome: FAO, 2004, pp. 34–6.

---

[12] Jean Dréze, Amartya Sen and Athar Hussain, eds., *The Political Economy of Hunger: Selected Essays* (NY: Oxford UP, 1995). Vaclav Smil, *Feeding the World: A Challenge for the Twenty-First Century* (Boston, MA: MIT, 2000). Phillips Foster, *The World Food Problem: Tackling the Causes of Undernutrition in the Third World* (Boulder, CO: Rienner, 1992).

[13] Food and Agriculture Organization, *The State of Food Insecurity in the World 1999* (Rome: FAO, 1999).

progress in South Asia had been very slow and Africa was not having success. A quarter of the world's children under age five—and nearly half those in India—were underweight in 2006. Of the world's 150 million underweight children, half lived in India, Pakistan and Bangladesh.[14]

The world has the potential to produce enough food to feed all people. The problem is not so much that there is an absolute shortage of food (though that condition does exist in some places) but that poor people do not have money to buy it.

Traditionally, rural communities have grown their own food—**subsistence farming.** Colonialism disrupted this pattern, and the disruption has continued in postcolonial times. States of the global South have shifted from subsistence to commercial agriculture, often at the insistence of international institutions such as the IMF or World Bank. Small plots have been merged into big plantations, often under the control of wealthy landlords. By concentrating capital and orienting the economy toward a niche in world trade, this process is consistent with liberal economics, but it displaces subsistence farmers from the land. Wars displace farmers even more quickly, with similar results.

subsistence farming Rural communities growing food mainly for their own consumption rather than for sale in local or world markets.

Commercial agriculture relies on machinery, commercial fuels and artificial fertilizers and pesticides, which must be bought with cash and often must be imported. To pay for these supplies, big farms grow **cash crops**—agricultural goods produced for export to world markets.[15] Cash crops typically provide little nutrition to local peasants; examples include coffee, tea and sugar cane. When a plantation is built or expanded, subsistence farmers end up working in the plantation at very low wages or migrating to cities in search of jobs. Often they end up hungry.

cash crops Agricultural goods produced as commodities for export to world markets.

Many governments support commercial agriculture with loans, subsidies, irrigation projects or technical help. Government support reflects both the political power of the big landowners and the government's ability to obtain hard-currency revenues from export crops, but not from subsistence crops.

International food aid can sometimes contribute to these problems.[16] Agricultural assistance may favour mechanized commercial agriculture. If an international agency floods an area with food, prices in local markets drop, which may force even more local farmers out of business and increase dependence on handouts from the government or international community. Also, people in a drought or famine often have to travel to feeding centres to receive the food, halting work on their own land.

Rural and Urban Populations

The displacement of peasants from subsistence farming contributes to a massive population shift that typically accompanies the demographic transition. More and more people move to the cities from the countryside—**urbanization.** This is hard to measure exactly; there is no standard definition of when a town is considered a city. Industrialized states report that close to 70 to 90 percent of their populations live in cities. By contrast, China is only 30 percent urbanized—a level typical for Asia and Africa. Most Middle Eastern states are slightly more urban (45 to 55 percent), and states in South America are 70 to 85 percent urban.

urbanization A shift of population from the countryside to cities that typically accompanies economic development and is augmented by displacement of peasants from subsistence farming.

[14] UNICEF, *Progress for Children: A Report Card on Nutrition*, Number 4, May 2006 (NY: UNICEF, 2006).

[15] David Barkin, Rosemary L. Batt and Billie R. DeWatt, *Food Crops vs. Feed Crops: Global Substitution of Grains in Production* (Boulder, CO: Rienner, 1990).

[16] Peter Uvin, "Regime, Surplus, and Self-Interest: The International Politics of Food Aid," *International Studies Quarterly* 36.3 (1992): 293–312.

Urbanization is not caused by higher population growth in cities than in the countryside. In fact, the opposite is true. In cities, the people are generally better educated with higher incomes. They are further along in the demographic transition, and have lower growth rates than people in the countryside. Rather, the growth of urban populations is caused by people moving from the countryside. They do so because of the higher income levels in the cities—economic opportunity—and the hope of greater chances for an exciting life. They also move because population growth in the countryside stretches available food, water, arable land and other resources—or because they have been displaced from subsistence farming as land is turned to commercial cultivation, or they have been displaced by war.

Capital accumulation is concentrated in cities. To some extent this makes urban dwellers more politically supportive of the status quo, especially if the city has a sizeable middle class. Governments extend their influence more readily to cities than to the countryside—Chinese government policies adopted in Beijing often have little bearing on village life. Urban dwellers may turn against a government, however: they are better educated and have rising expectations for their futures. Often rebellions arise from frustrated expectations rather than from poverty itself.

In many cities, the influx of people cannot be accommodated with jobs, housing or services. In slums, basic human needs often go unmet. Many states have considered policies to break up large land holdings and redistribute land to poor peasants for use in subsistence farming—**land reform.**[17] Socialists and other critical theorists almost always favour land reform, and some economic liberals also favour it in moderation. The standards of moderation change over time; for instance, the El Salvadoran land reform favoured by the United States in the 1980s was more sweeping than a program that U.S. officials considered a sign of communism in Guatemala when the United States intervened there militarily in 1954.

The main opponents of land reform are large landowners, who often wield great political power because of their wealth and international connections to markets, MNCs and other sources of hard currency. Landowners have great leverage in bargaining with peasants—from using the legal system to having virtual private armies.

land reform Policies that aim to break up large land holdings and redistribute land to poor peasants for use in subsistence farming.

Women in Development

Economic accumulation in poor countries is closely tied to the status of women in those societies.[18] This is a relatively recent revelation; most attention in the past was focused on men as the supposedly main generators of capital. Governments and international reports concentrated on work performed by male wage earners. Women's work, by contrast, often is not paid for in money and does not show up in financial statistics. As studies from the 1970s onward began to show, however, women in much of the world work harder than men and contribute more to the economic well-being of their families and communities. Women are key to efforts to improve the lot of children and reduce birthrates. In nutrition,

[17] Peter Dorner, *Latin American Land Reform in Theory and Practice* (Madison: U Wisconsin P, 1992). John D. Montgomery, ed., *International Dimensions of Land Reform* (Boulder, CO: Westview, 1984).

[18] Ester Boserup, *Women's Role in Economic Development* (London: Allen & Unwin, 1970). Martha Nussbaum and Jonathan Glover, eds., *Women, Culture, and Development: A Study of Human Capabilities* (NY: Oxford UP, 1996). Valentine M. Moghadam, ed., *Patriarchy and Economic Development: Women's Positions at the End of the Twentieth Century* (NY: Oxford UP, 1996). Irene Tinker and Gale Summerfield, eds., *Women's Rights to House and Land: China, Laos, Vietnam* (Boulder, CO: Rienner, 1999). Catherine V. Scott, *Gender and Development: Rethinking Modernization and Dependency Theory* (Boulder, CO: Rienner, 1994). Joycelin Massiah, ed., *Women in Developing Economies: Making Visible the Invisible* (NY: Berg, 1992).

education, health care and shelter, women are central to providing the basic needs of people in poor countries.

Even so, women hold inferior social status to men in the countries of the South (sometimes even more so than in the North). For instance, when food is in short supply, men and boys often eat first, with women and girls getting whatever is left. Because of this practice, of the world's malnourished children, 80 percent are female, according to Oxfam.

Discrimination against girls in education and literacy is widespread. Worldwide, nearly twice as many women as men are illiterate. Across the global South, only in Latin America do women's literacy rates approach those of men. In Pakistan, 50 percent of boys but fewer than 30 percent of girls receive pri-

LANDLESS
Subsistence farmers displaced from their land risk chronic hunger and sometimes starvation. In Sudan (1993), famine and war forced this starving girl to set out for a feeding centre, and she was at one point stalked by a vulture. She survived the incident, but the South African photographer committed suicide the next year, haunted by the photo (which had won a Pulitzer Prize).

mary education. Throughout Asia, Africa and the Middle East (though not in Latin America), more boys receive education, especially at the secondary level. At the university level, only 30 percent of students in China and the Middle East are women, and slightly more than 20 percent in South Asia and Africa (but 45 percent in Latin America). During the Taliban regime in Afghanistan (1996–2001), extreme measures were taken against women's education, with all girls banned from school and all women from work.

States and international agencies have begun to pay attention to ending discrimination in education, assuring women's access to health care and birth control, educating mothers about prenatal and child health and generally raising women's status in society (allowing them a greater voice in decisions). These issues occupied the 1995 UN women's conference in Beijing, China, attended by tens of thousands of state and NGO representatives. The United Nations also organized the Beijing +5 meetings in 2000 to review progress toward the Plan of Action adopted at Beijing.

International agencies help women organize small businesses, farms and other income-producing activities. For example, UNICEF has helped women get bank loans on favourable terms to start up small businesses in Egypt and Pakistan and cooperative farms in Indonesia. Women have organized cooperatives throughout the global South, often in rural areas, to produce income through weaving and other textile and clothing production, retail stores, agriculture and so forth.[19] In the slums of Addis Ababa, Ethiopia,

[19] Jill Bystydzienski, ed., *Women Transforming Politics: Worldwide Strategies for Empowerment* (Bloomington: Indiana UP, 1992). Amrita Basu, *Two Faces of Protest: Contrasting Modes of Women's Activism in India* (Berkeley: U California P, 1992). Helen Todd, *Women at the Center: Grameen Bank Borrowers after One Decade* (Boulder, CO: Westview, 1996).

WOMEN'S POWER
The status of women in countries of the global South affects their prospects for economic development. Women are central to rural economies, to population strategies and to the provision of basic human needs, including education. Here, a women's organization meets in a home in northern Pakistan.

female heads of household with no land for subsistence farming had been forced into begging and prostitution. Women taking part in the Integrated Holistic Approach Urban Development Project organized income-producing businesses from food processing to cloth weaving and garment production. These profitable businesses earned income for the women and helped subsidize health and sanitation services in the slums.

Migration and Refugees

The processes just outlined—basic-needs deprivation, displacement from land, urbanization—culminate in one of the biggest political issues affecting North-South relations—**migration** from poorer to richer states.[20] Millions of people from the global South have crossed international borders, often illegally, to reach the North.

Someone who moves to a new country in search of better economic opportunities, a better professional environment, or better access to their family, culture or religion is engaging in migration (emigration from the old state and immigration to a new state). Such migration is considered voluntary. The home state is not under any obligation to let such people leave, and, more important, no state is obligated to receive migrants. As with

migration Movement between states, usually emigration from an old state and immigration to a new state.

---

[20] Caroline Brettell and James Hollifield, eds., *Migration Theory: Talking across Disciplines* (NY: Routledge, 2000). Peter Stalker, *Workers without Frontiers: The Impact of Globalization on International Migration* (Boulder, CO: Rienner, 2000). Myron Weiner, *The Global Migration Crisis: Challenge to States and to Human Rights* (NY: HarperCollins, 1995).

any trade issue, migration creates complex patterns of winners and losers. Immigrants often provide cheap labour, benefiting the host economy overall, but also compete for jobs with (poor) citizens of the host country.

Most industrialized states try to limit immigration from the global South. Despite border guards and fences, many people migrate anyway, illegally. In the United States, such immigrants come from all over the world, but mostly from nearby Mexico, Central America and the Caribbean. In Western Europe, they come largely from North Africa, Turkey and (increasingly) Eastern Europe.[21] Some Western European leaders worry that the loosening of border controls under the process of integration (see pp. 379–381) will make it harder to keep out illegal immigrants. Indeed, fear of immigration is one reason why France and Denmark voted against the new 2005 EU constitution.

From 2004 to 2006, tens of thousands of migrants and refugees from sub-Saharan Africa came to Morocco and climbed over razor-wire fences to enter two tiny Spanish enclaves there. Once on Spanish soil, they could not be sent home if they kept authorities from determining their nationality. Canada is considered a country that is relatively open to foreign immigration. In 2005, the largest number of immigrants to Canada came from Asia and the Pacific followed by Africa and the Middle East. However, even in Canada

Focus on Canadian Scholarship

Scholars at Canadian universities who work on questions of North-South relations, poverty and imperialism include **Richard Sandbrook** at the University of Toronto, who examines basic needs and neoliberal development strategies with a particular focus on Africa. At the University of Toronto law school, **Audrey Macklin** examines Canadian immigration policy and issues of human trafficking. **Tim Shaw**, at Royal Roads University, has examined development in Southern Africa as well as peacebuilding and human development. At York University, **Liisa North** and **Judith Adler Hellman** focus on development in Latin America, and their colleague **Ananya Mukherjee-Reed** explores issues of human development with a particular focus on South Asia. At Dalhousie University, **David Black** is interested in questions of human rights and development in Africa. At the University of Windsor, **Tom Najem** is interested in the comparative politics of the developing world. At Simon Fraser University, **Sandra MacLean** focuses on comparative development. At Queen's University, **Abigail Bakan** researches development in the Caribbean and foreign domestic labour in Canada. **Cristina Rojas** at Carleton University's Norman Paterson School of International Affairs works on Latin American Politics, Development and Social Policy. At McGill University, **Baldev Raj Nayar** examines globalization and development. At Trent University, **Paul Shaffer** does work on interdisciplinary poverty analysis and development economics. **Craig Johnson** of the University of Guelph is interested in international development and the tensions between development theories and practice. At Ryerson University, **Sedef Arat-Koç** focuses on immigration policy and citizenship and the politics of imperialism, and her colleague **Tariq Amin-Khan** is interested in development and South Asian studies and the politics of colonialism. At the University of Ottawa, **Stephen Brown** focuses on North-South relations and the politics of aid in Africa. At the University of Montréal, **Dominique Caouette** examines revolutionary and anti-globalization movements in the global South. **Yasmine Shamsie** of Wilfrid Laurier University examines the political economy of development in Latin America. At the Université de Québec à Montréal, **Bonnie Campbell** focuses on questions of the post-colonial state and the political economy of development.

[21] Peter Nyers, *Rethinking Refugees: Beyond States of Emergency* (UK: Routledge, 2006). Alexander Aleinikoff and Douglas Klusmeyer, eds., *From Migrants to Citizens: Membership in a Changing World* (Washington, DC: Carnegie Endowment for International Peace, 2000). Stephen Castles and Alastair Davidson, eds., *Citizenship and Migration* (NY: Routledge, 2000). Mark J. Miller, ed., "Strategies for Immigration Control: An International Comparison," *Annals of the American Academy of Political and Social Science* 534 (July 1994).

the arrival of both legal and illegal immigrants has been met with incidents of the same kind of xenophobia witnessed elsewhere in the world.

International law and custom distinguish migrants from **refugees,** people fleeing to find refuge from war, natural disaster or political persecution.[22] (Fleeing from chronic discrimination may or may not be grounds for refugee status.) International norms obligate countries to accept refugees who arrive at their borders. Refugees from wars or natural disasters are generally temporarily housed in refugee camps until they can return home (though their stay can drag on for years). Refugees from political persecution may be granted asylum to stay in the new state. Acceptance of refugees—and the question of which states must bear the costs—is a collective goods problem.

The number of international refugees in the world grew from three million in 1976 to 10 million in 2004. In addition, seven million more people are currently displaced within their own countries. The majority of refugees and internally displaced people have been displaced by wars (see Table 12.2).

The political impact of refugees has been demonstrated repeatedly in recent years. After the Gulf War, Iraq's persecution of rebellious Iraqi Kurds sent large numbers of Kurdish refugees streaming to the Turkish border, where they threatened to become an economic burden to Turkey. Turkey closed its borders, and the hungry Iraqi Kurds were left stranded in the mountains. The United States and its allies then sent in military forces to protect the Kurds and return them to their homes in Iraq—violating Iraq's territorial integrity but upholding the Kurds' human rights. When the Kurdish-controlled area of Iraq became a base for Kurdish guerrillas in Turkey, the Turkish army invaded the area (another violation of Iraqi sovereignty) in 1995. The close connection of economics and international security is clear from this episode—a security-related incident (the war) caused an economic condition (starving Kurds) that in turn led to other security ramifications (U.S. military protection of Kurdish areas of Iraq; Turkish invasion of the area).

The connection of economics and security appears in other refugee questions as well. Palestinian refugees displaced in the 1948 and 1967 Arab-Israeli wars (and their children

refugees People fleeing their countries to find refuge from war, natural disaster or political persecution. International law distinguishes refugees from migrants.

Table 12.2 Refugee Populations, 2004

Region	Millions	Main Concentrations
Middle East and Asia	6	Afghanistan, Iran, Pakistan, and Sri Lanka
Africa	5	Tanzania, Liberia, Chad, Sudan
Latin America	2	Colombia
Western and Eastern Europe	6	Former Yugoslavia, Russia, Germany[a]
North America	1	United States[a]
World Total	20	

[a] Various regions of origin.

Note: Includes refugees, asylum-seekers, returned refugees, and internally displaced people. Excludes 4 million Palestinians under UN Relief and Works Agency (UNRWA).

Source: UN High Commissioner for Refugees (UNHCR).

---

[22] UN High Commissioner for Refugees, *The State of the World's Refugees* (NY: Oxford UP, annual). Gil Loescher, *The UNHCR and World Politics: A Perilous Path* (NY: Oxford UP, 2001). Aristide Zolberg, Astri Suhrke, and Sergio Aguayo, *Escape from Violence: Conflict and the Refugee Crisis in the Developing World* (NY: Oxford UP, 1989). Leon Gordenker, *Refugees in International Politics* (NY: Columbia UP, 1987).

HUMAN CARGO
Refugees are both a result of international conflicts and a source of conflict. In addition to those fleeing war and repression and those seeking economic opportunity, hundreds of thousands of people each year cross borders as sex and labour slaves. This truck X-rayed entering Mexico from Guatemala in 1999 may have held Central American migrants seeking work in Mexico or sex slaves from Asia or Eastern Europe en route to the United States.

and grandchildren) live in "camps" that have become long-term neighbourhoods, mainly in Jordan and Lebanon. Economic development is impeded in these camps because the host states and Palestinians insist that the arrangement is only temporary. The poverty of the refugees in turn fuels radical political movements among the camp inhabitants. The question of Palestinian refugees' right to return to what is now Israel was one of two issues that blocked agreement at the failed Camp David II summit in 2000.

It is not always easy to distinguish a refugee fleeing war or political persecution from a migrant seeking economic opportunity. Illegal immigrants may claim to be refugees in order to be allowed to stay, when really they are seeking better economic opportunities. At the same time, legitimate refugees may be subject to intense scrutiny and denied refugee status when in fact they should receive it. This has become a major issue in recent decades throughout the North.

In Germany, France, Austria and elsewhere, resentment of foreign immigrants has fuelled upsurges of right-wing nationalism in domestic politics. Germany, with lax regulations for asylum seekers (they could live for years at state expense while applications for refugee status were processed), became a favoured destination for growing numbers of immigrants—most of whom were not political refugees. At a time of economic difficulty following German reunification, around 1992, neo-Nazi youths staged violent attacks on foreigners and forced the government to tighten restrictions on immigration. (Hundreds of thousands of Germans then demonstrated against the neo-Nazis.) In 1999, Austria alarmed its EU partners by including a far-right party in a coalition government.

Trafficking In addition to migration and refugees, a growing number of persons—estimated at 900 000 annually—are trafficked across international borders against their will. They include sex and labour slaves, with each category including females and males, adults and children. An estimated half million women and children are thought to be trafficked into Western Europe each year, and some 50 000 women trafficked to the United States, as part of the sex trade alone.[23] Canadians tend to think that they are insulated from issues of human trafficking and smuggling, but Canada is a regular and growing destination of undocumented migrants (whether "voluntary" or forced). In fact, according to some observers, Canadian immigration policy directed

The Changing World Order
Engaging the South

Global poverty has become a problem of enormous concern in international relations. When the Cold War ended, it became easier to raise issues that had previously been submerged under the framework of "first world–second world conflict." Today scholars of IR can engage with questions of poverty in its own right, though some still link poverty to issues of security. For some observers, the attacks against the United States on September 11, 2001, demonstrated the increased interdependence of the global North and South. By this view (one largely shared by realist/mercantilists and some liberals), the extreme disparities of wealth and power between the North and South create conflicts and resentments in the South that can lead to punishment of the privileged citizens of the North who are oblivious to the problems of poor countries. To let a continent or even a country descend into despair may no longer be practical in an era of terrorism, by this view. Their fate ultimately may be the fate of the North that ignores them. This is the century in which desperate African states may be able to press their demands with weapons of mass destruction, and in which fanatics may destroy cities with nuclear weapons. To combat terrorism may require that poverty, repression and war be addressed throughout the poorest world regions. The need to address "root causes" of terrorism may

draw the United States and other Northern countries into close cooperation with the UN and other international institutions such as the IMF and World Bank in the years to come.

Others would argue that poverty needs to be addressed for its own sake, not simply because it is "impractical" to ignore because of the risk that "fanatics" will emerge bent on destroying the North. Poverty needs to be addressed because it destroys human potential and human lives, and also usually has a devastating effect on local culture and the environment. This view results from an analysis of poverty in the global South that sees it as inextricably related to the accumulation of wealth in the North. So, simply working with existing international institutions—especially those like the IMF and World Bank—will not by itself alleviate poverty. Many of the prescriptions suggested by these institutions may actually exacerbate poverty.

It is unclear how these views will play out in practice. Elites tend to emphasize the more instrumental approach to poverty (we want to address poverty in the South to ensure it does not come back to haunt the North), but that very attitude may be an example of the perceived arrogance that critics in both the South and North insist is part of the problem of global poverty and inequality.

---

[23] Joni Seager, *The Penguin Atlas of Women in the World*, rev. ed. (NY: Penguin, 2003). Barbara Ehrenreich and Arlie Russell Hochschild, eds., *Global Woman: Nannies, Maids, and Sex Workers in the New Economy* (NY: Holt, 2002). Anna M. Agathangelou, *The Political Economy of Sex: Desire, Violence and Insecurity in Mediterranean States* (NY: Palgrave Macmillan 2006).

at "exotic dancers" helps to facilitate the trafficking of women into Canada for sex work.[24]

In general, migration of all types creates problems that can seemingly be solved only by addressing the problems of the South. The following sections explore different accounts of global poverty.

THEORIES OF ACCUMULATION

How do we explain the enormous gap between income levels in the world's industrialized regions and those in the global South? What are the implications of that gap for international politics? There are several very different approaches to these questions; we will concentrate on two contrasting theories of wealth accumulation based on liberal and more critical world views.

Economic Accumulation

One view of the problem from the perspective of capitalism is based on economic liberalism—stressing overall efficiency in maximizing *economic growth*. This view sees the global South as merely lagging behind the industrialized North. More wealth creation in the North is a good thing, as is wealth creation in the South—the two do not conflict.

A more critical view is concerned with the distribution of wealth as much as the absolute creation of wealth. It sees the creation of wealth in the North most often coming at the expense of the South. Advocates of a socialist perspective would give politics (the state) a greater role in redistributing wealth and managing the economy than capitalism does. Socialism thus parallels mercantilism in some ways, but socialists see economic classes rather than states as the main actors in the political bargaining over the distribution of the world's wealth. Mercantilism promotes the idea of concentrating wealth (as a power element), whereas socialism promotes a broader distribution.

For socialists and other critical scholars of development studies, international exchange is shaped by capitalists' exploitation of cheap labour and cheap resources—using states to help create the political conditions for this exploitation. (Some focus on workers in countries of the global South, some on workers in richer industrialized countries and some on both.) Thus, whereas mercantilists see political interests (of the state) as driving economic policies, socialists see economic interests (of capitalists and of workers) as driving political policies.

Economic development is based on **capital accumulation**—the creation of standing wealth (capital) such as buildings, roads, factories and so forth. In order for human populations and their capital to grow, they must produce an **economic surplus** by using capital to produce more capital. This is done by investing money in productive capital rather than using it for consumption. The greater the surplus an economy produces, the more resources are available for investment above the minimum level of consumption needed to sustain human life.

Early human societies had a very simple stock of capital—mostly clothes and hand tools—and produced little surplus. With the development of agriculture about

capital accumulation
The creation of standing wealth (capital) such as buildings, roads, factories and so forth; such accumulation depends on investment and the creation of an economic surplus.

economic surplus Surplus created by investing money in productive capital rather than using it for consumption.

---

[24] Leslie Ann Jeffrey, "Canada and Migrant Sex-Work: Challenging the 'Foreign' in Foreign Policy," *Canadian Foreign Policy* 12.1 (Spring 2005): 33–48. Audrey Macklin, "Dancing Across Borders: 'Exotic Dancers,' Trafficking and Canadian Immigration Policy," *The International Migration Review* 37.2 (Summer 2003): 464–500. Alison Mountz, "Human Smuggling and the Canadian State," *Canadian Foreign Policy* 13.1 (2006): 59–80.

The Information Revolution
Sharpening Disparities?

The concentration of surplus tends to be self-reinforcing: the rich get richer. The information revolution is no exception in that richer countries and individuals tend to have much greater access to information technologies than do poorer ones. Will the information revolution give the industrialized West more power than ever, and increase the North-South gap in wealth?

To explore this question, go to www.pearsoned.ca/goldstein.

10 000 years ago, a group of people discovered they could produce a surplus—more grain than they could eat—decade after decade. The extra grain could feed specialists who made tools from metals, built houses and constructed irrigation works. Ever since, humans have been on an uninterrupted growth cycle based on economic surplus. More and more wealth has accumulated, and the human population has grown larger and larger.

The Industrial Revolution of several centuries ago greatly accelerated the process of world accumulation, drawing on large amounts of energy from fossil fuels. Industrialization has occurred very unevenly across the world regions, however. The North has accumulated vast capital. Though the South produces spurts of wealth and has pockets of accumulation, in most areas it remains a preindustrial economy—which explains why the North consumes nearly 10 times as much commercial energy per person as the South (see Table 14.1 on p. 521).

LOW-TECH
Production in the global South uses relatively little capital and much labour (at low wages), reflecting an early stage of industrialization. To develop economically, poor countries must generate self-sustaining capital accumulation. Agriculture, energy and textiles are classic export products from the global South; both require relatively low capital and are labour-intensive. Here, a weaver in Bangladesh, where textiles make up three-quarters of exports, dries cotton in the sun, 2004.

Information technology is now making a fuel-burning infrastructure relatively less important in the advanced economies. The countries of the global South may need to pass through a phase of heavy industrialization, as countries in the North did, or perhaps they can develop economically along different paths, using new technology from the start. The problem is that just as industrial infrastructure is located primarily in the North, so is the world's information infrastructure (see pp. 397–400). While a generation of students in industrialized countries access the internet, poorer countries still struggle to extend literacy to rural populations.

Nonetheless, neither the absolute size of a GDP nor its size relative to other countries indicates whether a national economy is growing or shrinking. Accumulation or profit in a national economy corresponds with the *economic growth rate*. States that operate profitably grow from year to year; those that operate at a loss shrink. (GDP and related concepts refer here to real values after adjusting for inflation.)

A state's economic growth rate does not indicate how much wealth it has accumulated in the past. In recent years, countries like Canada have grown only slowly—even shrinking slightly during times of recession (see "The Position of Canada" on p. 357). However, Canada has a considerable amount of standing wealth amassed over the past 150 years. By contrast, Mexico may have stronger economic growth, but because it does not have accumulated wealth, it still lags far behind in total wealth. On a global scale, the South will continue to lag behind the North in GDP (income) even if its economic growth rate continues to be higher than the North's, as it has been in the last few years. The concentration of surplus in the world economy—in the North—tends to be self-reinforcing for two reasons. First, concentrating wealth allows it to be invested more efficiently, which generates more wealth. Second, the more wealth is concentrated, the more power its owners gain. With 60 percent of the world's wealth, the North dominates world politics. Because critical theorists see a conflict of interest between rich and poor, they see the North's political power as oppressive to the South.

Ultimately, the distribution of the benefits of world accumulation is an issue for international bargaining, just as the distribution of benefits from trade is (see Chapter 9, pp. 327–331). In the bargaining between rich and poor regions over the process of world accumulation, the two sides have very unequal power.[25]

Capitalism

Previous chapters referred to capital in a general way as standing wealth. More precisely, *capital* is the set of goods that are used in producing other goods. Thus, a warehouse full of refined tin is capital, as is a tin can or a canning factory—all go into producing further goods. A stamp collection, a set of Lego toys and a pleasure boat are not capital in this sense, even though they have value; they are **consumption goods**. Their consumption does not contribute directly to the production of other goods and services.

A cycle of accumulation depends on capital goods more than consumption goods. Mines, factories, oil refineries, railroads and similar capital goods contribute directly to the cycle of surplus production by which more factories and oil refineries are produced.

Investment competes with consumption. Forgoing consumption for investment is another case where short-term costs produce long-term benefits (as in aspects of trade, environmental and population policies).

consumption goods Goods whose consumption does not contribute directly to the production of other goods and services, unlike some forms of investment.

investment Putting surplus wealth into capital-producing activities to produce long-term benefits rather than consuming it.

---

[25] David A. Lake, "Power and the Third World: Toward a Realist Political Economy of North-South Relations" [review article], *International Studies Quarterly* 31.2 (1987): 217–34.

capitalism An economic system based on private ownership of capital and the means of production (standing wealth and other forms of property). See also *socialism*.

Capitalism is a system of *private ownership of capital* that relies on market forces to govern distribution of goods. Under capitalism, the cycle of accumulation is largely controlled by private individuals and companies. When a surplus is produced, it is profit for the owners of the capital by which it was produced (after taxes). Private ownership encourages reinvestment of surplus because private individuals and companies seek to maximize their wealth. The concentration of capital ownership in few hands also allows investment to be shifted easily from less productive sectors and technologies to more productive ones. Capitalism concentrates wealth, promoting efficient and rapid accumulation; it does not seek an equitable distribution of benefits.

In reality, no state is purely capitalist. Almost all have some form of mixed economy that includes private and state ownership.[26] Also, in most capitalist countries the government balances the inhuman side of capitalism by redistributing some wealth downward (and regulating capitalists). A "welfare state" provides education, certain health benefits, welfare for the poor and so forth. The post–World War II period was one of a vastly expanding welfare state in many countries of the global North. However, scholars who examine capitalism in industrialized states now tend to focus on erosions in welfare state provisions, especially over the past two decades.

The principles of capitalism underlie the global economy and its great disparities of wealth. The concentration of capital in the global North furthers the development of global trade, technology and reinvestment for maximum profit (overall growth). The private ownership of companies and of currency makes international markets operate more efficiently. Capital can be moved around from less productive to more productive countries and economic sectors. If wealth were distributed equally across world regions, these efficiencies might be lost and world economic growth might be slower.

Socialism

socialism A term encompassing many political movements, parties, economic theories and ideologies, historical and present-day. Based on the idea that workers should have political power (or a larger share of power), socialism favours the redistribution of wealth toward the workers who produce it. In economic policy, socialists have favoured different combinations of planning and reliance on market forces, as well as various patterns of ownership.

Socialism—the idea that workers should have political power—favours the *redistribution of wealth* toward the workers who produce it. Because such redistribution does not naturally happen under capitalism, socialism generally endorses the use of the state for this purpose. It favours *governmental planning* to manage a national economy rather than leaving such management entirely to market forces. Often, socialists advocate *state ownership* of capital over private ownership so that the accumulation of wealth is controlled by the state, which can distribute it equitably.

Socialism describes many political movements, parties and ideologies, both historical and present-day. In Canada, the New Democratic Party has its roots in social democratic politics, and has held power in some provincial governments and held the balance of power in a number of minority governments at the federal level. Elsewhere in the global North, socialist or social democratic parties have also held important roles as governing parties in recent years (Britain, France), as parts of governing coalitions (Germany, Japan) or as main opposition parties (Russia). In the global South, where great poverty and disparities of wealth make the idea of redistributing wealth popular, most revolutionaries and many reformers consider themselves socialists of some sort.

Communist governments, including in China (and the former Soviet Union), also base their political philosophy on socialism. In practice, however, they tend to extract wealth toward the centre and have thus been described as practising a form of state capitalism. For example, in the Soviet Union under Stalin in the 1930s, there was a

---

[26] John R. Freeman, *Democracy and Markets: The Politics of Mixed Economies* (Ithaca, NY: Cornell UP, 1989).

tremendous concentration of capital, which allowed rapid industrialization but starved millions of people. This took place under dictatorial political control rather than workers' control. The term *democratic socialism* in part emerged out of a critique of policies like those of Stalin, and advocates instead that the economic principles of socialism be joined to democratic rather than authoritarian political principles.

Marxism is a theoretical and political approach that views capitalism as exploitative and advocates forms of governance based on socialism and communism. (Not all socialists, however, are Marxist.) (See Chapter 4, page 107.) In the mid-nineteenth century, *Karl Marx* emphasized labour as the source of economic surplus. At that time, the Industrial Revolution was accompanied by particular hardship among industrial workers (including children) in Europe. Marxists still believe that the surplus created by labour should be recaptured by workers through political struggle. Today, Marxism is most influential in countries where capital is scarce and labour conditions are wretched, most particularly in the global South. Some of the differences among Marxists and socialists focus on how political and economic transformation will be accomplished. For most Marxists, capitalism contains within itself the seeds of its own destruction—the transition to socialism and then communism is, in a sense, inevitable. For other Marxists and many socialists, the transition will need to be achieved through other means, for example by capturing state power and adopting policies that are socialist in principle and purpose.

Like capitalism, socialism does not exist anywhere in a pure form. There is an element of socialism in mixed economies. China now calls its economic system "market socialism"—a combination of continuing state ownership of many large industries, capitalism at the local level and openness to international investment and trade.

Marxism A theoretical and political approach that views capitalism as exploitative and emphasizes class struggle; includes socialism and communism and other approaches to social transformation.

RICH AND POOR
Disparity of wealth is a central aspect of global North-South relations. Marxists see international relations and domestic politics as shaped by a class struggle between the rich and poor. In São Paulo, Brazil, rich and poor neighbourhoods sit side by side.

Some socialist theories argue that state ownership of industry increases efficiency by avoiding problems that arise from the fragmentation of decision making under capitalism. In theory, central planners are supposed to use resources in a rational way that maximizes overall efficiency. After decades of experimentation, however, it is clear that whatever its benefits in equity, state ownership is not very efficient. State planners who set quotas for production at factories cannot adjust to economic conditions as efficiently as market-based prices can. State ownership is still promoted in many countries in order to redistribute wealth, to coordinate development of key industries or to maintain self-sufficiency in military production—but not because it is more efficient in general.

Russia and other Eastern European states are now in a difficult transition to market economies because of the failure of centrally planned economies. Many countries are also moving to sell off large state-owned industries—*privatization*—in hopes of increasing growth. Phone companies, oil companies, railroads—all are going on the auction block. This is happening a great deal in countries of the global South, but also in countries like Canada, where some provinces have moved to privatize hydroelectric services and the federal government has sold off its interests in some corporations, such as Petro-Canada.

Privatization has gone quickly in several Eastern European and former Soviet republics, where the state owned virtually the whole economy during decades of communism. Before Czechoslovakia split in two, citizens received coupons representing a small portion of stock in state-owned companies. They could sell the coupons for cash or invest them in any of several new mutual funds established by entrepreneurs. The mutual fund managers pooled the coupons and bought up state-owned companies they thought would be profitable. Lured by promises of large profits, most Czechoslovak citizens (as new capitalists) invested in this way. When a similar scheme was tried in Russia, citizens weary from economic depression did not put much value in the coupons. Many Russians invested in a leading mutual fund that promised high profits but then went bankrupt.

Thus, in Russia and Eastern Europe, communism had collapsed under the weight of inefficiency, but the beginning stages of capitalism were even more inefficient, leading to a reduction of economic activity by roughly half over several years. Some countries, including Russia, slowed the pace of reforms in response, while reformists argued that a speedup was needed to get through the transition. Some countries democratically threw out the reformers and brought back their old communist leaders. In coming years, it is likely that the various experiments being tried by the countries of Eastern Europe and the former Soviet Union will sort themselves out, making clearer the best routes of transition for former communist economies.

In any event, the collapse of Soviet communism has closed the books on a historic experiment in one type of socialism that failed—old-style **Stalinism,** as articulated and practised by *Joseph Stalin*, which was marked by totalitarian state control under the Communist party. The failures of state-owned enterprises do not mean that socialism is dead. Rather, other types of socialism are now more salient, and new mixes of socialism and capitalism are being created. In Latin America in recent years, several states have elected leftist presidents committed to changing course away from free-market capitalism toward a socialist philosophy with more state-owned industries. These countries include Venezuela, Bolivia, Ecuador and Nicaragua. The results of their changed economic policies were not yet known in early 2007.

Economic Classes

Socialists and Marxists argue that IR and domestic politics are both structured by unequal relationships between **economic classes.** (This emphasis on classes denies the

Stalinism The system that prevailed during Stalin's rule in the Soviet Union (1924–1953), which was marked by totalitarian state control under the Communist party and the ruthless elimination of the regime's opponents on a massive scale.

economic class
A categorization of individuals based on economic status (which in Marxism, for example, is determined by one's relationship to the means of production as either an owner of capital or worker).

realist dichotomy between domestic and international politics.) The more powerful classes oppress and exploit the less powerful by denying them their fair share of the surplus they create. The oppressed classes try to gain power in order to seize more of the wealth for themselves. This process, called **class struggle,** is one way of looking at the political relationships between rich and poor people and between rich and poor world regions.

Marx used a particular language to describe the different classes in an industrial economy. The **bourgeoisie** is the class of owners of capital—people who make money from their investments rather than from their labour. Under capitalism, they are also the ruling class (sometimes in concert with politicians, military officers or other powerful allies). The *petty bourgeoisie* are small-time owners of capital, such as shopkeepers. They tend to think like owners and identify with the bourgeoisie. *Intellectuals* (including university professors and students) are treated ambiguously in most Marxist analyses; they often see the world from the perspective of the rich, yet sometimes are radicalized and side with the oppressed.

The **proletariat**—industrial factory workers—are considered potentially the most powerful class because their labour is necessary for the production of surplus. They are supposed to lead the revolution against the bourgeoisie, but factories have changed since the time of Marx: they are more capital-intensive, and workers are better paid. Various Marxist theories try to come to terms with these changes. Marxists do not agree on how to categorize increasingly important classes such as technical workers and managers. Some Marxist theorists describe them as a class unto themselves (a technical managerial class). The class of economically unproductive people at the bottom of society is the *lumpenproletariat*—prisoners, criminals, drug addicts and so forth. They are so down-and-out that they seldom become effective political revolutionaries.

One very important class in revolutions during the past century (contrary to Marxist expectations) has been *peasants*.[27] Marxists traditionally consider peasants backward, ignorant, individualistic and politically passive as compared with the well-educated and class-conscious proletariat. In practice, however, the successful revolutions of the global South have been primarily peasant rebellions (often led by Marxists talking about the proletariat). The largest was the Chinese revolution in the 1930s and 1940s.

According to Marxism, capitalism is only one stage of social evolution, preceded by feudalism and followed by socialism (when workers seize the state and use it to redistribute wealth) and eventually by communism (when everyone is equal and the state withers away). Each stage has its own form of politics and culture, which make up society's **superstructure.** This superstructure is shaped by the **economic base** of society—its mode of production, such as slavery, feudalism or capitalism.

In their particulars, Marxist analyses have been insightful about the operation and effect of capitalist relations of production, though not always successful in their predictions about the stages of social development, class alliances and the results of revolutions. Marxist revolutions have occurred in many states of the global South, and Marxism (along with other forms of socialism) remains a force in development and North-South relations.

class struggle The process in which the more powerful classes oppress and exploit the less powerful by denying them their fair share of the surplus they create. The oppressed classes try to gain power, rebel and organize in order to seize more of the economic surplus for themselves.

bourgeoisie In Marxist terminology, the class of owners of capital—people who make money from their investments rather than from their labour.

proletariat In Marxist terminology, the class of workers who must sell their labour power to capitalists in order to survive and whose labour is needed to produce surplus value; more specifically, industrial factory workers. It was considered the class that would spearhead the socialist revolution.

superstructure In Marxist terminology, the forms of politics and culture that are shaped by the economic base or mode of production (slavery, feudalism, capitalism).

economic base A society's mode of production, such as slavery, feudalism or capitalism.

---

[27] Barrington Moore, *Social Origins of Dictatorship and Democracy: Lord and Peasant in the Making of the Modern World* (1966; Boston: Beacon, 1993). James C. Scott, *Weapons of the Weak: Everyday Forms of Peasant Resistance* (New Haven, CT: Yale UP, 1986).

IMPERIALISM

Marx's theories of class struggle were oriented toward *domestic* society in the industrializing countries of his time, not toward poor countries or international relations. Traditional Marxists looked to the advanced industrialized countries for revolution and socialism, which would grow out of capitalism. In their view, the global South would have to develop through its own stages of accumulation from feudalism to capitalism before taking the revolutionary step toward socialism. What actually happened was the opposite. Proletarian workers in industrialized countries enjoyed rising standards of living and did not make revolutions. Meanwhile, in the less-developed global South, oppressed workers and peasants have staged a series of revolutions, successful and failed, over the past 90 years.

The Globalization of Class

Why did revolutions occur in less-developed rather than industrialized countries? The answer largely shapes how one sees North-South relations today.[28] Marxists have mostly (but not exclusively) followed a line of argument developed by *V. I. Lenin*, founder of the Soviet Union, before the Russian Revolution of 1917.[29] Russia was then a relatively backward state, and most Marxists considered a revolution there unlikely (looking instead to Germany).

imperialism The acquisition of colonies by conquest or otherwise. Lenin's theory of imperialism argued that European capitalists were investing in colonies where they could earn big profits, then using part of those profits to buy off portions of the working class at home.

Lenin's theory of **imperialism** argued that European capitalists were investing in colonies where they could earn big profits, and then using part of these profits to *buy off* the working class at home. The only limit Lenin saw was that after the scramble for colonies in the 1890s, few areas of the world were left to be colonized. Imperialist expansion could occur only at the expense of other imperialist states, leading to inter-imperialist competition and wars, such as World War I. Seizing on Russia's weakness during that war, Lenin led the first successful communist revolution there in 1917.

Lenin's general theory still shapes a major approach to North-South relations—the idea that industrialized states exploit poor countries (through formal and informal colonization) and buy off their own working classes with the profits. Through this *globalization of class relations*, world accumulation concentrates surplus in the rich parts of the world and away from the poor ones. Revolutions, then, should be expected in poor regions.

Many revolutionaries of the global South have sought to break loose from exploitation by European colonizers. After colonization ended, the United States—the world's richest country (with large investments in the global South and a global military presence)—became the target of revolutionaries agitating against exploitation in poor countries. In a number of countries, imperialists were thrown out (often violently, sometimes not) and revolutionary nationalists took power.

One of the most important such revolutions was in China, where Mao Zedong's communists took power in 1949 on a Leninist platform adapted to their largely peasant-based movement. Mao declared that "China has stood up"—on its own feet, throwing off foreign domination and exploitation. At the same time in India, Gandhi's movement used a different means (nonviolence) to achieve similar ends—national independence from

---

[28] Anthony Brewer, *Marxist Theories of Imperialism: A Critical Survey* (Boston: Routledge, 1980). Vendulka Kubálková and Albert Cruickshank, *Marxism and International Relations* (Oxford: Clarendon, 1985).

[29] V. I. Lenin, "Imperialism the Highest Stage of Capitalism," *Essential Works of Lenin* (1916; NY: Bantam, 1966) 177–270. A.M. Eckstein, "Is There a 'Hobson-Lenin Thesis' on Late Nineteenth-Century Colonial Expansion?" *Economic History Review* XLIV, 4 (1991): 297–318.

colonialism. Indonesia threw out the Dutch. Lebanon threw out the French. Cuba threw out the Americans. This pattern was repeated, with variations, in dozens of countries.

According to the revolutionaries in these countries, exploitation by rich countries in the global South takes away economic surplus and concentrates the accumulation of wealth toward the rich parts of the world. By breaking free of such exploitation, developing states can retain their own surplus and begin to accumulate their own wealth. Eventually they may generate their own self-sustaining cycles of accumulation and lift themselves out of poverty.[30]

In reality, this approach has not worked well. A policy of autarky fosters growth for only a limited period of time, which then reaches a plateau (see p. 318). Within a single poor country, trade-offs arise between concentrating or distributing wealth. For former colonies, the realities of economic development after independence have been complex.

Not all Marxist approaches favour a policy of self-reliance after revolution. *Leon Trotsky,* a Russian revolutionary, believed that after the 1917 revolution Russia would never be able to build socialism alone and should make the spreading of revolution to other countries to build a worldwide alliance its top priority. Trotsky's arch-rival, Stalin, wanted to build *"socialism in one country,"* and prevailed (and had Trotsky killed).[31] Most revolutions since then, including China's, have had a strongly nationalist flavour.

The World-System

The global system of regional class divisions has been seen by some IR scholars as a **world-system** or a *capitalist world economy.*[32] This view is an elaboration of Marxist thinking (focusing on economic classes) and relies on a global level of analysis. In the world-system, class divisions are regionalized. Regions of the global South mostly extract raw materials (including agriculture)—work that uses much labour and little capital and pays low wages. Industrialized regions mostly manufacture goods—work that uses more capital, requires more skilled labour and pays workers higher wages. The manufacturing regions are called the **core** (or *centre*) of the world-system; the extraction regions are called the **periphery.**

The most important class struggle today, in this view, is between the core and the periphery of the world-system.[33] The core uses its power (derived from wealth) to concentrate surplus from the periphery, as it has done for about 500 years. Conflicts among great powers, including the two world wars and the Cold War, basically result from competition among core states over the right to exploit the periphery.

The core and periphery are not sharply delineated. Within the periphery, there are also centres and peripheries (for instance, the city of Rio de Janeiro compared with the Amazon rain forest), as there are within the core (such as New York City compared with

world-system theory
A view of the world in terms of regional class divisions, with industrialized countries as the core, poor global South countries as the periphery and other areas (for example, some of the newly industrializing countries) as the semiperiphery.

core The manufacturing regions of the world-system.

periphery The global South regions of the world-system that mostly extract raw materials (including agriculture).

---

[30] J. Ann Tickner, *Self-Reliance versus Power Politics* (NY: Columbia UP, 1987). Samir Amin, "Self-Reliance and the New International Economic Order," *Monthly Review* 29.3 (1977).

[31] Ernest Mandel, *From Stalinism to Eurocommunism: The Bitter Fruits of "Socialism in One Country,"* trans. Jon Rothschild (London: NLB, 1978). Irving Howe, *Leon Trotsky* (NY: Viking, 1978).

[32] Immanuel Wallerstein, *The Modern World-System,* 3 vols. (NY: Academic, 1974, 1980, 1989). Samir Amin, Giovanni Arrighi, André Gunder Frank and Immanuel Wallerstein, *Dynamics of Global Crisis* (NY: Monthly Review Press, 1982). André Gunder Frank, *World Accumulation, 1492–1789* (NY: Monthly Review Press, 1978). Sing C. Chew and Robert A. Denemark, eds., *The Underdevelopment of Development: Essays in Honor of André Gunder Frank* (Thousand Oaks, CA: Sage, 1996).

[33] Terry Boswell, ed., *Revolution in the World-System* (NY: Greenwood, 1989).

the Mississippi Delta or Toronto compared with the coastal towns and villages of Newfoundland). The whole global structure is one of overlapping hierarchies. The concentration of capital and the scale of wages form a continuum rather than a sharp division into two categories.[34]

semiperiphery The area in the world-system in which some manufacturing occurs and some capital concentrates, but not to the extent of the core areas.

In world-system theory, the **semiperiphery** is an area in which some manufacturing occurs and some capital concentrates, but not to the extent of the most advanced areas in the core. Eastern Europe and Russia are commonly considered to be semiperipheral, as are some of the newly industrializing countries (see pp. 455–458), such as Taiwan and Singapore. The semiperiphery acts as a kind of political buffer between the core and periphery because poor states can aspire to join the semiperiphery instead of aspiring to rebel against domination by the core.

Over time, membership in the core, the semiperiphery and the periphery changes somewhat, but the overall global system of class relations remains.[35] Areas once beyond the reach of Europeans, such as the interior of Latin America, became incorporated as periphery. Areas of the periphery can become semiperiphery and even join the core, as North America did. And core states can slip into the semiperiphery if they fall behind in accumulation, as Spain did in the late sixteenth and early seventeenth centuries. Because world-system theory provides only general concepts but not firm definitions of what constitutes the core, semiperiphery and periphery, it is hard to say exactly which states belong to each category.[36]

Actual patterns of world trade support world-system theory to some extent. Table 12.3 shows the net exports (exports minus imports) of each world region for several types of goods. As the boxed numbers indicate, different regions specialize in exporting different kinds of goods. In 1997, the industrialized West fit the profile of the core, exporting more than it imported in machinery, chemicals and similar heavily manufactured goods. All the other regions imported more than they exported in such goods. By 2002, as the table shows, manufacturing had shifted to Asia—including China, Taiwan, Hong Kong and South Korea (but not Japan)—which also became a net exporter of heavy manufactured goods. Asia also has a niche in exporting light manufacturing, including textile production. This pattern fits the semiperiphery category. The industrialized West imports light manufactured goods. The shift of export-oriented manufacturing from the industrialized countries to Asia reflects globalization.

The industrialized West's net imports of energy are an enormously important aspect of trade and another indication of globalization. Asia now also imports energy. The Middle East specializes in exporting oil, and Russia, Latin America and Africa all export energy on balance as well. This is an extraction role typical of the periphery. Latin America has net exports in food, agricultural products and minerals—also typical of the periphery. These regions' patterns of specialization must be kept in perspective, however. All regions import and export all these types of goods, and the net exports listed in the table amount to only a small part of the world's total trade.

---

[34] Terry Boswell and Christopher Chase-Dunn, *The Spiral of Capitalism and Socialism: Toward Global Democracy* (Boulder, CO: Rienner, 1999). Christopher Chase-Dunn, *Global Formation: Structures of the World-Economy* (Cambridge, MA: Blackwell, 1989).

[35] Edward Friedman, ed., *Ascent and Decline in the World-System* (Beverly Hills, CA: Sage, 1982). James M. Goldgeier and Michael McFaul, "A Tale of Two Worlds: Core and Periphery in the Post–Cold War Era," *International Organization* 46.2 (1992): 467–92.

[36] William R. Thompson, ed., *Contending Approaches to World System Analysis* (Beverly Hills, CA: Sage, 1983). Terence K. Hopkins and Immanuel Wallerstein, *The Age of Transition: Trajectory of the World-System, 1945–2025* (London: Zed, 1996). Albert Bergesen, ed., *Studies of the Modern World-System* (NY: Academic, 1980).

Table 12.3 Commodity Structure of World Trade by Region
Net Exports (Exports Minus Imports) for 2002, in Billions of 2004 Dollars

| | Manufactured Goods | | Raw Materials | |
Region[a]	Machinery/ Chemicals[b]	Textiles	Agriculture and Minerals	Energy
North America/Western Europe/Japan	121	−123	−4	−235
Russia and Eastern Europe	−19	0	3	35
Middle East	−73	3	−4	136
Latin America	−20	6	10	33
Asia[c]	105	119	−6	−25
Africa	−45	1	1	57

[a]Regions do not exactly match those used elsewhere in this book. World total imports do not equal exports owing to discrepancies in data from national government.

[b]Machinery, metal manufactures, and chemicals.

[c]China, Taiwan, Hong Kong, and South Korea are here included in Asia.

Source: Calculated from data in United Nations. *World Economic and Social Survey 2004.* NY: United Nations, 2004, pp. 156–9.

Semiperiphery regions, which export manufactured products, are those—China and South Asia—that have been growing very rapidly in recent years. Africa, the Middle East and Latin America, the three regions that engage with the globalizing world economy primarily as raw material exporters, are growing more slowly. Having exportable natural resources would seem a big plus for an economy, but in fact the problems of basing economic growth on resource exports have been called the *resource curse*. Even in a middle-income country such as Chile, the quadrupling of the price of copper, its main export commodity, from 2003 to 2006 was a mixed blessing. Protesters demanded that billions of dollars be spent on social services for the poor, but the president (although a socialist) warned against spending what could be a temporary windfall. Meanwhile, high export earnings strengthened Chile's currency, making it harder for other industries to export their products.[37]

European Colonialism

For most countries of the global South, a history of having been colonized by Europeans is central to their national identity, foreign policy and place in the world. For these states— and especially for those within them who favour socialist perspectives—international relations revolves around their asymmetrical power relationships with industrialized states. Economic liberal approaches tend to pay less attention to history and focus more on present-day problems in the South, such as unbalanced economies, unskilled work forces and corrupt governments. Their focus, in other words, looks at problems *internal* to Southern states to explain underdevelopment. Critical approaches look to more *global* and

[37] Richard M. Auty, *Sustaining Development in Mineral Economies: The Resource Curse Thesis* (London: Routledge, 1993). Jeffrey Sachs and Andrew M. Warner, "The Big Rush, Natural Resource Booms and Growth," *Journal of Development Economics* 59.1 (1999): 43–76. Larry Rohter, "Chile Copper Windfall Forces Hard Choices on Spending," *The New York Times* 7 Jan. 2007: 4.

historical explanations. For critical approaches in particular, the North plays a central role in creating, maintaining and perhaps someday helping to solve poverty in the South.

Today's global disparities did not exist until a few centuries ago. Eight hundred years ago there were a variety of relatively autonomous, independent civilizations in the world, none of which held power over each other—the Sung dynasty in China, the Arab empire in the Middle East, the Aztecs and Incas in Central America, the African kingdoms near present-day Nigeria, the shoguns in Japan, Genghis Khan's society in Siberia and the feudal society of Europe (see pp. 24–26).

Between the twelfth and fifteenth centuries, Europe saw the rise of capitalism, a merchant class, science and stronger states. Technological improvements in agriculture, industry and the military gave Europe an edge over other world civilizations for the first time. European states conquered and colonized different world regions at different times (see "Imperialism, 1500–the Present" on pp. 27–28). Decolonization in some regions (such as the United States in 1776) overlapped with new colonizing in other regions, but most of the world's territory was colonized by Europe at one time or another (see Figure 12.1).[38]

Decolonization occurred only 25 to 50 years ago in most of Asia, Africa and the Middle East. In Asia, the most important British colony was India (which included today's Pakistan and Bangladesh). Until 1997, Hong Kong was a British colony serving as the gateway to China. British possessions also included Malaysia, Singapore, New Guinea, Australia, New Zealand and others. Almost all the Asian colonies became independent around the time of World War II and the following two decades.

In Africa, European colonies included Portugal, the Netherlands, Britain, France, Belgium, Germany and Italy. In the late nineteenth century, European states rushed to grab colonies (with France and Britain gaining the most territory), and Africa then became a patchwork collection of colonies without coherent ethnic or geographic foundations.

The Middle East came under European influence as the Ottoman Empire disintegrated in the late nineteenth and early twentieth centuries—and as oil became a key fuel. Britain and France were most prominent in this region as well. Present-day Israel and Jordan were British-run until 1948. Syria and Lebanon were French. Iraq's claims on Kuwait stem from Britain's creation of Kuwait as an independent territory. The Arab-Israeli conflict is strongly influenced by the history of British rule.

European conquerors treated their colonies as possessions that could be traded, seized as booty in wars or given as mandates to new rulers. For instance, the island of Guam in the Pacific was once Spanish territory, then German, Japanese and American.

Being colonized has a devastating effect on a people and culture. Foreigners overrun a territory with force and install their own government, staffed by their own nationals. The inhabitants are forced to speak the language of the colonizers, to adopt their cultural and religious practices and to be educated at schools run under their guidance. The inhabitants are told that they are inherently racially inferior to the foreigners.

White Europeans in the colonies of Africa and Asia were greatly outnumbered by native inhabitants but maintained power through a combination of force and (more importantly) psychological conditioning. After generations under colonialism, most native inhabitants either saw white domination as normal or believed that nothing could be done about it. This is another way in which the Gramscian notion of hegemony (see p. 69) was exercised. Whites often lived in a "bubble world" separated from the lives of local inhabitants.

---

[38] David Strang, "Global Patterns of Decolonization, 1500–1987," *International Studies Quarterly* 35.4 (1991): 429–54.

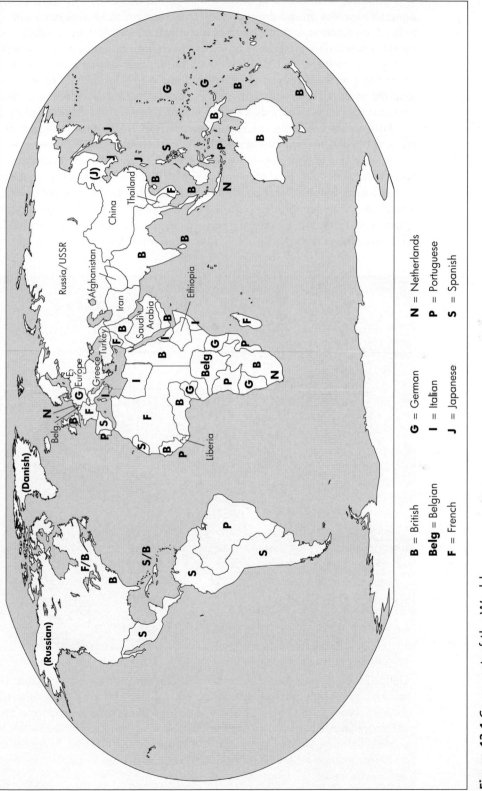

Figure 12.1 Conquest of the World

Former colonial territories of European states.

B = British   G = German   N = Netherlands

Belg = Belgian   I = Italian   P = Portuguese

F = French   J = Japanese   S = Spanish

Colonialism also had negative *economic* implications. The most easily accessible minerals were dug up and shipped away. The best farmland was planted with export crops rather than subsistence crops, and was sometimes overworked and eroded. The infrastructure that was built served the purposes of imperialism rather than the local population—for instance, railroads routed directly from mining areas to ports. The education and skills needed to run the economy were largely limited to whites. As a result, when colonies attained independence and many of the whites departed, what remained was an undereducated population with a distorted economic structure and depleted natural resources.

For economic liberals, the economic effects of colonialism were not all negative. It often fostered local economic accumulation (although controlled by whites). Cities grew. Mines were dug and farms established. It was in a colonial administration's interest to foster local cycles of capital accumulation. Much of the infrastructure that exists today in many countries of the global South was created by colonizers. In some cases, colonization united disparate communities into a cohesive political unit with a common religion, language and culture, thus creating more opportunities for economic accumulation. Local political cultures replaced by colonialism were sometimes themselves oppressive to the

FASHION STATEMENT
European colonialism worldwide promoted values and norms implying that a colonizer's culture was superior to the indigenous culture. Lingering effects remain in postcolonial societies. Evo Morales, Bolivia's first president born of indigenous rather than Spanish ancestry, makes a point of wearing a Bolivian alpaca sweater rather than a Western-style suit and tie. Here, Morales meets with Spain's prime minister, 2006. Almost all the countries of South America have recently elected leftist presidents committed to anticolonial values.

majority of the people. So, for economic liberals, colonialism established important economic infrastructure, while critical theorists see little that is positive coming out of colonialism. Mining and large-scale agriculture, for example, usually resulted in environmental degradation and massive displacement of local peoples.

Anti-Imperialism

Wherever there were colonizers, there were anti-colonial movements. Independence movements or revolutions throughout Africa and Asia gained momentum during and after World War II, when the European powers were weakened. Throughout the 1960s, a wave of successful independence movements swept from one country to the next as people stopped accepting imperialism as normal or inevitable (see Figure 12.2 on African decolonization).

Although many colonized countries gained independence around the same time, the methods by which they did so varied. In India, the most important colony of the largest empire (Britain), Gandhi led a movement based on nonviolent resistance to British rule, which resulted in Indian independence in 1947 (see "Nonviolence" on pp. 100–101). However, nonviolence failed in the subsequent Hindu-Muslim civil war, which split India into two states—India with mostly Hindus, and Pakistan (including what is now Bangladesh) with mostly Muslims.

The Chinese revolution of the 1930s and 1940s was the model of a successful communist revolution for decades thereafter. In Southeast Asia, communist guerrillas ultimately took power in South Vietnam, Cambodia and Laos, but lost in Thailand, Burma and Malaysia. In Latin America, Fidel Castro's forces took power in Cuba in 1959 after years of guerrilla war (though Castro declared the ideology of the revolution as "humanism," and neither communism nor capitalism). When Castro's comrade-in-arms, Che Guevara, tried to replicate the feat in Bolivia, he failed and was killed.[39]

Some colonies—for example, Algeria and Vietnam—won independence through warfare that ousted their European colonizers; others won it peacefully by negotiating a transfer of

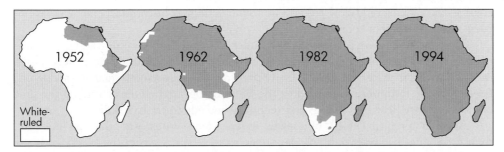

Figure 12.2 Areas of White Minority Rule in Africa, 1952–1994

Formal colonialism was swept away over a period of 40 years. However, postcolonial dependency lingers in many former colonies.

Source: Adapted from Andrew Boyd, *An Atlas of World Affairs,* 9th ed. (NY: Routledge, 1992) 91.

---

[39] Marifeli Pérez-Stable, *The Cuban Revolution: Origins, Course and Legacy,* 2nd ed. (New York: Oxford University Press, 1999) 71. Cynthia McClintock, *Revolutionary Movements in Latin America* (Washington, DC: U.S. Institute of Peace, 1998). Jorge Dominguez, *To Make a World Safe for Revolution: Cuba's Foreign Policy* (Cambridge, MA: Harvard UP, 1989). Forrest D. Colburn, *The Vogue of Revolution in Poor Countries* (Princeton NJ: Princeton UP, 1994).

power with weary Europeans. In Algeria, France abandoned its colonial claims in 1962 only after fighting a bitter guerrilla war. Some colonial liberation movements fought guerrilla wars based on communist ideology. The Viet Minh, for instance, defeated French occupiers in 1954 and established communist rule in all of Vietnam by 1975 after its war with the United States.

By the early 1990s, these communist revolutions seemed to have played themselves out—winning in some places, losing in others and reaching a stalemate in a few countries. The end of the Cold War removed superpower support from both sides, and the collapse of the Soviet Union and the adoption of capitalist-oriented economic reforms in China undercut some of the ideological appeal of communist revolutions.

Several Marxist revolutionary movements in Peru lingered after the Cold War, using brutal tactics of terrorism, which were answered with harsh repression by Peru's government. One group seized the Japanese embassy during a reception in 1996, and held hundreds of foreign hostages for months until a military attack ended the occupation.[40]

Throughout the various methods and ideologies of liberation movements in the global South, one common feature was reliance on nationalism for strong popular support. Nationalism was only one idea borrowed from Europe and used to undermine European control; others included democracy, freedom, progress and Marxism. Leaders of liberation movements had often gone to European universities. Under European control, many states developed infrastructures, educational and religious institutions, health care and military forces based on the European model. Europe's conquest of the global South thus contributed tools to undo their conquest.[41]

Postcolonial Dependency

If imperialism concentrated the accumulation of wealth in the core and drained economic surplus from the periphery, one might expect that accumulation in the South would take off once colonialism was overthrown. Generally this has not been the case. A few states, such as Singapore, have accumulated capital successfully since becoming independent, but others, including many African states, seem to be slipping even further behind, with little new capital accumulating to replace the old colonial infrastructure. Most former colonies are making only slow progress in accumulation. Political independence has not been a cure-all for poor countries.

One reason for these problems is that under colonialism the training and experience needed to manage the economy were often limited to white Europeans. A few native inhabitants went to Europe for university training, but most factory managers, doctors, bankers and so forth were whites. Often the white Europeans fled the country at the time of independence, leaving a huge gap in technical and administrative skills.

Another problem faced by newly independent states was that as colonies, their economies had been narrowly developed to serve the needs of the European home country. Many of these economies rested on the export of one or two primary products, called commodity concentration. For Zambia, it was copper ore; for El Salvador, coffee; for Botswana, diamonds; and so forth.

Such a narrow export economy would seem well suited to use a state's comparative advantage to specialize in one niche of the world economy, but it leaves the state vulnerable

---

[40] Ward Stavig, *The World of Túpac Amaru: Conflict, Community, and Identity in Colonial Peru* (Lincoln: U Nebraska P, 1999). Ellenbogen Gustavo Gorriti, *The Shining Path: A History of the Millenarian War in Peru* (Chapel Hill: U North Carolina P, 1999).

[41] Geoffrey Barraclough, *An Introduction to Contemporary History* (NY: Penguin, 1964), chap. 6.

to price fluctuations on world markets. Given North-South disparity in power, the raw materials exported by developing countries do not tend to receive high prices (oil, from the mid-1970s to the mid-1980s, was an exception). The liberal free trade regime based around the WTO only partially corrected for the North's superior bargaining position in North-South trade. And the GATT/WTO has allowed agriculture (exported by the periphery) to remain protected in core states (see pp. 332–335).

It is not easy to restructure an economy away from the export of a few commodities. Nor do state leaders generally want to do so, because leaders benefit from the imports that can be bought with hard currency (including weapons). In any case, coffee plantations and copper mines take time and capital to create, and represent capital accumulation—they cannot just be abandoned. In addition, local inhabitants' skills and training are likely concentrated in the existing industries. Furthermore, infrastructure such as railroads was most likely set up to serve the export economy. For instance, in Angola and Namibia the major railroads lead from mining or plantation districts to ports (see Figure 12.3). Political borders also may follow lines dictated by colonial economies. For example, an Angolan enclave (surrounded by Democratic Republic of the Congo) is home to the area's most profitable oil wells. A South African enclave, surrounded by Namibia, controls the best port in the area.

Newly independent states inherited borders that were drawn by foreign officers looking at maps in European capitals. As a result, especially in Africa, the internal rivalries of ethnic groups and regions made it very difficult for new states to implement coherent economic plans. In a number of cases, ethnic conflicts in countries of the global South contributed to civil wars, which halted or reversed capital accumulation.

In other instances, newly independent countries of Africa were little more than puppet governments serving their former colonizers. According to a recent memoir by a French official, France punished and even helped assassinate African leaders in the 1960s who opposed French policies. Those supporting France gave it open-ended permission for military intervention. French officials auditioned a potential president of Gabon before allowing him to take office, and the self-declared emperor of the Central African Republic (later accused of cannibalism) called President de Gaulle of France "Papa."[42]

Finally, governments of many postcolonial states did not function very effectively, creating another obstacle to accumulation. In some cases, corruption became much worse after independence (see "Corruption" on pp. 473–475). In other cases, governments tried to impose central

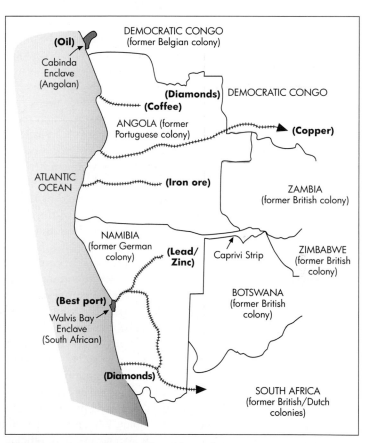

Figure 12.3 Borders, Railroads and Resources in Angola and Namibia

Despite the independence of Angola and Namibia, colonial times shaped the borders and infrastructure in the region.

[42] Howard W. French, "French Held the Strings in Africa," *New York Times* 28 Feb. 1995: A14.

control and planning on their national economy, based on nationalism, mercantilism or socialism.

In sum, liberation from colonial control did not change underlying economic realities. The main trading partners of newly independent countries were usually their former colonizers. The main products were usually those developed under colonialism. The administrative units and territorial borders were those created by Europeans. The state continued to occupy the same peripheral position in the world-system after independence as it had before, and in some cases continued to rely on its former colonizer for security.

neocolonialism
The continuation, in a former colony, of colonial exploitation without formal political control.

For these reasons, the period after independence is sometimes called **neocolonialism**—the continuation of colonial exploitation without formal political control (see p. xx). This concept is also used to refer to the relationship of the global South with the United States, which (with a few exceptions) was not a formal colonizer. And it also refers to the North-South international relations of Latin American states, independent for almost two centuries.

dependency theory
A Marxist-oriented theory that explains the lack of capital accumulation in the global South as a result of the interplay between domestic class relations and the forces of foreign capital.

Dependency Marxist IR scholars have developed **dependency theory** to explain the lack of accumulation in the global South.[43] They noticed that after World War II, Latin American states appeared to be on the verge of self-sustaining growth, in which a country's own capital would produce goods for its own markets. This did not happen, however. These scholars define dependency as a situation in which accumulation of capital cannot sustain itself internally. A dependent country must borrow capital to produce goods; its debt payments then reduce the accumulation of surplus. (Dependency is a form of international interdependence—rich regions need to loan out their money just as poor ones need to borrow it—but it is an interdependence with an extreme power imbalance.)

Dependency theorists focus not on the overall structure of the world-system (core and periphery) but on how a peripheral state's own internal class relationships play out. The development (or lack of development) of a state depends on its local conditions and history, though it is affected by the same global conditions as other countries located in the periphery. Recall that within the global South there are local centres and local peripheries. There are capitalists and a national government within a state in addition to external forces such as MNCs and governments of industrialized countries. These various forces can take on different configurations.

enclave economy
A historically important form of dependency in which foreign capital is invested in a global South country to extract a particular raw material in a specific place—usually a mine, oil well or plantation.

One historically important configuration of dependency is the **enclave economy,** in which foreign capital is invested in a country to extract a particular raw material in a specific place—usually a mine, oil well or plantation. Here, the cycle of capital accumulation is primed by foreign capital, fuelled by local resources and completes with the sale of products on foreign markets. Such an arrangement leaves a country's economy largely untouched except to give employment to a few local workers in the enclave and to provide taxes to the state (or line the pockets of some state officials). Over time, it leaves a state's natural resources depleted.

Angola's Cabinda province, located up the coast from the rest of Angola, is a classic enclave economy. Chevron pumps oil from a large field of offshore wells, with the money going to Angolan government officials who spend some on weapons for the civil war and

---

[43] Fernando Henrique Cardoso and Enzo Faletto, *Dependency and Development in Latin America*, trans. Marjory Mattingly Urquidi (Berkeley: U California P, 1979). Robert A. Packenham, *The Dependency Movement: Scholarship and Politics in Dependency Studies* (Cambridge, MA: Harvard UP, 1992). Mary Ann Tétreault and Charles Frederick Abel, eds., *Dependency Theory and the Return of High Politics* (NY: Greenwood, 1986). James Painter, *Bolivia and Coca: A Study in Dependency* (Boulder, CO: Rienner, 1994). Peter Evans, *Dependent Development: The Alliance of Multinational, State, and Local Capital in Brazil* (Princeton, NJ: Princeton UP, 1979).

Thinking Theoretically

Let us return to the example of genocide in Rwanda in 1994. We have discussed the theory that ethnic groups develop in-group biases that can lead to dehumanization of a rival group. Conservative realists might even say that violence of this type between ethnic groups is inevitable and natural, if deplorable. Since these conflicts are driven by "ancient ethnic hatreds," there is little the international community can do. Similar arguments were used, as we saw earlier, to justify the international community's feeble response in Bosnia.

Critical approaches provide different perspectives on the violence in Rwanda, pointing to different kinds of explanations and evidence. For starters, the position of a peripheral country such as Rwanda in the world-system can help explain its violence and social upheaval. Rwanda is one of the world's poorest countries, with a dense, fast-growing and extremely poor population, which is more than 90 percent rural. Typically for a peripheral state, Rwanda's main exports are tea and coffee; it imports machinery, fuel and other manufactured goods. Income from its exports pays less than half the costs of its imports. Before its recent troubles, the annual GDP was only US$1000 per person, and the land was depleted. Naturally such poverty drives a desperate struggle to survive.

Furthermore, dependency theories point to specific colonial histories as sources of explanation for the current problems of former colonies. Rwanda was colonized by Germany in the scramble for colonies by European powers at the end of the nineteenth century, then grabbed by Belgium as Germany lost World War I. Although the minority Tutsi group (about 10 percent of the population) had ruled the majority Hutu group for several centuries before colonialism, it was under Belgian rule that large-scale Hutu violence against Tutsis first erupted.

It might be hypothesized that Belgium's interest would be to undermine the strongest political powers in a colony and support rival political forces that would be dependent on Belgium. Ultimately, among other things, keeping Rwanda down in this way could keep coffee prices low for Belgian consumers (who would then, according to Lenin's theory, live more comfortable lives and not make trouble for their bosses and politicians). In 1959, the Tutsi king and hundreds of thousands of Tutsis were driven into exile (from where they fought back for 35 years). Rwanda under Hutu rule was then granted independence from Belgium in 1962. In the following decade, the government repeatedly massacred Tutsis in response to the efforts of their rebels in exile to return to power. As late as 1990, when Tutsi rebels advanced back into Rwanda, it was the Belgian army that showed up to save the Rwandan government—demonstrating the lasting nature of colonial ties. Ultimately, the government of Hutu extremists that perpetrated genocide against the Tutsis in 1994 must be understood in the context of Rwanda's colonial history. (This telling is of course highly simplified, but the point is that the colonial element, while not necessarily determinative of outcomes, must be a part of any useful explanation.)

pocket large sums in flagrant acts of corruption. The people of Cabinda, aside from a tiny number who work for Chevron, live in poverty with crumbling infrastructure, few government services, few jobs and recurrent banditry by unpaid soldiers. Inside the Chevron compound, however, U.S. workers drive on paved roads, eat American food and enjoy an 18-hole golf course. They spend 28 days there, working 12-hour days, then fly back to the United States for 28 days of rest. With the exception of travelling the 19 kilometres to the airport by helicopter, Americans rarely leave the fenced compound, which Chevron is believed to have surrounded with landmines.

A different historical pattern is that of nationally controlled production, in which a local capitalist class controls a cycle of accumulation based on producing export products. The cycle still depends on foreign markets, but profits accrue to local capitalists, building up a powerful class of rich owners. This class—the local bourgeoisie—tends to behave in a manner consistent with the interests of rich industrialized countries (on whose markets the class depends). They are not unpatriotic, but their interests tend to converge with those of foreign capitalists. For instance, they want to keep local wages as low as possible, to produce cheap goods for consumers in rich countries. Local capitalists, in alliance

Jobs in Nongovernmental Organizations

Summary

Jobs in NGOs provide personally rewarding experiences for those willing to work hard for a cause, but pay poorly and are hard to obtain.

Benefits and Costs Nearly 30 000 NGOs operate internationally, and their number grows daily. Thousands of individuals are interested in working in these organizations. Although all NGOs are different, many perform multiple functions: working in developing countries on a variety of issues; public outreach at home and abroad; lobbying governments to change their policies; designing projects to solve problems and attempting to find funding for their implementation.

Working for an NGO has many benefits. Workers often find themselves surrounded by others concerned with the same issues: improving the environment, protecting human rights, advancing economic development or promoting better health care. The spirit of camaraderie can be exhilarating and rewarding.

While working for an NGO can be extremely rewarding personally, it is rarely rewarding financially. Most NGOs are nonprofit operations that pay workers meagrely for long hours. Moreover, many smaller NGOs engage in a constant fight for funding from governments, think-tanks, private foundations or individuals. The process of fundraising can be very time consuming.

Despite the large number of NGOs and their relatively low pay and long hours, finding a job with an NGO can be difficult. The key is to be specific. Try to narrow your interests in terms of substantive areas (e.g., human rights, environment) and/or geographic region. Also think about whether you want to work in your own country or abroad. Positions abroad may be more rewarding, but the logistics of finding available openings can be daunting. A hint: subscribe to English-language newspapers in the countries where you are interested in finding employment or review the online versions if available (see "Weblinks" at the end of Chapter 1, p. 47). Just as in Canada, newspapers will often carry job advertisements placed by the local offices of national and international NGOs.

Skills to Hone NGOs are looking for self-starters. Most have little time and few resources for training. Basic office skills (e.g., computer expertise) are essential, but employees also need to perform a range of duties every day. Anything and everything is in your job description. Writing and communication skills are important, especially when fundraising is part of the job. Foreign language skills also matter, since many NGOs maintain or work with field offices abroad.

Often, NGOs ask potential employees to volunteer for a period while they train, before being hired. Increasingly, some companies place workers in an NGO or volunteer opportunity for a price. By paying to work, you can gain a probationary period in which to develop your skills and familiarize yourself with the operation so as to become efficient before going on the payroll. But there are obvious disadvantages to this approach, not least the lack of any salary.

Finally, in cities where NGOs cluster (e.g., Ottawa) personal networks play an important role in finding good opportunities. Workers often move from one organization to another. For this reason, many volunteer or accept jobs with NGOs not in their immediate area of interest in order to gain experience and contacts, which can help future career advancement.

Resources

Sherry Mueller. "Careers in Nonprofit and Educational Organizations" in *Careers in International Affairs,* 7th ed. Washington DC: Georgetown School of Foreign Service, 2003.

Richard M. King. *From Making a Profit to Making a Difference: How to Launch Your New Career in Nonprofits.* River Forest, IL: Planning/Communications, 2000.

Jennifer Bobrow Burns. *Career Opportunities in the Nonprofit Sector.* New York: Checkmark Books, 2006.

www.internships-usa.com

www.idealist.org

www.wango.org/resources/NGO_directory.htm

http://web.ncf.ca/dw413/rw_idlst.htm

http://www.acdi-cida.gc.ca/CIDAWEB/acdicida.nsf/En/NIC-56151554-QLN

http://www.cciorg.ca/

http://www.globalyouthnetwork.ca/

http://www.cwy-jcm.org/

http://www.afscanada.org/can_en/home

http://www.volunteer.ca/vol_contacts/voe_map/eng/flash_map.php

http://www.envision.ca/templates/resources.asp?ID=108

with political authorities, enforce a system of domination that ultimately serves foreign capitalists. This is another form of dependency.

After World War II a third form of dependency became more common—penetration of national economies by MNCs. Here the capital is provided externally (as with enclaves), but production is for local markets. For instance, a GM factory in Brazil would produce cars mostly for sale in Brazil. To create local markets for such manufactured goods, income must be concentrated enough to create a middle class that can afford them. This sharpens disparities of income within a country (most people remain poor). The cycle of accumulation depends on local labour and local markets, but because MNCs provide the foreign capital, they take out much of the surplus as profit.

According to dependency theory, the particular constellation of forces within a country determines which coalitions form among the state, the military, big landowners, local capitalists, foreign capitalists (MNCs), foreign governments and middle classes such as professionals and skilled industrial workers. On the other side, peasants, workers and sometimes students and the church form alliances to work for more equal distribution of income, human and political rights and local control of the economy. These class alliances and the resulting social relationships are not determined by any general rule but by concrete conditions and historical developments in each country. Like other Marxist theories, dependency theory pays special attention to class struggle as a source of social change.

Some think that under conditions of dependency, economic development is almost impossible. Others see development as possible under dependency, despite certain difficulties. Economic liberals argue that problems internal to countries of the global South explain their underdevelopment: corrupt governments, high government expenditures, poor educational systems and insufficient production geared toward the export market, among others. Critical theorists argue that it is the way Southern countries have been inserted into the global political economy that explains their underdevelopment, and that the legacies of colonialism in particular still shape what is possible in the global South. Chapter 13 examines practical strategies, suggested by both critical theorists and economic liberals, as means of promoting development in the global South.

Thinking Critically

1. In what ways does the North American Free Trade Agreement (NAFTA), discussed in Chapter 9, reflect the overall state of North-South relations as described in this chapter? How would economic liberalism and critical theory as general approaches to the theory of wealth accumulation differ in their views of the agreement?

2. The zones of the world economy as described by world-system theorists treat the North as a core and the South as largely a periphery. Can you think of exceptions to this formula? How seriously do such exceptions challenge the overall concept as applied to North-South relations generally? Be specific about why the exceptions do not fit the theory.

3. In North and South America, independence from colonialism was won by descendants of the colonists themselves. In Asia and Africa, it was won mainly by local populations with a long history of their own. How do you think this aspect has affected the postcolonial history of one or more specific countries from each group?

4. Suppose you lived in an extremely poor slum in the global South and had no money or job—but retained all the knowledge you now have. What strategy would you adopt for your own survival and well-being? What strategies would you reject as infeasible? Would you adopt or reject the idea of revolution? Why?

Chapter Summary

- Most of the world's people live in poverty in the global South. About a billion live in extreme poverty, without access to adequate food, water and other necessities.

- Wealth accumulation (including the demographic transition discussed in Chapter 14) depends on the meeting of basic human needs such as access to food, water, education, shelter and health care. States of the global South have had mixed success in meeting their populations' basic needs.

- War has been a major impediment to meeting basic needs and to wealth accumulation generally in poor countries. Almost all the wars of the past 50 years have been fought in the global South.

- Hunger and malnutrition are rampant in the global South. The predominant cause is the displacement of subsistence farmers from their land because of war, population pressures and the conversion of agricultural land into plantations growing export crops to earn hard currency, often at the insistence of international financial institutions like the IMF and World Bank.

- Urbanization is increasing throughout the global South as more people move from the countryside to cities. Huge slums have grown in the cities as poor people arrive and cannot find jobs.

- Women's central role in the process of accumulation has begun to be recognized. International agencies based in the North have started taking women's contributions into account in analyzing economic development in the South.

- Poverty in the South has led huge numbers of migrants to seek a better life in the North; this has created international political frictions. War and repression in the South have generated millions of refugees seeking safe haven. Under international law and norms, states are generally supposed to accept refugees but do not have to accept migrants.

- Moving from poverty to well-being requires the accumulation of capital. Capitalism and socialism take different views on this process. Capitalism emphasizes overall growth with considerable concentration of wealth, whereas socialism emphasizes a fair distribution of wealth.

- Most states have a mixed economy, with some degree of private ownership of capital and some degree of state ownership. However, state ownership has not been very successful in accumulating wealth. Consequently, many states have been selling off state-owned enterprises (privatization), especially in Russia and Eastern Europe.

- Marxists view international relations, including global North-South relations, in terms of a struggle between economic classes (especially workers and owners) that have different roles in society and different access to power.

- Since Lenin's time, many Marxists have attributed poverty in the South to the concentration of wealth in the North. In this theory, capitalists in the North exploit the South economically and use the wealth generated to buy off workers in the North. Revolutions thus occur in the South and are ultimately directed against the North.

- IR scholars in the world-system school argue that the North is a core region specializing in producing manufactured goods and the South is a periphery specializing in extracting raw materials through agriculture and mining. Between these are semiperiphery states with light manufacturing.

- Today's North-South gap traces its roots to the colonization of the countries of the global South by Europe over the past several centuries. This colonization occurred at different times in different parts of the world, as did decolonization.

- Because of the negative impact of colonialism on local populations, anticolonial movements arose throughout the global South at various times and using various methods. These culminated in a wave of successful independence movements after World War II in Asia and Africa. (Latin American states gained independence much earlier.)

- Following independence, states of the global South were left with legacies of colonialism, including basic economic infrastructures, that made wealth accumulation difficult in certain ways. These problems still remain in many countries.

Key Terms

developing countries   414
Millennium Development Goals   415
basic human needs   416
malnutrition   420
undernourishment   420
subsistence farming   421
cash crops   421
urbanization   421
land reform   422
migration   424
refugees   426
capital accumulation   429
economic surplus   429
consumption goods   431
investment   431
capitalism   432
socialism   432

Marxism   433
Stalinism   434
economic class   334
class struggle   435
bourgeoisie   435
proletariat   435
superstructure   435
economic base   435
imperialism   436
world-system theory   437
core   437
periphery   437
semiperiphery   438
neocolonialism   446
dependency theory   446
enclave economy   446

Research Navigator Question

Research Navigator.c⊕m
RESOURCES FOR COLLEGE RESEARCH ASSIGNMENTS

Use the Link Library for Sociology and explore some of the sites that focus on neocolonialism. Now use the Content Search in the History database and find scholarly articles using the keyword *colonialism*. In a small group discuss what these articles and websites tell you about the continuities and discontinuities between colonialism and neocolonialism.

Weblinks

The following links are a sampling of research centres, government departments and international organizations focused on North-South issues:

International Secretariat for Human Development:
http://www.yorku.ca/hddg

Maquila Solidarity Network:
http://www.maquilasolidarity.org

Mining Advocacy Network:
http://www.jatam.org/english/

Third World Network:
http://www.twnside.org.sg/index.htm

United Nations Development Programme:
http://www.undp.org

International Development

13

New Delhi bus stop, 2000.

WHAT IS DEVELOPMENT?

Chapter 12 discussed the situation in the global South and how it came to be, and this chapter examines the question of what to do about it. **Economic development** refers to the combined processes of capital accumulation, rising per capita incomes (with consequent falling birthrates), the increasing skills in the population, the adoption of new technologies and other related social and economic changes.[1] The most central aspect, especially for economic liberals, is the accumulation of capital (with its ongoing wealth-generating potential). Critical theorists would instead emphasize the distribution of wealth and quality of life indicators such as educational levels, nourishment, access to housing, clean water and the like.

The concept of development has a subjective aspect that cannot be measured statistically—the judgment of whether a certain pattern of wealth creation and distribution is good for a state and its people. A simple measure of economic development is the per capita GDP—the amount of economic activity per person.

economic development
The combined processes of capital accumulation, rising per capita incomes (with consequent falling birthrates), the increasing of skills in the population, the adoption of new technological styles and other related social and economic changes.

[1] Joseph Stiglitz and Gerald Meier, *Frontiers in Development* (NY: Oxford UP, 2000). Diane Stone, *Banking on Knowledge: The Genesis of the Global Development Network* (NY: Routledge, 2001). Robert H. Bates, *Prosperity and Violence: The Political Economy of Development* (NY: Norton, 2001). Uma Kothari and Martin Minogue, eds., *Development Theory and Practice: Critical Perspectives* (NY: Palgrave, 2002). Santosh Mehrota and Richard Jolly, eds., *Development with a Human Face: Experiences in Social Achievement and Economic Growth* (NY: Oxford, 1997). Robert J. Barro, *Determinants of Economic Growth: A Cross-Country Empirical Study* (Cambridge, MA: MIT P, 1997).

By this measure, we can trace the successes and failures of the South as a whole and, more importantly, its regions and countries. Most of the global South made progress in economic development in the 1970s, with real per capita GDP growth of almost 3 percent annually. This rate was a bit higher than in the global North (despite higher population growth in the South, which lowers per capita GDP). However, in the 1980s economic development came to a halt with the exception of Asia. Per capita GDP *decreased* from 1981 to 1991 in Latin America, Africa and the Middle East.[2] By contrast, China had 7 percent annual growth. In the 1990s, real economic growth returned across much of the South—about 5 to 6 percent annually as a whole, and even higher for China, compared with 2 to 3 percent in the global North. The 1997 Asian crisis curbed growth in that region, and the 2001 recession slowed growth globally, but China continued to grow rapidly, merely slowing somewhat during hard economic times. Thus, China stands out among the regions of the South as making rapid progress in economic development. All other areas of the global South had serious problems moving development forward.

In the new century, however, growth accelerated in the South and now outpaces the North in growth rate (see Figure 13.1 on p. 454). South Asia joined China with a rapid growth of 7 to 8 percent annually. Since China and South Asia together host the majority of the population in the global South, this development is very important. Other regions of the South have further to go, but this new growth shows that it is possible to rise out of poverty to relative prosperity. South Korea did so, followed by China, and India appears to be doing the same.

Rates of growth do not only vary between countries and regions, but also within countries. In countries with the greatest internal disparities in income, such as Brazil and Guatemala, the poorest fifth of the population lives on incomes one-tenth of the national average. The same is true in some Northern countries: in the United States, the income of the top 1 percent of families was 23 times that of median family income in 1995.[3]

The perspectives and prescriptions of economic liberalism and critical theory again diverge (see pp. 104–106) regarding how income is distributed and spent. Economic liberals tend to favour the concentration of capital as a way to spur investment rather than consumption (and to realize economies of scale and specialization). In line with liberalism, capitalists favour development paths that tie states of the global South closely to the world economy and international trade.[4] They argue that although such development strategies defer equity, they maximize efficiency. Once a developing state has a self-sustaining cycle of accumulation, it can better redress poverty in the broad population. To do so too early would choke off economic growth, in this view.

An alternative measure of development to per capita GDP is called the **Human Development Index (HDI).** The HDI measures a country's achievements in the areas of

Human Development Index (HDI) The HDI is an alternative measure of development to the gross domestic product (GDP). It measures a country's achievements in the areas of life expectancy at birth (as a measure of a long and healthy life), knowledge (including adult literacy and enrolment levels in primary, secondary and tertiary education) and standard of living (based on per capita GDP).

---

[2] South and East Asia here includes South Korea, Taiwan and Hong Kong. United Nations, *World Economic and Social Survey* (annual).

[3] United Nations, *Human Development Report 2003* (NY: United Nations, 2003). Paul Kennedy, *Preparing for the Twenty-First Century* (NY: Random House, 1993).

[4] William Easterly, *The Elusive Quest for Growth: Economists' Adventures and Misadventures in the Tropics* (Cambridge, MA: MIT P, 2001). Arthur McEwan, *Neo-Liberalism or Democracy? Economic Strategy, Markets, and Alternatives for the 21st Century* (NY: Zed/St. Martin's, 1999). Christopher Colclough and James Manor, eds., *States or Markets? Neo-Liberalism and the Development Policy Debate* (NY: Oxford UP, 1991).

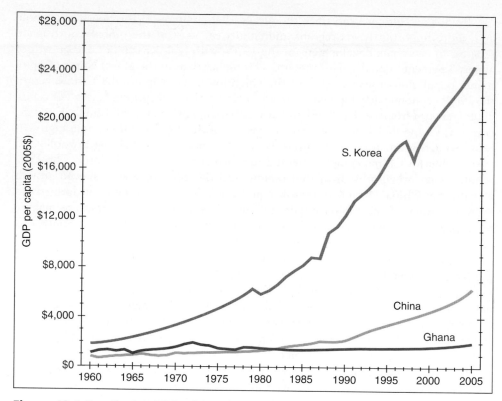

Figure 13.1 Per Capita GDP of South Korea, China and Ghana

Source: Based on Penn World Tables and World Bank and IMF data.

life expectancy at birth (as a measure of a long and healthy life), knowledge (including adult literacy and enrolment levels in primary, secondary and tertiary education) and standard of living (based on per capita GDP). The United Nations Development Programme (UNDP) publishes annual Human Development Reports that compare national HDI rankings. Using a broader scale than per capita GDP addresses some of the concerns raised by critical theorists about the distribution of wealth and quality of life indicators. While Nordic countries tend to be ranked high and most African countries quite low, many countries of the Middle East belong to high or medium human development categories (countries such as Kuwait and Qatar have high HDI measures; Libya, Saudi Arabia and Iran are in the middle categories). Others such as Cuba and Sri Lanka, with high literacy and life expectancy rates, compare favourably with countries like the United States (which despite high GDP per capita has enormous inequality between rich and poor, with some 32.9 million people living in absolute poverty in 2001).[5]

The same kinds of disagreement between critical theorists and economic liberals apply broadly to the world's development as a whole. From an economic liberal perspective, the North-South gap is a stage of world development in which capital accumulation is concentrated in the North. This unequal concentration creates faster economic growth,

---

[5] Ananya Mukherjee-Reed, "Human Development," *International Encyclopedia of Public Policy: Governance in a Global Age* (Routledge: London & New York, 2004). See also A.K. Sen, *Development as Freedom* (NY: Anchor, 1999).

which will ultimately bring more wealth to the South (a "trickle-down" approach). There is no practical way, in this view, to shift wealth from the North to the South without undermining the free market economics responsible for global economic growth.

In contrast, critical theorists argue that meaningful development should improve the position of the whole population and of the poor—sooner rather than later. Thus, critical theorists tend to advocate a more equitable distribution of wealth; they dispute the idea that greater equity will impede efficiency or slow economic growth. Rather, by raising incomes among the poor, a strategy based on equity will speed up the demographic transition and lead more quickly to sustained accumulation. Such a strategy seeks to develop a state's economy from the bottom up instead of the top down.

On a global level, critical theorists do not see the North-South disparities as justified by global growth benefits. They favour political actions to shift income from North to South in order to foster economic growth in the South. Such redistribution, in this view, would create faster, not slower, global economic growth that is balanced and stable.

In reality, most states in the South use a mix of the two strategies in their economic policies, as do industrialized states in shaping their roles in development. Welfare capitalism, practised by most industrialized states, distributes enough wealth to meet the basic needs of many while letting most wealth move freely in capitalist markets. Such a mix is harder to achieve in a state of the global South, where the smaller total amount of wealth may force a choice between welfare and capitalism.

The economic liberal theory that unequal income distributions are related to higher economic growth is only weakly supported by empirical evidence. Many states with fairly equitable income distributions have high growth rates (including South Korea, Taiwan, Singapore and Hong Kong); many with unequal distributions have grown slowly if at all (Zambia, Argentina and Ghana). There are also cases of relatively equitable countries that grow slowly (India) and inequitable ones that grow rapidly (Malaysia).

EXPERIENCES

The different levels of growth in various areas of the global South (whether measured by GDP or HDI) indicate that a single, simplified model of the South does not apply to all countries. One must consider the varied experiences of different countries as they try different approaches to development.

The Newly Industrializing Countries

One group of states in the global South has received considerable attention from development economists and scholars of IR. Called the **newly industrializing countries (NICs)**, these states have achieved self-sustaining capital accumulation, with impressive economic growth.[6] These semiperiphery states, which export light manufactured goods, posted strong economic growth in the 1980s and early 1990s (see "The World-System" on pp. 437–439). They encountered serious problems in the late 1990s because growth had been pushed too

newly industrializing countries (NICs) States of the global South that have achieved self-sustaining capital accumulation, with impressive economic growth.

---

[6] Alice Amsden, *The Rise of the "Rest": Challenges to the West from Late-Industrializing Economies* (NY: Oxford UP, 2001). Stephan Haggard, *Pathways from the Periphery: The Politics of Growth in the Newly Industrializing Countries* (Ithaca, NY: Cornell UP, 1990). Stephan Haggard, *Developing Nations and the Politics of Global Integration* (Washington, DC: Brookings, 1995).

fast with overly idealistic loans, speculative investments and corrupt deals (the 1997 financial crisis is described on pp. 361–363), but the NICs quickly resumed growth and have developed much further and faster than most of the global South.

The most successful NICs are the **"four tigers"** or **"four dragons"** of East Asia: South Korea, Taiwan, Hong Kong and Singapore. Each has succeeded in developing particular sectors and industries that are competitive in world markets.[7] These sectors and industries can create enough capital accumulation within each country to raise income levels not just among the small elite but across the population more broadly. However, income is not equitably distributed, and the NICs also tend to depend on quite authoritarian forms of government, which sometimes take a direct role in business decisions and impose severe restrictions on trade union activity and any forms of protest against the state.

Many countries of the global South have tried to apply the model of the NICs, but so far few have succeeded. Most poor states remain mired in poverty, with as many failures as successes. Scholars do not know whether the success of the NICs can eventually be replicated throughout the world. An important unanswered question has been whether authoritarianism is a necessary feature of their success.

"four tigers"/"four dragons" The most successful newly industrialized areas of East Asia: South Korea, Taiwan, Hong Kong and Singapore.

A "TIGER"

Singapore is one of the "four tigers" (with Hong Kong, Taiwan and South Korea). Even after the setback of a 1997 financial crisis, their growth has made them prosperous by the standards of the global South. Other countries are trying to emulate the success of these NICs, but no single, simple lesson applicable to other states has emerged.

[7] Ryoshin Minami, Kwan S. Kim and Malcolm Falkus, eds., *Growth, Distribution, and Political Change: Asia and the Wider World* (NY: St. Martin's, 1999). Robert Wade, *Governing the Market: Economic Theory and the Role of Government in East Asian Industrialization* (Princeton, NJ: Princeton UP, 1992).

South Korea, with iron and coal resources, developed competitive steel and automobile industries that export globally, creating a trade surplus (see "Balance of Trade" on p. 315). For example, Hyundai cars and trucks, sold in Canada and other countries, are produced by the giant South Korean MNC Hyundai. The state has been strongly involved in industrial policy, trying to promote and protect such industries. By the mid-1990s, South Korea had an income level per capita equivalent to that of Spain; Korean companies began to move manufacturing operations to Britain where production costs were lower. In 2004, South Korea and Canada announced plans to open up bilateral free trade negotiations, and by April 2007 they had conducted 10 such meetings, focusing on such issues as cross-border trade in services, financial services, investment, government procurement, intellectual property and e-commerce. Canadian-South Korean merchandise trade stood at $9 billion annually as of 2006 (Canada exported $3.3 billion and imported approximately $5.8 billion), and advocates of free trade argued that there were many benefits associated with establishing a free trade agreement with South Korea. Auto workers unions, however, raised concerns about the impact of such an agreement on Canadian employment in the automobile sector.[8]

Taiwan also has a strong state industrial policy. It specializes in the electronics and computer industries, in which Taiwanese products are very successful worldwide, and in other light manufacturing. Taiwan holds one of the world's largest hard-currency reserves.

Hong Kong—controlled by China since 1997—also has world-competitive electronics and other light industries, but its greatest strengths are in banking and trade—especially trade between southern China and the rest of the world. Hong Kong is a small territory with some of the world's highest real estate prices and great internal disparities of wealth. Its rich neighbourhoods are jammed with high-rise office buildings and expensive apartments, and Hong Kong is a financial centre for much of Asia.

Singapore is a trading city located at the tip of the Malaysian peninsula—convenient to the South China Sea, the Indian Ocean and Australia. Singapore has developed niches in light manufacturing, and like Hong Kong has attracted MNCs to locate their headquarters there. Canada is involved in negotiations with Singapore to establish a free trade agreement, though progress seems slower than in the discussions with South Korea. In 2005, Canadian merchandise exports to Singapore totalled some $637 million, while Canada imported $973 million.

For different reasons, each of these states holds a somewhat unusual political status in the international system. South Korea and Taiwan are hotspots of international conflict. South Korea and North Korea are separate states in practice, but have not recognized each other since fighting the Korean War from 1950 to 1953. Taiwan is formally part of China, but in practice operates independently. Both South Korea and Taiwan came under the U.S. security umbrella during the Cold War. Both were militarized, authoritarian states intolerant of dissent, although they later became democratic. U.S. spending in East Asia during the Cold War benefited South Korea and Taiwan. In these cases military conflict did not impede development; in fact, their geo-strategic significance to the United States benefited them significantly.

---

[8] Foreign Affairs and International Trade Canada, "Regional and Bilateral Initiatives: Canada-Korea Free Trade Agreement Negotiations," available at http://www.international.gc.ca/tna-nac/RB/korea-en.asp. Julian Bertram, "Canada-South Korea free trade talks a non-starter with auto sector," Canadian Press, 18 April 2007, available at http://www.bilaterals.org/article.php3?id_article=7936.

START YOUR ENGINES
China's rapid economic growth has dramatically raised incomes, especially for its growing middle class. These successes followed China's opening to the world economy and adoption of market-oriented reforms. China is emerging as a major producer and consumer of automobiles, and even luxury imported cars like these in 2003 are being bought by China's newly rich.

Hong Kong and Singapore have a different political profile. They are both former British colonies. They are more city-states than nation-states, and their cities are trading ports and financial centres. Although not as repressive or militarized as South Korea and Taiwan during the Cold War era, Hong Kong and Singapore were not democracies either. Hong Kong was ruled by a British governor (and since 1997 by the government in Beijing), Singapore by a dominant individual (who once banned sales of the *Asian Wall Street Journal,* hardly a radical newspaper, after it criticized him). Criticisms against state policy by citizens of both Hong Kong and Singapore are still highly restricted.

Beyond the "four tigers," other Southeast Asian countries have tried, since the 1980s, to follow in their footsteps. These include Thailand, Malaysia and Indonesia. Since their experiences vary, they are discussed below with other Asian economies. It is unclear whether there are general lessons to be learned from the success of the "four tigers." Hong Kong and Singapore are small trading cities located at the intersection of industrialized and third world regions (Japan/Pacific, South Asia and China). There are few equivalents elsewhere in the global South.

The Chinese Experience

Very few people of the global South live in NICs. The largest, South Korea, has approximately 50 million people. China's population is more than 20 times its size. Size alone makes China's efforts to generate self-sustaining accumulation worthy of study. It has also been one of the fastest-growing developing economies in the world, with average annual growth rates of over 9 percent over 25 years. China is Canada's second-largest trading partner and generates some 13 percent of world economic output in terms of purchasing parity, second only to the U.S. It is the world's largest consumer of commodities including copper, coal, steel and coal and one of the largest consumers of oil, second only to the U.S.[9]

Between the communist victory of 1949 and the Cultural Revolution of the late 1960s, Chinese economic policy emphasized national self-sufficiency and communist ideology. The state controlled all economic activity through central planning and state ownership. An "iron rice bowl" policy guaranteed basic food needs to all Chinese citizens (at least in theory).

After Mao died in 1976, China instituted economic reforms under Deng Xiaoping and transformed its southern coastal provinces (near Hong Kong and Taiwan) into **free economic zones** open to foreign investment and run on capitalist principles. Peasants work their own fields instead of collective farms and "get rich" (by Chinese standards) if they do well. Entrepreneurs start companies, hire workers and generate profits. Foreign investment has flooded into southern China, taking advantage of its location, cheap labour and relative political stability. Other areas of China have gradually opened up to capitalist principles as well. The state now requires more industries to turn a profit and gives more initiative to managers to run their own companies and spend the profits as they see fit. Economic growth has been rapid since these policies were instituted and standards of living are rising substantially.

free economic zones
The southern coastal provinces of China that were opened to foreign investment and run on capitalist principles with export-oriented industries in the 1980s and 1990s.

However, China is also recreating some of the aspects of capitalism that Mao's revolutionaries overturned. New class disparities are emerging, with rich entrepreneurs driving fancy imported cars while poor workers find themselves unemployed (earlier, socialism guaranteed everyone employment despite reduced efficiency). Unprofitable state-owned industries laid off 10 million workers in the 1990s, with more expected each year. In the countryside, areas bypassed by development still host 200 million desperately poor Chinese peasants. Social problems such as prostitution have returned, as have economic problems such as inflation. Most frustrating for ordinary Chinese is the widespread official corruption accompanying the get-rich atmosphere.

Popular resentment over such problems as inflation and corruption led industrial workers and even government officials to join students in antigovernment protests at Beijing's Tiananmen Square in 1989. Authorities used the military to violently suppress the protests, killing hundreds of people and signalling their determination to maintain tight political control while economic reform proceeded. This policy of combining economic reform with political orthodoxy was reaffirmed at the Party Congress in 1992 and again in 1997 and 2002.

The Information Revolution
China and the Net

China is emerging as a more globally oriented great power, one that can put astronauts in space, stabilize Asian financial crises and join the World Trade Organization. China's leaders need the internet to connect with the world economy, yet fear its political impacts. Can China open to the world as a great trading power without letting information in and out freely? Will new information channels affect China's form of government?

To explore this question, go to www.pearsoned.ca/goldstein.

---

[9] Paul Evans, "Canada, Meet Global China," *International Journal* 61.2 (Spring 2006): 283–97. Wendy Dobson, "China's Economic Transformation: Global and Canadian Implications," *International Journal* 61.2 (Spring 2006): 299–312.

China's leaders felt vindicated by subsequent economic performance. Foreign investors returned quickly after the political disruption of 1989, and economic growth roared ahead at 12 percent per year from 1992 to 1994. By 1997, Shanghai's mayor estimated that his city alone was using 18 percent of the world's construction cranes.[10] Since its currency was not convertible, China weathered the 1997 Asian financial crisis despite widespread problems with bad bank loans, money-losing state industries and corruption.

MNCs' foreign investments primed rapid growth in Chinese exports—to $250 billion in 2000 and nearly $1 trillion in 2006. In the coming years, China is poised to join the United States, Japan and Germany as a major automobile exporter. China's WTO membership has accelerated these trends since 2001.

By 2006, under a new generation of Chinese leaders led by President Hu Jintao, China had continued rapid economic growth (close to 10 percent annually) year after year with the help of large government infrastructure expenditures. President Hu consolidated his position in 2004 as his predecessor relinquished control of the military. Hu's top priority is to address the growing inequality between the country's newly rich strata and the hundreds of millions left in poverty in the countryside or laid off from jobs in state-owned industries in the cities (along with migrants from the countryside who cannot find work in the cities). In rural villages, hundreds of "mass incidents of unrest" took place every day in 2004, ranging from protests to full-scale riots put down by lethal force as peasants reacted to land seizures, taxes, pollution and corruption by local officials. The government suppressed news of these protests in the mass media and over the internet.

China's 2001 membership in the WTO raises new questions about how the ongoing opening of the Chinese economy to the world can coexist with continued political authoritarianism under communist rule. China's hundreds of millions of new internet users and cell phone subscribers will be able to communicate with overseas partners, monitor shipments and follow economic trends globally. They will also be able to bypass government-controlled sources of political information. Some observers expect economic integration in an information era to inexorably open up China's political system and lead to democratization, whereas others think that as long as Chinese leaders deliver economic growth, the population will have little appetite for political change.

China's economic success has given it more prestige in the international system and a more global perspective on international relations far from China's borders. From 2004 to 2006, President Hu and other Chinese leaders made high-profile visits to resource-rich areas of the global South, notably Africa and Latin America, making large-scale deals for minerals and energy to fuel China's growth while boosting China's foreign aid to these areas. In 2007, China announced $3 billion in preferential loans to Africa which, China emphasized, "carry no political conditions" (unlike Western loans, which often demand such policies as respect for human rights or fighting corruption). Several months earlier, China hosted a meeting of 48 African leaders. In recognition of China's new importance in the world economy, the G7 leading economies invited China to meet with them—a possible first step toward membership in the G7 (though China has been cool to full membership). China also has close economic ties with other Asian countries

---

[10] Nicholas R. Lardy, *China's Unfinished Economic Revolution* (Washington, DC: Brookings, 1998). Kenneth Lieberthal, *Governing China* (NY: Norton, 1995). Robert G. Kaiser, "China Rising: Is America Paying Attention?" *Washington Post* 26 Oct. 1997: C1.

🌐 Thinking Theoretically

China's economic growth in the 1980s and 1990s stands out (along with a few other East Asian countries) from the pattern of sluggish development (if any) elsewhere in the global South. Several different explanations can be offered for China's success. One is that China's traditional Confucian culture (shared to some extent by its East Asian neighbours) provides the discipline and social cohesion that allow rapid economic development and relative political stability. (China's path, then, would not apply to other areas of the global South.) The trouble with this explanation is that China's cultural traditions have been fairly fixed from decade to decade, yet its politics have careened from civil war to totalitarian stability to Cultural Revolution to reformism, and its economic development has varied from the disaster of the Great Leap Forward in the 1950s to the success of market socialism since the 1980s.

A more liberal approach—and the now-dominant one for explaining China's success—emphasizes the effect of market-oriented reforms in opening the way for rapid growth and rising incomes. Since liberals tend to favour open economies and free trade, they make much of the fact that when China moved its economic system in these directions, growth picked up rapidly. This explanation is appealing in that it can be widely applied to other countries of the South. However, the evidence that it actually works well across the board is not very strong. After all, economic reforms similar to China's have been implemented in many other countries, yet China's performance far exceeds most of those other cases. This line of thinking then suggests avenues for further refinement of this theoretical approach. For example, one could tease apart the various elements of China's economic reforms—ranging from agricultural reforms to privatization to allowing foreign investment and so forth—and see which ones coincide with other successful cases in the global South.

A different explanation can be found in world-system theory, a more critical approach. China can be viewed as moving from the periphery zone of the world economy to the semiperiphery (along with some East Asian neighbours). As we have seen, China's exports of light-industrial products support this characterization. In this theory, however, such a movement between zones does not change the overall structure of the world-system. Some regions, such as China, move up a zone; others like Russia and Eastern Europe move down a zone (from core to semiperiphery). The periphery itself must remain, and only a small part of the world can ever belong to the core. Thus, China's economic rise does not provide lessons or a viable path for states elsewhere in the global South. This theoretical approach, as compared with the liberal one, is somewhat vague in its predictions ("some move up, some move down"), but its main conclusion—that the success of one region does not indicate any overall convergence of the South with the North—is borne out by the data in Chapter 12. The global South is not, as a whole, catching up with the North. China is, so far, the exception to a persistent (even growing) North-South gap.

(see Figure 13.2 on p. 462) and its rising international standing is reflected in the selection of Beijing to host the 2008 Olympics.

For years it appeared that China's huge population would supply limitless cheap labour to foreign investors making goods in China. In recent years, however, its growth has begun to squeeze the available labour force and push wages somewhat higher. MNCs have begun to move some light manufacturing to other Asian countries with even cheaper labour, such as Vietnam.

It is unclear what lessons China's economic success over the past decade holds for the rest of the global South. The shift away from central planning and toward private ownership was clearly a key factor in its success, yet the state continued to play a central role in overseeing the economy (even more than in the NICs). These topics are being debated vigorously as China navigates its new era of rising prosperity and rising expectation, and as other poor states look to China's experience for lessons.

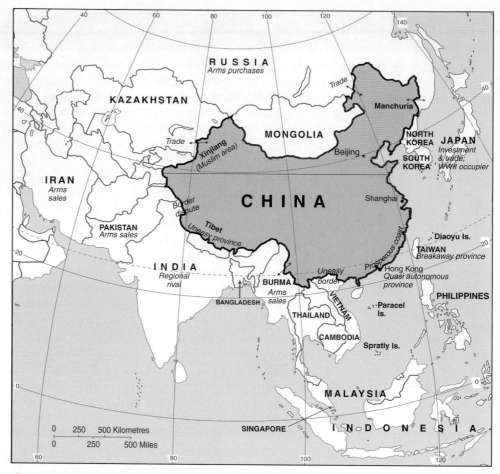

Figure 13.2 China's Neighbourhood

China's continuing growth is the leading success of economic development in the global South. China's future path will affect all of Asia.

India Takes Off

India, like China, deserves special attention because of its size. In the decade from 1996 to 2006, India's average annual growth rate exceeded 7 percent, with growth after 2003 accelerating to around 8 percent. India's one decade of success does not compare to China's nearly three decades, and India's GDP per person is still not much more than half of China's. However, India's successes have set it on a path toward what could be, in the coming years, a repetition of China's rise out of poverty.

Until recently, India's economy was based loosely on socialism and state control of large industries but on private capitalism in agriculture and consumer goods. The state subsidizes basic goods and gives special treatment to farmers. Unlike China, India has a relatively democratic government, but a fractious one, with various autonomy movements and ethnic conflicts. Elections in 2004 forced out of government the long-standing ruling party, the Hindu-nationalist Bharatiya Janata Party, widely considered corrupt.

Indian state-owned industries, like those elsewhere, are largely unprofitable. The prime minister of India, Manmohan Singh, pledged increasing privatization of state-owned enterprises and growth rates of 7–8 percent per year. Three years into his term progress has been slow and inflation is rising (elections are expected in 2009). Privatization and steady growth is needed to attract more foreign investment, which has lagged behind other large countries of the global South. In the 1990s, China received many times the foreign investment that India did.

The 1991 collapse of the Soviet Union—India's major trading partner—threw India into a severe economic crisis that nearly caused it to default on its international debts. India sought help from the IMF and the World Bank and committed itself to far-reaching economic reforms such as reducing bureaucracy and selling money-losing state-owned industries (see "IMF Conditionality," pp. 481–484). In the era of globalization, India's niche in the world economy is in the service and information sectors. Although the service sector accounts for less than 30 percent of India's labour force (most of which is still in agriculture), it contributes 60 percent of GDP. Whereas South Korea specializes in exporting heavy manufactured goods and China in light manufactured goods, India specializes in exporting information products such as software and telephone call centre services. Each country uses its labour force to add value to products that are exported worldwide, especially to the large American market. In India's case the labour force is well educated and speaks English. India also uses its location to its advantage by working during the nighttime hours in North America. Software companies can hand off projects daily for the India shift to work on overnight, and North American hospitals can send medical notes for overnight transcription. MNCs widely use India's labour force to answer phone calls from around the world, such as technical support calls for a company's products.

Other Experiments

Other sizeable states in the global South have pursued various development strategies, with mixed successes and failures. There is much variation in income level within the large countries of the South. The five highest-income countries (Turkey, Iran, Thailand, Mexico and Brazil) come from three of the four regions and are growing at 3–6 percent. At 7–9 percent, the fastest growing countries (India, Vietnam, Ethiopia and Democratic Congo) were at the lower end of the income scale. Clearly China is developing faster than the other 15 large countries of the global South, although all posted solid growth with an average of 5–9 percent.

In Asia, the first three regions to try to follow the NICs were Indonesia, Malaysia and Thailand. *Indonesia* set a goal in 1969 to become an NIC by 1994. It fell short, but made some progress in attracting foreign investment. With 250 million people and a GDP per capita near India's, Indonesia's major assets are cheap labour (a minimum wage below 50 cents per hour) and exportable natural resources, including oil. However, Indonesia has had to import oil since 2004 because of decreasing production. The December 2004 tsunami set the economy back, and inflation hit 13 percent in 2006. Reforms adopted in 2006 may help, if implemented. The position of the *Philippines* resembles that of Indonesia. After navigating the 1997 crisis smoothly, the Philippines developed a growth curve, currently about 5 percent a year, which is positive but not fast enough to address the widespread poverty in the country.

Malaysia also set out to follow closely in the footsteps of the "tigers." Although it also exports oil and gas, Malaysia focused its export industry heavily on electronics. It was hit hard by the information sector dot-com crash of 2001–2002, but came back with a growth rate of 5–7 percent a year in 2004 to 2006. With an average income per person of $13 000, Malaysia has successfully risen to a middle income level.

Thailand was often suggested as a potential "fifth tiger." It received enormous foreign investment in the 1980s (mostly from Japan) and created a sizeable middle class, but its growth masked serious problems that put Thailand at the centre of the 1997 financial crisis. Thailand recovered and posted strong growth, despite continuing problems with bad loans. A coup in 2006 showed troubling instability, however. Three months later the military government imposed controls on foreign investment (to curb currency speculation), and the stock market fell 15 percent in one day in December 2006 in response. With the military government emphasizing self-sufficiency rather than an export orientation, Thailand is somewhat less attractive for foreign investment.

Since 2001, several Southeast Asian countries have had to address problems of terrorism within their borders, and Indonesia faced simmering ethnic unrest on several islands (although the active secessionist war in Aceh province has ended). These factors prevented the economic development of would-be NICs in Southeast Asia.

Vietnam has found success similar to India's. Vietnam is a communist state following a reform model based on China's. Like China, Vietnam has few worries about terrorism and was largely unaffected by the 1997 crisis. Vietnam's growth since 1997 has averaged over 7 percent a year, accelerating to nearly 8 percent in 2005 and 2006. This period of fast growth follows liberalization of the economy, which had been held back by decades of devastating war and centralized communist rule. Vietnam, which exports textiles, joined the WTO in 2007. As with China, Vietnam did a good job of meeting basic human needs at very low average income levels, and has reduced extreme poverty despite remaining a poor country.

The large Asian states of *Bangladesh* and *Pakistan* are more deeply mired in poverty, have dimmer prospects for capital accumulation in the coming years and face problems with state bureaucracies and corruption. Nonetheless, they registered growth above 5 percent in 2006.

In Latin America, the major countries show higher income levels but lower growth rates than China and South Asia. *Brazil* and *Mexico* are the largest. Brazil built up a sizeable internal market by concentrating income in a growing middle and upper class, especially after a military coup in 1964. However, its cities are still ringed with huge slums filled with desperately poor people. In the 1980s, Brazil returned to democratic civilian rule and began economic reforms such as selling off unprofitable state-owned enterprises, promoting free markets and encouraging foreign investment.

Nonetheless, by the early 1990s, Brazil remained more than US$100 billion in debt (the largest foreign debt in the South). It had annual inflation of over 200 percent, causing the currency's value to fall drastically. The president was impeached in a corruption scandal. The positive side of this embarrassing episode for Brazil was a constitutional, civilian transfer of power. With faster economic growth and foreign investment, a bigger grain harvest and a substantial trade surplus, Brazil's primary problem by 1993 was inflation. The anti-inflation plan of finance minister Fernando Cardoso was so successful that he was elected president in 1995, and other countries tried to copy his methods. In the 1997 currency crisis, Cardoso was able to scare off currency speculators, though at the cost of a dramatic slowdown in Brazil's economy. Brazil received a US$41 billion IMF package in 1998, devalued its currency in 1999 and felt waves from next-door Argentina's financial meltdown in 2001. In 2002, the IMF provided a US$30 billion bailout loan, with few requirements for domestic reform because of worries that a financial collapse in Brazil would damage the world economy in a way that Argentina could not. The election of a leftist president, Lula da Silva, raised fears that free spending on social programs would undermine Brazil's financial position, but instead he reined in spending, brought down inflation and stabilized Brazil's financial position in 2003 at the short-term cost of economic recession. This belt-tightening lowered da Silva's popularity but improved Brazil's economic situation. Brazil grew about 3 percent in 2006, and has an average income of $8600 per person.

In Mexico, similar economic reforms were undertaken in the 1980s. Like Brazil, Mexico had pockets of deep poverty and a sizeable foreign debt. Unlike Brazil, however, Mexico had oil to export (a good source of hard currency, despite fluctuating world prices). Mexico has also enjoyed relative political stability, though corruption does exist. Leaders hoped NAFTA would accelerate foreign investment and create jobs and export opportunities. Mexico sold off more than US$20 billion of state-owned companies (sparing the strategic oil industry) to help lower its debt and bring down inflation. Assassinations and other political upheaval, including an armed rebellion in Chiapas that broke out in response to the NAFTA accord, complicated Mexico's development problems. In 1994 and 1995, Mexico's currency collapsed and standards of living for many consumers took a sharp drop. With help from the United States, Mexico undertook new economic reforms and began to rebuild the economy and restore international and domestic confidence. A reformist president, Vicente Fox, was elected from outside the long-standing ruling party in 2000 and a similarly minded president succeeded him after a contested election in 2006.[11] He faced a mass protest in 2007 when corn—a staple of the Mexican diet as tortillas—jumped in price after the United States, which supplies a quarter of Mexico's corn, began using a lot of it to make ethanol, driving the price up. In the 13 years since NAFTA, these upheavals have not been disastrous for Mexico, but nor have they brought a breakthrough. Mexico's economic growth has picked up after several years of sluggish growth from 2000–2003.

In Africa, *Nigeria* is the largest country and, with oil to export, one of the less impoverished. At $1400 per person, however, its income level is quite low, and corruption takes a steady toll on the economy. Nigeria seems to suffer from the "resource curse." Oil provides 95 percent of export earnings and pays two-thirds of the government's budget. In 1980, when oil prices were high, Nigeria began building a huge, Soviet-style steel plant, which leaders hoped would serve as the cornerstone of Nigerian economic development. In 1992, and US$5 billion later, the plant was ready to start producing steel. By 2003, with the steel complex still not in production, the Nigerian government signed an agreement with a U.S. company to take over management and provide billions of dollars in new foreign investment. The government brought in hundreds of Russian and Ukrainian experts to help, but the prospects for competitive steel production remain doubtful in the short term.

When world oil prices fell drastically in the 1980s, the country went into debt by US$35 billion. Corruption took a steady toll on the economy. This pattern of centralized industrialization under Nigeria's military government faces uncertain prospects at best, although oil exports provide continuing income.[12] Nigeria cancelled a planned experiment in democracy in the early 1990s, and a military dictatorship continued in power. African Americans began an unusual campaign to press for democracy in Nigeria in order to move Africa's largest country forward in both human rights and overall development. In 1995 Nigeria ignored international pleas and executed the popular leader of an oil-rich but impoverished region, Ken Saro-Wiwa. Finally, in 1999, the dictator died and his successor held elections in which a civilian president took power. Nigeria has enjoyed some political stability since then, but new ethnic conflicts have turned violent. Nigeria's economic condition remains fragile, though rising oil prices in 2007 may contribute to economic recovery.

---

[11] Nancy Neiman Auerbach, *States, Banks, Markets: Mexico's Path to Financial Liberalization in Comparative Perspective* (Boulder, CO: Westview, 2000).

[12] Kenneth B. Noble, "Nigeria's Monumental Steel Plant: Nationalist Mission or Colossal Mistake?" *New York Times* 11 July 1992: 3.

Elsewhere in Africa, matters hardly look better. The next largest countries, Ethiopia and Democratic Congo, are growing fast but starting from great poverty, with GDPs at or below $1000 per person. Democratic Congo is poised to recover from decades of war, but may need decades of growth just to regain its prewar income level. South Africa has a relatively high income ($13 000 per person) but tremendous inequality and high rates of HIV/AIDS. In the Middle East, *Israel* has developed economically in an unusual manner. It received sustained infusions of outside capital from several sources—German reparations, U.S. foreign aid and contributions from Zionists in foreign countries. This outside assistance was particular to the history of German genocide against Jews during World War II and the efforts of Jews world-wide to help build a Jewish state afterward. Few if any developing countries could hope to receive similar outside assistance (relative to Israel's small size). In common with other NICs, however, Israel maintained strong state involvement in key industries and carved out a few niches in world markets (notably in cut diamonds and military technology).

The small countries with large oil exports—such as *Saudi Arabia, Kuwait, Bahrain and the United Arab Emirates*—have done well economically. They are in a special class; their experience is not one that global South states without oil can follow. Iran began to grow robustly and to attract foreign investment after the Iran-Iraq War ended in 1988. Most of the economy is state-controlled, however. A reformist president of Iran opened new avenues to Western powers and their investment capital but lost power to conservatives, and U.S. sanctions have now been joined by UN sanctions.

Turkey has been fairly successful in developing its economy without oil revenues, but is a rare case. Like South Korea and Taiwan, Turkey was an authoritarian state for many years but has allowed political liberalization since the 1990s. It has developed under a Western security umbrella (NATO) and has received considerable U.S. foreign aid. Like Mexico, Turkey is trying to join its richer neighbours in the EU, and also hopes to develop strong ties with the five former Soviet Asian republics. A long-standing violent conflict hinders development in Turkey's Kurdish region. Turkey suffered recession in 2000 and 2001 and received a US$30 billion IMF bailout. Since 2003, Turkey's economy has grown solidly and its debt position has improved.

Egypt is mired in poverty despite substantial U.S. aid since the late 1970s. The state owns much of the industry, operates the economy centrally, imposes high import tariffs and provides patronage jobs and subsidized prices in order to maintain political power. A major portion of Egypt's foreign debt was forgiven after it helped the anti-Iraq coalition in the Gulf War, but Egypt remains highly indebted. Reforms in the 1990s brought economic growth, but remaining problems include high unemployment, a trade deficit and widespread corruption. Islamic militants have disrupted Egypt's economy (especially tourism) and politics in the past decade.

LESSONS

Clearly, the largest states of the global South are following somewhat different strategies with somewhat different results, but several common themes recur concerning trade, the concentration of capital, authoritarianism and corruption.

Import Substitution and Export-Led Growth

Throughout the global South, states are trying to use international trade as the basis of accumulation. For the reasons discussed in Chapter 9, a policy of self-reliance or autarky is at best an extremely slow method of building up wealth. Through the creation of a trade surplus, a state can accumulate hard currency and build industry and infrastructure.

One way to try to create a trade surplus, used frequently a few decades ago, is through **import substitution**—the development of local industries to produce items that a country had previously been importing. These industries may receive state subsidies or tariff protection. This might appear to be a good policy for reducing dependency—especially on a former colonial centre—while shrinking a trade deficit or building a trade surplus, but it goes against the principle of comparative advantage and tends to produce growth rates that plateau fairly quickly. Some scholars think that import substitution is a policy useful only at a very early phase of economic development, after which it becomes counterproductive. Others think it is never useful.

More and more states have shifted to a strategy of **export-led growth,** an approach used by the NICs. This strategy seeks to develop industries that can compete in specific niches in the world economy. These industries may receive special treatment, such as subsidies and protected access to local markets. Exports from these industries generate hard currency and create a favourable trade balance. The state can then spend part of its money on imports of commodities produced more cheaply elsewhere.

Export-led growth has risks, especially when a state specializes in the export of a few raw materials (see "Postcolonial Dependency" on pp. 444–449). It leaves poor countries vulnerable to sudden price fluctuations for their exports.[13]

The overall relationship between the prices of exported and imported goods—called the **terms of trade**—affects an export strategy based on raw materials. There is evidence that in the 1950s and 1960s, and again in the 1980s, the terms of trade eroded the value of raw materials, also called the declining terms of trade in raw materials and commodities. A state trying to create trade benefits by exporting such goods would have to export more and more over time in order to import the same amount of manufactured goods—a major obstacle to accumulation.

Because of both terms of trade and price fluctuations, states have looked to exporting manufactured goods rather than raw materials as the key to export-led growth. However, in seeking a niche for manufactured goods, a state of the global South must compete against industrialized countries with better technology, more educated work forces and much more capital. For example, Nigeria's steel exports are unlikely to provide the desired trade surplus (although South Korean steel did). Thus, countries of the global South need to be selective in developing export-oriented industrial strategies. It is not enough to subsidize and protect an industry until it grows in size; someday it has to be able to stand its own ground in a competitive world or it will not produce a trade surplus.

import substitution
A strategy of developing local industries, often conducted behind protectionist barriers, to produce items that a country had previously been importing.

export-led growth
An economic development strategy that seeks to develop industries capable of competing in specific niches in the world economy.

terms of trade The overall relationship between prices of imported and exported goods.

Concentrating Capital for Manufacturing

Manufacturing is a key factor in export-led growth and self-sustaining industrialization (home production for home markets). It is not surprising that states of the global South want to increase their own manufacturing bases and change the global division of labour based on manufacturing in the core and resource extraction in the periphery. A great obstacle in manufacturing is that capital is required to build factories at the outset. Most states in the South lack the funds to build competitive factories in technologically advanced industries.

---

[13] Willy Brandt et al., *North-South: A Programme for Survival* (Cambridge, MA: MIT P, 1980) 145.

To invest in manufacturing, these countries must *concentrate* whatever surplus their economies produce. Money spent building factories cannot be spent subsidizing food prices or building better schools. Thus the concentration of capital for manufacturing can sharpen disparities in income. A political price must often be paid in the short term for reducing public consumption, even in industrialized states. In states of the global South there is little margin for reducing consumption without causing extreme hardship. The result may be crowds rioting in the streets or guerrillas taking over the countryside.

The problem is compounded by the need to create domestic markets for manufactured goods. Because it is unlikely that a manufacturing industry in a poor country will be immediately competitive in world markets, a common strategy is to build the industry with sales to the home market (protected by tariffs and subsidies) before pursuing world markets. Home markets for manufactured goods are not generated by poor peasants in the countryside or unemployed youth in city slums. Rather, wealth must be concentrated in a *middle class* that has the income to buy manufactured goods.

The growing disparity of income often triggers intense frustration on the part of poor people, even those whose income is rising. (Political rebellion is fuelled by relative deprivation as much as by absolute poverty.) A common response to such problems is to crack down with force to stamp out the protests of the poor and of other political opponents of the government (see "Authoritarianism and Democracy" later in this chapter).

Such problems might be minimized by reducing the amount of capital that needs to be squeezed from a state's domestic economy. Capital for manufacturing can alternatively come from foreign investment or foreign loans, for instance. This strategy reduces short-term pain, but also reduces the amount of surplus (profit) available to the state in the long term. Another way to minimize the capital needs of manufacturing is to start out in low-capital industries. These industries can begin generating capital, which can in turn be used to move into somewhat more technologically demanding and capital-intensive kinds of manufacturing. A favourite starter industry is *textiles*, which is fairly labour-intensive, giving an advantage to countries with cheap labour, and does not require huge initial investments of capital. Many states in the South have built their own textile industries as a step toward industrialization. For this reason, many Northern states imposed high tariffs on textiles, which are among the least freely traded commodities. As of 2005, textile tariffs have been removed worldwide, and textile exporters in developing countries will now find both greater access to Western markets as well as intensified competition from China.

There are some problems with concentrating capital for manufacturing. One is that it creates conditions ripe for corruption (discussed shortly), a problem that is especially severe when authoritarian political control is used to enforce compliance with hardships that may accompany the concentration of wealth—currently an issue for China.

CAPITAL INTENSIVE
Foreign investment, international debt and domestic inequality can help concentrate the necessary capital for manufacturing. In recent years, microcredit—very small loans made directly to desperately poor people—has provided a more diffuse use of capital. These women in Bangladesh (1997) bought a cell phone with a loan and rented time on it to villagers.

An approach that received international attention in the 1980s is based on a Peruvian entrepreneur's analysis of the **informal sector** in Lima's economy—black markets (also called parallel markets or shadow markets), street vendors and other private arrangements.[14] These modes of business are often beyond state control and may not even show up in state-compiled economic statistics. Markets operate somewhat freely, and some scholars have begun to see such markets as the core of a new development strategy rather than large manufacturing industries.

A related approach to capitalization in very poor countries, growing in popularity in recent years, is **microcredit** (or *microlending*). Based on a successful model of the Grameen Bank in Bangladesh (which won the 2006 Nobel Peace Prize), microcredit involves giving small loans to poor people, especially women, to support economic self-sufficiency. Borrowers are organized into small groups and take responsibility for each other's success, including repayment. Repayment rates have been high, and the idea is spreading rapidly in several regions. In a high-tech twist, village women have begun using small loans to start businesses offering cellular phone booths (or huts) where people pay to make domestic or international calls. Rural farmers used phone time to find out market conditions before making a long trek to sell their products. Thus, bringing the information revolution to isolated villages raised incomes for both farmers and women, and the loans were repaid. Microcredit is now being applied on a macroscale. Tens of millions of families have received loans from thousands of institutions worldwide. Microcredit is the opposite of a trickle-down approach, instead injecting capital at the bottom of the economic hierarchy. A loan to buy a goat or cell phone may do more good, dollar for dollar, than a loan to build a dam.

Cartels

A **cartel** is an association of producers (or more rarely consumers, or both) of a certain product, formed to manipulate its price on the world market. It is an unusual but interesting form of trade regime, and one that has been used with limited success by developing countries in an effort to control the impact of fluctuating commodity prices on their economies, and to gain the most from their commodity exports. Producers are able to coordinate their actions so as to keep prices high. Cartels can use a variety of means to affect prices; the most effective of which is to coordinate limits on production by each member in order to lower the supply of the good relative to demand.

The most prominent cartel in the international economy is the **Organization of Petroleum Exporting Countries (OPEC).** Its member states control hundreds of billions of dollars in oil exports annually—about 60 percent of the world total and enough to significantly affect the price. (A cartel need not hold a monopoly on production of a good to be able to affect its price.) At OPEC's peak of strength in the 1970s, the proportion was even higher. OPEC maintains a headquarters in Vienna, Austria (which is not a member), and holds negotiations several times a year to set quotas for each country's production of oil in order to keep world oil prices in a target range. Saudi Arabia is by far the largest oil exporter, and therefore occupies a unique position in the world economy.

OPEC illustrates the potential that a cartel creates for serious collective goods problems. Individual members of OPEC can (and do) sometimes cheat by exceeding their production quotas while still enjoying the collective good of high oil prices. The collective

informal sector Those models of business, such as shadow markets and street vendors, operating beyond state control; some scholars see this sector as the core of a new development strategy.

microcredit The use of very small loans to small groups of individuals, often women, to stimulate economic development.

cartel An association of producers or consumers (or both) of a certain product, formed for the purpose of manipulating its price on the world market.

Organization of Petroleum Exporting Countries (OPEC) The most prominent cartel in the international economy; its members control over half the world's total oil exports, enough to significantly affect the world price of oil.

---

[14] Hernando De Soto, *The Other Path: The Invisible Revolution in the Third World* (NY: HarperCollins, 1989).

good breaks down when too many members exceed their quotas, as has happened repeatedly to OPEC, and world oil prices drop. (Iraq's accusations that fellow OPEC member Kuwait was exceeding production quotas and driving oil prices down was one factor in Iraq's invasion of Kuwait in 1990.)

OPEC may work as well as it does only because one member, Saudi Arabia, has sufficient oil to unilaterally manipulate supply enough to drive prices up or down. Saudi Arabia can take up the slack from some cheating in OPEC (cutting back its own production) and keep prices up. Or if too many OPEC members are cheating on their quotas, it can punish them by flooding the market with oil and driving prices down until the other OPEC members collectively come to their senses.

Consumers usually do not form cartels. However, in response to OPEC, the major oil-importing states formed their own organization, the *International Energy Agency (IEA)*, which has some of the functions of a cartel. The IEA coordinates the energy policies of major industrialized states—such as the maintenance of oil stockpiles in case of a shortage on world markets—in order to keep world oil prices low and stable. The largest importers of oil are the members of the G8 (large industrialized states). Considering the importance of oil to the world economy, and the existence of both producer and consumer cartels, the price of oil has been surprisingly unstable, with prices fluctuating over the years from barely above $10 per barrel to near $70. High oil prices in 2000 contributed to a world recession in 2001, which brought oil prices back down temporarily. By early 2006, with China driving up demand and continued instability in the Middle East, world oil prices neared $80 per barrel, dropping in early 2007 as a result of a decline in demand due to higher temperatures in parts of North America and Europe. Prices rose again at mid-year.

For a few commodities that are subject to large price fluctuations in world markets—detrimental to both producers and consumers—joint producer-consumer cartels have been formed. In order to keep prices stable, producing and consuming states use the cartel to coordinate the overall global supply and demand. Such cartels exist for coffee, several minerals and some other products. In the coffee cartel, Colombia argued in the late 1980s for a higher target price for coffee, so that Colombian peasants would have an incentive to switch from growing coca (for cocaine production) to coffee. The United States, as the major coffee-consuming state, would not agree to the proposal.[15] Coffee prices hit a 100-year low by 2002, forcing many coffee growers to switch to coca (or, in Africa, khat), before recovering modestly. NGOs have introduced fair trade certified coffee, guaranteeing farmers a price above their production costs through price booms and busts. By 2006, hundreds of companies sold fair trade certified products in North America, but whether fair trade coffee will address the various inequities involved in coffee production remains an open question.[16]

In general, the idea of cartels runs counter to liberal economics because cartels are deliberate efforts to distort free markets. However, for countries of the global South that rely on commodity exports and suffer price fluctuations or declining terms of trade, the creation of a cartel can be a means to take control of the impact of market forces on commodity prices. Cartels are not usually as powerful as market forces in determining overall world price levels: too many producers and suppliers exist, and too many substitute goods can replace ones that become too expensive, for a cartel to corner the market. The exceptions, such as OPEC, are rare.

---

[15] Robert H. Bates, *Open-Economy Politics: The Political Economy of the World Coffee Trade* (Princeton, NJ: Princeton UP, 1997).

[16] Gavin Fridell, *Fair Trade Coffee: The Prospects and Pitfalls of Market-Driven Social Justice* (Toronto: University of Toronto Press, 2007).

Authoritarianism and Democracy

Several decades ago, many scholars expected that states of the global South would follow European and North American states in economic and political development. The gradual accumulation of capital would be accompanied by the gradual extension of literacy and education, the reduction of class and gender disparities and the strengthening of democracy and political participation.

In reality, democracy has not accompanied economic development in a systematic or general way. In fact, the fastest-growing states have generally been authoritarian, not democracies. This observation has led to the theory that economic development is incompatible with democracy. Accordingly, political repression and the concentration of political control are necessary to start accumulation and to maintain order during the process of concentrating capital. Demands by poor people for greater short-term consumption must be refused. Class disparities must be sharpened. Labour discipline must be enforced at extremely low wage levels. Foreign investors must be assured of political stability—above all, that radicals will not take power and that foreign assets will not be nationalized in a revolution. A democracy may be inherently incapable of accomplishing these difficult and painful tasks, according to this theory.

The NICs did not achieve their success through free and open democratic politics, but through firm state rule permitting little dissent. Chinese leaders, for example, contrast their recent economic successes, achieved under tight political control, with failed Soviet efforts under Gorbachev to promote economic reform by first loosening political control.

It has been suggested that a strong state facilitates capital accumulation.[17] Only a strong state, in this view, has the power to enforce and coordinate the allocations of wealth required to start accumulation. However, scholars do not agree on the definition of a strong state; some refer to the size of a state bureaucracy or its ability to extract taxes, others to its legitimacy or its ability to enforce its will on a population. The idea of a strong state is often connected with economic nationalism or mercantilism (see pp. 303–305).

In reality, the theory that authoritarianism leads to economic development does not hold, just as the theory that democracy automatically accompanies economic development does not hold. Many authoritarian states have achieved neither political stability nor economic development. Others have realized political stability but have failed at economic accumulation. The many military dictatorships in Africa are among the least successful models in the global South. In Latin America, the poorest country, Haiti, had the most authoritarian government for decades.

Furthermore, authoritarian states can lead to greater political instability, not less. The harder a state cracks down, the more resentment its population feels. Instead of peaceful protests, violent insurgencies often grow out of such resentments. In Guatemala, a military government harshly repressed rural revolutionaries and their peasant sympathizers for decades until a peace agreement was reached in 1996. Since the 1960s, in this country of nine million, repression and war killed 100 000 people, and another 45 000 "disappeared"; most were killed and buried in mass graves.[18] At times, Guatemala's government received substantial U.S. aid (based on "anticommunism") and at other times was banned from receiving it (based on violations of human rights). Its decades of authoritarian rule did not

---

[17] Peter B. Evans, Dietrich Rueschemeyer and Theda Skocpol, eds., *Bringing the State Back In* (NY: Cambridge UP, 1985). Stephen D. Krasner, *Structural Conflict: The Third World against Global Liberalism* (Berkeley: U California P, 1985).

[18] Human Rights Watch World Report 1990. Cited in *Science* 257 (24 July 1992): 479.

stop dissent, bring political stability, attract much foreign investment or create much economic accumulation.

Meanwhile, elsewhere in Latin America a wave of civilian governments replaced military ones in the late 1980s.[19] Economic conditions there have improved, not worsened, as a result. In states such as South Korea and Taiwan, which began industrializing under authoritarianism but have since shifted toward democracy, economic progress was not harmed. Relatively free elections and some limited tolerance of dissent signalled greater stability and maturity and did not discourage investment or slow economic growth.

It has been suggested that authoritarian rule and the concentration of income in few hands represent a phase in the development process. First, capital must be concentrated to begin accumulation, and tight political control must be maintained during this painful phase. Later, more wealth is generated, income spreads to more people, the middle class expands and political controls can be relaxed.

Again, the empirical reality does not support this theory as a general rule. There is no guarantee that even in early phases of accumulation, authoritarian control leads to

ADDITIONAL CHARGES MAY APPLY
Corruption is a major impediment to economic development in rich and poor countries but is more devastating to economies in the global South and to transitional former communist economies. In 2005, Ukraine's new reformist president disbanded the entire 23 000-member traffic police force to break up widespread corruption in its ranks. Here a driver gets towed in the capital, 2005.

---

[19] Guillermo O'Donnell, Phillipe C. Schmitter and Lawrence Whitehead, eds., *Transitions from Authoritarian Rule: Prospects for Democracy* [series] (Baltimore: Johns Hopkins UP, 1986). Charles A. Reilly, ed., *New Paths to Democratic Development in Latin America: The Rise of NGO-Municipal Collaboration* (Boulder, CO: Rienner, 1995). Adam Przeworski, *Democracy and the Market: Political and Economic Reforms in Eastern Europe and Latin America.* (NY: Cambridge UP, 1991).

economic development. In fact, flagrant human rights abuses seem to cause political insta-bility at any stage of economic development. Some successful accumulators, such as Singapore, have maintained tight political control throughout the process. Others, such as South Korea and Turkey, have started with authoritarian rule and evolved into democra-cies. Still others, such as Costa Rica and Malaysia, have achieved good economic results while maintaining relative democracy and little repression. Similarly, the countries that have done poorly in economic accumulation include both authoritarian regimes and democratic ones. Therefore, a state's form of political governance does not determine its success in economic development.

Corruption

Corruption is an important negative factor in economic development in many states; it also plays a role in some of the theories just discussed about various strategies for using trade, industry and government to promote economic development. In the past decade, high-level corruption cases have become high-profile international news, knocking governments from power in Brazil, Italy, India, Pakistan, Indonesia and elsewhere, and sending two former South Korean presidents to jail.

Analyses of corruption look first and foremost to the governments of particular states, and to their relationship with foreign economic actors such as MNCs. Through foreign policy, government mediates a national economy's relationship to the world economy. It regulates the conditions under which MNCs operate in a country. It enforces worker discipline—calling out the army if necessary to break strikes or suppress revolutions. It sets tax rates and wields other macroeconomic levers of control over the economy. And in most states of the global South, it owns a sizeable stake in major industries—a monopoly, in some cases.

Corruption is a kind of privatization of politics in that it concerns the distribution of benefits from economic transactions (exchange and capital accumulation). For example, when a foreign MNC comes into a country to drill for oil, the surplus produced will be shared between the MNC (through profits), the state (through taxation and fees), the local capitalists who make money supplying the operation, the local workers who earn wages and the foreign consumers who use the oil (which, because of the added supply, will be slightly cheaper in world markets).

State officials will decide whether to let an MNC into their country, which MNC to give drilling rights to and what terms to insist on (leasing fees, percentages of sales, etc.). These are complex deals struck after long negotiations. Corruption merely adds another player, the corrupt official, to share the benefits. For instance, a foreign oil company can pay off an official to award a favourable contract, and both can profit. In 2003, U.S. prosecutors indicted a Mobil Oil executive and a New York banker for paying US$78 million to two senior officials in Kazakhstan—with a kick-back of $2 million for the Mobil executive—to secure Mobil's billion-dollar stake in a huge oil field.

Corruption is by no means limited to the global South, but for several reasons has a deeper effect in poor countries. First, there is simply less surplus to keep economic growth going; accumulation is fragile. Another difference is that in those countries dependent on exporting a few products, revenue arrives in a very concentrated form—large payments in hard currency. This presents a greater opportunity for corruption than in a more diversi-fied economy with more (smaller) deals. Furthermore, in developing countries, incomes are often so low that corrupt officials are more tempted to accept payments, and the redi-rection of services from the poor (who cannot pay bribes) has a devastating effect.

Corruption can also have a significant environmental impact: the World Bank estimates that some 80 percent of timber harvests in the Amazon are illegal.[20]

Corruption in the global South presents a collective goods problem for states and MNCs in the global North: individually, MNCs and their home states can profit by clinching a deal with a private payoff, but collectively MNCs and states of the North lose money by having to make these payoffs. Therefore, there is an incentive to clamp down on corruption only if other industrialized states do likewise. More often, governments will try to support their MNCs, even when convicted of corruption charges. For example, the Canadian multinational engineering company Acres International was convicted in the African country of Lesotho on bribery charges in a $12 billion water project (a conviction that was upheld on appeal). The Canadian government did not sanction Acres International, and also came to its defence at the World Bank. World Bank anti-corruption efforts entail barring companies engaged in corrupt or fraudulent practices from receiving World Bank contracts. Most companies that have been barred have been based in the South. The Acres case was considered an important test of World Bank resolve in addressing corruption committed by companies based in the global North. In a 2004 decision, the World Bank debarred Acres International for a three-year period.[21]

Focus on Canadian Scholarship

Scholars at Canadian universities who work on development practices, foreign aid and international financial institutions include **Laura Macdonald** at Carleton University, who has examined the political impact of nongovernmental assistance to Central America. At Carleton's Norman Paterson School of International Affairs, **Dane Rowlands** researches the impact of IMF lending. **Bessama Momani** at the University of Waterloo looks at IMF debt negotiations in Egypt and Turkey. At the University of British Columbia, **Paul Evans** has focused on Canada's relationship with China. **Henry Veltmeyer** of St Mary's University works on development and social movements. **Tanya Narozhna,** at the University of Manitoba, has examined international organizations and development aid. At Dalhousie University, **Rebecca Tiessen** examines Canadian foreign aid policies and NGO partnerships as well as gender mainstreaming and HIV/AIDS in Africa, and her colleague **Jane Parpart** has focused on questions of women in development as well as development and postmodernity.

At Carleton's Norman Paterson School of International Affairs, **Jean Daudelin** explores questions of development and conflict, land policy and property rights and violence. At York University, **John Saul** focuses on South Africa and his colleague, **Fahimul Quadir,** works on issues related to development, governance and microfinance. At Brock University, **Hevina Dashwood** conducts research on Canadian mining companies and has also worked on poverty alleviation policies in Zimbabwe. At Trent University, **Gavin Fridell** has explored fair trade coffee and the pitfalls of market-driven approaches to social justice. **Judith Teichman** of the University of Toronto has explored the politics of freeing markets and the role of the IMF and World Bank in Latin American policy reform. **Jean-Philippe Thérien** at the University of Montréal explores foreign aid, poverty and multilateral institutions. At Queen's University, **J. Andrew Grant** focuses on diamonds and foreign aid. **Andy Hira** of Simon Fraser University researches economic integration in Latin America and fair trade.

---

[20] World Bank, *World Development Report 2004: Making Services Work for Poor People* (Washington, DC: World Bank, 2004). World Bank, "How the Bank Helps Countries Fight Corruption" 8 April 2004.

[21] "World Bank Sanctions Acres International Limited," World Bank Press Release July 23, 2004, available at http://web.worldbank.org/WBSITE/EXTERNAL/NEWS/0, contentMDK:20229958~menuPK:34463~pagePK:6 4003015~piPK:64003012~theSitePK:4607,00.html. Lawrence Solomon, "Martin's Problem: Corruption at Home and Abroad," *National Post* 27 Mar. 2004. Emad Mekay, "Activists Prod World Bank on Canadian Corruption Case," *Inter Press Service* 23 Mar. 2004.

Transparency helps solve collective goods problems (see p. 82). The Berlin-based NGO Transparency International pushed successfully for action to stem corruption in international business deals. The group publishes annual surveys showing the countries considered most corrupt by business executives. The top five on the list in 2006 were Haiti, Burma, Iraq, Guinea and Sudan.

In 1997 the world's 29 leading industrialized states agreed to forbid their companies from bribing foreign officials (payments to political parties were not forbidden, however). The effect has been limited in practice. The Extractive Industries Transparency Initiative, a coalition of states, NGOs and MNCs launched by Britain in 2002, fights corruption in the especially vulnerable oil, gas and mineral sectors worldwide by getting companies to release information on payments they make to developing countries.

In Chad in 1999, a consortium led by Exxon Mobil and backed by World Bank loans struck a deal to build a $4 billion oil pipeline from the landlocked country, with oil revenues going through a Citibank account in London to avoid corruption. Chad promised to use 72 percent of the money to reduce poverty. In 2005, as the oil money flowed in, Chad's government—under attack by rebels based in Sudan—pulled out of the deal to use the money for its military, and the World Bank suspended its loans.

NORTH-SOUTH CAPITAL FLOWS

Capital from the global North moves to the South and potentially spurs growth in several forms—foreign investment, debt and foreign aid. The rest of this chapter discusses these capital flows.

Foreign Investment

Poor countries have little money available to invest in new factories, farms, mines or oil wells. Foreign investment—investment in such capital goods by foreigners (most often MNCs)—is one way to get accumulation started (see "Foreign Direct Investment" on pp. 365–367). Foreign investment has been crucial to the success of China and other Asian developing countries. Overall, private capital flows to the global South totalled more than US$500 billion in 2006—six times the amount given in official development assistance.

Foreigners who invest in a country then own the facilities; by virtue of ownership, the investor can control decisions about how many people to employ, whether to expand or shut down, what products to make and how to market them. The foreign investor can usually take the profits from an operation out of country (repatriation of profits). However, the host government can share in the wealth by charging fees and taxes or by leasing land or drilling rights (see "Host and Home Government Relations" on pp. 368–372).

Because of past colonial experiences, many governments in the global South have feared the loss of control that comes with foreign investment by MNCs. Sometimes the presence of MNCs was associated with the painful process of concentrating capital and the sharpening of class disparities in the host state. In other instances domestic legislation, tax rules and service provision are expected to adapt in order to attract foreign investment. The World Bank, for example, recommends that countries seeking foreign investment in the mining sector reduce or eliminate import taxes, release all land reserved for exploration by state-owned enterprises to foreign investors and reform the public service to enable administration of mining rights for investors.[22] Part of the argument of the World Bank, and others informed by an economic liberal perspective, is that any loss of sovereignty is counterbalanced by the ability of foreign investors to infuse capital and generate more surplus. By the 1980s and 1990s, as models based on autarky or state ownership were discredited and the NICs gained success, many poor states rushed to embrace foreign investment.

One way states have sought to soften the loss of control is through *joint ventures:* companies owned partly by a foreign MNC and partly by a local firm or the host government. Sometimes foreign ownership in joint ventures is limited to a percentage (often 49 percent) to ensure that ultimate control rests with the host country even though a large share of the profits goes to the MNC. The percentage of ownership is usually proportional to the amount of capital invested; if a host government wants more control it must put up more money. Joint ventures work well for MNCs because they help secure the host government's cooperation in reducing bureaucratic hassles and ensuring success (by giving the host government a direct stake in the outcome).

MNCs invest in a country because of some advantage of doing business there. In some cases, it is the presence of natural resources. Sometimes it is cheap labour. Sometimes geographical location is a factor. Some states have better *absorptive capacity* than others—the ability to put investments to productive use—because of more highly developed infrastructure and a higher level of skills among workers or managers. As these are most often middle-income states, the funnelling of investments to states with high absorptive capacity tends to sharpen disparities *within* the global South.

MNCs also look for a favourable *regulatory environment* in a host state, which will facilitate, rather than impede, the MNC's business. For example, Motorola decided to invest more than $1 billion in new facilities in India in the 1990s, but changed its mind after encountering India's bureaucracy and shifted its investments toward China instead.[23]

GM MOVES IN

Foreign investment is an important source of capital for economic development in the global South. The relationships between foreign investors and host countries transcend economics and draw in culture, politics and identity. General Motors built this US$1.5 billion Buick assembly line in Shanghai, the historical (and perhaps future) centre of foreign economic penetration in China, 1998.

---

[22] World Bank, *A Mining Strategy for Latin America and the Caribbean*, World Bank Technical Paper No. 345 (1996).

[23] Edward A. Gargan, "India's Rush to a Free Market Economy Stumbles," *New York Times* 15 Aug. 1992: 2.

MNC decisions about foreign investment also depend on prospects for *financial stability*, especially for low inflation and stable currency exchange rates. If a currency is not convertible into hard currency, an MNC will not be able to take profits back to its home state or reinvest them elsewhere.

Beyond these financial considerations, a foreign investor producing for local markets wants to know that a host country's *economic growth* will sustain demand for the goods being produced. Similarly, whether producing for local consumption or export, an MNC wants the local *labour* supply—whether semi-skilled labour or just cheap—to be stable. This means in part that an MNC is reluctant to invest in countries with strong legislation protecting workers' rights or active trade union activity. Foreign investors often look to international financial institutions, such as the World Bank and the IMF, and to private analyses to judge a state's economic stability before investing.

Beyond their usual role in providing foreign investment, technology transfer and loans (in the case of banks), MNCs also sometimes participate in more broadly conceived development projects in a host state. Such participation is a way of investing in political goodwill as well as helping provide political stability by improving conditions for the population. The attitude of the government and the goodwill of the population affect the overall business prospects of the MNC. However, the people most adversely affected by MNC activities (for example, peasant farmers displaced from their land in order to make way for bauxite mining) often have little influence with either the MNC or their own government. It is usually the middle classes, who benefit more immediately from enhanced economic growth, who are more willing to embrace foreign investment.

Technology Transfer

The productive investment of capital depends on the knowledge and skills—business management, technical training, higher education as well as basic literacy and education—of workers and managers. Of special importance are the management and technical skills related to the key industries in a state's economy. In many former colonies, whites with such skills left many states after independence (see "Postcolonial Dependency" on pp. 444–449). In other areas, the skills needed to develop new industries have never existed. A few states in the Persian Gulf with large incomes and small populations have imported whole work forces from foreign countries. This practice is rare.

Most states of the global South seek to build their own educated elite with the knowledge and skills to run the national economy. One way this is achieved is by sending students to industrialized states for higher education. This entails some risks, however. Students may enjoy life in the North and fail to return home. In most developing countries, every student talented enough to study abroad represents a national resource and usually a long investment in primary and secondary education, which is lost if the student does not return. The same applies to professionals (for example, doctors) who emigrate later in their careers. The problem of losing skilled workers to richer countries, called the **brain drain,** has impeded economic development in states such as India, Pakistan, the Philippines and China. It is even a concern in countries like Canada, which has seen many professionals leave for careers in the United States.

Technology transfer refers to a state's acquisition of technology (knowledge, skills, methods, designs and specialized equipment) from foreign sources, usually in conjunction with foreign direct investment or similar business operations. A state in the South may allow an MNC to produce certain goods in its country under favourable conditions, provided the MNC shares knowledge of the technology and design behind the product. The state may try to recruit its own citizens into the management and professional work

brain drain Poor countries' loss of skilled workers to rich countries.

technology transfer Global South states' acquisition of technology (knowledge, skills, methods, designs, specialized equipment, etc.) from foreign sources, usually in conjunction with direct foreign investment or similar business operations.

force of factories or facilities created by foreign investment. Not only can physical capital accumulate in the country, so can the related technological base for further development. However, MNCs are sometimes reluctant to share proprietary technology.

green revolution
The massive transfer of agricultural technology, such as high-yield seeds and tractors, to countries of the global South that began in the 1960s.

The **green revolution**—a massive transfer of agricultural technology coordinated through international agencies—deserves special mention.[24] This effort, which began in the 1960s, transplanted a range of agricultural technologies from rich countries to poor ones—new seed strains, fertilizers, tractors to replace oxen and so forth. The green revolution increased crop yields in a number of states, especially in Asia, and helped produce the food supplies to meet growing populations.

However, it did have drawbacks. Critics noted that the green revolution forced recipients to depend on imported technologies such as tractors and oil, that it damaged the environment with commercial pesticides and fertilizers and that it disrupted traditional agriculture (driving more people off the land and into cities). Environmental reactions to the green revolution—including the emergence of pesticide resistance in insect populations—have led to recent declines in crop yields, forcing changes.[25] For example, pesticides introduced in the green revolution in Indonesia created resistant strains of a rice parasite that killed off its natural predators while polluting water supplies. Recognizing the need to adapt imported technologies to local needs, the Indonesian government banned most pesticides in 1986 and instead adopted organic methods. In recent years, the Food and Agriculture Organization (FAO) has spread information about organic pest control through traditional village theatre plays. Pesticide usage has declined sharply while rice production has increased.

The green revolution also replaced local expertise with that of foreigners. On the Indonesian island of Bali, "water priests" traditionally controlled the allocation of scarce water resources to agriculture. In the green revolution, such practices were often dismissed as superstitious nonsense and replaced with modern water-allocation schemes. The water priests actually had more experience with local conditions over many years and more legitimacy with the local farmers than did the foreign experts. Over time, some attempts have been made to refocus on local expertise and return, at least in part, to indigenous agricultural practices.

In the 1990s, states in the North began to focus on technology transfer that promotes *environmentally sustainable development* (see pp. 503–504). Japan's MITI-funded International Center for Environmental Technology Transfer geared up to train 10 000 people from developing countries over 10 years in energy conservation, pollution control and other environmental technologies. Japan also hosts the International Environmental Technology Centre, a project of the UN Environment Program (UNEP). However, among other motives, Japan hopes these projects will encourage developing countries to choose Japanese technology and products.[26]

Debt

Borrowing money is an alternative to foreign investment as a way of obtaining funds to prime a cycle of economic accumulation. If accumulation succeeds, it produces enough

---

[24] Mohammed Alauddin and Clement Tisdell, *The "Green Revolution" and Economic Development: The Process and Its Development in Bangladesh* (NY: St. Martin's, 1991).

[25] *Science* 256 (22 May 1992): 1140. *Science* 256 (29 May 1992): 1272.

[26] *Science* 256 (22 May 1992): 1145.

surplus to repay the loan and still make a profit. Borrowing has several advantages. It keeps control in the hands of the state (or other local borrower) and does not impose painful sacrifices on local citizens, at least in the short term.

Debt also has disadvantages. The borrower must service the debt—making regular payments of interest and repaying the principal according to the terms of the loan. **Debt service** is a constant drain on whatever surplus is generated by the investment of the money. With foreign direct investment, a money-losing venture is the problem of the foreign MNC; with debt, it is the problem of the borrowing state, which must find the money elsewhere. Often, a debtor must borrow new funds to service old loans, slipping further into debt. Debt service has created a net financial outflow from South to North in recent years, as the South has paid billions more in interest to banks and governments in the North than it has received in foreign investment or development aid.

debt service An obligation to make regular interest payments and repay the principal of a loan according to its terms, which is a drain on many economies of the global South.

The failure to make scheduled payments, called a **default,** is considered a drastic action because it destroys lenders' confidence and results in the cutting off of future loans. Rather than defaulting, borrowers attempt **debt renegotiation**—a reworking of the terms on which a loan will be repaid. By renegotiating their debts with lenders, borrowers seek a mutually acceptable payment scheme to keep at least some money flowing to the lender. If interest rates have fallen since a loan was first taken out, the borrower can refinance. Borrowers and lenders can also negotiate to restructure a debt by changing the length of the loan (usually to a longer payback period) or the other terms. Occasionally state-to-state loans are written off altogether—forgiven—for political reasons, as happened with U.S. loans to Egypt after the Gulf War. In recent years, activists and NGOs have called for extensive debt forgiveness for the poorest countries.

default The failure to make scheduled debt payments.

debt renegotiation A reworking of the terms on which a loan will be repaid; frequently negotiated by global South debtor governments in order to avoid default.

Debt encompasses several types of lending relationships, all of which are influenced by international politics. The *borrower* may be a private firm or bank in a developing country, or it may be the government itself. Loans to the government are somewhat more common because lenders consider the government less likely to default than a private borrower. The *lender* may be a private bank or company or a state (both are important). Usually banks are more insistent on receiving timely payments and firmer in renegotiating debts than are states. Some state-to-state loans are made on artificially favourable *concessionary* terms, in effect subsidizing economic development in the borrowing state.

In the 1970s and 1980s, many states of the global South borrowed heavily from banks and states in the North, which engaged in sometimes quite aggressive lending policies, offering very favourable interest rates to borrowers. For banks, lending to a country was considered a good risk (countries do not normally disappear), but growth began to falter. In oil-exporting states such as Venezuela and Mexico, for instance, price declines reduced export earnings with which states planned to repay loans. Other exporting states found that protectionist measures in the North, combined with a slowing of the global economy, limited their ability to export. Sometimes borrowed funds were simply not spent wisely and produced too little surplus to service a debt.

GLOBALIZE THIS

Globalization is creating winners and losers while sharpening income disparities. Debt, currency crises, IMF conditionality and the privatization of state-owned enterprises are among the sources of upheaval and poverty in many countries in the global South. This beggar was caught in Argentina's financial collapse in 2001.

As a result, a *debt crisis* had developed by the 1980s, particularly in Latin America.[27] Many states in the South could not generate enough export earnings to service their debts, much less to repay them—not to mention the chance of retaining some surplus to generate sustained local accumulation. Major states of the global South, such as Brazil, Mexico and India, found foreign debt a tremendous weight on economic development. Although the "crisis" passed, and many debts were renegotiated to a longer-term basis, the weight of debt remains (see Table 13.1). The world banking system rode out the 1980s crisis, and some made sizeable profits during the worst of it, even when writing off a portion of the uncollectible debts each year.

Debt renegotiation has become a perennial occupation of states in the global South. Renegotiations are complex international bargaining situations, like international trade or arms control negotiations but with more parties. The various lenders—private banks and states—try to extract as much as possible, and the borrower tries to hold out for more favourable terms. If a borrowing government accepts terms that are too burdensome, it may lose popularity at home; the local population and opposition politicians may accuse it of selling out to foreigners, neocolonialists and so on. If the borrowing state does not give enough to gain the agreement of the lenders, it might be forced to default and lose out on future loans and investments, which could greatly impede economic growth.

For lenders, debt renegotiations involve a collective goods problem: they must all agree on the conditions of the renegotiation but each really cares only about getting back its own money. To solve this problem, state creditors meet together periodically as the **Paris Club,** and private creditors as the **London Club,** to work out terms.

Through renegotiations and the corresponding write-offs of debts by banks, developing countries have largely avoided defaulting. Some large states threatened to

Paris Club A group of global North governments that have loaned money to global South governments; it meets periodically to work out terms of debt renegotiations. Private creditors meet as the **London Club**.

Table 13.1 Debt in the Global South, 2005

Region	Foreign Debt		Annual Debt Service	
	Billion $	% of GDP[a]	Billion $	% of Exports
Latin America	800	36	140	26
Asia	800	23	100	7
Africa	300	39	30	11
Middle East	300	34	40	7
Total "South"	2,200	33	310	13

[a]GDP not calculated at purchasing-power parity.

Notes: Regions do not exactly match those used elsewhere in this book. Africa here includes North Africa. Asia includes China.

Source: IMF. Statistical Appendix to World Economic Outlook, September 2005, pp. 266–7.

---

[27] Antonio Jorge and Jorge Salazar-Carrillo, eds., *The Latin American Debt* (NY: St. Martin's, 1992). Jeffry A. Frieden, *Debt, Development, and Democracy: Modern Political Economy and Latin America, 1965–1985* (Princeton, NJ: Princeton UP, 1992). Miles Kahler, ed., *The Politics of International Debt* (Ithaca, NY: Cornell UP, 1986). York W. Bradshaw and Ana-Maria Wahl, "Foreign Debt Expansion, the International Monetary Fund, and Regional Variation in Third World Poverty," *International Studies Quarterly* 35.3 (1991): 251–72. Robert E. Wood, *From Marshall Plan to Debt Crisis: Foreign Aid and Development Choices in the World Economy* (Berkeley: U California P, 1986).

default—or even to lead a coalition of states all defaulting at once—but backed down. However, in 2001, Argentina in effect defaulted. By then, financial institutions had psychologically adjusted to the reality that Argentina could not pay its debt, so the default did not cause widespread panic. Indeed, Argentina recovered—growing 9 percent a year since 2001—and in 2005 offered its creditors a take-it-or-leave-it deal for repayment of less than 30 cents on the dollar. Most took it, which highlighted Argentina's strong position despite defaulting. Still, default is risky because of the integrated nature of the world economy, the need for foreign investment and foreign trade to accumulate wealth and the risks of provoking international confrontations. Lenders too have generally proven willing to absorb losses rather than push a borrower over the edge and risk financial instability.

Despite stabilization, states of the global South have not yet solved the debt problem. As shown in Table 13.1, the South owes US$2 trillion in foreign debt, and pays over US$300 billion a year to service that debt. The debt service (in hard currency) absorbs more than a third of the entire hard-currency export earnings in Latin America—the region most affected. Africa's debt is equal to 30 percent of its annual GDP. Many states in Asia are also vulnerable to debt problems.

Recent emphasis has focused on *Heavily Indebted Poor Countries (HIPCs)*, which international financial institutions like the IMF and World Bank began to identify in 1996 and target for certain levels of debt relief. In recent years, activists and NGOs have called for more extensive debt forgiveness for these poor countries, most of which are in Africa. Critics say that such cancellations just put more money in the hands of corrupt, inept governments. In 2004, Britain promised nearly $200 million a year for debt relief and urged other Western countries to contribute. Under this prodding, and with a history of successful bilateral debt forgiveness totalling tens of billions of dollars in recent years, G8 members agreed in 2005 to eliminate all debts owed by 37 very poor countries to the World Bank and IMF—cutting almost in half the poorest countries' estimated $200 billion in debt. The first $40 billion, owed by 18 countries, began to be written off in 2006. The IMF was considering a controversial plan to revalue its gold holdings (currently valued at $8 billion but worth ten times that at market prices) as a source of finance for this debt relief.

IMF Conditionality

The International Monetary Fund (IMF) and the World Bank have a large supply of capital from member states (see "The World Bank and the IMF" on pp. 350–352). This capital plays an important role in funding early stages of accumulation in developing countries and in assisting them through short periods of great difficulty. And, as a political entity rather than a bank, the IMF can make funds available on favourable financial terms (though normally with significant political and economic strings attached).

The IMF scrutinizes states' economic plans and policies, withholding loans until it is satisfied that the right policies are in place. It makes loans to help states through the transitional process of implementing the IMF-approved policies. The IMF also sends important signals to private lenders and investors. Its approval of a state's economic plans is a "seal of approval" used by bankers and MNCs to assess the wisdom of investing in that state. Thus, the IMF wields great power in influencing the economic policies of states in the global South.

An agreement to loan IMF funds on the condition that certain government policies are adopted is called an **IMF conditionality** agreement, and implementation of these

IMF conditionality
An agreement to loan IMF funds on the condition that certain government policies are adopted. Dozens of global South states have entered into such agreements in the past two decades. See also *International Monetary Fund (IMF)*.

conditions is referred to as a *structural adjustment program*.[28] Dozens of developing states have entered into such agreements in the past two decades. The terms insisted on by the IMF, called austerity measures, are usually painful for citizens (and hence for national politicians). The IMF demands that inflation be brought under control, which requires reducing state spending and closing budget deficits. These measures often spur unemployment and require that subsidies of food and basic goods be reduced or eliminated. Short-term consumption is curtailed in favour of longer-term investment. Surplus must be concentrated to service debt and invest in new capital accumulation. The IMF wants to ensure that money lent to a country is not spent for politically popular but economically unprofitable purposes (such as subsidizing food). It wants to ensure that inflation does not outweigh progress and that the economy is stable enough to attract investment. In addition, it demands steps to curtail corruption.

Because of the pain inflicted by a conditionality agreement—and to some extent by any debt renegotiation agreement—such agreements are often politically unpopular in

MIRACLE OF LOAVES
IMF conditionality agreements often call for reducing subsidies for food, transportation and other basic needs. In Egypt, bread prices are heavily subsidized, forcing the government to use hard currency to import wheat. Public resistance to bread price increases is so strong that the government has not been able to justify cutting the subsidy. Here, bread is delivered by bicycle in Cairo, 1996.

---

[28] Biplab Dasgupta, *Structural Adjustment, Global Trade, and the New Political Economy of Development* (NY: Zed/St. Martin's, 1999). David E. Sahn, Paul A. Dorosh and Stephen D. Younger, *Structural Adjustment Reconsidered: Economic Policy and Poverty in Africa* (NY: Cambridge UP, 1997). Jacques J. Polak, *The Changing Nature of IMF Conditionality*, Princeton Essays in International Finance, no. 184. (Princeton, NJ: Dept. of Economics, Princeton University, 1991). Erik Denters, *Law and Policy of IMF Conditionality* (The Hague and Boston: Kluwer, 1996).

the global South, as they would be anywhere.[29] On several occasions, a conditionality agreement has brought rioters into the streets demanding the restoration of subsidies for food, gasoline and other essential goods. Sometimes governments have backed out of an agreement or have broken promises under such pressure. Occasionally, governments have been toppled. In Peru, which in the early 1990s faced a violent leftist guerrilla war that fed on mass poverty, such a choice was especially difficult.

In Egypt, where the same word is used for both bread and life, cheap bread is vital to political stability, at least in the government's view. State-owned flour mills, and an annual subsidy of US$750 million, ensure a supply of bread at one-third its real cost for Egypt's large and poor population. For economic liberals, these costs distort the free market, encouraging Egyptians to eat (and waste) more bread than they otherwise would, and driving the need for imported wheat to more than US$1 billion per year. When the government tried to raise the price of bread in 1977, street riots forced a reversal. Instead, the government has subtly changed the size and composition of loaves, and in 1996 began secretly mixing cheaper corn flour into state-milled wheat flour. This example illustrates the political difficulties that many governments face in implementing typical IMF conditionality requirements.

The IMF formula for stability and success is remarkably universal from one country to the next. When the IMF negotiated terms for economic assistance to Russia and the former Soviet republics in the early 1990s, the terms were similar to those for any state in the global South: cut inflation, cut government spending, cut subsidies, crack down on corruption.

Critics of the IMF argue that it does not adapt its program adequately to account for differences in the local cultural and economic conditions in different states. The United States, for example, would not qualify for IMF assistance because of government deficits, but does not have to submit to IMF austerity measures because of an otherwise strong economy. More importantly, critics argue that the IMF prescription is an approach derived from another time and place, which may no longer apply to current problems of development and inequality. The IMF was created to assist the countries of Europe and Japan in their post–World War II recovery. In that case, short-term austerity measures made sense and were quite effective. Today's developing world does not suffer from short-term imbalances, but rather long-term structural conditions, resulting in part from historical legacies of colonialism. By this view, IMF diagnoses and prescriptions are misplaced and sometimes only exacerbate difficult economic conditions even further.[30]

A more recent innovation by the IMF and World Bank has been to shift to Poverty Reduction Strategy Papers (PRSPs). These are statements prepared every three years by Heavily Indebted Poor Countries seeking debt forgiveness, and are intended to be generated in greater consultation with the states than the more top-down approach of IMF conditionality. PRSPs are also expected to highlight a state's strategies not only to address its debt burden, but also to meet the UN's Millennium Development Goals (see Chapter 12), which include eradicating extreme poverty and hunger, achieving universal primary education, promoting gender equality and ensuring environmental sustainability, among other things. Some observers remain skeptical, however, and note that PRSPs and other

---

[29] Stephan Haggard and Robert R. Kaufman, eds., *The Politics of Economic Adjustment: International Constraints, Distributive Conflicts, and the State* (Princeton, NJ: Princeton UP, 1992). Fredoline O. Anunobi, *The Implications of Conditionality: The International Monetary Fund and Africa* (Lanham, MD: UP America, 1992).

[30] Joseph E. Stiglitz, *Globalization and Its Discontents* (NY: Norton, 2003).

measures to meet the Millennium Development Goals remain as "top-down" as ever, and continue to require the kinds of structural adjustment policies the IMF has always expected of indebted countries (and which, critics note, make it more rather than less difficult to achieve the UN's Millennium Development Goals).[31]

The South in International Economic Regimes

Because of the need for capital and the wealth created by international trade, most states of the global South nonetheless see their future economic development as resting on a close interconnection with the world economy, not on national autarky or regional economic communities. Thus they must play by the rules embedded in international economic regimes (see Chapters 9 and 10).

The WTO trading regime tends to work against developing states relative to industrialized ones. A free trade regime makes it harder for poor states to protect infant industries in order to build self-sufficient capital accumulation. It forces competition with more technologically advanced states. A poor state can be competitive only in low-wage, low-capital niches—especially those using natural resources that are scarce in the North, such as tropical agriculture, extractive (mining and drilling) industries and textiles.

Yet the economic sectors in which Southern states have a comparative advantage in world markets—agriculture and textiles in particular—were largely excluded from the free trade rules of the GATT (see pp. 332–335). The GATT instead concentrated on free trade in manufactured goods, for which states in the North have a comparative advantage. As a result, some states of the global South found that they were expected to open their home markets to foreign products that home industries are not competitive against while seeing their own export products shut out of foreign markets. Current WTO negotiations are attempting to address this inequity.

Another criticism levelled at the WTO centres on the trade dispute system, to which states may bring complaints of unfair trading practices. Legal trade disputes can cost millions of dollars to litigate, requiring expensive lawyers and a large staff at WTO headquarters in Geneva. Few states in the global South can afford this process and therefore few use it to help their own industries knock down unfair barriers to trade. Recall that even if a state wins a WTO dispute, it gains only the right to place tariffs on the offending country's goods in an equal amount. For small states, this retaliation can inflict as much damage on their own economy as on the economy of the offending state.

To compensate for these inequities and to help developing countries use trade to boost their economic growth, the WTO has a Generalized System of Preferences (p. 333). These and other measures—such as the Lomé conventions in which EU states relaxed tariffs on goods from the global South—are exceptions to the overall rules of trade, intended to ensure that participation in world trade advances rather than impedes global South development.[32] Nonetheless, critics claim that states of the global South are the losers in the overall world trading regime.

---

[31] IMF, "Poverty Reduction Strategy Papers," September 2005, available at http://www.imf.org/external/np/exr/facts/prsp.htm. Patrick Bond, "Global Governance Campaigning and MDGs: From Top-down to Bottom-up Anti-Poverty Work," *Third World Quarterly* 27.2 (2006): 339–54.

[32] Diana Tussie and David J. Glover, eds., *The Developing Countries in World Trade: Policies and Bargaining Strategies* (Boulder, CO: Rienner, 1993). John Ravenhill, *Collective Clientelism: The Lomé Conventions and North-South Relations* (NY: Columbia UP, 1985).

In past decades, critics have accused the World Bank of supporting authoritarian regimes and underwriting huge infrastructure projects that displaced poor people and had devastating environmental effects. Critics allege that the Bank's portfolio of loans in the global South, totalling more than US$100 billion, is more a hindrance than a help to true development. Bank officials respond that despite a few mistakes, the Bank and its mission are sound.

The tenuous position of the global South in international economic regimes reflects the role of power in IR. The global North, with nearly two-thirds of the world's wealth, clearly has more power—more effective leverage—than the South. The global disparity of power is accentuated by the fact that the South is split into more than a hundred actors whereas the North's power is concentrated in eight large states (the G8 members). Thus, when the rules of the world economy were created after World War II, and as they have been rewritten and adjusted over the years, the main actors shaping the outcome have been a handful of large industrialized states.

States in the South have responded to problems with world economic regimes in several ways. In the 1970s, OPEC shifted the terms of trade for oil—bringing huge amounts of capital into the oil-exporting countries. Some states hoped such successes could be repeated for other commodities, resulting in broad gains for the global South, but this did not occur (see "Cartels" on pp. 469–471, and "Minerals, Land, Water" on pp. 524–526).

Also in the 1970s, developing country states tried to form a broad political coalition to push for restructuring the world economy to make North-South economic transactions more favourable to the South. A summit meeting of the nonaligned movement (see p. 250) in 1973 called for a **New International Economic Order (NIEO).**[33] Central to the NIEO was a shift in the terms of trade to favour primary commodities relative to manufactured goods. The NIEO proposal also called for the promotion of industrialization in the global South and for increased development assistance from the North.

The NIEO never became much more than a rallying cry, partly due to the South's lack of power and partly because disparities within the South created divergent interests among its states. In the 1980s, the terms of trade for raw material exporters further deteriorated, and economic development slowed in much of the developing world. In China and some other Asian countries, however, development accelerated.

States of the global South continue to pursue proposals to restructure world trade to their benefit. These efforts now take place mainly through the *UN Conference on Trade and Development (UNCTAD)*, which meets periodically but lacks power to implement major changes in North-South economic relations.[34] Attempts to promote South-South trade (reducing dependence on the North) have proven largely impractical. However, Brazil's president, visiting China in 2004, referred to Brazil-China trade, which quadrupled in 1999–2003, as "a paradigm for South-South cooperation."[35] China sometimes uses the South-South solidarity argument in wooing new friends in Africa. And efforts

New International Economic Order (NIEO)
A global South effort begun in the mid-1970s, mainly conducted in UN forums, to advocate restructuring of the world economy to make North-South economic transactions less unfavourable to the South.

---

[33] R. W. Cox, "Ideologies and the New International Economic Order: Reflections on Some Recent Literature," *International Organization* 332 (Spring 1979): 257–302. Craig N. Murphy, *The Emergence of the NIEO Ideology* (Boulder, CO: Westview, 1984). Johan Galtung, *The North/South Debate: Technology, Basic Human Needs, and the New International Economic Order* (NY: Institute for World Order, 1980).

[34] Marc Williams, *Third World Cooperation: The Group of 77 in UNCTAD* (NY: St. Martin's, 1991). Thomas G. Weiss, *Multilateral Development Diplomacy in UNCTAD* (NY: St. Martin's, 1986).

[35] Larry Rohter, "China Widens Economic Role in Latin America," *The New York Times* 20 Nov. 2004: A1.

continue in boosting cooperation and solidarity among developing countries through a variety of groups such as the nonaligned movement and the UN.[36] Nonetheless, such efforts have done little to change the South's reliance on assistance from the North.

FOREIGN ASSISTANCE

foreign assistance Money or other aid made available to developing countries to help them speed up economic development or meet humanitarian needs. Most foreign assistance is provided by governments and is called official development assistance (ODA). See also *Development Assistance Committee (DAC)*.

Foreign assistance (or *overseas development assistance*) is money or other aid made available to developing countries to help them speed up economic development or simply meet basic humanitarian needs.[37] Along with the commercial economic activities just discussed (investments and loans), foreign assistance is a second major source of money for development. It is dedicated to a variety of programs—from individual volunteers lending a hand to massive government packages.

Different kinds of development assistance have different purposes. Some are humanitarian, some are political and others are intended to create future economic advantages for the giver (these purposes often overlap). The state or organization that gives assistance is called a *donor*; the state or organization receiving the aid is the *recipient*. Foreign assistance creates or extends a relationship between donor and recipient that is simultaneously political and cultural as well as economic.[38] Foreign assistance can be a form of power in which the donor seeks to influence the recipient, or it may be a form of interdependence in which the donor and recipient create a mutually beneficial exchange.

Patterns of Foreign Assistance

Development Assistance Committee (DAC) A committee whose members—consisting of states from Western Europe, North America and Japan/Pacific—provide 90 percent of official development assistance to countries of the global South. See also *foreign assistance*.

bilateral aid Government assistance that goes directly to global South governments as state-to-state aid.

multilateral aid Government foreign aid from several states that goes through a third party, such as the UN or another agency.

The majority of foreign assistance comes from governments in the North. Private donations provide a smaller and sometimes significant amount. In 1997, for instance, Ted Turner pledged US$1 billion for UN programs, George Soros contributed or pledged nearly US$2 billion in aid to Russia and other countries and Bill Gates's foundation contributed millions to world health campaigns.

Of the over $100 billion in governmental foreign assistance provided in 2005, more than 90 percent came from members of the **Development Assistance Committee (DAC),** consisting of states from Western Europe, North America and Japan/Pacific. Several oil-exporting Arab countries provided some foreign development assistance, and in 2003, transition economies became a net "exporter" of financial aid. Three-quarters of the DAC countries' government assistance goes directly to governments in the global South as state-to-state **bilateral aid;** the rest goes through the UN or other agencies as **multilateral aid.**

---

[36] Sheila Page, *Regionalism among Developing Countries* (NY: Palgrave, 2000). Steen Folke, Niels Fold and Thyge Enevoldsen, *South-South Trade and Development: Manufacturers in the New International Division of Labour* (NY: St. Martin's, 1993). Donald Bobiash, *South-South Aid: How Developing Countries Help Each Other* (NY: St. Martin's, 1992). H. Michael Erisman, *Pursuing Postdependency Politics: South-South Relations in the Caribbean* (Boulder, CO: Rienner, 1992).

[37] Michael O'Hanlon and Carol Graham, *A Half Penny on the Federal Dollar: The Future of Development Aid* (Washington, DC: Brookings, 1997). Steven W. Hook, *National Interest and Foreign Aid* (Boulder, CO: Rienner, 1995). Anne O. Krueger, Constantine Michalopoulos and Vernon W. Ruttan, *Aid and Development* (Baltimore: Johns Hopkins UP, 1989). Brian H. Smith, *More Than Altruism: The Politics of Private Foreign Aid* (Princeton, NJ: Princeton UP, 1990).

[38] Margee M. Ensign, *Doing Good or Doing Well? Japan's Foreign Aid Program* (NY: Columbia UP, 1992). Davis B. Bobrow and Mark A. Boyer, "Bilateral and Multilateral Foreign Aid: Japan's Approach in Comparative Perspective," *Review of International Political Economy* 3.1 (1996): 95–121.

The DAC countries set a goal to contribute 0.7 percent of their GNPs in foreign aid, but overall they give less than half this amount. Only Norway, Sweden, Denmark, the Netherlands and Luxembourg are close to the target. In fact, Oxfam International recently reported that industrialized countries' aid dropped from 0.48 percent of income in 1960–1965 to 0.34 percent in 1980–1985 and then to 0.24 percent in 2003.[39]

The United States gives the lowest percentage of GNP—about two-tenths of 1 percent—of any of the 30 states of the industrialized West that make up the Organisation for Economic Co-operation and Development (OECD). In total economic aid given (nearly $30 billion), the United States has recently regained the lead over Japan (which cut foreign aid to $13 billion). Germany, Britain and France have each given about $10 billion. Canada gave close to US$3.7 billion in 2005, or 0.34 percent of its Gross National Income.[40]

U.S. foreign assistance dropped by nearly half from 1992 to 1995, though it has since grown back, surpassing previous levels. This and other decreases brought the world total in foreign assistance down substantially in the 1990s. After the 2001 terrorist attacks, a number of Western states proposed raising foreign aid levels to tackle poverty that breeds extremism, and both the U.K. and the United States sharply raised their aid budgets. Whether poverty actually does breed extremism is an open question, but this view did result in rising aid levels in the early 2000s (see discussion in Changing World Order Box on Foreign Aid on p. 494).

Types of Aid   Bilateral aid takes a variety of forms. *Grants* are funds given free to a recipient state, usually for some stated purpose. *Technical cooperation* refers to grants given in the form of expert assistance on some project rather than just money or goods. *Credits* are grants that can be used to buy certain products from the donor state. For instance, Canada gives credits that can be used for purchases of Canadian grain. This is sometimes called "tied" aid. If people in a recipient country become accustomed to products from the donor state, they are likely to buy those same products in the future.

Loans are funds given to help economic development, which must be repaid in the future out of the surplus generated by the development process (they too are often tied to the purchase of products from a donor state). Unlike commercial loans, government-to-government development loans are often on concessionary terms, with long repayment times and low interest rates. Although still an obligation for the recipient country, such loans are relatively easy to service.

Loan guarantees, which are used only occasionally, are promises by a donor state to back up commercial loans to a recipient. If the recipient state services such debts and ultimately repays them, there is no cost to the donor. If the recipient cannot make payments, the donor must step in and cover the debts. A loan guarantee allows the recipient state to borrow money at lower interest from commercial banks (because the risk to the bank is much lower).

Military aid is not normally included in development assistance, but in a broad sense belongs there. It is money that flows from North to South, from government to government, and brings a certain amount of economic value into a developing country. If a country wants a certain size of army with certain weapons, getting them at no charge from a donor state frees up money that can be used elsewhere in the economy. However, of all the

---

[39] Arabella Fraser and Bethan Emmett, *Paying the Price: Why Rich Countries Must Invest Now in a War on Poverty* (Oxford, UK: Oxfam International, 2005) 6.

[40] Treasury Board of Canada, "Canada's Performance Report 2006, Annex 3—Indicators and Additional Information," 23 Nov. 2006, available at http://www.tbs-sct.gc.ca/report/govrev/06/ann303_e.asp.

forms of development assistance, military aid is certainly one of the least efficient and most prone to impede rather than help economic development. It is also geared almost exclusively to political alliances rather than actual development needs.

As of mid-2007 an increasing proportion of Canadian foreign aid had shifted to Afghanistan, intended specifically to complement Canada's military mission there. By the end of the 2006–2007 fiscal year, Canada was estimated to have invested some $600 million in Afghanistan since 2001, making it Canada's single largest recipient of development funding. This is part of the Canadian government initiative called a "3-D approach" to support Canada's interests in the world: the integration of defence, diplomacy and development. The strategy is controversial, since it can result in a redirection of support away from critical areas in the world and may even contradict other elements of Canadian aid policy. (Canada has also indicated that it will focus its aid initiatives in some of the poorest parts of Africa, not all of which have an accompanying military mission.) Aid agencies have observed that while there are instances where military and development agencies can work together, it can also be very dangerous for development personnel on the ground if the differences between development and military activities become blurred.[41]

The main agency dispensing foreign economic assistance in Canada (but not military aid) is the Canadian International Development Agency (CIDA). It supports projects in more than 100 countries and focuses on supporting sustainable development. Canada's Official Development Assistance (ODA) program emphasizes six priority areas: meeting basic human needs; gender equality; infrastructure support; human rights, democracy and good governance; private sector development; and the environment. CIDA normally works with international and local partners on a wide range of projects, which include the promotion of women and girls' literacy, HIV/AIDS awareness programs, desertification projects (planting trees with maize crops to prevent soil erosion), the provision of safe water and sanitation facilities, capacity-building in human rights monitoring and the criminal justice systems, microcredit programs and many others.

Canada has other publicly funded agencies involved in development issues. For example, the International Development Research Centre (IDRC) was created by an Act of Parliament in 1970 and is mandated to support and conduct policy-relevant research into problems faced by people in the global South. IDRC is innovative in that it aims primarily to support research (scientific and social scientific) produced by peoples in the South for the South. So, rather than bringing in northern "experts," IDRC attempts to support research capacity in the South. The aim is to fund research into issues deemed relevant by the very people the research aims to assist.

Canada also has a number of nongovernmental organizations that are involved in development assistance and are mandated to provide opportunities for Canadians to work in the field of international development. **World University Service of Canada (WUSC),** for example, is involved in development assistance projects in over 50 countries and also coordinates professional and volunteer positions in many of those projects.

In the United States, foreign assistance is administered through the State Department's *Agency for International Development (USAID)*, which works mainly through the U.S. embassy in each recipient country. The major recipients of U.S. foreign

World University Service of Canada (WUSC)
An agency involved in development assistance projects in over 50 countries that also coordinates professional and volunteer positions in many of those projects.

---

[41] John Elmer and Anthony Felton, "Canada: Development Aid as Counterinsurgency Tool," *Canadian Dimension* 23 Mar. 2007, available at http://canadiandimension.com/articles/2007/04/07/1019. David R. Black, "Canadian Aid to Africa: Assessing 'Reform,' " *Canada among Nations 2006: Minorities and Priorities*, ed. Andrew F. Cooper and Dane Rowlands (Montreal and Kingston: McGill UP, 2006) 319–38. Nancy Gordon, "Canada's Position on the Use of Force Internationally," *International Journal* 61.1 (Winter 2005/2006): 129–34.

aid are its important strategic allies in the Middle East, including Israel, Egypt and Turkey. The U.S., more than Canada, uses the promise of aid, or the threat of cutting it off, as leverage in political bargaining with recipients. For example, when Pakistan proceeded with a nuclear weapons program in the late 1980s despite U.S. warnings, a sizeable flow of U.S. aid was terminated. When Pakistan supported U.S. military action in neighbouring Afghanistan in 2001, U.S. aid was restored.

UN Programs Most multilateral development aid goes through *UN programs*. The position of these programs in the UN structure is described in Chapter 8 (see pp. 251–258). The overall flow of assistance through the UN is coordinated by the **UN Development Programme (UNDP),** which manages 5000 projects at once around the world (focusing especially on technical development assistance). Other UN programs focus on concentrating capital, transferring technology and developing work force skills for manufacturing. UNIDO works on industrialization, UNITAR on training and research. Most UN programs—such as UNICEF, UNFPA, UNESCO, WHO and others—focus on meeting basic needs.

UN programs have three advantages in promoting economic development. One is that governments and citizens tend to perceive the UN as a friend of the South, and not

UN Development Programme (UNDP)
UN agency that coordinates the flow of multilateral development assistance and manages 5000 projects at once around the world (focusing especially on technical development assistance).

JOINT EFFORT
Governments provide $55 billion annually in foreign assistance, with private donors giving over $10 billion more (1999 data). Here, a Canadian corporal helps load more than 20 000 kilograms of humanitarian relief supplies to be sent to Iran following a devastating earthquake that left more than 20 000 dead and another 30 000 injured.

an alien force, a threat to sovereignty or a reminder of colonialism. The UN can some-times mobilize technical experts and volunteers from other developing countries so that people who arrive to help do not look like white European colonialists. A team of Egyptian medical workers under a UN program may be more easily accepted in an African country than French or British workers, however well intentioned.

Second, UN workers may be more likely to make appropriate decisions because of their backgrounds. UN workers who come from the global South or have worked in other poor countries in a region may be more sensitive to local conditions and to the pitfalls of development assistance than are aid workers from rich countries.

A third advantage is that the UN can organize its assistance on a global scale, giving priority to projects and avoiding duplication and the reinvention of the wheel in each state. For some issues—such as the fight against HIV/AIDS or the integration of develop-ment objectives with environmental preservation—there is no substitute for global organ-ization linked to specific local circumstances.

A major disadvantage faced by UN development programs is that they are funded largely through voluntary contributions by rich states. Each program has to solicit con-tributions to carry on its activities, so contributions may be abruptly cut off if the program displeases a donor government—a strategy used regularly by the United States (see pp. 257–258). Also, governments that pledge aid may not follow through. For instance, the UN complained in early 2005 that only 5 percent of the $500 million pledged by the international community for southern Sudan five months earlier had actually been paid.

The Disaster Relief Model

The remainder of this chapter discusses three models of development assistance, which are distinguished by the type of assistance rather than the type of donor (all three models use both government and private aid).

First is the disaster relief model—the kind of foreign assistance given when poor people are afflicted by famine, drought, earthquakes, flooding or other natural disasters. (War is also a disaster and can compound naturally occurring disasters.) When disaster strikes a poor state, many people are left with no means of subsistence and often without their homes. **Disaster relief** is the provision of short-term relief in the form of food, water, shelter, clothing and other essentials.

disaster relief The provision of short-term relief in the form of food, water, shelter, clothing and other essentials to people facing natural disasters.

Disaster relief is very important because disasters can wipe out years of progress in economic development in a single blow. Generally, the international community tries to respond with enough assistance to get people back on their feet. The costs of this assis-tance are relatively modest, the benefits visible and dramatic. Having a system of disaster relief in place provides the global South with a kind of insurance against sudden losses that could otherwise destabilize economic accumulation.

Disasters generally occur quickly and without much warning. Rapid response is diffi-cult to coordinate. International disaster relief has become more organized and better coordinated in the past decade but is still a complex process that varies somewhat from one situation to the next. Contributions of governments, private charitable organizations and other groups and agencies are coordinated through the UN *Office of the Disaster Relief Coordinator (UNDRO)* in Geneva. In 2006, the UN set up a $500 million fund to enable it to respond quickly to disasters without waiting to raise funds each time disaster strikes. Typically, international contributions make up no more than about one-third of the total relief effort, with the remainder coming from local communities and national govern-ments in affected states.

Disaster relief is something of a collective good because the states of the North do not benefit individually by contributing, yet they benefit in the long run from greater stability in the South. Disaster relief is generally a positive example of international cooperation. Food donated by the World Council of Churches may be carried to a disaster scene in Canadian military aircraft and then distributed by the International Committee of the Red Cross (ICRC). Embarrassing failures in the past—of underresponse or overresponse, or of duplication of efforts or agencies working at cross-purposes—were much less common in the 1990s, and in the new century groups are attempting to coordinate their actions even more effectively.[42]

The new-found success of the international community in coordinating relief efforts was evident after the December 2004 tsunami disaster in Asia. Within hours, millions lost family members, homes, possessions, safe drinking water and ways of life. The World Health Organization estimated that five million people lacked basic supplies. The world community's response began quite modestly, but after the full extent of the disaster was beamed around the globe and the death toll climbed to staggering numbers, aid poured in to the region. More than $7 billion was pledged by states, IOs and private citizens across the globe. IOs and NGOs quickly mobilized to carry out what has been termed the "largest relief effort in human history." The efforts by these organizations were coordinated through a variety of relief agencies, including the International Committee of the Red Cross, the International Organization for Migration, the UNHCR and Oxfam.

The relationship between disasters and economic development is complex, and appropriate responses vary according to location, type and size of disaster and phase of recovery. For instance, refugees displaced from home communities have different needs from those of earthquake or hurricane victims whose entire communities have been damaged. Different resources are needed in the emergency phase (for example, food and medical supplies) than in the reconstruction phase (for example, earthquake-resistant housing designs). Responses that are too small in scale or too short-term may fail to meet critical needs, but those that are too large or prolonged can overwhelm the local economy and create dependency (reducing incentives for self-help). Thus, appropriate disaster relief can promote local economic development, whereas inappropriate responses can distort or impede such development.[43]

International norms regarding states' legal obligations to assist others in times of natural disaster and to accept such assistance if needed are changing.[44] In the 1990s—designated by the UN as the International Decade for Natural Disaster Reduction—a new international regime began solidifying, and passed its biggest test with the tsunami of 2004.

The Missionary Model

Beyond disaster relief, many governments and private organizations provide ongoing development assistance in the form of projects administered by agencies from the North in local communities in the South to help meet basic needs. Although efforts vary, the approach could be called a *missionary* model because it resembles the charitable works

---

[42] Kimberly A. Maynard, *Healing Communities in Conflict: International Assistance in Complex Emergencies* (NY: Columbia UP, 1999).

[43] Mary B. Anderson and Peter J. Woodrow, *Rising from the Ashes: Development Strategies in Times of Disaster* (Boulder, CO: Westview, 1989). Frederick C. Cuny, *Disasters and Development* (NY: Oxford UP, 1983).

[44] Jiri Toman, "Towards a Disaster Relief Law: Legal Aspects of Disaster Relief Operations," *Assisting the Victims of Armed Conflict and Other Disasters*, ed. Frits Kalshoven (Dordrecht, Netherlands: Martinus Nijhoff, 1989).

performed by missionaries in poor countries in past centuries. In fact, many of these private programs are still funded by churches and carried out by missionaries.

Charitable programs are helpful, though not without problems. They are a useful means by which people in the North funnel resources to people in the South. Even during the colonial era, missionaries did some good despite often perpetuating stereotypes of European superiority and native inferiority. Today's efforts to help poor people in the global South are helpful in giving local individuals and communities resources with which they may better contribute to national economic development.

However, most handout programs provide only short-term assistance and do not create sustained local economic development. They do not address the causes of poverty, the position of poor countries in the world economy or local political conditions such as military rule or corruption.

One version of "missionary" assistance—advertised widely in Canada—lets citizens in rich countries "adopt" poor children in the global South. Photos of a hungry child stare at the reader of a magazine while the accompanying text notes that a few cents a day can "save" the child. Although such programs raise awareness in the North of the extent of poverty in the South, at worst they tend to be exploitive and to reinforce racist and paternalistic stereotypes of the helplessness of people in the developing world.

There is a danger in the missionary model that people from the North may provide assistance inappropriate for a developing state's local conditions and culture, a danger illustrated by an experience in Kenya in the 1970s. Nomadic herders in the area of Lake

MOUTHWASH FOR MAURITANIA
The missionary model of foreign assistance contributes goods to economies of the global South, but often with little understanding of local needs or long-term strategies. Here, free supplies including cartons of mouthwash are delivered by a U.S. ambassador and the captain of a U.S. Navy ship participating in Project Handclasp, 1989.

Turkana near the Sahara desert—the Turkana tribe—were poor and vulnerable to periodic droughts. Northern aid donors and the Kenyan government decided that the herders' traditional way of life was not environmentally sustainable and should be replaced by commercial fishing of the abundant tilapia fish in Lake Turkana. Norway, with long experience in fishing, was asked to teach fishing and boat-building methods to the Turkana. To create a commercially viable local economy, Norwegian consultants recommended marketing frozen fish fillets to Kenya and the world. Thus, in 1981, Norway finished building a $2 million, state-of-the-art fish freezing plant on the shores of Lake Turkana and a US$20 million road connecting the plant to Kenya's transportation system.

There were three problems. First, with outside temperatures of 38 degrees Celsius (a contrast with Norway), the cost of operating the freezers exceeded the income from the fillets. So after a few days, the freezers were turned off and the facility became a dried-fish warehouse. Second, Turkana culture viewed fishing as the lowest-status profession, suitable only for those incompetent at herding. Third, every few decades Lake Turkana shrinks as drought reduces the inflow of water. Such a drought in 1984–1985 eliminated the gulf where the fishing operations were based. The Norwegians might have foreseen these problems by doing more homework instead of just transplanting what worked in Norway. When the drought hit, the 20 000 herders who had been brought to the lake to learn fishing were left in an overcrowded, overgrazed environment where every tree was cut for firewood and the majority of cattle died. Instead of becoming self-sufficient, the Turkana became totally dependent on outside aid.[45]

The NGO Model

A third model of development assistance can be found in the approach taken by nongovernmental organizations devoted to development aid, such as Oxfam and CARE. Originally devoted to short-term aid for famine victims, and still active in that effort, many development NGOs realized that in the long term, people needed not just handouts of food but the means to feed themselves—land, water, seed, tools and technical training.

The distinctive aspect of the NGO model is that it relies on local communities to determine the needs of their own people and to carry out development projects. NGOs such as Oxfam, for example, do not operate projects themselves but provide funding to local organizations. NGOs do not normally describe themselves as donors and these organizations as recipients. Rather, they call both sides "project partners"—working together to accomplish a task. In this model, a little outside money can go a long way toward building sustained local economic development. Furthermore, projects help participants empower themselves by organizing to meet their own needs.

For example, Oxfam America helped the Ethiopian women's cooperative mentioned in Chapter 12 (see p. 423). Oxfam did not design or organize the project; women in Addis Ababa did. When their garment-making workshop became profitable and was ready to expand and employ twice as many women, Oxfam gave the group a US$15 000 grant to construct a new building. This small grant helped to consolidate a new centre of accumulation in one of the world's poorest neighbourhoods.

CARE Canada (with assistance from CIDA) supported a charcoal stoves project in Zambia. Charcoal is the most common cooking and heating fuel among Zambia's poor and sometimes consumes as much as 90 percent of a family's income to acquire it. The

---

[45] Blaine Harden, *Africa: Dispatches from a Fragile Continent* (NY: Norton, 1990).

charcoal stoves project supported the manufacturing and sale of a fuel-efficient stove based on a model developed in Kenya. The stove itself resulted in savings of almost 50 percent of fuel costs and was produced and marketed by Zambians, eventually becoming a self-sustaining and profit-making enterprise (see http://carezambia.org).

The NGO approach seeks to reconceptualize development assistance to focus on long-term development through a bottom-up basic needs strategy. The measure of development adopted by most NGOs is similar to the Human Development Index (p. 453). Genuine development, in Oxfam's view, enables people to meet their own essential needs. This means extending beyond food aid and emergency relief, and instead attempting to reverse the process of impoverishment. Genuine development also enhances democracy; strikes a balance between populations and resources; aims to improve the well-being and status of women; respects local cultures; is environmentally sustainable; involves change, not just charity; requires the empowerment of the poor; and promotes the interests of the majority of people worldwide, in the North as well as the global South.[46]

The Changing World Order

Foreign Aid

In late 2001, Britain urged the United States to double global foreign aid to the South by spending US$50 billion more per year. The increase would almost equal, in inflation-adjusted terms, the Marshall Plan by which the United States helped rebuild Western Europe after World War II. The idea of a massive global increase in foreign aid has some support from Canada and the United Nations. It would mark a shift in the North-South dimension of world order, in which the North would more seriously engage in the task of progressively reducing poverty and despair in the South. This shift would also depart from the trend of the 1990s, which saw foreign aid fall sharply even as Northern countries got richer.

Britain's finance minister advanced the "instrumental" view described in the Changing World Order box in Chapter 12 (p. 428) when he argued that the 9/11 terrorist attacks demonstrated that the safety of people in the North depends in part on the well-being of people in the South. "Today what happens to the poorest person in the poorest country can affect the richest person in the richest country." Some observers suggested that increases to Canada's development cooperation would also support its security interests.*

The United States resisted the British proposal at first. U.S. critics of foreign aid say that programs are wasteful and even counterproductive. Bush administration officials say that market forces and foreign investment should drive development, not handouts. Overall, the U.S. share of GDP spent on foreign aid is the lowest of industrialized countries and major increases were not expected even after the terrorist attacks. The U.S. government hardly seemed inclined to radically increase foreign aid, especially to countries that did not pose a terrorist-related threat, at a time of sharp increases in military spending and other kinds of new expenditures in the war on terrorism. In 2002, however, the U.S. shifted its position and began to devote greater resources to foreign aid.

What do you think? Should Canada, the United States and other rich countries dramatically increase foreign aid? Is the threat of terrorist attacks the only argument that will persuade rich countries to finally begin to meet their foreign aid commitments? What is your view of the prospects of sustainable support for the South when it is justified on the basis of fear?

* Joseph Kahn, "Britain Urges U.S. to Expand Global Antipoverty Programs," *New York Times* 18 Dec. 2001: A10. Amitav Rath, "Canada and Development Cooperation," *International Journal* 59.4 (Fall 2004): 853–71.

---

[46] *Oxfam America News* (Boston: Oxfam America).

PARTNER IN DEVELOPMENT
The Oxfam model of foreign assistance emphasizes support for local groups that can stimulate self-sustaining economic development at a local level. A mutually beneficial North-South partnership is the global goal of such projects. These women show off a mill they purchased with microcredit from an Oxfam-affiliated group in Gambia, 2001.

The general goals of the NGO model of foreign aid are consistent with a broader movement in the global South toward grassroots **empowerment.** Efforts such as those of Oxfam and CARE are organized by poor people to gain some power over their situation and meet their own basic needs—not by seizing control of the state in a revolution but by means that are more direct, more local and less violent. The key to success is getting organized, finding information, gaining self-confidence and obtaining needed resources to implement action plans.

For example, women in Bangladesh have a very low status in rural society (see "Women in Development" on pp. 422–424). Often they cannot own property, participate in politics or even leave their houses without their husbands' permission. Now some women in rural Bangladesh have organized women's groups to raise women's self-esteem, promote their rights and mobilize them to change conditions. One woman reported, "Our husbands used to beat us—now they don't. They used to not let us in the fields—now we go with them. They used to not help us at home—now they do. . . . We now can do all this thanks to the group and the support it has given us." [47] In this example, economic development and the satisfaction of basic needs have been furthered not by violence or revolution, nor by the actions of the state, foreign governments or international agencies, but directly at the community level.

In India, local women's groups, using only the power of persuasion and logic, have convinced some landowners to give them land for cooperative income-generating projects such as vegetable farming and raising silkworms. Elsewhere in India, women working as

empowerment In a development context, it refers to the grassroots efforts of poor people to gain power over their situation and meet their own basic needs.

[47] Oxfam America, *Community*, video (Boston: Oxfam, 1995).

gatherers of wood and other forest products got organized to win the legal minimum wage for 250 000 female forest workers—three times what they were being paid before. In this case, government action was necessary, but the pressure for such action came from local organizing. The women took their case to the public and the press, staging protest marches and an art exhibit related to their cause in the provincial capital.

These examples do not mean that national and foreign governments are unimportant. To the contrary, government policies affect millions of people more quickly and more widely than do grassroots efforts. Indeed, grassroots organizing often has as an ultimate goal the restructuring of national political and social life so that policies reflect the needs of poor people. The successes of grassroots empowerment show that poor communities are not simply victims of poverty waiting to be saved or passive bystanders in North-South relations.

The NGO model has the advantage of promoting this trend toward grassroots empowerment, thereby overcoming the dangers of externally run programs under the disaster relief and missionary models. However, the NGO model has to date been tested on only a very small scale. Although the model may be effective in the local communities it reaches, it would have to be adopted widely and replicated on a much larger scale in order to influence the overall prospects for development in the global South. It is unclear whether the principles the model embodies, from a reliance on local community organizers to an avoidance of government involvement, would work on a massive scale.

Confronting the North-South Gap

It is imperative that people in affluent countries such as Canada become knowledgeable about questions of poverty and the different arguments and policies that are developed to explain poverty and to respond to it. It is increasingly difficult for citizens in rich countries to turn their backs and ignore these issues. North-South relations have become a part of everyday life. The integrated global economy brings to the North products and people from the South. The information revolution puts images of poverty on television sets in comfortable living rooms. The growing role of the UN brings the North and South together in a worldwide community. Security relations and political economies have shifted in the post–Cold War era to give new prominence to the global South.

The environment is another issue that impacts all regions of the world, and raises questions of political economy and security. Responses to environmental problems also cross many boundaries and range from efforts conducted at the local, national and global levels. These issues are the subject of Chapter 14.

Thinking Critically

1. How might the strong economic growth of the Asian NICs and China affect proposals for an Asian free trade area similar to NAFTA and the EU? What would be the interests and worries of Japan, China and the NICs and of the poor states of the region in such an arrangement?

2. Past successes in economic development have depended heavily on developing a manufacturing base, which requires access to scarce capital. How do you think the information revolution and the increasing role of services in the world economy might change this pattern? Might any countries of the global South find a niche in these growing sectors of the world economy and bypass manufacturing? What states or regions might be candidates for such an approach, and why?

3. How does the debt problem compare with debt accumulated in countries like Canada or the United States? Do the two debt problems arise from similar causes? Which of them do you consider the more serious problem, and why?

4. Some scholars criticize the IMF for imposing harsh terms in its conditionality agreements with poor states. Others applaud the IMF for demanding serious reforms before providing financial resources. If you were a leader of a developing country negotiating with the IMF, what kinds of terms would you be willing to agree to and what terms would you resist? Why?

5. If the states in North America, Western Europe and Japan/Pacific met the target of providing 0.7 percent of GNP in foreign assistance, what might the effects be? How much additional aid would be made available? To whom would it likely go? What effects might it have on recipient states and on global South economic development overall?

Chapter Summary

• Economic development in the global South has been uneven; per capita GDP increased in the 1970s but, with the exception of Asia, decreased in the 1980s. Growth in the 1990s was brisk in Asia but slow elsewhere, with parts of Africa sliding backward. The 2001 recession created further obstacles for development.

• Evidence does not support a strong association of economic growth with either internal equality of wealth distribution or internal inequality.

• The newly industrializing countries (NICs) in Asia—South Korea, Taiwan, Hong Kong and Singapore—show that it is possible to rise out of poverty into sustained economic accumulation. Other states are trying to emulate these successes, but it is unclear whether these experiences can apply elsewhere, and whether authoritarianism is a necessary element of the NICs' success.

• China has registered strong economic growth in the past 20 years of market-oriented economic reforms. Though still quite poor, China may be emerging as a leading success story in economic development.

• Economic development in other large countries of the global South, such as India, Brazil and Nigeria, has been slowed by the inefficiency of state-owned enterprises, corruption and debt.

• Import substitution has been largely rejected as a development strategy in favour of export-led growth. This reflects the experiences of the NICs and the theory of comparative advantage.

• Most poor states want to develop a manufacturing base, but this is a difficult task. Even when focused on low-capital industries, states have generally had to sharpen income disparities in the process of concentrating capital for manufacturing.

• The theory that democratization would accompany and strengthen economic development has not been supported by the actual experiences of developing countries. The opposite theory—that authoritarian government is necessary to maintain control while concentrating capital for industrialization—has also not been supported or refuted.

• Debate exists about the causes of underdevelopment. Liberals emphasize internal problems (such as government corruption), and critical theorists emphasize historical and global conditions (such as the structural relations of inequality that resulted from colonialism and continue to this day).

- Given the shortage of local capital in most poor states, foreign investment by MNCs is often courted as a means of stimulating economic growth. MNCs look for favourable local conditions, including political and economic stability, in deciding where to invest. Critics argue that MNCs take more out of a developing country than they bring in.

- States in the global South seek the transfer of technology to support future economic development. Technology transfer can be appropriate or inappropriate to local needs depending on the circumstances of each case.

- The green revolution of the 1960s was a massive North-South transfer of agricultural technology, which had good and bad effects. Today's "green" technologies being transferred to the South are techniques for environmentally sustainable development.

- Debt, resulting largely from overborrowing in the 1970s and early 1980s, is a major problem. Through renegotiations and other debt management efforts, the North and South have improved the debt situation in recent years. However, the South remains almost $2 trillion in debt to the North, and annual debt service consumes about one-sixth of all hard-currency earnings from exports of the South (much more in some regions and states).

- The IMF makes loans to states in the South conditional on economic and governmental reforms. These conditionality agreements often necessitate politically unpopular measures such as cutting food subsidies.

- The WTO trading regime works against the global South by allowing rich nations to protect sectors in which the South has advantages—notably agriculture and textiles. The Generalized System of Preferences (GSP) tries to compensate by lowering barriers to global South exports.

- Efforts to improve the South's solidarity, cooperation and bargaining position relative to the North—such as the New International Economic Order (NIEO)—have had little success.

- Foreign assistance, mostly from governments in the North, plays an important part in the economic development plans of the poorer states of the South.

- Only a few states in the North meet the goal of contributing 0.7 percent of their GNPs as foreign assistance to the South. The United States, at 0.1 percent of its GNP, contributes the smallest share of any industrialized state, and its contributions decreased sharply in the past decade.

- Most foreign aid consists of bilateral grants and loans from governments in the North to specific governments in the South. Such aid is often used for political leverage, and promotes the export of products from the donor state.

- About one-fifth of foreign aid is not bilateral but is funnelled through multilateral agencies—mostly UN programs.

- Disaster relief provides short-term aid to prevent a natural disaster from reversing a poor state's economic development efforts. Disaster relief generally involves cooperation by various donor governments, local governments, the UN and private agencies.

- Handouts to poor communities to meet immediate needs for food and supplies outside times of disaster—here called the missionary model—may be helpful but can have several drawbacks. Such aid may be inappropriate to local needs and can encourage dependence.

- Efforts to support local organizations working to empower poor people and generate community economic development—here called the NGO model—are promising but have been tried only on a small scale.

Key Terms

economic development   452

Human Development Index
   (HDI)   453

newly industrializing countries
   (NICs)   455

"four tigers"/"four dragons"   456

free economic zones   459

import substitution   467

export-led growth   467

terms of trade   467

informal sector   469

microcredit   469

cartel   469

Organization of Petroleum Exporting
   Countries (OPEC)   469

brain drain   477

technology transfer   477

green revolution   478

debt service   479

default   479

debt renegotiation   479

Paris Club, London Club   480

IMF conditionality   481

New International Economic Order
   (NIEO)   485

foreign assistance   486

Development Assistance Committee
   (DAC)   486

bilateral aid   486

multilateral aid   486

World University Service of Canada
   (WUSC)   488

UN Development Programme
   (UNDP)   489

disaster relief   490

empowerment   495

Research Navigator Question

Research Navigator.com
RESOURCES FOR COLLEGE RESEARCH ASSIGNMENTS

Log on to Research Navigator and find one or two articles using the keyword search: Human Development Index. Using the information you find in these articles, quickly summarize the main features of what human development means (you may want to think about how the HDI contrasts with a more standard measure of development—per capita Gross Domestic Product). Now search for visual images on websites or in newspapers. Find an image that you think best captures the idea of human development.

Weblinks

The following links are a sampling of research centres, government departments and international organizations focused on international development:

Canadian International Development Agency:
http://www.acdi-cida.gc.ca/index-e.htm

CARE Canada:
http://www.care.ca/care_e.asp

International Development Research Centre:
http://web.idrc.ca/en/ev-1-201-1-DO_TOPIC.html

Oxfam Canada:
http://www.oxfam.ca

United Nations Development Fund for Women:
http://www.unifem.org/

Women in Development Network:
http://www.focusintl.com/widnet.htm

Environment and Population

Windmill and nuclear power plant, Britain, c. 1984.

INTERDEPENDENCE AND THE ENVIRONMENT

As we have seen, world industrialization and technological development have increased international interdependence through functional economic integration and transnational communication. Industrialization has also intensified international interdependence in another way—through its impact on the world's natural environment. Actions taken by one state now routinely affect other states' access to natural resources and to the benefits of a healthy environment.[1] Global threats to the natural environment are thus a major new source of interdependence.

Because environmental effects tend to be diffuse and long term and because they spread easily from one location to another, international environmental politics creates difficult collective goods problems (see p. 82). A sustainable natural environment is a collective good, and states bargain over how to distribute the costs of providing that good. The technical, scientific and ethical aspects of managing the environment are complex, but the basic nature of states' interests is not. A collective goods problem arises in every issue area concerning the environment, natural resources and population.

For example, the world's major fisheries in international waters are not owned by any state; they are a collective good. Various fishing states must cooperate (partly by regulating nonstate actors such as MNCs) to avoid depleting stocks of fish. If too many states fail to cooperate, fish populations are wiped out and everyone's catch is much reduced. In fact, this has already happened in many of the world's largest fisheries, such as Canada's.

---

[1] Jyrki Käkönen, ed., *Perspectives on Environmental Conflict and International Politics* (London: Pinter, 1992).

Fish catches worldwide dropped sharply in the early 1990s and the global fishing industry started losing more than $50 billion a year, relying increasingly on government subsidies. Cod in North American waters were wiped out in the early 1990s, with the North Sea cod likely to follow. The EU cut quotas for cod fishing by 80 percent in 1998–2003 after long political negotiations, but scientists do not expect stock to recover short of a total ban. Worldwide, according to a 2003 study, the oceans' population of large fish including cod has dropped by 90 percent in the past 50 years.[2] As of 2007, global catches of all fish species had declined by about 15 percent in a decade, with only further declines projected.

Depletion has occurred because each additional fishing boat—and its owners as well as its state of origin—gains by catching an additional fish. The benefits of that fish go entirely to the catcher, whereas the eventual costs of depleted stocks will be shared by all. What is a state's fair quota of fish? There is no world government to decide, so states must enter into multilateral negotiations, agreements and regimes. Such efforts create new avenues for functionalism and international integration, but also new potentials for conflict and "prisoner's dilemmas."

States negotiate complex agreements to try to manage the fisheries dilemma. In 1999, a UN-sponsored agreement among all the world's major fishing states set goals to reduce fleet overcapacity. (There are four million fishing boats worldwide, of which 40 000 are ships larger than 90 tonnes.) Participating nations are capping the size of fishing fleets and scaling them back gradually while reducing subsidies. The pain of unemployment and economic adjustment would thus be shared. However, the agreement is voluntary, and its effect on collapsing fisheries is probably too little, too late.

This type of collective goods dilemma has been called the **tragedy of the commons.**[3] Centuries ago, the commons was shared grazing land in Britain. As with fisheries, if too many people kept too many sheep, the commons would be overgrazed, yet adding one more sheep was profitable to that sheep's owner. Britain solved the problem (although creating other problems) by **enclosure of the commons**—splitting it into privately owned pieces on which a single owner would have an incentive to manage resources responsibly. The world's states are gradually taking a similar approach to fisheries by extending territorial waters to put more fish under the control of single states (see "Minerals, Land, Water" later in this chapter). The *global commons* refers to shared parts of the earth, such as the oceans and outer space.

The solution of environmental collective goods problems is based on achieving shared benefits that depend on overcoming conflicting interests.[4] *Regimes* are an important part of this solution, providing rules to govern bargaining over who gets the benefits and bears the costs of environmental protection. Functional IOs that specialize in technical and management aspects of the environment are also vital.[5]

tragedy of the commons
A collective goods dilemma created when common environmental assets (such as the world's fisheries) are depleted or degraded through the failure of states to cooperate effectively. One solution is the enclosure of the commons (splitting them into individually owned pieces); international regimes can also be a (partial) solution.

enclosure of the commons
The splitting of a common area or good into privately owned pieces, giving individual owners an incentive to manage resources responsibly.

---

[2] Ransom A. Myers and Boris Worm, "Rapid Worldwide Depletion of Predatory Fish Communities," *Nature* 423 (15 May 2003): 280–283.

[3] Garrett Hardin, "The Tragedy of the Commons," *Science* 162 (16 Dec. 1968): 1243–48. Elinor Ostrom, *Governing the Commons: The Evolution of Institutions for Collective Action* (NY: Cambridge UP, 1991). Robert O. Keohane and Elinor Ostrom, eds., *Local Commons and Global Interdependence: Heterogeneity in Two Domains* (Thousand Oaks, CA: Sage, 1995).

[4] Dimitris Stevis and Valerie J. Assetto, eds., *The International Political Economy of the Environment: Critical Perspectives* (Boulder, CO: Rienner, 2001). Miranda A. Schreurs and Elizabeth Economy, eds., *The Internationalization of Environmental Protection* (NY: Cambridge UP, 1997). Benedict Kingsbury and Andrew Hurrell, eds., *The International Politics of the Environment* (NY: Oxford UP, 1992).

[5] Oran R. Young, ed., *The Effectiveness of International Environmental Regimes: Casual Connections and Behavioral Mechanisms* (Cambridge, MA: MIT P, 1999). Lynne M. Jurgielewicz, *Global Environmental Change and International Law: Prospects for Progress in the Legal Order* (Lanham, MD: UP America, 1996). Robert O. Keohane, Marc A. Levy and Peter M. Haas, *Institutions for the Earth: Sources of Effective International Environmental Protection* (Cambridge, MA: MIT P, 1993).

TOO MANY COOKS
Management of environmental issues is complicated by the large numbers of actors involved, which make collective goods problems hard to resolve (individuals may be more tempted to free-ride). The 1992 Earth Summit (UN Conference on Environment and Development) in Rio de Janeiro, Brazil, was the largest gathering of state leaders in history.

epistemic communities
Transnational communities of experts who help structure the way states manage environmental and other issues.

Increasingly, IOs overlap with broader communities of experts from various states that structure the way states manage environmental issues; these have been called **epistemic communities** (knowledge-based communities). For example, the transnational community of experts and policy-makers concerned with pollution in the Mediterranean is an epistemic community.[6]

In global environmental politics, it is hard to manage collective goods problems because of the large number of actors. Collective goods are easier to provide in small groups, where individual actions have more impact on the total picture and where cheating is more noticeable. The opposite is true with the environment. The actions of nearly 200 states (albeit some more than others) aggregate to cause indirect but serious consequences throughout the world. This large number of actors was seen in the 1992 *UN Conference on Environment and Development* (the "*Earth Summit*") in Rio de Janeiro, Brazil; it was the largest summit meeting of state leaders ever, 153 in all.

With a few exceptions, only in the last few decades has the global environment become a major subject of international negotiation and IR scholarship.[7] Interest in the environment has grown rapidly since the first "Earth Day" was held by environmental

[6] Peter M. Haas, "Introduction: Epistemic Communities and International Policy Coordination," spec. issue of *International Organization* 46.1 (1992): 1–36. Peter M. Haas, *Saving the Mediterranean: The Politics of International Environmental Cooperation* (NY: Columbia UP, 1990).

[7] Elizabeth R. DeSombre, *Domestic Sources of International Environmental Policy* (Cambridge, MA: MIT P, 2000). Harold Sprout and Margaret Sprout, *The Ecological Perspective on Human Affairs, with Special Reference to International Politics* (Princeton, NJ: Princeton UP, 1965).

activists in 1970. The energy crises of the 1970s seemed to underline the issue in industrialized regions. Oil spills, urban air pollution, pesticide residues and difficulties at nuclear power plants elevated the environment on the international agenda.

The first UN conference on the international environment took place in Stockholm, Sweden, in 1972. It adopted general principles—that one state's actions should not cause environmental damage to another, for instance—and raised awareness about international aspects of environmental damage. A second conference was held, with less publicity, in 1982 in Nairobi, Kenya (headquarters of the UN Environment Programme). The larger and more ambitious 1992 Earth Summit was the third conference. The fourth was held in Johannesburg, South Africa, in 2002.

Sustainable Economic Development

At the 1992 Earth Summit, the major theme was *sustainable* economic development, which refers to economic growth that does not deplete resources and destroy ecosystems so quickly that the basis of that growth is itself undermined. The concept applies to both industrialized regions and the global South.[8]

In the past, the growth of population, industry, energy use and the extraction of natural resources on the planet has been exponential—growing faster and faster over time. Such rapid growth cannot continue indefinitely, almost by definition. Several possibilities emerge. First, new tech-

NOT SUSTAINABLE
Pollution from industrialization caused great environmental damage in the Soviet Union, its unsustainable path contributing to the stagnation and collapse of the Soviet economy. Many environmental problems remain in post-Soviet states, such as this heavily polluting nickel plant in Siberia. Today's developing countries will have to industrialize along cleaner lines to realize sustainable development.

nologies may allow *unabated economic growth*, but will shift the basis of that growth away from the ever-increasing use of energy and other resources. This is what optimists with faith in technology expect. Goods and services would continue to multiply, raising the global standard of living, but would do so more efficiently to reduce strains on the environment.

A second possibility is a *collapse* of population and living standards in the world as excessive growth leads to ecological disaster. Pessimists worry that the present course will overshoot the **carrying capacity** of the planetary ecosystem and cause it to break down because of long-term environmental problems such as species depletion and global warming. By the time such problems produced severe short-term effects, it would be too late to correct them.

carrying capacity The limits of the planetary ecosystem's ability to absorb continual growth in population, industry, energy use and extraction of natural resources.

---

[8] Paul Harrison, *The Third World Revolution: Population, Environment, and a Sustainable World* (NY: Penguin, 1994). Lester R. Brown et al., *State of the World* (NY: Norton/Worldwatch Institute, annual). Richard N. Cooper, *Environment and Resource Policies for the World Economy* (Washington, DC: Brookings, 1995).

A third possibility is that the past curve of exponential growth will flatten out into an *S-curve*. The curve rises from a fairly flat slope to an exponential growth curve before levelling back off into a flat slope at a higher level. Instead of overshooting the planet's limits of human population and energy (triggering collapse), human beings would adapt to those limits in time to achieve a *steady-state* economy in which population, food production, energy use and other key processes would be stable from year to year. It has been argued that our generation is the "hinge of history," just past the middle point of the S-curve. If so, we are experiencing the most rapid change of any generation in the past *or* future.[9]

The Earth Summit produced an overall plan, called *Agenda 21*, whereby large states of the global South promised to industrialize along cleaner lines (at a certain cost to economic growth) and industrialized states promised to funnel aid and technology to assist in that process.[10]

Commission on Sustainable Development
An organization established at the 1992 UN Earth Summit that monitors states' compliance with their promises and hears evidence from environmental nongovernmental organizations (NGOs).

The Earth Summit also established the **Commission on Sustainable Development**, which monitors states' compliance with the promises they made at the summit and hears evidence from environmental NGOs such as Greenpeace. However, it lacks powers of enforcement over national governments—again reflecting the pre-eminence of state sovereignty over supranational authority (see pp. 378–379). The commission has 53 members. Its ability to monitor and publicize state actions is supposed to discourage states from cheating on the Earth Summit plan (and the follow-up 2002 Johannesburg Plan of Implementation, see below), but progress has been slow.[11]

In 2002, the Johannesburg World Summit on Sustainable Development involved 22 000 participants, including 100 heads of state and government. The summit was also attended by 8000 NGO representatives and 4000 members of the media, and resulted in the Johannesburg Plan of Implementation, which attempted to outline concrete actions and measures to achieve the goals outlined in Agenda 21. For example, the Plan of Implementation calls for countries to employ the globally harmonized system for the classification and labelling of chemicals as soon as possible, with a view to having it fully operational by 2008. It also promotes the idea of supporting sustainable tourism, and in particular eco-tourism, and suggests ways to provide technical support for countries of the global South that are attempting a transition into more sustainable forms of tourism.

China and other developing countries in Asia stood at the centre of the debate over sustainable development. In the drive for rapid economic growth, these countries have cut corners environmentally, resulting in the world's worst air pollution and other serious problems. Because of China's size, any success in developing its economy along Western industrialized lines (for example, with mass ownership of automobiles) creates shocks to the global environment. In recent years China has been scouring the planet for raw materials—with imports of 200 million tons of iron a year—to fuel its extraordinary growth. China has begun to switch away from dirty coal, helping ease air pollution, but its thirst for imported oil and gas drove up world oil prices from 2003 to 2006. Some of its clean energy options, such as the Three Gorges Dam, have damaged a large river ecosystem, and human rights advocates have been concerned about the massive displacement of people resulting from the 600-kilometre-long reservoir created by the dam.

---

[9] John R. Platt, "The Step to Man," *Science* 149 (6 Aug. 1965): 607–13.

[10] Tim O'Riordan and Heather Voisey, eds., *Sustainable Development in Europe: Coming to Terms with Agenda 21* (Ilford, UK: Cass, 1997). Marian A. L. Miller, *The Third World in Global Environmental Politics* (Boulder, CO: Rienner, 1995).

[11] Paul Lewis, "UN Implementing the Earth Summit," *New York Times* 1 Dec. 1992: A16.

Rethinking Interdependence

We have thus far treated international environmental issues as problems of interstate bargaining, an approach that reflects a neoliberal theoretical orientation. This approach has been challenged in recent years by an emerging theoretical framework that is more critical in orientation, seeking more fundamental change in the nature of the international community's approach to environmental problems. The more critical approach is well reflected in the grassroots activism of Greenpeace and other environment-related NGOs. Environmentalists object to free trade provisions that weaken environmental standards by empowering international bureaucrats who care more about wealth generation than eco-preservation (see p. 325). Similarly, environmental groups have objected to management of economic development in the global South by international institutions, in particular the World Bank.

Thus the more critical theoretical perspective rejects the liberal goal of maximizing wealth (see pp. 104–106). Although liberal concepts of rationality are longer-term than realist ones (see p. 49), environmentalists take an even broader and longer-term view. From this perspective, the collective goods issue among states is not the problem; it is the growth of industrial civilization out of balance with the planetary ecosystem that must ultimately support it. True rationality, for environmentalists, must include very long-term calculations about how the self-interest of humanity itself is undermined by a greedy drive to exploit nature—that is, interdependence and the collective goods problem are broadened to include humanity versus nature, not just state versus state.

The remainder of this chapter will focus on a series of environmental issues of interest to state leaders and environmental activists alike.

The Atmosphere

Preserving the health of the earth's atmosphere is beneficial to people throughout the world without regard for their own state's contribution to the problem or its solution. Two problems of the atmosphere have become major international issues—global warming and depletion of the ozone layer.

Global Warming Global climate change, or **global warming,** is a slow, long-term rise in the average world temperature. Scientists are not certain that such a rise is occurring, or if so how fast, but there is growing evidence that global warming is a real problem caused by the emission of carbon dioxide and other gases, and that it will get worse in the future. Many scientists believe it prudent to address the issue soon, because once the symptoms become obvious it will be too late to prevent disaster. The time frame is unclear: the issue of global warming rose high on political agendas in 2005–2007 because of a string of warm years, massive melt-offs of Arctic ice, high oil prices and the devastation of Hurricane Katrina in the U.S.

Over the next few decades, according to most estimates, global temperatures may rise by between one and five degrees Celsius if nothing is done. The high end of this temperature range corresponds with the difference between today's climate and that of the last ice age: it is a major climate change. Possibly within a few decades the polar ice caps would begin to melt and cause the sea level to rise by as much as a few feet. This rise could flood many coastal cities and devastate low-lying areas, such as the heavily populated coastal areas of Bangladesh and China. Urgent calls for action to avert global warming come from island states in the Pacific that are likely to disappear this century.

global warming A slow, long-term rise in the average world temperature caused by the emission of greenhouse gases produced by burning fossil fuels—oil, coal and natural gas. See also *greenhouse gases.*

The Information Revolution

Silicon versus Fossil Fuels?

The Industrial Revolution, which harnessed fossil fuels to power machinery, changed IR profoundly (see pp. 30–32). Now, perhaps, a comparable revolution in technology is driving world events in new directions. Some call information- and service-based economies "postindustrial." Is the information revolution the endpoint of industrialization? And if so, can the global South bypass industrialization and the global North decrease its energy use, thus reducing global warming?

To explore this question, go to www.pearsoned.ca/goldstein.

fossil fuels Oil, coal and natural gas, burned to run factories, cars, tractors, furnaces, electrical generating plants and other things that drive an industrial economy.

greenhouse gases Carbon dioxide and other gases that, when concentrated in the atmosphere, act like the glass in a greenhouse, holding in energy and leading to global warming.

Global climate change could also change weather patterns in many regions, causing droughts, floods and widespread disruption of natural ecosystems. It is possible also that climate changes (at least mild ones) could *benefit* some regions and make agriculture more productive. Nobody knows for sure, but sudden environmental changes are usually much more destructive than helpful.

It is very difficult to reduce the emissions of gases—mainly carbon dioxide—that cause global warming. These gases result from the broad spectrum of activities that drive an industrial economy. They are a byproduct of burning **fossil fuels**—oil, coal and natural gas—to run cars, tractors, furnaces, factories and so forth. These activities create **greenhouse gases**—so named because when concentrated in the atmosphere these gases act like the glass in a greenhouse: letting in energy in the form of short-wavelength solar radiation but reflecting it back when it tries to exit as longer-wavelength heat waves. The greenhouse gases are *carbon dioxide* (responsible for two-thirds of the effect), *methane gas*, *chlorofluorocarbons* (CFCs) and *nitrous oxide*. The concentration of these gases in the global atmosphere is slowly increasing, though the rates and processes involved are complicated (carbon is exchanged among the atmosphere, oceans and trees).

Thus the costs of reducing the greenhouse effect are high, because solutions entail curbing economic growth or shifting it to entirely new technological paths.[12] The political costs of such actions—which would likely increase unemployment, reduce corporate profits and lower personal incomes—could be severe. For example, in Canada, the government of Alberta—Canada's largest energy-producing province—and representatives from industry have argued that efforts to address global warming will have a detrimental impact on the Canadian economy. Not only will industry bear the burden of the costs of reducing the emissions, but because Canada's largest trading partner, the United States, has refused to set limits on greenhouse gas emissions, Canadian industry would be at a distinct disadvantage vis-à-vis U.S. exporters.

For individual states, the costs of reducing greenhouse emissions are almost unrelated to the benefits of a solution. If one state reduces its industrial production or makes expensive investments in new technologies, it will have little effect on the long-term outcome unless other states do likewise. And if most states took such steps, a free rider that did not go along would save money and still benefit from the solution.

Global warming thus presents a triple dilemma. First, there is the problem of short-term (and predictable) costs to gain long-term (and less predictable) benefits. Second, specific constituencies such as oil companies and industrial workers pay the costs, whereas the benefits are distributed more generally across domestic society. Third, there is the collective goods dilemma among states: benefits are shared globally but costs must be extracted from each state individually.

---

[12] Urs Luterbacher and Detlef F. Sprinz, *International Relations and Global Climate Change* (Cambridge, MA: MIT P, 2001). Ian H. Rowlands, *The Politics of Global Atmospheric Change* (NY: St. Martin's, 1995). Matthew Paterson, *Global Warming and Global Politics* (NY: Routledge, 1996). Edward S. Rubin et al., "Realistic Mitigation Options for Global Warming," *Science* 257 (10 July 1992): 148.

This third dilemma is complicated by the North-South divide, which creates divergent expectations about fair allocation of costs. Specifically, how can the industrialization of today's poor countries take place without pushing greenhouse emissions to unacceptable levels? Greenhouse gases are produced by each state roughly in proportion to its industrial activity. Eighty percent of greenhouse gases now come from the industrialized countries—25 percent from the United States alone. (U.S. carbon dioxide emissions amount to 18 tonnes per person annually, about twice the European rate and ten times China's.) Yet the most severe impacts of global warming are likely to be felt in the global South. Thus, serious international conflicts exist over who should pay the bills to avert global warming.

All these elements make for a difficult multilateral bargaining situation, one not yet resolved. The *Framework Convention on Climate Change* adopted at the 1992 Earth Summit set a nonbinding goal to limit greenhouse emissions to 1990 levels by the year 2000; that goal was not met. The treaty did not commit the signatory states to meet target levels of greenhouse emissions by a particular date, owing to U.S. objections.

Western Europe and Japan have been more willing to regulate greenhouse emissions than the United States (which burns more fossil fuel per person). Europe and Japan later proposed a binding treaty requiring all states to stabilize their emissions at 1990 levels by the year 2000, and then to reduce them by a further 15 percent by 2010. The United States modified its position in 1996, supporting a binding treaty, but with a target date of 2010 to reach 1990 levels and no subsequent targets.

The 1997 *Kyoto Protocol* adopted a complex formula for reducing greenhouse emissions to 1990 levels in the global North over about a decade. Countries in the global South received preferential treatment, however, since their levels (per capita) were much lower. China is the world's second-largest producer of carbon dioxide (after the United States), and India the sixth largest (after Russia, Japan and Germany). Objecting to this "free ride," the U.S. Congress promptly declared that it would not ratify the treaty. President Bush then dropped out of follow-up negotiations to Kyoto, declaring the treaty "dead." China, meanwhile, started lowering its carbon emissions, independently of the treaty, as it began switching away from its predominant fuel, coal.[13]

Moving forward without U.S. support, 160 countries agreed in 2001 to implement the Kyoto Protocol. Canada ratified in 2002. The needed ratifications to put the treaty into effect (from states totalling 55 percent of world emissions) came when Russia finally ratified in 2004. The Kyoto Protocol entered into effect in 2005, and mandatory carbon cuts under the treaty are to begin in 2008. The agreement calls for 40 industrialized countries to reduce emissions to 5 percent below 1990 levels by 2012, with binding penalties for failure. States will be able to buy and sell carbon emission credits and will get credit for forests that absorb carbon dioxide. For example, a venture in Brazil earned carbon credits by burning methane gas from a garbage dump (to generate electricity) instead of venting it as a strong greenhouse gas. European investors bought the credits and could then sell them to, say, a polluting factory in Eastern Europe where reducing carbon might be especially expensive.[14] The EU has pledged US$400 million per year to help the global South reduce its emissions.

---

[13] David G. Victor, *The Collapse of the Kyoto Protocol and the Struggle to Slow Global Warming* (Princeton, NJ: Princeton UP, 2001). Michael Grubb and Duncan Brack, eds., *The Kyoto Protocol: A Guide and Assessment* (London: Royal Institute of International Affairs, 1999).

[14] Deborah Stowell, *Climate Trading: Development of Greenhouse Gas Markets* (Basingstoke, UK: Palgrave, 2005).

MELTING AWAY
International treaties have been much more successful at addressing ozone depletion than global warming, mostly because the costs of the latter are much higher and the results are further in the future. A 1997 conference in Kyoto, Japan, set goals for industrialized countries to reduce their output of carbon dioxide and related gases modestly over the following decade, but the goals will probably not be met. If global warming melts polar ice caps in the new century, sea levels could rise and devastate many cities. This crack in the Antarctic ice shelf in 1997 suggests that this process is underway.

In some ways, Canada's position on Kyoto has shifted since the protocol was ratified in 2002. Kyoto received strong support, in principle, under a Liberal federal government when it was originally ratified. However, even with that strong support, the Canadian government made little concrete progress toward achieving Kyoto targets. A newly elected minority Conservative government in 2006 pledged to scrap Canada's commitment to Kyoto entirely. However, in 2007, public opinion polls indicated that the environment was a number-one priority for most Canadians, and a UN report signalled a wider consensus within the scientific community on the causes of climate change. The Conservative government then promised to strengthen its position on global warming, but stated that Canada would still be unable to meet its Kyoto commitments without adversely affecting industry. Some observers were pleased with the rhetorical shift of the Conservative government and its greater attention to climate change, but environmental activists have pointed out that carbon emissions can be cut without affecting industry, as the U.K. has demonstrated in having already reached its Kyoto targets.[15]

In 2006, 180 states negotiated on the question of what should happen after 2012 when Kyoto expires. With the United States still opposed, negotiations stalled as participants waited to see whether changes in U.S. domestic politics might lead it to join a follow-on treaty. The dilemma of global warming remains fundamentally unsolved, though, and with weak enforcement mechanisms, even the states that signed the Kyoto Protocol may not meet their targets by 2012, if ever. Technology may help make the bargaining somewhat easier in future. Many technical experts now argue that dramatic gains can be made through energy efficiency measures and other solutions that do not reduce the amount of economic activity but do make it cleaner and more efficient. Although costly, such investments would ultimately pay for themselves through greater economic efficiency. If this approach succeeds, international conflicts over global warming will be reduced.

[15] Daniel Schwanen, "Canada and the Kyoto Protocol: When Reality Sets In," *Canada Among Nations 2006: Minorities and Priorities*, ed. Andrew F. Cooper and Dane Rowland (Montreal and Kingston: McGill-Queen's University Press, 2006) 292–317. Sierra Club of Canada, "Kyoto Report Card 2007," available at http://www.sierraclub.ca/national/kyoto/kyoto-report-card-2007.pdf.

Focus on Canadian Scholarship

Scholars working at Canadian universities who examine questions of the environment include **Jennifer Clapp** at the University of Waterloo, who focuses on global environmental politics, the transfer of hazardous wastes and agricultural biotechnology. **Peter Dauvergne,** at the University of British Columbia, researches environmental theory in international relations and the political economy of globalization and the environment. **Steven Bernstein** of the University of Toronto is interested in the evolution of international environmental norms and the compromises of liberal environmentalism, and his colleague **Matthew J. Hoffman** focuses on ozone depletion and climate change. At Concordia University, **Peter Stoett** studies global biosecurity and ecopolitics. At York University, **Rodney Loeppky** examines the political economy of the human genome project, and at York's Faculty of Environmental Studies, **Bonnie Kettel** focuses on the environment and development. Also at York, **Deborah Barndt** focuses on women, globalization and food. **Robert Boardman** of Dalhousie University is interested in pesticides in world agriculture and the political economy of nature. At the University of Ottawa, **Matthew Paterson** focuses on global environmental and climate change politics. At Carleton's Norman Paterson School of International Affairs, **Inger Weibust** studies international and comparative environmental policy. **Melissa Gabler** at the University of Guelph is interested in intellectual property protection and the conservation of biodiversity. At Ryerson University, **Christopher Gore** focuses on the tensions between local, national and global interests in urban and environmental management. **Jeremy Wilson** of the University of Victoria is interested in global climate change and biodiversity loss. At the University of Western Ontario, **Radoslav S. Dimitrov** focuses on global environmental politics and law. **Jamey Essex** at the University of Windsor studies biotechnology, development and food security.

The **UN Environment Programme (UNEP),** whose main function is to monitor environmental conditions, works with the World Meteorological Organization to measure changes in the global climate. Since 1989, the UN-sponsored *Intergovernmental Panel on Climate Change* has served as a negotiating forum for this issue.

Ozone Depletion A second major atmospheric problem being negotiated by the world's governments is the depletion of the **ozone layer.**[16] Ozone high in the atmosphere screens out harmful ultraviolet rays from the sun. Chemicals expelled by some industries float to the top of the atmosphere and interact with ozone in a way that causes it to break down. The chief culprits are CFCs, widely used in refrigeration and in aerosol sprays. (Unfortunately, ozone produced by burning fossil fuels does not replace high-level ozone but only pollutes the lower atmosphere.)

As the ozone layer thins, more ultraviolet radiation is reaching the Earth's surface. Over Antarctica, where the ozone is thinnest, a hole appears to be growing larger and lasting longer year by year. Depleted ozone levels over North America were detected in the early 1990s, and people have been warned to limit exposure to the sun to lower their risk of skin cancer. Eventually, increased radiation could begin to kill vegetation, reduce agricultural yields and disrupt ecosystems.

Clearly, this is another collective goods problem in that one state benefits from allowing the use of CFCs in its economy provided that most other states prohibit their use. The costs of replacing CFCs are much lower than the costs of addressing global warming: CFCs can be replaced with other chemicals at relatively modest costs. Furthermore, the consequences of ozone depletion are better understood and more immediate than those of global warming.

UN Environment Programme (UNEP) UN agency that monitors environmental conditions and, among other activities, works with the World Meteorological Organization to measure changes in the global climate.

ozone layer The part of the atmosphere that screens out harmful ultraviolet rays from the sun. Certain chemicals used by some industries, in particular chlorofluorocarbons (CFCs), break down the ozone layer.

---

[16] Richard Elliot Benedick, *Ozone Diplomacy* (Cambridge, MA: Harvard UP, 1991). Karen Litfin, *Ozone Discourses: Science and Politics in Global Environmental Cooperation* (NY: Columbia UP, 1993).

Montreal Protocol (1987)
An agreement on the protection of the ozone layer in which states pledged to reduce and then eliminate use of chlorofluorocarbons (CFCs). It is the most successful environmental treaty to date.

Therefore, states have had more success negotiating agreements and developing regimes to manage the ozone problem. In the 1987 **Montreal Protocol,** 22 states agreed to reduce CFCs by 50 percent by 1998. In 1990, the timetable was accelerated and the signatories expanded: 81 states agreed to eliminate all CFCs by 2000. In 1992, as evidence of ozone depletion mounted, the schedule was again accelerated, with major industrial states phasing out CFCs by 1995. The signatories agreed in principle to establish a fund (of unspecified size and source) to help countries of the global South pay for alternative refrigeration technologies not based on CFCs. Without this help, developing-country states would be tempted to free-ride and could ultimately undermine the effort. These countries were also given until 2010 to phase out production. The Montreal Protocol was revised and strengthened again in 1997 and 1999. Rich countries stopped making CFCs in 1996, and ultimately contributed $2 billion to the fund as of 2006, at a current rate of about $500 million a year. This money, which supports about 5000 projects in 139 countries, has helped the global South reduce emissions over the past decade. The ozone hole continued to grow larger in 2006, but was projected to slowly shrink over the coming 50 years if current arrangements continue.

The Montreal Protocol on CFCs is the most important success yet achieved in international negotiations to preserve the global environment. Indeed, then–UN Secretary-General Kofi Annan called it "perhaps the single most successful international agreement to date." It showed that states can agree to take action on urgent environmental threats, can agree on targets and measures to counter such threats and can allocate (and pay) the costs in a mutually acceptable way. International cooperation on the ozone problem has not been widely repeated on other environmental issues.

Biodiversity

biodiversity The tremendous diversity of plant and animal species making up the earth's (global, regional and local) ecosystems.

Biodiversity refers to the tremendous diversity of plant and animal species making up the earth's (global, regional and local) ecosystems.[17] Biologists believe that the 1.4 million species that have been identified and named are only a small fraction of the total number of species in existence (most of which are micro-organisms). Some species, such as humans, are distributed broadly around the world, whereas others live in just one locale.

As a result of human destruction of ecosystems, large numbers of species are already *extinct* and others are in danger of becoming so. Extinct species cannot return. The causes of their extinction include overhunting, overfishing and introducing nonnative species that crowd out previous inhabitants. The most important cause is *loss of habitat*—the destruction of rain forests, pollution of lakes and streams and loss of agricultural lands to urban sprawl. Because ecosystems are based on complex interrelationships among species, the extinction of a few species can cause deeper changes in the environment. For example, the loss of native micro-organisms can lead to chronic pollution of rivers or to the transformation of arable land into deserts.

Because ecosystems are so complex, it is usually impossible to predict the consequences of a species' extinction or of the loss of a habitat or ecosystem. Generally the activities that lead to habitat loss are economically profitable, so there are real costs associated with limiting such activities. For example, logging in the U.S. northwest has been restricted to save the northern spotted owl from extinction. Less extensive restrictions have been attempted in British Columbia, and by some estimates there are fewer than

---

[17] Timothy M. Swanson, ed., *The Economics and Ecology of Biodiversity Decline: The Forces Driving Global Change* (NY: Cambridge UP, 1998).

50 spotted owls remaining in Canada. Nobody can be sure what effect the owl's extinction would have, but the costs to loggers are clear and immediate.

Species preservation is thus a collective good resembling global warming; the costs are immediate and substantial but the benefits are long term and ill defined. As for biodiversity, the effects of policies tend to be more local than those of global warming, so the problem can to some degree be enclosed within the purview of states. To a surprising extent, the biodiversity in one state affects the quality of the environment in others. Topsoil blown away in Africa is deposited in South America; monarch butterflies that failed to breed in Mexico in 1991 did not appear in Ontario in 1992.

It has been difficult to reach international agreement on sharing the costs of preserving biodiversity. A UN convention on trade in endangered species has reduced but not eliminated such trade. At the 1992 Earth Summit, a treaty on biodiversity was adopted that committed signatories to preserving habitats, forcing rich states to pay poor ones for the rights to use commercially profitable biological products extracted from rare species in protected habitats (such as medicines from rain forest trees). However, because of fears that it could limit U.S. patent rights in biotechnology, the United States did not sign the treaty. It signed in 1993, with stipulations, but did not ratify the treaty. As of 2007, the treaty had 189 member states, including Canada.

Biodiversity issues also include problems of invasive species—the accidental or intended introduction of life forms into new habitats, with sometimes disastrous environmental consequences. This occurred in Canada after the introduction of insects (the Asian long-horned beetle in wooden shipping crates), shellfish (zebra mussels in the ballast water of ships), plant life (purple loosestrife imported as ornamental plants) and amphibians (non-native bullfrogs in British Columbia). These species sometimes destroy or alter local habitats, prey on native species or carry disease. Invasive species also include micro-organisms—diseases such as West Nile, transmitted by infected mosquitoes native to parts of Africa, and the avian bird flu, originating in Asia. In an increasingly globalized world, the means for the transmission of alien species and diseases is compounded, but the resources to address their impact remain quite limited.[18]

Many environmentalists have a special concern for whales and dolphins, which, like humans, are large-brained mammals. In the past 20 years, environmental activists have persuaded states to agree to international regimes to protect whales and dolphins. The **International Whaling Commission** (an IGO) sets quotas for hunting certain whale species. Participation is voluntary, and Norway dropped out in 1992 when it decided unilaterally that it could increase its catch without endangering the species. The *Inter-American Tropical Tuna Commission* (another IGO) regulates methods used to fish for tuna, aiming to minimize dolphin losses.

The United States, which consumes half the world's tuna catch, has gone further and unilaterally requires that "dolphin-safe" methods be used for tuna sold on U.S. territory under the Marine Mammal Protection Act. In 1990, the United States banned imports of tuna from Mexico and Venezuela under this law. These countries, which could not comply as easily as the U.S. tuna industry could, took their case to the GATT (see pp. 332–335) and won. Species protection lost out to free trade in the GATT ruling. The United States did not comply with the GATT ruling, however, despite appeals from the EC and dozens of other states, including Canada.[19]

International Whaling Commission
An intergovernmental organization (IGO) that sets quotas for hunting certain whale species; states' participation is voluntary.

---

[18] Peter Stoett, "Biosecurity: The Next Public Policy Imperative for Canada and the World," *Policy Options* (February 2006): 24–30. Roger Keil and S. Harris Ali, "The Avian Flu: Some Lessons Learned from the 2003 SARS Outbreak in Toronto," *Area* 38.1 (2006): 107–09.

[19] James Brooke, "America—Environmental Dictator?" *New York Times* 3 May 1992: F7.

Such conflicts portend future battles between environmentalists and free trade advocates.[20] Free traders argue that states must not use domestic legislation to seek global environmental goals. Environmentalists do not want to give up national laws that they worked for decades to enact over the opposition of industrial corporations. Canadian efforts to prohibit the gasoline additive MMT (see p. 336) were rejected by NAFTA and the restriction was eventually abandoned by the Canadian government. Environmentalists adopted the sea turtle as a symbol of their opposition to the WTO after the WTO overturned U.S. regulations that required shrimp to be caught in nets from which sea turtles (an endangered species) can escape. NAFTA and the WTO's actions in cases such as the gasoline or shrimp disputes are based on unfair *application* of environmental rules to domestic versus foreign companies. In practical terms, however, from environmentalists' perspective the effect is negative.

In recent years, most spectacularly at the WTO's failed 1999 Seattle summit, a coalition of environmental groups campaigned against the "faceless bureaucrats" at the WTO who override national laws such as the tuna act. These bureaucrats are portrayed as agents of MNCs, out to increase profits with no regard for the environment. (Note the similarity to earlier popular European resistance to "faceless Eurocrats.") Recent conflicts have arisen over U.S. laws restricting the import of foods with pesticide residues and over European laws on imports of genetically engineered agricultural and pharmaceutical products, which the United States wants to export worldwide. Environmentalists fear that the successful Montreal Protocol on ozone protection (see p. 510), which relies on trade sanctions for enforcement, could be threatened by WTO agreements.

Thus, unilateral approaches to biodiversity issues are problematic because they disrupt free trade; multilateral approaches are problematic because of the collective goods problem. It is not surprising that the international response to species extinction has been fairly ineffective to date.

Forests and Oceans

Two types of habitat—tropical rain forests and oceans—are especially important to biodiversity *and* the atmosphere. Both are also reservoirs of commercially profitable resources, such as fish and wood. They differ in that forests are located almost entirely within state territory, while oceans are in the global commons, largely beyond any state territory.

Rain Forests As many as half the world's species live in *rain forests*. Rain forests replenish oxygen and reduce carbon dioxide in the atmosphere—slowing global warming and thus benefiting all the world's states. They are collective goods.

International bargaining on the preservation of rain forests has made considerable progress, probably because most rain forests belong to a few states. These few states have the power to speed up or slow down the destruction of forests—and international bargaining involves agreements that shift costs from those few states onto the broader group of

---

[20] W. Bradnee Chambers, ed., *Inter-Linkages: The Kyoto Protocol and the International Trade and Investment Regimes* (Washington, DC: Brookings, 2001). Dani Rodrik, *Has Globalization Gone Too Far?* (Washington, DC: Institute for International Economics, 1997). Daniel C. Esty, *Greening the GATT: Trade, Environment and the Future* (Washington, DC: Institute for International Economics, 1994). H. Jeffrey Leonard, *Pollution and the Struggle for the World Product: Multinational Corporations, Environment, and International Comparative Advantage* (NY: Cambridge UP, 1988). Thomas J. Schoenbaum, "International Trade and Protection of the Environment: The Continuing Search for Reconciliation," *American Journal of International Law* 91.2 (1997): 268–313.

states benefiting from the rain forests. This collective goods problem is simpler and has fewer actors than global warming.

Although some rich states (including Canada) have large forests, most of the largest rain forests are in poor states, such as Brazil, Indonesia, Malaysia and Madagascar. These states can benefit economically from exploiting the forests—by freely cutting lumber, clearing land for agriculture and mining.[21] Until recently (and still to an extent), leaders of rich states have been interested in encouraging maximum economic growth in poor states so that foreign debts could be paid—with little regard for environmental damage. The World Bank, for example, has been criticized by environmentalists for providing technical assistance and investment to build large dams in environmentally sensitive areas of the global South.

Now that rich states have an interest in protecting rain forests, they are using money and development assistance as leverage to induce poorer states to protect their forests rather than exploiting them maximally. Under international agreements of the early 1990s, rich countries are contributing hundreds of millions of dollars in foreign aid for this purpose. In some countries of the global South, burdened by large foreign debts, environmentalists and bankers from rich countries have worked out "debt-for-nature swaps" in which a debt is cancelled in exchange for a state's agreement to preserve forests.

Brazil in particular has responded to these agreements with significant steps. A major government-sponsored drive to settle and exploit the Amazon basin had begun in the 1960s. In the early 1990s, the government adopted sweeping new policies to balance economic exploitation of the basin with the needs of environmental preservation and the rights of indigenous peoples. In 2005, Brazil announced that deforestation had fallen 50 percent since 2003, though environmentalists perceive the figure as overly optimistic.

DEVELOPMENT OR DESTRUCTION?
Some environmentalists criticize the World Bank and other international institutions promoting economic development in poor countries for interfering destructively in local ecosystems such as rain forests. The green revolution increased yields but shifted patterns of agriculture in complex ways, such as by increasing pesticide and fertilizer runoff. Now genetically engineered crops promise further increases in agricultural productivity—more food on the table—but with environmental consequences that are not fully understood. This corporate president holds a genetically modified seedling, 2001.

Oceans The *oceans*, covering 70 percent of the earth's surface, are (like rain forests) a key to regulating the climate and preserving biodiversity. Oceans, like forests, are attractive targets for short-term economic uses that cause long-term environmental damage. Short-term uses include overfishing, dumping toxic and nuclear waste (and other garbage) and long-distance oil shipments (with their recurrent spills). Unlike rain

---

[21] Peter Dauvergne, *Shadows in the Forest: Japan and the Politics of Timber in Southeast Asia* (Cambridge, MA: MIT P, 1997). Roberto P. Guimãraes, *The Ecopolitics of Development in the Third World: Politics and Environment in Brazil* (Boulder, CO: Rienner, 1991).

forests, however, oceans belong to no state but are a global commons.[22] This makes the collective goods problem more difficult because no authority exists to enforce regulations. Preserving oceans depends on the cooperation of more than a hundred states and thousands of nonstate actors.

Free riders have great opportunities for profit. For example, *drift nets* are huge, kilometres-long fishing nets that scoop up everything in their path. They are very profitable but destructive of a sustainable ocean environment. Most states have now banned their use (under pressure from the environmental movement). However, no state has the authority to go onto the **high seas** (nonterritorial waters) and stop illegal use of these nets.

One solution that states have pursued involves "enclosing" more of the ocean. Territorial waters have expanded to hundreds of kilometres off coasts (and around islands) so that state sovereignty encloses substantial resources (fisheries and offshore oil and mineral deposits). This solution has been pursued in the context of larger multilateral negotiations on ocean management.

The **UN Convention on the Law of the Sea (UNCLOS),** negotiated from 1973 to 1982, governs the use of the oceans. The UNCLOS treaty established rules on territorial waters—12 nautical miles (22.2 kilometres) for shipping and a 200–nautical mile (370.4 kilometres) exclusive economic zone (EEZ) for economic activities such as fishing and mining. The 200–nautical mile limit put a substantial share of the economically profitable ocean resources in the control of about a dozen states (see Figure 14.1).

Varying interpretations leave economic rights in dispute in a number of locations. In the East China Sea in 2005, China sent five warships to back up its claim to an undersea gas field partly claimed by Japan, where China had begun drilling and Japan had granted drilling rights to a Japanese company. China's claim under a Continental Shelf treaty conflicts with Japan's claim of an EEZ.

Another conflict developed over a small piece of the continental shelf off Newfoundland that was just beyond the 200–nautical mile range controlled by Canada. The Canadian Navy harassed Spanish fishing ships there, which the Canadians claimed were overfishing and thus endangering fish populations that were mostly within their 200–nautical mile limit. Although the European Union accused Canada of "piracy" on the high seas, the two sides reached an agreement on fishing levels and practices in 1995. The agreement in turn stimulated progress in UN talks on developing global rules and norms for ocean fishing. (These talks did not reach a quick breakthrough, however.) In 1994, Russian warships drove away dozens of foreign fishing ships in the Sea of Okhotsk (in the centre of which is a small hole created by the 200–nautical mile limit). Similar conflicts may develop near Norway, West Africa, the South Pacific and the Indian Ocean.

UNCLOS also developed the general principle that the oceans are a common heritage of humankind. A mechanism was created, through an International Sea-Bed Authority, for sharing some of the wealth that rich states might gain from extracting minerals on the ocean floor (beyond 200 nautical miles).

Private environmental groups have been active players on the subject of oceans, just as with rain forests—pressuring governments and MNCs to change policies and activities. Tactics include direct action (such as Greenpeace ships shadowing garbage barges), lobbying, lawsuits and public education. These tactics have effectively used global communications

high seas That portion of the oceans considered common territory, not under any exclusive state jurisdiction. See also *territorial waters*.

UN Convention on the Law of the Sea (UNCLOS)
A world treaty (1982) governing use of the oceans. The UNCLOS treaty established rules on territorial waters and a 200–nautical mile exclusive economic zone (EEZ). See also *territorial waters*.

---

[22] Elisabeth Mann Borgese, *The Oceanic Circle: Governing the Seas as a Global Resource* (NY: UN UP, 1999). Giulio Pontecorvo, ed., *The New Order of the Oceans* (NY: Columbia UP, 1986).

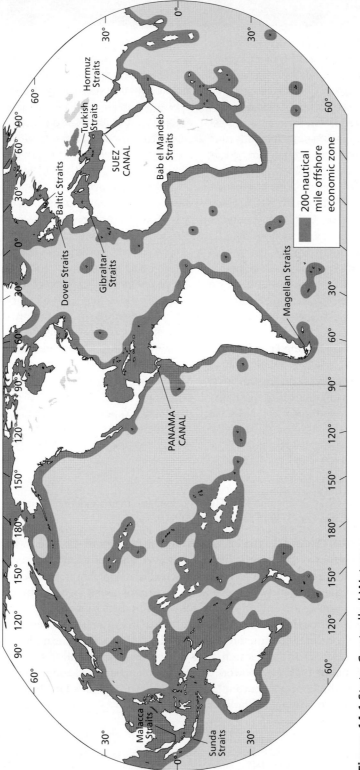

Figure 14.1 State-Controlled Waters

Overfishing and similar problems of managing the "commons" of world oceans have been addressed by enclosing the most important ocean areas under the exclusive control of states. Shaded areas are within the 200–nautical mile economic zones controlled by states under terms of the UNCLOS treaty.

Source: Adapted from Andrew Boyd, *An Atlas of World Affairs*, 9th ed. (NY: Routledge, 1992).

Thinking Theoretically

In 1995, Canada began unilaterally enforcing fishing rules just outside its 200–nautical mile exclusive economic zone, using military force several times to threaten Spanish fishing ships, once even seizing one. The actions appeared to be setting the stage for a nasty confrontation between allies (Canada and the European Union). Instead, an agreement was reached that limited fishing methods and catches in the area, as Canada had wanted. How might we explain this episode in theoretical terms? Realists would note the effectiveness of Canada's resort to military leverage, which drove the cost of European resistance way up and made it worthwhile for the EU to come to terms with Canadian demands. Since treaties such as UNCLOS are viewed with some skepticism by realists, they would attribute Canada's success to its proximity—the greater ease with which its navy could deploy to the disputed area—and a stronger will to prevail (reflecting the fact that the issue affected Canada's national interests much more than those of the EU).

Liberals could note, however, that the EU is far more powerful than Canada overall, so sheer power politics does not provide a very good starting point for explaining the outcome. Rather, liberals might emphasize the collective goods problem involved in overfishing, and note that Canada's willingness to unilaterally take on the enforcement costs effectively resolved the dilemma. Only the

negotiation of the terms of what was being enforced (the specific rules for fishing) remained, and there the conflicts of interest were small compared with the overall range of mutual benefits produced by close economic cooperation between Canada and the EU. The idea that unilateral enforcement could resolve collective goods dilemmas is supported by the comments of the chairman of a UN conference working on an international fishing treaty. He noted that the Canadian-EU agreement "will help our discussions here because it establishes the principle that there can be boarding and monitoring on the high seas." Critical theorists would be less concerned about the question of enforcing norms, and might instead ask why "enforcement" became the important question when thinking about overfishing. Focusing on enforcement, as liberals and realists do, redirects our attention away from larger questions such as the role of global capitalism in species depletion. Critical theorists are concerned that problem-solving responses like the creation of treaties and questions of their enforcement keep us from applying deeper analyses and considering more radical solutions. Most critical theorists, for example, do not think that capitalism can be "managed" to produce better environmental outcomes; rather, capitalism would need to be transformed in order to get to the root causes of environmental degradation.

(see Chapter 11, pp. 406–410)—a dramatic event videotaped in a remote location on the high seas can be seen on millions of television sets.

Antarctic Treaty of 1959
One of the first multilateral treaties concerning the environment, it forbids military activity in Antarctica as well as the presence of nuclear weapons or the dumping of nuclear waste there, sets aside territorial claims on the continent for future resolution and establishes a regime for the conduct of scientific research.

Antarctica Like the oceans, *Antarctica* belongs to no state.[23] The continent's strategic and commercial value is limited, however, and not many states care about it. Thus, states have been successful in reaching agreements on Antarctica because the costs were low and the players few. The **Antarctic Treaty of 1959**—one of the first multilateral treaties concerning the environment—forbids military activity as well as the presence of nuclear weapons or the dumping of nuclear waste in Antarctica. It sets aside territorial claims on the continent for future resolution and establishes a regime under which various states can conduct scientific research. The treaty was signed by all states with interests in the area, including both superpowers. By 1991, Greenpeace had convinced the treaty signatories to turn the continent into a "world park." Antarctica is largely a success story in international environmental politics.

---

[23] Olav Schram Stokke and Davor Vidas, eds., *Governing the Antarctic: The Effectiveness and Legitimacy of the Antarctic Treaty System* (NY: Cambridge UP, 1997). Gail Osherenko and Oran R. Young, *The Age of the Arctic: Hot Conflicts and Cold Realities* (NY: Cambridge UP, 1989).

Pollution

Pollution generally creates a collective goods problem, but one that is not often global in scale. Pollution is more often a regional or bilateral issue. With some exceptions—such as dumping at sea—the effects of pollution are limited to the state where it occurs and its close neighbours—U.S. industrial smokestack emissions affect acid rain in Canada but do not directly affect distant states. Even when pollution crosses state borders, it often has its strongest effects closest to the source. This localized effect makes for a somewhat less intractable collective goods problem, because a polluting state can seldom get an entirely free ride and there are a limited number of actors. The effects of pollution are also more tangible than global warming or the ozone hole.

In several regions—notably Western and Eastern Europe and the Middle East—states are closely packed in the same air, river or sea basins. In such situations, pollution controls must often be negotiated multilaterally. In Europe during the Cold War, the international pollution problem was exacerbated by the inability of Western European states to impose any limits on Eastern ones, whose pollution was notorious. These problems are only now being addressed.

Several regional agreements seek to limit **acid rain,** caused by air pollution. Acid rain often crosses borders. European states—whose forests have been heavily damaged—have agreed to limit air pollution and acid rain for their mutual benefit. In 1988, 24 European states signed a treaty to limit nitrogen oxide emissions to 1988 levels by 1995. After long negotiations, the United States and Canada signed bilateral agreements to limit such pollution as well. These regional agreements have worked fairly well.

Water pollution often crosses borders, especially because industrial pollution, human sewage and agricultural fertilizers and pesticides tend to run into rivers and seas.

Long-standing international regional agencies that regulate shipping on heavily used European rivers now also deal with pollution. The Mediterranean basin is severely polluted and difficult to manage because it is bordered by so many states.[24] The Great Lakes on the U.S.-Canadian border were heavily polluted by the 1970s. Because the issue affected only two countries, it was easier to address through the Great Lakes Water Quality Agreement of 1978, which is monitored by the International Joint Commission (IJC)—a binational body established in 1909 to monitor and resolve transboundary water issues between Canada and the U.S. As a result of IJC efforts—as well as those of federal, provincial and state governments on both sides of the border—water quality in the Great Lakes has improved in recent years.[25]

Sometimes water pollution results not from industrial effluent but from accidents. One of the worst occurred in 1989 when the Exxon Valdez, a supertanker carrying over a million barrels of crude oil, rammed a reef and dumped its cargo into Prince William Sound, Alaska, destroying local habitat, animal and sea life. Blame was soon laid with the ship's captain, who was not on the bridge at the time of the accident and had allegedly been drinking. Critical theorists point out that the Exxon Valdez incident is a good illustration of the way in which, given the nature of the corporate drive for profit, environmental "accidents" are inevitable. Investigations into the accident showed that years of cost-cutting efforts by large oil companies had resulted in personnel reductions on oil tankers (with a corresponding increase in stress levels and a persistent problem of

acid rain Rain that contains acids caused by air pollution; it damages trees and often crosses borders. Limiting acid rain (via limiting nitrogen oxide emissions) has been the subject of several regional agreements.

---

[24] Peter M. Haas, *Saving the Mediterranean* (see footnote 6 in this chapter).

[25] Alan M. Schwartz, "The Canada-US Environmental Relationship: Calm Waters but Slow Sailing," *International Journal* 60.2 (Spring 2005): 437–48.

alcoholism); the use of ever-larger supertankers (which made them increasingly difficult to manoeuvre); and a refusal, on the part of oil companies, to switch to double-hulled ships to transport oil (which would have reduced the amount of the Alaska spill by as much as 60 percent, according U.S. Coast Guard estimates). In the drive to be more efficient and earn larger profits, corporate decisions, according to critical theorists, set the stage for environmental catastrophes.[26]

In other cases, it is not accidents that result in environmental damage and adverse health effects but simply the production of particular products. Canada, for example, is a large producer of asbestos—a known carcinogen. Because of restrictions on its use, most of Canada's asbestos (between 95 and 97 percent) is exported. In recent years, a number of European countries have banned asbestos imports (bans that have been supported by the WTO) and there is a push to establish a global ban. Currently, most of Canada's asbestos is exported to countries of the global South, including India, Thailand and Indonesia. The Canadian government promotes its use abroad because asbestos manufacturing is an important and profitable industry (especially to the province of Québec). It argues that safe handling can eliminate the health effects. Critics argue that safe handling of asbestos is possible only with the most advanced protective measures—often unavailable in poorer countries where health and safety regulations tend to be more lax. Critics, in other words, point out that profit takes precedence over the known adverse health effects of a product destined for the global South.[27]

Toxic and *nuclear wastes* are a special problem because of their long-term dangers. States occasionally try to ship such wastes out of their countries. International agreements now ban the dumping of toxic and nuclear wastes at sea (an obvious collective goods problem). However, waste has been sent to countries of the global South for disposal for a fee. For instance, toxic ash from Pennsylvania became material for bricks in Guinea, and Italian nuclear waste was shipped to Nigeria.

Norms have developed in recent years against exporting toxic wastes—a practice seen as exploitive of the receiving country. In 1989, 100 states signed a treaty under UN auspices to regulate shipments of toxic and nuclear wastes and to prevent their secret movements under corrupt deals. Forty more countries in Africa did not sign the treaty but called for a complete halt of toxic waste shipments to Africa. Nonetheless, in 2006 a multinational company tried to dispose of toxic waste from a tanker ship in the Netherlands, but changed its mind on finding it would cost hundreds of thousands of dollars. Six weeks later, the ship unloaded the toxic sludge in Abidjan, Ivory Coast, where a local company dumped it from tanker trucks at multiple locations around the city. Thousands of residents got sick and eight people died.[28]

Chernobyl A city in Ukraine that was the site of a 1986 meltdown at a Soviet nuclear power plant.

In 1986, a meltdown at a Soviet nuclear power plant at **Chernobyl,** in Ukraine, created airborne radioactivity that spread over much of Europe, from Italy to Sweden. The accident exemplified the new reality—that economic and technical decisions taken in one state can have grave environmental consequences for others. Soviet leaders made matters worse by failing to promptly notify neighbours of the accident.

On the various issues of water and air pollution, unilateral state actions and international agreements have often been feasible and effective. In recent decades, river water

---

[26] Joni Seager, *Earth Follies: Coming to Feminist Terms with the Global Environmental Crisis* (NY: Routledge, 1993).

[27] Department of Foreign Affairs and International Trade, "Canada Disappointed with WTO Appellate Body's Decision" (news release), 12 March 2001.

[28] Lydia Polgreen and Marlise Simons, "Global Sludge Ends in Tragedy for Ivory Coast," *The New York Times* 2 Oct. 2006: A1.

POISONED WATERS
Pollution easily crosses national borders. In this picture, industrial waste and sewage in the New River crosses from Mexico into California, 2003.

quality has improved in most industrialized regions. Market economies have begun to deal with pollution as just another cost of production that should be charged to the polluter instead of to society at large. Some governments have begun to allocate "pollution rights" that companies can buy and sell on a free market.

In the former Soviet bloc, decades of centrally planned industrialization have created severe environmental problems, which may prove more intractable.[29] With staggering environmental damage and human health effects, the economically strapped former Soviet republics must now bargain over limiting pollution and repairing damage. For example, the severely polluted Aral Sea, formerly belonging to one state, the Soviet Union, is now shared by two, Kazakhstan and Uzbekistan. Once the world's fourth largest inland sea, it shrank in half and its huge fisheries were destroyed after a Soviet-era mega-irrigation project to grow cotton in the desert diverted the Aral Sea's inlet rivers and polluted them with pesticides. Former fishing towns found themselves dozens of kilometres away from the shoreline. In the 1990s, environmentalists gave up efforts to save the Aral Sea after local and international political leaders failed to implement plans to address the problem. Local populations suffered from widespread health effects of the disaster. Decisions by the former Soviet republics to keep operating old and unsafe nuclear power reactors, as well as the problems associated with dismantling nuclear weapons, also add to the region's long environmental agenda.

---

[29] Murray Feshbach, *Ecological Disaster: Cleaning Up the Hidden Legacy of the Soviet Regime* (Washington, DC: Brookings, 1995). Klaus Schleicher, ed., *Pollution Knows No Frontiers: A Reader* (NY: Paragon, 1992). Joan DeBardeleben, ed., *To Breathe Free: Eastern Europe's Environmental Crisis* (Baltimore: Johns Hopkins UP, 1991). Fred Singleton, ed., *Environmental Problems in the Soviet Union and Eastern Europe* (Boulder, CO: Rienner, 1987).

NATURAL RESOURCES

The natural environment is not only a delicate ecosystem requiring protection, it is also a repository of natural resources. Because the extraction of resources brings states wealth (and hence power), they are a regular source of international conflict.[30] Mostly located within individual states, they do not present a collective goods problem. Rather, states bargain (with leverage) for these vital resources.

Three aspects of natural resources shape their role in international conflict. First, they are required for the operation of an industrial economy (sometimes even an agrarian one). Second, their sources—mineral deposits, rivers and so forth—are associated with particular territories over which states may fight for control. Third, natural resources tend to be unevenly distributed, with plentiful supplies in some states and an absence in others. These aspects mean that trade in natural resources is extremely profitable; much additional wealth is created. They also mean that trade in resources is fairly politicized—creating market imperfections such as monopoly, oligopoly, price manipulation and so on (see "Politics of Markets" on pp. 312–315).

World Energy

Energy resources (fuels) are central to the various natural resources required by states. The commercial fuels that power the world's industrial economies are oil (about 40 percent of world energy consumption), coal (30 percent), natural gas (25 percent) and hydroelectric and nuclear power (5 percent). Fossil fuels (coal, oil, gas) thus account for 95 percent of world energy consumption. Some energy consumed as electricity comes from hydroelectric dams or nuclear power plants, but the majority of it comes from burning fossil fuels in electric-generating plants.

Imagine a pile of coal weighing 75 pounds. The energy released by burning that much coal is equivalent to the amount of energy North Americans use per person every day. Wealthier people, of course, consume more energy than do poorer people, but 75 pounds is the average. A North American's pile of coal would be 10 times the pile of a person in China, 20 times that of someone in Africa.

Table 14.1 shows energy consumption per person in the nine world regions. The four industrialized regions of the North use much more energy per person than those of the South. Because Asia and Africa have little industry, North America uses approximately 20 to 25 times as much as Asia or Africa. Among industrialized countries there are differences in the *efficiency* of energy use—GDP produced per unit of energy consumed. The least efficient are Russia and Eastern Europe (even before that region's current economic depression). North America is also rather inefficient, and Europe and Japan are the most energy efficient.

International trade in energy plays a vital role in the world economy. As Table 14.1 shows, the regions of the industrialized West are net importers of energy (though considered alone, Canada is a net exporter). Together the industrialized West imports the energy equivalent of more than a billion tonnes of coal from the rest of the world each year. The other six world regions are net exporters of energy.

---

[30] Mark W. Zacher, ed., *The International Political Economy of Natural Resources* (Brookfield, VT: Elgar, 1993). Lim Teck Ghee and Mark J. Valencia, eds., *Conflict over Natural Resources in South-East Asia and the Pacific* (NY: Oxford UP, 1991). Ronnie D. Lipschutz, *When Nations Clash: Raw Materials, Ideology, and Foreign Policy* (NY: Ballinger, 1989). Dennis Pirages, *Global Technolopolitics: The International Politics of Technology and Resources* (Pacific Grove, CA: Brooks/Cole, 1989).

Table 14.1 Per Capita Energy Consumption and Net Energy Trade, 2003

	Per Capita Consumption (million BTU)	Total Net Energy Exports[a] (quadrillion BTU)
North America	380	−25
Western Europe	150	−30
Japan/Pacific	170	−21
Russia & Eastern Europe	140	+16
China	35	−5
Middle East	100	+38
Latin America	55	+7
South Asia	20	−2
Africa	15	+17
World as a whole	70	

[a]Net exports refers to production minus consumption. Net exports worldwide do not equal net imports for technical reasons.

Source: Calculated from data in U.S. Department of Energy. Energy Information Administration. See www.eia.doe.gov/iea/.

Although all forms of energy are traded internationally, the most important by far is oil, which is the cheapest to transport over long distances. Russia and Eastern Europe receive vital hard currency earnings from exporting oil. Venezuela and Mexico (in Latin America) and Nigeria and Angola (in Africa) are important oil exporters, as is Canada. By far the largest source of oil exports is the Middle East—especially the countries around the Persian Gulf (Saudi Arabia, Kuwait, Iraq, Iran and the small sheikdoms of United Arab Emirates, Qatar, Bahrain and Oman). Saudi Arabia is the largest oil exporter and sits atop the largest oil reserves. The politics of world energy revolve around Middle East oil shipped to Western Europe, Japan/Pacific and North America.

The importance of oil in the industrialized economies helps to explain the importance of the Middle East in world politics. Iraq's 1990 invasion of Kuwait (and the mere possibility that Iraq's army could move into Saudi Arabia) threatened the West's access to stable, inexpensive supplies of oil. Immediately, world oil prices more than doubled. Saudi Arabia could have increased its own rate of oil exports massively enough to compensate if both Kuwaiti and Iraqi exports had been cut off by the invasion and the UN sanctions against Iraq. When it became clear that Saudi exports would not be disrupted, the price of oil dropped again on world markets. Thus, not only is energy a crucial economic sector (on which all industrial activity depends), but also one of the most politically sensitive (because of the dependence of the West on energy imported from the Middle East and other regions of the global South). Some commentators have also noted the strategic importance of Canadian energy exports, especially as a stable supplier of oil and natural gas to the U.S.[31]

---

[31] Isidoro Morales, "The New Strategic Positioning of Canada within North America: The Energy Factor," *Canada among Nations 2006: Minorities and Priorities*, ed. Andrew F. Cooper and Dane Rowlands (Montreal and Kingston: McGill-Queen's University Press 2006) 269–91. Ethan B. Kapstein, *The Insecure Alliance: Energy Crises and Western Politics since 1944* (NY: Oxford UP, 1990).

To secure a supply of oil in the Middle East, Britain and other European countries colonized the area early in the twentieth century, carving up territory into protectorates in which European power kept local monarchs on their thrones. (Iraq, for instance, argues that Kuwait is part of Iraq, and that it was cut off and made into a separate state by the British.) The United States did not claim colonies or protectorates, but U.S. MNCs were heavily involved in the development of oil resources in the area from the 1920s through the 1960s—often wielding vast power. Local rulers depended on the expertise and capital investment of U.S. and European oil companies. The "seven sisters"—a cartel of Western oil companies—kept the price paid to local states low and their own profits high.

After World War II the British gave up colonial claims in the Middle East, but Western oil companies kept producing cheap oil there for Western consumption. Then in 1973, during an Arab-Israeli war, the oil-producing Arab states of the region decided to punish the United States for supporting Israel. They cut off their oil exports to the United States and curtailed overall exports. This supply disruption sent world oil prices skyrocketing. OPEC realized its potential power and the high price the world was willing to pay for oil. After the war ended, OPEC agreed to limit production to keep oil prices high.

The 1973 **oil shock** had a profound effect on the world economy and world politics. Huge amounts of hard currency accumulated in the treasuries of the Middle East oil-exporting countries, which in turn invested them around the world (with what were called *petrodollars*). High inflation plagued the United States, Canada and Europe for years afterward.

In 1979, the revolution in Iran led to another major increase in oil prices. This second oil shock further weakened the industrialized economies. However, these economies were already adjusting to the new realities of world energy. Higher oil prices led to the expansion of oil production in new locations outside of OPEC—in the North Sea (Britain and Norway), Alaska, Angola, Russia and elsewhere. By the mid-1980s, the Middle East was rapidly losing its market share of world trade in oil. At the same time, industrialized economies learned to be more *energy efficient*. With supply up and demand down, oil prices dropped in the late 1980s to historic lows below US$20/barrel, and stayed low into the new century except for a price surge around 2000 and again in 2004. As a result of the market adjustments that followed high oil prices, the industrialized West is now somewhat less dependent on Middle East oil and the power of OPEC has been greatly reduced. Still, energy continues to be a crucial issue in which the Middle East plays a key role.

In the late 1990s, the Caspian Sea region beckoned as a new and largely untapped oil source (see Figure 14.2). However, international politics and geography hampered the development of this zone. The oil must travel overland by pipeline to reach world markets (the Caspian is an inland sea), but the main pipeline from oil-producing Azerbaijan to the Black Sea (where tanker ships can load) travels through war-torn Chechnya in southern Russia. Russia built a bypass route around Chechnya that carries a large and growing amount of Caspian oil for export through the Black Sea.

Western powers sought other pipeline routes that did not cross Russia, while Turkey sought to control a larger market share and to reduce environmental damage to the Bosporus waterway (through which Russian tankers must travel). After long negotiations, in 2002–2004 states and oil companies spent billions of dollars on a large-capacity pipeline through Azerbaijan and Georgia to Turkey's Mediterranean coast.

Violent conflicts make pipeline routes particularly complex. All three countries on the new pipeline route were at war in the past decade. A dozen other existing and proposed oil pipelines for Caspian Sea oil are no easier. Across the Caspian Sea, Turkmenistan wants to export natural gas to Pakistan, and from there to Asia, but a

oil shocks The two sharp rises in the world price of oil that occurred in 1973–1974 and 1979.

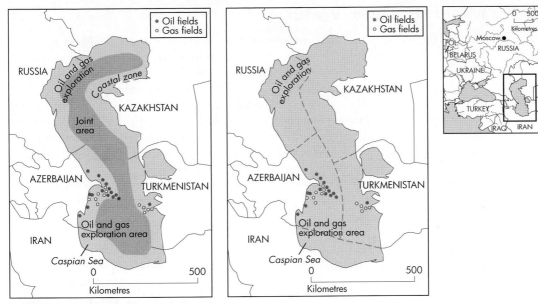

FIGURE 14.2 Dividing the Caspian Sea

The Caspian Sea is the world's largest inland body of water. It could be defined under international law as either a lake or a sea. The middle of a lake (beyond territorial waters) is a joint area (see left panel), which can be exploited only if countries agree on terms. As a sea less than 644 kilometres (400 miles) wide, it is split up by bordering countries' Exclusive Economic Zones (EEZs) (right panel).

After a 1912 treaty, the Soviet Union and Iran treated the Caspian as a lake and made agreements on fishing. Later, substantial oil deposits were found offshore. When the Soviet Union broke up a decade ago, the Caspian was suddenly bordered by five countries instead of two, with most of the oil and gas in or near Azerbaijan and Turkmenistan, not Russia. Under the "lake" interpretation, however, Russia could share in revenues from some of the offshore oil. In the past few years, more oil and gas has been discovered, including some potentially big fields near Russia. This makes Russia more inclined to accept a "sea" interpretation and begin drilling, without waiting to negotiate a complex deal with contentious neighbours.[a] The negotiations dragged on into 2002, and Iran sent a warship in 2001 to drive away an Azerbaijan-based oil exploration ship (owned by British Petroleum) from disputed waters.

[a]Elaine Sciolino, "It's a Sea! It's a Lake! No. It's a Pool of Oil!" *New York Times* 21 June 1998.

pipeline has to cross war-torn Afghanistan. Meanwhile, in 2003, a new $4 billion pipeline began carrying oil from Chad through Cameroon for export, promising to help both countries alleviate poverty, but as rebels based in Sudan attacked Chad, oil money was diverted for military purposes. Although borders and geography may be less and less important in communications and business, they still matter greatly in international economic transactions, such as oil pipelines.

Oil prices have been relatively high since 2000, reaching nearly $80 a barrel in 2006 and pushing U.S. gas prices above $3 a gallon at one point. High oil prices hurt industrialized economies, but have two major benefits. First, burning oil contributes to global warming, and high prices make it profitable to burn less oil and be more energy efficient. Second, high oil prices increase the export earnings of oil-producing states. Countries such as Venezuela and Mexico count on oil revenues in their economic development plans and for repayment of foreign debts, and higher prices have helped these countries ease their debt problems. High oil prices in recent years have also played a crucial part in the economic recovery of Russia, an oil exporter, and have also been important for countries such as Iran, Saudi Arabia and Venezuela.

Minerals, Land, Water

To build the infrastructure and other manufactured goods that create wealth in a national economy, states need other raw materials in addition to energy. These include metals, other minerals and related materials extracted through mining.

The political economy of minerals—iron, copper, platinum and so forth—differs from that of world energy. The value of international trade in oil is many times greater than that of any mineral. Mineral production is distributed more evenly than oil production—supply is not as concentrated in one region of the world. Industrialized countries have reduced their vulnerability by stockpiling strategic minerals (easier to do with minerals than with energy because of smaller quantities and values).

Nonetheless, industrialized countries do have certain vulnerabilities with regard to mineral supply, which affect international politics. Among the industrialized regions, Japan and Europe are most dependent on mineral imports; Canada and the United States are more self-sufficient. The former Soviet Union was a leading exporter of key minerals—a role that Russia may continue in the future. Despite its economic problems, one great strength of the Russian economy is its self-sufficiency in energy and mineral resources.

Another major exporter of key minerals is South Africa. For a few strategic minerals, notably manganese and chromium, South Africa controls three-quarters or more of the world's reserves. Western leaders worried that political instability in South Africa (where the black majority struggled for years under white minority rule) could disrupt the supply of these minerals. This is one reason why industrialized countries were reluctant to impose trade sanctions on South Africa over human rights issues. South Africa's leading position in supplying diamonds, gold and platinum to world markets provided a valuable source of income, but in the end the West did apply economic sanctions that hurt the South African economy and helped end apartheid.

The minerals that go into making industrial equipment are vital to industrialized economies. Traditionally most important is iron, from which steel is made. The leading producers of steel are Russia, Japan, the United States, China and Germany, followed by Brazil, Italy, South Korea, France and Britain. Thus, major industrialized countries produce their own steel (Germany and Japan are the leading exporters worldwide). As of 2005, Canada was ranked fifteenth among major steel producing countries (producing 15.6 million tonnes of crude steel annually). To preserve self-sufficiency in steel production, the United States and others have used trade policies to protect domestic steel industries.

Some industrialized countries, notably Japan, depend heavily on importing iron ore for their steel industries. Unlike oil, iron ore is not concentrated in a "Persian Gulf" but is exported from both global South and industrialized countries around the world. There is an *Association of Iron Ore Exporting Countries (AIOEC)*, but it is limited to consultation, and the United States, Canada and the former Soviet Union are exporters that are not among its 12 members.

For other important industrial minerals such as copper, nickel and zinc, the pattern of supply and trade is much more diffuse than for oil, and industrialized countries are largely self-sufficient. Even when states of the global South are the main suppliers, as with tin and bauxite, they have not gained the power of OPEC. There is a producer cartel for some goods (copper), a producer-consumer cartel for others (tin) and separate producer and consumer cartels for still others (bauxite).

Certain agricultural products have spawned producer cartels, such as the Union of Banana Exporting Countries (UBEC) and the African Groundnut Council. Like minerals, some export crops come mainly from just a few countries. These include sugar (Cuba), cocoa (Ivory Coast, Ghana, Nigeria), tea (India, Sri Lanka, China) and coffee (Brazil, Colombia). Despite the concentrations, producer cartels have not been very successful in boosting prices of these products, which are less essential than energy.

Water Disputes In addition to energy and minerals, states need water. The need for water increases as a society industrializes, intensifies agriculture and as its population grows. World water use is 35 times higher than just a few centuries ago, and grew twice as fast as population in the twentieth century. Yet water supplies are relatively unchanging, and are becoming depleted in many places. One-fifth of the world's population lacks safe drinking water, and 80 countries suffer water shortages. Water supplies—rivers and water tables—often cross international boundaries,

WATER, WATER EVERYWHERE

As population growth and economic development increase the demand for water, more international conflicts arise over water rights. Many important rivers pass through multiple states, and many states share access to seas and lakes. The Aral Sea, once part of the Soviet Union but now shared by Kazakhstan and Uzbekistan, was among the world's largest lakes until it was decimated by the diversion of its water sources to irrigate cotton. This scene shows the former seabed, now 113 kilometres from shore, in 1997.

and thus access to water is increasingly a source of international conflict. Sometimes—as when several states share access to a single water table—these conflicts are collective goods problems.

Canada has an abundance of fresh water reserves: by some estimates, close to 20 percent of the world's total supply. An issue that has arisen in Canada concerns bulk water exports. On one hand, it might make sense for Canada to export water, in particular to the United States, which has a demand for fresh water. However, the bulk export of water from Canada would have a number of environmental impacts, such as altering ecosystems and changing groundwater levels. Critics of bulk water exports also point out that exporting water would result in its being treated as a commodity rather than a natural resource under trade agreements such as NAFTA or the WTO. This would mean that Canada could lose control of its water supplies; for example, in times of shortage, or if exports seriously depleted reserves, Canada's obligations to export water would be determined by its trade commitments and not national policies (Canada would be required to treat signatories to NAFTA in the same manner it treats domestic users of Canadian water). In order to retain control over fresh water, amendments to the International Boundary Waters Treaty Act (IBWTA) between Canada and the U.S. prohibiting water exports came into force in 2002 (see Environment Canada's Freshwater website: http://www.ec.gc.ca/water/e_main.html).

Water problems are especially important in the Middle East. For instance, the Euphrates River runs from Turkey through Syria to Iraq before reaching the Persian Gulf. Iraq objects to Syrian diversion of water from the river, and both Iraq and Syria object to Turkey's diversion.

The Jordan River originates in Syria and Lebanon and runs through Israel to Jordan. In the 1950s, Israel began building a canal to take water from the Jordan River to "make the desert bloom." Jordan and its Arab neighbours complained to the UN Security Council, which failed in efforts to mediate the dispute, and each state went ahead with its own water plans (Israel and Jordan agreeing, however, to stay within UN-proposed allocations). In 1964, Syria and Lebanon tried to build dams and divert water before it reached Israel, rendering Israel's new water system worthless. Israeli air and artillery attacks on the construction site forced Syria to abandon its diversion project, and Israel's 1967 capture of the Golan Heights precluded Syria from renewing such efforts.[32]

Water also contains other resources, such as fish and offshore oil deposits. The UNCLOS treaty enclosed more of these resources within states' territory—but this enclosure created new problems. Norms regarding territorial waters are not firmly entrenched; some states disagree on who owns what. Additionally, control of small islands now implies rights to surrounding oceans and their fish, offshore oil and minerals. A potentially serious international dispute has been brewing in the Spratly Islands, where some tiny islands are claimed by China, Vietnam and other nearby countries (see p. 170). With the islands come nearby oil drilling rights and fisheries. China has invited a U.S. company to explore for oil, promising protection by the Chinese navy. For similar reasons, Iran and the United Arab Emirates dispute control of several small islands in the Persian Gulf.

A common theme runs through conflicts over fuels, minerals, agricultural products and territorial waters. They are produced in fixed locations but traded to distant places. Control of these locations gives a state both greater self-sufficiency (valued by mercantilists) and market commodities generating wealth (valued by liberals). However, the exploitation of these products can have severe environmental impacts (a concern raised by critical theorists).

International Security and the Environment

In recent years, IR scholars have expanded their studies of environmental politics to systematically include the relationship of military and security affairs with the environment.[33] One side of this relationship is the role of the environment as a source of international conflict. We have seen how environmental degradation can lead to collective goods problems among large numbers of states, and how competition for territory and resources can create conflicts among smaller groups of states. Environmental damage from the oil industry in the very poor river delta region of Nigeria has inflamed a local insurgency, which attacked oil installations and kidnapped foreign oil workers in 2006 and 2007.

The other side of the environment-security relationship concerns the effect of activities in the international security realm of the environment. Military activities—especially warfare—are important contributors to environmental degradation, above and beyond the degradation caused by economic activities such as mining and manufacturing.

These damaging effects were spotlighted during the Gulf War. Iraqi forces spilled large amounts of Kuwaiti oil into the Persian Gulf—either to try to stop an amphibious

---

[32] Miriam L. Lowi, *Water and Power: The Politics of a Scarce Resource in the Jordan River Basin* (NY: Cambridge UP, 1993). United Nations, *Comprehensive Assessment of the Freshwater Resources of the World* (NY: United Nations, 1997).

[33] Daniel H. Deudney and Richard A. Matthew, eds., *Contested Grounds: Security and Conflict in the New Environmental Politics* (Albany: SUNY P, 1999). Thomas F. Homer-Dixon, "On the Threshold: Environmental Changes as Causes of Acute Conflict," *International Security* 16.2 (1991): 76–116.

WAR IS NOT GREEN
Wars often bring environmental destruction, sometimes deliberately and sometimes as a byproduct. Military operations in peacetime also contribute to environmental problems. Here, U.S. forces pass a sabotaged oil pipeline near Fallujah, Iraq, in November 2004.

invasion or simply to punish Saudi Arabia (in whose direction the oil was pushed by currents). Then, before retreating from Kuwait, the Iraqis blew up hundreds of Kuwaiti oil wells, leaving them burning uncontrollably and blanketing the country with thick black smoke. Air pollution and weather effects lasted more than a year and were felt in other countries around the Gulf. Iraq's environment also suffered tremendous damage from the massive bombing campaign. After the war, Iraq built a giant canal to drain marshes used for refuge by rebels—another environmental disaster.

The deliberate environmental destruction seen in the Gulf War is not without precedent. Armies sometimes adopt a "scorched earth policy" to deny sustenance to their adversaries. Fields are burned, wells poisoned and villages levelled. In World War II, the Soviets left a scorched earth behind as they retreated before the Nazi invasion. Japan used incendiary devices carried in high-altitude balloons to start forest fires in the U.S. northwest. The United States massively sprayed defoliants in Vietnam to destroy jungles in an attempt to expose guerrilla forces. The Vietnamese countryside still shows effects from these herbicides, as do U.S. veterans and Vietnamese citizens who suffer lingering health effects due to contact with chemicals such as *Agent Orange*.

Military activity short of war also tends to damage the environment. Military industries pollute. Military forces use energy less efficiently than civilians do. Military aircraft and missiles contribute to ozone depletion. Their bases contain many toxic-waste dumps.

The greatest *potential* environmental disaster imaginable would be a large nuclear war. Ecosystems would be severely damaged throughout the world by secondary effects of nuclear weapons alone—radioactive fallout and the breakdown of social order and technology. Some scientists also think that global climate changes, leading to famine and environmental collapse, could result—the "nuclear winter" mentioned on page 211.

POPULATION

The global population reached a record high today, as it does every day. World population, 6.7 billion in 2007, is growing by 75 million each year—more than 200 000 additional people per day.

Forecasting future population is easy in some respects. Barring a nuclear war or environmental catastrophe, today's children will grow up and have children of their own. The projected world population in 2030 will be around 8 billion people, and there is little anyone can do to change that projection.

Of the increase in population in that period, 96 percent will be in the global South. Currently, half the world's population growth occurs in just six countries—India, China, Pakistan, Nigeria, Bangladesh and Indonesia. Among the world's poorest countries, population is expected to triple in the next 50 years, whereas many rich countries will see population shrinkage.[34]

Forecasting beyond 25 years is difficult. When today's children grow up, the number of children they bear will be affected by their incomes (because of the "demographic transition," discussed shortly). To the extent that countries of the global South accumulate wealth—a subject that was discussed in Chapter 13—their population growth will likely slow. A second factor affecting the rate of population growth will be government policies regarding women's rights and birth control.

Because of these two uncertainties, projections beyond a few decades have a range of uncertainty (see Figure 14.3). By 2050, world population could be 8 or 9 billion, with a final levelling out around 9 to 10 billion in the next 200 years. In the 1980s the decline in birth rates stalled in a number of countries and economic growth in the global South fell below expectations, pushing population projections up. However, successes in regions of the South outside Africa—in raising incomes and lowering birth rates in the 1990s—brought projections down again. New data in 2002 showed that higher women's status and literacy rates are reducing population growth more than expected in large, poor countries.[35] The actions of states and IOs *now* will determine the earth's population in 200 years.

Two hundred years ago, British writer *Thomas Malthus* warned that population tends to increase faster than food supply and predicted that population growth would limit itself through famine and disease. Today, experts and officials who warn against world overpopulation are sometimes called *Malthusian*. Critics point out that technology has kept pace with population in the past, allowing more food and other resources to be extracted from the environment even as the population keeps growing.

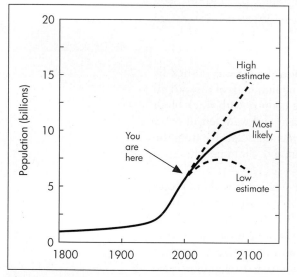

Figure 14.3 World Population Trends and Projections

Source: Based on data from the UN Population Office.

---

[34] UNFPA data. See United Nations, *State of World Population Report 2004* (NY: UN, 2004).

[35] Shiro Horiuchi, "Stagnation in the Decline of the World Population Growth Rate during the 1980s," *Science* 257 (7 Aug. 1992): 761–65. Barbara Crossette, "Population Estimates Fall as Women Assert Control," *New York Times* 10 March 2002.

The Demographic Transition

Population growth results from a difference between rates of birth (per 1000 people) and rates of death. In agrarian (pre-industrial) societies, both birth and death rates are high. Population growth is thus slow—even negative at times when death rates exceed birth rates (during a famine or plague, for instance).

The process of economic development—of industrialization and the accumulation of wealth on a per capita basis—brings about a change in birth and death rates that follows a fairly universal pattern called the **demographic transition** (see Figure 14.4). First, death rates fall as food supplies increase and access to health care expands. Later, birth rates fall as people become educated, more secure and more urbanized, and as the status of women in society rises. At the end of the transition, as at the beginning, birth and death rates are fairly close to each other, and population growth is limited. During the transition, when death rates have fallen more than birth rates, population grows rapidly.

One reason poor people tend to have many children is that under harsh poverty a child's survival is not assured. Disease, malnutrition or violence may claim the lives of many children, leaving parents with no one to look after them in their old age. Having many children helps ensure that some survive. (The collective goods problem appears again, because each family wants more children but when all pursue this strategy the economic development of the whole community or state is held back.)

As a state makes the demographic transition, the structure of its population changes dramatically. At the beginning and middle of the process, most of the population is young. Families have many children and adults do not have a long life expectancy. Because children are not very productive economically, the large number of children in poor countries tends to slow down the accumulation of wealth. By the end of the demographic transition, because adults live longer and families have fewer children, the average age of the population is much older. Eventually a substantial section of the population is elderly—a different nonproductive population that the economy must support.

demographic transition The pattern of falling death rates, followed by falling birth rates, that generally accompanies industrialization and economic development.

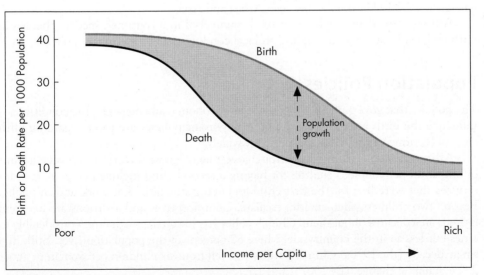

Figure 14.4 The Demographic Transition

As income rises, first death rates and then birth rates fall. The gap between the two is the population growth rate. Early in the transition, the population contains a large proportion of children; later it contains a large proportion of elderly people.

Industrialized countries have been through the demographic transition and now have slow population growth. Europe and Japan are experiencing negative growth that could double by 2015. Most countries of the global South are in the middle of the transition and have rapid population growth.

The dilemma of the demographic transition is that rapid population growth and a child-heavy population are powerful forces that lower per capita income, yet the best way to slow population growth is to raise per capita income.

Population growth thus contributes to a vicious cycle in many poor states. Where population rises at the same rate as overall wealth, the average person is no better off over time. Even when the economy grows faster than the population, so that the *average* income rises, the total *number* of poor people may increase.

The demographic transition tends to widen international disparities of wealth. States that manage to raise incomes enter an upward spiral—as population growth slows, income levels per capita rise more, which further slows population growth, and so forth. Meanwhile, states that do not raise incomes have unabated population growth; per capita incomes stay low, which fuels more population growth—a downward spiral.

Globally, this disparity contributes to the gap in wealth between the North and South (see Chapter 12). Within the South disparities are also sharpened, as a few countries manage to slow population growth and raise incomes while others fail. Even within a single country, the demographic transition sharpens disparities. Cities, richer classes, richer ethnic groups and richer provinces tend to have low birth rates compared with the countryside and the poorer classes, ethnic groups and provinces. In countries such as France, Israel and the United States, wealthier ethnic groups (often white) have much slower population growth than poorer ethnic groups (often nonwhite).

In recent decades, countries of the global South seem to be splitting into two groups of states. The first group, including China and India, entered the phase of the demographic transition marked by falling birth rates in the 1970s. In nearly 70 other poor states, death rates kept falling faster than birth rates, leading to accelerating population growth. These population trends contributed to disparities in the global South that emerged in the 1990s, notably between Africa and Asia.

Although the demographic transition is universal in its outlines, specific changes in birth and death rates vary depending on local conditions and government policies.

Population Policies

The policies that governments adopt—not just economic and demographic conditions—influence the birth rate. Among the most important policies are those regarding birth control (contraception). State policies vary widely.

At one extreme, China uses strong government control to try to enforce a limit of one child per couple. Penalties for having a second child include being charged for services that were free for the first child and being stigmatized at work and in public. Beyond two children, the penalties escalate. Contraceptives and abortions are free, and citizens are educated about them. China's policy has lowered growth rates considerably in cities but less so in the countryside, where 80 percent of the population lives. Still, in a single decade (the 1970s) China's fertility rate fell from six children per woman to about 2.5, a dramatic change. (By 2007 it was 1.7.)

The Chinese policy has enormous drawbacks. It limits individual freedom in favour of government control. Forced or coerced abortions are widespread. In traditional Chinese society (as in some other countries), sons are valued more than daughters. Couples who have a daughter may keep trying until they have a son. Chinese peasants have reportedly killed newborn daughters so they could try for a son. Simply bribing or paying fines became more common routes around the one-child policy in the 1990s. Most often, parents in China (and some places in India) are using information technology—ultrasound scans—to determine the gender of their fetus and abort it if female. China's 2000 census showed the percentage of female births at 0.85 per boy, rather than the normal 0.95, a difference that amounts to a million "missing" girls per year. In the countryside, the sex differential is twice as high as in the cities, reaching 140 men per 100 women in some areas where the one-child policy is strictly enforced. In recent years, hundreds of thousands of young women have been kidnapped and sold as brides.[36]

India's policies are less extreme but have been slower. The birth rate fell from just under six per woman to about 4.7 in the 1970s to 2.7 in 2006. India's government, strongly committed to birth control, has tried to make information and means widely available, but as a democracy it does not have China's extreme government control over society. However, India does resort to economic incentives, a practice that was particularly widespread during the 1970s. Monetary rewards or livestock were offered to men and women who agreed to be sterilized. Doctors and nurses who convinced patients to undergo the operations were also provided with incentives. Such methods may seem less overtly forceful than China's approach, but using incentives to persuade people to be sterilized is also considered a coercive approach to birth control and family planning.

Countries with somewhat higher incomes than India or China can succeed more easily. Mexico's strong but noncoercive family-planning program, adopted in 1974, cut birth rates in half over 15 years to 2.7 per woman (and to 2.4 as of 2007).[37]

Family planning programs have had at best a mixed history, and many have been accused of very questionable practices. International NGOs such as the International Planned Parenthood Federation had their early origins in eugenicist movements—organizations aimed at the "betterment" of the races through selective breeding. Although that connection no longer exists, family planning is sometimes still viewed with suspicion by many people around the world. In addition to incentive programs, birth control programs sometimes recommended unsafe or unproven methods of birth control. For a long time, the injectable contraceptive Depo-Provera was not approved for use in the United States or Canada, for example, but was widely available in countries of the global South.[38]

At the other extreme from China are governments that encourage or force childbearing and outlaw or limit access to contraception. Such a policy is **pronatalist** (pro-birth). Traditionally, many governments have adopted pronatalist policies because population was seen as an element of national power. More babies today meant more soldiers later.

pronatalist policy
A government policy that encourages or forces childbearing and outlaws or limits access to contraception.

Today, only a few governments have strongly pronatalist policies, but many do not make birth control or sex education available to women. In some states, population is not considered a problem (and may even be seen as an asset); in other states, the government simply cannot afford effective measures to lower birth rates. (Again, birth control has short-term costs and long-term benefits.) According to the UNFPA, 300 million women do not have access to effective contraception.

---

[36] Celia W. Dugger, "Modern Asia's Anomaly: The Girls Who Don't Get Born," *New York Times* 6 May 2001. Elisabeth Rosenthal, "Harsh Chinese Reality Feeds a Black Market in Women," *New York Times* 25 June 2001: A1.

[37] John Ward Anderson, "Six Billion and Counting—But Slower," *Washington Post* 12 Oct. 1999: A1.

[38] Linda Gordon, *The Moral Property of Women: A History of Birth Control Politics in America* (Champaign, IL: U Illinois P, 2002). Betsy Hartmann, *Reproductive Rights and Wrongs: The Global Politics of Population*, rev. ed. (Boston: South End, 1995).

Industrialized states have provided financial assistance for family planning programs in poor countries. One reason the drop in birth rates slowed in the 1980s is that international financial assistance slowed dramatically. The U.S. government, providing more than a quarter of the voluntary contributions that finance the UNFPA's annual budget of US$225 million, terminated contributions in 1976 after U.S. anti-abortion activists protested that some UNFPA funds were financing abortions. The United States did the same to the International Planned Parenthood Federation in the 1980s.[39] Some U.S. funding was restored in the 1990s.

Women's Status Perhaps most important, birth rates are influenced by the status of women in society. In cultures that traditionally see women as valuable only in producing babies, great pressures exist against women who stop doing so. Many women do not use birth control because their husbands will not allow them to. Their husbands may think that having many children is proof of manliness. As women's status improves and they can work in various occupations, own property and vote, women gain the power as well as the education and money necessary to limit the size of their families.

According to the UNFPA, improving the status of women is one of the most important means of controlling world population growth. Government policies about women's status vary from one state to another. International programs and agencies, such as the UN Commission on the Status of Women, are working to address the issue on a global scale. International economic aid programs have been criticized for paying insufficient attention to the status of women, focusing on economic development in isolation from population growth (see "Women in Development" on pp. 422–424).

Disease

Population growth is determined by the death rate as well as the birth rate. In a way, the death rate is more complicated: births have only one source (involving women of childbearing age), whereas people die from many different causes at different ages. In poor countries, people tend to die younger, often from infectious diseases; in rich countries, people live longer and die more often from cancer and heart disease. The proportion of babies who die within their first year is the **infant mortality rate.** This rate is an excellent indicator of overall health, since it reflects a population's access to nutrition, water, shelter and health care. Infant mortality is 5 percent worldwide, 1 percent or less in rich countries but over 10 percent in the poorest countries and even higher in local pockets of extreme poverty (especially in Africa and in recent war zones).

Although death rates vary greatly from one state or region to another, the overall trends are stable from decade to decade. Wars, droughts, epidemics and disasters have an effect locally but hardly matter globally. In the poorest countries, which are just beginning the demographic transition, the death rate declined from nearly 30 deaths per thousand in 1950 to less than 15 since 1990. In the *industrialized countries*, the death rate bottomed out around 10 per thousand by 1960, and now stands near 7 in the West. However, Russia's death rate *rose* from 11 in 1980 to 15 in 1995 (and rates are high elsewhere in Eastern Europe and central Asia). In the *midtransition* countries (including China and India), the death rate fell from 25 in 1950 to 10 in 1980 and has equalled that of rich countries since then. (Between 1980 and 1995, China's death rate rose from

infant mortality rate The proportion of babies who die within their first year of life.

---

[39] Sandra Whitworth, "Planned Parenthood and the New Right: Onslaught and Opportunity?" *Studies in Political Economy* 35 (Summer 1991): 73–101.

6 to 7; India's fell from 13 to 9.) In this middle group of developing countries, infant mortality is generally much lower than in the poorest countries.[40]

Stable trends in mortality mean that the death rate is not a means by which governments or international agencies can affect population growth—worsening poverty may cause famine and a rising death rate, but this is obviously not a realistic way to control population growth. Nor do wars kill enough people to reduce population growth (short of global nuclear war). Even a major famine or war, one killing a million people, hardly alters world population trends because every year about 56 million people die—150 000 every day. In short, most of the world is already at or near the end of the transition in *death* rates; the key question is how long birth rates will take to complete the transition.

Three mortality factors, however—AIDS, other infectious diseases and smoking—deserve special attention because they have begun to exact very high costs even if they do not much affect global population trends. In these cases, actions taken in the short term have long-term and often international consequences, and once again there are short-term costs and long-term benefits.

AIDS   In the worldwide AIDS epidemic, one state's success or failure in limiting the spread of HIV (human immunodeficiency virus) affects infections in other states. There is a delay of five to ten years after infection by the virus before symptoms appear, and during this period an infected individual can infect others (through sex or blood). AIDS spreads internationally—through business, tourism, migration and military and peacekeeping operations—reflecting the interdependence of states.

By 2007, the HIV/AIDS epidemic had already killed more than 30 million people, and an estimated 40 million more were infected—though most of them did not know it. Two-thirds of infected people live in Africa and half of the rest in South Asia (see Table 14.2 on p. 534). The epidemic has also left 15 million orphans. Every year, four million people are newly infected with HIV and three million die from AIDS, including half a million children. About 85 percent of people with AIDS are in the global South. Because of systematic underreporting, none of the totals are firm, and other estimates revise them upward.[41]

In Africa, already the world's poorest and most war-torn region, AIDS has emerged as one of several powerful forces driving the region into deeper poverty. About 8 percent of adults are infected with HIV, more than half of them women. In the most affected African countries in southern Africa, one in six adults has HIV (one in three for Botswana, the worst case). Infection is also rampant in central African armies, with direct implications for international security in a war-torn zone. In Angola, the *end* of a long civil war opened borders and increased traffic with neighbouring states, which created high HIV infection rates. As Angola's infection rate began to climb, military officers took the initiative to set up education programs and comprehensive HIV testing within the army. In contrast to other African states with high military infection rates, Angola's aggressive program kept the rate as low as in the general population, below 10 percent.

In North America and other industrialized regions, new drug therapies (which could keep the virus in check for years) dramatically lowered the death rate from AIDS in the late 1990s. These treatments were too expensive to provide much help in Africa and other poor regions, however. India and Brazil began to export cheap generic versions of

---

[40] Tatyana P. Soubbotina and Katherine Sheram, *Beyond Economic Growth: Meeting the Challenges of Global Development* (Washington, DC: World Bank, 2000).

[41] UN data (see footnote 34 in this chapter). *Washington Post* 24 Nov. 1999: A3. Jonathan Mann, Daniel J. M. Tarantola and Thomas W. Netter, eds., *AIDS in the World 1992* (Cambridge, MA: Harvard UP, 1992).

Table 14.2 Population and AIDS by World Region, 2005

Region[a]	Population (millions)	Population Growth Rate 1991–2004	HIV Infections (millions)
World	6,200	1.3%	40
Global North	1,300	0.3	2
Global South of which:	4,900	1.6	37
China/East Asia	1,300	1.0	1
Middle East	400	2.3	1
Latin America	500	1.6	2
South Asia	2,100	1.9	7
Africa (sub-Saharan)	600	2.6	26

[a]Regions do not exactly match those used elsewhere in this book.

Source: Calculated from World Bank. *World Development Indicators.* World Bank, 2005. UNAIDS. *AIDS Epidemic Update.* UN, December 2005.

these drugs, violating patent rights of Western drug companies. The U.S. government threatened to punish South Africa and other countries if they allowed the import of these drugs without compensating U.S. corporations holding patents. It filed a complaint against Brazil with the WTO. In response, AIDS activists demonstrated loudly and mobilized public opinion to get these policies changed. The United States withdrew its complaint against Brazil in 2001. Meanwhile, drug companies began offering lower prices to poor countries, though many critics claim the costs are still too high for most countries of the global South.

In 2001, during a special UN session on AIDS, Kofi Annan proposed a US$7 to $10 billion per year global budget to combat AIDS (a five-fold increase in funding). The G8 states responded with pledges of US$1.2 billion—"laudable" but "not enough" in Annan's view—and the large funding target became more even difficult to reach as the global recession unfolded and the war on terrorism absorbed attention and resources.[42] In 2006, five countries—France, Britain, Norway, Brazil and Chile—agreed to raise $300 million a year to buy medications for children with AIDS, TB and malaria. Most of it would come from taxing airline tickets (typically $5 for coach and $50 for first class).

Overall, of worldwide spending on AIDS, less than 10 percent has been in countries of the global South, where more than 80 percent of infected people live. Thus, AIDS has deepened the global North-South division. The 2001 UN session also revealed sharp differences between Western secular states and a number of Islamic states that objected to any reference to gay people. Furthermore, Catholic authorities worldwide objected to programs that encourage condom use.

States can adopt policies to slow the spread of AIDS. It is primarily a sexually transmitted disease; its transmission can be prevented by using condoms. Drug users and medical

---

[42] Kofi A. Annan, "We Can Beat AIDS," *New York Times* 25 June 2001: A21. David E. Sanger, "Rich Nations Offer a Hand, but the Poor Hope for More," *New York Times* 21 July 2001: A6.

personnel can use only new or disinfected needles; hospitals can screen blood. Although there is a massive scientific effort to develop a vaccine, a cure has not yet been produced. The most effective measures, then, are public education and the distribution of condoms (especially to prostitutes) and clean needles to drug users. All of these are culturally and politically sensitive issues, however.

States have little choice but to cooperate to try to bring the epidemic under control. International efforts are coordinated primarily by the WHO and funded mainly by industrialized countries. However, the entire WHO budget is equivalent to that of a midsize hospital in the global North. The WHO depends on national governments to provide information and carry out policies, and governments have been slow to respond. Governments falsify statistics to underreport the number of cases (lest tourists be driven away), and many governments are reluctant to condone or sponsor sex education and distribution of condoms because of religious or cultural taboos.

In recent years, HIV has spread rapidly in South Asia, China and Russia/Eastern Europe, where prostitution and drug use are growing. Thailand was especially vulnerable because of its huge prostitution industry, acceptance of male promiscuity and large tourism industry. "Sex tours" attract thousands of foreign men to visit brothels in Thailand and other Southeast Asian countries each year. In addition, hundreds of thousands of young women are trafficked across international borders in the growing sex slave trade. However, Thailand was one of the first developing countries to adopt an effective anti-AIDS program, which focuses on public education. Condom use among prostitutes increased from 20 percent to 90 percent in four years (1988–1992), and cases of sexually transmitted diseases among men (an indicator of HIV spread) dropped by 80 percent. Thailand still faces serious problems with AIDS, but dramatically lowered the infection rate in the 1990s.[43]

In China, the government has been slow to act, and a stigma still prevents effective identification or treatment of the rapidly growing HIV-positive population. Unscrupulous cash-for-blood businesses, especially in one rural region, caused massive HIV infection. In rural China, medical practice relies heavily on injections—often with poorly sterilized needles—when other forms of treatment would be as effective. As a result, 60 percent of China's population has Hepatitis B, compared with 1 percent in the United States and Japan—a danger sign for the future growth of HIV in China.[44] There were an estimated 1 million infected people in China in 2005, with projections of 10 million or more by 2010.

Overall, worldwide, the AIDS epidemic is on track to kill more people in this decade than died in both world wars together—about 100 million people. The international response to the AIDS epidemic is crucial in determining its ultimate course. AIDS illustrates the transnational linkages that make international borders less meaningful than in the past. Effective international cooperation could save millions of lives and significantly enhance prospects for economic development in poor countries in the coming decades. However, there is once again a collective goods problem regarding the allocation of costs and benefits from such efforts. A dollar spent by the WHO has the same effect regardless of which country contributed it.

---

[43] Leslie Ann Jeffrey, *Sex and Borders: Gender, National Identity, and Prostitution Policy in Thailand* (Vancouver: U British Columbia P, 2002). Philip Shenon, "Brash and Unabashed, Mr. Condom Takes on Sex Death in Thailand," *New York Times* 20 Dec. 1992. Lawrence K. Altman, "AIDS Surge Is Forecast for China, India, and Eastern Europe," *New York Times* 4 Nov. 1997.

[44] Elisabeth Rosenthal, "Doctors' Dirty Needles Spreading Disease in China," *New York Times* 20 Aug. 2001: A1.

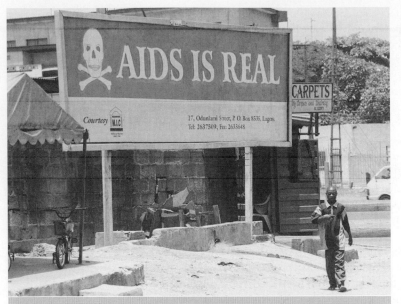

BE CAREFUL OUT THERE

AIDS is spreading rapidly in Southeast Asia and Africa. The worldwide effort to slow AIDS, coordinated by the World Health Organization (WHO), illustrates how global-level problems like AIDS are making IOs like WHO more important. Pictured is an AIDS poster in Nigeria, 2001.

Other Infectious Diseases AIDS is the most severe epidemic of infectious disease in the world, but not the only concern. Tuberculosis (TB), malaria, hepatitis, dengue fever and cholera have all re-emerged or spread in recent decades, often mutating into drug-resistant strains that are increasingly difficult to treat. TB now kills 1.5 million people per year (in addition to AIDS patients who also contract TB). Meanwhile, new and poorly understood diseases have emerged, among them HIV, Ebola virus, hantavirus, SARS and Hepatitis C. Pneumonia, influenza, diarrhea-causing diseases and measles all continue to be major problems but are not growing or spreading to the same extent. Vaccination programs have reduced the incidence of polio and measles in recent years. Epidemics among animals have major economic effects. In the late 1990s, Britain lost billions of dollars during an outbreak of mad-cow disease and foot-and-mouth disease in livestock, while bird flu shut down poultry exports from several Asian countries.[45] Canada's beef exports were curtailed as a result of a case of mad cow disease in 2003, and poultry on British Columbia farms was slaughtered as a result of avian flu in 2004. Currently, scientists fear that bird flu could mutate and spread person-to-person, sparking a global pandemic that could potentially kill millions.

Smoking In the case of smoking, which kills four million people a year, states that fail to curb the spread of nicotine addiction face high future costs in health care—costs that are just beginning to surface in many poor countries. The costs are largely limited to the state itself; its own citizens and economy pay the price. Nonetheless, the tobacco trade makes smoking an international issue. Worldwide, more than a billion people smoke, five-sixths of them in developing countries, and five million people a year die from tobacco-related diseases. Tobacco companies' new marketing campaigns targeting women in the global South could encourage a huge increase in smokers in that group, according to the WHO. With some U.S. support, tobacco companies sought to weaken a new proposed treaty in 2001—the Framework Convention on Tobacco Control—but in 2003 the U.S. dropped its objections and WHO member states adopted the treaty. After ratification by 40 signatories, including Canada, the treaty entered into force in 2005. Parties to the treaty will ban tobacco advertising within five years and will be encouraged to raise taxes on tobacco by 5 percent a year above the inflation rate.

---

[45] U.S. Central Intelligence Agency, *The Global Infectious Disease Threat and Its Implications for the United States, National Intelligence Estimate 99-17D* (Washington, DC: CIA, 2000). Laurie Garrett, *The Coming Plague: Newly Emerging Diseases in a World Out of Balance* (NY: Farrar, Straus & Giroux, 1994). See also footnote 34 in this chapter.

Population and International Conflict

Population issues are sometimes portrayed as simply too many people using too little food and natural resources. This is too simplified. In particular, the idea that overpopulation is the cause of hunger in today's world is not really accurate. Poverty and politics more than population are the causes of malnutrition and hunger (see "World Hunger" on pp. 420–421). There is enough food in the world to feed all people. There is also enough water, petroleum, land and so forth—but the resources are unequally distributed.

Nonetheless, growing populations do put more strain on resources, regionally and globally. Though resources do not usually run out, it costs more to extract them as the

The Changing World Order
The Return of Smallpox

The world order influences levels of analysis down the ladder—interstate relations, domestic societies and individuals—as we have seen in previous chapters. Nor does it stop there. The quality of international political cooperation shapes global public health, reaching down to the level of analysis of microscopic viruses and up to the global level of humanity's relationship with the natural environment (e.g., global warming).

The Cold War world order did not put priority on world health. Poor countries became proxy battlegrounds for the superpowers, and political differences dampened cooperation on health issues. For example, the AIDS virus gathered force in Africa (then a zone of great power rivalry for influence) and spread globally before the international community had galvanized a credible international response. Nonetheless, a limited regime of international cooperation in health matters—centred on the World Health Organization (WHO)—took form during the Cold War.

One of the greatest achievements of this health regime was wiping out smallpox, a virus that had historically killed about one billion people—in particular, decimating Native American populations after its arrival from Europe. Scientists learned how to inoculate against smallpox (using cowpox) 200 years ago, and during the Cold War years the WHO organized a worldwide campaign using the modern vaccine. The baby boom generation of North Americans still carry small scars on their shoulders where they were vaccinated as children. Today's university students, however, were not vaccinated because in 1980 the WHO declared smallpox as having been eliminated globally, three years after the last case was reported in Somalia.

Since then, smallpox has existed officially in two frozen test tubes in Atlanta and Moscow. An increasing share of the world's population has no immunity to the virus, since vaccinations stopped decades ago. After the Cold War, defectors revealed that the Soviet Union had secretly developed smallpox for weapons, perhaps genetically modifying it to make vaccination ineffective. These programs have reportedly closed down, but nobody can be sure that a sample of smallpox has not made it into other hands. In the wake of the 2001 terrorist attacks, the Canadian and U.S. governments scrambled to begin large-scale production of the vaccine again, in case of a terrorist attack with smallpox, which is highly contagious, not treatable and sometimes fatal. (The vaccine itself causes a few rare deaths, so it would probably not be used until needed.)

The world order that emerged in the 1990s and early 2000s, with its growing interdependence and quickening pace of interactions, is one that allows the rapid spread of viruses and bacteria. Overuse of antibiotics (such as in livestock feed) produced drug-resistant strains of bacteria that threatened to outpace the development of new antibiotics. Meanwhile, the AIDS epidemic defied control by the international community. Viruses cross borders with ease, whereas doctors and vaccines can go only where allowed by host governments (and pharmaceutical companies).

Does the world need a stronger form of governance with the power to impose global health regulations and interventions without regard for national sovereignty? If so, how would it work? If not, how else would you stop global epidemics from ravaging societies and economies?

quantity needed increases. New agricultural land is less productive than existing plots; new oil or water supplies must come from greater depths; and so on. For example, food production grew more slowly than population in two-thirds of the developing countries in the 1980s.[46] In the 1960s and 1970s, the "green revolution" increased yields enough to stay ahead of population growth, but had a negative impact on the environment (see "Technology Transfer" on pp. 477–478). Other forms of environmental damage—such as soil erosion and water table depletion—have reduced agricultural productivity in some areas. The faster populations grow, the more pressing world food problems will become.

Growing populations exacerbate all the international conflicts over natural resources discussed earlier. Conflicts over water, which are very serious in several regions, become worse as populations grow. So do a range of issues such as overfishing, deforestation and the loss of agricultural land to urban sprawl. Although it does not cause these problems, population growth affects how severe they become and how quickly they develop.

There is not a simple linear relationship between the number of people in a state and its need for resources. Rather, as an economy develops, population growth slows but the demand for resources continues to rise. The resources are then needed to raise incomes (industrialization) rather than just to feed more mouths. The type of resources needed also changes—less food and more petroleum—as the state's technological needs evolve. Overall, while more states moving through the demographic transition more quickly will slow population growth, it will not decrease the quantity of resources used or the environmental damage caused. More likely the opposite is true.

If population growth can be limited at lower income levels—shifting the demographic curve by using government policies to encourage lower birth rates—strains on the environment will be less. A country would then not only increase its per capita income sooner and faster but it would do so at lower total population levels. This outcome would reduce the load on the environment and resources as compared with industrializing at a higher level of population. Presumably, international conflicts would also be reduced.

Some IR scholars have argued that population growth leads states to expand outwardly in search of resources (the theory of lateral pressure mentioned on p. 174). During the rise of Germany from the mid-nineteenth century through World War II, a consistent theme of German expansionists was the need for "living space" for the growing German population. This need was as much psychological as physical, but was used to justify German territorial expansion, imperialism and aggression.

Another source of international conflict connected with demographics is migration from poor states with high population growth to rich states with low population growth. For example, illegal immigration from Mexico to the United States is an irritant in U.S.-Mexican relations. Refugees are also a recurrent source of interstate conflict. Migration and refugees are population issues, but are discussed in Chapter 12 (pp. 424–429) in the context of North-South relations.

Thus, population pressures are not a simple explanation for the world's problems but do contribute in various ways to international conflicts. Demographic and environmental factors play a large role and are receiving more attention from IR scholars.

As we have seen, the implications of population issues differ greatly in the world's North and South. Strains on the environment and on natural resources are global in scope, yet in the North they arise from industrialization (growing GDP per capita), whereas in the South they are more affected by growing populations.

---

[46] See footnote 35 in this chapter.

These differences in environmental impacts are by no means the only North-South discrepancy. In many ways the world seems to be splitting in two, with different realities in rich and poor regions—a trend running contrary to the integration theme of the previous few chapters.

Thinking Critically

1. Given the collective goods problem in managing environmental issues—heightened by the participation of large numbers of actors—what new international organizations or agreements could be created in the coming years to help solve this problem? Are there ways to reduce the number of actors participating in the management of global problems like ozone depletion? What obstacles might your proposals face regarding issues such as state sovereignty?

2. Few effective international agreements have been reached to solve the problem of global warming. Given the multiple difficulties associated with managing this problem, what creative international solutions can you think of? What would be the strengths and weaknesses of your solutions in the short and long term?

3. Does the record of the international community on environmental management reflect the views of mercantilists, liberals or critical theorists? In what ways?

4. Some politicians call for the Western industrialized countries to be more self-sufficient in energy resources in order to reduce dependence on oil imports from the Middle East. In light of the overall world energy picture and the economics of international trade, what are the pros and cons of such a proposal?

5. Dozens of poor states appear to be stuck midway through the demographic transition; death rates have fallen, birth rates remain high and per capita incomes are not increasing. How do you think these states, with or without foreign assistance, can best get unstuck and complete the demographic transition?

Chapter Summary

- Environmental problems are an example of international interdependence and often create collective goods problems for the states involved. The large numbers of actors involved in global environmental problems make them more difficult to solve.

- To resolve collective goods problems, states have used international regimes and IOs, and have in some cases extended state sovereignty (notably over territorial waters) to make management a national rather than international matter.

- International efforts to solve environmental problems aim to bring about sustainable economic development. This was the theme of the 1992 UN Earth Summit.

- Global warming results from burning fossil fuels—the basis of industrial economies today. Industrialized states are much more responsible for the problem than are states of the global South. Solutions are difficult to reach because the costs are substantial and dangers are somewhat distant and uncertain.

- Damage to the earth's ozone layer results from the use of specific chemicals, which are now being phased out under international agreements. In contrast to global warming, the costs of solutions are much lower and the problem is better understood.

- Many species are threatened with extinction due to loss of habitats such as rain forests. An international treaty on biodiversity and an agreement on forests aim to reduce the destruction of local ecosystems, with costs spread among states.

- The UN Convention on the Law of the Sea (UNCLOS) establishes an ocean regime that puts most commercial fisheries and offshore oil under the control of states as territorial waters. The United States signed the treaty after a decade's delay.

- Pollution—including acid rain, water and air pollution and toxic and nuclear waste—tends to be more localized than global and has been addressed mainly through unilateral, bilateral and regional measures rather than global ones.

- The economies of the industrialized West depend on fossil fuels. Overall, these economies import energy resources, mostly oil, whereas other world regions export them. Oil prices rose dramatically in the 1970s but declined in the 1980s as the world economy adjusted by increasing supply and reducing demand. After spiking in 1991 and again around 2000, prices dropped again. Such fluctuations undermine world economic stability.

- The most important source of oil traded worldwide is the Persian Gulf area of the Middle East. Consequently, this area has long been a focal point of international political conflict, including the 1991 Gulf War.

- States need other raw materials such as minerals, but no such materials have assumed the importance or political status of oil. Water resources are a growing source of local international conflicts, however.

- War and other military activities cause considerable environmental damage—sometimes deliberately inflicted as part of a war strategy.

- World population—now at 6.2 billion—will reach 7 to 8 billion within 25 years and may eventually level out around 10 billion. Virtually all of the increase will occur in the global South.

- Future world population growth will be largely driven by the demographic transition. Death rates have fallen throughout the world, but birth rates will fall proportionally only as per capita incomes rise. The faster the economies of poor states develop, the sooner their populations will level out.

- The demographic transition sharpens disparities of wealth globally and locally. High per capita incomes and low population growth make rich states or groups richer, whereas low incomes and high population growth reinforce one another to keep poor states and groups poor.

- Within the overall shape of the demographic transition, government policies can reduce birth rates somewhat at a given level of per capita income. Effective policies are those that improve access to birth control and raise the status of women in society. Actual policies vary, from China's very strict rules on childbearing to pronatalist governments that encourage maximum birth rates and outlaw birth control.

- Death rates are stable and minimally affected in the large picture by wars, famines and other disasters. Raising the death rate is not a feasible way to limit population growth.

- Although the global AIDS epidemic may not greatly slow world population growth, it will impose huge costs on many poor states in the coming years. Currently 36 million people are infected with HIV, and 22 million more have died. Most are in Africa, and new infections are growing rapidly in Asia.

- AIDS demonstrates that growing international interdependence—the shrinking world—has costs and not just benefits. Because states cannot wall themselves off from the outside world, international cooperation in addition to unilateral state actions will be necessary to contain AIDS.

- Population pressures do not cause, but do contribute to, a variety of international conflicts including ethnic disputes, economic competition and territorial disputes.

Key Terms

tragedy of the commons   501
enclosure of the commons   501
epistemic communities   502
carrying capacity   503
Commission on Sustainable
   Development   504
global warming   505
fossil fuels   506
greenhouse gases   506
UN Environment Programme
   (UNEP)   509
ozone layer   509
Montreal Protocol   510

biodiversity   510
International Whaling Commission   511
high seas   514
UN Convention on the Law of the Sea
   (UNCLOS)   514
Antarctic Treaty of
   1959   516
acid rain   517
Chernobyl   518
oil shocks   522
demographic transition   529
pronatalist policy   531
infant mortality rate   532

Research Navigator Question

Use the Link Library for Sociology on Research Navigator and explore several of the sites that focus on global warming. In small groups, examine some of the contending arguments concerning the state of knowledge on global warming. What are the arguments both for and against the Kyoto Protocol in light of these arguments?

Weblinks

The following links are a small sampling of the many sites devoted to the environment and population:

Amazon Watch:
http://www.amazonwatch.org

Environment Canada:
http://www.ec.gc.ca/envhome.html

Greenpeace:
http://www.greenpeace.org/homepage

United Nations Environment Programme:
http://www.unep.org

United Nations Population Fund:
http://www.unfpa.org

World Wildlife Fund:
http://www.panda.org

Postscript

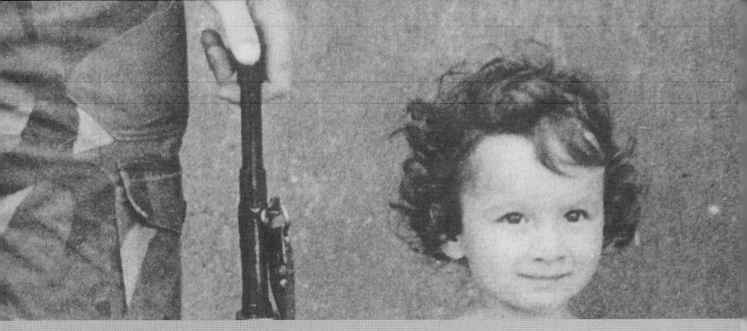

Soldier and child, Sarajevo, 1993.

Ultimately, the conflicts and dramas of international relations are not much different from those of other spheres of political and social life. The problems of IR are the problems of human society—struggles for power and wealth, efforts to cooperate despite differences, social dilemmas and collective goods problems, the balance between freedom and order, the costs of efficiency versus equity and of long-term versus short-term outcomes. These themes are inescapable in human society, from the smallest groups to the world community. In this sense, the subject of international relations is an extension of everyday life and a reflection of the choices of individual human beings. IR belongs to all of us—North and South, women and men, citizens and leaders—who live together on this planet.

Technological development is just one aspect of the profound yet incremental changes taking place in international relations. New actors are gaining power, long-standing principles are becoming less effective and new challenges are arising for states, groups and individuals. The post–Cold War era, just over a decade old, remains undefined. Will it, like past "postwar" eras, lapse slowly into the next "prewar" era? Or will it lead to a robust and lasting "permanent peace"?

Consider a few aspects of these changes discussed in this book. One major theme was the nature of the international system, which for some observers operated on a well-developed set of rules based on state sovereignty, territoriality and "anarchy"—a lack of central government. Others argued that the international system was far more complex, more nuanced and more interconnected with other aspects of planetary society, and that this complexity is becoming ever more apparent. State sovereignty is challenged by the principle of self-determination. International norms have begun to limit the right of government to rule a population by force and to violate human rights, but at the same time the new war on terror has subjected more people to surveillance and control. Territorial integrity is also problematic, since national borders do not stop information, environmental changes or missiles. Information allows actors—state, substate and supranational—to know what is going on in the world and to coordinate actions globally.

Technology is profoundly changing the utility and role of military forces. The power of defensive weaponry makes successful attacks more difficult, and the power of offensive weaponry makes retaliation an extremely potent deterrent. Twentieth-century superpowers could not attack each other without destroying themselves, and a large force cannot reliably defeat a small one (or, to be more accurate, the costs of doing so are too high), as demonstrated in Vietnam, Afghanistan and now Iraq. Nonmilitary forms of leverage, particularly economic rewards, have become much more important power capabilities.

In IPE, we see conflicting trends toward integration and disintegration among states. People continue to speak their own language, fly their own flag and use their own currency with its pictures and emblems. Nationalism continues to be an important force. At the same time, however, although people identify with their state, they also now hold competing identities based on ethnic ties, gender and sometimes region. In international trade, liberal economics prevails but sometimes at a great cost to those on the periphery of the global political economy. States have learned that in order to survive they must help, rather than impede, the creation of wealth by MNCs and other economic actors, which means sometimes siding with foreign economic interests over local citizens.

Meanwhile, North-South relations are moving to the centre of world politics. Demographic and economic trends are sharpening the global gap, with the North continuing to accumulate wealth while much of the South lingers in great poverty. Ultimately, the North will bear a high cost for failing to address the economic development of the South. Perhaps, with the use of computerization and biotechnology innovations, poor states can develop their economies much more efficiently than did Europe or North America.

Environmental damage may become the single greatest obstacle to sustained economic growth in the North and South. Because of high costs, the large number of actors and collective goods problems, international bargaining over the environment is difficult. However, the 1992 Earth Summit's call for sustainable economic growth that does not deplete resources and destroy ecosystems may be supported by new technology that moves information, instead of materials, to accomplish the same goals. The traditional technological style of industrialization cannot be sustained environmentally on the giant scale of countries like China and India.

The future is unknowable, but as it unfolds it can be compared—at mileposts along the way—to the worlds you desire and expect. A comparison of divergent futures may be facilitated by examining a range of possible branch points where alternative paths diverge. For example, you could ask the following questions (asking yourself, for each one, why you answer the way you do for your desired and expected future):

1. Will state sovereignty be eroded by supranational authority?
2. Will norms of human rights and democracy become global?
3. Will the UN evolve into a quasi-government for the world?
4. Will the UN be restructured?
5. Will World Court and International Criminal Court judgments become enforceable?
6. Will the number of states increase?
7. Will China become democratic? Will it become rich?

8. What effects will information technologies have on IR?

9. Will military leverage become obsolete?

10. Will weapons of mass destruction proliferate?

11. Will disarmament occur?

12. Will women participate more fully in IR? With what effect?

13. Will there be a single world currency?

14. Will there be a global free trade regime?

15. Will nationalism fade out or continue to be strong?

16. Will many people develop a global identity?

17. Will world culture become more homogeneous or more pluralistic?

18. Will the EU or other regional IOs achieve political union?

19. Will global environmental destruction be severe? How soon?

20. Will new technologies avert environmental constraints?

21. Will global problems create a stronger or weaker world order?

22. Will population growth level out? If so, when and at what level?

23. Will the poorest countries accumulate wealth? How soon?

24. What role will NGOs play in development in the South?

The choices you make and actions you take will ultimately affect, in some way, the world you live in. You cannot opt out of involvement in international relations. You are involved, and year after year the information revolution and other aspects of interdependence are drawing you more closely into contact with the rest of the world. You can act in varied ways, on a large or small scale, to bring the world you expect more into line with the world you desire. You can empower yourself by finding the actions and choices that define your place in international relations.

Now that you have completed the studies covered in this book, don't stop here. Continue learning about the world beyond your country's borders. Keep thinking about the world that might exist. Be a part of the changes that will carry this world through the coming decades. It's your world: study it, care for it, make it your own.

Studying International Relations in Canada: Relevant Links

Students interested in pursuing the study of International Relations at the graduate level may find the following links helpful. They are the websites of various programs in International Relations or Political Science across the country. The list is not exhaustive, and further research may be worthwhile (especially for college programs of IR or those located within departments other than Political Science). The list is intended to provide interested students with a good place to start exploring the possibilities for continued study of IR in Canada.

British Columbia

University of British Columbia
http://www.politics.ubc.ca (Department of Political Science)
http://www.arts.ubc.ca/International_Relations_Program.4630.0.html (International Relations Program)

University of Northern British Columbia
http://www.unbc.ca/internationalstudies (International Studies)
http://www.unbc.ca/politicalscience/index.html (Political Science Program)

University of Victoria
http://web.uvic.ca/polisci (Department of Political Science)

Simon Fraser University
http://www.sfu.ca/internationalstudies (School for International Studies)
http://www.sfu.ca/polysci (Department of Political Science)

Alberta

University of Alberta
http://www.uofaweb.ualberta.ca/polisci (Department of Political Science)

University of Calgary
http://www.poli.ucalgary.ca (Department of Political Science)

University of Lethbridge
http://www.uleth.ca/fas/pol/index.html (Political Science)

Saskatchewan

University of Regina
http://www.uregina.ca/arts/political-science/index.html (Department of Political Science)

University of Saskatchewan
http://www.usask.ca/politic (Department of Political Studies)

Manitoba

Brandon University
http://www.brandonu.ca/academic/arts/Departments/PoliticalScience/politicalscience.htm
(Political Science)

University of Manitoba
http://umanitoba.ca/faculties/arts/departments/political_studies (Political Studies)

University of Winnipeg
http://www.uwinnipeg.ca/academic/as/polsci/polsci.html (Department of Politics)

Ontario

Brock University
http://www.brocku.ca/politicalscience/index.html (Department of Political Science)

Carleton University
http://www.carleton.ca/polisci (Department of Political Science)
http://www.carleton.ca/npsia/index.html (Norman Paterson School of International Affairs)

Lakehead University
http://politicalscience.lakeheadu.ca/index.php (Department of Political Science)

Laurentian University
http://www.laurentian.ca/Laurentian/Home/Departments/Political+Science (Department of Political Science)

McMaster University
http://www.socsci.mcmaster.ca/polisci/index.cfm (Political Science Department)

Nipissing University
http://www.nipissingu.ca/politicalscience (Political Science)

Queen's University
http://www.queensu.ca/politics/index.php (Department of Political Studies)

Royal Military College of Canada
http://www.rmc.ca/academic/poli-econ/index_e.html (Department of Politics and Economics)

Ryerson University
http://www.ryerson.ca/politics/pogv (Politics and Governance)

Trent University
http://www.trentu.ca/academic/politics/Titlepage.html (Politics at Trent)

University of Guelph
http://www.polisci.uoguelph.ca/index.shtml (Department of Political Science)

University of Ottawa
http://www.politicalscience.uottawa.ca (Faculty of Social Sciences)

University of Toronto
http://www.chass.utoronto.ca/polsci (Department of Political Science)
http://webapp.mcis.utoronto.ca (Munk Centre for International Studies)
http://www.trinity.utoronto.ca/Academics/Programs/IR (International Relations Degree Program—Trinity College)

University of Waterloo
http://globalgovernance.uwaterloo.ca/index.html (Global Governance Program)
http://politicalscience.uwaterloo.ca (Politics Department)
http://grebel.uwaterloo.ca/academic/undergrad/pacs (Peace and Conflict Studies Program)

University of Western Ontario
http://politicalscience.uwo.ca (Department of Political Science)

University of Windsor
http://web4.uwindsor.ca/units/polsci/political.nsf/inToc/2E06663687DF782A8525710D007AD930 (Political Science)

Wilfred Laurier University
http://www.wlu.ca/homepage.php?grp_id=166 (Politics Department)
http://www.wlu.ca/homepage.php?grp_id=1678 (Laurier Centre for Global Relations)

York University
http://www.arts.yorku.ca/politics/index.html (Department of Political Science)

Quebec

Bishop's University
http://www.ubishops.ca/ccc/div/soc/pol/programme.html (Political Studies)

Concordia University
http://politicalscience.concordia.ca/about/whats_in_it/index.shtml (Department of Political Science)

McGill University
http://www.mcgill.ca/politicalscience (Political Science)

Université de Montréal
http://www.pol.umontreal.ca (Département de Science Politique)

Université du Québec à Montréal
http://www.politis.uqam.ca (Département de Science Politique)

Université Sherbrooke
http://www.usherbrooke.ca/dhsp (Département d'Histoire et de Sciences Politiques)

Université Laval
http://www.pol.ulaval.ca/site/index.asp (Département de Science Politique)

New Brunswick

Mount Allison
http://www.mta.ca/faculty/socsci/polisci/index.html (Political Science Department)

Université de Moncton
http://www.umoncton.ca/scpol (Département de Science Politique)

University of New Brunswick
http://www.unbsj.ca/arts/polsci/index.html (Saint John) (Political Science)
http://www.unbf.ca/arts/Poli (Fredericton) (Political Science)

Prince Edward Island

University of Prince Edward Island
http://www.upei.ca/politicalstudies (Department of Political Studies)

Nova Scotia

Acadia University
http://ace.acadiau.ca/polisci/homepage.htm (Department of Political Science)

Dalhousie University
http://politicalscience.dal.ca/index.htm (Department of Political Science)
http://internationaldevelopmentstudies.artsandsocialsciences.dal.ca/index.php (Department
of International Development Studies)

Mount St. Vincent University
http://www.msvu.ca/PAX/index.asp (Peace and Conflict Studies)
http://www.msvu.ca/political-canadian/index.asp (Political and Canadian Studies Department)

St. Francis Xavier University
http://www.stfx.ca/academic/political-science/welcome.htm (Department of Political Science)

St. Mary's University
http://www.smu.ca/academic/arts/pscience/welcome.html (Political Science Department)

Newfoundland

Memorial University of Newfoundland
http://www.mun.ca/posc/welcome (Department of Political Science)

Glossary

acid rain Rain that contains acids caused by air pollution; it damages trees and often crosses borders. Limiting acid rain (via limiting nitrogen oxide emissions) has been the subject of several regional agreements. *(p. 517)*

airspace The space above a state that is considered its territory, in contrast to outer space, which is considered international territory. *(p. 172)*

alliance cohesion The ease with which members hold together an alliance; it tends to be high when national interests converge and when cooperation among allies becomes institutionalized. *(p. 247)*

Amnesty International An influential nongovernmental organization that operates globally to monitor and try to rectify glaring abuses of political (not economic or social) human rights. *(p. 295)*

anarchy In IR theory, the termimplies not complete chaos but the lack of a centralgovernment that can enforce rules. *(p. 60)*

Antarctic Treaty of 1959 One of the first multilateral treaties concerning the environment, it forbids military activity in Antarctica as well as the presence of nuclear weapons or the dumping of nuclear waste there, sets aside territorial claims on the continent for future resolution and establishes a regime for the conduct of scientific research. *(p. 516)*

Anti-Ballistic Missile (ABM) Treaty (1972) Treaty that prohibited either the United States and the Soviet Union from using a ballistic missile defence as a shield, a tactic that would have undermined mutually assured destruction and the basis of deterrence *(p. 275)*. See also *mutually assured destruction (MAD)* and *Strategic Defense Initiative (SDI)*.

arms race A reciprocal process in which two (or more) states build up military capabilities in response to each other. *(p. 74)*

autarky (self-reliance) A policy of avoiding or minimizing trade and trying to produce everything one needs (or the most vital things) by oneself. *(p. 318)*

balance of payments A summary of all the flows of money into and out of a country. It includes three types of international transactions: the current account (including the merchandise trade balance), flows of capital and changes in reserves. *(p. 352)*

balance of power The general concept of one or more states' power being used to balance that of another state or group of states. The term can refer to (1) any ratio of power capabilities between states or alliances, (2) a relatively equal ratio, or (3) the process by which counterbalancing coalitions have repeatedly formed to prevent one state from conquering an entire region. *(p. 63)*

balance of trade The value of a state's exports relative to its imports. *(p. 315)*

ballistic missiles The major strategic delivery vehicles for nuclear weapons; they carry awarhead along a trajectory (typically rising at least 80 kilometres high) and let it drop on a target. *(p. 211)* See also *intercontinental ballistic missiles* (ICBHs)

basic human needs The fundamental needs of people for adequate food, shelter, health care, sanitation and education. Meeting such needs may be thought of as both a moral imperative and a form of investment in the "human capital" essential for economic growth. *(p. 416)*

bilateral aid Government assistance that goes directly to global South governments as state-to-state aid. *(p. 486)*

biodiversity The tremendous diversity of plant and animal species making up the earth's (global, regional and local) ecosystems. *(p. 510)*

Biological Weapons Convention (1972) Treaty that prohibits the development, production and possession of biological weapons, but makes no provision for inspections. *(p. 217)*

blue helmets UN peacekeeping forces, so called because they wear helmets or berets in the UN colour, blue, with UN insignia. *(p. 263)*

bourgeoisie In Marxist terminology, the class of owners of capital—people who make money from their investments rather than from their labour. *(p. 435)*

brain drain Poor countries' loss of skilled workers to rich countries. *(p. 477)*

Bretton Woods system A post–World War II arrangement for managing the world economy, established at a meeting in Bretton Woods, New Hampshire, in 1944. Its main institutional componentsare the World Bank and the International Monetary Fund (IMF). *(p. 350)*

burden sharing The distribution of the costs of an alliance among members; the term also refers to the conflicts that may arise over such distribution. *(p. 247)*

bureaucratic politics model A decision-making model that sees foreign policy decisions as flowing from a bargaining process among various government agencies that have somewhat divergent interests in the outcome ("where you stand depends on where you sit"). Also called the *government bargaining model*. *(p. 140)*

capital accumulation The creation of standing wealth (capital) such as buildings, roads, factories and so forth; such accumulation depends on investment and the creation of an economic surplus. *(p. 429)*

capitalism An economic system based on private ownership of capital and the means of production (standing wealth and other forms of property). See also *socialism*. *(p. 432)*

carrying capacity The limits of the planetary ecosystem's ability to absorb continual growth in population, industry, energy use and extraction of natural resources. *(p. 503)*

cartel An association of producers or consumers (or both) of a certain product, formed for the purpose of manipulating its price on the world market. *(p. 469)*

cash crops Agricultural goods produced as commodities for export to world markets. *(p. 421)*

central bank An institution common in industrialized countries whose major tasks are to maintain the value of a state's currency and to control inflation. *(p. 348)*

centrally planned (or command) economy An economy in which political authorities set prices and decide on quotas for production and consumption of each commodity according to a long-term plan.   (*p. 311*)

Chemical Weapons Convention (1992) Treaty banning the production and possession of chemical weapons, which includes strict verification provisions and the threat of sanctions against violators, including nonparticipants in the treaty.   (*p. 216*)

Chernobyl A city in Ukraine that was the site of a 1986 meltdown at a Soviet nuclear power plant.   (*p. 518*)

civil war A war between factions within a state trying to create or prevent a new government for the entire state or some territorial part of it.   (*p. 159*)

class struggle The process in which the more powerful classes oppress and exploit the less powerful by denying them their fair share of the surplus they create. The oppressed classes try to gain power, rebel and organize in order to seize more of the economic surplus for themselves.   (*p. 435*)

Cold War The hostile relations, punctuated by occasional periods of improvement, or détente, between the two superpowers—the U.S. and the U.S.S.R.—from 1945 to 1990.   (*p. 35*)

collective goods problem The problem of how to provide something that benefits all members of a group regardless of what each member contributes to it.   (*p. 82*)

collective security The formation of a broad coalition of most major actors in an international system for the purpose of jointly opposing aggression by any actor; sometimes seen as presupposing the existence of a universal organization (such as the United Nations) to which both the aggressor and its opponents belong. See also *League of Nations*.   (*p. 86*)

Commission on Sustainable Development An organization established at the 1992 UN Earth Summit that monitors states' compliance with their promises and hears evidence from environmental *nongovernmental organizations* (NGOs).   (*p. 504*)

Common Agricultural Policy (CAP) A European Union policy based on the principle that a subsidy extended to farmers in any member country should be extended to farmers in all member countries.   (*p. 383*)

common market A zone in which labour and capital (as well as goods) flow freely across borders.   (*p. 383*)

comparative advantage The principle that states should specialize in trading those goods that they produce with the greatest relative efficiency and at the lowest relative cost (relative, that is, to other goods produced by the same state).   (*p. 308*)

compellence The use of force to make another actor take some action (rather than refrain from taking one); sometimes used after *deterrence* fails.   (*p. 73*)

Comprehensive Test Ban Treaty (CTBT) (1996) Treaty that bans all nuclear weapons testing, thereby broadening the ban on atmospheric testing negotiated in 1963.   (*p. 276*)

conflict A difference in preferred outcomes in a bargaining situation.   (*p. 161*)

conflict resolution The development and implementation of peaceful strategies for settling conflicts.   (*p. 94*)

constructivism A recently popular approach in IR that focuses on the nature of norms, identity and social interaction between various actors in global politics.   (*p. 91*)

consumption goods Goods whose consumption does not contribute directly to the production of other goods and services, unlike some forms of investment.   (*p. 431*)

containment A policy adopted in the late 1940s by which the United States sought to halt the global expansion of Soviet influence on several levels—military, political, ideological and economic.   (*p. 35*)

Conventional Forces in Europe (CFE) Treaty (1990) A U.S.-Soviet agreement that provided for asymmetrical reductions in Soviet forces in Europe and limited the forces of both sides.   (*p. 277*)

convertible currency The guarantee that the holder of aparticular currency can exchange it for another currency. Some states' currencies are nonconvertible. See also *hard currency*.   (*p. 343*)

core The manufacturing regions of the world-system.   (*p. 437*)

cost-benefit analysis A calculation of the costs incurred by a possible action and the benefits it is likely to bring.   (*p. 56*)

Council of the European Union (formerly known as the Council of Ministers.) The main legislative and decision-making body in the European Union, composed of relevant ministers (foreign, economic, agriculture, finance, etc.) from the 27 member countries. When a meeting takes place, it is called the "European Council."   (*p. 386*)

counterinsurgency Counterinsurgency warfare often includes programs that try to "win the hearts and minds" of populations so that they stop sheltering guerrillas. While battling armed factions of an insurgency, a government must essentially conduct a public relations campaign to convince the population to abandon the movement, while providing public services (such as education and welfare programs) to show their responsiveness to the population.   (*p. 198*)

counterinsurgency An effort to combat guerrilla armies, often including programs to "win the hearts and minds" of rural populations so that they stop sheltering guerrillas.   (*p. 160*)

coup d'état French for "blow against the state"; the seizure of political power by domestic military forces—that is, a change of political power outside the state's constitutional order.   (*p. 234*)

crimes against humanity A category of legal offences created at the Nuremberg trials after World War II to encompass genocide and other acts committed by the political and military leaders of the Third Reich (Nazi Germany). See also *dehumanization* and *genocide*.   (*p. 286*)

critical theory Theory that questions the very framework (the very world) that problem-solving theory takes for granted, and is concerned with relations of inequality and the issues that are unexplored or made invisible within more mainstream approaches to IR.   (*p. 105*)

cruise missile A small, winged missile that can navigate across thousands of kilometres of previously mapped terrain to reach a particular target; it can carry either a nuclear or a conventional warhead.   (*p. 212*)

Cuban Missile Crisis (1962) A superpower crisis, sparked by the Soviet Union's installation of medium-range nuclear missiles in Cuba, that marks the moment when the United States and the Soviet Union came closest to nuclear war.   (*p. 36*)

cultural imperialism A critical term for Western (especially U.S.) dominance of the emerging global culture.   (*p. 409*)

customs union A common external tariff adopted by members of a free trade area; that is, participating states adopt a unified set of tariffs with regard to goods coming in from outside.   (*p. 383*)

debt renegotiation A reworking of the terms on which a loan will be repaid; frequently negotiated by global South debtor governments in order to avoid default.   (*p. 479*)

debt service An obligation to make regular interest payments and repay the principal of a loan according to its terms, which is a drain on many economies of the global South.   (*p. 479*)

Declaration of Human Rights (UDHR) Adopted by the UN General Assembly in 1948, the UNDHR is considered the core international document concerning human rights.   (*p. 292*)

default The failure to make scheduled debt payments.   (*p. 479*)

dehumanization Stigmatization of enemies as subhuman or nonhuman, leading frequently to widespread massacres or, in the worst cases, destruction of entire populations. See also *crimes against humanity* and *genocide*.   (*p. 182*)

democratic peace The proposition, strongly supported by empirical evidence, that democracies almost never fight wars against each other (although they do fight against authoritarian states).   (*p. 89*)

demographic transition The pattern of falling death rates, followed by falling birth rates, that generally accompanies *industrialization* and *economic development*.   (*p. 529*)

dependency theory A Marxist-oriented theory that explains the lack of capital accumulation in the global South as a result of the interplay between domestic class relations and the forces of foreign capital.   (*p. 446*)

deterrence The threat to punish another actor if it takes a certain negative action (especially attacking one's own state or allies).   (*p. 73*)

devaluation A unilateral move to reduce the value of a currency by changing a fixed or official exchange rate. See also exchange rate.   (*p. 347*)

developing countries States in the global South, the poorest regions of the world—also called third world countries, less-developed countries and underdeveloped countries.   (*p. 414*)

Development Assistance Committee (DAC) A committee whose members—consisting of states from Western Europe, North America and Japan/Pacific—provide 90 percent of official development assistance to countries of the global South. See also *foreign assistance*.   (*p. 486*)

digital divide The gap in access to information technologies between and within countries.   (*p. 399*)

diplomatic immunity Refers to diplomats' activity being outside the jurisdiction of the host country's national courts.   (*p. 283*)

diplomatic recognition The process by which the status of embassies and that of an ambassador as an official state representative are explicitly defined.   (*p. 282*)

disaster relief The provision of short-term relief in the form of food, water, shelter, clothing and other essentials to people facing natural disasters.   (*p. 490*)

discount rate The interest rate charged by governments when they lend money to private banks. The discount rate (called the bank rate in Canada) is set by countries' central banks.   (*p. 348*)

dumping The sale of products in foreign markets at prices below the minimum level necessary to make a profit (orbelow cost).   (*p. 320*)

economic base A society's mode of production, such as slavery, feudalism or capitalism.   (*p. 435*)

economic class A categorization of individuals based on economic status (which in Marxism, for example, is determined by one's relationship to the means of production as either an owner of capital or worker).   (*p. 434*)

economic conversion The use of former military facilities and industries for new civilian production.   (*p. 226*)

economic development The combined processes of capital accumulation, rising per capita incomes (with consequent falling birthrates), the increasing of skills in the population, the adoption of new technological styles and other related social and economic changes.   (*p. 452*)

economic liberalism An approach to IPE that emphasizes the gains made through trade and that, in practice, is committed to free trade, free capital flows and an "open" world economy. See also *mercantilism* and *neoliberalism*.   (*p. 303*)

economic surplus Surplus created by investing money in productive capital rather than using it for consumption.   (*p. 429*)

electronic warfare The use of the electromagnetic spectrum (radio waves, radar, infrared, etc.) in war; employing electromagnetic signals for one's own benefit while denying their use to an enemy.   (*p. 203*)

elite model (or its more critical variant, instrumental Marxism) The view that decision-makers within governments or state agencies share a common business or class background, and that their decisions will reflect their business or class interests.   (*p. 151*)

empowerment In a development context, it refers to the grassroots efforts of poor people to gain power over their situation and meet their own basic needs.   (*p. 495*)

enclave economy A historically important form ofdependency in which foreign capital is invested in a global South country to extract a particular raw material in a specific place—usually a mine, oil well or plantation.   (*p. 446*)

enclosure of the commons The splitting of a common area or good into privately owned pieces, giving individual owners an incentive to manage resources responsibly.   (*p. 501*)

epistemic communities Transnational communities of experts who help structure the way states manage environmental and other issues.   (*p. 502*)

ethnic cleansing Forced displacement of an ethnic group or groups from a particular territory, accompanied by massacres and other human rights violations; it has occurred after the breakup of multinational states, notably in the former Yugoslavia.   (*p. 168*)

ethnic groups Large groups of people who share ancestral, language, cultural, or religious ties and a common identity.   *(p. 178)*

ethnocentrism (in-group bias) The tendency to see one's own group (in-group) in favourable terms and an out-group in unfavourable terms.   *(p. 181)*

Euratom An organization created in the Treaty of Rome in 1957 to coordinate nuclear power development by pooling research, investment and management.   *(p. 382)*

euro Also called the ECU (*European Currency Unit*), the euro is a single European currency used by 12 members of the *European Union (EU)*.   *(p. 390)*

European Commission A European Union body whose members, while appointed by states, are supposed to represent EU interests. Supported by a multinational civil service in Brussels, the commission's role is to identify problems and propose solutions to the *Council of the European Union*.   *(p. 385)*

European Court of Justice A judicial arm of the European Union, based in Luxembourg. The court has actively established its jurisdiction and the right to overrule national law when it conflicts with EU law.   *(p. 387)*

European Parliament The quasi-legislative body of the European Union that operates mainly as a watchdog over the *European Commission* and has little real legislative power.   *(p. 386)*

European Union (EU) The official term for the European Community (formerly the European Economic Community) and associated treaty organizations. The EU has 27 member states and is negotiating with other states that have applied for membership. See also *Maastricht Treaty*.   *(p. 381)*

exchange rate The rate at which one state's currency can be exchanged for the currency of another state. Since 1973, the international monetary system has depended mainly on flexible (or floating) rather than fixed exchange rates. See also *convertibility fixed exchange rates; Exchange Rate Mechanism* (ERM); and managed float.   *(p. 342)*

export-led growth An economic development strategy that seeks to develop industries capable of competing in specific niches in the world economy.   *(p. 467)*

fiscal policy A government's decisions about spending and taxation, and one of the two major tools of macroeconomic policy-making (the other being monetary policy).   *(p. 356)*

fissionable material The elements uranium-235 and plutonium, whose atoms split apart and release energy via a chain reaction when an atomic bomb explodes. See also *fusion weapons*.   *(p. 208)*

fixed exchange rates The official rates of exchange for currencies set by governments; not a dominant mechanism in the international monetary system since 1973.   *(p. 344)*

floating exchange rates The rates determined by global currency markets; used by private investors and governments alike to buy and sell currencies.   *(p. 344)*

foreign assistance Money or other aid made available to developing countries to help them speed up economic development or meet humanitarian needs. Most foreign assistance is provided by governments and is called official development assistance (ODA). See also *Development Assistance Committee (DAC)*.   *(p. 486)*

foreign direct investment The acquisition by residents of one country of control over a new or existing business in another country. Also called direct foreign investment.   *(p. 353)*

foreign policy process The process by which foreign policies are arrived at and implemented.   *(p. 130)*

fossil fuels Oil, coal and natural gas, burned to run factories, cars, tractors, furnaces, electrical generating plants and other things that drive an industrial economy.   *(p. 506)*

"four tigers"/"four dragons" The most successful newly industrialized areas of East Asia: South Korea, Taiwan, Hong Kong and Singapore.   *(p. 456)*

free economic zones The southern coastal provinces of China that were opened to foreign investment and run on capitalist principles with export-oriented industries in the 1980s and 1990s.   *(p. 459)*

free riders Those who benefit from someone else's provision of a collective good without paying their share of costs.   *(p. 82)*

free trade The flow of goods and services across national boundaries unimpeded by tariffs or other restrictions; in principle (if not always in practice), free trade was a key aspect of Britain's policy after 1846 and of U.S. and Canadian policy after 1945.   *(p. 31)*

free trade area A zone in which there are no tariffs or other restrictions on the movement of goods and services across borders.   *(p. 383)*

fusion weapons Extremely destructive, expensive and technologically sophisticated weapons in which two small atoms fuse together to form alarger atom, releasing energy. Also referred to as "thermonuclear weapons "or" hydrogen bombs." See also *fissionable material*.   *(p. 208)*

game theory A branch of mathematics concerned with predicting bargaining outcomes. Games such as Prisoner's Dilemma and Chicken have been used to analyze various sorts of international interactions.   *(p. 57)*

gender gap Refers to polls showing women lower than men on average in their support for military actions (as well as for various other issues and candidates).   *(p. 117)*

General Agreement on Tariffs and Trade (GATT) A world organization established in 1947 to work for freer trade on a multilateral basis; the GATT has been more of a negotiating framework than an administrative institution. It became the World Trade Organization (WTO) in 1995.   *(p. 332)*

Generalized System of Preferences (GSP) Amechanism by which some industrialized states began to give tariff concessions to global South states on certain imports in the 1970s; an exception to the most-favoured nation (MFN) principle.   *(p. 333)*

genocide The intentional and systematic attempt to destroy a national, ethnic, racial or religious group, in whole or part. It was confirmed as a crime under international law by the UN Genocide Convention (1948). See also *crimes against humanity* and *dehumanization*.   *(p. 34)*

geopolitics The use of geography as an element of power, and the ideas about it held by political leaders and scholars.   *(p. 55)*

global culture Worldwide cultural integration based on a massive increase in satellite television, radio and internet communication.   *(p. 406)*

global social movements Non-state groups that organize transnationally, usually to protest around an issue or event (such as the environment, peace, women's issues, human rights and globalization).   *(p. 12)*

global warming A slow, long-term rise in the average world temperature caused by the emission of greenhouse gases produced by burning fossil fuels—oil, coal and natural gas. See also *greenhouse gases*.   *(p. 505)*

globalization The increasing integration of the world in terms of communications, culture and economics; may also refer to changing subjective experiences of space and time that accompany this process.   *(p. 305)*

gold standard A system in international monetary relations, prominent for a century before the 1970s, in which the value of national currencies was pegged to thevalue of gold or other precious metals.   *(p. 342)*

Gramscian hegemony A view that contrasts with realist definition of hegemony; recognizes that those with power rule through a mixture of coercion and consent and that hegemony functions when the relations of power that sustain a given social order recede into the background of consciousness.   *(p. 110)*

great powers Generally, the half dozen or so most powerful states; the great-power club was exclusively European until the twentieth century. See also *middle powers*.   *(p. 65)*

green revolution The massive transfer of agricultural technology, such ashigh-yield seeds and tractors, to countries of the global South that began in the1960s.   *(p. 478)*

greenhouse gases Carbon dioxide and other gases that, when concentrated in the atmosphere, act like the glass in a greenhouse, holding in energy and leading to *global warming*.   *(p. 506)*

gross domestic product (GDP) The size of a state's total annual economic activity.   *(p. 10)*

Group of 20 (G20) The G20 is composed of the G7 states, plus Australia, Argentina, Brazil, China, India, Indonesia, Mexico, Korea, Russia, Saudi Arabia, South Africa and Turkey, along with the European Union, International Monetary Fund and World Bank. Members of the G7 realized that even acting together, they were not sufficient in number to manage world financial markets.   *(p. 357)*

Group of 7 (G7) The world's seven largest industrial market economies: the United States, Japan, Germany, France, Britain, Italy and Canada. The leaders of G7 countries meet in annual summits, and G7 finance ministers meet several times a year. When the group includes Russia, as it has done at summits since 1998, it is called the G8. On some issues, particularly monetary matters, the G7 acts without Russia (primarily because Russia's currency is not yet fully convertible).   *(p. 345)*

groupthink The tendency of individual members of a group to go along with ideas they think other group members support, leading to the adoption of decisions that conform to group sentiment but not necessarily to the available evidence (and in extreme cases, that contravene legal or ethical norms).   *(p. 142)*

guerrilla war Warfare without front lines and with irregular forces operating in the midst of, and often hidden or protected by, civilian populations.   *(p. 160)*

hard currency Money that can be readily converted to leading world currencies. See also convertible currency.   *(p. 344)*

hegemonic stability theory The argument that regimes are most effective when power in the international system is most concentrated. See also *hegemony*.   *(p. 84)*

hegemonic war War for control of the entire world order— the rules of the international system as a whole. Also known as world war, global war, general war, or systemic war.   *(p. 159)*

hegemony The holding by one state of a preponderance of power in the international system, so that it can single-handedly dominate the rules and arrangements by which international political and economic relations are conducted. See also *hegemonic stability theory*.   *(p. 69)*

high seas That portion of the oceans considered common territory, not under any exclusive state jurisdiction. See also *territorial waters*.   *(p. 514)*

historical materialism A unique contribution of Marxist thought which understands societies in terms of the ways in which relations of production are organized and eventually transformed.   *(p. 108)*

home country The state where a *multinational corporation* (MNC) has its headquarters.   *(p. 367)*

host country A state in which a foreign *multinational corporation* (MNC) operates.   *(p. 367)*

Human Development Index (HDI) The HDI is an alternative measure of development to the gross domestic product (GDP). It measures a country's achievements in the areas of life expectancy at birth (as a measure of a long and healthy life), knowledge (including adult literacy and enrolment levels in primary, secondary and tertiary education) and standard of living (based on per capita GDP).   *(p. 453)*

human rights Rights of all persons to be free from abuses such as torture or imprisonment for their political beliefs (political and civil rights), and to enjoy certain minimum economic and social protections (economic and social rights).   *(p. 290)*

human security Expands the notion of security away from a focus on states to one that examines all the complex ways in which people are made secure, including through human rights protections; access to education, food and shelter; availability of health services; and a sustainable environment.   *(p. 88)*

humanitarian intervention Armed intrusion into a state, without its consent, to prevent or alleviate widespread or severe human rights violations.   *(p. 243)*

hyperinflation An extremely rapid, uncontrolled rise in prices, such as occurred in Germany in the 1920s and some global South countries more recently.   *(p. 343)*

idealism An approach that emphasizes international law, morality and international organization, rather than power alone, as key influences on international relations.   *(p. 49)*

IMF conditionality An agreement to loan IMF funds on the condition that certain government policies areadopted. Dozens of global South states have entered into such agreements in the past two decades. See also *International Monetary Fund (IMF).*   (*p. 481*)

immigration law National laws that establish the conditions under which foreigners may travel within a state's territory, work within the state and become citizens of the state (naturalization).   (*p. 282*)

imperialism The acquisition of colonies by conquest or otherwise. Lenin's theory of imperialism argued that European capitalists were investing in colonies where they could earn big profits, then using part of those profits to buy off portions of the working class at home.   (*p. 436*)

import substitution A strategy of developing local industries, often conducted behind protectionist barriers, to produce items that a country had previously been importing.   (*p. 467*)

industrial policy The strategies by which a government works actively with industries to promote their growth and tailor trade policy to their needs.   (*p. 324*)

industrialization The use of fossil-fuel energy to drive machinery and the accumulation of such machinery along with the products created by it.   (*p. 30*)

infant mortality rate The proportion of babies who die within their first year of life.   (*p. 532*)

infantry Foot soldiers who use assault rifles and other light weaponry (mines, machine guns and the like).   (*p. 198*)

informal sector Those models of business, such as shadow markets and street vendors, operating beyond state control; some scholars see this sector as the core of a new development strategy.   (*p. 469*)

information screens The subconscious or unconscious filters through which people screen information about the world around them.   (*p. 135*)

intellectual property rights The legal protection of the original works of inventors, authors, creators and performers under patent, copyright and trademark law. Such rights became a contentious area of trade negotiations in the 1990s.   (*p. 325*)

intercontinental ballistic missiles (ICBMs) The longest-range ballistic missiles, able to travel 8000 kilometres.   (*p. 211*)

interdependence A political and economic situation in which two or more states are simultaneously dependent on one another for their well-being. Degrees of interdependence are sometimes designated in terms of "sensitivity" or "vulnerability."   (*p. 316*)

interest groups Coalitions of people who share a common interest in the outcome of some political issue and whoorganize themselves to try to influence the outcome.   (*p. 146*)

intergovernmental organizations (IGOs) Organizations (such as the United Nations and its agencies) whose members are state governments.   (*p. 13*)

Intermediate Nuclear Forces (INF) Treaty (1987) Treaty that banned an entire class of missiles that both the Soviet Union and the United States had deployed in Europe.   (*p. 276*)

International Committee of the Red Cross (ICRC) An organization based in Geneva, Switzerland, that provides practical support, such as medical care, food and letters from home, to civilians caught in wars and to prisoners of war(POWs). The ICRC works with national societies of the Red Cross or Red Crescent. Exchanges of POWs are usually negotiated through the ICRC.   (*p. 289*)

International Criminal Court (ICC) Permanent tribunal for war crimes and crimes against humanity.   (*p. 286*)

international integration The process by which supranational institutions come to replace national ones; the gradual shifting upward of sovereignty from the state to regional or global structures.   (*p. 379*)

International Monetary Fund (IMF) An *intergovernmental organization (IGO)* that coordinates international currency exchange, the balance of international payments and national accounts. Along with the *World Bank*, it is a pillar of the international financial system. See also IMF *conditionality.*   (*p. 350*)

international norms The expectations held by participants about normal relations among states.   (*p. 242*)

international organizations (IOs) Institutions including *intergovernmental organizations (IGOs)* such as the UN and *nongovernmental organizations (NGOs)* such as Médecins Sans Frontières or Amnesty International.   (*p. 244*)

international political economy (IPE) The study of the politics of trade, monetary and other economic relations among nations, and their connection to other transnational forces.   (*p. 3*)

international regime A set of rules, norms and procedures around which the expectations of actors converge on a certain international issue (such as oceans or monetary policy).   (*p. 83*)

international relations (IR) The relationships among the world's state governments and the connection of those relationships with other actors (such as the United Nations, multinational corporations, and individuals), with other social relationships (including economics, culture and domestic politics) and with geographic and historical influences.   (*p. 1*)

international security A subfield of *international relations (IR)* that focuses on questions of war and peace.   (*p. 3*)

international system The set of relationships among the world's states, structured by certain rules and patterns of interaction.   (*p. 8*)

International Whaling Commission An *intergovernmental organization (IGO)* that sets quotas for hunting certain whale species; states' participation is voluntary.   (*p. 511*)

investment Putting surplus wealth into capital-producing activities to produce long-term benefits rather than consuming it.   (*p. 431*)

irredentism A form of nationalism whose goal is to regain territory lost to another state; it can lead directly to violent interstate conflicts.   (*p. 166*)

Islam/Muslims A broad and diverse world religion whose divergent populations include Sunni Muslims, Shiite Muslims and many smaller branches and sects; practised by Muslims from Nigeria to Indonesia, and centred in the Middle East.   (*p. 185*)

just war doctrine A branch of international law and political theory that defines when wars can be justly started (*jus ad bellum*) and how they can be justly fought (*jus in bello*). See also *war crimes.*   (*p. 285*)

Keynesian economics The principles articulated by British economist John Maynard Keynes, which were used successfully in the Great Depression of the 1930s and include the view that governments should sometimes use deficit spending to stimulate economic growth. *(p. 356)*

land reform Policies that aim to break up large land holdings and redistribute land to poor peasants for use in *subsistence farming.* *(p. 422)*

landmines Concealed explosive devices that kill or maim civilians after war's end. Such mines number more than 100 million, primarily in Angola, Bosnia, Afghanistan and Cambodia. A movement to ban landmines is underway, and nearly 100 states have agreed to do so. *(p. 198)*

lateral pressure (theory of) The theory that the economic and population growth of states fuels geographic expansion as they seek natural resources beyond their borders, which in turn leads to conflicts and sometimes war. *(p. 174)*

League of Nations Established after World War I and a forerunner of today's United Nations, the League of Nations achieved certain humanitarian and other successes but was weakened by the absence of U.S. membership and its own lack of effectiveness in ensuring collective security. See also *collective security.* *(p. 33)*

liberal feminism A strand of feminism that emphasizes gender equality and views the "essential" differences in men's and women's abilities or perspectives as trivial or nonexistent. *(p. 113)*

limited war Military actions that seek objectives short of the surrender and occupation of the enemy. *(p. 159)*

Maastricht Treaty Signed in the Dutch city of Maastricht in 1992, this treaty committed the European Union to monetary union (a single currency and European central bank) and to a common foreign policy. See also *European Union (EU).* *(p. 388)*

malnutrition A lack of needed foods, including protein and vitamins; about 10 million children die each year from malnutrition-related causes. *(p. 420)*

managed float A system of occasional multinational government interventions in currency markets to manage otherwise free-floating currency rates. *(p. 345)*

Marxism A theoretical and political approach that views capitalism as exploitative and emphasizes class struggle; includes socialism and communism and other approaches to social transformation. *(p. 433)*

mediation The use of a third party (or parties) in *conflict resolution.* *(p. 94)*

mercantilism An economic theory and a political ideology opposed to free trade; it shares with *realism* the belief that each state must protect its own interests without seeking mutual gains through international organizations. See also *liberalism.* *(p. 74)*

microcredit The use of very small loans to small groups of individuals, often women, to stimulate economic development. *(p. 469)*

middle powers States that rank somewhat below the great powers in terms of their influence on world affairs (for example, Canada, Brazil and India). See also *great powers.* *(p. 66)*

migration Movement between states, usually emigration from an old state and immigration to a new state. *(p. 424)*

militarism The glorification of war, military force and violence and the structuring of society around war—for example, the dominant role of a military-industrial complex in a national economy. *(p. 96)*

military-industrial complex A huge, interlocking network of governmental agencies, industrial corporations and research institutes, all working together to promote and benefit from military spending. *(p. 152)*

military governments States in which military forces control the government; more common in countries of the global South, where the military may be the only large modern institution. *(p. 234)*

Millennium Development Goals Targets established by the UN in 2000 for meeting basic human needs around the world by 2015. The first of the eight goals is to cut in half the proportion of the world's population living in "extreme poverty," defined as income below $1 per day. *(p. 415)*

misperceptions and selective perceptions The selective or mistaken processing of the available information about a decision; one of several ways—along with affective and cognitive bias—in which individual decision-making diverges from the *rational model.* *(p. 135)*

Missile Technology Control Regime A set of agreements through which industrialized states try to limit the flow of missile-relevant technology to states of the global South. *(p. 214)*

monetary policy A government's decisions about printing and circulating money, and one of the two major tools of macroeconomic policy-making (the other being *fiscal policy*). *(p. 356)*

Montreal Protocol (1987) An agreement on the protection of the ozone layer in which states pledged to reduce and then eliminate use of chlorofluorocarbons (CFCs). It is the most successful environmental treaty to date. *(p. 510)*

most-favoured nation (MFN) concept The principle that one state, by granting another state MFN status, promises to give it the same treatment given to the first state's most-favoured trading partner. *(p. 333)*

multilateral aid Government foreign aid from several states that goes through a third party, such as the UN or another agency. *(p. 486)*

multinational corporations (MNCs) Companies based in one state with affiliated branches or subsidiaries operating in other states. See also *home country* and *host country.* *(p. 363)*

multipolar system An international system with typically five or six centres of power that are not grouped into alliances. *(p. 68)*

Munich Agreement A symbol of the failed policy of appeasement, this agreement, signed in 1938, allowed Nazi Germany to occupy a part of Czechoslovakia. Rather than appease German aspirations, it was followed by further German expansions, which triggered World War II. *(p. 33)*

mutually assured destruction (MAD) The possession of second-strike nuclear capabilities by two adversaries, which ensures that neither could prevent the other from destroying it in an all-out war. See also *deterrence*.   *(p. 223)*

national debt The amount a government owes in debt as a result of deficit spending.   *(p. 357)*

national interest The interests of a state overall (as opposed to particular parties or factions within the state).   *(p. 56)*

nationalism The identification with and devotion to the interests of one's nation. It usually involves a large group of people who share a national identity and often a language, culture, or ancestry.   *(p. 28)*

nation-states States whose populations share a sense of national identity, usually including a language and culture.   *(p. 9)*

neocolonialism The continuation, in a former colony, of colonial exploitation without formal political control.   *(p. 446)*

neofunctionalism The theory that holds that economic integration (functionalism) generates a "spillover" effect, resulting in increased political integration.   *(p. 380)*

neoliberalism Short for "neoliberal institutionalism," an approach that stresses the importance of international institutions in reducing the inherent conflict that realists assume in an international system; with reasoning based on the core liberal idea that seeking long-term mutual gains is often more rational than maximizing individual short-term ones. See also *liberalism*.   *(p. 81)*

neorealism A version of realist theory that emphasizes the influence of the system's structure on state behaviour, and particularly the international distribution of power. See also *realism*.   *(p. 51)*

New International Economic Order (NIEO) A global South effort begun in the mid-1970s, mainly conducted in UN forums, to advocate restructuring of the world economy to make North-South economic transactions less unfavourable to the South.   *(p. 485)*

newly industrializing countries (NICs) States of the global South that have achieved self-sustaining capital accumulation, with impressive economic growth.   *(p. 455)*

nonaligned movement Movement of states, largely from the global South, led by India and the former Yugoslavia, that attempted to stand apart from the U.S.-Soviet rivalry during the Cold War.   *(p. 250)*

nongovernmental organizations (NGOs) Transnational groups or entities (such as the Catholic Church, Greenpeace and the International Olympic Committee) that interact with states, multinational corporations (MNCs), other NGOs and intergovernmental organizations (IGOs).   *(p. 12)*

Non-Proliferation Treaty (NPT) (1968) Treaty that created a framework for controlling the spread of nuclear materials and expertise, including the International Atomic Energy Agency (IAEA), a UN agency based in Vienna that is charged with inspecting the nuclear power industry in NPT member states to prevent secret military diversions of nuclear materials.   *(p. 220)*

nonstate actors Actors other than state governments who operate either below the level of the state (that is, within states) or across state borders.   *(p. 11)*

nontariff barriers Forms of restricting imports other than tariffs, such as quotas (ceilings on how many goods of a certain kind can be imported).   *(p. 321)*

nonviolence/pacifism A philosophy based on a unilateral commitment to refrain from using any violent forms of leverage. More specifically, *pacifism* refers to a principled opposition to war in general rather than simply to particular wars.   *(p. 100)*

normative bias The personal norms and values that IR scholars bring to their studies, such as a preference for peace rather than war.   *(p. 94)*

norms (of behaviour) Shared expectations about what behaviour is considered proper.   *(p. 61)*

North American Aerospace Defense Command (NORAD) A binational military organization established in 1958 by Canada and the U.S. to monitor and defend North American air space.   *(p. 249)*

North American Free Trade Agreement (NAFTA) A free trade zone encompassing the United States, Canada and Mexico established in 1994.   *(p. 329)*

North American Monetary Union (NAMU) A proposed currency union between Canada and the U.S. The NAMU has become a regular feature in some policy discussions but has never been endorsed by a federal political party.   *(p. 396)*

North Atlantic Treaty Organization (NATO) A U.S.-led military alliance, formed in 1949 with mainly West European members, to oppose and deter Soviet power in Europe. It has recently expanded into the former Soviet bloc. See also *Warsaw Pact*.   *(p. 247)*

North-South gap The disparity in resources (income, wealth and power) between the industrialized, relatively rich countries of the West (and the former Communist bloc) and poorer countries in Africa, the Middle East and much of Asia and Latin America.   *(p. 16)*

oil shocks The two sharp rises in the world price of oil that occurred in 1973–1974 and 1979.   *(p. 522)*

optimizing Picking the very best option; contrasts with *satisficing*, or finding a satisfactory but less than best-solution to a problem. The model of "bounded rationality" postulates that decision-makers generally satisfice rather than optimize.   *(p. 137)*

organizational process model A decision-making model in which policy-makers or lower-level officials rely largely on standardized responses or standard operating procedures.   *(p. 139)*

Organization of Petroleum Exporting Countries (OPEC) The most prominent cartel in the international economy; its members control over half the world's total oil exports, enough to significantly affect the world price of oil.   *(p. 469)*

ozone layer The part of the atmosphere that screens out harmful ultraviolet rays from the sun. Certain chemicals used by some industries, in particular chlorofluorocarbons (CFCs), break down the ozone layer.   *(p. 509)*

Paris Club A group of global North governments that have loaned money to global South governments; it meets periodically to work out terms of debt renegotiations. Private creditors meet as the **London Club.**   *(p. 480)*

peace movements Movements against specific wars or against war and militarism in general, usually involving large numbers of people and forms of direct action, such as street protests.   *(p. 100)*

periphery The global South regions of the world-system that mostly extract raw materials (including agriculture).   *(p. 437)*

positive peace A peace that resolves the underlying reasons for war; not just a ceasefire but a transformation of relationships, including elimination or reduction of economic exploitation and political oppression.   *(p. 98)*

post-positivism Entails reflecting on the assumptions and political commitments that inform our theories and acknowledging that theories help to constitute the world as we know it.   *(p. 107)*

post-positivist feminism An effort to combine feminist and postmodernist perspectives with the aim of uncovering the hidden influences of gender in IR and showing how arbitrary the construction of gender roles is.   *(p. 113)*

postmodernism An approach that denies the existence of a single fixed reality, and pays special attention to texts and discourses—that is, how people write and talk about a subject.   *(p. 123)*

power The ability or potential to influence others' behaviour, as measured by the possession of certain tangible and intangible characteristics.   *(p. 52)*

power projection The ability to use military force in areas far from a country's region or sphere of influence.   *(p. 199)*

prisoners of war (POWs) Soldiers who are captured or have surrendered (and who thereby receive special status under the laws of war).   *(p. 289)*

problem-solving theory Theory that takes the world as it is and attempts to make institutions and relationships work more smoothly within that given framework. Problem-solving theory is usually contrasted with critical theory, which stands apart from the prevailing order of the world and asks how that order came about.   *(p. 105)*

proletariat In Marxist terminology, the class of workers who must sell their labour power to capitalists in order to survive and whose labour is needed to produce surplus value; more specifically, industrial factory workers. It was considered the class that would spearhead the socialist revolution.   *(p. 435)*

proliferation The spread of weapons of mass destruction (nuclear, chemical or biological weapons) into the hands of more actors.   *(p. 218)*

pronatalist policy A government policy that encourages or forces childbearing and outlaws or limits access to contraception.   *(p. 531)*

protectionism The protection of domestic industries against international competition by trade tariffs and other means.   *(p. 319)*

proxy wars Wars in the global South—often civil wars—in which the United States and the Soviet Union jockeyed for position by supplying and advising opposing factions.   *(p. 36)*

public opinion In IR, the range of views on foreign policy issues held by the citizens of a state.   *(p. 148)*

rally 'round the flag syndrome The public's increased support for government leaders during wartime, at least in the short term.   *(p. 151)*

rational actors Actors conceived as single entities that can "think" about their actions coherently, make choices, identify their interests and rank the interests in terms of priority.   *(p. 56)*

rational actor model (of decision-making) A model in which decision-makers calculate the costs and benefits of each possible course of action, then choose the one with the highest benefits and lowest costs.   *(p. 132)*

realism (political realism) A broad intellectual tradition that explains international relations mainly in terms of power.   *(p. 49)*

reciprocity A response in kind to another's actions; a strategy of reciprocity uses positive forms of leverage to promise rewards and negative forms of leverage to threaten punishment.   *(p. 73)*

refugees People fleeing their countries to find refuge from war, natural disaster or political persecution. International law distinguishes refugees from migrants.   *(p. 426)*

reserves Hard-currency stockpiles kept by states.   *(p. 344)*

Responsibility to Protect (R2P) A report issued by the International Commission on Intervention and State Sovereignty and formed under the sponsorship of the Canadian government. It focuses on the responsibilities states have to protect populations suffering serious harm or human rights abuses as a result of conflict.   *(p. 296)*

risk assessment The pre-investment efforts by corporations (especially banks) to determine how likely it is that future political conditions in a target country will change so radically as to disrupt the flow of income.   *(p. 369)*

satisficing The act of finding a satisfactory or "good enough" solution to a problem.   *(p. 137)*

secular (state) A state created apart from religious establishments and in which there is a high degree of separation between religious and political organizations.   *(p. 184)*

security community A situation in which low expectations of interstate violence permit a high degree of political cooperation.   *(p. 380)*

security dilemma A situation in which states' actions taken to assure their own security (such as deploying military forces) are perceived as threats to the security of other states.   *(p. 62)*

semiperiphery The area in the world-system in which some manufacturing occurs and some capital concentrates, but not to the extent of the core areas.   *(p. 438)*

service sector The part of an economy that concerns services (as opposed to the production of tangible goods); the key focus of this sector in international trade negotiations is on banking, insurance and related financial services.   *(p. 326)*

settlement The outcome of a bargaining process.   *(p. 161)*

Single European Act (1985) A revision of the Treaty of Rome that set a target of the end of 1992 for the creation of a *true common market* (free cross-border movement of goods, capital, people and services) in the European Community (EC).   *(p. 387)*

Sino-Soviet split A rift in the 1960s between the communist powers of the Soviet Union and China, fuelled by

China's opposition to Soviet moves toward peaceful coexistence with the United States. *(p. 35)*

socialism A term encompassing many political movements, parties, economic theories and ideologies, historical and present-day. Based on the idea that workers should have political power (or a larger share of power), socialism favours the redistribution of wealth toward the workers who produce it. In economic policy, socialists have favoured different combinations of planning and reliance on market forces, as well as various patterns of ownership. *(p. 432)*

sovereignty A state's right, at least in principle, to do whatever it wants within its own territory; traditionally sovereignty is the most important international norm. *(p. 61)*

Special Drawing Right (SDR) A world currency created by the *International Monetary Fund (IMF)* to replace gold as a world standard. Valued by a "basket" of national currencies, the SDR has been called "paper gold." *(p. 351)*

Stalinism The system that prevailed during Stalin's rule in the Soviet Union (1924–1953), which was marked by totalitarian state control under the Communist party and the ruthless elimination of the regime's opponents on a massive scale. *(p. 434)*

standpoint feminism A strand of feminism that believes gender differences are not just socially constructed and that views women as inherently less warlike than men (on average). *(p. 112)*

state An inhabited territorial entity controlled by a government that exercises its sovereignty. *(p. 8)*

state-sponsored terrorism The use of terrorist groups by states, usually under control of a state's intelligence agency, to achieve political aims. *(p. 207)*

stealth technology The use of special radar-absorbent materials and unusual shapes in the design of aircraft, missiles and ships to scatter enemy radar. *(p. 203)*

Strategic Arms Limitation Treaties (SALT) SALT I (1972) and SALT II (1979) put formal ceilings on the growth of U.S. and Soviet strategic weapons. SALT II was never ratified by the U.S. Senate (due to the subsequent Soviet invasion of Afghanistan). *(p. 276)*

Strategic Arms Reduction Treaties (START) START I (1991) called for a reduction inthe superpowers' strategic arsenals by about 30 percent. START II (1992) proposes to cut the remaining weapons by more than half in the next decade. START III is under discussion. *(p. 276)*

Strategic Defense Initiative (SDI) A U.S. effort, also known as "star wars," to develop defences that could shoot down incoming ballistic missiles, spurred by President Ronald Reagan in 1983. Critics call it an expensive failure that would violate the ABM Treaty. See also *Anti-Ballistic Missile (ABM) Treaty*. *(p. 224)*

structural violence A term used by some scholars to refer to poverty, hunger, oppression and other social and economic sources of conflict. *(p. 98)*

subsistence farming Rural communities growing food mainly for their own consumption rather than for sale in local or world markets. *(p. 421)*

subtext Meanings that are implicit or hidden in a text rather than explicitly addressed. See also *postmodernism*. *(p. 122)*

summit meeting A meeting between heads of state, often referring to leaders of great powers, as in the Cold War superpower summits between the United States and the Soviet Union or today's meetings of the Group of Eight on economic coordination. *(p. 36)*

superstructure In Marxist terminology, the forms of politics and culture that are shaped by the economic base or mode of production (slavery, feudalism, capitalism). *(p. 435)*

supranationalism The subordination of state authority or national identity to larger institutions and groupings, such as the European Union. *(p. 378)*

tariff A duty or tax levied on certain types of imports (usually as a percentage of their value) as they enter a country. *(p. 321)*

technology transfer Global South states' acquisition of technology (knowledge, skills, methods, designs, specialized equipment, etc.) from foreign sources, usually in conjunction with *direct foreign investment* or similar business operations. *(p. 477)*

terms of trade The overall relationship between prices of imported and exported goods. *(p. 467)*

territorial waters The waters near states' shores, generally treated as part of national territory. The UN Convention on the Law of the Sea provides for a 12-nautical mile territorial sea (and exclusive national jurisdiction over shipping and navigation) and a 200-nautical mile exclusive economic zone (EEZ) covering fishing and mineral rights (but allowing for free navigation by all). See also *high seas* and UN *Convention on the Law of the Sea (UNCLOS)*. *(p. 171)*

tit for tat A strategy of strict reciprocity (matching the other player's response) after an initial cooperative move; it can bring about mutual cooperation in a repeated Prisoner's Dilemma game, since it ensures that defection will not pay. *(p. 81)*

total war Warfare by one state waged to conquer and occupy another; modern total war originated in the Napoleonic Wars, which relied on conscription on a mass scale. *(p. 159)*

tragedy of the commons A collective goods dilemma created when common environmental assets (such as the world's fisheries) are depleted or degraded through the failure of states to cooperate effectively. One solution is the *enclosure of the commons* (splitting them into individually owned pieces); international regimes can also be a (partial) solution. *(p. 501)*

transitional economies Countries in Russia and Eastern Europe that are trying to convert from communism to capitalism, with varying degrees of success. *(p. 311)*

Treaty of Rome (1957) The founding document of the European Economic Community (EEC) or Common Market, now subsumed by the European Union. *(p. 382)*

truth commissions Commissions used by new governments to hear testimony from periods of war; used to find truthful accounts of past occurrences in exchange for asylum from punishment for participants. *(p. 182)*

United Nations (UN) An organization of nearly all world states, created after World War II to promote collective security.   *(p. 8)*

UN Charter The founding document of the United Nations; it is based on the principles that states are equal,have *sovereignty* over their own affairs, enjoy independence and territorial integrity and must fulfill international obligations. The Charter also lays out the structure and methods of the UN.   *(p. 252)*

UN Conference on Trade and Development (UNCTAD) A structure established in 1964 to promote development in the global South through various trade proposals.   *(p. 271)*

UN Convention on the Law of the Sea (UNCLOS) A world treaty (1982) governing use of the oceans. The UNCLOS treaty established rules on territorial waters and a 200–nautical mile exclusive economic zone (EEZ). See also *territorial waters*.   *(p. 514)*

UN Development Programme (UNDP) UN agency that coorpdinates the flow of multilateral development assistance and manages 5000 projects at once around the world (focusing especially on technical development assistance).   *(p. 489)*

UN Environment Programme (UNEP) UN agency that monitors environmental conditions and, among other activities, works with the World Meteorological Organization to measure changes in the global climate.   *(p. 509)*

UN General Assembly Comprising representatives of all states, it allocates UN funds, passes nonbinding resolutions and coordinates development programs and various autonomous agencies through the Economic and Social Council (ECOSOC).   *(p. 252)*

UN Secretariat The UN's executive branch, led by the secretary-general.   *(p. 252)*

UN Security Council A body of five great powers (which can veto resolutions) and 10 rotating member states; it makes decisions about international peace and security, including the dispatch of UN peacekeeping forces.   *(p. 252)*

undernourishment A lack of needed foods; a lack of calories.   *(p. 420)*

urbanization A shift of population from the countryside to cities that typically accompanies economic development and is augmented by displacement of peasants from *subsistence farming*.   *(p. 421)*

Uruguay Round A series of negotiations under the *General Agreement on Tariffs and Trade (GATT)* that began in Uruguay in 1986, and concluded in 1994 with agreement to create the World Trade Organization. The Uruguay Round followed earlier GATT negotiations such as the Kennedy Round and the Tokyo Round. See also *World Trade Organization (WTO)*.   *(p. 334)*

war crimes Violations of the law governing the conduct of warfare, such as mistreating prisoners of war or unnecessarily targeting civilians. See also *just war doctrine*.   *(p. 286)*

Warsaw Pact A Soviet-led Eastern European military alliance founded in 1955 and disbanded in 1991. It opposed the NATO alliance. See also *North Atlantic Treaty Organization (NATO)*.   *(p. 248)*

weapons of mass destruction Nuclear, chemical and biological weapons, distinguished from conventional weapons by their enormous potential lethality and by their relative lack of discrimination in whom they kill.   *(p. 208)*

World Bank Formally the International Bank for Reconstruction and Development (IBRD), it was established in 1944 as a source of loans to help reconstruct the European economies. Later, the main borrowers were countries of the global South and, in the 1990s, Eastern European states.   *(p. 350)*

World Court (International Court of Justice) The judicial arm of the UN; located in The Hague, it hears only cases between states.   *(p. 278)*

world government A centralized world governing body with strong enforcement powers.   *(p. 99)*

World Health Organization (WHO) Based in Geneva, an that provides technical assistance to improve health conditions primarily in the global South (but can address health concerns anywhere around the world) and conducts major immunization campaigns.   *(p. 271)*

world-system theory A view of the world in terms of regional class divisions, with industrialized countries as the *core*, poor global South countries as the *periphery* and other areas (for example, some of the newly industrializing countries) as the *semiperiphery*.   *(p. 437)*

World Trade Organization (WTO) An organization begun in 1995 that expanded the GATT's traditional focus on manufactured goods and created monitoring and enforcement mechanisms.   *(p. 332)*

World University Service of Canada (WUSC) An agency involved in development assistance projects in over 50 countries that also coordinates professional and volunteer positions in many of those projects.   *(p. 488)*

zero-sum games A situation in which one actor's gain is by definition equal to the other's loss, as opposed to a non-zero-sum game, in which it is possible for both actors to gain (or lose).   *(p. 58)*

Photo Credits

Author Index

Subject Index

REFERENCE MAPS

North America

Scale 1:38,700,000

Lambert Conformal Conic Projection,
standard parallels 37° N and 65° N

0   500 Kilometres

0   500 Nautical Miles

Boundary representation is
not necessarily authoritative.

802374 (B01267) 5-95

Central America and the Caribbean

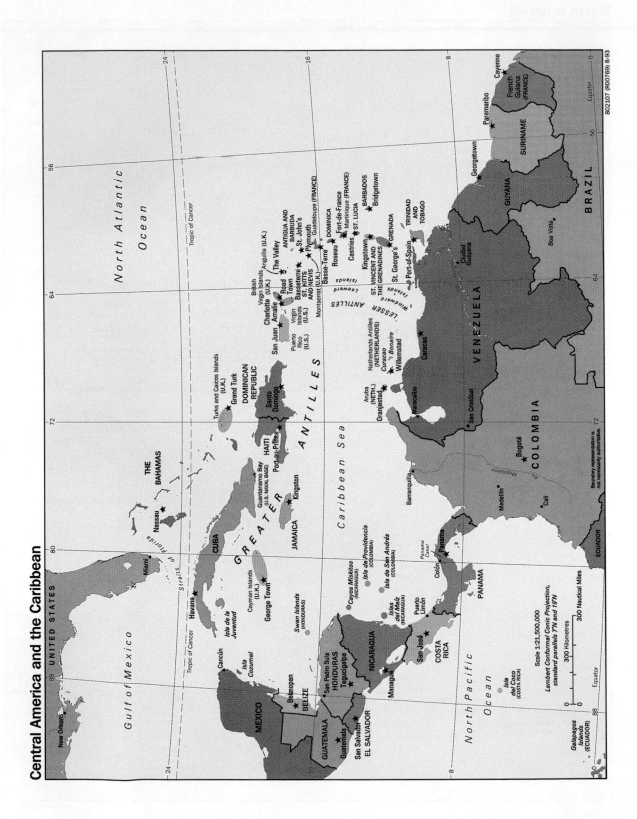

South America

North
Atlantic
Ocean

Caribbean Sea

HONDURAS
Puerto
Lempira
Tegucigalpa
Puerto
Cabezas
NICARAGUA
Isla de San Andrés
(COLOMBIA)
Managua
Liberia
San José
COSTA RICA
David
Colón
Panama
PANAMA
Barranquilla
Maracaibo
San
Cristóbal
Caracas
Port-of-Spain

Guadeloupe
(FRANCE)
DOMINICA
Martinique
(FRANCE)
ST. LUCIA
ST. VINCENT AND
THE GRENADINES
BARBADOS
GRENADA
TRINIDAD AND
TOBAGO

VENEZUELA
Río Orinoco
Ciudad
Guayana
Georgetown
GUYANA
Paramaribo
French Guiana
(FRANCE)
SURINAME
Cayenne

Medellín
Bogotá
COLOMBIA
Cali
Isla de Malpelo
(COLOMBIA)
Mitú
Boa Vista
Macapá

Equator

ECUADOR
Quito
Guayaquil
Iquitos
Río Negro
Amazon
Fonte Boa
Manaus
Santarém
Belém
São Luís

Piura
Fortaleza
Teresina

Trujillo
PERU
Huánuco
Pôrto Velho
Rio
Branco
BRAZIL
Palmas
Natal
Recife

Lima
Ica
Cuzco
Aracaju
Salvador

South
Pacific
Ocean

Arequipa
Trinidad
Lago
Titicaca
La Paz
BOLIVIA
Cochabamba
Santa
Cruz
Cuiabá
Goiânia
Brasília

Arica
Potosí
Sucre
Rio São Francisco

Belo
Horizonte
Vitória

Tropic of Capricorn
Antofagasta
PARAGUAY
Rio de Janeiro
São Paulo

Isla San Félix
(CHILE)
Isla San Ambrosio
(CHILE)
San Miguel
de Tucumán
Asunción
Curitiba
Resistencia
Florianópolis

South
Atlantic
Ocean

CHILE
Córdoba
Rosario
Rio Paraná
Pôrto Alegre
URUGUAY

Valparaíso
Mendoza
Buenos Aires
Montevideo

Santiago
ARGENTINA

Concepción
Bahía Blanca
Mar del Plata

Archipiélago
Juan Fernández
(CHILE)

San Carlos
de Bariloche

Puerto Montt

Comodoro Rivadavia

Scale 1:35,000,000

Azimuthal Equal-Area Projection

0   250   500 Kilometres
0   250   500 Nautical Miles

Boundary representation is
not necessarily authoritative.

Strait of
Magellan
Punta Arenas
Ushuaia

Stanley
Falkland Islands
(Islas Malvinas)
(administered by U.K.,
claimed by Argentina)

South Georgia and the
South Sandwich Islands
(administered by U.K.,
claimed by Argentina)

802376 (545528) 5-95

Africa

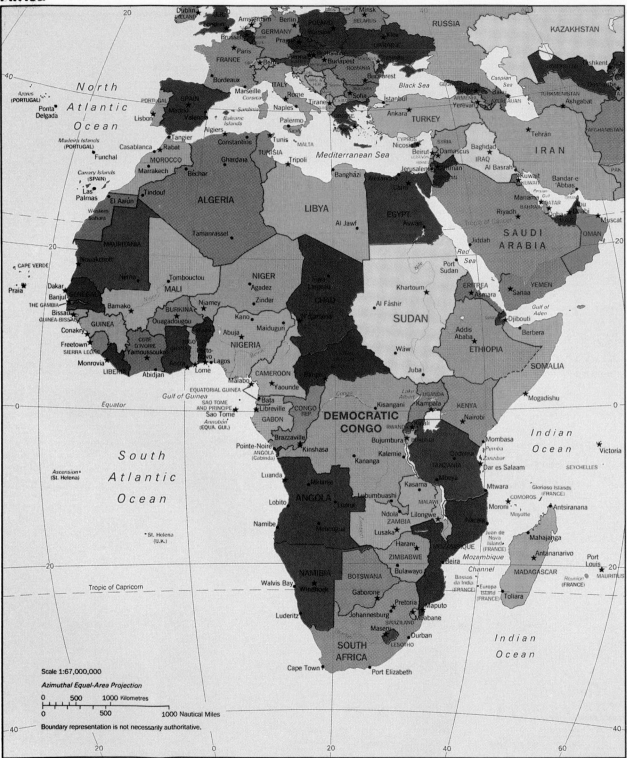

Scale 1:67,000,000

Azimuthal Equal-Area Projection

0   500   1000 Kilometres

0   500   1000 Nautical Miles

Boundary representation is not necessarily authoritative.

802380 (R00475) 5-95

Northern Africa and the Middle East

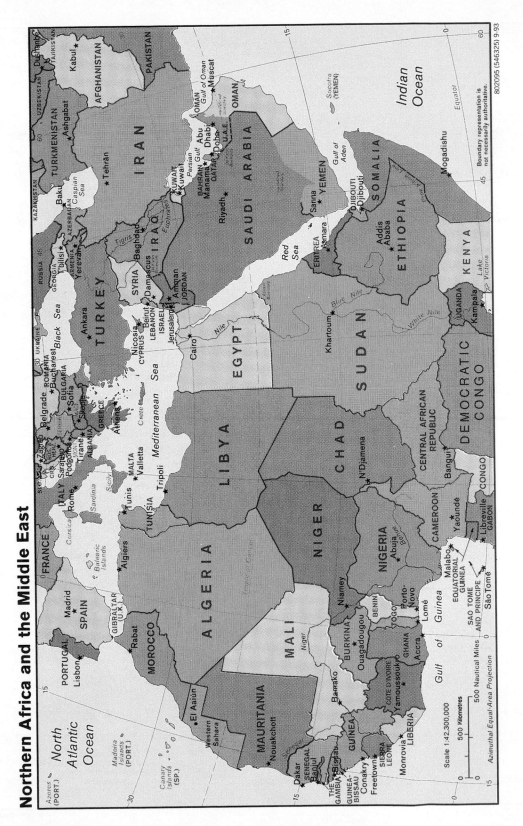

802095 (546325) 9-93

Europe

Serbia and Montenegro have asserted the formation of a joint independent state, but this entity has not been formally recognized as a state by the United States.

Scale 1:19,500,000

Lambert Conformal Conic Projection, standard parallels 40°N and 56°N

300 Kilometres

300 Nautical Miles

802377 (R01083) 5-95

Asia